Britain's Declining Empire:
The Road to Decolonisation, 19

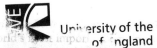

University of the
of England

Hyam offers a major reassessment of the end o
study of British policy-making with case studies on the   nce of
decolonisation across Africa, Asia, and the Caribbean. He describes the
often dysfunctional policies of an imperial system coping with postwar,
interwar, and wartime crises from 1918 to 1945 but the main emphasis
is on the period after 1945 and the gradual unravelling of empire as a
result of international criticism and of the growing imbalance between
Britain's capabilities and its global commitments. He analyses the transfers of power from India in 1947 to Swaziland in 1968, the major crises
such as Mau Mau and Suez, and assesses the role of leading figures from
Churchill, Attlee, and Eden to Macmillan and Wilson. This is essential
reading for scholars and students of empire and decolonisation.

RONALD HYAM is Emeritus Reader in British Imperial History at the
University of Cambridge, and a Fellow and former President of
Magdalene College. He is the author of several books on the British
Empire, including most recently (with Peter Henshaw) *The Lion and the
Springbok: Britain and South Africa since the Boer War* (Cambridge,
2003).

The Viceroy's Palace, New Delhi, designed by Sir Edwin Lutyens

Britain's Declining Empire:
The Road to Decolonisation,
1918–1968

Ronald Hyam

CAMBRIDGE
UNIVERSITY PRESS

CAMBRIDGE UNIVERSITY PRESS

Cambridge, New York, Melbourne, Madrid, Cape Town, Singapore, São Paulo

Cambridge University Press
The Edinburgh Building, Cambridge CB2 8RU, UK

Published in the United States of America by Cambridge University Press,
New York

www.cambridge.org
Information on this title: www.cambridge.org/9780521685559

First published 2006

Printed in the United Kingdom at the University Press, Cambridge

A catalogue record for this publication is available from the British Library

ISBN-13 978-0-521-86649-1 hardback
ISBN-10 0-521-86649-9 hardback

ISBN-13 978-0-521-68555-9 paperback
ISBN-10 0-521-68555-9 paperback

Contents

Illustrations

Acknowledgements: Royal Commonwealth Society Photographic
Collection, by permission of the Syndics of the Cambridge University
Library, including mostly Crown Copyright pictures, by permission of
the Controller of HM Stationery Office (1.2, 2.1–2.3, 3.1, 3.3, 4.1–4.8);
Associated Press (5.1); Swaziland Information Service (5.2); Magdalene
College Archives (1.1, 3.2), by permission of the Master and Fellows.

Maps

Preface

Dismantling the wardrobe

The house-clearance people refused to take my parents' huge wardrobe. So I set about breaking it up before burning it. The job was much harder than I expected. A good friend of mine, who knows a thing or two about furniture-making, later commented that of course dismantling a wardrobe is not easy – the secret is to know how it was put together. Something I had not known. It struck me that he was making an essential point not just about pulling a wardrobe to pieces, but about my field of study: that you cannot properly understand the dismantling of the British empire unless you know how it was constructed. Explanations of end and decline must show a continuity and congruence with the beginnings and the heyday, the dynamics of empire-building and the principles of imperial management. The empire is itself to be defined by the manner of its dismantling.

Although this book takes up more or less where *Britain's imperial century, 1815–1914* leaves off, it is a sequel with a different character, focused more upon a single theme, 'the end of empire' in its political aspects. And it is more closely based on archival research. In a sense it is the finished product: *Britain's imperial century* can be regarded as the user's handbook.[1]

There are already many books on the general theme of the decline, fall, eclipse, end, liquidation, collapse, dissolution, or decolonisation of the British empire. The main excuse for this one is that we now have before us the massive documentation of several major projects operating between 1970 and 2005: the Transfer of Power series for India (TOPI: twelve volumes) and for Burma (BSI: two volumes), the British Documents on the End of Empire Project (BDEEP: to be completed in eighteen volumes in thirty-eight parts),[2] and the *Official History of*

---

[1] R. Hyam, *Britain's imperial century, 1815–1914: a study of empire and expansion* (3rd edn, 2002).

[2] At the time of going to press, the following BDEEP volumes still await publication: *Fiji* (ed. Brij Lal), *Malta* (ed. Simon Smith), *Southern Africa* (ed. Peter Henshaw), *Cyprus* (ed. Robert Holland), and *Kenya* (ed. John Lonsdale and David Throup).

Colonial Development (five volumes).[3] Together, these can form the foundation for a more authoritative version of British policy than has previously been possible. These large-scale compilations take time to get absorbed into general accounts, but the impact they can make is already evident in illuminating work published by D. G. Boyce,[4] L. J. Butler,[5] and F. Heinlein,[6] on government action between 1945 and 1956. My aim is to carry the historiography a stage further, taking advantage of the fact that I have edited two volumes for BDEEP, on the Labour government 1945–51, and the Conservative government 1957–64. I owe a great deal to discussions with my fellow-editors on the BDEEP, especially Stephen Ashton, Roger Louis, David Goldsworthy, John Kent, Tony Stockwell, and Peter Henshaw. In addition I have a general acquaintance with some at least of the Colonial Office records for the sixty-year period since 1905. Writing this book has impressed on me just how rich is the material now available, even though only a small proportion of it can actually be used in a volume of this size.[7]

The emphasis here is on the twenty years or so after the Second World War, but a scene-setting introduction and the first chapter aim to give

---

[3] The India and Burma documentary series were official government projects, as were the War Histories and the *Documents on British policy overseas* (Foreign Office). On 18 December 1969, the prime minister, Mr Harold Wilson, announced an official 'Peacetime Series' of documents, commissioned by an inter-party group of Privy Counsellors: on colonial development (edited by D. J. Morgan), on environmental planning (by J. B. Cullingworth), and on nationalism (by D. N. Chester) (*PD, Commons* vol. 793, cols. 411–12). Of these, only Morgan's volume came to fruition. When the British Documents on the End of Empire Project was launched in 1987, Mrs Thatcher's government refused to follow precedent and adopt it as an official project, with the result that editors were able to draw only on those documents already in the public domain; they were, however, granted special privileges of access at The National Archives, and The Stationery Office undertook publication.

[4] D. George Boyce, *Decolonisation and the British empire, 1775–1997* (1999).

[5] L. J. Butler, *Britain and empire: adjusting to a post-imperial world* (2002), chs. 3 and 4, drawing on the published documents for 1945 to 1956.

[6] F. Heinlein, *British government policy and decolonisation, 1945–1963: scrutinising the official mind* (2002), with similar documentary coverage.

[7] Other general collections of documents include Nicholas Mansergh's *Documents and speeches on Commonwealth affairs, 1931–1962*, three vols. (1953, 1963), and A. N. Porter and A. J. Stockwell, eds., *British imperial policy and decolonisation, 1938–1964*, 2 vols. (1987–9); and Frederick Madden's lifetime project, *Select documents on the constitutional history of the British empire and Commonwealth*, 8 vols. (Westport, Conn.), particularly vol. VI: *The Dominions and India since 1900* (1993), vol. VII: *The dependent empire, 1900–1948: colonies, protectorates and mandates* (1994) – these two edited with John Darwin – and vol. VIII: *The end of empire: dependencies since 1948* (2000). Unfortunately, as Madden ruefully admitted in his final 'editor's note', the BDEEP project has 'to a degree made this exercise of mine irrelevant' (vol. VIII, p. xxxii). His volumes are in any case hard to use, because of the Greenwood Press's unattractive format, typography, and layout, and the density of learned technical notes and paraphrasing. Madden hoped his scheme would be completed with a ninth volume, to be edited by J. Darwin and R. Holland.

some idea of what the empire was about, and what some of the central preoccupations were during the period immediately before decline began to register. The four core chapters which follow deal with successive ministries, from Attlee to Wilson, rather than a country-by-country analysis. They are not constructed on a uniform template, but have enough flexibility to make it possible to highlight the aspects of policy and areas of concern which seem most significant in the changing phases of government. The chronological sequence of these chapters allows developments in individual territories to be seen in context, and provides a sense of accumulating problems over time. Chapter 4 draws heavily on my introduction to *The Conservative government and the end of empire, 1957–1964*, published in 2000, but now out of print. The political and constitutional (but not the economic) sections of its editorial commentary are mostly reproduced here, with additional material on Nigeria and on the departure of South Africa from the Commonwealth. The notes to it have been comprehensively revised and extended. Finally, an epilogue provides a kind of de-briefing.

Historians have offered four main options for explaining the end of empire. These may be put in the form of a cricketing analogy. Either the British were bowled out (by nationalists and freedom-fighters), or they were run out (by imperial over-stretch and economic constraints), or they retired hurt (because of a collapse of morale and 'failure of will'), or they were booed off the field (by international criticism and especially United Nations clamour). Except for unregenerate Marxists and nationalist patriots, few historians think the violent assaults of freedom-fighters were decisive or can provide a sufficient overall explanation of imperial retreat. Equally, however, few would try to write out entirely nationalist protest in the broader sense. After all, not many states got independence without asking for it. The important question perhaps is how the British government arrived at the point where they were prepared to open the door to whoever knocked. Plainly, it would be silly to ignore the implications of scarce resources and the continuing metropolitan need for financial economies. Although this motive was not much in evidence for African territories, it clearly was influential in Cyprus, in Malaysia, in the West Indies, and ultimately 'East-of-Suez', where policy was driven by the requirement for military and other cut-backs. 'Failure of will' is perhaps the weakest of the explanations; some historians even postulate periods of 'revival' for the imperial dream. More persuasive is the theory that international pressures and constraints were highly significant, even if not operating uniformly.

Ever wary of monocausal theories, most historians opt for a judicious balance or interlock of metropolitan, colonial-nationalist, and international influences ('all are important').[8] My particular angle of vision leads me to the conclusion that the international dimension was the most important of all. It may be objected that an account based mainly on British government records is likely to be skewed, and to underestimate the role of colonial nationalism. In fact, the documentary record takes us deep into the heart of complex policy-making processes, and, as has been rightly argued, it is 'certainly an authentic slice of the past, even if it is not the whole of the past'.[9] It may be conceded that this book does not explore as fully as it might the nature of nationalist movements and local politics in the colonial territories. However, this aspect of decolonisation is certainly not ignored, nor I hope misrepresented, even if it occupies the background rather than the foreground, appearing mainly as it was perceived and assessed by British decision-makers, with whom the final word lay.

Throughout I have tried to convey a sense of history made through personal agency. People make policy, so it is important to understand ministers and officials (as far as possible) as individuals with differing views – views which are also influenced by discussion and events, and may change.[10]

For their responses – uniformly courteous and candid – to enquiries, I must thank the following former government ministers and officials, all of them, alas, now dead: Lord Wilson of Rievaulx, Lord Listowel, Sir Evelyn Shuckburgh, Sir John Le Rougetel, and Ian Winchester. Four colleagues, who also count as friends, have shown me how to improve my drafts. Roger Louis, Tony Stockwell, and Tim Harper nobly read the entire typescript, and Philip Murphy brought his expertise to bear on chapter 3. They have each made significantly helpful suggestions, and

---

[8] This historiographical consensus can be seen clearly operating in the contributions to the *Oxford History of the British Empire*, vol. IV: *The twentieth century* (1999), edited by Judith M. Brown and Wm Roger Louis.

[9] H. Tinker, review of *TOPI*, vol. IX, *Times Literary Supplement* (26 Sept 1980).

[10] Some readers may be surprised to learn that, despite my book *Empire and sexuality: the British experience* (1990, 1991, 1998), I do not believe that we have to know about the private lives of politicians in order to assess their policies and performance. We all make mistakes in our private lives, and occasionally lose control of our emotions; nor are we defined by our sexuality, since sexual life belongs – or should do – to the realm of the *parergal*, that is, subsidiary to the main business of life, the recreational realm which we inhabit with characteristics often divergent from our public 'persona'. Bad decisions in the private sphere do not necessarily reflect upon our judgment, trustworthiness, and competence in the public sphere. As C. S. Lewis shrewdly observed, 'one can paddle every canoe except one's own' (*Collected letters*, vol. II: *1931–1949*, ed. W. Hooper, 2004, p. 953). The two spheres should be kept separate. This was easier in the period covered by this study, before media attention, with all its hypocrisy, infantilism, and prurience, began to insist on a vicious blurring of the dividing line between them. I give examples in the footnotes of policy-makers who in this period were lucky to escape such destructive attention.

I am most grateful to them. I should also like to record my thanks to Andrew Brown and Michael Watson at the Cambridge University Press for their support, and to Magdalene College for generous contributions towards the costs of researching and preparing this book.

R. H.

16 May 2006
Laus Deo

Abbreviations

AFPFL	Anti-Fascist People's Freedom League (Burma)
AIOC	Anglo-Iranian Oil Company
AKEL	Reform Party of Working People (Communist Party of Cyprus)
ANC	African National Congress
BDEEP	British Documents on the End of Empire Project

	IPCP:	*Imperial policy and colonial practice, 1925–1945*
	BDEEP:	*Labour government and the end of empire, 1945–1951*
	Goldsworthy:	*Conservative government and the end of empire, 1951–1957*
	CGEE:	*Conservative government and the end of empire 1957–1964*
	ESC:	*East of Suez and the Commonwealth, 1964–1971*

BP	British Petroleum
CAB	Cabinet

Codes alternate with changes of prime minister:

CP	Cabinet memoranda	Attlee/Eden/
CM	Cabinet conclusions	Douglas-Home
CC	Cabinet memoranda	Churchill/Macmillan/
C	Cabinet conclusions	Wilson

CO	Colonial Office
COS	Chiefs of Staff
CPP	Convention People's Party (Gold Coast)
CSM	Church of Scotland Mission
CRO	Commonwealth Relations Office
DO	Dominions Office
EEC	European Economic Community
EFTA	European Free Trade Area
EOKA	National Organisation of Cypriot Fighters (Greek initials)

FCO	Foreign and Commonwealth Office
FLOSY	Front for the Liberation of South Yemen (Aden)
FO	Foreign Office
GNP	Gross national product
HMG	Her Majesty's Government
ICS	Indian Civil Service
INA	Indian National Army
INM	[I]Mbokodvo National Movement (Swaziland)
JICH	*Journal of Imperial and Commonwealth History*
Leg Co.	Legislative Council
memo	memorandum
MoD	Ministry of Defence
MP	Member of Parliament
NATO	North Atlantic Treaty Organisation
NCNC	National Council of Nigeria and the Cameroons
NLF	National Liberation Front (Aden)
NNLC	Ngwane National Liberatory Congress (Swaziland)
ODNB	*Oxford Dictionary of National Biography* (2004)
OHBE	*Oxford History of the British Empire* (1999)
PD	*Parliamentary Debates* (Hansard, 5th series)
PPP	People's Progressive Party (British Guiana)
PREM	Prime Minister's Office
PRO	Public Record Office: The National Archives
QC	Queen's Counsel (KC)
SPP	Swaziland Progressive Party
T	Treasury
TANU	Tanganyika African National Union
TOPI	*Transfer of Power in India* (documents, ed. N. Mansergh *et al.*)
TUC	Trades Union Congress
UDI	Unilateral Declaration of Independence (Rhodesia)
UK	United Kingdom
UMNO	United Malays National Organisation (Malaya)
UN(O)	United Nations Organisation
US(A)	United States of America

Introduction

1. The essence of the empire

Describing the British empire at the time of Queen Victoria's jubilee in 1897, the brilliant young journalist and imperial propagandist, G. W. Steevens, declared it to be a 'world-shaping force'.[1] Steevens with these words captured the very essence of the Victorian empire, a cosmoplastic enterprise not defined by mere territorial extent, even though this was coterminous with a considerable portion of the earth's surface. The British dominance – 'Britain's imperial century', the Pax Britannica, economic and cultural hegemony – was, however, effectively over by the end of the First World War. As the 1920s opened, Britain was weaker, its rivals stronger and more worrying, its challengers more determined, its policies increasingly uncertain and confused. It had become, in short, a declining, dysfunctional empire on the road to liquidation. This was not, of course, immediately apparent. In 1927 a young professor of history at the University of Toronto concluded his lecture-course on the history of the British empire:

> It is with confidence that I look a hundred years ahead to a classroom of earnest, eager young faces, their pens moving with lightning rapidity, to catch the fleeting word, that flows from the lips of an ambitious young lecturer, who is giving a course on 'The successful solution of Britain's Imperial problems in the twentieth century'.[2]

This prediction was made by Lester Pearson, later prime minister of Canada (1963–8). However, 'success' is not a theme or prediction that history can endorse for the twentieth-century British empire.

To most British people between the 1920s and the 1950s, 'the empire' meant those outposts of colonial settlement to which relatives had migrated, the four self-governing dominions of Canada, Australia,

---

[1] R. T. Stearn, 'G. W. Steevens and the message of empire', *JICH*, vol. 17 (1989), pp. 210–31, quoting Steevens in the *Daily Mail*, 23 June 1897.
[2] I owe this quotation to Ged Martin. It comes from John English, *The shadow of heaven: the life of Lester Pearson*, vol. I: *1897–1948* (1990), p. 125.

New Zealand and South Africa. Some, who had served in the army or navy, had imperial port-cities lodged in the memory, those vital maritime nodal-points of empire and transit, like Gibraltar, Cape Town, Aden, Bombay, Singapore, and Hong Kong. Even the most cynical can hardly have failed to be stirred by the sight of the Union Jack flying over the Rock of Gibraltar, or, at the opposite end of the world, to be amazed at relieving himself against the familiar porcelain fittings of 'Doultons of London' in the lavatories of the Seamen's Club of Shanghai, long after the portraits on the wall had been changed to those of Mao Tse-tung in 1949. Some were acquainted with Port Said and Cairo (headquarters of the British Middle East Command throughout the Second World War), and therefore with Egyptian brothels and bazaars and – in the words of G. W. Steevens – their 'incessant cries of "baksheesh, baksheesh", the national anthem of Egypt'.[3] There was no particular enthusiasm for empire in Britain,[4] still less for Egyptians. The Wembley Exhibition of 1924, which

---

[3] Stearn, 'G. W. Steevens', p. 219.

[4] The current debate about the impact of empire on British society is between 'integralists' and 'minimalists'. The 'integralists' include a whole phalanx of recent 'post-colonialist' writers who think Britain was 'steeped', 'saturated', even 'imbricated' (really?) in 'imperialism', that empire played an integral part in values, thoughts and ideas. John MacKenzie also propagates the view that imperial resonances and paraphernalia mattered and were ubiquitous in mid-twentieth-century Britain: see, for example, his euphoric chapter, 'The popular culture of empire in Britain', in J. M. Brown and W. R. Louis, eds., *The Oxford History of the British Empire*, vol. IV: *The twentieth century* (1999), pp. 212–31. David Cannadine lends some cautious support to MacKenzie, recalling 'An imperial childhood?' (*Ornamentalism: how the British saw their empire* (2001), pp. 181–99). A powerfully devastating attack on the 'integralists' has been launched by Bernard Porter, *The absent-minded imperialists: empire, society and culture in Britain* (2004). Porter has examined hundreds of magazines, memoirs, and school textbooks to establish 'what the British really thought about empire', and concludes, with scholarly caveats, that they were 'relatively unaffected'. This is certainly in line with what intelligent contemporaries always said was the case. Noel Annan, for example, writes that 'the country had always been bored with the empire: on this matter a gulf yawned between the mass of the population and the ruling class. There were few imperialists among Our Age' (*Our age: portrait of a generation* (1990), p. 32; Annan was born in 1916). Then there is R. G. Casey: 'I do not believe that the Empire or the Commonwealth has ever in the past aroused any broad-based emotional enthusiasm among the people of Britain, high or low' (*The future of the Commonwealth* (1963), p. 85). If I may add a personal comment it would be this: empire was important to those families who made a career or a living out of it. Otherwise it was merely accepted (and not widely questioned until the trauma of the Suez Crisis in 1956). Red on the class-room wall-map was not a source of pride, merely a fact, as neutral as blue for the sea and brown for the mountains. Much of what might seem enthusiasm for empire was in reality no more than enthusiasm for the monarchy, which always had a starring role in any 'imperial' ceremonial. With a memory that goes back to 1939, I can recall nothing which would suggest that the empire permeated the general consciousness. Or to put it another way, I believe that Porter has enabled those who believe the impact was minimal to win the argument. Meanwhile, for a calm and thoughtful discussion of 'imperial identity', see P. J. Marshall, 'Imperial Britain', in Marshall, ed., *The Cambridge illustrated history of the British Empire* (Cambridge, 1996), pp. 318–37.

was meant to celebrate it, did little to increase awareness: 'I've brought you here to see the wonders of the empire', says one of Noel Coward's characters, 'and all you want to do is go on the dodgems.'[5] The Queen's doll's house (designed by Sir Edwin Lutyens) also attracted the Wembley crowds. Few people in the 1940s could have named any 'empire' figures except Gandhi, famous for his skeletal appearance, and Don Bradman, the Australian batsman, knighted in 1949. But there was so much more to the empire than most Britons knew.

The empire – Kipling's 'dominion over palm and pine' – was a global mosaic of almost ungraspable complexity and staggering contrasts. At one end of the scale there was India, an ancient civilisation and an empire in its own right, where the British ruled grandly, *Leviathan Indicus*, as heirs to the Mughals.[6] At the other end, there was Pitcairn, remote and tiny, 1.75 square miles in extent, with a peak population of 233 in 1937, descendants of eighteenth-century mutineers. There were great capitals like neo-classical Calcutta (not at all deserving without qualification of its epithet as 'the arsehole of the world') and twentieth-century New Delhi; and sleepy, dusty ones like Maseru in Basutoland, with its single-storey buildings and tin roofs; or, in another variation, Jamaica's Kingston, rebuilt entirely of reinforced concrete after the terrible earthquake of 1907. Some countries were dauntingly big artificial complexes like Nigeria, 350,000 square miles, made up of hundreds of 'tribes', each with its own language, animists in religion, of elegant Muslim emirs in the north, and entrepreneurial Ibos in the south, and, in between, minuscule clans lost deep in rain-forests.[7] By contrast, Gambia was little more than the banks of a 200-mile stretch of river, embedded in French Senegal. One quarter of Nyasaland was a lake, while British Guiana was held in the embrace of four mighty rivers, with spectacular rapids and falls. Fiji was made up of 844 islands, about one hundred of them permanently inhabited. There was, perhaps, a certain uniformity about the scatters of lush tropical islands. Few were large enough to be profitable economically, yet small enough to be manageable politically. Ceylon (Sri Lanka, 'Taprobane') headed the list, moulded into what the British regarded as a model colony. Coffee had been introduced and failed, but then came cocoa, tea, and rubber, so there were hundreds of thousands of acres in

---

[5] Quoted in J. Morris, *Farewell the trumpets: an imperial retreat* (1978), p. 302, and Porter, *The absent-minded imperialists*, p. 265.

[6] J. S. Furnivall, *The fashioning of Leviathan: the beginnings of British rule in Burma* (Canberra, 1991), repr. from *Journal of Burma Research Society*, vol. 29 (1939), p. 2.

[7] Readers will recognise here echoes of Morris, *Farewell the trumpets*: they are inevitable and I make no apology for them. Further inspiration is derived from the FCO's *Yearbook of the Commonwealth* (1980, etc.).

plantation estates – cocoa pleasant to behold (rather like olive trees), rubber growing in majestic avenues (rather like young birches), and tea, its bushes of too-vivid green (and about as attractive visually as a field of cabbages). Politically Ceylon had an anglicised elite almost sycophantic in its attitude to foreign overlords: a famous instance was the naming of Solomon W. R. D. Bandaranaike, prime minister (1956–9), who inherited from his father a biblical forename, combined with a Singhalese surname, 'West Ridgeway', after the governor at the time of his birth in 1899 (Sir Joseph West Ridgeway), and 'Dias' from the era of Portuguese rule.

Britain left its mark in ways great and small. Bombay boasted the finest swathe of Victorian buildings anywhere, including the high court, secretariat, university, museum, and culminating in the breathtaking railway terminus. But there were tiny barren outcrops like Tristan da Cunha (in the South Atlantic) and Perim (near the Red Sea), which had little to boast about. Tristan kept its spirits up with a Golf Club, though it was only a one-hole affair, while Perim designated an area as 'the racecourse', though it was never raced on by anything. In Palestine and elsewhere, they rode in hunting-pink after jackals instead of foxes. There were countries with thousands of miles of railway (India pre-eminently), but Basutoland with just three-quarters of a mile, and some without even that, such as Cyprus, the Bahamas, and British Honduras. Nevertheless, railways were an emblematic source of pride, with some remarkable technological achievements. The line in the hill country near Kandy in Ceylon wound round with a bridge over itself. In Kenya the gradients of the Rift Valley were ingeniously conquered. The line connecting the two Rhodesias crossed the Zambesi within range of the spray from the Victoria Falls. It was no doubt symptomatic that there was no uniform imperial gauge. Even the Australian colonies built to three different ones, which meant five changes of train between Perth and Brisbane, and no through-train between Sydney and Melbourne until 1965.

The British milled about the world in all their multifarious guises: fresh-faced district officers, hymn-singing missionaries, eccentric engineers, elegant diplomats, drunken sailors. Atmospheres varied enormously. Not everywhere thrived. Newfoundland sank into a strange depression, its community of fishermen and loggers mired in sectarian strife and vestry corruption. It became a 'dead dominion' when in 1937 Britain withdrew self-government and put the receivers in, the only failure of the British people to govern themselves. On the other hand, there were buzzing commercial centres like Shanghai and Hong Kong, where a private firm, Jardine, Mathieson, employed 113,000 people (more than the strength of the Royal Navy), but also capital cities where next to nothing happened – Belize, perhaps. Many colonies had a cosmopolitan mix, and few were as homogeneous as Basutoland. Malaya was genuinely multi-racial: European civil servants and estate managers, Malayo-Muslim farmers and fishermen, Indian rubber-tappers, Chinese tin-miners, Japanese prostitutes. There were places where Europeans could sleep with the natives, like Sarawak and the Solomon Islands, and places where they most definitely could not, like Simla and Salisbury.

Inheritances, jurisdictions and functions were bewildering in their variety and strangeness. In India, there was a parallel administration, with some 560 princely states left largely to their own devices and desires, ruling one-fifth of the population: half-a-dozen considerable states, including Hyderabad and Kashmir, but some minute and insignificant. Northern Nigeria in the early nineteenth century had been the site of a sophisticated empire, the Sokoto caliphate, a reformist jihad state expanding to control 180,000 square miles, ruled by a family triumvirate of warrior-scholars who between them are said to have written 250 books in Arabic. Their descendants were treated with respect by the British; the great-great-grandson of the founder of Sokoto became premier of the Northern Region of Nigeria. Elsewhere there were protectorates and paramountcies, League of Nations mandates, plantation economies and fortress colonies, military bases and cantonments, entrepots and coaling-stations, spheres of influence, treaty-ports and consulates,[8] enclaves and extra-territoriality privileges (in China until 1943). Structures of government were equally varied. The administration of the New Hebrides was shared with France, and the Sudan, in theory, with Egypt; the 'Anglo-Egyptian Sudan' had its own separate Political Service. The military administration of the Palestine Mandate started off with 'a cashier from a bank in Rangoon, an actor-manager, two assistants from Thomas Cook, a picture-dealer, an army coach, a land valuer, a bo'sun from the Niger, a Glasgow distiller, an organist, an Alexandria cotton-broker, an architect, a junior service London postal official, a taxi-driver from Egypt, two schoolmasters, and a missionary'.[9] Of course some of their skills were useful, but by any standard they were a rum lot. Hong Kong was reckoned

---

[8] A fifth of consulates were in China, twenty in number. T. A. Dunlop, inspector-general of consulates, told the FO in 1937 that consuls wore out quicker in China than anywhere else: in twenty-five years, eight had died in their posts, three had committed suicide, four had retired for health reasons and died shortly afterwards, three were certified insane and confined to asylums, four were invalided out, ten were compulsorily retired for 'eccentricity' (including two who had married Chinese women), one was killed in a motor accident, and nine resigned (S. L. Endicott, *Diplomacy and enterprise: British China policy, 1933–1937* (1975), p. 5).

[9] Ronald Storrs (governor of Jerusalem), *Orientations* (1943, 1945), p. 375; quoted in T. Segev, *One Palestine, complete: Jews and Arabs under the British Mandate* (transl. H. Watzman, 2000, 2001), p. 62.

Illustration 1 Sir Charles Vyner Brooke, 3rd 'white raja' of Sarawak, 1917–46. The portrait was painted by Margaret Noble in 1938 and hangs in Magdalene College, where he was an undergraduate, mid-1890s.

to be ruled by the Jockey Club, Jardine, Mathieson, the Hongkong and Shanghai Banking Corporation (HSBC), and the governor – in that order. The Bahamas, essentially a playground for American tourists, were governed during the Second World War by an ex-king, the duke of Windsor. In Dubai, even into the 1960s, the 'political agent' to the Trucial States was like an oriental potentate, ruling as a sheikh in all but name.[10] There was a 'white raja' in Sarawak, where 'Brooke rule' was in

[10] See the astonishing description by A. J. M. Craig, the political agent to the Trucial States (now the United Arab Emirates), 27 September 1963, in S. R. Ashton and W. R. Louis, eds., *East of Suez and the Commonwealth, 1964–1971* (BDEEP, 2004), pt 1, pp. 395–7 (document no. 116).

effect a sub-contracted private dynasty until after the Second World War. The raja of the third generation, Sir Charles Vyner Brooke (ruling from 1917 to 1946), described himself in *Who's Who* as having 'led several expeditions into the far interior of the country to punish head-hunters; understands the management of natives'; while his wife cruelly wrote that 'he made love just as he played golf – in a nervous unimaginative flurry'. Brooke rule was undoubtedly eccentric, but not without a certain conservative altruism, and a genuine concern for the populace.[11] A rather smaller private fiefdom was the Cocos (Keeling) Islands in the Indian Ocean, granted by Queen Victoria in 1886 to John Clunies Ross and his heirs and successors in perpetuity: Ross was a Scottish pirate who as a young man had in dubious circumstances landed several boatloads of Malay seamen on the main coral atoll. The supervising authority was successively the government of Ceylon, Straits Settlements, Singapore, and finally, from 1955, the government of Australia, which eventually bought out most of the family's interests.

The Brookes and the Rosses kept themselves to themselves. By contrast, among the more rabid advocates of white settlement there were outrageous speculative ambitions: for Southern Rhodesia as a white 'fifth dominion' (despite Europeans being outnumbered 25:1 by blacks), for Argentina as the 'sixth' (often regarded as the leading component of 'informal empire', never under the flag), and even for Palestine as 'the seventh dominion'.

The empire, according to Lord Macaulay in 1833, was 'a pacific triumph of reason over barbarism', and there would be 'an empire exempt from all natural causes of decay . . . an imperishable empire of our arts and our morals, our literature and our laws'.[12] The rule of law was certainly a most important legacy, literacy too. Later generations saw an ecological empire, of wheat and daisies, of rubber, cocoa, bananas, maize, and cotton transplanted across continents. Sheep were introduced into New Zealand, and, less happily, rabbits into Australia. There was an empire of sport: everywhere there was football and cricket, horse-racing and golf. The empire was a web of submarine cables (according to Kipling), supplemented by wireless, telegraphs, and shipping. The empire might become 'an empire of the air', as Imperial Airways (the forerunner of British Airways) struggled to get dominion of the skies in

---

[11] Sylvia, Lady Brooke, *Queen of the head-hunters: autobiography* (1970), pp. 134–5. For Vyner Brooke as 'an unwilling raja', see *ODNB*, vol. VII, pp. 916–17 (by R. H. W. Reece). For contrasting views on Brooke rule in the twentieth century, see R. Pringle, *Rajahs and rebels: the Ibans of Sarawak under Brooke rule, 1841–1941* (1970), pp. 331–49 (critical) and Ooi Keat Gin, *Of free trade and native interests: the economic development of Sarawak, 1841–1941* (Singapore, 1997) (rather more favourable).

[12] *PD, Commons, Hansard* 3rd series, vol. 19, c. 536, 10 July 1833: the final words of the peroration of his great speech on the East India Company's Charter.

the interwar period. The empire was a set of prostitution-networks.[13] The empire was a great Muslim power. The empire was a great Christian domain, embracing the world-wide Protestant missionary movement, and the Anglican Communion,[14] within which 'the voice of prayer is never silent/Nor dies the strain of praise away' (though Roman Catholics predominated in Dominica and Trinidad, claimed three-quarters of the population of Gibraltar, 95 per cent in Malta, and 99 per cent in St Lucia). The Anglican Bishop of Gibraltar had a diocese which extended from the Portuguese Atlantic to the Caspian Sea; the pope was said to be one of his parishioners.

Perhaps above all else, the empire was a field of migration, abounding in diasporas. There were Scots in the Falkland Islands, Welsh in Patagonia, Irish in Australia (27 per cent of the population by 1900), Arabs around the Indian Ocean, Chinese in British Columbia. The empire spread Indian communities into fifty-three countries, often there originally with indentured labour contracts, brought into exploit tropical resources: sugar, cotton, tea, rubber, tin, and guano. By 1921, 2.5 million Indians lived in other parts of the empire, about 4 million by 1947, and this despite the ending of indentured labour in 1917. They accounted for 12 per cent of the population of Ceylon, 3 per cent of South Africa (mostly in Natal), 35 per cent of Trinidad, 42 per cent of British Guiana, 47 per cent of Fiji, nearly 70 per cent of Mauritius. There were also hundreds of thousands of Indians in Burma and Malaya, a significant presence in Jamaica, Kenya, Uganda, Tanganyika, and Zanzibar – and there were Gurkhas in the British army, Sikh policeman in Hong Kong, and turbaned Pathan servants in Dubai.[15] Soon there would be many thousands of South Asian shopkeepers in Britain itself.

In all these ways, and many others too, the empire had indeed been 'a world-shaping', cosmoplastic force. In some ways it continued to be so, but in the twentieth century the essential characteristic was to be dysfunction, as responsibilities simply overwhelmed it: collapsing under the pressure of its own weight, perhaps. Almost none of the plans and policies

---

[13] R. Hyam, *Empire and sexuality: the British experience* (1990, 1991, 1998), map, p. 144, or *Britain's imperial century, 1815–1914: a study of empire and expansion* (2nd or 3rd edn, 1993, 2002), p. 293.

[14] It is important to stress that missionaries did not see themselves as *agents* of empire, but as frequently criticising it and trying to dissociate themselves from it; however, conversions were often enough made on the principle of assimilating to the colonial power. See Andrew N. Porter, *Religion versus empire? British Protestant missionaries, 1700–1914* (2004).

[15] H. Tinker, 'Colour and colonisation', *Round Table*, vol. 240 (1970), pp. 405–16; and *Separate and unequal: India and Indians in the British Commonwealth, 1920–1950* (1976), pp. 36, 313; Adam McKeown, 'Global migration, 1846–1940', *Journal of World History*, vol. 15 (Hawai'i, 2004), pp. 155–89.

developed after 1918 were without flaws, and several were seriously embarrassing failures.

Symptomatic – and at the highest level of planned action – was the failure of the geopolitical blue-print for a final tidying up of the map of empire (or a post-imperial configuration). As envisaged by the Colonial Office (CO) after 1909, there would be a series of regional federal units: a 'great American group' led by Canada, absorbing Newfoundland and the West Indies; a 'great Pacific group' headed by Australia and New Zealand, with responsibility for the islands of Polynesia and Micronesia; and a 'great African group', with the South African state expanding to include Basutoland, Bechuanaland, Swaziland, Southern Rhodesia, and perhaps Northern Rhodesia and Nyasaland, and maybe even Kenya.[16] An East African federation was another possibility: Sir Herbert Baker built a grand house suitable for a governor-general in Nairobi. In South-East Asia, North Borneo (Sabah), Sarawak, Brunei, and Singapore could be brought into a Greater Malaya, an idea first suggested in the CO in 1892.[17] Talks were held in 1884–5, 1911–12, and 1919 about a possible Canadian–West Indian union; a royal commission had been set up in 1910 under Lord Balfour of Burleigh to investigate a closer trading relationship. Canada, however, lost interest in the political project.[18] Some Pacific Islands were ruled from Australia (Papua New Guinea and Norfolk Island), and New Zealand (the Cook Islands, Samoa, and Niue), but both showed a marked reluctance to acquire further responsibilities (see below, p. 315). South Africa was increasingly distrusted from the later 1920s, so that part of the blue-print also collapsed, and when a Central African Federation was eventually set up (1953) the intention was mainly to block South African expansion. A West Indies Federation came briefly into being (1958) but soon broke up. A Malaysian Federation (1963) had to defend itself against external aggression from Indonesia, and Singapore quickly seceded, while resentment continued to fester in Sabah and Sarawak.

Despite all the official hopes naively vested in the theoretical rationality and convenience of 'the federal panacea', the truth is that federations have to evolve organically, and require positively dynamic local pressures to stand any chance. The failure rate is very high. They remain one of the more spectacular imperial mirages.

---

[16] *PD, Lords* vol. 2, c. 767, 27 July 1909, speech by Lord Crewe on the Union of South Africa Act; R. Hyam, *The failure of South African expansion, 1908–1948* (1972), p. 2.

[17] Jagjit Singh Sidhu, *Administration in the Federated Malay States, 1896–1920* (Kuala Lumpur, 1980), p. 38, memo by C. P. Lucas.

[18] R. W. Winks, *Canadian–West Indian union: a forty-year minuet* (University of London Commonwealth Papers, no. 11, 1968); A. R. Stewart, 'Canadian–West Indian union, 1884–1885', *Canadian Historical Review* vol. 31 (1950), pp. 369–89.

Meanwhile, whatever simplifications might be contemplated for the future, a huge empire had to be governed. This was done with astonishingly small inputs of manpower and force. India was governed by an administrative civil service of 1,200 posts. Before 1939 the Indian army of some 200,000 men, together with a British garrison of about 60,000, kept the peace on land from Suez to Hong Kong. The police-force was exiguous – in Bihar, just a dozen constables for a hundred square miles. There were very few police in Ceylon, and outside Colombo and Kandy not a single soldier. And yet huge gatherings for the annual pearl-fisheries, or religious processions with elephants, were orderly.[19] One traveller noted of the Kandy *perahera*: 'It is a wonderful sight: for me the most wonderful part of it is the crowd. I have never seen such a happy and considerate crowd.'[20] There was in the empire widespread traditional respect for government officials, whether alien or not, and perhaps particularly if actual conquerors. This acquiescence was striking. In the 1880s, and for long after, 'not a dog wags his tail against us among these 260 millions of Indians'.[21] In the Gilbert Islands, their most famous governor wrote: it was the 'natives' not 'the officials who were the truly intransigent imperialists in that part of the world'. But as he rightly noted, it was 'the greatness of the men, not of the system'.[22] That the empire functioned at all was mainly because hundreds of individual colonial officers did their often lonely jobs faithfully, fairly, and humanely.

Generalisation about the nature of the imperial administrative elite, post-1918, is difficult, for individuals varied in their temperamental approaches. It has been claimed that they were all 'prisoners of the values they absorbed in youth',[23] but this seems to allow too little for learning through experience. Service in India and the colonial empire often ran in families through the generations; a proper prosopography awaits its compilation.[24] Perhaps it is remarkable that of those who rose to be colonial governors, almost a third of them had fathers who were Anglican clergy.[25] And there seems no denying that the generic district officer was usually

[19] Leonard Woolf, *Growing: an autobiography of the years 1904–1911* (1961), pp. 92–3, 135.
[20] R. Raven-Hart, *Ceylon: history in stone* (Colombo, 1964, 1973), p. 266.
[21] H. A. L. Fisher, *James Bryce* (1927), vol. I, p. 270 (1889); Bryce went on to complain that it was very different in Ireland.
[22] Arthur Grimble, *Return to the islands* (1957), pp. 153, 211–15.
[23] C. Dewey, *Anglo-Indian attitudes: the mind of the Indian Civil Service* (1994), presents a contrast between F. L. Brayne, an evangelical with doctrinaire insistence on self-help, and Sir Malcolm Darling, more worldly, and sympathetic.
[24] Kirk-Greene, *British imperial administrators*, p. 100; Porter, *Absent-minded imperialists*, p. 43.
[25] I. F. Nicolson and C. A. Hughes, 'A provenance of proconsuls: British colonial governors, 1900–1960', *JICH*, vol. 4 (1975).

a practitioner of the public-school code and cultural ethos, even though not always from a public school. The admired characteristics in the formation of a self-confident *esprit de corps* were 'go and grit', 'stiff upper lip', loyalty to the system, monogamous sexual restraint (if not total sexual denial), 'straightforward dogged perseverance', combined with common sense, pluck, and 'moral strength'.[26] These district officers regarded themselves as protectors, and the prevention of injustice as their primary task. In many ways they did form a distinct middle-class club, mostly graduates (though seldom with good degrees). They had to look the part, and have a firm handshake. Probably a majority of them were circumcised.[27] Recruitment interviewing was not searching, but based on forming an impression about character. When Arthur Tedder was interviewed in the CO for a colonial service cadetship in 1913, two officials sat behind large desks in the same room, 'each interviewing a victim'. Both were obviously 'university men'. Interviewer A asked mostly about health and whether the candidate 'could swim, shoot, walk far, etc., etc.'. After an interval of about five minutes, A handed over to B, having given his impressions to the second interviewer, and B engaged in 'mostly general chat' ('why do you want to join the colonial service?').[28] The famous Ralph Furse controlled interviewing as director of recruitment for the whole of the critical period from 1931 to 1948, ensuring agreed standards of judgment.

Colonial Service officers were not well-trained in the formal sense. Even the Cambridge Colonial Service courses were distinctly amateurish, a secondary chore for the lecturers, and seldom taken seriously by the cadets. Partly for this reason government on the ground was a haphazard business, but on the whole it did what was necessary in terms of keeping the peace. Critics of the system pointed to the lack of much sense of innovation or entrepreneurship.

---

[26] George Orwell, *Burmese days* (1934); S. Orwell and I. Angus, eds., *The collected essays, journalism and letters of George Orwell* (1968), vol. I, pp. 239, 288, 393, 403.

[27] A. H. M. Kirk-Greene, *Britain's imperial administrators, 1858–1966* (2000), esp. pp. 11–12; Ashley Jackson, 'Governing empire: colonial memoirs', review article, *African Affairs*, vol. 103 (2004), pp. 471–92. Pioneering studies by R. Heussler now have a dated air: *Yesterday's rulers: the making of the British Colonial Service* (Syracuse, 1963) and *The British in Northern Nigeria* (1968). Heussler was confused about British social class, labelling most members of the colonial services wrongly as 'upper class' with 'aristocratic' values (they were upper-*middle* class). He also failed to tackle properly issues of sexual behaviour, even in the rich field of Malaya (*British rule in Malaya: the Malayan Civil Service and its predecessors, 1867–1942* (1981)), despite having collected evidence, which T. N. Harper has located, he tells me, in the Heussler Papers in Rhodes House, Oxford.

[28] A. W. Tedder to his future wife, Rosalind MacLardy, 18 November 1913 (Magdalene College Archives, F/OMP/X).

What gave a degree of coherence to the management of the empire was its oversight by officials in Whitehall, though several government departments were involved and they sometimes differed among themselves: principally, the Colonial Office, the Dominions Office (renamed the Commonwealth Relations Office in 1947) and the Foreign Office (FO).[29] The mandarins of the civil service could sometimes determine main lines of policy, and they made possible a strong element of continuity of policy through changes of government. This is one of the central themes of this book. Politicians came and went, and were allocated portfolios almost haphazardly; in any case, 'a career in politics is no preparation for government'.[30] Few ministers ever drafted the papers issued in their name, and they depended heavily on the expert advice of their permanent staff, an expertise partly inherited from a previous generation, but also built up through long experience. The FO had a persistent elitist tradition, with a conservative understanding of what constituted 'the national interest'. Even a strong minister like Ernest Bevin did not challenge this.[31] Though it would be wrong to postulate a monolithic 'official mind', nevertheless certain broad principles were generally subscribed to, and gave imperial administration its overall character, detectably similar over decades.

2. The futility and the irony

Evidence of the dysfunctional nature of the empire after 1918 will emerge in these pages. There were many mistaken policies, and control was gradually beginning to slip away. To set the scene, five flawed projects are considered, into which a great deal of effort was poured, ultimately in most cases to no enduring purpose. The five are: Indirect Rule, a white man's country, an imperial palace, an international language, and the 'special relationship' with the USA. 'Indirect Rule' was the widely preferred method of imperial administration, but had to be abandoned

---

[29] R. Hyam, 'Bureaucracy and "trusteeship" in the colonial empire', in Brown and Louis, *Oxford History of the British Empire*, vol. IV. *Twentieth Century*, pp. 255–79.

[30] J. Lynn and A. Jay, *The complete 'Yes minister': the diaries of a Cabinet minister, by the Rt Hon James Hacker, MP* (rev. edn, 1984), p. 30; see also pp. 336–7, where 'Sir Bernard Woolley' reflects that governments have at the very most two years (in a five-year parliament) for serious activity, between an initial eighteen months learning ('especially that electoral commitments cannot be kept'), and a final eighteen months running up to the next election – 'this gave us [the officials] the maximum freedom from control by Ministers, who, if they stayed too long in office, were likely to begin to think that they knew how to run the country!'

[31] J. Saville, *The politics of continuity: British foreign policy and the Labour government, 1945–1946* (1993), pp. 10–40; Raymond Smith, 'Introduction' to J. Zametica, ed., *British officials and British foreign policy, 1945–1950* (Leicester, 1990), pp. 4–5.

in the 1940s for failing to meet modern requirements. The idea that Kenya, despite its black majority, might become a 'white man's country' was an exotic fantasy that fizzled out. A new imperial city at Delhi and a palace for the viceroy came too late to be of much use, and the latter was in any case a grand conception flawed in execution. The failure of the attempt in the 1930s and 1940s to establish a simplified form of English ('Basic') as an international medium was highly ironic, granted that English in the twenty-first century has emerged as the world's dominant language. And accommodating to the emergence of the United States to world-power status was full of frustration, and by the 1960s, ironically, Britain could no longer fulfil the expectations the USA wanted to place upon it.

(1) Indirect Rule

A formidable problem was involved in governing so many places with so few trained administrators and exiguous funding. Almost nowhere was closely governed, while indigenous collaborators were everywhere essential. The full apparatus of direct rule could not be afforded, thus 'British rule in Africa between the wars was predicated on the assumption that routine tasks of local government should be delegated to "traditional" African authorities.'[32] There were never many theorists of empire, so when F. D. Lugard worked out an ideology in Nigeria he was accorded guru-like respect. 'Indirect Rule' as he formulated it meant 'ruling native peoples on native lines'. It was not a new idea, but acquired first a stricter form and ultimately a mystique. Traditional rulers in Africa were not to be treated as semi-sovereign princes in the Indian and Malayan fashion, but as integral parts of a single administration, recognised, respected, regulated. The aim was to 'maintain and develop all that is best in indigenous methods and institutions of native rule'. Native law and custom would be strengthened.[33]

Lugard was governor of Northern Nigeria (1899–1906) and of Nigeria (1912–18). He was dedicated to the empire and entered its pantheon of heroes, a little man, rather headmasterly, and under the thumb of his formidable wife, Flora Shaw, a columnist for *The Times*. In 1922 Lugard published *The dual mandate in tropical Africa*. Drawing upon some of the themes of Joseph Chamberlain, secretary of state for the colonies, 1895–1903, it enunciated the policy of 'trusteeship' with dual responsibilities

---

[32] A. D. Roberts, 'The imperial mind', in *The Cambridge History of Africa*, vol. VII: *From 1905 to 1940*, ed. A. D. Roberts (1986), pp. 49–52.
[33] M. Perham, *Lugard*, vol. II: *The years of authority, 1898–1945* (1960); *ODNB* (2004), 'Lugard, Frederick D', vol. XXXIV, pp. 727–32 (by A. H. M. Kirk-Greene).

and reciprocal benefits. Britain was to be a trustee 'to civilisation for the development of resources, to the natives for their welfare', with Indirect Rule providing for the latter.[34] The book was instantly welcomed as authoritative, offering 'at once a sop to the liberal conscience and a prod to the wavering imperialists'. But as he sought 'to conserve African civilisation, all the more vigorous of the Africans did their best to escape it',[35] noting the statement that 'complete independence is not as yet visible on the horizon of time'.[36] Yet for all its limitations, *The dual mandate* was an epoch-making book, influential far beyond Africa. With it, said Sir Arthur Grimble, a governor in the South Pacific islands, 'the Heaven-born Big-White-Master theory of colonial administration began to crack up'.[37]

Indirect Rule started out as an expedient in Northern Nigeria. It was applied to Western Nigeria in 1916, next in Tanganyika (by Sir Donald Cameron, and to over 400 authorities), then to Eastern Nigeria, Sierra Leone, Northern Rhodesia, Nyasaland, Ashanti, the Northern territories of the Gold Coast, and Sudan. In the 1930s, the CO was generally encouraging governors to introduce the system. It seemed an ideal solution: a sensible, moderate, generous-spirited compromise, intellectually and morally defensible, economical and inevitable – in a word, highly plausible.[38] To some advocates, it seemed obvious that most Africans would prefer to be even indifferently governed by their own chiefs than well-governed by an alien race.[39] In any case, 'where would lie the moral justice, let alone the purely political expediency, of sweeping away the rule of the natural rulers of a country?' (E. D. Morel.)[40] African types of government were incorporated into imperial administration without too much anxiety. These were seen as 'rural' styles of government, which fitted in well with interwar British romantic myths about the superiority of 'countryside' over industrialised cities, the idealisation of rustic values common to the prime ministers of the 1920s, to both Stanley Baldwin on the right and Ramsay MacDonald on the left.[41] Indirect Rule also had its

---

[34] F. D. Lugard, *The dual mandate in tropical Africa* (1922, 2nd edn 1929), p. 391.

[35] Morris, *Farewell the trumpets*, pp. 386–90.   [36] Lugard, *Dual mandate*, p. 198.

[37] Grimble, *Return to the islands*, p. 209.

[38] Two of the best discussions of early Indirect Rule are: J. E. Flint, 'Nigeria: the colonial experience, 1800–1914', in L. H. Gann and P. Duignan, eds., *Colonialism in Africa, 1870–1960*, vol. I: *History and politics of colonialism* (Cambridge 1969), esp. pp. 250–2, and M. Bull, 'Indirect Rule in Northern Nigeria, 1906–1911', in K. Robinson and A. F. Madden, eds., *Essays in imperial government presented to Margery Perham* (1963), pp. 47–87.

[39] C. W. Orr, *The making of Northern Nigeria* (1911), pp. 214, 229.

[40] E. D. Morel, *Nigeria: its peoples and problems* (2nd edn 1912), p. 139.

[41] Roberts, 'The imperial mind', pp. 49–52; M. J. Wiener, *English culture and the decline of industrial spirit, 1850–1950* (1981).

affinities with prefectorial systems in British public schools, concurrently being copied in state grammar schools. Lugard was conscious of the analogy, hoping chiefs would acquire public-schoolboy ideas of 'team spirit' and responsibility, of 'playing the game'.[42]

There were fatal flaws in the system. The first was that Africa had a baffling dispersal of authority. Societies which were acephalous – that is, stateless, uncentralised, minimalist and without a single head, mostly Nilotic and East African – cohered as political entities through an intermeshing of 'vertical' kin and clan allegiances, and 'horizontal' agemate-set obligations and adjudications. These societies did not need 'heads' in order to work, but head-men were essential in the Indirect Rule chain of command. Chiefs had to be created through 'invented tradition'. Unsuitable characters often emerged. The process of searching for chiefs was sometimes little short of ludicrous. For the Galla (of eastern Kenya) in 1925, two out of four designated chiefs were not Galla but former Galla slaves, one from Nyasaland, one a Kamba.[43]

But there was another flaw too. From the beginning, the motto of Indirect Rule was '*festina lente*', reflecting the assumption that Africans disliked being hurried and hustled. It assumed a static situation. It assumed 'that we had an indefinite time ahead during which the system could grow and develop under our guidance'.[44] It was designed to deal with people under tribal conditions. It was not concerned with towns. It was not concerned with nation-building. It was designed to facilitate control rather than constructive change, law and order rather than effective modernisation. It was assumed there would be few changes, just the abolition of slavery and the collection of tax. It focused 'too much on the experience of the past and too little on the exigencies of the future'.[45] In significant ways it was an evasion rather than a policy, an uncertainty principle. It relied too much on the personality and efficiency of the chief. As traditional authorities were increasingly weakened by 'detribalisation', it became ever more apparent that at the heart of Indirect Rule was a serious miscalculation as to with whom the future was to lie. The British backed the wrong horse by preferring strong traditional authorities, and snubbing the newly emerging Western-educated elites, seen as unrepresentative, self-seeking agitators. This was the final irony in an imperial ideology once lauded as so finely attuned to the dual needs of African peoples and European rulers.

---

[42] Lugard, *Dual mandate*, p. 132.
[43] J. Middleton, 'Kenya: changes in African life, 1912–1945', in V. T. Harlow and E. M. Chilver, eds., *History of East Africa*, vol. II (1965), p. 350.
[44] *Dual mandate*, p. 199; A. B. Cohen, *British policy in changing Africa* (1959), pp. 22–8.
[45] R. Hyam, ed., *The Labour government and the end of empire, 1945–1951* (BDEEP, 1992), pt 2, pp. 153–7 (no. 49), memo by R. E. Robinson, 1947.

(2) A white man's country

Having by 1908 formally secured the reservation of the 'white highlands' of Kenya to European settlement, the settlers there had notions of obtaining self-government. They were frustrated not just by Indian counter-claims, but by the commitment of the imperial government to trusteeship for the African majority.

Kenya lies astride the equator. Most of its population lives on the high plateau of the south-western quarter. The Africans consist of four main groups: Bantu (such as the Kikuyu), Nilotic (Luo), Nilo-Hamitic (Masai, Nandi, Kipsigis), and Hamitic (Somali). Of these the Kikuyu and Luo are numerically the largest (about 2.2 million and 1.5 million respectively at the time of independence). Agricultural peoples like the Kikuyu tended to be less resistant to cultural change than the conservative pastoral societies, especially proud nomads like the Masai. Both the Bantu and the Nilotics valued cattle highly, but the pastoralists had a much deeper cattle-focus to economic life, and a more uncompromising resistance to European influence. Cattle possession was not merely a source of food, but a form and measure of wealth, the ritual medium (through sacrifice) for ensuring ancestral goodwill, the means of obtaining wives and ratifying marriage, as well as a prized source of aesthetic pleasure and essential subject of men's conversation. Cattle were so important that any man with ten head could be considered 'poor', and a man with none was 'dead' (in much the same way as a Christian without 'charity' is 'counted dead before Thee').[46]

These Africans had suffered grievously in the ecological catastrophe of the 1890s. The rinderpest (cattle-plague) pandemic brought a whole complex and interwoven religio-socio-political-cultural edifice crashing down amid hideous cattle-lowing and deathly stench.[47] This disaster was followed by droughts, famines, sleeping sickness, and smallpox, all of which together took a dreadful toll of life – anything up to 50 per cent. The consequence was exhaustion and a certain weary resignation which facilitated European conquest. When Europeans took the land, many Africans affected not to regard it as permanent alienation, but the sense that their old gods had failed them provided a fertile field for Christian conversions.

Christian missions proved hard taskmasters, and very soon they were attacking the practice of clitoridectomy. This remains a deeply emotive subject.[48] As the counterpart of male circumcision, it can be seen as an

---

[46] H. K. Schneider, 'Pakot resistance to change', in W. R. Bascom and M. J. Herskovits, eds., *Continuity and change in African cultures* (Chicago, 1959), pp. 144–67.
[47] P. Phoofolo, 'The Rinderpest pandemic in late 19th-century Africa', *Past & Present*, no. 138 (1993), pp. 112–43.   [48] Hyam, *Empire and sexuality*, pp. 189–97.

act of gender differentiation, even of cosmetic surgery ('done for beauty and cleanliness'), but it was also a patriarchal attempt to control female sexuality by reducing the sensitivity of the woman's sexual response. Its sociological functions were profound. Without circumcision women were not adult and not members of society, and therefore not able to marry, nor own property, nor take public office. Circumcision was the focal point of initiation ceremonies, and all initiation ceremonies were integral mechanisms for the assertion of tribal unity and loyalty, the most important of all traditional customs. By about 1915 the Protestant missions had decided that clitoridectomy was the 'sexual mutilation of women', undesirable on medical and moral grounds. (The Catholics more sensibly decided to leave it alone.) A confrontation was forced by the Church of Scotland Mission (CSM) in 1929, barring the attendance at their schools of children whose parents did not denounce it, and sacking teachers who subscribed to it. The reaction, directed chiefly by the emergent Kikuyu Central Association, was angry. Early in 1930 an elderly missionary, Hulda Stumpf (not from the CSM) died as a result of rape, forcible circumcision, and mutilation. The British government thought the missions had been foolish, and was determined not to over-react. The missionary campaign was a failure. Devotion to the practice probably increased. By the 1960s 90 per cent of the women of rural Kenya were still being circumcised. The campaign was not only counterproductive, but had far-reaching political consequences. More independent schools and separatist churches were founded, and the former became a focus of Kikuyu political activity for the next twenty years. Clitoridectomy became a spur to politics. As the Kikuyu spokesman Kenyatta wrote: 'The overwhelming majority of Gikuyu believe that it is the secret aim of those who attack this centuries-old custom to disintegrate their social order and thereby hasten their Europeanisation.'[49] Kenyatta was expelled from the CSM, and later became president of Kenya (1964–78).

The Kikuyu also had severe grievances over land. They suffered alienation between 1903 and 1909 as the 'white highlands' were occupied by European farmers. Small areas of land had been 'owned' by kin-groups, and much larger ones by non-kin-related syndicates. Under the latter system there were some twenty different interpretations of what 'land ownership' actually was and who was involved in it (ancestors might be included, who would have to be consulted), so it was not clear precisely who had lost what to the Europeans. Ferocious conflicts resulted.[50]

[49] Jomo Kenyatta, *Facing Mount Kenya: the tribal life of the Gikuyu* (1938), pp. 130–5.
[50] Greet Kershaw, *Mau Mau from below* (1997); M. P. K. Sorrenson, *Origins of European settlement in Kenya* (Nairobi, 1968); 'Land policy in Kenya, 1895–1945', in Harlow and Chilver, eds., *History of East Africa*, vol. II, app. I, pp. 672–89.

White settlement in Kenya owed its existence primarily to the need to pay for the Uganda Railway, built in the 1890s at a cost of £5.5 million (£9,500 a mile). Nobody was quite sure what this 'lunatic line' was for, but there were vague strategic notions about protecting the headwaters of the Nile. The railway could only be made to pay for itself by putting freight on it. But who would supply the freight? Certainly not the Nandi, who pinched the track-bolts and made them into necklaces and chopped up the telegraph-wires for earrings.[51] Only the introduction of white farmers, it seemed, could put freight on the railway. And so, to fill an economic vacuum, and against the better judgment of officials in London, the settlement of the 'white highlands' began in 1903. At first, the European community was composed mainly of migrants from Australia, New Zealand, and Canada, and above all from South Africa. A considerable number of Afrikaners trekked to Kenya after the Anglo-Boer War, settling around the town of Eldoret, in what became virtually an Afrikaner province. In 1908, 280 Boers arrived in a single week. Settlers picked up vast acreages at derisory prices. By 1920, when the total European population was about 10,000, fewer than 2,000 farmers owned 10,000 square miles between them. Nairobi was a true frontier town, where wild behaviour was explained away by the effects of high-altitude climate.[52]

'A sunny place for shady people' was how one British army officer, General Erskine, described Kenya in 1954, while the governor of the day, Sir Evelyn Baring, commented, 'The Europeans have made this country; they also make most of the trouble.'[53] Aristocrats and upper classes – the Cavendish-Bentincks and Finch-Hattons – were not the majority, but they defined the ethos, the fast living and social antics of boisterous public-school types or subalterns.[54] Hugh Cholmondeley (pronounced 'Chumley'), Lord Delamere, an old Etonian, was known as 'the uncrowned king of Kenya'. He grew his hair outrageously long, and

---

[51] M. F. Hill, *Permanent way: the story of the Kenya and Uganda Railway* (Nairobi, 2nd edn, 1961), pp. 282–3.

[52] G. Bennett, 'Settlers and politics, up to 1945', in Harlow and Chilver, *History of East Africa*, vol. II, pp. 265–332.

[53] C. Douglas-Home, *Evelyn Baring: the last proconsul* (1978), pp. 242, 271.

[54] For general background: Edward Paice, *Lost lion of empire: the life of 'Cape-to-Cairo' Grogan* (2001), pp. 196–210 (ch. 3: 'The battle-lines are drawn'); Dane Kennedy, *Islands of white: settler society and culture in Kenya and Southern Rhodesia, 1890–1939* (Duke, 1987). There are several older histories, too, the best of which is W. McGregor Ross, *Kenya from within: a short political history* (1927) – the author was director of public works, 1905–1923 and an official member of the Legislative Council, 1916–1923; his book is well documented; he criticised the 'noisy minority' of settlers; he was not sentimental about the Africans, or disaffected towards government, but recognised that injustice and oppressive policies towards the Africans were creating dangerous social unrest.

regularly shot out the street-lamps in Nairobi. Once he locked a hotel manager into his refrigerator, along with several dead sheep, for refusing to serve him more liquor. Exuberant and excessive, Delamere was also an entrepreneur extraordinary, who developed rust-resistant wheat and supported processing industries.[55] Capt. E. S. Grogan was famous for having walked from Cape-to-Cairo, carrying a union flag, after having been sent down from Jesus College Cambridge for excessive rowdiness. In Kenya he was imprisoned for a month, found guilty of taking the law into his own hands in 1907 against some Kikuyu who had jolted a rickshaw, flogging them on the steps of the Nairobi court-house itself. Grogan wanted a 'second New Zealand' here. He constantly criticised the Colonial Office as 'remote from realities' and taking insufficient notice of settler demands for constructive action. He was described as 'sexually over-engined'.[56]

Kenya was soon out of control. The settlers ridiculed governors like James Hayes Sadler (1905–09), demonstrating in 1908 outside Government House, calling for his resignation. They nicknamed him 'Flannel-Foot', joking about 'pacification by phonograph' when he tried to calm and impress Africans by playing them gramophone records.[57] His successor, Sir Percy Girouard (1909–12), disappointed the CO by falling willingly into settler clutches. Girouard decided to move all the Masai into one reserve, to make Kenya more convenient for the settlers. (He castigated the Masai for their 'extraordinary lack of any commercial instinct'.) The move began before the CO had a chance to give or refuse permission. Officials were aghast. Girouard was recalled. But it was too late to stop the Masai move.[58] By 1921–3 the settlers were openly threatening rebellion in order to prevent a common-roll electoral franchise for Indians. Many of them were prepared to defy the British government with force. Sanctions against them were considered.[59]

The Asians were the second and much larger alien community, 23,000 of them by 1920, though much divided among themselves. They had been brought in to build the railway to Uganda (which may explain the

[55] *ODNB* (2004), 'Cholmondeley, Hugh, 3rd Baron Delamere', vol. XI, pp. 508–9 (by A. Clayton); Elspeth Huxley, *White man's country: Lord Delamere and the making of Kenya* (2 vols.), vol. I: *1870–1914* (1953).

[56] Paice, *Lost lion of empire* p. 282; see also 'Grogan, Ewart S.', *ODNB*, vol. XXIV, pp. 60–1 (by R. Davenport-Hines).

[57] R. Hyam, *Elgin and Churchill at the Colonial Office, 1905–1908* (1968), pp. 405–17.

[58] CO 533/63, no. 39400; CO 533/72, no. 9075; CO 533/74, no. 22070 (1909–10).

[59] D. Wylie, 'Confrontation over Kenya: the Colonial Office and its critics, 1918–40', *Journal of African History*, vol. 18 (1970), pp. 427–47. C. P. Youé, 'The threat of settler rebellion and the imperial predicament: the denial of Indian rights in Kenya, 1923', *Canadian Journal of History*, vol. 12 (1978), pp. 347–60.

anomaly of its Indian metre-gauge instead of the more usual African 3'6"). Many remained after the expiry of their contracts. Indians began to look to Kenya as a possible area of Indian colonisation, the 'America of the Hindu' perhaps. Some Indians longed for a country to which they could emigrate without being treated as inferiors. This complicated the debate about the future of Kenya as a 'white man's country'. Was it to be, in Winston Churchill's words (speaking as secretary of state for the colonies 1921–2), 'a white daughter colony or an Asian grand-daughter colony'?[60] Was it to be the northern-most link in a chain of settlement from the Cape to Ethiopia (as South Africa's Jan Smuts dreamed), or the funnel through which an Asian horde would pour into Africa? Or was it to be designated as 'primarily an African country'? By 1921–3 the Indians were campaigning vigorously for a common-roll franchise under the slogan 'Kenya lost, everything lost.' Success for Indians in Kenya would mean even larger claims in the Indian diaspora – in British Guiana, Fiji, and Natal. Kenya thus became a testing-ground for imperial policy towards all Indians overseas.[61] The difficulty was that the settlers opposed Indian claims, and what was conceded to Indians must surely in the long run be conceded to Africans. Reconciling these conflicting interests with 'trusteeship' was an impossible task, and, however well-intentioned, successive British governments were unequal to the challenge.

But in the long run, white settlers failed to dominate Kenya, and an African government did its best to get rid of the Asians. Delamere's statue in the middle of Nairobi was pulled down and Delamere Avenue renamed in honour of Jomo Kenyatta.

(3) An imperial palace

In a rare act of repentance, the British government decided to reverse Curzon's partition of Bengal (1905: Curzon was viceroy, 1899–1905) after only six years. Viceroy Lord Hardinge (1910–16) saw it as his mission to promote the cohesion of India, and in this spirit the reversal was coupled with an announcement by the king at the coronation *durbar* in 1911 that the capital of the Raj would be moved from Calcutta to the historic Mughal capital of Delhi, where a new city would be built.[62] This would be a

---

[60] Huxley, *White man's country: Lord Delamere*, vol. I, p. 267.
[61] Tinker, *Separate and unequal*; R. G. Gregory, *India and East Africa: a history of race relations within the British empire, 1890–1939* (1971).
[62] R. J. Moore, *Liberalism and Indian politics, 1872–1922* (1966); G. Johnson, 'Partition, agitation and Congress: Bengal, 1904–1908', in J. Gallagher, G. Johnson, and A. Seal, eds., *Locality, province and nation: essays on Indian politics, 1870–1914* (Cambridge, 1973), repr. from *Modern Asian Studies*, vol. 7 (1973), pp. 213–67.

garden-city on the evolving English model, but 'imbued with the spirit of the East'. The British had not planned on this scale very often. Canberra – a compromise new capital for Australia (1901), side-stepping rivalry between Sydney and Melbourne – was designed (rather unimaginatively) by an American architect. South Africa in 1909 decided against a new city, but split capital functions between Cape Town, Pretoria, and Bloemfontein.

There was plenty of opposition to the transfer from Calcutta and to the grandiose scheme proposed for New Delhi, the centre-piece of which was to be a huge palace for the viceroy. Sir Edwin Lutyens was appointed the architect in 1913, assisted by his old friend Herbert Baker. Lutyens was known for grand country houses, while Baker had left his architectural mark on South Africa. Lutyens moved in snobbish circles and had married the daughter of a former viceroy, Lord Lytton. Baker was of different temperament: less clever, more reserved, and much more athletic. Patron for the project was in effect Viceroy Hardinge, and he was to prove difficult. The resulting clash of personalities and ideals became one of the classic conflicts of architectural history, comparable with that of Michelangelo and Pope Julius II or Sir John Vanbrugh and the Duchess of Marlborough over Blenheim. Animosity developed between the two architects. Baker was always prepared to defer to political and financial constraints. Lutyens was not. But the main cause of their falling out was a cock-up over site layout.[63]

The viceroy wanted majestic buildings but continually demanded economies. The viceroy wanted buildings of an oriental character. Lutyens was equally determined that this was out of the question. The ancient architecture of India was as far as he was concerned little more than the 'antics of adolescents', hideous barbarities, the product of 'a childish ignorance', 'with occasional flukes into great charm such as the Taj', but 'as architecture, nil', only 'a mad riot' of indiscriminate decoration, buildings deficient in sublime order, proportion, and line of beauty. Mughal pointed arches he dismissed with the argument that God had not made a pointed rainbow. His early disparagement modulated somewhat: 'East and West can and do meet, with mutual respect and affection', and he was prepared to learn. At New Delhi he fused Mughal and Hindu elements into his architectural language, and the central dome of the viceroy's palace was based on a famous Buddhist *stupa*.

---

[63] C. Hussey, *The life of Sir Edwin Lutyens* (1950: The Lutyens Memorial); G. Stamp, 'Lutyens, Edwin', *ODNB* (2004), vol. XXXIV, pp. 817–25; R. G. Irving, *Indian summer: Lutyens, Baker and imperial Delhi* (1981). There is an important essay by Jane Ridley, 'Edwin Lutyens, New Delhi, and the architecture of imperialism', in P. Burroughs and A. J. Stockwell, eds., *Managing the business of empire: essays in honour of David Fieldhouse* (1998), pp. 67–83, repr. from *JICH*, vol. 26 (1998).

The long horizontal emphasis of the palace was 'eastern', but its vertical emphasis – the classical columns – was 'western'. Conceptually this was bungalow-as-palace. It covered about 200,000 square feet, slightly more than Versailles, though not quite as much as the Palace of Westminster. There were about 285 rooms. It required 7,000 employees to service. It had twelve enclosed courtyards. There were fountains on the roof. Carpets for the three principal state-rooms were based on sixteenth-century Persian designs, woven by 500 weavers taking two years and using 7,000 miles of wool. The attached 'Mughal garden' was like a vast 'living carpet': here Lutyens created out of terraces, waterways, and sunken courts 'ten acres of brilliant mosaic compacted on intersecting canals, fountains splashing on tiers of red sandstone water-lily leaves, paved alleys, squares of lawn, plats of flowers, and geometrical groves of trees' – and a sandstone pergola.[64]

Such extravagance was bound to attract criticism. Newspaper headlines at the time of the visit of the Prince of Wales in 1922 included 'Historical Monument of Folly', 'Delhi's Ghostly Glories', and 'Marble Halls and Bad Government'. Perhaps in response, it was decided that the great building should be officially known simply as 'the viceroy's house'. It was finished at the end of 1929. It had taken eighteen years to build and cost a million pounds. New Delhi as a whole came in – over budget – at £10 million. It was officially opened two years later.

One of the subsequent complaints made about the viceroy's house and Baker's secretariat buildings was that their walls stored and reflected heat to an uncomfortable degree. This seems to have been because the way the local red sandstone was back-filled proved to be particularly absorbent of heat. Ironically, Lutyens had wanted marble cladding, which would certainly have given the requisite coolness, and he only abandoned it reluctantly under pressure. If this change was mistaken, it was as nothing compared with the tragi-comedy of the vista.

The viceroy's palace was meant to dominate the layout of New Delhi, and to be continuously visible along the central processional avenue, 800 feet wide and 2 miles long. This vista was to be the principal visual excitement of the entire conception. It was ruined by a misunderstanding between the architects over the gradient of the ascending processional avenue. It was not easy to fit a large and complex symmetrical building-pattern to an irregular physical conformation, but the intention was clear. Lutyens inadvertently put his signature to the crucial order for landscaping the gradient, without

---

[64] Hussey, *Life of Sir Edwin Lutyens*, p. 368.

checking the angle of ascent. The result was to mask the palace over a considerable part of the approach. When this became apparent, Lutyens accused Baker of deceiving him by not alerting him to the departure from the original intention. Baker said he assumed his colleague's signature meant he had no objection. Lutyens said he was entitled to assume Baker was proceeding as originally agreed, and not altering things to suit his own technical preferences for the secretariat buildings. The committee with overall responsibility for New Delhi rejected Lutyens's plea for rectification, on grounds of cost – what else? Baker refused to go to arbitration. Lutyens admitted he had made a mistake, but had done so in good faith. The effect, he told the viceroy, would be 'clumsy and ugly'. Privately his view was much less measured. This was his 'Bakerloo' and he never forgave Baker. He felt humiliated as well as betrayed, his greatest masterpiece 'spoiled by a silly slope'.[65]

Nevertheless, Lutyens had designed one of the world's finest buildings, vast, serene, imaginative, and sublime. Even Le Corbusier respected it, when coming to build his own Indian capital for the Punjab at Chandigarh. But as one of Parkinson's Laws states – or is it a pseudo-Parkinson? – institutions only acquire headquarters worthy of their function once they are already in decline.[66] It is one of the greater ironies of history that the only city with which the British, 'never distinguished for monumental conceptions', resolved to challenge the builders of Greece and Rome, should have served its intended imperial purpose for little more than a decade. After independence there was even talk of turning the viceroy's palace – the supreme temple to the British idea of empire – [67] into a medical school and museum. It is now 'Rashtrapati Bhavan', the president's house, isolated from the centres of political power.

[65] *Ibid.*, pp. 322–5, 344–58, 522.
[66] Actually, Parkinson expressed it much more elegantly: that 'a perfectly planned layout is achieved only by institutions on the point of collapse', a perfect headquarters being planned only 'when all the important work has been done'. The proof? No other example of British building 'can match in significance New Delhi': 'the stages of its progress towards completion correspond to so many steps in political collapse . . . what was achieved was no more and no less than a mausoleum' (C. Northcote Parkinson, *Parkinson's Law, or the pursuit of progress* (1958), pp. 83–94, 'Plans and plants: the administrative block'). Parkinson was Professor of History at the University of Singapore during the years 1950 to 1958. The original 'law' (published in *The Economist*, 19 November 1955) stated that 'work expands so as to fill the time available for its completion', leading to an inevitable expansion in the number of staff regardless of workload. He particularly fastened upon the example of the Colonial Office, where the number of officials more than quadrupled between 1939 and 1954 while the number of colonies was shrinking.
[67] Morris, *Farewell the trumpets*, pp. 373–80 gives, as you'd expect, a fine evocation.

(4) An international language

'Make everybody speak English' was the four-word slogan suggested by Henry Ford. A Cambridge scholar in the 1920s determined to show how it could be done. C. K. Ogden was a radical polymath who invented 'Basic English' and published his scheme in 1929. The name was a punning acronym, 'British American Scientific Industrial Commercial' English. Unlike previous failed attempts at an international language, it was not an artifical construct, but a system which reduced the 20,000 English words in common use to 850, plus a few more scientific terms. The entire list and the operational rules could be legibly printed on a sheet of notepaper 7" × 10", and because the language could be seen at a glance, Ogden (a latter-day Benthamite) sometimes called it 'panoptic'. Ogden reckoned that there were only twenty-nine languages spoken by more than ten million people, twelve of them European. He believed English was the only language sufficiently adaptable and already simplified enough to permit 'the final step', a language 'universalised by simplification'. It had a 'fundamental practicality' for his purpose of 'debabelization', while French was too nationalistic and Latin too religious. He expressly denied Basic was 'cultural propaganda' ('nation' was one of the 850 words, 'empire' was not).[68] Nor was its inception connected with 'the administrative class'. Quite the reverse: he expected opposition from officialdom, with what he described as its 'stereotyped academic background, its dislike of change, and its literary pride'. (He was right: Basic was 'not very popular with the Colonial Office', reported Victor Purcell sadly in 1938.)[69]

Ogden's particular concerns were the failure of English teaching in Japan under the existing method, the rectification of 'the local Babel' of India's hundreds of languages, and the lifting of Africa culturally 'out of virtual isolation in a single generation'. He dismissed 'kitchen vernaculars' as a basis for a proper education, and he hoped to rescue East Africans from the misguided attempt to introduce Swahili (mainly the language of the coastal Arabs) as a lingua franca. The general framework of Ogden's motivation was, however, of a decidedly left-wing, post-world-war kind. The absence of a common universal language was, he

---

[68] C. K. Ogden, *Debabelization: with a survey of contemporary opinion on the problem of a universal language* (1931), is the main exposition. For background, see J. W. Scott and W. T. Gordon, 'Ogden, Charles Kaye', *ODNB*, vol. XLI, pp. 558–9; P. Sargant Florence and J. R. L. Anderson, eds., *C. K. Ogden: a collective memoir* (1977); T. N. Harper, 'Diaspora and the languages of globalisation', in A. G. Hopkins, ed., *Globalisation in world history* (2002), pp. 141–66.

[69] Magdalene College Archives, I. A. Richards Papers, F/IAR/50, Victor Purcell to I. A. Richards, 19 December 1938.

thought, the 'chief obstacle to international understanding, and therefore the chief underlying cause of war', as well as the most formidable obstacle to the global progress of science. He called upon 'all internationally-minded persons to make Basic English part of the system of education in every country, so that there may be less chance of war, and less learning of languages – which, after all, for most of us, are a very unnecessary waste of time'. What the world needs, he wrote, was 'about a thousand more dead languages – and one more alive'. Basic would enable people to learn quickly as much as would be needed 'for all the purposes of everyday existence', in talk, trade, and travel, but for good measure he claimed that Shakespeare was a practitioner of Basic.[70]

Ogden was fortunate in getting the commitment of his college colleagues, I. A. Richards and William Empson, the influential literary critics, respected in China and America, to publicise it. Richards devoted much of his life to its promotion, especially – if intermittently – in China.[71] H. G. Wells was intrigued, but thought it would take time to catch on; he predicted a revival between 2000 and 2100, when Basic would become 'the common language for use between nations'; by 2200 'almost everyone was able to make use of Basic for talking and writing'.[72]

Initially, interest was shown in many countries, from Argentina to China, Poland to the Philippines. Ogden established in Cambridge the Orthographical Institute, which set up agencies in thirty countries. The time seemed propitious at last for a successful and effective universal language. The new inventions of the international telephone, 'talkie' films, and above all radio, would help its adoption as well as making it the more necessary. Unfortunately, in other respects the timing could not have been worse. It was hard to rebut the charge of 'linguistic imperialism'. In this regard the support of Prime Minister Winston Churchill proved to be the kiss of death. In 1943 Churchill formed a Cabinet committee, which reported favourably, and in January 1944 the government agreed to encourage officially (through the Foreign Office and British Council) the use of Basic as an 'auxiliary international language'. Churchill himself announced this in the House of Commons. He believed it 'would be a gain to us far more durable and fruitful than the annexation of great provinces', while it would also help to promote closer relations with the United States, by making it even more worthwhile for America to belong to 'the English-speaking club'. This was in the best manner of Macaulay's

---

[70] Ogden, *Debabelization*, pp. 12–13.
[71] John Haffenden, *William Empson: among the mandarins* (2005), pp. 304–9, 439–42, 530–3; Rodney Koeneke, *Empires of the mind: I. A. Richards and Basic English in China, 1929–1979* (Stanford, CA, 2004).   [72] H. G. Wells, *The shape of things to come* (1933).

vision for British cosmoplasticism, but it was seriously open to misinter-pretation.[73]

After the war, Prime Minister Clement Attlee was lukewarm: 'I have no strong opinion on this' – which meant there was no real steam behind the Labour government's formal endorsement in June 1946 of governmental encouragement of the use of Basic, which it saw particularly as the medium for international commerce. Ogden offered to assign copyright to the Crown, and this was agreed for the considerable sum of £23,000, a figure chosen as the same as Bentham received for his 'panopticon prison' design.[74] A Basic English Foundation was half-heartedly set up under the Ministry of Education in 1947. Funding stopped in 1953.

Basic thus failed to make any real progress after 1945. The war was a fatal interruption, and the 1930s agencies were never fully restored. The project was not helped by Ogden's truculent mismanagement and obsti-nacy. There was an Asian intellectual resistance to what seemed to be 'a short cut'. The inevitable association with 'colonialism' was calamitous. As Richards's biographer observes, 'Basic lay under a dark historical shadow during the break-up of the British colonial empire.' When the shutters came down after the Chinese communist take-over in 1949, it was a fatal blow in a critical area of the globe, since more people spoke Chinese languages than any other language in the world.[75]

Ogden undoubtedly had one of mankind's 'big ideas'. His principles in formulating Basic were sound. His intentions were simple and humanis-tic: improved communication between all peoples on the planet. He and Richards tried to solve a fundamental problem or requirement, and had they successfully promoted it they would probably have won the Noble Prize for peace. Ironically, even tragically for them, the twenty-first-century world recognises English – or perhaps more strictly American-English – as its most serviceable language (even French is in world-wide retreat), but the world has got there without benefit of Basic. Perhaps the ubiquitous transistor-radio made it redundant.

(5) A special relationship

Throughout the period from 1918 to 1968 – and of course beyond – makers of British external policy had the possible reactions of the United States always at the back of their mind. The 'special relationship' was not

---

[73] *PD, Commons* vol. 397, cc. 2187–90, 9 March 1944; W. S. Churchill, *The Second World War*, vol. V (1952), p. 571.

[74] PREM 8/180, minute by Attlee, 5 June 1946; CAB 128/5, CM 61(46)6, 24 June 1946.

[75] J. P. Russo, *I. A. Richards: his life and work* (Baltimore, 1989), pp. 404, 469.

entirely mythical, and acquired some reality, though it was decidely ambivalent and intermittent. There was a vague sense of affinity based on the Victorian notion that the USA was simply 'forty Englands rolled into one' (Lord Derby, 1880). A similar misconception may have influenced Kipling's invitation in 1899 for the Americans to 'take up the White Man's Burden'. But there was also a sense of competition, of alarm about this power moving into the ascendant, threatening a possible 'Americanisation of the world'. America projected a confusing image. As the first of Britain's colonials to break free, Americans were supposed to be champions of colonial independence, but the USA was from the outset an inherently expansionist state. The conquest of the Philippines from 1898 was a bloodthirsty business in the worst tradition of European military adventurism.[76] For much of the twentieth century there was a major uncertainty: would the United States emulate the British in shouldering the 'White Man's Burden', or retreat into isolationism? And if at times the Americans seemed high-mindedly hostile to the British empire, was this entirely altruistic? So it was an uncomfortable relationship rather than a 'special' one, 'competitive co-operation' at best.[77]

Historians have a spectrum of interpretation to choose from. At one extreme there is A. N. Wilson who argues that President Roosevelt was indeed fighting the Second World War to rid Europe of a dangerous German dictatorship, but did so believing that 'they could also reduce British power to negligible levels'; he would help Britain, 'but only on condition that Britain surrendered any claim to be a world power and handed that role to the Americans'. The special relationship during the 1940s, according to Wilson, 'was in part, like a lot of outwardly successful marriages, an abusive relationship'.[78] A completely different kind of relationship is suggested by Roger Louis and R. E. Robinson. For them, the postwar British empire was 'regenerated on Anglo-American wealth and power', 'nationalised and internationalised', transformed as part of 'an Anglo-American coalition, modulated strategically into an Anglo-American field of influence'. They even argue that this reinforcement was so valuable that compared with it the loss of India 'seems almost derisory' – a debatable proposition.[79] The truth is probably somewhere between these alternatives. The United States was neither so calculating

[76] Hyam, *Britain's imperial century*, pp. 231–5, 327–9.
[77] D. Reynolds, 'Competitive co-operation: Anglo-American relations in World War Two', *Historical Journal*, vol. 23 (1980), pp. 233–45, and *The creation of the Anglo-American alliance, 1937–1941: a study in competitive co-operation* (1981), esp. pp. 9–16, 292–4.
[78] A. N. Wilson, *After the Victorians* (2005), esp. pp. 382–7, 438.
[79] W. R. Louis and R. E. Robinson, 'The imperialism of decolonisation', *JICH*, vol. 22 (1994), pp. 462–511.

nor so co-operative as suggested. In any case, the crucial fact is that American anti-colonialism was brought to an end by the cold war, when communism became a far more serious bogey than colonialism. It was an astonishing paradox, and a supreme irony, that by the time the British government was ready in the 1960s to reduce significantly its world role, the Americans did not want it to do so, Secretary of State Dean Rusk pleading for a continuation of the British presence East-of-Suez on the grounds that the Americans could not act alone as policeman of the world (unconsciously echoing what Churchill and Bonar Law had said in 1921–2). Yet by 1967 the British ambassador was bold enough to dismiss the 'so-called Anglo-American special relationship' as 'little more than sentimental terminology'.[80]

A feeling of disillusionment was never far away. Joseph Chamberlain had said that the British and Americans were 'branches of one family' (1887). If so, it was a dysfunctional family, with the USA regarded by many of the British elite as only an illegitimate offspring. Their histories and geopolitical concerns certainly intersected to an extent, and they shared a broad range of values. One of the most extraordinary features of British cosmology, however, was the widespread condescension towards and distrust of America, an ingrained suspicion in Whitehall. Americans were regarded as brash, immature, woolly idealists, far too unpredictable. Quotations to support these apprehensions, and resentment of the wealth and competitive power of the USA, are easily multiplied through the decades. To Lloyd George in 1921 the Japanese were loyal and gallant, 'unlike fickle Americans'.[81] Neville Chamberlain in the 1930s complained that America was 'a nation of cads', completely unreliable, without a scrap of moral courage.[82] Any co-operation, he feared, would come at too high a price, and – according to Maurice Cowling – one element in his desire to reach a political agreement with Hitler was that it might reduce British dependence on the USA.[83] In 1941 R. A. Butler (under-secretary in the FO) penned a stinging denunciation of America: 'she may in her turn yet rat on us'.[84] The Foreign Office's 'stocktaking memorandum' at the end of the war in 1945 warned that American foreign policy was fluctuating, emotional, and uncertain: 'the Americans are a mercurial people, unduly swayed by sentiment and

[80] Matthew Jones, *Conflict and Confrontation in South-East Asia 1961–1965* (2002), pp. 293, 304.
[81] W. R. Louis, *British strategy in the Far East, 1919–1939* (Oxford, 1971), p. 48.
[82] C. Thorne, *Allies of a kind: the United States, Britain and the war against Japan, 1941–1945* (1978), pp. 295, 354.
[83] M. Cowling, *The impact of Hitler: British politics and British policy, 1933–1940* (1975), pp. 299, 397. [84] V. Rothwell, *Britain and the Cold War, 1941–1947* (1982), pp. 7, 364.

prejudice'.[85] Labour ministers agreed. Attlee was notably wary. By 1950 Bevin had concluded they were crude, noisy, boastful, and materialistic.[86] He worried that the Americans might gradually alienate Asians from the West. Their policy over China and Japan seemed to him dangerously lacking in direction, taking too little account of Asian opinion and nationalist susceptibilities, a policy which he believed was in sharp contrast to Britain's encouragement of 'the legitimate aspirations' of the people of South-East Asia for independence, which would provide the 'best possible counter to communist subversion and penetration'.[87] Towards the end of the life of the Labour government, one of the younger ministers noted what he believed was the 'lack of understanding and anti-Americanism displayed in the Cabinet'. Hugh Gaitskell thought it was a 'poor-relation' attitude bred of relative weakness.[88] Misunderstanding of the American attitude was to plunge the relationship into unprecedented depths during the Eden government's 1956 Suez venture, marking the lowest point of the Anglo-American relationship. Despite Macmillan's efforts to repair the damage, misperceptions, tensions, and disagreements persisted.[89]

[85] Hyam, *The Labour government and the end of empire, 1945–1951* pt 2, pp. 297–304 (no. 138), memo by Sir Orme Sargent, August 1945.
[86] M. R. Gordon, *Conflict and consensus in Labour's foreign policy, 1914–1965* (Stanford, CA, 1969), p. 37.
[87] CAB 129/41, CP(50)200, 30 August 1950, memo, 'Review of the international situation in Asia in the light of the Korean conflict'.
[88] Philip M. Williams, ed., *The diary of Hugh Gaitskell, 1945–1956* (1983), p. 230 (2 February 1951), and 316 (memo, July 1952).
[89] N. J. Ashton, 'Anglo-American revival and empire during the Macmillan years', in M. Lynn, ed., *The British empire in the 1950s: retreat or revival?* (2006), pp. 164–85.

1 'The whole world is rocking': British governments and a dysfunctional imperial system, 1918–1945

'Our born leaders are dead.'[1] Of course we cannot prove that the British empire would have been better run if so many young men had not died in the First World War, which claimed the lives of over 37,000 officers, many of whom would have gone into politics and imperial administration. What we can say is that those who fought and survived and moved into public life and the service of the empire believed themselves to be merely the runts of what had promised to be 'a great generation': 'the better chaps were gone'.[2] They were, as one Cambridge don put it, 'most of them not meant to be our leaders at all. They are only the last and worst of our war substitutes.' Almost all of them were marked by 'moral and psychological shock', haunted by memories, guilty in their survival. Almost all intelligent young men of whatever political party were active supporters of the League of Nations, and attracted by disarmament. Many turned to pacifism, or something like it.[3] Some turned to communism. Another war was something to be avoided at all costs. They felt driven to serve, specifically 'to strive for the creation and organisation of peace, above all things', and to forge a better world.[4] The war caused at least one serious defection from the colonial service. Arthur Tedder, who had been posted to Fiji early in 1914, joined the Royal Flying Corps and remained in the RAF, rising to become Lord Tedder, Marshal of the Royal Air Force, deputy allied commander on 'D'-day, Chief of the Air Staff, and Chancellor of the University of Cambridge.[5]

If the immediate postwar years were ones of painful adjustment for individuals, they were near-nightmares for those in charge of the empire. The 'Great War' destroyed empires, the Muslim Caliphate, and ancient

---

[1] Quoted in R. Hyam, *Britain's imperial century, 1815–1914: a study of empire and expansion* (3rd edn, 2002) pp. 336–7; J. M. Winter, *The Great War and the British people* (1985), ch. 3, 'The lost generation', pp. 65–99.

[2] R. Vansittart, *The mist procession: the autobiography of Lord Vansittart* (1958), p. 187.

[3] Harold Macmillan, *Memoirs*, vol. I: *Winds of change, 1914–1939* (1966) pp. 9, 78, 95, 98, 582. M. Ceadel, *Pacifism in Britain, 1914–45: the defining of a faith* (Oxford, 1980).

[4] D. McLachlan, *In the chair: Barrington-Ward of 'The Times', 1927–1948* (1971), p. 6 (diary of Robin Barrington-Ward, 23 February, 1941).

[5] V. Orange, 'Tedder, Arthur W.', *ODNB*, vol. LIV, pp. 14–19.

European dynasties. It led to the Bolshevik revolution. It created new states out of the ruins of the Ottoman empire. It transferred ex-German colonies to League of Nations mandates. It removed the centre of financial power after two centuries from London to New York. In Ireland, the first step towards the creation of the Irish Free State was launched by the Easter Rising of 1916. There was a revolt in Egypt led by the charismatic Saad Zaghlul; it was put down relatively easily but led to qualified independence and the end of protectorate status in 1922. In 1920 there was a large-scale Arab uprising in Iraq. It took six months and the lives of 2,300 British and Indian troops to repress, while 8,000 Iraqis died. In Ceylon there were Buddhist-inspired riots in 1915, leading to martial law. In India, quite apart from Gandhi's stirring up of riots and disorders, there were other violent protests: in 1919–24 the Muslim Khalifat movement (the most serious protest against British rule since the Mutiny-rebellion of 1857), the 1921 Moplah peasant uprising in Kerala, in 1922 the Akali Sikh movement. More portentous still, in China in 1919 there was the 'May 4th movement', which began in student protest in Peking (against the transfer of German holdings to Japan) but grew to involve nation-wide strikes by industrial workers; it saw the emergence of Mao Tse-tung, and was recognised as evidence of mounting rejection of Western ways and 'imperialism'. And although much less in the public consciousness, there were worrying disturbances in Africa: the epoch-making Chilembwe uprising in Nyasaland (1915), the continuing jihad of Muhammad Abdullah (Abdille Hassan) in Somaliland (1899–1920), another jihad in South Darfur in the Sudan (1921) in response to British taxation schemes, and a Dinka uprising (1919).[6] There were anti-white riots in Trinidad, Jamaica, and British Honduras.

The Great War also led to an intellectual revolt against the European colonial order. The barbaric horrors it revealed 'did much to break the psychological bondage of the colonised elite', whose writers now began to produce critiques of the 'civilising mission', rejecting Western models, and giving greater credence to Gandhi's contention that the industrialised West had not opened up a morally and socially sustainable path for humanity. The most famous critic was Rabindranath Tagore (1861–1941), Indian poet, philosopher, and guru. This new world-wide discourse was to form a critical prelude to the struggles of decolonisation.[7]

For British politicians, the gravest situation of all was in Ireland. 'If we lose Ireland we have lost the empire', declared that Jeremiah,

[6] Wm Roger Louis, *Great Britain and Germany's lost colonies, 1914–1919* (Oxford, 1967); *Cambridge History of Africa*, vol. VII (ed. A. D. Roberts, 1986), pp. 196, 764.

[7] M. Adas, 'Contested hegemony: the Great War and the Afro-Asian assault on the civilising mission ideology', *Journal of World History*, vol. 15 (Hawai'i, 2004) pp. 31–63.

Field-Marshal Sir Henry Wilson, Chief of the Imperial General Staff. In the Easter Rising of 1916, 64 Irish rebels and some 300 civilians were killed in Dublin, and 130 British soldiers died. Fifteen rebels were executed under martial law. This attempt to assert Irish nationality sent shock-waves well beyond the colonial empire. Even Lenin wrote half-a-dozen pages about it; one historical account is entitled *Six days to shake an empire*.[8] In January 1919 Sinn Feiners gathered in Dublin to set up their own assembly, both they and it soon proscribed. A two-and-a-half-year guerilla war began, as the British government dithered, agonised, and vacillated. To the more extreme right-wing officials there was no such thing as genuine politics in Ireland, only 'flagrant disloyalty'.[9] A truce and a 'treaty' in 1921 preceded the establishment of the Irish Free State, with sovereignty over twenty-six of Ireland's thirty-two counties, a compromise which not all regarded as permanent, and a precedent for partition which was to reverberate down the decades.[10]

Former prime minister and now foreign secretary, A. J. Balfour in 1919 detected 'a world movement which takes different forms in different places, but is plainly discernible on every continent and in every country. We are only at the beginning of our troubles.' It was not clear how they were going to deal with these forces of 'social and international disintegration'.[11] Lord Milner as secretary of state for the colonies (1919–21) was overwhelmed with the scale of problems which extended far beyond imperial issues, though these were bad enough. 'The whole world is rocking', he wrote in 1919.[12] With the Middle East 'in a state of raging chaos', Milner was 'quite at the end of my tether'. The conjunction of rebellions and troubles in Ireland, Egypt and India constituted a 'crisis of empire, 1919–1922'. Gandhi's new recklessness in 'non-cooperation' (*satyagraha*) put the rulers of the Raj 'at wit's end'. Everything interlocked. As the secretary of state for India, E. S. Montagu, explained: 'The concessions which look likely to be necessary in Ireland harden public opinion against any new concessions in Egypt. Anything that is done as to complete independence in Egypt might

[8] D. W. Harkness in *Oxford History of the British Empire*, vol. V: *Historiography* (ed. R Winks, 1999), pp. 123–4; C. Duff, *Six days to shake an empire* (1966).

[9] Deirdre McMahon, 'Ireland and the Empire-Commonwealth, 1900–1948', in *Oxford History of the British Empire*, vol. IV: *Twentieth century* (ed. J. M. Brown and W. R. Louis, 1999), pp. 143–6.

[10] N. Mansergh, *The prelude to partition: concepts and aims in Ireland and India* (1976), repr. in *Independence years: the selected Indian and Commonwealth papers of Nicholas Mansergh* (ed. Diana Mansergh, New Delhi, 1999), pp. 3–41. See also Mansergh's magisterial chapter in *The Commonwealth experience* (1982 edn, 2 vols.), vol. I: *The Durham Report to the Anglo-Irish treaty*, ch. 7, 'Ireland: the Dominion settlement', pp. 215–43.

[11] Quoted by Lawrence James, *The rise and fall of the British empire* (1994), p. 371.

[12] Sydney Buxton Papers, Milner to Buxton, 8 April 1919.

Illustration 1.1 The Imperial Conference, 1923.
This was the first gathering of dominion representatives after the forma-
tion of the Irish Free State in 1921. Desmond Fitzgerald, the Irish min-
ister of external affairs, and J. MacNeill, Irish minister of education, are
both shown centrally seated. In the back row, standing left to right:
Mr W. F. Massey (New Zealand), the Maharaja of Alwar (India),
Mr W. R. Warren (Newfoundland), and General Smuts (South Africa).
In the front row, seated: Mr S. M. Bruce (Australia), Mr Stanley
Baldwin (UK), Mr Mackenzie King (Canada). The scene in the confer-
ence room at No. 10 Downing Street, was painted by Douglas Chandor.
The painting was exhibited at the 1924 Wembley Exhibition.

appear to encourage Indian extremists.'[13] Sir Henry Wilson repeatedly drew attention to the dangers of 'being spread all over the world, strong nowhere, weak everywhere, and with no reserve', the 'desperately weak and narrow margin of troops on which we are running the empire'. In December 1921 at Camberley he lectured on 'The passing of the British empire.' Inability to deal with internal discontents strongly, as illustrated by Ireland, seemed to him certain to lead to imperial decline.[14]

When Winston Churchill became secretary of state for the colonies in 1921, he felt, like his predecessor, that 'the whole future of the world' was in the melting-pot. Despite severe-enough problems in Ireland and Iraq, Palestine and Kenya, he worried that the issues which really should preoccupy him were Russia and Turkey, America and Japan. Ireland he described as suffering an 'enormous retrogression of civilisation and Christianity'. Egypt and India were in revolt, on the edge of a blind and heedless plunge back into 'primordial chaos'. 'The whole accumulated greatness of Britain is under challenge', he wrote in 1922. Every separate foreign or nationalist embarrassment, created by the 'rascals and rapscallions of mankind', he saw as a threat to the crumbling global position. Straitened economic circumstances meant that 'the British empire cannot become the policeman of the world'. Yet there was trouble everywhere, and so 'we may well be within measurable distance of universal collapse and anarchy throughout Europe and Asia'. All over the world, countries were 'relapsing in hideous succession into bankruptcy, barbarism or anarchy', and not least within the ambit of the Pax Britannica.[15] Iraq presented him with a particular challenge. It was, he said, 'an ungrateful volcano': 'we live on a precarious basis in this wild land, filled with . . . extremely peppery well-armed politicians'. In an ominous new development, Churchill

---

[13] The most attractive introduction to the post-war period remains J. A. Gallagher, *The decline, revival and fall of the British empire: The Ford Lectures and other essays* (ed. A Seal, Cambridge, 1982), pp. 73–141. Although making the fairly obvious point that decline was discontinuous, and that India made important contributions to the 1939–45 war-effort (pp. 135–41), the theme of 'revival' is not all that significant: Gallagher introduced the word into the title in order mainly to avoid too direct an echo of Edward Gibbon's *Decline and fall of the Roman empire* (1776–88). See also J. A. Gallagher, 'Nationalism and the crisis of empire, 1919–1922', in C. Baker, G. Johnson, and A Seal, eds., *Power, profit and politics: essays on imperialism, nationalism and change in twentieth-century India* (1981), pp. 355–68, repr. from *Modern Asian Studies*, vol. 15.

[14] K. Jeffery, 'Sir Henry Wilson and the defence of the British empire, 1918–1922', *JICH*, vol. 5 (1977), pp. 270–93 and *The British Army and the crisis of empire, 1918–1922* (Manchester, 1984), esp. pp. 50, 143–9, and *Field Marshal Sir Henry Wilson: a political soldier* (Oxford, 2006), pp. 229–55 ('Defending the empire').

[15] M. Gilbert, *Winston S. Churchill*, vol. IV: *1917–1922* (1975), pp. 859, 898, 912–15, and *Companion*, vol. IV, pt 3, *Documents, April 1921 to November 1922* (1977), pp. 2080–94.

authorised aerial bombardment and intimidation in order to control Iraqi rebels.[16]

Meanwhile, worse things still were occurring in India, with the horrendous catastrophe of the Amritsar massacre in 1919.[17] Rioting had broken out in this Sikh holy city in the Punjab. There was looting, arson, and the wrecking of property, including Christian churches; a lady missionary doctor was seriously assaulted (*not* raped) and almost died. A huge crowd gathered at a prohibited but peaceful meeting in the Jallianwala Bagh, an enclosure near the Sikh Golden Temple, partly to mark the beginning of a major festival. On the orders of General Dyer, 1,650 rounds of ammunition were fired into the crowd. At least 379 Indians were killed in the massacre. In the aftermath, martial law served to facilitate punishment rather than control order; 108 Indians were sentenced to death; there were public floggings, and collective punishments – water and electricity supplies were shut off in Amritsar, and there was some aerial bombing of surrounding villages. The British devised ritualistic humiliations. Wells were polluted by soldiers pissing in and near them. Most notoriously, Dyer closed off the lane where the missionary had been attacked, so that for some two weeks while the 'crawling order' remained in force, access to homes could only be obtained by crawling through the gutter-filth of a street without sanitation. Dyer believed he was doing no more than his duty: 'I thought it would be doing a jolly lot of good and they would realise that they were not to be wicked.' Regarding Indians as mere 'naughty boys', they had to be 'taught a lesson'. (Sir Harry Smith used to talk like this in South Africa in the 1830s and 40s.) Secretary of state Montagu condemned Dyer's actions as rule 'by terrorism, racial humiliation and subordination, and frightfulness'. When Dyer was forced to resign from the army there was a staggering demonstration of public support, raising money for him as if for a sporting hero's testimonial. Both

---

[16] Gilbert, *Companion*, vol. IV, pt 3, p. 1511, Churchill to Lloyd George, 17 July 1921. Churchill has acquired a certain notoriety for the decision over air-power in Iraq. However, what he was trying to do was reduce the impact and enormous costs of the post-war military garrison, without a 'policy of scuttle', and to put British relations with turbulent Iraq on a footing more like that of an Indian princely state, with a treaty; in other words to apply the classic mid-Victorian theory of 'informal empire' – the difference being that instead of gunboats in the background there would be aircraft overhead. More than anything else, perhaps, he was promoting nascent 'but proven aerial power' (CAB 24/128, CP 3328, memo, 'Policy and finance in Mesopotamia, 1922–1923', 4 August 1921; Gilbert, *Companion*, vol. IV, pt 3, pp. 1577–80). It should also be noted that, true to his lifelong defence of minorities, Churchill laid it down as a matter of principle that they should not put the Kurds under Arab control (*Companion*, vol. IV, pt 3, p. 1547).

[17] D. Sayer, 'The British reaction to the Amritsar Massacre, 1919–1920', *Past and Present*, no. 131 (1991), pp. 130–64.

Gandhi and Nehru sat on the Congress committee of inquiry. It confirmed their despair of the Raj. Gandhi asked how could they possibly compromise when the British lion 'shakes its claws at us'? Indians now united behind the campaign of civil disobedience and non-cooperation.[18]

Pertinent comment on events like Amritsar comes from George Orwell, who as Eric Blair served in Burma with the Indian Imperial Police from 1922 to 1927, an experience which turned him into a critic of the 'evils of imperialism'. The dreadful thing about such brutalities, he wrote, 'is that they are quite unavoidable': 'in order to rule over barbarians, you have got to become a barbarian yourself'. If there was revolt, rulers had got to suppress it, 'and you can only do so by methods which make nonsense of any claims for the superiority of Western civilisation' (1930). It was hard for those in charge to remember that they were ruling human beings as opposed to 'a kind of undifferentiated brown-stuff, about as individual as bees or coral insects'. Soldiers in particular, he had observed at first hand, could be brutal, but perhaps of necessity: 'you cannot hold down a subject empire with troops infected by notions of class solidarity' (1939).[19]

Imperial Britain survived the 'crisis of empire', if not with naval superiority, or honour, intact. Horns were drawn in. Some of the overblown apparatus of immediate postwar territorial reponsibility was dismantled. America retreated into isolation.[20] But it remained 'a very distracted world' (Lloyd George), a world 'completely out of joint', in which crisis succeeded crisis (Neville Chamberlain, 1931).[21] It would also become painfully apparent that the survivors of the First World War were to live out their careers through yet another world war and in economic decline. New enemies emerged just when Britain was greatly weakened in its crucial economic underpinnings.

The Wall Street crash in the autumn of 1929 suddenly triggered an accumulating contraction of world trade which we know as the Great Depression. There was a major British recession which Ramsay MacDonald called an 'economic blizzard', marked by spiralling unemployment, and a financial crisis culminating in the replacement of the Labour government by a National coalition and the decision to abandon the gold standard in 1931. The Depression was a traumatic experience.

---

[18] Judith M. Brown, *Nehru: a political life* (2003) or *Nehru* (1999), p. 33.
[19] George Orwell, *The collected essays, journalism and letters of George Orwell*, ed. S. Orwell and I. Angus (1968), vol. I, pp. 235, 388, 403.
[20] J. Darwin, 'Imperialism in decline?' *Historical Journal*, vol. 23 (1980), pp. 657–78; see also Darwin's remarkable essay on the Middle East, 'An undeclared empire: the British in the Middle East, 1918–1939', *JICH*, vol. 27 (1999), pp. 159–76, repr. in R. D. King and R. W. Kilson, eds., *The statecraft of British imperialism: essays in honour of Wm Roger Louis* (1999).
[21] W. R. Louis, *British strategy in the Far East, 1919–1939* (1971), p. 58; C. Thorne, *The limits of foreign policy: the West, the League and the Far Eastern crisis of 1931–1933* (1972), p. 90.

Economic decline was relative to the United States and to Japan. The Japanese launched a dazzling period of economic expansion, which in China and India was at the expense of British interests. Critical was what happened to British manufacture of cotton goods. Total exports of cotton piece-goods declined from 7,035 million square yards in 1913 to 1,448 million in 1938, from 58 per cent of the world's total to 28 per cent. Exports of cotton goods to India dropped rapidly from 1,248 million square yards in 1929 to 376 million in 1931, a loss in value from £26 million to £5.5 million. Exports to China fell from £71.25 million in 1929 to £300,000 in 1936. India's imports from Japan rose from 18.4 per cent in 1928/9 to 47.3 per cent in 1932–3, while Britain's share declined from 75.2 per cent to 48.7 per cent.[22]

The account of the 1920s and 1930s which follows must inevitably be compressed and selective. It is organised around certain key ideas and the dominant preoccupations of the period: racism (especially as it affected Africa), Zionism and the Palestine Mandate, nationalism, Commonwealth idealism, and geopolitical problems. The final section of the chapter – new directions and the impact of the Second World War – forms a narrative bridge from 1937 to the post-war period which must be the main focus of our attention.

1. Racism

'The problem of the twentieth century is the problem of the colour-line – the relation of the darker to the lighter races of man in Asia and Africa, in America and the islands of the sea.' This was the prediction of the Afro-American writer W. E. B. Du Bois in 1903.[23] From a different perspective, Professor James Bryce, Liberal theorist and politician (chief secretary for Ireland, 1905–7 and then ambassador to the USA) came to similar conclusions. Relations between the dominant and backward races, declared Bryce in 1902, were 'a great secular process' which transcended everyday 'political and commercial questions' and had entered a critical phase.[24] Both Du Bois and Bryce were wrong. Race was not the critical problem of the twentieth century, even if it was an underlying reality. The defining problem of the twentieth century for Europeans, the chief preoccupation, which gives it an over-arching historical framework, was totalitarian aggression, the 'seventy-five years' war' from 1914 to

---

[22] S. Pollard, *The development of the British economy, 1914–1967* (2nd edn, 1969), pp. 121–2; B. R. Mitchell and P. Deane, eds., *Abstract of British historical statistics* (1962), pp. 182–3.

[23] W. E. B. Du Bois, *The souls of black folk* (1903), ch. 3, 'Of the dawn of freedom.'

[24] James Bryce, *The relations of the advanced and backward races of mankind* (Romanes lecture, Oxford, 1902), pp. 45–6.

1989 when the Berlin Wall fell. There were hot and cold phases and shifting enemies. Although it was driven from Europe, or the Eurasian heartland, the whole world became caught up in it. If, alternatively, the twentieth century is defined as 'the century of genocide', this was not fundamentally racial in character, for exterminations were directed against any group seen as a threat to dominant economic or nationalistic projects, and for whom racial, ethnic, or social tags were found.[25]

Even if 'race' was therefore not the central focus of metropolitan concern, it was bound to be an issue for the British empire. Writing in 1937, Professor W. K. Hancock, its leading historian, drew attention to 'the inescapable and intractable issues of race and nationality which constitute the supreme challenge to the British Commonwealth', especially as they affected Indians, and particularly, perhaps, those in the diaspora created largely by indentured labour migration. Problems arose, suggested Hancock, from the way nineteenth-century liberalism had been 'distorted and impoverished by an unconscious philistinism which ignored all values except those of European bourgeois society' and showed 'profound indifference to the anthropological and historical individuality of the communities in which men actually lived'.[26] There were continuing problems, too, in the sometimes nasty way individual army officers and soldiers treated non-Europeans in their everyday contact.[27] So was the British empire 'racist'?

The question is increasingly posed in these querulous days. It is difficult to refute because non-Europeans were invariably seen as basically different. This assumption generated emotional attitudes: difference meant inferiority. Race was seen as biological proof of difference, an elemental category of belonging. The 'idea of race' was integral to the mentality of post-Victorian generations in a way that is repudiated in the twenty-first century. Unfortunately, too, there is no agreed definition of 'racism'. Sometimes it is equated with racial prejudice and said to be an ideology, a theory of biological racial superiority. This seems too vague and all-embracing. There is no human community which is incapable of racial prejudice and many are afflicted with ethnic hatreds. It is surely more satisfactory to distinguish between 'racism' and 'racial prejudice' and restrict 'racism' to the abnormal

---

[25] M. Levine, 'Why is the 20th century the century of genocide?' *Journal of World History*, vol. 11 (2000), pp. 305–36.

[26] W. K. Hancock, *Survey of British Commonwealth affairs*, vol. I: *Problems of nationality*, pp. 22, 177–8.

[27] Orwell, *Collected essays, journalism and letters* vol. I: 'Democracy in the British army', p. 403. He frequently noted in Burma that soldiers were 'the best-hated section of the white community, and, judged simply by their behaviour, they certainly deserved to be'.

systematisation of racial prejudice into institutionalised (legalised) discrimination or exploitation.[28] By this tight definition it is clear that certain states are undoubtedly 'racist' by deliberate intent: the United States before the victory of civil rights, Australia in the days of 'White Australia' immigration policy, South Africa in the era of apartheid, Nazi Germany, Rhodesia between 1965 and 1979. These were all independent states (or claimed to be) over which Britain had no real control. In this sense, then, and by comparison, the British empire as a whole can only dubiously be called racist, and to the extent that it was, not by deliberate aim. The dynamic aim was not racial domination *per se*, but geopolitical security or commercial profit. By contrast the aim of racist states is ethnic survival, since they feel threatened by an alien 'other'. For this reason, settler communities were always more likely to be seriously racially prejudiced than politicians and officials sitting in the comfort of London, simply because settlers were in closer contact with other races. Fear was always at the bottom of settler racial prejudice, just as it was for racist states. Many factors may be involved: fear of the unfamiliar, fear bred by the memory of historic conflict, fear of demographic swamping by the superior numbers of a culture perceived as alien and inferior, fear of disease, fear of economic competition for limited resources or specialised markets, and fear arising out of sexual jealousies and insecurities. There was 'pressure from the inner core of colonial society to maintain social distance and to keep in line any Europeans who threatened to blur the margin' by 'going native', that is, taking a local mistress or wife. There was no legal racial separation, but an insidious hierarchical social convention.[29]

The attitudes of settler communities, however, were never built into an imperial system. The most that can be said is that race was a useful supporting mechanism for the imperial structure, or justification for the cosmoplastic (world-moulding) project. A sense of racial difference certainly permeated many aspects of colonial practice. It explains, for example, the general absence of inter-marriage with non-whites, the prohibition (after the Crewe Circular of 1909) of local concubinage for district officers, the segregation of non-Europeans into separate townships, the misbehaviour of soldiers towards local populations, the absence of

---

[28] I find the discussion in Robert Miles, *Racism* (1989), helpful, though I do not draw exactly the same conclusions. Historians who have tried to address these issues include R. Ross, ed., *Racism and colonialism* (Leiden, 1982); R. W. Winks, 'A system of commands: the infrastructure of race conflict', in G. Martel, ed., *Studies in British imperial history: essays in honour of A. P. Thornton* (1986), pp. 19–30; and P. B. Rich, *Race and empire in British politics* (1986, 2nd edn, Cambridge, 1990).

[29] C. Bayly and T. Harper, *Forgotten armies: the fall of British Asia, 1941–1945* (2004, 2005), pp. 62, 120–1, 168.

African diocesan bishops in the Anglican Church between 1890 and 1953 – and so forth. Categorising people by race or ethnic origin tended to harden divisions and make them seem more dependent on colonial rule, but it is not the case that this was its purpose. Making categories is what administrators do: it is a function of bureaucracy, and not normally evidence of political manipulation. The difference is sharply exemplified by the Afrikaner-nationalist regime in South Africa, which after 1948, did indeed use racial classification as a basis for European domination. That is true racism. So let us not exaggerate the mere shortcomings of the British empire when tested against genuinely evil regimes or the criteria of later generations. Racism certainly cannot be blamed on empire. It has more to do with antecedent class attitudes and snobberies exported from Britain itself. Moreover, meeting non-Europeans in an imperial context could sometimes make people less contemptuous.

None of this is to say that we may also acquit the empire of racial prejudice. In a society consumed and permeated with class consciousness, obsessed with snobbish codes of behaviour bordering on the ridiculous, and conditioned to the need to have social inferiors to look down upon, these attitudes were inevitably magnified when thinking about and treating Asians and Africans.[30] British attitudes were awash with cultural chauvinism, at least between the Indian Mutiny-Rebellion of 1857 and the collapse of Hitler's Germany. Derogatory terms were bandied about even by the elite: wogs, niggers, nig-nogs, 'Gypos, Chinks, and Japs – but also in reference to Europeans as Huns, Frogs, Wops, Dagoes, and Jugs. It is important to stress again that this cultural arrogance is not to be confused analytically with institutionalised racism, otherwise the whole charge-sheet dissolves in a dangerous miasma. In assessing what – if anything – 'racial prejudice' as a cultural phenomenon might mean in practice, we need to distinguish between words and actions, ideas and their implementation. Does it really matter – beyond affronting our own politically correct susceptibilities – if government ministers of an earlier generation used these terms in private, in their table-talk, family letters and diaries? Churchill inevitably comes under the spotlight here. As a central actor in 'the end of empire' – secretary of state for war and air 1919–21, for the colonies 1921–2, chancellor of the Exchequer 1924–9, opponent of Indian constitutional reform 1929–35, first lord of the Admiralty 1939–40, and prime minister 1940–5 and 1951–5 – if the charges that he was 'a malignant racist' practising a 'virulent Anglo-Saxon triumphalism' can be made to stick, then that will affect our perception of the mentality

---

[30] V. G. Kiernan, *The lords of human kind: European attitudes towards the outside world in the imperial age* (1969), p. 214.

of the British elite and its performance overall.[31] In arguing against such charges it needs to be said that too much focuses on what Churchill *said*, mostly when relaxing with cronies, rather than what he *did* or decided.[32] Churchill himself was strict in observing the boundaries. He might joke with his private secretary about sending a telegram to Dr Malan, the Afrikaner prime minister, urging him to 'keep on skelping the kaffirs'[33] – but it was inconceivable that he would ever do so. Also, it is important to realise that, above all else, Churchill was a wordsmith, and proud of it, a master of the English language, delighting in everything from overblown rhetoric to earthy slang. Of course Churchill believed in British superiority over non-Europeans (and most Europeans), and thought the empire was a good thing. But he loathed racial exploitation ('racism' by our definition). He was incensed as a young man by Kitchener's disrespectful cavalier behaviour towards 'lion-hearted' opponents with 'legitimate motives' in the Sudan in 1898;[34] shocked by the Amritsar massacre in India in 1919 ('monstrous . . . sinister'), appalled by Mussolini's cynical invasion of Ethiopia in 1935. As first lord of the Admiralty in 1939 he wrote: 'there must be no discrimination on grounds of race or colour . . . I cannot see any objections to Indians serving in HM ships where they are qualified or needed, or, if their virtues so deserve, rising to be Admiral of the Fleet.'[35] His performance as a minister was invariably directed towards fairness, justice, pragmatism, and racial reconciliation. He had a genuine sympathy for 'subject races', and believed in trying to 'measure the weight of the burden they bear' in being ruled by alien administrators.[36] Paul Addison, while he also believes too much should not be read into Churchill's derogatory private utterances, thinks I have perhaps offered too generous a verdict. He points out that as a professional politician Churchill would have been constantly aware of the parliamentary danger of abuses in colonial administration.[37] But whether dictated from

---

[31] C. Thorne, *Allies of a kind: the United States, Britain and the war against Japan, 1941–45* (1978), pp. 669, 725, 750; see also Andrew Roberts, 'Churchill and the "magpie society"', in *Eminent Churchillians* (1994), pp. 211–41.

[32] Paul Addison, 'The political beliefs of Winston Churchill', *Transactions of the Royal Historical Society*, 5th ser., vol. 30 (1980), pp. 23–47.

[33] Roberts, *Eminent Churchillians*, p. 214, quotation from Sir D. Hunt.

[34] Winston S. Churchill, *The River War: an historical account of the reconquest of the Soudan* (1st edn, 1899).

[35] M. Gilbert, ed., *The Churchill War Papers*, vol. I (New York, 1993): *At the Admiralty, September 1939–May 1940*, p. 240, memo of 14 October 1939.

[36] R. Hyam, *Elgin and Churchill at the Colonial Office, 1905–1908* (1968), pp. 503–5; and 'Churchill and the British empire', in R. Blake and W. R. Louis, eds., *Churchill* (1993), pp. 167–86.

[37] P. Addison, *Churchill: the unexpected hero* (2005), p. 38. This admirable short introduction to Churchill is based upon Addison's long entry on Churchill in the *ODNB* (2004), vol. XI, pp. 653–85.

the head or the heart, Churchill's record is good. 'Racially prejudiced' perhaps, but certainly not a 'malignant racist'.

Churchill was not alone in his careless private racial attitudes. Prejudice was typical of the governing elite of his generation. Why was this? In a word, they had little real knowledge and less understanding. They belonged to a more naive, more juvenile, more introverted private world, a world incomparably less well-informed about human nature and human societies, the cosmos, the flesh, and the devil than those who came after them, innocent of multi-culturalism, and much more prone to poke thoughtless fun at foreigners and every kind of outsider. Post-1918 British cosmologies inherited a late-Victorian racial stereotyping which was harsher than anything which had preceded it. Even Edwardian socialist progressives and humanitarian campaigners shared the notions of a pseudo-scientific racial hierarchy. They allowed themselves to be unduly influenced by aspects of non-European life that should have been irrelevant to any sensible assessment of capacity, such as nudity in tropical climes, or sexual activities. 'Nakedness is a grievous sin', declared Sir Harry Smith in the Eastern Cape in 1836, and he was still being echoed by the recently retired governor of British East Africa in 1905, Sir Charles Eliot. Although prepared to exempt the stylish Masai, Eliot thought 'most natives appear to be simply in the state of Adam and Eve before the Fall, which is also that of the animals, to have no idea of indecency'. (Sir Charles believed the distance between man and beasts was 'minimised in Africa.')[38] The other problem was male-to-male sex, widespread in China and Japan and many other societies untouched by the Judaeo-Christian tradition which – quaintly – regarded anal intercourse as unnatural. A major reason for virulent Sinophobia was the realisation that sodomy was very popular among the Chinese. The Webbs, Sidney and Beatrice, after a visit to China in 1911, dismissed the Chinese as 'essentially an unclean race', physically and mentally rotten, 'a horrid race' devastated by drugs and 'abnormal sexual indulgence'.[39] To an extraordinary extent, promiscuity, prostitution, and sodomy were depicted as central characteristics of Asian and other societies, and it was this which was said to make them

---

[38] Sir C. Eliot, *The East Africa Protectorate* (1905), pp. 92–3. Few things are more puzzling today about Victorian and Edwardian attitudes to Afro-Asian peoples than this unreasoning and obsessive horror of nakedness, the equation of nudity not only with irredeemable savagery but with grievous sin; the gravamen of Churchill's charge against Gandhi, of course, was that he was 'half-naked'. Was Churchill unaware of the German *wandervogel* movement or the *nacktbaden* cult, or the early British and American nudist and sunbathing organisations, later transmuted into 'naturism', that most genteel of respectable bourgeois pastimes?

[39] J. M. Winter, 'The Webbs and the non-white world: a case of socialist racialism', *Journal of Contemporary History*, vol. 9 (1974), pp. 181–92.

inferior and unfit for self-rule. The differential was reduced to a simple equation: licentiousness + indiscipline = primitive, sexual restraint + rationality = modern.[40]

A further influential presupposition was that races must be inferior if they lacked industrial enterprise. The reputation of the Chinese – especially in comparison with the Japanese – suffered in this respect. It might be conceded that they had once invented useful things, but they stood accused of having done very little with them. The stereotype of Chinese society was essentially that it was stagnant, foolish and fatalistic, chaotic, amorphous and unmanageable: 'an inept, torpid polity' (Lord Curzon). It was annoyingly hard to know what was going on 'inside the ant-hill' (Sir John Simon), impossible to stir it up with gunboats: 'punishing China is like flogging a jellyfish' (Churchill).[41] Africans were regarded as indolent, lacking in initiative, thrift, and honesty. They had, it was argued, invented nothing – founded no civilisation, built no stone cities, or ships, or produced a literature, or suggested a creed. This, said the governor of the Gold Coast, Sir Alan Burns (1941–7), was a poor record. But he did at least realise that 'lack of achievement was no real test of capacity in different conditions', and he disliked colour prejudice enough to write a book about it.[42]

In the 1930s Europeans still tended to think they could do what they liked with Africa. Although during the Ethiopian crisis (1935–6) frontier changes and 'corridors for camels' were planned with scant regard for Ethiopian, Somali, or Eritrean feelings, the most shocking – but lesser known – example of European high-handedness was a massive proposed re-partition of Central Africa. The records lie in an extremely fat file innocently entitled 'Colonial policy 1938', but in fact discussions had been going on for a couple of years before that. There was some initial moral repugnance expressed in Cabinet committee, but this had become muted by 1937–8, mainly because the proposal was by then being presented as a 'new deal' or 'new conception', in order to head off public criticism. An area was designated for de-militarisation and governments within it would have to subscribe to certain principles about 'modern standards' concerning African rights and freedom of trade. But the essence of the scheme was Neville Chamberlain's plan as prime minister

[40] Philippa Levine, *Prostitution, race and politics: policing venereal disease in the British empire* (2003), pp. 177, 322–5, and 'Sexuality, gender and empire' in Levine, *Oxford History of the British empire*, Companion series: *Gender and empire* (2004), p. 151. See also, more generally, Hyam, *Empire and sexuality*, esp. pp. 200–15.

[41] Louis, *British strategy in the Far East*, pp. 18–19, 133, 186; S. L. Endicott, *Diplomacy and enterprise: British China policy, 1933–1937* (1975), p. 14.

[42] A. R. Burns, *Colour prejudice* (1948), p. 82. This book is mainly a history of the subject within the empire.

(1937–40) to restore to Germany the former Togoland and Cameroon colonies, and in addition to create for Germany a completely new colony. Britain and France would each surrender their colonies in Togoland and Cameroon; the British would add in bits of Nigeria around the Adamaoua Massif; Belgium would surrender a portion of the southern Congo; Portugal would be compelled to give up a part of northern Angola, and in compensation would receive from Britain a chunk of south-eastern Tanganyika (which one day became the site of the ground-nuts fiasco). The rationale for this farcical and elaborate reconstruction, admitted to be 'a patchwork solution', was that Britain was not prepared, for strategic reasons, to give back the whole of Tanganyika, which would mean severing the air-route to South Africa and giving up relatively large economic interests. Chamberlain did not entirely accept this reasoning. He did not believe he could purchase peace and a lasting settlement by handing over the whole of Tanganyika, but would not have hesitated for a moment to do so ('It would be of more value to them than to us'). Colonial secretary W. G. Ormsby-Gore (1936–8) also refused to toss in Sierra Leone or the Gambia, because this would lead to serious risings.

This bizarre scheme thus went beyond mere retrocession to involve a general adjustment of the African map. It was fundamentally unrealistic. It failed not because of ethical doubts but simply because Hitler rejected it, being unwilling to enter into the essential quid pro quo, a general settlement in Europe, including co-operation over Austria and Czechoslovakia.[43]

Despite low-grade racial prejudice and some high-handed politics, the empire had a definite countervailing doctrine of trusteeship – the idea that African territories were held in trust, and the interests of the ward should be carefully considered.

The doctrine of trusteeship between the wars was played out mainly in eight separate pronouncements about the future of East and Central Africa, especially Kenya and Southern Rhodesia, which had the largest and most vociferous settler communities, seeking self-rule.[44] The most famous

[43] PREM 1/247. See also S. R. Ashton and S. E. Stockwell, eds., *Imperial policy and colonial practice, 1925–1945* (BDEEP, 1996), pt 1, pp. 136–49 (no. 20), meeting of Cabinet committee on foreign policy, 24 January 1938; W. R. Louis, 'Appeasement and the colonies, 1936–1938', *Revue Belge de Philologie et d'Histoire*, vol. 49 (1971), pp. 1175–91; A. J. Crozier, 'Imperial decline and the colonial question in Anglo-German relations, 1919–1939', *European Studies Review*, vol. 11 (1981), esp. pp. 229–31.

[44] R. E. Robinson, 'The moral disarmament of African colonial empire', *JICH*, vol. 8 (1979), pp. 86–104, repr. in N. Hillmer and P. G. Wrigley, *The first British Commonwealth: essays in honour of Nicholas Mansergh* (1980); R. Hyam, 'Bureaucracy and "trusteeship" in the colonial empire', in J. M. Brown and W. R. Louis, eds., *The Oxford History of the British Empire*, vol. IV: *The twentieth century* (1999), pp. 255–79, esp. pp 265–7.

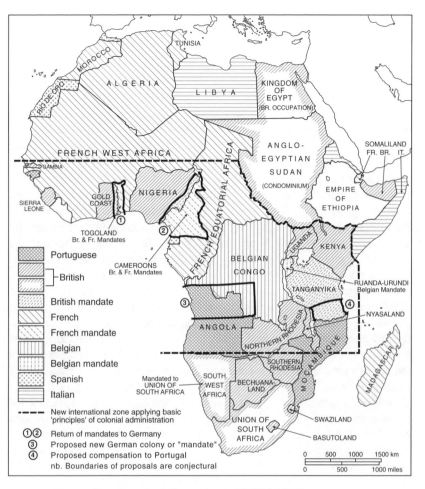

Source: Based on the information in PREM 1/247

Map 1.1 Appeasement in Africa: Neville Chamberlain's 'New Deal' for the re-partition of tropical Africa, 1938.

pronouncement was the Devonshire declaration of 1923, which said that the object of the trust was 'the protection and advancement of the native races': 'primarily Kenya is an African country and . . . the interests of the African natives must be paramount' – that is, prevail over the interests of immigrant races, whether Indian or European (23,000 Asians, 10,000 Europeans). The policy of the metropolitan government was thus clear, but constantly had to be adjusted to keep the settlers, or the government of

India, happy. It was in practice hard to implement the policy against the machinations of strong-willed settlers, who even threatened rebellion.[45] The various White Papers and declarations achieved little beyond a certain holding of the line. Too often the government felt let down by the governors they had chosen in the hope that they would stand firm on African interests, such as Girouard, Coryndon, and Mitchell, who were all either intimidated or 'captured' by the settlers. Even Lord Passfield (Sidney Webb) as Labour colonial secretary (1929–31) could not apply progressive Fabian principles, and had to water down his White Paper pronouncements, since a common-roll franchise could not be enforced without provoking a settler rebellion in kenya.[46]

Another equally important battle for trusteeship concerned the three High Commission Territories, Basutoland, Bechuanaland, and Swaziland, in which South Africa had a reversionary interest under the South Africa Act of 1909. The Union of South Africa was an expansionist state and pressed its claims. Its increasingly harsh native policies made it hard to square any acquiescence in South African ambitions with the British protection of African interests. There was no doubt about African opposition to a transfer out of the area of British responsibility. To the Tswana, Sotho, and Swazi, South Africa was feared like a lion and distrusted like a snake, or as one chief put it, 'Our prayer is that our mother may keep her baby on her back and that she will not drop the blanket for a stranger to pick up.' The case against transfer was skilfully articulated by Tshekedi Khama, regent of the Bangwato in Bechuanaland (1925–50). This hard-headed, stocky, and persistent man was the favourite son of Khama the Great. He was intelligent and well-read, with a library which included British parliamentary blue-books as well as *How to play Association Football* and Kingsley's *Water babies*. Tshekedi was probably the outstanding African leader of the interwar years. In June 1938 he submitted to the British government a powerful statement of the case against transfer, based on a formidable indictment of Union policies. Civil servants in the Colonial and Dominions Offices stood firm on trusteeship, and managed to stave off any concession without provoking a large-scale row with the South African government. It was a victory for trusteeship which eventually made possible the emergence of three independent African states in the 1960s.[47]

[45] Edna Bradlow, 'The evolution of "trusteeship" in Kenya', *South African Historical Journal*, vol. 4 (1972), pp. 64–80; J. G. Kamoche, *Imperial trusteeship and political evolution in Kenya, 1923–1963: a study of official views and the road to decolonisation* (Washington, 1981); R. M. Maxon, *The struggle for Kenya: the loss and reassertion of imperial initative, 1912–1923* (1993).

[46] Robinson, 'The moral disarmament of African colonial empire' pp. 97–8.

[47] R. Hyam and P. Henshaw, *The lion and the springbok: Britain and South Africa since the Boer War* (Cambridge, 2003), ch. 5, ' "Greater South Africa": the struggle for the High

In so far as governments followed, or tried to follow, an ethical imperial policy, where did this come from? The fundamentals of an ethical policy were laid out by the Liberal governments before the First World War,[48] and progressive attitudes were self-generating within the Colonial Office in the 1930s. Fabian theorists made their contribution, though it is important not to exaggerate it. Passfield was quite unable to provide the charter of empire citizenship the Fabians hoped for, to outlaw colour-bars and grant all races equal rights to franchises. Moreover, even Fabians did not jettison hierarchical views of racial superiority. A Fabian who had worked in the Colonial Office, Sydney Olivier, believed, however, that 'the Bantu stand very much higher in the scale of human intelligence than the typical Boer statesmen': J. B. M. Hertzog, the South African prime minister from 1924 to 1939, was a 'hysterical dunderhead' and his regime one of 'pestilential obscurantism and reaction'.[49] Their feelings about empire were ambivalent. This is vividly seen in one of its most scholarly 'advanced' thinkers, J. S. Furnival, an experienced ex-ICS officer, who married a Burmese, converted to Buddhism (for ten years, at any rate), and supported Burmese nationalism. But Furnivall could not shake off a paternalist nostalgia for imperial rule in Burma, nor a belief that imperial rule could only be effectively dismantled and Burma freed by British administrators.[50] He wanted to preserve the 'established political connections between Europe and the tropics'.[51]

The ethnographers of the 1860s had played a big part in developing late-Victorian racial stereotypes, so it is appropriate that it was the social anthropologists of the 1930s who began a more positive and favourable intellectual reconstruction. Bronislaw Malinowski arrived in London from Poland in 1910 and taught at the London School of Economics, where he was a professor from 1927 to 1938. He was a

---

Commission Territories, 1910–1961', pp. 102–17; Hyam, *The failure of South African expansion, 1908–1948*; W. Henderson, 'Khama, Tshekedi', *ODNB* (2004), vol. XXXI, pp. 507–9.

[48] Hyam, *Elgin and Churchill at the Colonial Office*, pp. 525–45, and 'The Colonial Office mind, 1900–1914', *JICH*, vol. 8 (1979), pp. 30–55, repr. in Hillmer and Wrigley, *The first British Commonwealth*.

[49] M. Olivier, ed., *Sydney Olivier: letters and selected writings* (1948), p. 164, Olivier to H. G. Wells, 8 April 1929.

[50] Julie Pham, 'Ghost-hunting in colonial Burma: nostalgia, paternalism, and the thought of J. S. Furnivall', *South-East Asia Research*, vol. 12 (2004), pp. 237–68, and 'J. S. Furnivall and Fabianism: interpreting the plural society in Burma', *Modern Asian Studies*, vol. 39 (2005), pp. 321–48. See also W. K. Hancock's comment on Furnivall in *The wealth of colonies* (1950), pp. 28–34. For Fabianism in its setting, see P. S. Gupta, *Imperialism and the British Labour movement, 1914–1964* (1975).

[51] J. S. Furnivall, *Colonial policy and practice: a comparative study of Burma and Netherlands India* (1948), p. 550.

pioneer of fieldwork involving 'participant observation', working in the Trobriand Islands of the South Pacific. Among his pupils was Jomo (Johnstone) Kenyatta, who wrote *Facing Mt Kenya* (1938), which although in part it had a polemical purpose, was a revealing analysis of the Kikuyu world, one of the first ethnographic studies produced by an African of his own people. Another student was Evans-Pritchard, who made highly significant contributions, such as *Witchcraft, oracles and magic among the Azande* (1937) and *The Nuer* (1940), fascinating and marvellous works.[52] A. R. Radcliffe-Brown was also an important pioneer, who published his revised study of the Andaman Islanders in 1933, though his other influential books appeared only after the Second World War.[53] As the respected commentator Margery Perham wrote in 1934: 'We begin to understand how African cultures were integrated, and so to recognise the functions of certain customs which seemed to our grandfathers the perverse aberrations of the heathen.'[54] What the social anthropologists were achieving was in many ways only a recovery of understandings which had been clear enough to Captain Cook on his South Pacific voyages in the eighteenth century, insights which had stopped him being censoriously shocked by anything, from courtship customs to cannibalism.[55] Be that as it may, in the interwar years anthropological studies had their impact in the Colonial Office. It became apparent to the 'recruiting officer', Sir Ralph Furse, that the one charge they could not escape was 'that of insensitivity, even obtuseness on the spiritual and aesthetic values of other peoples'. He was thinking mainly of Africans, but it was equally true of Arabs.[56]

---

[52] E. Evans-Pritchard, *The Nuer: a description of the livelihood and the political institutions of a Nilotic people* (1940).

[53] See especially *Structure and function in primitive society: essays and addresses* (1952).

[54] Margery Perham, 'A re-statement of Indirect Rule', *Africa*, vol. 7 (1934), p. 322.

[55] J. C. Beaglehole, ed., *The journals of Captain James Cook on his voyages of discovery*, vol. I: *The voyage of the 'Endeavour', 1768–1771* (1955); vol. II: *Voyage of the 'Resolution' and 'Adventurer'* (1961). When Cook found a 'young fellow' lying with a girl of ten or twelve, who was being instructed by a woman, his comment was, 'it appeared to be done more from Custom than Lewdness' (vol. I, p. 94). 'Youthful incontinency', he observed, 'can hardly be called a vice, since neither the state nor individuals are the least injured by it'; in any case, societies should not be judged by their prostitutes, any more 'than England by Covent Garden or Drury Lane' (vol. II, pp. 236–59.). The islanders' cooking pleased him: entertained by Chief Oreo at Raiaka, he ate roast pig tasting 'far sweeter than it would have done had it been dressed by any of our methods' (vol. II, p. 226). As to cannibalism, that was an ancient tradition, restricted to eating enemies slain in war, and 'we know that it is not an easy matter to break a nation of its ancient customs' (vol. II, p. 294). It is hard to imagine any Englishman even of the 1920s writing from such an enlightened perspective.

[56] R. Furse, *Aucuparius: recollections of a recruiting officer* (1962), p. 286.

2. Zionism

Theodor Herzl, a Hungarian journalist, in a pamphlet entitled *Judenstaat*, in 1896 called for a world council to discuss the question of a homeland for the Jews. He convened the first Zionist Congress at Basle in the following year, and became first president of the World Zionist Organisation. Zionism was a creed which set out its own national solution to the 'problem' of the Jewish diaspora. It saw itself, in modern parlance, as the national liberation movement of the Jewish people. It was in fact a pure example of 'invented tradition', with no roots in existing Jewish tradition, of which it was a drastic rejection. In October 1902 Herzl approached Joe Chamberlain (secretary of state for the colonies, 1895–1903) and asked if the CO would agree to a Jewish colony in Sinai peninsula. Chamberlain, after a trip on the Uganda railway, preferred to offer a site on the Uasin Gishu plateau near Nairobi. Although the Zionist commissioner reported unfavourably, East Africa remained of interest to Zionists for a few years more.[57] In 1904 Chaim Weizmann arrived at the University of Manchester as a lecturer in chemistry, and made the acquaintance of his local MP, Winston Churchill, who was fascinated by him and his Palestine project. In 1908 Churchill wrote of his belief that

The establishment of a strong Jewish state astride the bridge between Europe and Africa, flanking the land routes to the East, would not only be an immense advantage to the Empire, but a notable step towards a harmonious disposition of the world among its peoples.[58]

This was probably more a romantic Churchillian rhetorical flourish than a serious political commitment.[59] Weizmann continued to cultivate many British politicians and officials.

However, in 1917, Lloyd George's foreign secretary from 1916 to 1919, A. J. Balfour, issued a famous – and fateful – statement, which said:

His Majesty's Government view with favour the establishment in Palestine of a National Home for the Jewish people, and will use their best endeavours to facilitate the achievement of this object, it being clearly understood that nothing shall be done which may prejudice the civil and religious rights of existing non-Jewish communities in Palestine.

[57] J. Amery, *The life of Joseph Chamberlain*, vol. IV: *1901–1903* (1951), pp. 256–70; Hyam, *Elgin and Churchill at the Colonial Office, 1905–1908*, p. 407.

[58] I. Friedman, *The question of Palestine, 1914–1918: British–Jewish–Arab relations* (1973), p. 7. There is a good account of Chaim Weizmann in *ODNB* (2004), vol. LVII, pp. 959–63, by N. Rose.

[59] N. Rose, 'Churchill and Zionism', in R. Blake and W. R. Louis, eds., *Churchill* (1993), pp. 147–66.

The wording was almost entirely derived from Weizmann, though he had wanted 'the National Home of the Jews'.[60] In accordance with the Balfour Declaration, the British government accepted the Palestine Mandate from the League of Nations in April 1920, thus saddling themselves with one of the most difficult problems Britain ever had to face, and to which no British politician would find a solution. Unlike almost all other problems, it was not one which arose naturally or ineluctably out of the circumstances of, or challenges to, imperial power, but was actually created, a gratuitous piece of self-inflicted harm, if you like. Palestine developed into the world's most portentous dispute.[61]

How did this extraordinary involvement come about? Churchill's statement quoted above gives us one clue, for he had identified a geopolitical idea which was formally articulated in 1917 by L. S. Amery (a Conservative MP, soon to be the under-secretary of state for the colonies, in January 1919). Amery contemplated the possibility that the Germans might install themselves in Palestine, and try to link it up to their colony in East Africa, with a railway from Hamburg to Lake Nyasa, as a Germano-Islamic empire, 'the greatest of all dangers which can confront the British Empire in the future'. The Germans must therefore be removed from Tanganyika and from any possible influence in the Middle East, which alone would give an imperial strategical security, enabling 'that Southern British world, which runs from Cape Town through Cairo, Baghdad, and Calcutta to Sydney and Wellington, to go about its peaceful business without constant fear of German aggression'. The keystone of this geopolitical arch would be in Palestine. This would protect the British position in Egypt and India, as 'a central pivot of support for our whole Middle East policy as well as assuring the effective control of our sea and air communications with the East'.[62]

This geopolitical concept was, then, the first and long-term reason for the patronage of Zionism by the British government. Zionism provided a means of acquiring informal control without annexation.[63] Zionism played into British hands, making it possible to realise a strategic objective – an

[60] J. Reinharz, 'The Balfour Declaration and its maker: a reassessment; *Journal of Modern History*, vol. 64 (1992), pp. 455–99. The declaration was made in the form of a letter to Lord Rothschild.

[61] T. Segev, *One Palestine, complete: Jews and Arabs under the British Mandate* (transl. H Watzman, 2000, 2001): pp. 33–50 on the Balfour Declaration. This work is both controversial Jewish revisionism and an epic evocation of the three communities.

[62] L. S. Amery, *My political life*, vol. II: *War and peace, 1914–1929* (1953), p. 115; M. Howard, *The continental commitment: the dilemma of British defence policy in the era of the two world wars* (1972), pp. 65–8.

[63] M. Vereté, 'The Balfour Declaration and its makers', *Middle Eastern Studies*, vol. 6 (1970), pp. 48–67, repr. in E. Kedourie and S. G. Haim, eds., *Palestine and Israel in the nineteenth and twentieth centuries* (1982).

imperial bastion on the cheap – without offending the USA. (It has been said that if Zionism had not existed it would have been necessary to invent it.) For prime minister Lloyd George, the attraction of the Palestine project was as a pre-emptive measure against the French, who wanted to be a major power in the Middle East. Asquith believed Lloyd George 'does not care a damn for the Jews or their past or their future, but thinks it will be an outrage to let the Holy Places pass into the possession of "agnostic, atheistic France"'. Palestine would be a buffer between the Suez Canal and French Syria to the north. (As late as 1923 Curzon said that if Britain abandoned Palestine, 'the French would step in and then be on the threshold of Egypt and on the outskirts of the Canal'.)[64]

There was, however, a much more important reason why Britain became the patron of Zionism. The short-term aim was to use it as a wartime device to rally the allies. When Churchill in 1922 explained the reason for the Balfour Declaration, he said 'it was considered that the support which the Jews could give us all over the world, and particularly in the USA, and also in Russia, would be a definite, palpable advantage' in the conduct of the war.[65] Or as Balfour himself argued, it would enable Britain to 'carry on extremely useful propaganda both in Russia and America'. There were reckoned to be two important groups of Jews who could be rallied. One was in Russia, where the revolutionary leaders were threatening to take Russia *out* of the war (it was assumed Jews were directing the Revolution and needed to be diverted from communism). The other was in America, which still had to be brought *into* the war, and where American Jews were antagonistic to the Allied cause. There were five million Jews in America, the largest single concentration of Jews anywhere – up to 1914 they had been entering the USA at the rate of 100,000 a year. Supposedly, a gesture to Zionism might unlock legendary Jewish millions in Wall Street, or at least divide the huge neutralist minority of the German-descended American Jews. Lloyd George probably saw British support as having a quid pro quo: in return he hoped the Jewish leaders would promote support throughout the world for the Allied war effort.[66] But contrary to folklore, there was no bargain. Folklore has suggested that he wanted to reward Weizmann for his contribution to the war effort: Weizmann's bulk-produced acetone process (making acetone from conkers) saved the British armaments industry. But as Weizmann himself recognised, governments do not operate like that, and 'history does not deal in Aladdin's lamps'.[67] The truth is, as the government said in

[64] J. J. McTague, *British policy in Palestine, 1917–1922* (Lanham, USA, 1983), pp. 25, 39, 56, 252.   [65] Gilbert, *Winston S. Churchill*, vol. IV: *1917–1922*, pp. 652–3.
[66] Friedman, *The question of Palestine*, pp. 168–71.
[67] M. Cohen, *Churchill and the Jews* (1985), p. 34.

1923: the Balfour Declaration was a 'war measure . . . designed to secure tangible benefits which it was hoped could contribute to the ultimate victory of the Allies' at a time of 'extreme peril'.[68] The power of world Jewry was, however, vastly over-estimated. It simply was not true that Jewish minorities were all of the same mind or coherently linked, let alone active supporters of Zionism. Belief in the 'international power' of the Jews was sometimes ludicrously exaggerated. In the final analysis, it was a damaging absurdity.[69]

One other interpretation of the Palestine project is possible: that it was to forestall German competition for the patronage of Zionism, the pre-emption of a possible German initiative to sponsor her own sort of pro-Zionist gesture. This, it was argued, would have won over a great deal of the Jewish support that the British were aiming at. There were fears that the war might end in stalemate, and that a German protectorate in the Middle East might be the outcome. 'The Balfour Declaration was meant to torpedo the supposed German–Turkish move and to undermine their negotiating position at the peace conference' (Friedman). The fear was that Turkey would be 'teutonised' and play a new role in the Middle East after the withdrawal of Russian influence. Curzon (lord president of the council, former viceroy of India, and foreign secretary from 1921), noting the infection of the Turkish empire with German militarism, said that a 'Teutonised Turkey' in possession of Syria and Palestine would be 'an extreme and perpetual menace to the empire' – the kind of language Wellesley had used about Mysore in India in the 1790s. Many German-orientated and Turkophile Jews, especially in America, would perhaps have been happy to see a Jewish settlement in Palestine under German protection.[70]

Ironically, the Balfour Declaration was passionately denounced by the only Jewish member of the Cabinet, E. S. Montagu, the secretary of state for India (1917–22). He opposed a Zionist homeland as the reconstruction of the tower of Babel: 'Palestine will become the world's ghetto.' He claimed that most influential British Jews (including Sir Matthew Nathan, the leading colonial governor) were against it, and that it was, after all, a 'foreign' cosmopolitan movement which Britain was not obliged to support. He worried especially about the Muslim reaction in India.[71]

Nevertheless, Zionism was vaguely supported by many Britons, and the government did not renege on its promise after the war was over, so the policy must have touched roots beyond simple wartime short-term

[68] D. Ingrams, ed., *Palestine papers, 1917–1922: the seeds of conflict* (1972), p. 173.
[69] N. Shepherd, *Ploughing sand: British rule in Palestine, 1917–1948* (1999), pp. 5–19.
[70] Friedman, *The question of Palestine*, pp. 285–6.
[71] R. M. Basheer, *Montagu and the Balfour Declaration* (Arab League pamphlet, 1966).

expediency. To some, sympathy for the Jewish cause was of interest to them as Christians. The idea of a return of the Jews to Jerusalem fascinated them. The number of 'biblical tourists' and pilgrims to the Holy Land was increasing. Biblical romanticism had a hold on Lloyd George and many Welshmen: 'I was taught in school far more about the history of the Jews than about the history of my own land.'[72] The South African leader, General Jan Smuts, said the Jewish cause appealed to him 'with peculiar force', because something was due from Christians to Jews in the interests of historic justice, compensation for 'unspeakable persecutions' of the people who had in fact 'produced Christ'; 'moral and religious motives thus reinforced the political considerations', security in the eastern Mediterranean.[73] In many ways support for a Jewish homeland was a specifically Edwardian emotion. Zionism had its appeal as a Jewish version of the idea behind the phenomenally successful boy-scout movement from 1908 in leading deprived boys, bare-kneed, out of Europe's crammed smoky cities into a healthier life outdoors (or overseas). The healthiness of British Jewish men was discovered and admired, and circumcision was becoming remarkably popular, especially with higher social groups.[74]

Certainly the idea bit deep with the empire-minded political elite. Many of the key figures were Zionists to some degree, including not only Joe Chamberlain, Balfour, Lloyd George, Churchill, Milner, Amery and Smuts, but also John Buchan, Malcolm MacDonald, William Ormsby-Gore, and, in the next generation, Harold Wilson. It was not supported to anything like the same extent by Middle East experts, such as General Sir Edmund Allenby or governor Sir Ronald Storrs, nor by those concerned with India. Field-Marshal Sir Henry Wilson could see no strategic value in it, and urged abandonment of the Mandate. Initially the project was actively opposed by Curzon, who in Cabinet in 1917 said the government 'should have nothing to do with it': Palestine was 'an unpropitious place', too poor, and what about its Muslims?; to aim at the repatriation of the Jews was 'sentimental idealism', and he felt 'cordial distrust' for the intoxicating 'fumes of Zionism'; on the principle of 'historic rights', Curzon added, 'we have a stronger claim to parts of France'. But Curzon allowed himself to be overruled, and, like other objectors, out-manoeuvred by those putting the strategic arguments.[75]

---

[72] Segev, *One Palestine, complete*, p. 43; Wilson, *After the Victorians*, pp. 99–104.

[73] Jean van der Poel, ed., *Selections from the Smuts Papers*, vol. VI (1973), p. 315, speech in honour of Dr Weizmann, president of Israel (27 November 1949).

[74] Hyam, *Britain's imperial century, 1815–1914*, pp. 276–9.

[75] Ingrams, *Palestine papers*, pp. 12, 96–7.

It was widely felt that the British could have it both ways. Jewish and Arab interests not only should but could be reconciled. Probably few British officials took the Jewish side, but they did not much care for Arabs either: a parity of disesteem, perhaps. Ormsby-Gore (secretary of state for the colonies, 1936–8) came to regard the Jews as greedy and aggressive, the Arabs as 'treacherous and untrustworthy',[76] equally devious, equally loathsome. Or as haughty Storrs wrote, after nine years as governor of Jerusalem: 'I am not wholly for either, but for both. Two hours of Arab grievances drive me into the synagogue, while after an intensive course of Zionist propaganda, I am prepared to embrace Islam.'[77] High Commissioner Sir John Chancellor (appointed in 1928) concluded that the Jews were ungrateful, the Arabs impertinent, and the Balfour Declaration a 'colossal blunder'.[78]

Patronage of Zionism reflected non-comprehension and contempt for nationalist movements which were general in the 1920s. Arab nationalism was not regarded as an identifiable factor at all until the Arab revolt of 1936. In 1919 Balfour – pressing the cause with uncharacterstic energy and commitment – recognised that the Arabs would oppose Britain's policy, and that it was indeed not consistent with principles of self-determination, but:

we do not propose to go through the form of consulting the wishes of the present inhabitants of the country . . . The four Great Powers are committed to Zionism. And Zionism be it right or wrong, good or bad, is rooted in agelong traditions, in present needs, in future hopes, of far profounder import that the desires and prejudices of the 700,000 Arabs who now inhabit that ancient land.

The question of the Jews, he added, was one of 'world importance'.[79] It would be hard to find a more shocking illustration of the extent and depth of the West's complacency in the early twentieth century about the supposedly inevitable decline of Islam, of the West's contempt for Muslim interests – its backing of Zionism 'right or wrong' – than Balfour's statement here. The British government was largely oblivious to the terrible nature of the provocation it was giving to the Muslim world.

In other ways, too, Zionism was underpinned by deep attitudes within the British ruling elite. The Victorian belief in 'the immorality of the economic status quo' was well to the fore. This goes right back to Charles Kingsley in the 1850s (if no further), castigating the people of Paraguay for their immoral unawareness that they could not remain in 'a stationary state': 'the human species has a right to demand . . . that each people

---

[76] Ormsby-Gore to N. Chamberlain, 9 January 1938, quoted in M. J. Cohen, *Palestine: retreat from the Mandate: the making of British policy, 1936–1945* (1978), p. 49.

[77] R. H. A. Storrs, *Orientations* (1943, 1945), p. 340.

[78] Segev, *One Palestine, complete*, pp. 334–5.

[79] Ingrams, *Palestine papers* (Balfour to prime minister, 19 February 1919).

should either develop the capabilities of their own country, or make room for those who will develop them'. Half a century later, the future Labour leader Ramsay MacDonald believed 'the world is the inheritance of all men' and no nation could deny its produce to the world; this economic reason justified the acquisition of territory.[80] Churchill was strongly moved by this kind of reasoning. 'Inefficient and out-of-date' Turks must be bought out, having misruled one of the most fertile areas in the world.[81] A new Palestine would be created by the Jews, which would bring prosperity and 'a higher economic and social life to all', a great experiment, in conformity with the empire's 'great estates' policy. The Arabs, insisted Churchill, 'should see them as their friends and helpers, not as expellers and expropriators'. After all:

Left to themselves, the Arabs of Palestine would not in a thousand years have taken effective steps towards the irrigation and electrification of Palestine. They would have been quite content to dwell – a handful of philosophic people – in the wasted sun-scorched plains, letting the waters of the Jordan continue to flow unbridled and unharnessed into the Dead Sea.

Churchill tactlessly reproached the Arabs for being guilty of a 'breach of hospitality'.[82]

Zionism also reflects the obsession of the interwar generation with declarations, definitions, legalistic pronouncements, paper solutions – what George Orwell called the 'time of labels, slogans and evasions' – and what a permanent under-secretary at the Foreign Office, Sir Robert Vansittart, recalled as a time when 'we paddled in a puree of words and hoped to catch a formula'.[83] Words tided over short-term crises without providing real solutions. The reports of nineteen Palestine commissions of inquiry piled up. The Balfour Declaration was subjected to interpretation and modification in no fewer than three White Papers: in 1922, in 1930, and in 1939.[84] Officially a Jewish state was not envisaged by British policy, but unofficially none could say. There was really no unequivocally clear policy before 1939. Churchill's glosses in his White Paper of 1922 were a careful balancing of allegedly incompatible earlier promises. The Balfour Declaration did *not* mean 'that Palestine as a whole should be converted

---

[80] Charles Kingsley, *Miscellanies* (2 vols., 1859) vol. II, pp. 21–2; J. R. MacDonald, *Labour and the empire* (1907), pp. 65, 98.   [81] `Friedman, *The question of Palestine*, pp. 17–18.

[82] *PD, Commons* vol. 156, cc. 334–5, 4 July 1922. See also Gilbert, *Winston S. Churchill*, vol. IV, pp. 531–662, and *Companion*, vol. IV, pt 3, *Documents, April 1921–November 1922* (1977), esp. pp. 1610–18.

[83] Orwell, *Collected essays, journalism and letters*, vol. I: *1920–1940*, p. 519 ('Inside the whale', 1940); Vansittart, *The mist procession*, p. 484.

[84] Segev, *One Palestine, complete*, p. 9; B. Wasserstein, *The British in Palestine: the mandatory government and the Arab-Jewish conflict, 1917–1929* (1978).

into a Jewish National Home, but that such a Home should be founded *in* Palestine'. There was to be a Jewish 'centre' in Palestine, 'internationally guaranteed and formally recognised to rest upon ancient historic connection'. On the other hand the future development of the Jewish community must not lead to the imposition of a Jewish nationality on the inhabitants of Palestine as a whole; and Jewish immigration should not be so great as to go beyond the economic capacity of the country to absorb it. There must be no subordination of the Arab population, or its language or its culture. There ought, in his view, to be a shared bi-national state. Neither side was in fact really interested in such an outcome.[85]

There was some attempt to get off the hook, or at least spread the load. Alternative sites for Zion were investigated, all of them more fantastic – if that is possible – than Palestine itself. Tanganyika, Madagascar, and British Guiana were all looked at by Neville Chamberlain. Another possibility was satellite settlements in Eritrea and Tripolitania (Libya), as Jewish colonies affiliated to the National Home in Palestine. By 1943 Churchill thought this a possibility, and Professor Arnold Toynbee was working out possible plans.[86]

Palestine, however, had – in some evaluations at least – become too important strategically to be given up. As Colonel Wedgwood (a minister in the 1924 Labour government) put it, Palestine was 'the Clapham Junction of the Commonwealth'. It was argued that its evolving strategic significance was two-fold: as the 'strategic buffer of Egypt', the north-east buttress defending Egypt, the Red Sea, and the Suez Canal; and as an easily accessible land link with Iraq and the Persian Gulf, necessary for the protection of the British position at Baghdad. In the 1920s communications were developed to make the Haifa–Baghdad route a viable alternative route to India if the Canal was threatened. In fact this second strategic consideration developed at the expense of the Egyptian function. Haifa was developed as a deep-water harbour, with oil pipe-lines laid from Kirkuk. Haifa was also a railway terminus. There was even consideration after 1936 of turning Haifa into a substitute for Malta, as a base, and for building up a local strategic reserve. In this way Palestine came to be regarded as an indispensable geopolitical link between British interests in Egypt and Iraq, and an irreducible strategic requirement of policy from the 1920s.[87]

---

[85] W. S. Churchill, memo, 3 June 1922 (Cmd 1700); McTague, *British policy in Palestine*, pp. 259–60.

[86] R. Ovendale, *'Appeasement' and the English-speaking world: Britain, the United States and the Dominions, and the policy of 'appeasement' 1937–1939* (Cardiff, 1975), p. 196; W. R. Louis, *Imperialism at bay, 1941–1945: the United States and the decolonisation of the British empire* (1977), pp. 58–62.

[87] N. Rose, *The gentile Zionists: a study in Anglo-Zionist diplomacy, 1929–1939* (1973), pp. 73–103.

The tricky thing about strategic requirements is that they have an awkward propensity to change, and in any case can be subverted by local instability. And just such a dramatic change of evaluation about Palestine was expressed in the White Paper of 1939, marking a decisive shift to a greater sympathy with the Arab predicament, and in the context of growing disillusionment about the Mandate. There were disturbances in 1928–9, and by the mid-1930s the British were thoroughly sick of Palestine. It was never easy to rule. Too little money was available to the administration. Almost nothing was done to improve Arab backwardness. Officials felt frustrated. Sir Douglas Harris (for many years special commissioner in Palestine) complained 'that one is ploughing sand'.[88] Immigration and border control was a nightmare: not just illegal entrants, whether Jews or Arabs, but smugglers and bandits, nomadic shepherds and salesman, pilgrims and archaeologists all milling about. Guns poured in. From 1936 the Arab revolt gathered momentum, as strikes turned into sabotage. By 1938 the government had lost control of large areas of the country, and order was only restored by drastic counter-terrorist measures. The death penalty was extended to rebels merely carrying arms, and sometimes to simple arsonists. The suppression of this proto-*intifada* can only be described as cruel. Between August and October 1938, thirty death sentences were pronounced (six were commuted). Villages were razed to the ground as collective punishment, 2,000 houses were destroyed, and there were countless floggings. Protests at the latter merely mystified Britons who had been routinely caned at their public schools and even enjoyed it as sexually exciting. High Commissioner Sir Alan Cunningham asked what all the fuss was about: 'one shouldn't take these things so seriously'. However, there were unauthorised abuses not so airily dismissed. Soldiers robbed and vandalised, looted, and destroyed food in revenge attacks. There was widespread official refusal to believe such things could be done by British soldiers. Surely reports were 'fabricated by Nazi agents'? The truth is, though, that the abuses were well authenticated, often by Anglican clergy.[89] The suppression of the Arab revolt thus falls into place as one of the links in that deplorable chain of excessive retribution which runs from the Indian Mutiny, through 1865 Jamaica, Dinshawai 1906, and Amritsar, to the Mau Mau revolt in Kenya. The Israeli successor regime picked up many tips and tactics. (Indeed, the Mandate Emergency Regulations remained unchanged on

---

[88] Shepherd, *Ploughing sand*, pp. 76–80, 226 (Harris made his comment in 1945).
[89] Segev, *One Palestine, complete*, pp. 415–26; Shepherd, *Ploughing sand*, pp. 211–21, 246–7; C. Smith, 'Communal conflict and insurrection in Palestine, 1936–1948', in D. Anderson and D. Killingray, eds., *Policing and decolonisation: politics, nationalism and the police, 1917–1965* (Manchester, 1992), esp. pp. 66–71.

the statute books and have been frequently invoked as a basis for Israeli destruction of property, collective punishment, and the confiscation of land in Gaza and the West Bank.)

The Arab revolt of 1936 was an expression of disgust for British policy perceived as pro-Zionist, and a protest against the levels of Jewish immigration, and the threat of partition, which now seemed to be the favoured solution of an inquiry headed by Lord Peel. The reaction of the British government to the revolt was in part a rediscovery of an underlying imperial policy alive to the need for an understanding with the Arab world. Zionism disrupted this, and thus imperilled imperial communications in the Middle East and the flow of oil.[90] For this reason the White Paper of 1939 should not perhaps be seen quite so much as it sometimes is as part of the policy of 'appeasement' (which was being abandoned at this date).

The White Paper of 1939 did four things. (1) It declared that the British government's 'ultimate objective is the establishment of an independent Palestine State, possibly of a federal nature, in such treaty relations with Great Britain as would provide satisfactorily for the commercial and strategic interests of both countries'; it was not the objective 'that Palestine should become a Jewish state or an Arab state; nor do they regard their pledges to either Jews or Arabs as requiring them to promote either of these alternatives'; the state envisaged would be a shared state, which, with the co-operation of both, it was hoped might emerge within ten years. (2) It severely restricted the opportunities for Jewish land purchase. (3) It severely restricted opportunities for Jewish immigration: a fixed quota of 75,000 Jewish immigrants over the next five years was set forth, to be made up of 10,000 a year, plus 25,000 refugees over the period as a whole. (This was a formidable restriction, because even assuming that Arabs would agree to 10,000 a year, it would then have taken a hundred years to bring in a million Jews.) (4) After five years, immigration was made 'subject to the acquiescence of the Arabs'.[91]

The reason for these changes was a realistic, or cynical, belief that the Jews would have no alternative but to be anti-Nazi in a German war, whatever Britain did. As Neville Chamberlain expressed it to Malcolm MacDonald (secretary of state for the colonies) in April 1939: 'we are now compelled to consider the Palestine problem mainly from the point of view of its effect on the international situation'; if they must offend one side, 'let us offend the Jews rather than the Arabs'. Thus the White

[90] Y. Bauer, *From diplomacy to resistance: Jewish Palestine, 1939–1945* (1970), pp. 411–12.

[91] M. J. Cohen, 'Appeasement in the Middle East: the British White Paper on Palestine, 1939', *Historical Journal*, vol. 16 (1973), pp. 571–96, and *Palestine: retreat from the Mandate: the making of British policy, 1936–1945*.

Paper showed a fundamental recognition that there was growing up an increasingly anti-British brand of Arab nationalism, and aimed to prevent its becoming contagious. Peace in Palestine was essential for three reasons: to release troops tied up to defend the Suez Canal in war; to bring Indian reinforcements to Egypt if Italy blocked the Red Sea exit of the Canal in war, reinforcements which would have to come overland via the Persian Gulf and Palestine on a guaranteed route; and to secure, in the long run, the important oil interests. There was a feeling with some that since the Jews had waited two thousand years they could afford to be made to wait a little longer.

As prime minister, Churchill in 1943 privately denounced the White Paper as 'a gross breach of faith'. The Arabs were, he believed, proving bad allies (unlike in the First World War), and Britain owed them nothing.[92] But as the Foreign Office officials pointed out, Churchill had missed the point:

The question is . . . not whether we owe [sympathy to the sufferings of the Jews, or the] Arabs a debt of gratitude, but whether we have important interests centring in the Arab world. The answer must be emphatically that we have; and in particular our oil interests.[93]

Churchill did not get matters very much back into a Zionist direction. By 1944 the Coalition government was moving towards the partition of Palestine as a solution, that is to say, a reversion to the abortive partition policy already proposed by Viscount Peel and the CO in 1937. Probably the trend towards partition resulted from growing American interest and Jewish terrorism, and from the administrative difficulty of implementing the White Paper in wartime conditions; and perhaps it was a means of sustaining old-fashioned and co-operative Weizmann at the head of the Zionist movement. But the White Paper policy was not overthrown. The Foreign Office saw to that.[94]

3. Nationalism

'Nationalism is essentially an anti-feeling . . . especially against the foreign rulers in a subject country.' Jawaharlal Nehru's uncomplicated definition of colonial nationalism is entirely serviceable. It *is* best

---

[92] M. J. Cohen, 'The British White Paper on Palestine, May 1939: part 2, The testing of a policy, 1942–1945' *Historical Journal*, vol. 19 (1976), pp. 727–57.

[93] Cohen, *Palestine: retreat from the Mandate*, p. 163.

[94] A. S. Klieman, 'The divisiveness of Palestine: the Foreign Office versus the Colonial Office on the issue of partition, 1937', *Historical Journal*, vol. 22 (1979) pp. 423–42; R. W. Zweig, 'The Palestine Mandate', *Historical Journal*, vol. 24 (1981), pp. 243–51 and *Britain and Palestine during the Second World War* (1986).

conceived of as a political instrument for articulating a change in the power structure, by organising an alternative allegiance.[95] Definitions suited to Europe, about nationalisms as cultural phenomena, dependent on industrialisation, or 'things remembered in common', do not help us much when considering Asian and African nationalisms, though D'Azeglio's assertion (1871) 'we have made Italy – now we have to make Italians' has a definite relevance.[96] To Nehru 'nationalism pure and simple' was 'the feeling of humiliation of India and a fierce desire to be rid of it and to put an end to our continuing degradation'. This humiliation he likened to a subservient mentality: 'For many years the British treated India as a kind of enormous country-house (after the old English fashion) that they owned. They were the gentry owning the house and occupying the desirable parts of it, while the Indians were consigned to the servants' hall and pantry and kitchen.' And the terrible thing was that 'most of *us* accepted the hierarchical order as inevitable' and impassable. Of course there were benefits, but the imposed Pax Britannica was not enough: 'even peace can be purchased at too great a price, and we can have the perfect peace of the grave, and the absolute safety of a cage or prison'. Peace might also be 'the sodden despair of men unable to better themselves'. Nationalism aimed to change that, for a nation which was subject to another 'and hedged and circumscribed and exploited can never achieve inner growth'.

Indian nationalism developed strong religious and cultural elements, most evident in Gandhi's use of Hindu spiritual rhetoric, symbols, and practices. Gandhi acquired an awesome reputation for saintliness, but he was also an astute politician. 'Non-co-operation' was a skilful tactic to employ against the British.

African nationalism drew inspiration from Indian nationalism in general and Gandhian principles in particular, as well as from the Caribbean propagandists for 'negro improvement' like Marcus Garvey. In 1952 Kwame Nkrumah, graduate of American universities, founder of the Convention People's Party in the Gold Coast, said they had 'India,

[95] Jawaharlal Nehru, *An autobiography* (1936, 1938), pp. 66, 75, 379, 417, 436; it became a best-seller in Britain – see B. R. Nanda, 'Nehru and the British', *Modern Asian Studies* vol. 30 (1996), pp. 469–79. For nationalism as essentially 'a political instrument', see J. Breuilly, *Nationalism and the state* (2nd edn, 1993), and as 'colonial political growth', Gallagher, *The decline, revival and fall of the British empire*, pp. 101–12.

[96] D'Azeglio's remark was quoted as having contemporary relevance in *Nationalism: a report by members of the Royal Institute of International Affairs*, (ed. E. H. Carr, 1939), p. 88. It reminds us that 'nationalism' can operate at two levels and speak to different concerns and agendas. The external interface debate with the colonial power is what concerns us here, but nationalism is at another level a form of identity politics, an internal debate about the nature and intent of the post-colonial state, for example whether secular or not.

Ceylon and Burma to draw inspiration from'. His 'positive action' campaign was a continuation of Gandhi's non-violent methods, based on strikes and boycotts, with a more disciplined and effectual political activity, manipulating newspaper and educational campaigns. Nkrumah's slogan was 'seek ye first the political kingdom and all things shall be added unto you'. There were echoes of Nehru in his belief that 'it is only when people are politically free that other races can give them the respect that is due to them', for 'no race, no people, no nation can exist freely and be respected at home and abroad without political freedom'. And of course, he proclaimed, 'it is far better to be free to govern, or misgovern, yourself than be governed by anybody else'.[97]

Everywhere, 'resentment of racial contempt was a primary source of nationalist thought and action' (Iliffe). Nationalism drew support by evoking African traditions of defiant heroic leadership, and stories of early resistance to the white man.[98] Nelson Mandela recalled: 'In my youth in the Transkei I listened to the elders of my tribe telling . . . of wars fought by our ancestors in defence of the fatherland . . . their freedom struggle.'[99]

The British were not short of experience and memory either, in dealing with nationalist protests, ever since the Home Rule movement in Ireland. In a speech in 1886, Charles Stewart Parnell (leader of the Irish Parliamentary Party, 1880–90) threw down the challenge with the immortal words: 'No man has a right to fix the boundary to the march of a nation.' The British technique for dealing with nationalism was first worked out in Ireland, applied to India, carried to Egypt by Lord Cromer (administrator, 1883–1907), and thence on to Africa. Viscount Goschen (chancellor of the Exchequer, 1886–92)[100] had dismissed the

---

[97] Kwame Nkrumah, *The autobiography of Kwame Nkrumah* (1957, 1964), pp. ix–x; G. Shepperson, 'Notes on Negro-American influences on the emergence of African nationalism', *Journal of African History* vol. 1 (1960), p. 303. Other pioneering studies of African nationalism include T. Hodgkin, *Nationalism in Colonial Africa* (1956), Ndabaningi Sithole, *African nationalism* (Cape Town, 1959), and H. Kohn and W. Sokolsky, *African nationalism in the twentieth century* (Princeton, NJ, 1965). On African nationalism as 'the rejection of European control in the first instance', see B. T. G. Chidzero, 'African nationalism in East and Central Africa', *International Affairs*, vol. 36 (1960), pp. 465–74. Because colonial nationalism is essentially an 'anti' phenomenon, African nationalism functioned within the parameters of the colonial state, and this is why the successor states were defined exclusively by colonial boundaries rather than by ethnic or religious cohesion: see D. Birmingham, *The decolonization of Africa* (1995), p. 86.   [98] J. Iliffe, *Honour in African history* (2005), pp. 306–8.

[99] Nelson Mandela, *No easy walk to freedom: articles and speeches* (1973 edn), p. 26; T. O. Ranger, 'Connexions between "primary resistance" movements and modern mass nationalism in East and Central Africa', pts 1 and 2, *Journal of African History*, vol. 9 (1968), pp. 437–53, 631–41.

[100] L. P. Curtis, jnr, *Coercion and conciliation in Ireland, 1880–1892: a study in Conservative Unionism* (Princeton, NJ, 1963), pp. 408–10.

Irish Home Rule agitation as a fraud, 'a bastard nationalism', thus setting the precedent for tackling early nationalist movements – not least in India – [101] simply by denying their validity. To Cromer, Egypt was not and never could be a nation – it was just a 'fortuitous concourse of international atoms'. To Lord Curzon as viceroy from 1898 to 1905, the Indian National Congress was 'an unclean thing', absurdly unrepresentative of the people, led by a 'microscopic minority'.[102] Or, in Churchill's words, Congress was a 'highly artificial and restricted oligarchy', merely representing those who had acquired 'a veneer of civilisation'. Churchill could dismiss India as 'an abstraction . . . a geographical term . . . no more a united nation than the Equator'.[103] 'Voiceless millions' everywhere were alleged to be content with the Pax Britannica, in which – said Churchill in expansively indignant mood – 'an Indian maid with bangles on can travel from Travancore to Punjab all alone without fear of molestation', whereas in wartime Britain women service personnel 'cannot go two miles with the same feeling of safety'.[104] Non-Europeans in general, and Egyptians in particular, were held to be incompetent and lacking in character: every experiment in transferring administrative departments to their control seemed only to prove it. What was good as a system of government for white dominions was said not to be necessarily suitable for universal export. Analogies from Canada and South Africa were expressly ruled out for India, where administration required an exceptional degree of 'technical' ability. The British might be able to do business with 'moderates', but most nationalists seemed to be 'extremists', and these, whether in Dublin, Cairo, Delhi, or Lagos, it was simply not possible to conciliate, 'save on terms which in India and Ireland spell political suicide, and in Egypt would involve a relapse into all the misgovernment and disorder of the past' (Cromer).[105]

All this psychological blockage was cemented together by a personal dislike, a derogatory rhetoric against nationalist leaders. Again, this went back to Unionist vilification of the Irish leader Parnell. Curzon

---

[101] The classic study is A. Seal, *The emergence of Indian nationalism: competition and collaboration in the late nineteenth century* (Cambridge, 1968).

[102] S. Gopal, *British policy in India, 1885–1905* (1965); R. L. Tignor, *Modernisation and British colonial rule in Egypt, 1882–1941* (Princeton, NJ, 1966); Roger Owen, *Lord Cromer: Victorian imperialist and Edwardian proconsul* (2005).

[103] W. S. Churchill, *India: speeches and an introduction* (1931), p. 139.

[104] N. Mansergh and E. W. R. Lumby, eds., *India: the transfer of power, 1942–7*, vol. III: *Reassertion of authority, 21 Sept 1942–12 June 1943* (1971), p. 3 (no. 2), enclosure, Sir A. R. Mudaliar to Sir G. Laithwaite, 21 September 1942.

[105] Quoted in R. Hyam, 'The British empire in the Edwardian era', in Brown and Louis, *The Oxford History of the British Empire*, vol. IV: *The twentieth century*, p. 62.

denounced Surendranath Banerjea as 'that vitriolic windbag'. Cromer
blamed all protest in Egypt on 'weak' Khedive Abbas personally. Sheikh
Muhammad Abdille Hassan of Somaliland was referred to by everybody
in Britain as 'the Mad Mullah'. Churchill called Indian leaders 'men of
straw'. 'Fanatics' like Gandhi should be crushed: 'it is no use trying to
satisfy a tiger by feeding him with cat's-meat'. And this is Churchill's best-
known denunciation: 'It is alarming and also nauseating to see Mr
Gandhi, a seditious Middle Temple lawyer, now posing as a fakir of a type
well-known in the East, striding half-naked up the steps of the viceregal
place . . . to parley on equal terms with the representative of the King-
Emperor.'[106] L. S. Amery (secretary of state for India, 1940–5), who
regarded himself as considerably more liberal than Churchill in his views
on India, described Nehru and Gandhi as 'niggling unpractical crea-
tures', commenting on Nehru's 'complete intransigence' and 'unreasoning bitterness'. He was not sure, he wrote, 'that these people really want
responsibility, and if we offered them the moon they would probably
reject it because of the wrinkles on its surface'.[107]

Churchill in 1930 believed that independence for India was not going
to happen 'in any period which we can even remotely foresee'. In a series
of speeches at around this time he stressed two big objections: the danger
to Britain and the danger to India. 'The loss of India . . . would be final
and fatal to us. It could not fail to be part of a process which would reduce
us to the scale of a minor power . . . The British Empire would pass at a
stroke out of life into history.' This was entirely in the Curzonian mode.
But Churchill also had the concerns of a Lancashire constituency MP.
Two million Englishmen, he foretold, could become unemployed as a
result of Indian self-government, because Gandhi the bogeyman might
stop cotton imports from Lancashire. There could be famine in the
north-west. Churchill placed no faith in leaving everything to the chance
of ties of tradition, 'which in India is adverse, and sentiment, which in
India is hostile'. Churchill's second big theme was the danger to India
itself. Drawing upon the late-Victorian themes adumbrated by his father
Randolph Churchill and Sir John Seeley, he stressed the chaos which
would ensue upon a British withdrawal: 'Hideous disaster to hundreds of
helpless millions . . . and immediate resumption of medieval wars.'[108] In
sum, Churchill believed two things were at stake: 'British authority and

[106] Churchill, *India: speeches and an introduction*, pp. 46, 94.
[107] N. Mansergh and E. W. R. Lumby, eds., *The transfer of power*, vol. I: *The Cripps Mission,
Jan.–April 1942* (1970), L. S. Amery to Viceroy Lord Linlithgow, p. 108 (2 February
1942), 632 (3 April), 867 (29 April), and 840 (no. 681: 'Notes on the Indian situation',
April, 1942); vol. II: *'Quit India', 30 Apr.–21 Sept. 1942* (1971), p. 43 (29 May 1942, to
Linlithgow).   [108] *India: speeches*, pp. 35, 47, 82, 139.

Indian tranquillity.' The policy leading to self-government 'will bring a fatal disaster upon the British Empire and entail endless misery to hundreds of millions of harmless Indian[s]'.[109]

In all this, there is an awful substratum of truth. It is probably true to say that Britain as a great power suffered a mortal blow on 15 August 1947 when India became independent, and there was great misery for millions of Indians in the immediate post-partition upheaval.

In the light of this Churchillian analysis – strong or substantially correct in diagnosis, but hopelessly impracticable in prescription (the maintenance of an Edwardian status quo) – it is easy to see why the Government of India Act of 1935, not in itself a great liberal measure, has been regarded as 'a great liberal victory' over the Churchill-led diehard opposition to constitutional advance in India.[110] The diehard MPs numbered about eighty, and Churchill got about one-third of the votes at the Conservative Party Conference in 1933, attracting support from Lancashire cotton interests, and retired Indian army officers and administrators in the home counties, together with those impatient with Prime Minister Baldwin's general policy.[111]

The Government of India Act conceded provincial autonomy (that is, responsible self-government for the provinces), in the hope of diverting Congress politicians away from the central government, where British rulers still wished to remain in exclusive control of foreign and defence policy and most of the revenue. The Act also promised a federation at the all-India level, including princely states. This was an abortive chimera, not least because the princes were slow to accede and in effect exercised a veto. But provincial autonomy was established and proved to be a useful step forward, though perhaps more for the Muslim League than Congress. Churchill memorably denounced the Act as 'a monstrous monument of sham [sic] built by the pygmies'. ('Sham' because he was – rightly – sceptical of the federation's ever being set up;[112] the 'pygmies'

---

[109] Ibid., p. 11. Historians should treat Churchill's volume of speeches seriously. He said of it, 'I have taken much more trouble with them than with any book I have ever written': M. Gilbert, Winston S. Churchill, vol. V: 1922–1939 (1976), p. 400. For general accounts of Churchill on India, see R. Rhodes James, Churchill: a study in failure, 1900–1939 (1970), and S. Gopal, 'Churchill and India', in R. Blake and W. R. Louis, eds., Churchill (1993), pp. 457–71.

[110] D. A. Low, 'Sapru and the First Round Table Conference', in Low, ed., Soundings in modern South Asian history (1968), pp. 294–329.

[111] G. Peele, 'The revolt over India', in G. Peele and C. Cook, eds., The politics of reappraisal, 1918–1939 (1975), pp. 114–44.

[112] 'Sham' is too often incorrectly rendered as 'shame' by biographers who should know better, e.g. Gilbert, Winston S. Churchill, vol. V, p. 595, and Rhodes James, Churchill: a study in failure, p. 212. The inaccuracy destroys the whole point of Churchill's criticism, which was not that the federal proposals were unworthy but that they were unworkable.

were its architects, Hoare, Simon, and Halifax.) The act was the culmination of a huge debate. In the Commons there were nearly 1,200 speeches, while a select committee had 159 meetings. This debate on the future of the Raj was never again equalled in the history of the demission of imperial power.

The essence of the Act – the reason why it was not a great liberal measure – is that its authors all saw it was possible 'to give a semblance of responsible government and yet retain in our hands the realities and verities of British control'. It was a grand device for 'holding the commanding heights of the Raj while gaining imperial kudos for giving away inessentials', a mechanism 'for ensuring the survival of the Raj by creating a buffer of collaborators'.[113] The underlying strategy went back to the Edwardian Morley–Minto package of 'order plus reforms', of cautious concessions. 'The imprint of ambiguity' was all over the Act. The policy, as one historian describes it, was ambidextrous, dualist, disingenuous, delusory: there was 'a pervasive dualism immersed in ambiguity', a vulnerable ambiguity which Gandhi understood only too well how to exploit. It was not really a workable solution at all.[114] As the Labour leader Clement Attlee said, it offered insufficient scope to 'the living forces of India', the politically minded; and whatever doubts there might be about it – and he was under no illusions – 'the nationalism of India is a force you cannot ignore'.[115]

Within five years British policy in India was in disarray, the whole situation was deadlocked, and imperial prestige in India at its nadir. Thus British Indian policy in the 1930s is unequivocal evidence of a dysfunctional empire. The transfer of power in 1947 was, on any objective criterion, at least ten years too late.[116]

The exigencies of war, dependence on or deference to the US, and pressure from the Labour leadership, led to the mission of Sir Stafford Cripps in 1942. The Cripps offer was in effect a promise of independence (with the option to leave the Commonwealth) after the war, in return for wartime co-operation and a political freeze meanwhile. Dissenting provinces might achieve freedom separately, and the princes could stand aside. There would be a treaty and a constituent assembly. It was a sharp departure in policy, in that it was entirely unambiguous and unqualified. Nevertheless, the Cripps mission failed, mainly and quite

---

[113] Carl Bridge, *Holding India to the empire: the British Conservative Party and the 1935 Constitution* (1986), esp. pp. 156–64.
[114] D. A. Low, *Britain and Indian nationalism: the imprint of ambiguity, 1929–1942* (1997), esp, pp. 1–40; R. J. Moore, *Endgames of empire: studies of Britain's Indian problem* (New Delhi, 1988), pp. 37–85. [115] *PD, Commons* vol. 276, cc. 730–1, 27 March 1933.
[116] Mansergh, *Independence years*, p. 234 ('The partition of India in retrospect', 1965–6).

simply because it was unacceptable to Indian leaders, Muslim League as well as Congress. It had too little to offer in the short-term. Gandhi (it was said) famously dismissed it as 'a post-dated cheque on a crashing bank'. Cripps expostulated that viceroy Linlithgow was as wooden as he was impossible, no help at all. Linlithgow must bear much of the responsibility for failure.[117] This makes it unnecessary to lay the blame on Churchill's lack of enthusiasm – once he had impressed the Americans by dispatching the mission – however sardonic his observations.[118] Churchill was in fact privately rude about the 'bluff and sob-stuff' of Gandhi's hunger-strike 'antics' in February 1943: 'the old rascal' had not 'the slightest intention of dying'. (Churchill had heard that Gandhi had 'cheated' by taking glucose in his water, and was slipped the occasional orange juice when he looked groggy – nine doctors remained in attendance.)[119]

With more than a little of the English gentleman about him,[120] Gandhi looked and sounded remarkably like Attlee, though the latter was not so emaciated. Gandhi's influence became transcendent. It was his preaching of non-violence 'more than any other single factor that stood between India and bloodshed on a frightful scale'. The other dominant figures were Nehru, Jinnah, and Vallabhbhai Patel. Nehru was always the devoted disciple of Gandhi, but with all the easy confidence, charm, and eloquence of a born leader. Educated at Harrow and Trinity College, Cambridge, he was also a 'prison graduate', and long years of imprisonment left him with some bitterness. Muhammad Ali Jinnah was a brilliantly able man who resented the British presence partly because he felt he was cleverer than most British ministers and governors. As the Anglicised and secular leader of a religious party, the Muslim League, he had a difficult position to sustain, which perhaps explains why he kept his ideas about the future close to his chest. He was utterly dismissive of British notions of unity in India, believing Hindus and Muslims could not evolve

---

[117] P. F. Clarke, *The Cripps version: the life of Sir Stafford Cripps, 1889–1952* (2002), pp. 250–3, 276, 318–30.

[118] Mansergh, *Independence years*, pp. 42–50, 'The Cripps Mission to India, March–April 1942'; R. J. Moore, *Churchill, Cripps and India, 1939–1945* (1979).

[119] Mansergh and Lumby, eds., *The transfer of power (TOPI)*, vol. III: *21 September 1942–12 June 1943* (1971), pp. 659, 738, 744, Churchill to viceroy, 13 February 1943, and to Smuts, 26 February 1943. It was also reported that Gandhi was massaged for 1¼ hours a day with mustard-oil and lemon-juice, and was given frequent enemas: *ibid.*, vol. VI: *1 August 1945–22 March 1946* (1976), p. 679.

[120] J. M. Brown, 'Gandhi – a Victorian gentleman: an essay in imperial encounter', *JICH*, vol. 27 (1999), pp. 68–85, repr. in R. D. King and R. W. Kilson, eds, *The statecraft of British imperialism: essays in honour of Wm Roger Louis*. For an incisive contemporary vignette of Gandhi, see *TOPI*, vol. VI, pp. 616–17 (no. 272), diary of R. G. Casey (6 December 1945).

a common nationality: 'they have two different religions, philosophies, social customs, literature. They neither inter-marry, nor even inter-dine.' They also, he might have added, treat penises and corpses differently. Sardar Vallabhbhai Patel was a somewhat brooding presence, but the most hard-nosed of senior Congress Party leaders, determined, with realism and a ruthless sense of purpose, not to unleash social revolution.[121]

The backdrop to the evolution of British policy for India was that India's importance was declining. Before 1914 the imperial value of India was manifest: 'she provided opportunities for export, professional employment, exported indentured labour through the empire, was crucial for imperial security, important for British trade and investment, [and made] sterling remittances to London' (which paid for ICS training and pensions).[122] Within twenty years, however, the position was very different. Indianisation of military, police, and civilian services reduced British career prospects. Indentured labour had been voluntarily given up in 1917. India no longer provided an 'oriental barrack', a standing army on the cheap, as the government of India stood its ground on the need for Britain to pay the costs of the overseas deployment of the Indian army, after concern that nearly one million Indians had fought in the First World War in major theatres abroad, and almost 65,000 were killed. British exports to India were dramatically declining. India was no longer the largest single market for British goods or its biggest single buyer. Import-substitution was proceeding apace. Investment was flagging. Tariff manipulation in the interest of Lancashire was interdicted. Sterling balances were problematic. In short, India's economic value was severely disrupted.[123]

None of this made a transfer of power inevitable, but it did make it easier to contemplate.

The nationalism that confronted Britain in India in the 1930s had aspirations to be broadly based. A specifically Muslim nationalism was an emerging force, however, registering mounting successes in gaining support.

[121] Mansergh, *Independence years*, pp. 51–70, 'The last days of British rule in India: some personal impressions', 1948.

[122] The quotation is from J. M. Brown, 'India', in Brown and Louis, *The Oxford History of the British Empire*, vol. IV: *The twentieth century*, pp. 421–46, at p. 439.

[123] For analysis of 'decline', see B. R. Tomlinson, 'India and the British empire, 1880–1935', *Indian Economic and Social History Review*, vol. 12 (1975), and pt 2, '1935–1947', *ibid.*, vol. 13 (1976), pp. 331–52, and *The political economy of the Raj, 1914–1947: the economics of decolonisation in India* (1979), esp. pp. 1–56, 104–41, and *The Indian National Congress and the Raj, 1929–1942: the penultimate phase* (1976), ch. 1, 'British policy and the Indian problem 1919–1935'. See also C. Dewey, 'The end of the imperialism of free trade: the eclipse of the Lancashire lobby', in C. Dewey and A. G. Hopkins, eds., *The imperial impact: studies in the economic history of Africa and India* (1978).

The Muslim League in India, founded at the end of 1906, more than twenty years after Congress, had a low profile and limited constituency, until Muslim politics were integrated and galvanised under Jinnah, with a new slogan, 'Pakistan'. The fissures which opened up in India in 1937 with the failure of Congress to form coalitions with the League politicians had their potential parallels elsewhere. The tectonic plates between Muslim and Christian (or other religious) worlds were uneasily aligned in Nigeria and Sudan, Iraq and Palestine, and in Malaya. British rulers had to keep the peace. Christian missions made little progress where they were in competition with Islam, in Africa particularly – at a disadvantage because Islam was not 'the colonial religion', did not insist on monogamy, and generally seemed closer to African styles and expectations. The British rulers also worried about the possibility of Pan-Islamic *jihad*. Not all Muslim ideology was driven, however, by 'fundamentalists' (Islamists), like the Muslim Brotherhood founded in Egypt in 1928. Islamic 'modernists', ill at ease with the traditional rigidities of the rural *ulama* ('religious institution') were reformists who preferred to seek an accommodation with Western ideas and promote a secular nationalism. The ideological divergences, tensions, and competition between modernisers and traditionalists (themselves of various kinds) could be profound and intense, and characterised the whole Muslim world in this period.[124]

In the Middle East these tensions were especially evident. Arab nationalism was stirring even before the First World War, marking a decidedly hostile reaction to increasing Western influence, questioning early more favourable images of the West. By 1919, the whole Arabic-speaking world was under European domination except parts of the Arabian peninsula. In response to this situation, the secular nationalism of reformist Islam was what most Arab-Muslims wanted, even if religion was an activating force in that nationalism. Pan-Arab sentiment certainly existed, but regional loyalties and rivalries remained strong. The disparity between British and nationalist forces was gradually shifting in the region towards a more even balance from the 1920s, and especially from the 1940s, when there was ever-increasing hostility. The creation of the state of Israel in 1948 became a Muslim rallying-point throughout the region and beyond.[125] A passionate reassertion of Islamic beliefs gained momentum,

[124] F. Robinson, 'The British empire and the Muslim world', in Brown and Louis, *The Oxford History of the British Empire*, vol. IV: *The twentieth century*, pp. 398–419; M. G. S. Hodgson, *The venture of Islam: conscience and history in a world civilisation*, vol. III: (Chicago, 1974); C. C. Stewart, 'Islam', in A. D. Roberts, ed. *Cambridge history of Africa*, vol. VII, pp. 191–222.

[125] J. Abu-Lughod, *Arab discovery of Europe: a study in cultural encounters* (Princeton, 1963), pp. 157–63; A. Hourani, *A history of the Arab peoples* (1991); Chatham House Study Group Report, *British interests in the Mediterranean and Middle East* (1958).

much more in touch with the masses than earlier nationalist movements had been, and all the more potent for that. In Egypt, the 'Free Officers' group from 1939 were from the lower-bourgeois class, dedicated within the army to an ultra-nationalist and anti-British programme quite different from the now torpid Wafd nationalism of landed plutocrats and high-ranking bureaucrats. In the Sudan 'Abd al-Rahman emerged in the mid-1920s as a nationalist leader, but was challenged, and soon there were two opposing factions, a sectarian schism (neo-Mahdists and anti-Mahdists) which weakened the nationalist movement.[126]

4. Idealism: the British Commonwealth

The white Dominions also had their nationalist aspirations, which their costly contributions to the First World War had intensified. Between the wars, the British Commonwealth was essentially an arrangement by which the more independent-minded pushed for a clarification of their status and were prevented from breaking away completely from Britain.[127] South Africa and Canada were the leaders in this process, while the discontented Irish Free State was less prominent before 1936 when republicanism became more definite.[128] Britain was especially concerned to prevent the secession of South Africa, a course which seemed to be vaguely threatened by its prime minister, General J. B. M. Hertzog (1924–39). The centre-piece of Commonwealth evolution was a formula known as the Balfour Definition,[129] arrived at by the Commonwealth prime ministers meeting in an inter-imperial relations committee at the Imperial Conference of 1926, and chaired by Lord Balfour, by then

[126] P. J. Vatikiotis, *Nasser and his generation* (1978); M. W. Daly and G. N. Sanderson, 'Egypt and the Anglo-Egyptian Sudan', in *Cambridge History of Africa*, vol. VII, pp. 742–879; G. N. Sanderson, 'Sudanese nationalism and the independence of Sudan', in M. Brett, ed., *Northern Africa, Islam and modernisation* (1973), pp. 97–109.

[127] N. Mansergh, *The Commonwealth experience* (2nd edn, 1982), vol. II: *From British to Multi-racial Commonwealth*, 'Status seeking and tariff reform, 1921–1936', pp. 3–42.

[128] In a field always at risk from constitutional stulification, the liveliest essay is by Ged Martin, 'The Irish Free State and the evolution of the Commonwealth, 1921–1949', in R. Hyam and G. W. Martin, *Reappraisals in British imperial history* (1975), pp. 201–23, which takes apart the contention of Harkness that the Irish Free State radically made the running for a decade in transforming the empire into a Commonwealth: D. W. Harkness, *The restless Dominion: the Irish Free State and the British Commonwealth of Nations, 1921–1931* (1969), and related essays. On the 1926 formula, Martin writes: 'At best, it can only be a question of Irish spin-bowling's mopping up after the South African and Canadian pace-attack had broken through the batting'; and, the Irish were not genuine contributors, 'hardly even genuine members'.

[129] D. Judd, *Empire: the British imperial experience from 1765 to the present* (1996), ch. 22, 'The Balfour Definition of Dominion status, 1926'. It is of course important not to confuse the Balfour Definition, or Report, with the 'Balfour Declaration', which was on Zionism (1917), as some historians have done, though I will not embarrass them by naming them.

Britain's elder statesman as lord president of the Council. The famous formula defined dominion status – that is, Commonwealth membership – as follows:

They are autonomous communities within the British Empire, equal in status, in no way subordinate to one another in any aspect of their domestic or external affairs, though united by a common allegiance to the Crown, and freely associated as members of the British Commonwealth of Nations.

Much of the initiative for this statement had come from L. S. Amery as dominions secretary, and it reflected theories going back to Edwardian liberalism. The aim was to recognise reality and avoid needless confrontation. It represented a genuine compromise. Hertzog, determined to see off any lingering suggestion that Britain was a 'super-state superior', objected to the term 'British Empire' – but New Zealand would not subscribe to a formula which omitted it. Mackenzie King of Canada objected to anything which seemed like an American-style 'declaration of independence', so Hertzog lost the word 'independent'. Balfour himself objected to 'freely associated', because it might imply they could be freely dissociated, which was a bit like stating in a marriage ceremony the possibility of divorce.[130] The reference to autonomy pleased the South Africans and the Irish; the reference to the Crown placated the Australians and New Zealanders; and there was a sizeable qualification to the substance – 'But the principles of equality and similarity, appropriate to status, do not universally extend to function' – which reassured some of the British sceptics.

Subtle, but essentially bland, for five years the Balfour Definition had no legal force. However, the next imperial conference in 1930 agreed that legislation should give effect to the formula, and the Statute of Westminster was enacted in 1931. Henceforth the British parliament could not legislate on behalf of a dominion (except with its consent), and no law passed in the dominions could be invalidated on the grounds of repugnance to English law (thus repealing an act of 1865). Governors-general would no longer act in any way as the agent of the UK government. Dominions were now as independent as they chose to be. (New Zealand did not enact the statute until 1947.)[131] Each would remain the sole judge of the nature and extent of its co-operation with Britain, though in practice some dependence in diplomacy and defence remained until the Second World War.

---

[130] P. Wigley and N. Hillmer, 'Defining the first British Commonwealth: the Hankey memoranda on the 1926 Imperial Conference', in H. Hillmer and P. Wigley, eds., *The first British Commonwealth: essays in honour of Nicholas Mansergh* (1980), pp. 105–16, repr. from *JICH*, vol. 8 (1979).

[131] A. Ross, 'New Zealand and the Statute of Westminster', in *ibid.*, pp. 136–58.

The Balfour Definition opened the way for a torrent of idealism about the Commonwealth, not least among academics, such as Alfred Zimmern, Duncan Hall, and Arnold Toynbee,[132] and even the more austere specialists such as Keith Hancock and the Cambridge historians E. A. Benians and Eric Walker. To the Australian Hancock – who began publishing his magisterial *Survey of British Commonwealth affairs* in 1937 – the empire had now commendably reconciled *imperium* and *libertas*. To Benians, the British, after 'making a shipwreck' of the 'first empire' by the loss of the American colonies, and after the tragedy of the 'ill-starred events' of the Boer War, had achieved the emergence of the Commonwealth – 'a union of states and nations in a free and peaceful co-operation' – in a way which was little short of miraculous, especially considering its heterogeneous membership and racial and geographical diversity. It was, as Benians described it, 'a moral conception, a great partnership', whose justification was 'to teach the way of freedom, to teach nations to live together in society'.[133] This idea – that the Commonwealth could be a model for larger international organisations, such as the League of Nations – was particularly important when it came to trying to estimate its significance and potential.

Those who thought along these lines were enthusiastic idealists. There were also visionary idealists. The visionaries wanted to use the Commonwealth in a quite different way. Some of them would have preferred a much more organic structure.[134] Most influential of them was L. S. Amery, Conservative under-secretary at the CO (1919–21), then first lord of the Admiralty, and secretary of state for the colonies between 1924 and 1929, and finally secretary of state for India and Burma during the Second World War.[135] Amery was a politician of unusually clear economic and geopolitical insight, who disagreed with Churchill more often than not. (They first met at Harrow School, when Churchill, his junior, pushed him fully clothed into the swimming pool.) Amery was short, and he talked too often and too much: it was said of

---

[132] J. D. B. Miller, 'The Commonwealth and world order: the Zimmern vision and after', in *ibid.* pp. 159–74; W. D. McIntyre, 'Clio and Britannia's dream: historians and the British Commonwealth of Nations in the first half of the twentieth century', *Round Table*, vol. 93, no. 376 (2004), pp. 517–40.

[133] R. Hyam, 'The study of imperial and Commonwealth history at Cambridge, 1881–1981: founding fathers and pioneer research students', *JICH*, vol. 29 (2001), pp. 76–9. For Hancock, see W. R. Louis, 'Sir Keith Hancock and the British empire: Pax Britannica and the Pax Americana', *English Historical Review*, vol. 120 (2005), pp. 937–62.

[134] I. M. Drummond, *British economic policy and the empire, 1919–1939* (1972), esp, pp. 36–87, 'The imperial vision', and *Imperial economic policy, 1917–1939: studies in expansion and protection* (1974).

[135] W. R. Louis, '*In the name of God, go!': Leo Amery and the British empire in the age of Churchill* (1993); 'Amery, Leopold', in *ODNB*, vol. I, pp. 932–6 (by Deborah Lavin).

him that he might have been prime minister if he had been half-a-head taller and his speeches half-an-hour shorter. He was a dynamo of energy. He created the Dominions Office in 1925 by splitting it off from the CO. He prepared the first Colonial Development Act, 1929. He promoted Zionism, and the Singapore base. Geopolitical visions intoxicated him: he would use air-power, he would consolidate a 'Southern British world', a great territorial arc around the Indian Ocean, and he would 'take the lead in shaping the course of world economics', as Britain had done in the nineteenth century. He found money for modest improvements in colonial transport and research. The CO, he liked to say, was 'very essentially, a ministry of health for the tropics'.[136] In Treasury circles he was feared as 'the Mad Mullah of colonial finance', and in the War Office as 'the most dangerous amateur strategist we have got'.[137] Amery wanted to use the empire to develop not only primary production, but also patriotic settler communities in eastern and southern Africa. Introducing the Empire Settlement Bill in 1922, with provision for subsidised emigration, he declared that they had 'three-quarters of our people penned, confined and congested in this little corner of the Empire, and millions of square miles of the richest lands in the world – boundless plains, forests without end, water and coal-power without computation', which could be used to build up 'new centres of British power'.[138]

Other visionary idealists included Lord Beaverbrook, the Canadian who bought the *Daily Express* in 1921 and made it the most-read newspaper in the world; Philip Cunliffe-Lister (president of the Board of Trade for much of the 1920s, and secretary of state for the colonies, 1931–5, and later, as Lord Swinton, for Commonwealth relations, 1952–5); and J. H. Thomas, secretary of state for dominion affairs (1930–5). A leading Labour politician, former errand-boy and trade unionist, and inveterate dropper of aspirates (newspapers once reported him as having spoken of the 'islands of Kenya'), Thomas approached empire development with romantic idealism, supposing it could cure unemployment at home. Generally, the idealists looked to economic regeneration in the empire, sending out capital and labour, in order to stimulate the British share of the empire market. There was an enormous gap between vision and achievement. A great deal of extravagant nonsense was talked, not least about land settlement schemes, project-mongering full of homely gardening metaphors. South Africa

---

[136] L. S. Amery, *My political life*, vol. II; *War and peace, 1914–1929* (1953), p. 338.
[137] Louis, '*In the name of God, go!*', pp. 26 and 69 n 99.
[138] *PD, Commons* vol. 153, cc 575–9, 26 April 1922.

consistently refused to participate in any of this. Canada was lukewarm. Even New Zealand was cautious.

The visionary idealists looked to imperial mutual tariff preferences, a form of protection within the empire as a single economic unit. As a result of the Great Depression, the Conservative Party, supported by Beaverbrook, launched a campaign for imperial preference, a revamped version of Joseph Chamberlain's 'tariff reform' programme from the early years of the century, now confusingly renamed as 'Empire Free Trade'. The British position within the Commonwealth was still strong enough to bring members together to discuss how to stabilise the economic situation, but proved not strong enough to secure a single unified agreement. There was much squabbling over meat and margarine quotas. The result was the Ottawa Agreements of 1932, operating a protectionist system through a series of voluntary bi-lateral trading treaties between Britain and the various countries of the empire. They did succeed in substantially increasing trade within the empire during the remainder of the 1930s.[139]

Over a third of a million emigrants received assisted passages under the empire settlement scheme, until it more or less collapsed after 1931. Politically, by 1937 the Irish had side-stepped dominion status through the External Relations Act.[140] But by-and-large the main achievement of the Commonwealth idealists between the wars was to have held it together in a disrupted world. This made it possible for the dominions to co-operate spectacularly well (with the exception of the Irish) in the Second World War, despite the absence of binding commitments. Postwar, the Commonwealth proved to be adaptable enough to produce another phase of idealistic hope placed in it.

5. Geopolitics

Geopolitics is a politico-strategic concept which relates a state's global position and its inter-state contacts to the configurations of world space, geography, resources, capacities, and military requirements. A more reductionist definition might simply be 'taking a global-political view'. It assumes the essential competitiveness of the international system, of states locked into an almost Darwinian struggle. Strategy is what is deduced from these considerations. Among British twentieth-century politicians, the most geopolitically aware were Curzon, L. S. Amery,

[139] R. Holland, *Britain and the Commonwealth alliance, 1918–1939* (1981).
[140] See the important essay by Deirdre McMahon, 'A larger and noisier Southern Ireland: Ireland and the evolution of Dominion Status in India, Burma and the Commonwealth, 1942–1949', in M. Kennedy and J. M. Skelly, eds., *Irish foreign policy, 1917–1966: from independence to internationalism* (Dublin, 2000), pp. 155–91.

Churchill, and the post-1945 Labour ministers, Bevin and Gordon Walker.[141]

The First World War notably increased geopolitical perceptions and alarms, and in 1919 Halford Mackinder ('the father of geopolitics') published his *Democratic ideals and reality: a study of the politics of reconstruction*, pointing out some of the dangers in the relations between land and sea-power, and air-power. Two of the main aims of the British government in peace-making were to strengthen security in the Middle East (in Egypt and through Palestine) and around the Indian Ocean rim. The geopolitical problems of an over-extended empire can explain all the overseas policies of the 1920s and 1930s, from appeasement to the Singapore naval base.[142]

(1) Appeasement

In a much-quoted metaphor, an Edwardian official had described the British empire as like 'some huge giant sprawling over the globe, with gouty fingers and toes stretching out in every direction, which cannot be approached without eliciting a scream'. By the 1920s the gouty giant had become (in the eyes of one historian) 'a brontosaurus with huge, vulnerable limbs which the central nervous system had little capacity to protect, direct or control'.[143] The British empire reached its greatest extent yet after the First World War, and thereafter suffered problems of acute strategic over-extension. Financial stringency meant it was increasingly impossible to balance resources and requirements. Throughout the whole period from 1918 to 1968 the central problem of British government was the fundamental conundrum of matching ends and means, of paying for a global imperial and defence system.[144] The Depression left Britain weak and demoralised, and the ruling elite half-paralysed.

One of the compounding problems of the interwar years was the soft-centredness of attitudes towards the realities of power politics, the hope that international difficulties would simply go away or resolve themselves

---

[141] Geoffrey Parker, *Western geopolitical thought in the twentieth century* (1985), p. 175; B. W. Blouet, *Geopolitics and globalisation in the twentieth century* (2001).

[142] R. Hyam, 'The primacy of geopolitics: the dynamics of British imperial policy, 1763–1963', *JICH*, vol. 27 (1999), pp. 42–5.

[143] Howard, *The continental commitment*, pp. 11 and 75. Sir T. Sanderson quoted from G. P. Gooch and H. Temperley, eds., *British documents on the origin of the War, 1898–1914*, vol. III, p. 430 (23 February 1907).

[144] P. M. Kennedy, 'Strategy versus finance in twentieth-century Great Britain', *International History Review*, vol. 3 (1981), pp. 44–61, repr. in *Strategy and diplomacy, 1870–1945: eight studies*, ch. 3. See also P. M. Kennedy, *The realities behind diplomacy: background influences on British external policy, 1865–1980* (1981), pp. 285–312.

through disarmament. In the 1920s and 1930s, the Labour Party saw itself as the residuary legatee of the dissenting foreign-policy tradition and Gladstonian Liberal moralising internationalism, which the horrible experience of the war had only reinforced. The Labour leader George Lansbury was an extreme pacifist, 'whose notion of a diplomatic initiative was to propose going to pray for peace with Hitler'. The Party remained opposed to disarmament until 1937. Throughout the 1930s governments seemed to submit too passively to difficulties. Cabinets seemed awash with baronets, ministers of the Crown as short-sighted as they were second-rate. It was Edmund Burke who said 'a great empire and little minds go ill together' (1775).[145]

There was an air of unreality, only dispelled by the outbreak of another war: 'we lived in a world of imagination', wrote a leading official, 'trying to pierce the veil of the future', obsessed with paper solutions and juggling with formulas.[146] There were four foreign secretaries in the 1930s, all of them irresolute. Sir John Simon was a frigid, congenital fence-sitter, 'a serpentine lawyer . . . a snake in snake's clothing'. After four years, in June 1935 he was succeeded by Sir Samuel Hoare (previously secretary of state for India), who lasted just six months. Hoare would have been more convincing as an Anglican clergyman of the primmer Anglo-Catholic kind. (One of his senior advisers did not trust his ambitiousness, and decided he was 'the stuff from which a British quisling could be fashioned'.)[147] Then there was Anthony Eden (1935–8), to some a charming diplomat, but also vain and light-weight, a prima donna prone to vacillation and addicted to clichés. (Eden was to prove more successful as a breeder of cows than as a prime minister.) Lastly there was Viscount Halifax (1938–40), brilliantly nicknamed 'Holy-Fox', which tells you all you need to know about him: remote and religious, essentially mysterious, dismissed by some historians as an old-fashioned aristocrat with a speech impediment and a passion for fox-hunting, and clearly 'not encumbered by any particular intellectual subtlety'. He took his chaplain with him on his honeymoon, and leapt at the chance to visit Hermann Göring's hunting-lodge. As Lord Irwin he had been viceroy of India from 1926 to 1931. For Halifax the empire was 'a rallying point of sanity for a mad civilisation'.[148]

Stanley Baldwin was prime minister from 1923 until January 1924, and again from November 1924 until 1930, and from 1935 to 1937, and in

---

[145] My views on the 1930s were formed early, strongly influenced by Harry Hinsley, who gave pioneering lectures in the Cambridge History Faculty in the late 1950s on 'British foreign policy, 1870–1939'.   [146] Vansittart, *The mist procession*, p. 487.

[147] R. J. Q. Adams, 'Hoare, Samuel', *ODNB*, vol. XXVII, p. 368.

[148] D. J. Dutton, 'Wood, Edward F., earl of Halifax', *ODNB*, vol. LX, pp. 81–9.

between he was second-in-command as lord president of the Council in the National government, from 1931 to 1935. Except for India, he had little interest in the empire. He was preoccupied with domestic issues, and although not as lazy as his reputation usually suggests, he was a nervous fidget prone to neurasthenic collapse. The other two prime ministers of the period both seemed out of their depth in external policy. Ramsay MacDonald fascinated people, with his grave Scottish pseudo-aristocratic manner – which did nothing to dispel the (unfounded) rumours that he was the illegitimate son not of a ploughman but of a marquis; a decent man, but more likely to wring his hands than to give a lead. He was a radical rather than a socialist, committed to a non-sectarian progressivism, and he seemed to slide all too effortlessly from running a Labour government into heading a National coalition from 1931. Neville Chamberlain took over from Baldwin in May 1937, and, like him, wanted to concentrate on domestic issues. Cold and corvine, an arrogant autocrat, a charmless, 'earnest, opinionated provincial', he 'hugged his illusions tightly' and 'was bound to err in diplomacy'. In September 1938 after his first meeting with Hitler he told a friend, 'I got the impression that here was a man who could be relied upon when he had given his word.' He complained like a petulant schoolboy that 'Mussolini has behaved to me like a sneak and a cad.' The Americans were cads, too, he thought. In short, in Lloyd George's immortal words, this son of Joseph Chamberlain was 'a retail mind in a wholesale business'.[149]

For nearly ten years from 1929 the country scarcely had any foreign policy worth the name, as more and more a vague reliance was placed on the League of Nations. Almost everybody thought the League would preserve peace, and disarmament would prevent war. This malaise led to a lack of clear-sighted policy, while an obsessive governmental anxiety about imperial weakness went hand-in-hand with a penchant for isolationist inaction and undue reliance on a clamorous but ill-informed public opinion consumed by an emotional surge of moralising idealism. In an unprecedented episode in 1935, the foreign secretary, Sir Samuel Hoare, was dismissed by a supine Cabinet in order to placate a protesting public opinion, when it was realised that the government was trying to secure peace with Italy by the dismemberment of Abyssinia (Ethiopia),

---

[149] Piers Brendon, *The dark valley: a panorama of the 1930s* (2000) ch. 24, 'Churchill, Chamberlain and appeasement', pp. 604–32, wonderfully full of sharp characterisations including the quotation about Lansbury on the previous page. For the quotation from Lloyd George, see Thomas Jones, *Whitehall diary*, ed. K. Middlemas, vol. II, *1926–1930* (1969), p. 422. There is a careful reassessment of Chamberlain by A. J. Crozier in *ODNB*, vol. X, pp. 934–55, but the fact remains that for all his commitment to social reform, 'he knew nothing of the real world' (Attlee) and would not listen to advice (*A prime minister remembers*, ed. F. Williams (1960), p. 19).

which Mussolini had invaded. Then, as Hitler became more menacing, Neville Chamberlain and Anthony Eden placed their faith in God and the good sense of their enemies. Halifax thought Hitler could be treated like a European Gandhi, never grasping his capacity for evil until it was too late. The result of this dysfunctional foreign and defence policy was that in September 1939 Britain entered war against Germany in almost uniquely unfavourable circumstances, worse prepared than at any time in the last two hundred years.[150] So what had happened about rearmament?

Ramsay MacDonald exemplified much of the ambivalence of the period. He was a man who would place his faith in any panacea, but discovered the dilemmas of disarmament. He was so confused by the emotional desire to disarm and the difficulty of implementing it as a policy that he paralysed himself into inaction. In 1930 he declared that 'we must never underestimate the effectiveness of moral bulwarks with no bayonet nor bludgeon behind them', but increasingly he realised that it was not as simple as that. Although he began to question the old assumptions, he could not bring himself to drop them, or even to decide what the alternative to a League-and-disarmament policy should be, or how he could communicate his realisation of the dangers of disarmament to his colleagues. By 1935 he was in failing health, a despairing and ineffectual figure earning the Churchillian epithet of 'a boneless wonder'.[151]

Again, Neville Chamberlain as prime minister dithered over rearmament – because of its cost.[152] The dilemma was real and we need not doubt it. The agonising that went on at Cabinet level echoes through the decades. At the end of 1937 Chamberlain's splendidly titled but ineffectual minister for the co-ordination of defence, Sir Thomas Inskip, produced a Cabinet memorandum supporting the prime minister and Treasury in their argument that economic stability was Britain's 'fourth arm of defence', alongside the three fighting services, and without it purely military effort would be of no avail. Fundamental truths and anxieties were propounded:

financial resources and economic strength more generally are essential components in the defence structure . . . Nothing operates more strongly to deter a potential aggressor . . . than our stability . . . But were other countries to detect in us signs of strain, this deterrent would at once be lost. The question is how are we to reconcile the two desiderata, first to be safe, secondly to be solvent.

[150] For the 1935 Ethiopian crisis see R. A. C. Parker, 'Great Britain, France and the Ethiopian crisis, 1935–1936', *English Historical Review*, vol. 89 (1974), pp. 293–332, supplemented by J. A. Cross, *Sir Samuel Hoare: a political biography* (1977), pp. 180–265. For Halifax on Gandhi, see Roy Jenkins, *Nine men of power* (1974), p. 149.

[151] D. Marquand, *Ramsay MacDonald* (1977), pp. 748–95, and in *ODNB*, vol. XXXV, pp. 268–82; Lord Strang, *Home and abroad* (1956), pp. 65, 153–4.

[152] A. J. Crozier, 'Chamberlain, (A) Neville', *ODNB*, vol. X, pp. 934–55; Vansittart, *The mist procession*, pp. 429–30.

With chilling flabbiness, Inskip confessed: 'I can find no solution of the problem presented.' To spend too much money in 1937–8 would exhaust British financial resources and undermine Britain's war capacity even before Germany moved against the UK.[153]

Appeasement had its roots in the economic depression, the financial anxieties which so worried Chamberlain, and in geopolitical evaluations and constraints. It is well understood today that appeasement rested in part on the need to defend an over-extended exhausted empire which could not in the final analysis be properly defended, and certainly not against three enemies so geographically spread apart as Germany and Japan, with fascist Italy having a stranglehold on the vital communications-link between the two theatres of war. 'The global dilemma was thus the forcing-house of appeasement', especially with respect to Italy. The imperial imperatives of appeasement dictated the essential outlines of much of Chamberlain's policy.[154] Italy, it was argued, had to be kept neutral, since the maintenance of the Far Eastern position against the Japanese was thought to be essential. If Singapore fell, Australia, New Zealand, Borneo, Malaya, Burma, and India would all be at risk; the whole Indian Ocean would be at the mercy of Japan; and if Japan got hold of Indonesian oil, and Malayan tin, iron, and rubber, the British empire might well be doomed. Despite their recognition that the number of enemies must be reduced, the Chiefs of Staff persisted in the strategy of building a Singapore naval base, provoking to Japan. In trying to sort out the priorities, the Chiefs of Staff decided that their basic aim was the security of imperial communications throughout the world, and that this was followed in order of priority by the security of the UK against Germany, the security of the empire in the Far East against Japan, the security of the Mediterranean and the Middle East, and finally the security of India against Russia. This was a daunting and unrealistic programme.[155]

Policy was not of course determined solely by the Chiefs of Staff, but also by civil servants, often with different concerns and different solutions. There was no one 'official mind' on appeasement. There were complexities and contradictions.

---

[153] N. H. Gibbs, *Grand strategy*, vol. I: *Rearmament policy* (History of the Second World War, UK military series, 1976), pp. 283–7, report to Cabinet, 15 December 1937 (CAB 24/273, CP(37)316).

[154] L. R. Pratt, *East of Malta, West of Suez: Britain's Mediterranean crisis, 1936–1939* (1979); R. Quartararo, 'Imperial defence in the Mediterranean, 1935', *Historical Journal*, vol. 20 (1977), pp. 185–220. S. Roskill, *Hankey: man of secrets*, vol. III: *1931–1963* (1974), pp. 270–82.

[155] Gibbs, *Grand strategy*, vol. I: *Rearmanent policy*, pp. 410–18, Chiefs of Staff review, February 1937.

Whether or not Chamberlain's appeasement scheme for co-existence with Hitler's Germany – allegedly not in principle wanting to destroy the British empire – should be accepted as rational, or whether the true rationalism and realism was to accept the necessity of fighting against Germany, need not detain us here. The truth is that Hitler made co-existence impossible and forced on the war. Whatever Britain did, the results would be disastrous. Chamberlain was right that the war would wreck the empire – but Churchill was even more right in seeing that the empire could not survive as part of a German-dominated world.[156] Moreover, if you are in the frying-pan it is natural to jump into the fire. It is surely hard to believe that Britain had any option but to fight a war – a ruinous war, admittedly – for total security against the evils of Naziism, even at the risk of awakening the slumbering giants of Moscow and Washington, even at the expense of the future viability of the economy. High Tories have always been reluctant to accept these propositions, and denounced them as leading to the needless destruction of the old Establishment and empire.[157] As Dean Inge ('the gloomy Dean' of St Paul's) wrote in his diary: it was an incredible, insensate, fatuous, idiotic, suicidal war, which would 'ruin all who have anything to lose' and possibly end in 'national disaster' even if Britain won.[158]

As to the longer-term geopolitical conflict known as the cold war, it is presumably the case that Naziism had to be treated as the prior enemy to communism, and therefore a cautious alliance with the Soviet Union had to be adopted in order to defeat Hitler, costly and embarrassing though this was.[159] Churchill of course was under no illusions. Asked in 1942 by the new ambassador (Sir Archie Clark Kerr) for a directive on policy towards the Soviet Union, Churchill replied, 'I don't mind kissing Stalin's bum but I'm damned if I'll lick his arse.' To which the ambassador replied, 'Thank you, prime minister: now I quite understand.'[160]

(2) Anglo-Japanese relations and the Singapore base

The crumbling of the British position in the Far East seems to register all its significant set-backs in ten-year intervals. In 1911 came the definitive

---

[156] J. Kent, *British imperial strategy and the origins of the Cold War, 1944–1949* (1993), p. 212.

[157] M. Cowling, *The impact of Hitler: British politics and British policy, 1933–1940* (1975); N. Annan, *Our age: portrait of a generation* (1990), pp. 190–204, 441–3.

[158] Magdalene College Archives, Dean Inge Papers, F/WRI/36 and 37, diary, 1939–43.

[159] D. Carlton, *Anthony Eden: a biography* (1981), p. 482.

[160] LSE, Hugh Dalton Papers, I/36, f. 49, diary, end of 1948. After four years in the Soviet Union, Clark Kerr became, as Lord Inverchapel, ambassador in the USA, 1946–8.

confirmation of the decision in 1905 to rely on Japan as an ally (using the alliance of 1902) to keep the peace in the region, and thus to withdraw five battleships from the China Seas in order to make three-quarters of British battleships available against Germany.[161] In 1921 came the termination of the Japanese alliance, followed by the Washington Naval Conference (1922) which marked the surrender of British supremacy at sea. In 1931 the Manchurian and Shanghai crises demonstrated the post-1921 inability to stop Japanese expansion in China, and highlighted the significance of the Singapore naval base, which project was reactivated. In 1941 came the loss of the battleships *Prince of Wales* and *Repulse* and the fall of Singapore to the Japanese in 1942.

In 1921 Britain had a terrible choice to make: between the useful Japanese alliance and the wishes of Canada and the United States, one of the most crucial decisions Britain ever made on strategic policy. The USA was obsessed with the Japanese 'yellow peril' menace. (American revulsion against the Japanese was so strong that all Japanese immigration was halted in 1924.) Curzon was concerned that the loss of the Japanese alliance would revive a colour prejudice which Britain had been trying to obliterate: 'you again revive the old position in the Far East – the white men against the dark men or the yellow men'.[162] Canadian opposition to the Japanese alliance was probably decisive. Canada's prime minister Arthur Meighen (1920–1) emphasised the need for good relations with the USA. He said that for Britain to maintain a 'special confidential relationship' with Japan to which America was not a party would be regarded as an 'unfriendly exclusion and as a barrier to an English-speaking accord'. For all practical purposes Canada's Mr Meighen exercised a veto on the renewal of the Japanese alliance, while the Americans made abrogation a condition for a naval agreement which was meant to control the 'arms race' and end naval rivalry. The effect was that Britain lost a Far Eastern ally (and the possibility of exercising some restraining influence over Japanese expansion) without gaining any effective American support.[163]

Under the terms of the Washington Treaty (1922), for the first time the Royal Navy had mere parity with rivals, not superiority, and its size was determined by international treaty rather than by assessment of Britain's own strategic needs. A ratio of capital ships (battleships and

[161] C. Northcote Parkinson, *East and West* (1963), pp. 230–4; I. H. Nish, *The Anglo-Japanese alliance: the diplomacy of two island empires, 1894–1907* (1966).

[162] Louis, *British strategy in the Far East, 1919–1939*, pp. 61, 94–5.

[163] I. H. Nish, *Alliance in decline: a study of Anglo-Japanese relations, 1908–1923* (1972); P. G. Wigley, *Canada and the transition to Commonwealth: British–Canadian relations, 1917–1926* (1977), p. 141; Louis, *British strategy in the Far East*, pp. 1–49.

battle-cruisers) was fixed in the proportion: USA 5, Britain 5, Japan 3, France 1.75, Italy 1.75. It was doubtful whether Britain could have afforded a more favourable ratio, but the aim in agreeing to it was basically to conciliate the Americans, who wished to build up their strength, and to eliminate friction. The British could accept these terms because they were less apprehensive of the Japanese, but also, no doubt rightly and sensibly, did so out of an overriding conviction that naval competition and war with the Americans was unthinkable; in any case the British could not afford the money for keeping ahead of the Americans if the Americans were determined to have a navy 'second to none'.[164]

As a result of the ending of the Japanese alliance and the Washington Naval Conference, and the problems which followed from them, Britain had neither alignment with Japan nor a navy strong enough to defend its imperial interests against the Land of Rising Sun.[165] Financial stringency seemed to make it impossible to maintain a sufficient fleet. And so they built a naval base instead.

Why was Britain building a huge base at Singapore?[166] The project began in 1921. It cost £25 million. The idea was that it would defend itself for the time it was estimated it would take the fleet to get there. The estimate got progressively longer, from 42 days to 90 days (June 1939) to at least 180 days (September 1939).[167] Singapore was chosen as less peripheral than Sydney, less vulnerable than Hong Kong. The project dominated strategic planning between the wars. Although coherent and plausible at first, it became increasingly obsolete and unviable as a strategy, partly because it depended as an essential precondition on peace in Europe and on free movement through the Mediterranean, and partly because the development of air-power upset all calculations. Singapore became a symbol, in which too much emotional capital was invested. The irony was that the Singapore naval base fell to overland attack, and capital ships were sunk by air-power. By the thirties it was essentially a bogus policy, a symbol of Britain's (unrealisable) commitment to protect

---

[164] S. Roskill, *Naval policy between the wars*, vol. I: *The period of Anglo-American antagonism, 1919–1929* (1968), pp. 318–30; Louis, *British strategy in the Far East*, pp. 52–108.

[165] For Japanese background: N. J. Brailey, 'Southeast Asia and Japan's road to war', review article, *Historical Journal*, vol. 30 (1987), pp. 995–1011, and I. Hata, 'Continental expansion, 1905–1941', in P. Duus, ed., *Cambridge History of Japan*, vol. VI: *The twentieth century* (1988), pp. 299–314.

[166] There are three books on the Singapore base: W. D. McIntyre, *The rise and fall of the Singapore naval base, 1919–1942* (1979), P. Haggie, *Britannia at bay: the defence of the British empire against Japan, 1931–1941* (1981) and J. Neidpath, *Singapore naval base and the defence of Britain's eastern empire, 1919–1941* (1981) – and the best of these is McIntyre's.

[167] K. Hack and K. Blackburn, *Did Singapore have to fall? Churchill and the impregnable fortress* (2004), p. 32.

Australia and New Zealand from Japanese attack, as a cardinal link in the Commonwealth geopolitical structure.

Of course there was always a case against such a base. General Smuts and Admiral Richmond made prescient criticisms. There was strategic uncertainty (would battleships be effective and what about air-power?), financial-economic and diplomatic worries (don't bankrupt yourself and antagonise Japan at the same time), and moral questioning (queering the disarmament pitch). But a Singapore base nevertheless seemed to be essential in terms of Britain's total imperial role, geopolitical, technical, and diplomatic. Geopolitically, the defensive integrity of British territory and commerce had to be maintained and clearly demonstrated; the mere existence of Japan's 'New Order' and burgeoning naval power in the East required a response of a kind not necessary in the nineteenth century. There was a technical imperative too. Because warships were bigger now and oil-fired they were more dependent on major base facilities; therefore, not to provide the logistical framework for the operation of large naval units in the East would have been tantamount to accepting the hollowness of imperial pretensions. The project also seemed essential in terms of the relationship with the United States. Unless Britain could claim to have a convincing naval policy and an impressive base, Australia and New Zealand might increasingly have looked to America – which of course actually happened after 1942. (Singapore was especially important to New Zealand as a centre for oil supplies and air-links.) Even if people thought Britain would have to co-operate with the United States to preserve empire in the Far East, there were still three formidable reasons from the perspective of Anglo-American relations why a base was needed. The first was the overriding unlikelihood of obtaining a binding American commitment to act in alliance with Britain if only British territory were attacked by Japan. Secondly, the Washington Naval Conference had excluded the Americans from building any new base in the West and South Pacific, so that the American navy would not be able to interpose its main forces between Japan and the British possessions in South-East Asia. Thirdly, it followed that, in order to appear a worthwhile political ally for the Americans in the Far East, Britain must have a major base, which possibly the Americans could also use.[168]

The fall of Singapore on 15 February 1942 was described by Churchill as 'the worst disaster and largest capitulation in British history'.[169] British

---

[168] J. P. D. Dunbabin, review of Haggie, Neidpath, and related books by I. C. McGibbon and A. J. Marder, *English Historical Review*, vol. 98, no. 386 (1983), pp. 170–6; C. Thorne, review of Neidpath, *Times Literary Supplement* 4 December 1981, 1409; S. Roskill, review of Haggie, *ibid.*, 12 June 1981, p. 675.

[169] W. S. Churchill, *The Second World War*, vol. IV: *The hinge of fate* (1951), p. 81.

troops numbering 130,000 surrendered to Japanese forces of only a quarter of that number, fighting 3,000 miles from base. As one British soldier quipped, 'Never have so many been fucked about by so few.'[170] Why did Singapore collapse? Perhaps the isolationist Americans could have given more enthusiastic co-operation in defence of the British empire. More certainly, Malaya should have been better prepared against Japanese attack. This was not given the high political priority it deserved in 1940–1. Not to have done more to provide Singapore with static defences to the north was lamentably unsound militarily and politically. Churchill was partly to blame, because he wanted to reinforce Middle East Command instead.[171] In a memorandum on sea-power, in March 1939, he had declared 'how vain is the menace that Japan will send a fleet and army to conquer Singapore', which was as far from Japan as Southampton was from New York; it would be 'a wild adventure', and he was quite certain that the 'sensible' Japanese would not run such a risk, or, if undertaken at all, then not until after Britain had been beaten in Europe.[172] Japanese military abilities were seriously underestimated by many others besides Churchill. It was supposed they could not fly aeroplanes properly on account of their slit eyes ('they wouldn't be able to see in the dark') and poor sense of balance ('as a result' of having been carried on their mother's backs as babies), and that their aircraft were of shoddy construction.

But it also has to be said that the British in Malaya were unlucky, and faced with a resourceful enemy. The Japanese by contrast were lucky, and brilliant risk-takers. They came through the monsoon, which the British never expected. They came with astonishing speed in an epic advance of fifty-five days, hurtling down the Malay peninsula at the rate of twenty miles a day, cycling on good British roads, wearing shorts and plimsolls, peddling like mad, fighting all the way, repairing 250 bridges.[173]

The effects of the fall of Singapore are not in dispute. If the British were disabused of their belief that the Japanese were myopic midgets, the Japanese were confirmed in their belief that the British were indeed, as Darwin said, descended from monkeys, but *they* were descended from gods. Psychologically it was the end of many British illusions, while Asians were given a vision of the future without European over-lords. British prestige suffered a mortal blow.[174] The Japanese made white

[170] Bayly and Harper, *Forgotten armies*, p. 132.
[171] Neidpath, *Singapore naval base*, pp. 214–22.
[172] PREM 1/345, memo 25 Mar 1939; Gilbert, *Winston S Churchill* vol. IV *Companion*, p. 1415.   [173] Bayly and Harper, *Forgotten armies*, pp. 106–55.
[174] Mansergh and Lumby, eds., *India: Transfer of power*, vol. I: *January to April 1942* (1970), p. 110 (no. 60) Attlee, 2 February 1942; *ibid*, vol IX. *4 November 1946–22 March 1947* (1980), p. 803, Wavell to the king, 24 February 1947.

troops sweep the streets to prove that the reign of the Western man was over. No-one forgot the ease with which the rottenness of Britain's eastern empire was exposed.[175] The fall of Singapore destroyed the myth that Britain was capable of protecting Australia and New Zealand, and thus disposed them to look to the United States for protection. The Australian prime minister John Curtin said that Australia turned to America now, 'free of pangs as to traditional links'. There was a serious and rapid decline in relations between Britain and Australia, leading ultimately to the ANZUS pact of 1952 from which Britain was excluded.[176] At the same time it increased British dependence on America. Only through the USA could Britain get back some of the lost possessions. As to the effect on India, the nationalist movement received a boost. Churchill feared now a 'pan-Asian malaise spreading through all the bazaars of India'.[177] The failure of local populations in Malaya to rally to the imperial flag caused a mixture of pained surprise and disgusted recrimination. Full administrative control was never properly re-established after the war, which provided the conditions for the emergence of the Chinese communist insurrection of 1948.

On the more positive side, the wartime loss of South-East Asia did at least enable planning in Whitehall to break with the past. As the CO's Sir Ralph Furse commented: 'The change was coming anyhow; Singapore precipitated it.'[178]

6. New directions – and war

The lack of dynamism in foreign policy in the 1930s was paralleled by the lack of a forward-looking colonial policy. Britain's colonial record up until 1938 can only be described as deplorable. The historian Hancock, engaged on his Commonwealth survey, described the interwar period as one in which there was a disposition to draw too heavily on the capital of past achievements, an inability to strike out on new and adventurous policies, a passivity and out-of-date conventionality about economic and social policy, a general failure of imagination, initiative, and confidence. At the same time he recognised the moment of change, the 'explicit and deliberate purpose that is new', heralded by the Colonial Development

---

[175] Thorne, *Allies of a kind*, pp. 7–10, 701–2.
[176] T. Reese, *Australia, New Zealand and the United States: a survey of international relations, 1941–1968* (1969), pp. 126–49; Thorne, *Allies of a kind*, pp. 252–3.
[177] D. Dilks, ed., *The diaries of Sir Alexander Cadogan, 1938–1945* (1971), pp. 431–2.
[178] S. R. Ashton and S. E. Stockwell, eds., *Imperial policy and colonial practice, 1925–1945* (BDEEP, 1996), pt 1, intro., p. lix, and p. 15 (no. 5) Sir R. Furse, 27 February 1943.

and Welfare Act of 1940.[179] From within the Colonial Office, Sir Ralph Furse broadly agreed. There was, he admitted, no general colonial policy between the wars; the CO was fumbling, daunted by the bewildering and kaleidoscopic variety of problems. Concurrently there was a degree of public apathy and ignorance which Furse found unbelievable. Press and parliament were inattentive. Academics were largely indifferent. Worse still, most of the commentators were female (Margery Perham, Elspeth Huxley, Ruth Hinden), which Furse regarded as seriously unhealthy. But then, from about 1940, 'an embryonic policy' emerged. According to W. M. Macmillan, too, changes 'on a seismic scale' were then begun.[180]

Malcolm MacDonald was thirty when he was appointed a junior minister in the Dominions Office in 1931. His father was the prime minister. After being head prefect at the 'progressive' school Bedales, and studying history at Oxford, he went on a debating tour of the USA, Canada, Hawaii, Fiji, New Zealand, and Australia, and then on a trip to Kyoto as secretary of a British delegation. He became a Labour MP in 1929. At the Dominions Office he achieved the not inconsiderable feat of getting on well with the Irish prime minister de Valera, though he was perhaps less successful with South Africa's prime minister General Hertzog (1924–39) in delicate discussions about the future of the High Commission Territories. Acquiring a reputation for 'quiet efficiency', MacDonald was appointed as secretary of state for the colonies by Neville Chamberlain in May 1938. He still had to prove that he owed his fast promotion to merit and not to his father.[181]

MacDonald was determined to inaugurate a more active policy of colonial development, alerted to the potential salience of colonial questions by the plans for a deal with Germany (see above, pp. 43–5) and by major strikes and protests in the West Indies from the middle of 1937, looked upon askance by the Americans. Within weeks he had penned a memorandum arguing that the social and economic conditions in some West Indian colonies were 'at least fifty years behind the times'. 'It is in my view imperative that, at a time when the "colonial question" is being ventilated at home and abroad, we should ourselves be as far as possible above reproach', which plainly was not the case. The eyes of the world were watching Britain, and more money must be spent if British reputation 'was

---

[179] W. K. Hancock, *Argument of empire* (1943), pp. 134–5, and *Survey of British Commonwealth affairs*, vol. II: *Problems of economic policy, 1918–1939*, pt 2, p. 267.

[180] Furse, *Aucuparius*, pp. 301–5; W. M. Macmillan, *The road to self-rule: a study in colonial evolution* (1959), p. 205.

[181] Clyde Sanger, *Malcolm MacDonald: bringing an end to empire* (Canada/Liverpool, 1995), ch. 15, 'Moyne, Hailey and a new view on colonies, 1935–1940', pp. 143–58; P. Lyon, 'MacDonald, Malcolm', *ODNB* (2004), vol. XXXV, pp. 260–3; for MacDonald at the Dominions Office, see Hyam, *The failure of South African expansion*, pp. 153–60.

not to suffer irretrievable damage'. A few months later he told his officials, 'in future, criticism of Great Britain will be directed against her management of the Colonial Empire and . . . it was an essential part of her defence policy that her reputation as a colonial power should be unassailable'.[182] MacDonald was aware of foreign criticisms about a neglected 'slum empire', not just in Nazi propaganda, but also in French, Italian, and even Polish commentaries. Lord Moyne (formerly a junior minister at the Treasury) was appointed in July 1938 to head a royal commission on the West Indies; he reported in December 1939 and was very critical of 'defects of policy'. Meanwhile, plans were pressed ahead for a new colonial development act. By the end of 1938 MacDonald was also planning a new social services department in the CO, which began work in March 1939. Then, about a week after war broke out, MacDonald urged that they ought immediately 'to be formulating definite principles of future policy', otherwise they might get side-tracked 'from what ought to he our broad objective'. And, a month later, at a meeting in the CO, he gave details of a big ten-point plan which he hoped would impress colonies and enemies alike, identifying three main areas for investigation. These were the fundamental issue of land policy, the provision of more technical and social services, and political development which did not irrevocably give more power to settlers. He wanted more staff in the CO, and better office accommodation. He wanted to see a 'seething of thought' in the African division of the CO, with even the most junior members contributing.[183] The proposed inquiry into land policy was not implemented. In January 1940, in the context of a fight to keep 'welfare' in the title of the new Colonial Development and Welfare Act, he recorded his opinion that 'if we are not now going to do something fairly good for the Colonial Empire, and something which helps them to get proper social services, we shall deserve to lose the colonies and it will only be a matter of time before we get what we deserve'.[184] In introducing the new Act in May 1940 he explained that its funds could be spent on economic development, and 'everything which ministers to the physical, mental or moral development of the colonial peoples of whom we are the trustees'.[185]

---

[182] Ashton and Stockwell, *Imperial policy and colonial practice, 1925–1945*, hereafter cited as *IPCP*, pt 1, intro pp. lxvii–lxxii, and pt 2, pp. 61–5 (nos. 93 and 94), 27 June and 9 December 1938.

[183] Ashton and Stockwell, *IPCP*, pt 1, pp. 294–5 (nos. 55–7), September–November 1939.

[184] Ashton and Stockwell, *IPCP*, pt 2, p. 111 (no. 101), 14 January 1940.

[185] H. Johnson, 'The British Caribbean from demobilisation to constitutional decolonisation', in Brown and Louis, eds., *The Oxford History of the British Empire*, vol. IV: *The twentieth century*, pp. 608–11, and 'The West Indies and the conversion of the British official classes to the development idea', *Journal of Commonwealth and Comparative Politics*, vol. 15 (1977), pp. 58–83.

MacDonald thus widened the vision behind trusteeship. His 'seething of thought' laid the foundations during the war for fundamental changes in British policy in Africa and the Caribbean, tackling economic stagnation, building up 'moral prestige', questioning hitherto sacrosanct doctrines of minimal government interference, colonial self-sufficiency in finance, and the almost ubiquitous system of Indirect Rule. Many specialist and advisory bodies were set up in and around the CO, including research and public relations, and helped the dynamic. MacDonald believed it to be 'essential to get away from the old principle that Colonies can only have what they themselves can afford to pay for'. Rather cleverly, he used the device of a royal commission in the West Indies as a lever to open the tight-fisted Treasury's coffers, for they would have to be impressed by such a high-level report. The ploy was successful. Whereas the Colonial Development Act of 1929 was a neo-mercantilist measure primarily aimed at stimulating British exports for British economic benefit, the Colonial Development and Welfare Act of 1940 was quite different in its motivation.[186] It was the first step in a positive and constructive policy which led on to the postwar policy of 'political advancement'.[187] In 1940, £5 million was provided as pump-priming. In 1945 this was increased to £120 million over ten years. Despite Britain's financial difficulties, MacDonald's successor Oliver Stanley entered fully into MacDonald's vision. He commended the new act as showing gratitude for the participation of colonies in the war effort, which had 'increased our awareness of past deficiencies in our administration', but added: 'the overriding reason why I feel that these proposals are essential is the necessity to justify our position as a Colonial power'. The end of the war, said Stanley, was the psychological moment to have 'a dynamic programme of colonial development' which would demonstrate 'the permanence and adequacy of our policy'.[188]

Roger Louis has commented that 'the Second World War witnessed a moral regeneration of British purpose in the colonial world'.[189] Although it is true that war was a catalyst, the 'new direction' was in origin not a response to war or even to the Moyne report on the West Indies. MacDonald had taken the initiative in advance of both.[190]

---

[186] S. Constantine, *The making of British colonial development policy, 1914–1940* (1984), pp. 232–61; see also M. Havinden and D. Meredith, *Colonialism and development: Britain and its tropical colonies, 1850–1960* (1993), pp. 195–205; D. J. Morgan, *Official history of colonial development* (1980), vol. I: *The origins of British aid policy, 1924–1945*, pp. 64–88.   [187] A. Cohen, *British policy in changing Africa* (1959), pp. 32–3.

[188] PREM 4/43A, no. 8; *IPCP*, pt 2, pp. 203–5 (no. 120).

[189] W. R. Louis, *Imperialism at bay, 1941–1945: the United States and the decolonisation of the British empire* (1977), pp. 101–3.

[190] J. E. Flint, 'Planned decolonisation and its failure in British Africa', *African Affairs*, vol. 82 (1983), pp. 390–410; but see also a cautionary 'addendum' by R. D. Pearce, 'The Colonial Office and planned decolonisation in Africa', *African Affairs*, vol. 83 (1984), pp. 77–93.

Although we must not exaggerate the practical effects of all this, the change in atmosphere is palpable. The demand for a 'seething of thought' certainly encouraged officials to clarify their ideas. On the West African desk, O. G. R. Williams pointed to the importance of retaining the initiative politically, forestalling African demands for progress 'rather than allowing ourselves to be forced into the position of making concessions to the "clamour of demagogues" '. Not that he expected progress to be fast: 'a good many years (perhaps a good many generations, though it would not be politic to say so openly) must elapse' before there was much advance to self-government in West Africa.[191] Sydney Caine, the financial adviser, called for 'a much greater development of initiatory power at the centre', giving much more informed thought to economic prospects. He believed colonial development required such specialised scientific and technical expertise that they should allow foreigners in, with contracts. This would be 'a big break with the past', but should be welcomed if it would help to attain their ideals more quickly. It might, he added, divert 'the surplus energy of European peoples to a co-operative task'.[192] Another assistant under-secretary, A. J. Dawe, insisted that Indirect Rule was outmoded, and it was 'absurd to erect what was an ephemeral experiment into a sacrosanct principle'; 'it was not handed down on Mt Sinai'.[193] After the war, he predicted, Africa was going 'to become a scene of a great contest for power'. In a major memorandum on Kenya, Dawe implied that MacDonald's economic and social initiatives would not be enough:

A marked transformation is taking place. Forces released by the war are gathering great velocity . . . The old nineteenth-century concepts are dead. The African territories can no longer be regarded as appendages of the European powers . . . There will be an increasing urge towards the self-government which Colonial peoples, under the British system, have been led to expect. These forces are not likely to be contained for long by any policy of material development and social welfare directed from London. Improved health services and education will not be accepted by these peoples as a substitute for the freedom to develop according to their own political consciousness. The problem for the British government, therefore, is to find a method by which these inexorable African forces can be reconciled with future British interests. How are we to bind these people to us in such a way that their moral and material sources of strength will continue to be ranged on the side of Great Britain?

It was to be expected that after the war Britain would be 'much exhausted and weakened by its long ordeal'. While there was weakness at the centre,

---

[191] R. Rathbone, ed., *Ghana* (BDEEP, 1992), pt 1: *1941–52* intro, p. xxxvi.
[192] J. M. Lee and M. Petter, *The Colonial Office, war and development policy: the organisation and planning of a metropolitan initiative, 1939–1945* (1982), pp. 169–73.
[193] *IPCP*, pt 1, p. 350 (no. 68), 17 July 1943.

it would be natural for colonies 'to seek to widen control of their own affairs'.[194]

Dawe was especially concerned about Kenya, 'an inflammable country', where the prestige of the British government had never recovered from the potential settlers' rebellion in 1923. Imperial power was sharply limited here, and difficulties had ever since been pushed aside as far as possible. The move towards settler domination had been much speeded up by the war. Dawe wondered whether the solution might be to curtail settler power by absorbing the Europeans into an East African federation of five provinces, Kenya, Tanganyika, Zanzibar, Uganda, and 'a White Highlands state'.

Harold Macmillan as a CO under-secretary of state in 1942 was now seized with his own 'seething of thought'. He challenged Dawe's assumption that Kenya had proved to be a 'white man's country'. Instead of a federation, Macmillan suggested 'a quite different and much more radical policy', one which at first sight 'may seem quite fantastic; perhaps it is': 'let us nationalise all or some of the land in the Highlands', buying out decadent and unserious European farmers, putting control of African interests back in the hands of the British government, and allowing African access to the land. This would be very expensive, 'but it will be less expensive than a civil war', for a clash between black and white 'is bound to come'. The words were prophetic.[195]

In the field, too, some governors responded enthusiastically to the call for a new direction. Sir Charles Dundas in Uganda (1940–4) commented on a 'rather too narrow and unimaginative attitude in certain local quarters', a stultifying ultra-conservatism; but the empire had to be justified now by 'impeccable and progressive rule'. Britain could no longer determine policy dictatorially 'according as it seems best to us', but must accommodate to African demands, otherwise there was 'a danger that it will not be the Africans but ourselves who are backward'. The CO was pleased with this despatch. Sir Alan Burns had little difficulty in persuading the CO to approve the appointment of the first African district commissioners in the Gold Coast.[196]

In the 1940s, new universities were established in Legon, Ibadan, Makerere, Khartoum, and the West Indies, which it was hoped would produce more professional groups who could run their countries. This was a creditable achievement. The crucial impetus came from Earl De La

---

[194] CO 967/57, memo by Dawe, July 1942, 'A federal solution for East Africa'; *IPCP*, pt 1, pp. 322–37 (no. 65); N. Westcott, 'Closer union and the future of East Africa, 1939–1948', *JICH*, vol. 10 (1981), pp. 67–88.

[195] Macmillan to Sir G. Gater, 15 August 1942; *IPCP*, pt 1, pp. 337–40 (no. 66).

[196] *IPCP*, pt 1, intro., p. xci, and pt 2, pp. 319–21 (no. 154), June 1942.

Warr's report in September 1937, the first published exposition of university policy for British Africa, recommending a synthesis of both African and European cultural elements. Oliver Stanley in 1943 declared his belief that higher education would be 'one of the most important questions in connection with the post-war reconstruction and development of the Colonial Empire'.[197]

One new contextual element was South Africa's wartime emergence as an African power. This was perceived as something which could be dangerous to British interests. Dawe was acutely aware of the insidious seductiveness of Smuts, so close to the British war establishment, but pursuing his own agenda: 'there is always the danger that we may be deluded by the ephemeral magnetism of General Smuts's personality into taking a step which would have grave consequences to our long-term interests in Africa'. South African expansion northwards, he realised, would be only too acceptable to many official and unofficial elements in British African communities, not least in Kenya. Other officials feared Swaziland might be transferred to South African rule.[198]

'Partnership' became the new slogan, though it was uncertain precisely what it involved. It was employed (though not invented) by Lord Hailey, who had published his much admired *African survey* in 1938, a vast compendium which provided useful information rather than innovative ideas. Macmillan then publicised 'partnership' in a parliamentary speech in June 1942.[199] The paternalism of the old trusteeship was supposed to be over. However that may be, it was clearly understood in the CO that colonial problems must be dealt with from 'a new angle of vision', collaborating with colonial peoples instead of merely directing them.[200]

The war saw a huge increase in the importance of Africa. Africans made heroic exertions on behalf of, and mostly at the behest of, the Allies. Some 400,000 African soldiers were mobilised by Britain alone, and by the end of their service 70 per cent of them were literate. Black soldiers served in North Africa, Madagascar, Egypt, Palestine, and Burma. Most parts of Africa also felt the pressure of the demand for labour. Many millions of men, women, and children were set to work. Freetown, Cape Town, and Mombasa became vital bases guarding the trade routes and

---

[197] Flint, 'Planned decolonisation', p. 403; E. Ashby, *Universities; British, Indian and African: a study in the ecology of higher education* (with M. Anderson, 1966), pp. 197–223, 233.

[198] *IPCP*, pt 1, p. 350 (no. 68), minute, 17 July 1943, and p. 343 (no. 72), Stanley, 5 August 1943. See also Hyam, *The failure of South African expansion*, pp. 163–83.

[199] *IPCP*, intro, p. lii; Lee and Petter, *The Colonial Office, war and development policy*, p. 126.

[200] Sir John Shuckburgh quoted by K. Jeffery, 'The Second World War', in *Oxford History of the British Empire*, vol. IV, p. 327.

supply-lines for war matériel and essential foodstuffs for the army. A West Africa supply-route ferried aircraft from the USA to the Middle East via Takoradi and Kano. By 1945 a chain of forty airfields existed across Africa, linking Nigeria and Egypt. West Africa was a scene of intense activity, especially in Sierra Leone, where the strategic harbour of Freetown was much improved, palm-oil production was greatly increased, iron ore, timber, rubber, bauxite (for aluminium), and above all tin (after the loss of Malaya) were sought. There was such urgency that forced labour was used to get the tin. The most notorious example of forced labour occurred in Northern Nigeria, where over 100,000 peasants were conscripted into tin-mines between 1942 and 1944. In the Gold Coast a 46-mile branch railway was built to open up sources of bauxite.[201]

In East Africa as well, food and raw materials were produced on a large scale for the war effort, especially for troops in the Middle East. As in West Africa, bulk-purchasing and marketing boards were established to enable the British government to buy raw materials more cheaply. The Japanese war caused a major restructuring of the world economy, halving the amount of hard fibres available to the West, cutting off America's sources of twine in the Philippines. The effect was felt in Tanganyika, where 84,500 Africans were conscripted for agricultural work, mainly on the sisal plantations, or in rubber estates reactivated after a generation of neglect. In Kenya, coffee and sisal production increased, and pyrethrum daisies were produced for the insecticides so vital in the jungle warfare of South-East Asia. The white farmers of Kenya for the first time could be regarded as useful, and not dismissed as a bunch of 'aristocratic playboys giving in to altitude, alcohol and adultery'.[202]

With a few individual exceptions, the vast majority of demobilised African soldiers were re-absorbed without trouble into the rural communities from which they came. Hundreds of thousands of Africans successfully uprooted for their labour were also quietly repatriated. So the impact of returning ex-soldiers and others – contrary to some accounts – did not fuel post-war nationalist agitation or political

---

[201] Viscount Swinton, *As I remember* [n.d.,? 1949], pp. 191–207; D. Killingray and R. Rathbone, eds., *Africa and the Second World War* (1986), intro., pp. 1–17; M. Crowder, 'The 1939–1945 War and West Africa', in J. F. A. Ajayi and M. Crowder, eds., *History of West Africa*, vol. II (1974), pp. 596–621; G. O. Olusanya, *The Second World War and politics in Nigeria, 1939–1953* (Lagos, 1973).

[202] N. Westcott, 'The impact of the Second World War on Tanganyika', in Killingray and Rathbone, eds., *Africa and the Second World War*, pp. 143–59; J. M. Lonsdale, 'The Depression, the Second World War and the transformation of Kenya', *ibid.*, esp. pp. 119–36; D. A. Low and J. M. Lonsdale, in *A History of East Africa*, vol. III (ed. D. A. Low and A. Smith, 1976), pp. 1–64, intro, 'Towards the new order, 1945–1963'.

turmoil. The roots of imperial decline are not to be looked for in this particular process.[203]

This is not to say that the Second World War did not have a profound impact in Africa. New economic, social, and political forces were set in motion. Expectations changed and the whole milieu was different. Sylvia Leith-Ross, the widow of a colonial service officer, who had been in Nigeria since 1907, commented on this with extraordinary perception. Britain had ruled 'by prestige and with only a handful of rifles'. The only whites the Africans knew seemed to have not just wealth, but superior knowledge and skills entitling them to rulership. Before the war – according to her understanding – Nigerians believed all whites were one race, treating each other as 'brothers' ('with all the implications connoted in the African mind by that term'). But now:

Perhaps for the first time, except in individual cases, an element of contempt had crept into their minds: these 'civilised' white men could nevertheless kill each other in great numbers, their rich towns could be destroyed, their expensive homes burnt down, they could be tortured and starved, they could cringe and beg for help and for money. And, a curious sidelight emerging from conversations with observant Africans who had been in contact with our troops or sailors, for the first time in their lives these Africans had met a number of Europeans *less educated than themselves*, speaking a less grammatical English than themselves. They were careful to show no disdain, only sheer amazement that they should have been mistaken . . . You could not help feeling that this discovery was perhaps the final insidious blow which shattered the crumbling edifice of white superiority.[204]

An early African study of African nationalism confirms this analysis, arguing that 'after four years hunting white enemy soldiers the Africans never regarded them again as gods'; if Europeans could legitimately struggle against the domination of Hitler, they could legitimately continue their own struggle against alien domination.[205]

The war also brought portentous changes to the international scene, and tensions between Britain and the United States. The Americans had not fought to uphold the British empire. They thought Hong Kong should be given up. Conversely, Churchill told them 'I have not become the king's first minister in order to preside over the liquidation of the

---

[203] A. Jackson, 'Supplying war: the High Commission Territories military-logistical contribution to the Second World War', *Journal of Military History* vol. 66 (2002), pp. 719–60. Ashley Jackson, *The British empire and the Second World War* (2006) is a major new reassessment, redefining the role of the empire.

[204] Sylvia Leith-Ross, *Stepping-stones: memoirs of colonial Nigeria, 1907–1960* (ed. M. Crowder, 1983), pp. 116–17; quoted (not quite in full) by M. Crowder, 'The Second World War: prelude to decolonisation in Africa', in M. Crowder, ed., *The Cambridge History of Africa*, vol. VIII: *From c 1940 to c 1975* (1984), p. 40.

[205] Sithole, *African nationalism*, pp. 19–24, 156.

British Empire.' The Americans had schemes for an 'international trusteeship', to be superintended by the new United Nations Organisation. Churchill was sceptical. ' "Hands off the British Empire" is our maxim and it must not be weakened or smirched to please sob-stuff merchants at home or foreigners of any hue.' He would not have the empire 'jockeyed or edged nearer the abyss'. He would not consent to forty or fifty nations 'thrusting interfering fingers' into the vitals of the British Empire. He would not have 'one scrap of British territory flung into that arena' (the international organisation): 'I will have no suggestion that the British empire is to be put into the dock', and 'asked to justify our right to live in a world we have tried to save'. But for all his rhetoric, Churchill was insufficiently vigilant at the Yalta conference (in the Crimea, February 1945). The 'trusteeship formula' agreed there by the 'Big Three' was that it would apply only to existing League of Nations Mandates, conquered territory, and any other territory voluntarily placed under trusteeship. Churchill did not examine the proposal closely enough. The Americans explicitly but not very honestly said it had nothing to do with the British empire. But Britain *was* involved in respect of League of Nations Mandates, and Churchill unwittingly gave the future international organisation, the Trusteeship Council of the UN, a basis for putting the empire 'in the dock'. It was to lead to a great deal of trouble and anxiety as decolonisation unfolded.[206]

---

[206] Louis, *Imperialism at bay*, pp. 433–5, 454–60; *IPCP*, pt 1, pp. 216–18 (no. 38), minutes, 31 December 1944–24 January 1945. The UN's trusteeship formula required 'progressive development towards self-government or independence'.

2 'British imperialism is dead': the Attlee government and the end of empire, 1945–1951

Some years before he became prime minister, probably in 1942 when he was secretary of state for dominion affairs, Attlee set down his thoughts on post-war colonial policy. 'The colonial problem will not be solved', he wrote, 'by a combination of an eye to business and humanitarian sentiment. Nor on the other hand will it be solved by looking backwards and imagining that we can recreate the conditions of a past age.' Britain must therefore, he concluded, 'set aside sentimental imperialism and take a realist view of our problems'. He believed they were committed to giving India self-government (treating India as 'a political entity with which an accommodation has to be reached'). As far as the rest of Asia was concerned, he considered that it consisted of 'a group of peoples on the way towards self-government requiring tutelage for many years yet and susceptible to much economic development which should be directed primarily to the welfare of the indigenous populations and to the general service of the world'. He did not mention Africa.[1]

Four years later, in August 1946, an official Labour government publicity hand-out declared 'British "Imperialism" is dead, in so far as it ever existed, except as a slogan used by our critics'; colonial policy was being approached in a way that was 'both liberal and dynamic'.[2] By this date, the government was well on the road to reducing the imperial grip on India and Burma, and more reluctantly Ceylon and Palestine, but these reductions did not amount to a 'decolonisation' strategy. They were a set of revaluations about the more developed parts of the empire, made pragmatically to meet changing realities. Elsewhere there were reassertions of empire, notably in Africa. Old-style 'imperialism' may indeed have been dead, but there was still much constructive work for an imperial power to do. The sense of providing tutelage remained strong, and the

---

[1] CAB 118/73; see also PREM 8/59, Attlee to Cripps and Pethick-Lawrence, 22 December 1945.
[2] CAB 124/1007, no. 62, 'Projection of Britain overseas'; R. Hyam, ed., *The Labour government and the end of empire, 1945–1951* (British Documents on the End of Empire Project, 1992), hereafter cited as *BDEEP*: pt 1, p. 309 (document no. 68).

Labour government's years in control coincided with a creative period in the history of the Colonial Office.

As prime minister Attlee did indeed prove to be a 'realist'. He was committed to the maintenance of British global interests where they could still be justified after rigorous re-examination. Two quintessential themes dominated postwar colonial policy: economic recovery and Russian expansion. Almost all overseas policy-making evolved within the fundamental parameters provided by the dollar shortage and the cold war. Both problems predicated enhanced interest in the empire in general and Africa in particular. The minister of defence (A. V. Alexander) in October 1949 defined the three main policy objectives as (i) to secure 'our people against aggression', (ii) to sustain a foreign policy dominated by global 'resistance to the onrush of communist influence', and (iii) to achieve 'the most rapid development practicable of our overseas possessions, since without such colonial development there can be no major improvement in the standard of living of our own people at home'.[3] A Colonial Office minister might have added some rather more altruistic goals, but there is no doubt that Alexander reflected the sense of priorities held by the majority of his Cabinet colleagues. The increased importance they attached economically and geopolitically to Africa was in part a direct consequence of disengagement from India, the replacement of a lost Indian empire in Africa. In the words of Jack Gallagher: 'Africa would be a surrogate for India, more docile, more malleable, more pious.'[4] Field-Marshal Lord Montgomery, Chief of the Imperial General Staff, hoped Africa would be a military manpower-reserve, replacing the Indian Army.[5]

It was in 1945 still plausible to regard the empire as having some future – though not an indefinite one – in some places. 'Imperial Britain' still had some reality, and it was not just Churchill who did not want to preside over the liquidation of the British empire: it was true of Attlee, and even of Harold Wilson. The very mechanisms of British government imposed constraints on ministers, guided by permanent officials into accepting principles of continuity of policy and realistic pragmatism. For some Labour ministers there had to be a sharp cessation of doctrinaire commitments to pacificism, disarmament, anti-capitalism, working-class solidarity, anti-militarism, and anti-imperialism.[6] The inclination of the Labour Party to question principles of continuity between 1924 and 1939

[3] CAB 129/37/3, CP(49)245, annex A, 18 October 1949.
[4] Gallagher, *Decline, revival and fall of the British empire*, pp. 145–6.
[5] FO 800/435, f. 10, Montgomery to Bevin, 10 September [1947].
[6] M. A. Fitzsimons, 'The continuity of British foreign policy', *Review of Politics*, vol. 21 (1959), esp. pp. 302–4.

came to a definitive stop at Cabinet level.[7] As minister of food, the Marxist (former communist) John Strachey superintended the ground-nuts scheme in Tanganyika to improve British margarine supplies, and then became secretary of state for war, responsible for full-scale counter-insurgency in Malaya.

Yet for all the limitations, reservations, and disappointments, the Labour government did see major changes of approach, and its claim that 'British "Imperialism" is dead' was not a hollow one. Much of the credit must go to the prime minister. In Asia, reflected perspicacious Attlee, 'an attempt to maintain the old colonialism would I am sure have immensely aided communism'.[8] As far as the Gold Coast and Nigeria were concerned, 'It was clear to me that the wave of nationalist feeling and the desire for an enhancement of the status of the darker-coloured races which we had had to meet in India had now spread to Africa.' Macmillan was famously to say something similar, though it may be conceded that 'the wave of nationalist feeling' does not have quite the same resonance as the 'wind of change' blowing through Africa. Attlee added that it was also clear that 'a failure to meet reasonably these aspirations led to an ever-worsening position', as could be seen in the fruits of delay in French Indo-China and the danger only narrowly averted by the Dutch in Indonesia.[9] Indian example had been crucial in bringing him to see that a sufficient outlet must be allowed to nationalism but Attlee applied stringent tests; the wave must be 'tide rather than froth', and in Africa, which 'was not as developed in civilisation', there was a danger of too rapid a transition.[10] But, above all, Attlee understood the wisdom of 'accepting the inevitable pleasantly'.[11]

The world that the new Labour ministers confronted in August 1945 was hugely disrupted by the ravages of war. As after the First World War there was a 'crisis of empire' and 'the whole world was rocking'. Not all British subjects had remained loyal to the king. Many Indians and Burmese had latched on to the Japanese invader. Gurkha and Tamil troops also defected to the Indian National Army (INA) led by Chandra Subhas Bose. Imperial control was quite hard to re-establish in Malaya. Egyptians would never forget the humiliation of Sir Miles Lampson's tanks rumbling around the gates of the royal palace in February 1942, an event which set

---

[7] M. R. Gordon, *Conflict and consensus in Labour's foreign policy, 1914–1965* (Stanford, CA, 1969).

[8] Compare Andrew Cohen: 'co-operation with nationalism is our greatest bulwark against communism in Africa', *British policy in changing Africa* (1959), p. 61.

[9] C. R. Attlee, *As it happened* (1954), pp. 189–91.

[10] CO 1015/144, no. 15, observations of Sir G. Rennie, 20 August 1952.

[11] Compare Edmund Burke, 'not the least of the arts of diplomacy is to grant graciously what one no longer has the power to withhold'.

Colonel Nasser on his revolutionary path. Arabs enjoyed seeing their 'haughty governess' fighting for survival.[12] The economic effects of the war were even more disruptive. There was a world food shortage. In Europe food production was 25 per cent below average, 12 per cent in the world as a whole, with rice down 15 per cent. An Asian famine, Attlee realised, would have 'far-reaching political effects on maintaining the stability of the empire', and he took the initiative in averting a widespread catastrophe, deliberately deciding that 'Britain would have to go without in order to help'.[13] The empire was more over-extended than ever. Troops were deployed across the globe from the West Indies to Hong Kong, with other garrisons in West Germany, Gibraltar, Malta, Libya, Cyprus, Greece, Turkey, Egypt, Palestine, Aden, the Persian Gulf, India, East Africa, Singapore and Malaya, and there were naval bases in the West Indies, Gibraltar, Malta, Simon's Town, Aden, Singapore, and Hong Kong. Above all things, there was the new communist menace to be resisted. The head of the FO, Sir Orme Sargent, warned ministers, 'If we cease to regard ourselves as a World Power we shall gradually cease to be one.'[14]

The postwar retrenchment and adjustment was similar in character to that of 1919–22 but more dramatic. In February 1947 British troops were withdrawn from Greece and Turkey (to be followed by Palestine). President Truman responded decisively and America took over defence of the 'northern tier' (Greece, Turkey, Iran, and Afghanistan), the ring of countries on or near the Soviet border.[15]

1. Who was in charge?

Attlee, according to Churchill's famous jibe, was just a 'sheep in sheep's clothing', a genuinely modest man, but 'plenty to be modest about'. It was a deceptive modesty. Attlee may have been unprepossessing and shy, but he was not in the least lacking in authoritative assertiveness when required (even towards Churchill himself). He had indeed many of the attributes of a typical clerkly, middle-class army major, terse of speech, honest, interested in cricket, boys' clubs, bishops, and furniture repairs.[16]

---

[12] Vatikiotis, *Nasser and his generation*, p. 113; E. S. Atiyah, *An Arab tells his own story: a study in loyalties* (1946), pp. 198–9.

[13] Francis Williams, ed., *A prime minister remembers* (1960, repr. as *Twilight of empire: memoirs of Prime Minister Clement Attlee*, Connecticut, 1978) pp. 135–48.

[14] Hyam, ed., *BDEEP*, pt 2, p. 303 (no. 138), memo by Sir O. Sargent, 11 July 1945, 'Stocktaking after VE-Day.'

[15] B. R. Kuniholm, *The origins of the Cold War in the Near East: great power conflict and diplomacy in Iran, Turkey and Greece* (Princeton, NJ, 1980).

[16] K. Harris, *Attlee* (1982); T. Burridge, *Clement Attlee: a political biography* (1985); R. C. Whiting, 'Attlee, C. R.', *ODNB* (2004), vol. II, pp. 875–84.

As K. O. Morgan has put it, he had the useful if limited talents of a public-school headmaster and country solicitor, 'transmuted into a kind of genius'.[17] He was happily married, and chauffeured about by his wife, though it was a miracle that he was not killed by her notoriously danger-ous driving. During the war he was an unobtrusive but ubiquitous minis-ter, learning all there was to know about executive efficiency and the arts of government. His instinctive good judgment was honed to a fine art. Briefly dominions secretary, he took a great interest in the problems of Newfoundland prior to its entry into the Canadian Confederation. As prime minister he dominated a clever but difficult team of prima donnas, showing commonsense in small matters and statesmanship in large ones. As chairman of the Cabinet, he steered it time and again to appropriate and unambiguous decisions, summing up concisely, getting right to the heart of the matter.

Indian independence and continuing membership of the Common-wealth was perhaps his greatest achievement overseas, but Attlee also made one of the most remarkable attempts to rethink the fundamentals of policy in any field, the whole rationale of 'holding' the Middle East.[18] Incoming ministers do sometimes fire off radical, corruscating memo-randa, from Churchill on Nigeria in 1906 to Macmillan's 'profit and loss' call in 1957, but few touched off such a scorching debate as Attlee. He argued that air-power and the atomic bomb had subverted existing strate-gic doctrine. They should therefore give up a 'hopeless attempt' to defend the Middle East oil-producing areas, and work routinely in future round the Cape to the east and Australia, instead of continuing to rely on an ever-more problematic Mediterranean route. He wanted to see an inter-nationalist approach based on making the United Nations really effective. Attlee was supported by his chancellor of the Exchequer, Hugh Dalton, but opposed by the whole weight of Bevin and the Foreign Office, and by the Chiefs of Staff (in the end apparently threatening resignation). The battle of the titans lasted for almost eighteen months, as point-scoring batted to and fro, Attlee always unhesitatingly tenacious in counter-attack.[19] It ended with a victory for the traditionalists, aided by the devel-

---

[17] K. O. Morgan, review of Harris, *Attlee*, in *Times Literary Supplement*, 24 September 1982, p. 1026.

[18] *BDEEP*, pt 3, pp. 207–29 (nos. 273–82). There is a good account in Saville, *The politics of continuity: British foreign policy and the Labour government, 1945–1946* (1999), pp. 112–48, and another in R. J. Aldrich and J. Zametica, 'The rise and decline of a strategic concept: the Middle East, 1945–1951' in R. J. Aldrich, ed., *British intelligence, strategy, and the Cold War, 1945–1951* (1992), pp. 236–74.

[19] R. Smith and J. Zametica, 'The cold warrior: Clement Attlee reconsidered, 1945–1947', *International Affairs*, vol. 61 (1985) pp. 241–50; J. Kent, *British imperial strategy and the origins of the Cold War, 1944–1949* (1993), pp. 98–109.

opment of the cold war. Withdrawal from the Mediterranean route, it was said, would leave a vacuum, into which the Soviet Union (even if not bent on world domination) would move, since 'the bear could not resist pushing its paw into soft places'. This would at the very least make a gift to Russia of Middle East oil and manpower. The traditionalists rejected Attlee's concept of a disengagement from a 'neutral zone' which would put a 'wide glacis of desert and Arabs between ourselves and the Russians'. Attlee's eventual defeat under overwhelming pressure does not mean he was not right in many ways: the need for more coherent thought about geopolitics, a more realistic appreciation of economic constraints, and of nationalist opposition to overseas bases, and of their international vulnerability. Nor does it detract from his ability to 'think the unthinkable', and to look further ahead than most could contemplate. The tragedy of the Central African Federation could also have been avoided had Attlee remained in power and sent the process into reverse. With the utmost clarity by 1952 he discerned its fatal flaw: that it froze the pace of African political advancement by making it dependent on European settler concurrence, and in the long run it would turn African nationalism sour.[20]

Ernest Bevin took charge of the Foreign Office. This 'working-class John Bull' looked like a lumbering elephant ('the size of three Buddhas, hardly hewn at all', according to Diana Cooper), and behaved like an ebullient emperor.[21] A Bristolian of the poorest possible origins, he started life working as a waiter, and as a tram conductor, and he spent five years delivering mineral-water from a horse-and-cart, then rose by way of Baptist preaching and trades-union leadership, to become an almost Curzonian figure in the Foreign Office, where, as Roy Jenkins once observed, there were only two roles he could have filled, either foreign secretary, or a rather truculent lift-man on the verge of retirement.[22] Of masterful temperament, but with the common touch, vain, brutal and kind, sullen and exuberant, patient and impatient – every paradox abounds. His education and skills were minimal, although his excruciatingly bad handwriting was mainly the result of an injury which had almost entirely destroyed the nerves in his index finger.[23] He had travelled widely and made many contacts as a trades-union delegate, not just across America, but to Hawaii, Fiji, Australia, and New Zealand.[24]

---

[20] CO 1015/770, no. 43, August 1952; Hyam and Henshaw, *The lion and the springbok: Britain and South Africa since the Boer War* (2003) p. 221.

[21] I. Kirkpatrick, *Inner circle: memoirs* (1959), p. 202; P. Ziegler, *Diana Cooper* (1981), pp. 249–52.   [22] Roy Jenkins, *Nine men of power* (1974), p. 63.

[23] M. Stephens, *Ernest Bevin: unskilled labourer and world statesman, 1881–1951* (1981), p. 133.

[24] A. Bullock, *Life and times of Ernest Bevin*, vol. I: *Trade Union leader, 1881–1940* (1960).

An excellent memory was another important asset. His instinct rather than his brain was the precision instrument. He was much loved and respected. Bevin was not impressed by moves towards a united Europe ('if you open that Pandora's Box you never know what Trojan 'orses will jump out').[25] But he took the Commonwealth seriously, as the basis of a continuing British claim to be a power with world-wide interests. 'I am not imperialist', he declared, but saw the need to move beyond a traditional socialist 'anti-imperialism'.[26] He even publicly declared that the fall of the British empire would be a disaster.[27] His dream was the 'conquest of hunger and misery', an 'international policy and effort for the rehabilitation of the world'. The Colombo Plan for South-East Asia and the Far East (1950) – encouraging improvement of living standards – was his idea.

When Bevin's health finally gave out he was succeeded by Herbert Morrison. This Cockney fixer had 'an almost Kiplingesque reverence for empire'; as a Little England jingo, he admired Palmerston and thought foreign policy 'would be okay but for the bloody foreigners'. He was ignorant of foreign affairs and seemed unwilling to learn. Attlee quickly came to regret his appointment: 'a terrible flop', as bad a foreign secretary 'as any in living memory'.[28]

One of the 'big five' ministerial heavyweights was Hugh Dalton, chancellor of the Exchequer. Although not directly concerned with overseas affairs, he was an astringent observer of them, and in 1949 Attlee relied on him closely during the Hong Kong crisis (see below, p. 139. Dalton's diary is full of intelligent if contemptuous comment about their colleagues, so he will be quoted. A loud, exhausting, egotistical extrovert, he was deeply unpopular with all but his youthful political protégés. Conservatives especially disliked him as a renegade from his Windsor and Eton upbringing.[29]

At the Colonial Office, Arthur Creech Jones was probably the best qualified secretary of state Britain ever had. He had been imprisoned during the First World War as a conscientious objector, which debarred him from a career as a junior clerk in the civil service. There followed years of work and study on the Anti-Slavery Committee, the Labour Party's advisory committee on imperial affairs, and as founder-chairman

---

[25] Bullock, *Ernest Bevin*, vol. III: *Foreign secretary, 1945–1951* (1983), p. 659.

[26] Francis Williams, *Ernest Bevin: portrait of a great Englishman* (1952), pp. 153–4.

[27] Saville, *The politics of continuity*, p. 4. He gives a helpful assessment, pp. 81–111.

[28] Attlee talking to Dalton: Dalton Diary, vol. 42, p. 18 (24 September 1951), p. 40 (27 October 1951). See also B. Donoughue and G. W. Jones, *Herbert Morrison: portrait of a politician* (1973), pp. 498, 610.

[29] B. Pimlott, *Hugh Dalton* (1985); H. Dalton, *Memoirs*, vol. III: *High tide and after, 1945–1960* (1962).

of the Fabian Colonial Bureau.[30] In 1943 he visited West Africa as a member of the commission on higher education. He was determined to make policy 'less paternal and ungenerous' as the 'brittle foundations of imperial power begin to crack'.[31] He was dismayed at having to start as under-secretary to George Hall, formerly himself an under-secretary (1940–42), a worthy but uninspiring MP for Merthyr Tydfil since 1922, who had gone down the mines at twelve and was now approaching retirement. Sadly, for all Creech Jones's innovative work at the Colonial Office, he was bullied by Bevin, his fellow Bristolian, and Attlee never valued him, concluding that he was 'perhaps hardly strong enough for the position', appearing to have 'no real grip of administration'; he was bad in the Commons, and did not contribute in Cabinet.[32] The truth was, Attlee could not stand Creech Jones, particularly on account of his prolixity.[33] An uncharismatic blatherer no doubt, Creech Jones nevertheless left his mark, with the help of officials, shifting colonial policy away from paternalism into something much more positive.

His successor was James Griffiths, a former president of the South Wales Miners' Federation. He had all the Welsh eloquence without the egotism which often seems to go with it. Courageous, loyal, charming and warm-hearted, firmly in and respected by the Labour mainstream, he could have been a leadership contender in the 1950s, but was thought too old (though he did become deputy leader).[34] The future, he wrote, was as likely to be determined not in what they were pleased to call the corridors of power, but 'on the paddy-fields of Asia and the *shambas* of Africa'.[35]

At the Dominions Office (later the Commonwealth Relations Office) Lord Addison was the first of the secretaries of state, a veteran of substance, but nothing much happened during his tenure. Then there was Philip Noel-Baker. His concerns were peace movements, disarmaments, and sport. He had done short stints in the Foreign Office and Air Ministry. 'He has not enhanced his reputation', was Attlee's verdict on his time at the CRO. Despite his many qualities, Attlee believed he 'did not inspire much confidence', his judgment was poor (especially on Kashmir), and 'he was talkative but not illuminating in Cabinet'.[36] In

[30] R. D. Pearce, *The turning-point in Africa: British colonial policy, 1938–1948* (1982), pp. 95–9; P. M. Pugh, 'Jones, Arthur Creech-' *ODNB*, vol. XXX, pp. 443–5.
[31] A. Creech Jones, intro. to R. Hinden, ed., *Fabian colonial essays* (1945), pp. 17–18.
[32] Attlee Papers, Churchill Archives Centre, Cambridge, ATLE 1/17, pp. 8 and 16.
[33] Earl of Listowel to the author, 16 April 1993.
[34] D. Jay, *Change and fortune: a political record* (1980), p. 249; Philip M. Williams, ed., *The diary of Hugh Gaitskell, 1945–1956* (1983).
[35] James Griffiths, *Pages from memory* (1969), p. 121.
[36] ATLE 1/17, pp. 8 and 16; Gordon Walker Papers, Churchill Archives Centre, GNWR 1/6, diary, 21 Apr 1948.

his stead he appointed Patrick Gordon Walker, who had shown 'exceptional ability'. Bevin also thought him 'good and reliable'.[37] He was a right-winger, son of an Indian Civil Service judge, trained as an Oxford historian, but attracted to politics, though he kept on writing. It was his misfortune to combine a lugubrious face and an unlucky career.[38] He staked rather too much on an idealistic belief in the Commonwealth as a major force in world affairs, although not as an Anglo-centric construct, but 'in truth and without inhibition as an Euro-Afro-Asian Commonwealth'.[39] He was highly regarded by officials. Sir Percivale Liesching wrote to him on losing office – not of course an occasion for insults – 'we have lost a grand leader . . . in 31 years I have served many Ministers, but none with a wholer heart or with more conviction about the value of what had been done'.[40] This was in stark contrast to Liesching's opinion of Noel-Baker, 'an intellectual mosquito', an ineffective busybody.[41]

Among officials, Liesching himself stood out as a permanent head of the CRO, tough, decisive, aggressive, a good delegator as well as a good mixer.[42] His opposite number at the Colonial Office was Sir Thomas Lloyd, highly experienced and liberal-minded. The most famous historically, however, was (Sir) Andrew Cohen, head of the CO African Department. Cohen was highly congenial to the Labour leadership, and even to extreme left-wing critics of empire like Fenner Brockway.[43] His background was a privileged one in cosmopolitan Hampstead Jewry, though his mother was English. Large, excitable, and unconventional, his minutes were written in a spiky hand, difficult to read, like gothicised Hebrew with the diacriticals left out; it had caused his demotion in the civil service entry examination from a close second place to fourth (60 marks deducted).[44] As an undergraduate at Trinity College Cambridge he had successfully acted Dionysus in the Greek Play, and joined the Apostles; a friend of Anthony Blunt, he was investigated by MI5 in 1964 shortly before his early death. As his biographer-manqué described him,

[37] ATLE 1/17, p. 16; Williams, *A prime minister remembers*, p. 167.
[38] R. D. Pearce, ed., *Patrick Gordon Walker: political diaries, 1932–1971* (1991), pp. 29–32.
[39] P. Gordon Walker, *The Commonwealth* (1962), p. 380.
[40] GNWR 1/9, 29 October 1951.
[41] J. S. Garner, *The Commonwealth Office, 1925–1968* (1978), p. 292. This is a semi-autobiographical work. Saville Garner became more generally known as 'Joe', after a Labour secretary of state, 'Jimmy' Thomas in 1930, had insisted the new recruit drop 'Saville': 'What sort of a name is that?' (see Alex May, 'Garner, Joseph John Saville', *ODNB*, vol. XXI, pp. 482–3). Garner was an assistant under-secretary of state, 1948–51, deputy under-secretary, 1952–6, and permanent under-secretary, 1962–8.
[42] L. Lloyd, 'Liesching, Percivale', *ODNB*, vol. XXXIII, pp. 746–7.
[43] A. Fenner Brockway, *Towards tomorrow: autobiography* (1977), p. 195.
[44] Magdalene College Archives, F/REB/5, Broadbent diary, 28 September 1932.

he was 'the proconsul of African nationalism', with 'a heroic image of himself as the future in action'.[45]

Other influential voices in the CO included Sir Sydney Caine, a deputy under-secretary of state specialising in economic affairs (vice-chancellor of the University of Malaya from 1952), and H. T. Bourdillon, son of a colonial governor, an assistant secretary who moved to Singapore in 1959 as deputy UK commissioner. Of the rising stars, John Bennett seemed most likely to shoot to the top. After a Cambridge double-starred-first in history (the sort of result which put him in the category of future Regius professors and Eric Hobsbawm), he quickly attracted attention during the war whilst working on Palestine and the Middle East with the minister of state, R. G. Casey. He swiftly rose to an assistant secretaryship in the CO by 1946, prominent particularly on the Cyprus desk, and always a keen radical advocate of self-government there and indeed almost everywhere else.[46]

Among the governors, Sir Evelyn Baring stands out, as the key man in British African affairs between 1942 and 1959.[47] He was a patrician figure, with snobbish attitudes, Christian beliefs, and vice-regal pretensions, having been brought up to revere the work in Egypt of his father, the great Lord Cromer (who died when he was thirteen). With a first-class history degree (Oxford) behind him, he started out with the Indian Civil Service. Despite poor health, he was successively governor of Southern Rhodesia (1942), high commissioner in South Africa (1944, with responsibility for the High Commission Territories), governor of Kenya (1952), and finally (with the title Lord Howick) chairman of the Colonial Development Corporation (1960). In all of these assignments Baring made valuable contributions to rural development, especially for Swaziland and Kenya, both of which saw economic transformation. Two controversies dogged him: Seretse Khama's marriage – although much of the criticism was unjustified, he did under-estimate Seretse (see below, pp. 164–5) – and the treatment of Kikuyu detainees. The

---

[45] R. E. Robinson, 'Sir Andrew Cohen, 1909–1965', in L. H. Gann and P. Duignan, eds., *African proconsuls: Europeans in Africa* (Stanford and New York, 1972), pp. 353–64, and 'Andrew Cohen and the transfer of power in tropical Africa, 1940–1951', in W. H. Morris-Jones and G. Fischer, eds., *Decolonisation and after; the British and French experience* (1980), pp. 50–72, and in *ODNB*, vol. XII (2004), pp. 418–19, where 'the future in action' of Robinson's original *DNB* entry is amended to 'idea in action'. Robinson abandoned the intention of writing a full-scale biography of Cohen, I think in part because of the difficulty of recovering his minutes and memoranda from the scattered archival records.

[46] For J. S. Bennett, I draw on Albert Hourani, 'Thoughts on the writing of the history of the Middle East', first John Bennett Memorial Lecture, Cambridge, 1992 (unpublished).

[47] C. Douglas-Home, *Evelyn Baring: the last proconsul* (1978); *ODNB* (2004), vol. III, pp. 828–9, by A. Clayton.

rehabilitation of former Mau Mau supporters was a major blot on British reputation in the twentieth century.[48] It was all too reminiscent of the savage retribution indulged in after the Indian Mutiny-Rebellion of 1857, and Baring ought to have exercised closer supervision of locally recruited police and guards (see below, pp. 191–2). Rescuing a girl from drowning in the sea during the last days of his Kenya governorship was much admired, however.

2. The transfer of power in Asia: India, Burma, and Ceylon

The transfer of power in Asia was an astonishing development, the most epoch-making part of the process of ending the empire. Labour leaders travelled a long way intellectually to achieve it. As late as 1943 Bevin believed Burma might be polished into 'an Empire gem'.[49] Even Attlee spoke of Indian nationalism in the 1930s as 'the illegitimate offspring of patriotism, out of inferiority complex'; he was pessimistic about Indian leadership, particularly (having it observed it at first hand) the local administration, which he found corrupt, inefficient, and irresponsible.[50] The war of course changed everything. By October 1946 Bevin was telling the House of Commons 'we have to take into account the rising of nationalism all over the world and, while recognising it, guide it into the world organisation, or it may become a danger of conflict'. Since December 1945 the Labour government had been trying 'vigorously' (his word) to reconcile the Indonesian nationalists with the Netherlands overlord. Lord Inverchapel and Lord Killearn had both tried to mediate between the two sides and get an agreement on Indonesian autonomy within a framework of co-operative partnership. The role of British troops was praised by the Indonesian prime minister, Mr Sjahrir, for showing 'a just appreciation' of their nationalism and of the Indonesian national revolution. Bevin quoted this with satisfaction.[51]

Having committed themselves in this way in Indonesia, it was going to be hard to take a less sympathetic line in Britain's own Asian territories.

---

[48] D. Anderson, *Histories of the hanged: Britain's dirty war in Kenya and the end of empire* (2004); and for an even more damning indictment, Caroline Elkins, *Britain's Gulag: the brutal end of empire in Kenya* (2005).

[49] N. Tarling, *The sun never sets: an historical essay on Britain and its place in the world* (New Delhi, 1986) p. 105.

[50] Burridge, *Clement Attlee*, pp. 270–5; *PD, Commons* vol. 276, cc. 718–31, 27 March 1933.

[51] *PD, Commons* vol. 427, cc. 1490–1 (22 October 1946) and vol. 440, cc. 1205–10 (23 July 1947).

(1) India

Attlee had an unusually strong background in Indian affairs. His schc was Haileybury, traditionally associated with India. He was a member of the Simon Commission, 1927–30, visiting India twice. He was chairman of the wartime Cabinet India Committee. In 1943, secretary of state for India, L. S. Amery, would have been pleased enough to see him made viceroy in succession to Linlithgow, a pukka Conservative Scottish aristocrat (nicknamed 'Linlith*slow*').[52] Early in 1942 Attlee wrote a crucially important memorandum denouncing the 'crude imperialism' of Linlithgow as 'fatally shortsighted and suicidal' and ugly: 'to mark time is to lose India'. Attlee argued that the balance of prestige had changed: the reverses sustained at the hands of the Japanese had continued a process begun in 1905, while acceptance of China in the war against the Axis powers meant that Indians asked why they could not be accepted as equals too, as masters in their own house. Then, overtly but cheekily appealing to Churchill: 'the increasingly large contribution in blood and tears and sweat made by Indians will not be forgotten and will be fully exploited by Indians who have not themselves contributed'. There was a British obligation to see that they would share in the 'things for which we and they are fighting'.[53] Attlee was almost alone at this time in seeing the necessity of real accommodation with the Indian nationalists. His initiative was effective to the extent that the Cripps Mission was sent to India in 1942. This mission had failed (see above, pp. 65–6).

The postwar Attlee administration promised a more propitious atmosphere.[54] Cripps remained a key player in Indian policy, and hoped to nurse Gandhi along. Indeed, as himself a clever lawyer, Christian ascetic, vegetarian, teetotal (though not non-smoking), Cripps often seemed to be 'the English Gandhi'.[55] Attlee's first problem was what to do with the viceroy who had succeeded Linlithgow in 1943, Field-Marshal Lord Wavell. Wavell was a man of ability and integrity, with some of the attributes of a scholarly Manchu warlord, such as writing poems. But he lacked political skills. He was also rather intimidating, with a glass eye and no small-talk. By the end of 1945 he and the commander-in-chief,

[52] N. Mansergh, E. W. R. Lumby, P. Moon *et al.*, eds., *Constitutional relations between Britain and India: the transfer of power, 1942–1947* (12 vols., 1970–83), cited hereafter as *TOPI*: vol. III, *21 September 1942–12 June 1943* (1971), pp. 243, 896, L. S. Amery to Churchill, 13 November 1942 and 16 April 1943.   [53] *TOPI* vol. I, pp 110–12 (no. 60).

[54] R. J. Moore, *Escape from empire: the Attlee government and the Indian problem* (Oxford, 1983).

[55] P. F. Clarke, *The Cripps version: the life of Sir Stafford Cripps, 1889–1952* (2002), pp. 387–457, provides a compellingly fresh perspective, based on sources not used before.

General Auchinleck, were advising that there was a real threat in 1946 of large-scale anti-British disorders, amounting even to a well-organised rising aiming to expel the British by paralysing the administration. Combined with communal strife between Hindus and Muslims this could be very serious, and disaffection might spread to Indian troops in the Middle East, with alarming repercussions.[56] After reading this analysis, it was clear to Attlee that everything depended on the reliability and spirit of the Indian Army: 'provided that they do their duty, armed insurrection in India would not be an insoluble problem. If, however, the Indian Army were to go the other way, the picture would be very different.'[57] Wavell warned that, commanding practically the whole of Hindu articulate opinion, Congress could undoubtedly bring about a most serious revolt against British rule, which Britain could probably still suppress, but it would mean nothing short of a campaign for the reconquest of India.[58]

India could not, however, be ruled by the British alone, because the necessary number of officials simply did not exist, and collapsing British prestige left a nakedly exposed situation. For example, Indian National Army trials had to be reduced after an explosion of opposition in Calcutta from November 1945. In the Central Provinces there were no troops, and only seventeen British ICS officials and only nineteen British police.[59] Given the state of public opinion both at home and in the world at large, a policy of martial law and repression was not really an option. Moreover, British soldiers were war-weary, and would not want to remain in India in large numbers in order to hold the country down.[60] Thus, Wavell concluded, if the army and police 'failed' Britain would be forced to go. In theory it might be possible to revive and reinforce the services, and rule for another fifteen to twenty years, but: 'it is a fallacy to suppose that the solution lies in trying to maintain the status quo. We have no longer the resources, nor I think the necessary prestige and confidence in ourselves'.[61]

It was decided to send a Cabinet Mission to India in order to try to get Indians – specifically the Congress and the Muslim League – to agree on constitution-making machinery for independence and to set up an interim government. The 'three magi' consisted of Stafford Cripps ('Sir Stifford Crapps', Churchill called him – 'there but for the grace of God,

[56] *TOPI* vol. VI, pp. 576–82, memo by Auchinleck, 1 December 1945.
[57] *Ibid.* p. 616, Attlee to Pethick-Lawrence, 6 December 1945.
[58] *Ibid.* pp. 686–9, memo, 27 December 1945.
[59] *Ibid.* p. 604, Wavell to Pethick-Lawrence, 5 December 1945.
[60] *TOPI* vol. V, pp. 131–2 (no. 64), Wavell to Churchill, 24 October 1944; *TOPI* vol. VII, pp. 734–5, memo, 30 May 1946.
[61] *TOPI* vol. VII, pp. 1084–9 (no. 641), note, 29 January 1946.

goes God'), Lord Pethick-Lawrence, Attlee's tame and somewhat woolly secretary of state ('Pathetic' Lawrence), and A. V. Alexander ('King Albert Victorious' to his detractors), the minister of defence, of working-class credentials (a supporter of Chelsea FC and a wizard at billiards), with an affability bordering on becoming a bore, but not at all 'anti-colonialist' in outlook. (In an unguarded moment he let slip his opinion of the Indians: 'truth is, they are all buggers'.) In three months, and between bouts of diarrhoea, the team interviewed 472 Indian political leaders, but, in Wavell's clever comment, achieved little, despite 'the frankincense of goodwill, the myrrh of honeyed words, the gold of promises'. Gandhi, he knew only too well, was difficult to deal with: 'double-tongued but single-minded'.[62] Gandhi was indeed a tough negotiator. It proved impossible to bring Congress and the Muslim League together. Neither the plan for a coalition government, nor the constitutional scheme, came off. And there matters stalled.

After the failure of the Cabinet Mission, the Cabinet had some hard thinking to do. The main debates among ministers were in June and December 1946. Attlee thought the central problem was how to convince Indian politicians that the British really were going, and Indians must therefore hammer out a future for their country. The main worry of the Labour ministers was appearing to be weak, and to head off Churchillian jibes about 'scuttle'. They had a positive fixation about this. In the words of the Cabinet minutes: 'having regard to current difficulties in Palestine and Egypt, it was important to avoid any course which could be represented as a policy of "scuttle". This would provoke very strong reactions in this country and in the Dominions, and would have a most damaging effect on our international position.' It must not seem as if they were being forced out, but 'for economic, military and political reasons like, we could not face a situation which involved committing British troops to a long series of operations in India'.[63] Cripps took the view that neither repression nor scuttle were tenable propositions. Repression was beyond British resources, while scuttle would lead to chaos, causing general consternation in the Commonwealth. Bevin argued that any suggestion of 'abandoning our position in India without obtaining a solution' would be interpreted 'as evidence of a decline in British power and resolution', and would upset the Americans.[64] If India broke down, Russia might step in and the seeds of a world conflict could be sown.[65] But equally worrying

---

[62] P. Moon, ed., *Wavell: the viceroy's journal* (1973), p. 249 (18 April 1946); *TOPI* vol. VII, p. 1092. For A. V. Alexander's indiscretion: Clarke, *The Cripps version*, p. 441.

[63] CAB 128/7, CM 55(46), Cabinet minutes annex, 5 June 1946; *TOPI* vol. VII, pp. 812–19 (no. 455).   [64] *TOPI* vol. VII, pp. 571–2, Cabinet meeting, 16 May 1946.

[65] Cabinet memoranda: CAB 129/10, CP(46)222; *TOPI* vol. VII, pp. 930–3 (no. 528).

was the conclusion of the Chiefs of Staff: to remain might permanently antagonise the Indians, which would militate against long-term British strategic requirements, the need for bases and airfields and access to the industry and manpower of India in war. The reliability of Indian forces was now, they believed, seriously open to doubt, and to rely on them might mean being forced to withdraw ignominiously.[66]

What the Chiefs of Staff said was of course enormously important. The whole outcome in India would have been different if the service Chiefs had mounted a strong case for staying on. Arguments still continued – and were frequently put by A. V. Alexander – about the feasibility of 'continuing for fifteen years'. In November 1946 Attlee set out with typical trenchancy his reasons for rejecting this:

(a)   In view of our commitments all over the world we have not the military force to hold India agst [sic] a widespread guerilla movement or to reconquer India.
(b)   If we had, public opinion especially in our Party would not stand for it.
(c)   It is very doubtful if we could keep the Indian troops loyal. It is doubtful if our own troops would be prepared to act.
(d)   We should have world opinion agst [sic] us and be placed in an impossible position at UNO.
(e)   We have not now the administrative machine to carry out such a policy either British or Indian.[67]

The Cabinet on 10 December 1946 accepted much of his reasoning. It was agreed that the Army could not be expected to prove a reliable instrument for maintaining public order in conditions which would be tantamount to civil war. One thing was quite certain, 'that we could not put the clock back and introduce a period of firm British rule'. Simply leaving Indians to solve their own problems, probably in conditions of chaos, was equally unrealistic, if only because 'world opinion would regard it as a policy of scuttle unworthy of a great Power', and it would indeed be an inglorious end if Britain had not guaranteed fair treatment for Muslims and other minorities.[68]

On the last day of 1946 the Cabinet considered the question of whether an announcement of withdrawal from India would be regarded as the beginning of the liquidation of the British empire. The general feeling of ministers was that withdrawal need not appear to be forced upon them by weakness, or be the first step in the dissolution of the empire; on the contrary, it was the logical conclusion of the policy of

---

[66]   CAB 129/10, CP(46)229; *TOPI* vol. VII, pp. 889–900 (no. 509).
[67]   *TOPI* vol. XI, p. 68 (no. 35).
[68]   CAB 128/8, CM 104(46)3, and CM 108(46) annexes, 10 December 1946; *TOPI* vol. XI, pp. 319–20; *BDEEP* pt 1, pp. 31–2 (no. 13).

successive governments. Their main objective now was to bring the principal Indian communities into co-operation – and the announcement of a withdrawal date might promote this.[69] The chancellor of the Exchequer, Hugh Dalton, pressed for an early withdrawal; as he wrote in his diary, 'I am quite clear that we cannot think of holding India by force, and that means that we must let them have the freedom to run their own show – even if this should unhappily include a Hindu–Muslim civil war.'[70] Dalton was glad the new viceroy, Mountbatten, was to be given a fixed terminal date, June 1948:

This was by far the best chance of making these wretched Indians work together while letting us out of a situation which was rapidly becoming quite untenable. If you are in a place where you are not wanted, and where you have not got the force, or perhaps the will, to squash those who do not want you, the only thing to do is to come out. This very simple truth will have to be applied to other places too, e.g. Palestine.[71]

One hopes that Dalton pronounced his splendidly monosyllabic dictum at the Cabinet table. His diary-vignette of the proceedings is not, however, edifying:

I supported fixed date now to India: Cripps very strong for this, and so (after some long intervals of speechlessness, a growing tendency, I fear) was PM. King Albert always kept making same speech over and over again, objected strongly, would have stayed 10–15 years, no matter the cost, but realised it was impossible. Pethick goes to sleep. Addison very long-winded, and unusually tiresome. Smuts had expressed grave doubts but as usual accepts no responsibility except offering advice; other Dominions didn't feel strongly about a fixed date; A[ddison] was obstructive and unusually indecisive. Mountbatten (we couldn't say publicly) wouldn't take it without a fixed date. Wavell has become increasingly tired and mentally unresilient.[72]

Mountbatten's appointment was urged by Cripps, but he was not Attlee's first choice for the last viceroy. He had wanted Tom Johnston, sometime secretary of state for Scotland. As so often with candidates who do not get the job, he seems now an extraordinary alternative. Whatever criticisms attach to Mountbatten, his was at least one of those appointments which has a wide appeal. Glamorous, a high-profile (if not exactly heroic) wartime commander, a left-wing patrician with royal connections, and an ego to match, he was hugely self-important and not a

---

[69] CAB 128/8, CM 108(46) annex, 31 December 1946; *TOPI* vol. XI, pp. 427–31 (no. 235); *BDEEP*, pt 1, pp. 34–7 (no. 15).

[70] Dalton, *High tide and after*, p. 172 (20 December 1946).

[71] *Ibid*, p. 211 (24 February 1947).

[72] London School of Economics, Library of Political Science Archives, Dalton Papers, section I, Diary, vol. 35, p. 15 (24 February 1947).

little eccentric. The American General Stilwell called him a 'childish pisspot';[73] one knows what he meant – though Stilwell himself was known as 'Vinegar Joe' – and as Churchill might have said, 'some child, some pisspot'. Mountbatten arrived in Delhi on 22 March 1947, taking just four and a half months to complete an unavoidable transfer of power. As Lord Ismay, Mountbatten's right-hand man, recognised, 'We had lost the initiative. We had lost all authority. The sawdust was running out of the doll hour by hour . . . You can't bluff if you've nothing to bluff with. We hadn't anything.'[74]

In assessing the Mountbatten viceroyalty, it has to be remembered that Attlee remained ultimately in charge of policy throughout, having put Mountbatten 'in to bat on a very sticky wicket to pull the game out of the fire'.[75] (He did not in any legal sense have 'plenipotentiary powers'.) What Mountbatten provided was the essential brokerage, negotiating the agreement which had hitherto eluded Britain. There were two main elements: a decision to speed things up, and a decision to concede Pakistan, and thus to partition India. Both decisions were taken in April–May 1947. The acceleration of the timetable to 15 August 1947 was intended to forestall a civil war, granted the shocking deterioration into communal violence.[76] Better, it was thought, to have disorders consequent upon the implementation of a plan, than civil war without a plan. A quick decision might also 'give Pakistan a greater chance to fail on its demerits' (Mountbatten). There may also have been a hope that it was a way of holding India in the Commonwealth.[77]

As to Pakistan, the fundamental issue facing Mountbatten was unity or division of the Indian sub-continent. Unity was his primary goal, the ideal, the reasonable solution, and the British held to it until it was plain for all the world to see that Jinnah's intransigent insistence on Pakistan left no alternative but partition. The Cabinet Mission of 1946 had boldly rejected Pakistan: as in Palestine, partition was to be avoided.[78] But by May 1947 the government had to accept it, though placing upon Indians the full responsibility of working out its extent.[79] Pakistan represented a stumbling-block to a tidy and desirable solution. It owed everything to Jinnah, who (according to Mountbatten) was a psychopath who had 'lost

---

[73] C. Thorne, *Allies of a kind: the United States, Britain and the war against Japan, 1941–1945* (1978), p. 267.

[74] H. V. Hodson, *The great divide: Britain–India–Pakistan* (1969), p. 534.

[75] *TOPI* vol. XII, p. 214 (no. 153), Attlee to Mountbatten, 17 July 1947.

[76] *TOPI* vol X, p. 533.   [77] *Ibid.* p. 251 (15 April 1947).

[78] *Ibid.* p. 49 (31 March), and p. 540 (1 May 1946), no 276.

[79] W. R. Louis, 'British imperialism and the partitions of India and Palestine', in C. Wrigley, ed., *Warfare, diplomacy and politics: essays in honour of A. J. P. Taylor* (1986), pp. 189–209.

the art of saying yes'.[80] British ministers regarded Jinnah's maximal Pakistan as a horrible prospect; intrinsically mad, a negation, an illogical monster, ruinous, and impracticable, strategically a geopolitical disaster, a deadly blow against the defence security of the whole area as it was the most liable to be attacked, and yet ill-equipped to withstand a Soviet drive. To divide India was to the British a confession of failure and a retrograde step. There were serious doubts about the viability of Pakistan, including its economic viability. Especially there were concerns about East Pakistan (now Bangladesh). But the reasoning behind the capitulation to Pakistan was that Muslim determination to have it was so great that chaos and maybe civil war would follow its denial.[81] To unite India against Muslim wishes would necessarily involve force, while dividing India against the wishes of the Hindus would not. And that was in the end the deciding consideration. Moreover, Britain could not afford to antagonise the Muslims.[82] Unlike the Hindus they were not yet deeply estranged (they had been friendly for decades and were keen to trade). Potential Pakistan lay across a major imperial line of air communication. Nor did Britain want to upset Muslims in the Middle East, who also bestrode a line of Commonwealth communications.[83] Shrewdly, Jinnah made an early announcement that Pakistan would remain in the Commonwealth. Of course, Mountbatten's recommendation to bring forward the date of the transfer of power without the Muslim League's acceptance of a united India left the British government with no alternative but to hand over to 'more than one authority'. This was acceptable to Congress because it would give them the strong central government they wanted. There was tragic loss of life as a consequence of partition – up to a million dead – especially in the Punjab, but probably less than would have occurred if the process had been significantly slower. The Sikhs were spoiling for a fight, but accepted partition.

What is our judgment of these decisions to be? Mountbatten was always boastful about his role ('What I did in India in 1947 was one of the three most important events in the world in this [twentieth] century, equalled in significance only by the Russian revolution of 1917 and the Chinese Communist take-over of 1949 . . .')[84] As far as Pakistan is concerned, it is no doubt true that there was no option, despite the appalling

---

[80] For a more favourable view of Jinnah, see Fenner Brockway, *Towards tomorrow: autobiography* (1971), p. 96.

[81] *TOPI* vol. XI, p. 958; Moore, *Escape from empire*, p. 62; *TOPI* vol. VII, p. 69 and 591.

[82] Note by Pethick-Lawrence, 14 February 1946, *TOPI* vol. VI, p. 979.

[83] R. G. Casey (governor of Bengal) to Wavell, 6 November 1944, *TOPI* vol. V, p. 183 (no. 91).

[84] Earl Mountbatten of Burma, *Reflections on the transfer of power and Jawaharlal Nehru*, 2nd Nehru Memorial Lecture (Cambridge, 1968), p. 1.

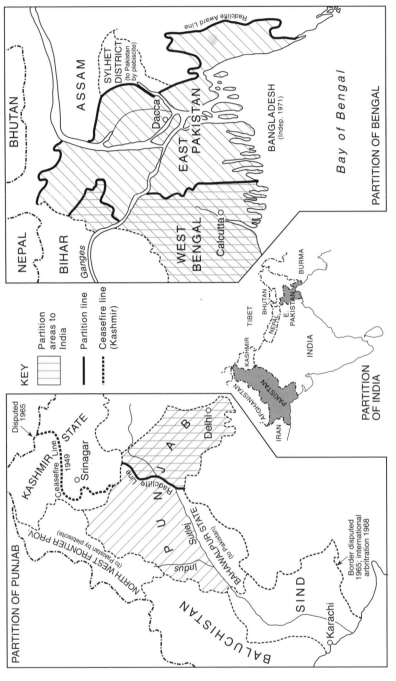

Map 2.1 Partition of India, 15 August 1947

problem of dividing the Sikhs in the Punjab and the irrigation systems of Bengal.[85] It was the only means of reconciling 'irreconcilable people'. Mountbatten did not hold the scales even between Congress and Muslim League, being close to Nehru (Lady Mountbatten was said to be even closer). He convinced himself that if he 'fell foul of Congress it would be impossible to continue to run the country'.[86] Mountbatten's anti-Jinnah and anti-Pakistan attitude compromised his impartiality. He interfered with the Radcliffe boundary line in favour of India, and pushed the mapping forward. This is the crucial specific charge against him. It rankled with Pakistanis, particularly as they were accepting a 'moth-eaten' Pakistan, which many considered did not serve their interests well. It was a country not of six great provinces, but only those administrative districts which had actual Muslim majorities, and thus including only about three-fifths of the Muslims in India.[87]

As to the question of acceleration of the timetable, this is an open question. Did Mountbatten rush it too much? The situation was highly inflammable, but could it not have been held for half a year more? After all, it would be smart work to complete a house-sale in seventy-two days, let alone liquidate an empire, and yet that is all it took from 3 June 1947 until agreement was reached. At the most favourable judgment, he was surely going a bit too fast. Put more harshly, it was absurd and reckless.

Nevertheless, Mountbatten probably achieved the best that was available in difficult circumstances. Events were probably already beyond control, and if so, he rode the whirlwind not just flamboyantly but in an overall sense correctly, whatever the serious flaws in the detail.[88]

What were the essential dynamics of the Attlee government's transfer of power in India? How important were changing economic circumstances? Manifestly, India had been declining in its economic importance to Britain, and this removed some of the inhibitions to constitutional change, although these did not necessarily lead to a transfer of power. From the economic standpoint, the position was simply one of *nihil obstat*. As Amery had expressed it to the Cabinet in 1945: 'In surrendering control from here we should not be sacrificing anything that mattered.'[89] Policy was constructed with more than a few glances over

[85] *TOPI* vol. X, p. 643.

[86] A. Jalal, *The sole spokesman: Jinnah, the Muslim League and the demand for Pakistan* (Cambridge, 1983), p. 262.

[87] *Ibid.* pp. 243–4: 'the timetable dramatically opened Pandora's box'. 'Pakistan' means 'pure land': 'P' for Punjab, 'A' for Afghania (i.e., Pathan, North-West Frontier Province), 'K' for Kashmir, 'S' for Sind, and Baluchis-TAN.

[88] W. Morris-Jones, '36 years later: the mixed legacies of Mountbatten's transfer of power' *International Affairs*, vol. 59 (1983), pp. 621–8.

[89] *TOPI* vol. V, p. 620, 28 February 1945. See p. 67 above for more detail.

the shoulders. One aim was to impress the United States; the 'three wise men' had been sent out partly to demonstrate internationally the importance attached to solving the Indian problem.[90] Strong, well-disposed inheritor regimes were essential geopolitically. A power vacuum must be avoided at all costs. The Chiefs of Staff thought Russia would at least try to influence independent India, and, if Britain were at war with Russia, India could be easily overrun by Russia. Such a policy would, it was thought, have great attractions for Russia and devastating effects for Britain, because India was the lynchpin of Commonwealth air communications, the strategic protecting-flank for Persian Gulf oil supplies, and it had important deposits of thorium in Travancore (thorium was needed to make atomic bombs). The Great Game cast a long shadow.[91]

Then there is the question of morale and manpower.[92] In parliamentary debate Churchill said the real reason for withdrawal from India was the British lack of will-power and moral strength. For Britain could, he argued, have gone on for some fifteen to twenty years more, though it would not have been easy. Therefore, he denounced Labour policy as a 'premature and hurried scuttle . . . with the taint and smear of shame . . . the clattering down of the British Empire.'[93] This of course was the very last thing the government wanted said. Churchill underestimated the moral courage involved in transferring power. It was, however, not really a matter of will at all, for everything turned at the last stage upon calculations about governability. The number of Europeans in the Indian Civil Service (ICS) had been run right down, and there was 'a descent into inefficiency.'[94] Europeans were in a clear minority, and a quarter of them were over fifty years old and thus near retirement. Recruitment had dried up totally in 1943, and by December 1946 there were only 608 ICS Europeans left. Even if replacements could be recruited, it would take three to four years' training before they were any real use. 'To govern India on anything approaching modern or efficient standards would require a considerable new European element in the services' – which just did not seem to be forthcoming.[95] As a result, Britain faced 'a crisis of the colonial state' (J. M. Brown).[96] The police were discontended; there were police strikes in 1946 in Malabar and

[90] *TOPI* vol. VI, pp. 192 and 834.   [91] *TOPI* vol. VIII, pp. 57 and 640.

[92] D. C. Potter, 'Manpower shortage and the end of colonialism: the case of the Indian Civil Service', *Modern Asian Studies*, vol. 8 (1973), pp. 47–73 and *India's political administrators, 1918–1983* (1986), pp. 121–49 (ch. 3).

[93] *PD. Commons* vol. 434, cc. 663–78 (6 March 1947).

[94] *TOPI* vol. IX, p. 269, note by Pethick-Lawrence, 5 December 1946.

[95] *TOPI* vol. VIII, p. 551, Pethick-Lawrence to Attlee, 20 September 1946 (no. 342).

[96] Judith M. Brown, 'India', in J. M. Brown and W. R. Louis, eds., *The Oxford History of the British Empire*, vol. IV *Twentieth century* (1999), pp. 443–5.

Bihar. The armed services could no longer be relied upon. In six years the number of Indian NCOs and officers increased from 1,000 to 15,740, and they were not instilled with the traditional sort of loyalty to the Raj. There were mutinies of Royal Navy ratings at Bombay and Karachi, from 18 to 23 February 1946.

All this was against a backdrop of peasant revolt and armed resistance in Bengal, Travancore and Hyderabad: these were sporadic, localised, but extremely militant and committed mass actions.[97] Penderel Moon, a senior civil servant, described the British as on 'the edge of a volcano'. Between August 1946 and March 1947 there were communal riots on an unprecedented scale in Calcutta, East Bengal, Bihar, the United Provinces and Punjab. To this extent Britain was 'on the run', although it may also be the case that the hideous spectre of social revolution created fears in Indian elites which made them prepared to settle for a realistic but compromise independence.[98]

One other dynamic determined the shape of the outcome. This was the determination to preserve a British connection. Most British politicians wished to see India held in the Commonwealth, or at least friendly, in the context that 'the threat of Communist encroachment in South-East Asia was very real' (Attlee).[99] Nowhere, perhaps, was Attlee's domination of the process more apparent than in his efforts to keep India in the Commonwealth as a republic in 1949.[100] Neither the Foreign Office nor the foreign secretary really wanted this outcome, the Chiefs of Staff did not insist on it, and the constitutional lawyers argued that it would be a nonsense for a republic to be a member of an association headed by a monarch. Attlee would have none of it: 'There is . . . nothing inherently impossible in a republic forming part of a monarchy.' He and Gordon Walker brilliantly solved the problem by simply declaring, in effect, that there *was* no problem.[101] Attlee's appeal to Nehru – a theological appeal to the national status of the Christian 'holy family', who were not

---

[97] S. Sarkar, *Modern India, 1885–1947* (1989), pp. 414–54.

[98] H. V. Brasted and C. Bridge, 'The transfer of power in South Asia: an historiographical review', *South Asia: A Journal of South Asian Studies*, vol. 17 (1994), pp. 93–114.

[99] CAB 128/15, CM 17(49)2, 3 March 1949; *BDEEP*, pt 4, pp. 201–3 (no. 401); *TOPI* vol. VI, p. 324.

[100] Anita I. Singh, 'Keeping India in the Commonwealth: British political and military aims, 1947–1949', *Journal of Contemporary History*, vol. 20 (1985), pp. 469–81. For an important essay on the contrast with Ireland, see Deirdre McMahon, 'A large and noisier Southern Ireland: Ireland and the evolution of Dominion Status in India, Burma and the Commonwealth, 1942–1949', in M. Kennedy and J. M. Skelly, eds., *Irish foreign policy, 1919–1966: from independence to internationalism* (Dublin, 2000), pp. 155–91.

[101] CAB 134/119, CR 1(49), 7 January, and CR 3(49), 9 February 1949; *BDEEP*, pt 4, pp. 180–3, 192–6 (nos. 396 and 399); see also pp. 146–55 (nos. 382–5); GNWR I/7; R. J. Moore, *Making the new Commonwealth* (1987), pp. 160–73.

considered Jews, but Welsh in Wales, Dutch in Holland, etc.[102] – was not perhaps quite so effective, although the future would demonstrate that the dynastic principle was not without its attraction to Indians.

Historians debate the relative balance in the triangle of forces which brought about the transfer of power: the British government, Jinnah and his Muslim League, and the Congress high command. From the perspective of imperial history the positive contribution of the Labour government is not to be underestimated. Attlee was genuinely instrumental in making the settlement. His getting rid of Wavell made a friendly transition possible, rather than a fraught military evacuation. His appointment of Mountbatten kept Nehru 'on side'. There was no equivocation, and no 'fine print'. The exchange between Attlee and Bevin in January 1947 shows that it might have been very different. On New Year's Day Bevin wrote despondently that they seemed to be 'trying nothing except to scuttle out of it', instead of trying to find young men who could carry on a British administration. He was opposed to fixing a date for withdrawal. He begged Attlee 'to take a stronger line and not give way to this awful pessimism.' Attlee scornfully and confidently rejected all this. Yes, Wavell had a defeatist mind, but 'I am not defeatist but realist'. He was seeking to fulfil pledges given by successive British governments in the last twenty-five years, and 'avoid an ignominious scuttle'. The idea that people could suddenly and quickly be trained in such intricacies as 'the collection of land revenue, the backbone of Indian finance', without even Indian clerical assistance and in the face of the active opposition of the whole of the politically-minded body of Indians – this was an impossibility. 'If you disagree with what is proposed, you must offer a practical alternative. I fail to find one in your letter.'[103]

Despite all the imperfections, the transfer of power in India must be considered a geopolitically prudent response to the realities of declining power, a response which Attlee brought about quicker than would otherwise have been the case.

(2) Burma

The transfer of power in Burma shows many parallels with India, including the Labour government's replacement of the incumbent governor.

---

[102] PREM 8/950, no. 3, 20 March 1949. For Nehru's reasons for staying in the Commonwealth, see S. Gopal, *Jawaharlal Nehru: a biography* (1975), vol. II, pp. 45–55 and M. Brecher, 'India's decision to remain in the Commonwealth', *Journal of Commonwealth and Comparative Politics*, vol. 12 (1974), pp. 62–90.

[103] PREM 8/564; *TOPI* vol. IX, pp. 431–33, Bevin to Attlee, 1 January 1947, and pp. 445–6, Attlee to Bevin, 2 January 1947.

Illustration 2.1 Mr Attlee with Commonwealth prime ministers in the garden of No. 10 Downing Street, 23 April 1949.

The prime ministers had gathered for the Commonwealth Prime Ministers' Meeting. Back row, left to right: Sir Stafford Cripps (chancellor of the Exchequer), Mr Lester Pearson (Canadian secretary of state for external affairs), Liaquat Ali Khan (Pakistan), Mr Peter Fraser (New Zealand), Dr Malan (South Africa), Mr Don Senanayake (Ceylon), Mr Noel-Baker (secretary of state for Commonwealth relations). Seated: Mrs Attlee, Pandit Nehru (India), Lady Cripps, Mrs Malan, Mr Attlee, Begum Ali Khan, Mr Joseph Chifley (Australia). The main business of the conference was India's membership of the Commonwealth as a republic.

Sir 'Reggie' Dorman-Smith had gone to Burma in 1941 without any relevant previous experience – he had been a Conservative minister for agriculture and fisheries. He was an aloof and blimpish character, typical of a certain type of an ineffably awful Old Harrovian, with Irish citizenship, which made for 'an interestingly ambivalent view of empire and nationalism'.[104] On resuming office after the departure of the Japanese, he recognised that Burma 'would be a political volcano for some time to come'.[105] His task was not made easier by the machinations of Mountbatten, still Supreme Allied Commander South-East Asia. As a result, by May 1946 Attlee had decided 'the sooner he [Dorman-Smith] comes home the better': he was vacillating, incoherent, and 'had lost his grip'.[106] His replacement was Sir Hubert Rance, an army staff officer who was director of civil affairs. Rance's diagnosis was that 'the time for equivocation is past'; the Burmese nationalists were 'determined to have nothing less in any way than India', and further delay 'might mean harder terms.'[107] Attlee was perhaps a little slow to move into decisive gear, at first being anxious above all to keep things as quiet as possible. But he recognised General Aung San and the Anti-Fascist People's Freedom League (AFPFL) as 'the most important single political force', and that it would be 'unrealistic to fail to adjust our policy accordingly.' What would be Aung San's terms for co-operation?[108] As in India, Attlee realised that 'the question is one of timing'; there was 'an obvious risk in moving so fast but an equal risk of disturbances'.[109]

Exactly as in India too, there were fears of police unreliability and a shortage of manpower to cope with serious trouble. There were fears of a police strike in Rangoon. A widespread rebellion could not be dealt with effectively. It would become impossible to maintain government without

[104] C. Bayly and T. Harper, *Forgotten armies: the fall of British Asia, 1941–1945* (2004), pp. 85–6.

[105] N. Tarling, 'Lord Mountbatten and the return to civil government in Burma', *JICH*, vol. 11 (1983), p. 216. See also, generally, N. Tinker, 'Burma's struggle for independence: the transfer of power thesis re-examined', *Modern Asian Studies*, vol. 20 (1986), pp. 461–81 and 'The contraction of empire in Asia, 1945–1948: the military dimension', *JICH*, vol. 16 (1988), pp. 218–31).

[106] PREM 8/143, Attlee to Pethick-Lawrence, 7 May 1946; N. Tinker, ed., *Burma: the struggle for independence, 1944–1948*, vol. I: *From military occupation to civil government, 1 Jan. 1944–31 August 1946* (1983) and vol. II: *From general strike to independence, 31 August 1946–4 January 1948* (1984), hereafter cited as *BSI*: vol. I, p. 773 (no. 489), and p. 806 (no. 522), minute 23 May 1946.

[107] *BSI* vol. II, p. 175 (no. 127), and pp. 202–3 (no.143), 7 and 12 December 1946, Rance to Pethick-Lawrence.

[108] *BSI* vol. II, p. 806 (no. 522), minute by Attlee, 23 May 1946; and *BSI* vol. I, pp. 867–8 (no. 584), 29 June 1946, to acting governor.

[109] *BSI* vol. I, p. 479 (no. 276), Attlee to Pethick-Lawrence, minute M 65/45, 20 Sept. 1946.

the use of force, and there would be 'great military difficulty' in doing so. Rance stressed there was no other party than the AFPFL with whom to come to terms, 'the only horse to back'. AFPFL were quite prepared to seize freedom forcibly, but Britain could not afford to take suppressive action, if only for the damage it would do to its international prestige. They could not, Rance said, 'afford to concede by force later what they could concede with dignity now'.[110] The Cabinet accepted that humiliating withdrawal might ensue if they held back. Nor was it clear 'what useful result' could come from an attempt to rule by force, as it would probably only strengthen nationalist and secessionist feeling. Britain had persuaded the Dutch to accept a settlement involving almost complete independence for Indonesia, and it was undesirable British policy should be inconsistent with this.[111]

There was hesitation and heart-searching. Some Ministers regretted the pressure of events, but India had now been informed that they could decide whether or not to remain in the Commonwealth, and Burma expected the same treatment. Probably it was Attlee himself who advanced the opinion that 'if the principle of independence was sound for India it was also sound for Burma'.[112] Nevertheless he thought it of the utmost importance that the realisation of independence should be orderly as well as rapid.[113] In February 1947 he announced that British rule would end before June 1948. Much reliance was placed on Aung San, but in July 1947 he was murdered. Nevertheless independence was achieved in January 1948. Burma immediately left the Commonwealth. Attlee believed this might not have happened if Aung San – for whom he had considerable admiration – had still been in charge.[114]

(3) Ceylon

The case of Ceylon (renamed Sri Lanka in 1972) demonstrates considerable reluctance on the part of the Labour government to extend Indian 'precedent'. The governor, Sir Henry Moore, was keen to move ahead in September 1945, believing there was 'a golden opportunity by the exercise of a little courage now, of making a generous and spontaneous

---

[110] BSI vol. II, p. 197 (no. 140), Rance to Pethick-Lawrence, 17 December 1946.

[111] CAB 128/6, CM 107(46)2, 19 December 1946; BSI vol. II, pp. 206–7 (no. 145); BDEEP pt 1, pp. 32–4 (no. 14).

[112] BSI vol. II, p. 205 (no. 144), Cabinet India and Burma Committee, IB 10(46), 19 December 1946.

[113] BSI vol. II, pp. 209–10 (no. 147); PD, Commons vol. 431, cc. 2341–43 (20 December 1946).

[114] Williams, A prime minister remembers, pp. 213–15. Aung San's daughter is Aung San Suu Kyi (b. 1945).

gesture to Ceylon which, in the long run, would pay a handsome dividend'. The Labour government was sceptical and decided to wait for the report of Lord Soulbury, a former Conservative minister, appointed to chair a commission in 1944 to give advice on constitutional reform. Lord Soulbury formulated the doctrine which was to run like the proverbial scarlet thread through the history of decolonisation: 'in the long run giving too much and too soon will prove to be wiser than giving too little and too late'. The truth of this insight was not yet understood, however, and Soulbury's feeling that 'to hit the golden mean between caution and magnanimity is perhaps impossible' also proved pertinent.[115] In a country which had had universal suffrage since 1931 (twenty years ahead of India), a population which was barely one-fiftieth the size of India, with an elite more Anglophile than in Burma,[116] and, as yet, none of the communal violence of either, transition to independence should not have been too difficult. Although Tamils made up about 20 per cent of the mainly Singhalese population, relations were at this time good enough to allow the Tamil Congress from 1948 to support the ruling United National Party until 1956. The issue of protection for minorities was raised vaguely in the British Cabinet in 1947, but it was felt constitutional safeguards would only lead to a deterioration of relations with the Singhalese leaders, and would be a cause of complication and delay.[117]

Although it was peaceful and orderly, the transfer of power in Ceylon was far from straightforward.[118]

In October 1945 British ministers were prepared to contemplate full internal self-government and dominion status for Ceylon, but only to be reached in six years' time. The moderate Singhalese leader D. S. Senanayake – flamboyant but shrewd – accepted this reluctantly, but when in December 1946 Burma was offered independence, and in the spring of 1947 a withdrawal date was announced for India, he maintained that he would be seriously embarrassed to accept a greatly inferior status to that of India and Burma. The argument struck home because it was hard to deny that Ceylon's behaviour had been everything that Burma's had not: it was not only geopolitically and economically important but

[115] CO 54/986/6, no. 3, Moore to CO, 25 September 1945, and no. 174, Soulbury to Hall, 5 October 1945; *BDEEP* pt 1, pp. 4–5 (no. 3); K. M. de Silva, ed., *Sri Lanka* (also BDEEP, 1997), pt 2: *Towards independence, 1945–1948*, no. 295 and no. 300 (p. 113).

[116] Ged Martin, *Past futures: the impossible necessity of history* (Toronto, 2004), p. 200, makes the point forcibly that 'size matters'.   [117] CAB 128/10, CM 51(47)4, 3 June 1947.

[118] S. R. Ashton, 'Ceylon' in Brown and Louis, ed., *Oxford history of the British empire* vol. IV, pp. 447–64, gives an admirable account. F. Heinlein, *British government policy and decolonisation, 1945–1963: scrutinising the official mind* (2002), pp. 42–53, is good on Burma and Malaya as well as Ceylon.

loyal and helpful in war, friendly and correct in its post-war politics. Sir Henry Moore, recalled 'frankly I was aghast' at the Burma announcement.[119] Ceylon could hardly be treated less favourably than Burma, which would otherwise seem to be rewarded for bad behaviour.

Creech Jones regarded presentation as all-important:

I have given anxious thought to this matter, more particularly in view of the accusation which has been made against the present government of 'scuttle' and of 'squandering the empire'. It seems to me, that, on the contrary, if this matter is rightly handled, we have not only an excellent opportunity of keeping Ceylon within the British Commonwealth and of securing our vital defence interests here, but of demonstrating to the world that our proclaimed policy for the Colonial peoples is not an empty boast, and that an independent status in the Commonwealth is not, in practice, reserved for people of European descent.[120]

Bevin thought the colonial secretary's draft reply went too far, implying that an unconditional promise of independence would be given 'later on' if not immediately. If the whole of the Indian Ocean was 'going', then, thought Bevin, the 'British empire is considerably weakened':

I do not like the repetition of the word 'independence' the whole time . . . in all these matters the countries of the Middle East and Far East are watching every move we make and if we go any further with this policy than we have done already then the moral authority of Great Britain in that area will be lost. This constant desire to make further pronouncements in these territories I think should be resisted.[121]

Creech Jones in reply pointed out that Senanayake was only narrowly being persuaded to co-operate, and they had to try to hold Ceylon in the Commonwealth. But it seems Attlee backed Bevin, and all reference to an advance commitment on independence disappeared.[122] The Chiefs of Staff also thought immediate unconditional independence would be a gamble, and were very worried. Gradually, the Cabinet recognised that although to accept most of Senanayake's demands and to collaborate with him was indeed to risk everything on his good faith and continuation in power, to refuse him would strengthen the 'extremists' pressing for immediate complete independence and freedom to leave the Commonwealth, and it might prejudice the new constitution and British defence requirements.[123] It was decided that a new constitution must come into operation. Once it was properly functioning, Britain would then discuss the reserved subjects so as to advance the status of Ceylon.[124]

---

[119] Sir Henry Monck-Mason Moore, in H. A. J. Hulugalle, *British governors of Ceylon* (Colombo, 1963), p. 232.

[120] CAB 129/18, CP(47)144, 29 April 1947; de Silva, *Sri Lanka*, pt 2, pp. 283–6 (no. 388).

[121] CAB 118/29, letter to 'Arthur', 20 May 1947; *BDEEP* pt 1, pp. 71–3 (no. 26).

[122] CAB 129/18, CP(47)147, 5 May 1947; de Silva, *Sri Lanka*, pt 2, pp. 286–7 (no. 389).

[123] CAB 128/9, CM 44(47)2, 6 May 1947; *BDEEP* pt 1, pp. 70–1 (no. 25); de Silva, pt 2, pp. 288–90 (no. 390).   [124] CAB 129/19, CP(47)171, 1 June 1947.

The government was willing to see 'fully reponsible status' for Ceylon, but this fell short of Senanayake's demand for independence, which was bypassed for about eighteen months. As constitutional advance for Ceylon was speeded up, the Cabinet insisted that it would be inadvisable to suggest publicly that events in India and Burma had been responsible.[125] In other words, a line was being drawn. The government had reluctantly extended the precedent of India and Burma, but, especially influenced by Bevin, was in no mood to let it go any further.

However, Senanayake won the election as Ceylon's first prime minister in November 1947. For his part, he was prepared to meet British anxieties over strategic facilities, and fair treatment for ethnic minorities (mainly Tamil), and to play down the 'Buddhist' policies of his rival, the ex-Christian S. W. R. D. Bandaranaike. Negotiations were fairly easy. Of course they could not be certain Senanayake would be returned to power, but his chances, Creech Jones argued, would be seriously damaged if they attempted to qualify the grant of independence or to make it conditional on prior acceptance of terms stipulated by Britain (such as the Chiefs of Staff wanted). Nor would it be easy, he said, to enforce them on a government indifferent or hostile to the maintenance of a British connection. And so a collaborative bargain was struck with Senanayake and a Singhalese elite with recognisably British attributes, even if with a somewhat eighteenth-century oligarchical outlook. Many of the professional politicians had been at British universities.[126] Senanayake was anxious not 'to be drawn from Britain into the Indian sphere', and so he allowed continued British use of extensive bases. The Chiefs of Staff were satisfied.[127]

When Ceylon became independent, on 4 February 1948, the presentation was again to deny that it constituted a precedent for others to follow. Ceylon, it was said, was unique, the most advanced, the premier colony on the British books.[128] Senanayake was also unusually well-liked. When in 1952 he fell off his horse and was dying from his injuries, Prime Minister Churchill immediately insisted on dispatching Sir Hugh Cairns, the leading neuro-surgeon – and himself terminally ill – to try to save him.[129]

[125] CAB 128/10, CM 51(47)4, 3 June 1947.
[126] Swinton Papers, Churchill Archives Centre, SWIN I/6/6, Swinton to his wife, December 1953; H. Macmillan, *Memoirs*, vol. IV: *Riding the storm, 1956–1959* (1971), p. 395 (19 January 1958).
[127] R. J. Aldrich, 'British strategy and the end of empire: South Asia, 1945–1951', in Aldrich, ed., *British intelligence, strategy and the cold war* (1992), pp. 285–90.
[128] de Silva, *Sri Lanka* pt 1, intro, pp. lxxxiv–lxxxvi.
[129] R. Hyam and W. R. Louis, eds., *The Conservative government and the end of empire, 1957–1964* (BDEEP, 2000), pt 2, pp. 647–8.

3. Palestine

Most Labour Party leaders, including Bevin, had been pro-Zionist. Soon after taking office, however, Bevin went to the prime minister and said, 'Clem, about Palestine. According to my lads in the [foreign] office, we've got it wrong. We've got to think again.'[130] Palestine policy, as it was evolved by Attlee and Bevin, was determined by two main considerations operating in parallel:[131] (1) good Anglo-American relations, to which the Cabinet attached pre-eminent importance, pointed to a pro-Jewish solution, since the United States government was, by and large (swayed by strong pressure-groups), pro-Zionist; and (2) an appropriate Middle East strategy, perhaps with a base, certainly protecting oil supplies, which pointed to a pro-Arab solution. The two aims conflicted. The latter took preference,[132] though not without some determined resistance from the Cabinet's principal pro-Zionists, Dalton, Bevan, Shinwell and – to some extent – Creech Jones. Almost every historian has heaped condemnation upon the government's Palestine policy.[133] Such criticism perhaps forgets the complexity of the problem, or indeed the rationality of the way they cut through it by withdrawal in 1948.[134]

Why did the Foreign Office help to make Bevin change his mind? The essence of the situation was categorically set out by the Chiefs of Staff in the middle of 1946:

All our defence requirements in the Middle East, including maintenance of our essential oil supplies and communications, demand that an essential feature of our policy should be to retain the co-operation of the Arab states, and to ensure that the Arab world does not gravitate towards the Russians . . .

We cannot stress too strongly the importance of Middle East oil resources to us both in peace and war. We consider that this factor alone makes the retention of Arab friendship essential. The vulnerability of our existing sources of oil makes it

[130] Harris, *Attlee*, p. 390.

[131] W. R. Louis, *The British empire in the Middle East, 1945–1951: Arab nationalism, the United States and post-war imperialism* (Oxford, 1984), pp. 383–572; R. Ovendale, 'The Palestine policy of the British Labour government', pt 1, '1945–1946' and pt 2, '1947: The decision to withdraw', *International Affairs*, vols. 55 and 56 (1979, 1980), pp. 409–31, 73–93.

[132] According to Harold Wilson, Attlee 'was improving Arab relations at the expense of relations with the United States, particularly Truman. This was a point Truman frequently mentioned to me, once during his Presidency, when I had dinner with him, and again when I used to see him in Washington and New York after his retirement' (Sir Harold Wilson to the author, 2 March 1978).

[133] Martin Jones, *Failure in Palestine: British and United States policy after the Second World War* (1986) is perhaps an extreme example.

[134] As a Zionist, Harold Wilson remained convinced that Attlee and Bevin had pressed Arab relations to the point 'to the extent that they did mean in effect repudiating the Balfour Declaration, or at least setting it aside' (to the author, 2 March 1978).

imperative that we should seek to develop areas more remote from possible attack, but our ability to do this will be seriously prejudiced if we incur the hostility of the Arabs.[135]

Bevin was persuaded of the vital importance of Middle East oil. In 1947, 60 per cent of all British oil came from the area, and it was expected to become 70 per cent by 1955.[136]

The attempt to conciliate and propitiate the United States, and work together, only in fact made matters worse.[137] The government set up an Anglo-American committee of inquiry, which made sensible suggestions, but coupled them with concern about Jewish refugees. President Truman seized upon this, and began demanding that 100,000 Jewish refugees be admitted at once. He repeated this demand over and over again. Attlee was furious, adamant that this would never do. His reasons were as follows: putting the Jews at the head of the queue for the resettlement of East Europeans would be a disastrous form of 'racial discrimination' (or 'positive discrimination' as we might now call it); the Arabs and Indian Muslims would be dismayed, and the Jews would take it as the 'thin end of the wedge' and press for more concessions.[138] Other countries, including the USA, were reluctant to open their doors. Bevin was thought to have been tactless in publicly complaining that the Americans 'did not want too many Jews in New York', but as was recognised in the British embassy, he had 'not only hit the nail on the head, but driven it woundingly deep'. Truman was almost unashamedly motivated by domestic and personal electoral considerations.[139] Almost all American official experts were in disagreement with him, whether in the State Department, the Pentagon, or most US embassies in Europe – all recognised that Jewish immigration needed to be restricted. It is hardly too much to say that Truman's intransigence sabotaged the British government's policy.[140]

The other disheartening factor was the sudden and very violent emergence of Jewish terrorism. At the end of October 1945, the Haganah

---

[135] CAB 129/11, CP(46)267, 10 July 1946, 'Anglo-American report: military implications'; *BDEEP*, pt 1, pp. 21–2 (no. 10).

[136] CAB 129/16, CP(47)11, memo by Bevin and Shinwell, 3 January 1947.

[137] W. R. Louis: 'Anglo-American co-operation over Palestine proved to be the single most frustrating and elusive goal of the Labour government in imperial and colonial affairs', *Middle East*, p. 386. See also A. Nachmani, ' "It is a matter of getting the mixture right": Britain's post-war relations with America in the Middle East', *Journal of Contemporary History*, vol. 18 (1983), pp. 117–35.

[138] PREM 8/89, Attlee to Truman, telegram 16 September 1945.

[139] N. Bethell, *The Palestine triangle: the struggle between the British, the Jews and the Arabs, 1935–1948* (1979), p. 244.

[140] J. Marlowe, review of R. Ovendale, *Britain, the United States and the end of the Palestine Mandate, 1942–1948* (1989), in *English Historical Review*, vol. 108 (1993), pp. 536–7.

organisation caused several hundred explosions throughout Palestine, including 242 breaks in the railways. In February 1946, twenty-two British aircraft were destroyed. In July 1946, a wing of the King David Hotel (closely associated with British administration) was blown up, killing ninety-one people, including some senior British officials. Palestine became a nightmare even for the army. In order to deal with a Jewish population of barely 600,000, apparently totally lacking in 'moderates', Britain drafted in 80,000 troops and 20,000 police. The Irgun terrorists captured two unarmed sergeants and hanged them, with booby-traps for those who approached their bodies. The British were outraged. Soldiers and policemen in Palestine went on the rampage, and in Britain anti-semitic riots broke out in Liverpool, Manchester, Glasgow, and London.[141]

The Labour government had no intention of being trapped for ever in a situation rapidly becoming intolerable. Palestine drained resources and had become a degrading death-trap. There were three basic alternatives considered for the future of Palestine: provincial autonomy, a unitary state, and partition.[142]

Provincial autonomy was sometimes referred to as a bi-national solution, with elements rather like Swiss cantons. This was no doubt a typical British preference for a compromise, a civilised adaptation. Unfortunately it was unacceptable to Jews, Arabs and Americans alike: to the Jews because it would lead to an Arab majority, to the Arabs because it would lead to partition, and to both because it required them to get on together with people of a different culture.[143]

A *unitary independent state* was what the Arabs wanted, but was of course anathema to the Jews, so the principal objection to this solution was that the Jews would step up their terrorist campaign in order to thwart it. The Cabinet decided that the cost of enforcing this plan against the organised opposition of all Jews would be civil war and 'disorder and bloodshed on a scale which we could never contemplate', with all the adverse reaction it would cause in the USA and the British empire. In any case, it was simply too profoundly anti-Jewish.[144]

The third possibility was *partition*, and this was what the Zionists demanded. The trouble with this solution was that any scheme of partition which would satisfy the Jews would be demonstrably unfair to

---

[141] Bethell, *The Palestine triangle*, pp. 215–27.
[142] CAB 129/16, CP(47)30, 14 January 1947, memo by Bevin on main policy options; *BDEEP*, pt 1, pp. 39–44 (no. 17).
[143] CAB 129/16, CP(47)32, 16 January 1947, memo by Creech Jones; and CAB 129/17, CP(47)59, 13 February 1947, memo by Bevin and Creech Jones; *BDEEP*, pt 1, pp. 51–5 (no. 19).
[144] CAB 129/16, CO(47)30, 14 January 1947, memo by Bevin, and CP(47)32, 16 January 1947, memo by Bevin and Creech Jones; *BDEEP*, pt 1, pp. 43–4, 51–5 (nos. 17 and 19).

the Arabs.[145] Partition, then, seemed to mean incurring Arab hostility without being able to count on the support of the Jews, since the size of a Jewish state the British would think fair would almost certainly be too small to be acceptable to the Jews. Attlee, Bevin, the Foreign Office and the Chiefs of Staff were all opposed to partition as incompatible with strategic needs. It was easy to foresee that each state would oppose the establishment of British bases in the other. The Colonial Office, however, had several advocates of partition, and there were powerful voices in its favour in the Cabinet, making some resurgence in mid-January 1947.[146] But Bevin put great pressure on his colleagues to accept his analysis. Partition would mean, he argued, the establishment of a Jewish state, which had not been promised by the Balfour Declaration and was not required of the mandated authority; it would involve serious injustices to the Arabs; it was feared a Jewish state would be expansionist, and that the very threat of partition would provoke an Arab rising. As Bevin explained:

The certainty of Arab hostility to partition is so clear, and the consequences of permanently alienating the Arabs will be so serious, that partition must on this ground alone be regarded as a desperate remedy. The risk cannot be excluded that it would contribute to the elimination of British influence from the whole of the vast Moslem area lying between Greece and India. This would have not only strategic consequences; it would also jeopardise the security of our interest in the increasingly important oil production of the Middle East.[147]

If we aroused Arab hostility, he warned, the Russians would align themselves with the Arabs in the UN, and 'we should thus have helped to bring about a diplomatic combination which it should be one of the first aims of our policy to prevent'.[148]

Thus by February 1947 the Labour government after prolonged uncertainty concluded that there was no prospect whatever of any agreed solution, that it was 'impossible to arrive at a peaceful settlement in Palestine on any basis whatsoever'. The only hope was to get the backing of the United Nations.[149]

The problem was therefore referred to the UN, who established a commission on Palestine, UNSCOP – improbably including Czechoslovakia, Peru, Canada, Guatemala, Uruguay, Sweden, Iran, India, Australia, Jugoslavia and the Netherlands – to draw up a plan. Their majority report proved to be in favour of partition, but with an economic union between

[145] CAB 129/16, CP(47)49, memo by Bevin and Creech Jones, 6 February 1947; *BDEEP*, pt 1, pp. 57–60 (no. 21).   [146] Bethell, *Palestine triangle*, p. 282.
[147] CAB 128/11, CM 6(47) 3 and 4, 15 January 1947; *BDEEP*, pt 1, pp. 44–51 (no. 18).
[148] CAB 129/16, CP(47)30, 14 January 1947; *BDEEP*, pp. 39–44 (no. 17).
[149] CAB 129/17, CP(47)59, 13 February, 1947, memo by Bevin and Creech Jones; *BDEEP*, pt 1, pp. 63–6 (no. 23).

the two successor states. The proposed division was more favourable to the Jews than any plan ever contemplated by Britain: half the Jewish state would be non-Jew, and with a third of the population but half the land.[150] Each state would have three asymmetric segments joined by narrow corridors, a pattern derided as the 'two fighting serpents' or a 'Picasso drawing'. It was completely impracticable, and even the Labour 'Zionists' would not support it.[151] (See map 2.2(2) overleaf.)

Bevin had been confident the UN would never recommend partition, so another strategy back-fired. The UN had assumed that the British would hold the ring for a two-year transitional period. The United States backed the plan. The British government, however, would not enforce this plan, chiefly because it would be opposed by the Arabs. Bevin declared in the House of Commons: 'I don't want the Arabs to be dismissed as if they were nobody.'[152] Indeed it was unlikely a Palestinian state could even be set up. The only answer for Britain was to withdraw, which, whatever the immediate resultant chaos and bloodshed, would have two major advantages. First, British lives would not be further lost, nor British resources expended, in suppressing one Palestinian community for the advantage of the other. Second, Britain would not be pursuing a policy destructive of its own interests in the Middle East.[153] The government argued that the Mandate was to establish a Jewish home without prejudicing non-Jewish rights. This was proven to be an impossibility. Therefore Britain could lay down an unworkable mandate without too much dishonour. Britain had never undertaken to establish any state by force or to coerce either party in the interests of the other.[154]

Accordingly the decision to withdraw was taken on 20 September 1947, on the grounds that there was no prospect of an agreed settlement, and Britain was unwilling to enforce a settlement unacceptable to either.[155] It would hand over to a UN commission, consisting improbably this time of Czechoslovakia, Panama, Bolivia, Denmark, and the Philippines. The costs of Palestine between January 1945 and November 1947 were put at £100 million. In the three-year conflict, 338 Britons had died violently at Jewish hands.[156] There were vague hopes that

---

[150] CAB 129/21, CP(47)259, 18 September 1947, memo by Bevin; *BDEEP*, pt 1, p. 75 (no. 29).

[151] A. Bullock, *Life and times of Ernest Bevin*, vol. III: *Foreign secretary, 1945–1951* (1983), p. 476; Ovendale, 'Palestine policy', *International Affairs*, vol. 56 (1980), p. 90.

[152] *PD, Commons* vol. 445, cc. 1394–5, 12 December 1947.

[153] CAB 129/21, CP(47)259, 18 September 1947, memo by Bevin.

[154] CAB 129/22, CP(47)320, 3 December 1947, memo by Bevin and Creech Jones; *BDEEP*, pt 1, p. 79 (no. 31).

[155] CAB 128/10, CC 76(47)6, 20 September 1947; *BDEEP*, pt 1, pp. 76–8 (no. 30).

[156] Bethell, *Palestine triangle*, p. 358.

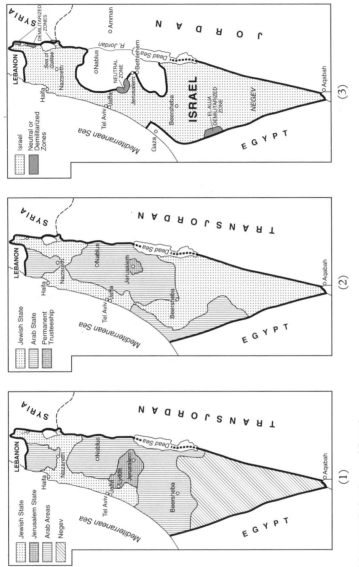

Map 2.2 Palestine and Israel
(1)   The Cabinet committee's porposal of partition, 1944.
(2)   The UN General Assembly's proposal of partition, 1947.
(3)   Boundaries of Israel, 'agreed' 1949.

announcing a withdrawal might, as in India, contribute towards a settlement.[157] Attlee pointed to close parallels with India: to leave India but continue fighting in Palestine in unreasonable conditions was simply incongruous.

One principal disadvantage of withdrawal was that it made even greater difficulties between the British and US governments. And it won the gratitude of neither Arabs nor Jews.[158] But despite the criticism to which it has been subject, then and subsequently, the Labour government's Palestine policy made good sense from its own point of view. Attlee and Bevin had in an impossible situation attempted to hold the balance evenly between the two sides. They refused to be deflected from a pragmatic policy. They guided the Cabinet into the following position: (1) try to get a just settlement by agreement of both parties; (2) if this was impossible – as it proved to be – then get the best solution for British interests; (3) British interests, especially strategic interests, would be best served by pursuing Arab friendship, since antagonising the Arabs would almost certainly drive them into the arms of the Russians, and because a Jewish state could never provide Britain with useful base facilities, since it would be surrounded by implacably hostile Arabs.[159] Or as Dalton put it, 'you cannot have a secure base on top of a wasps' nest'.[160]

The merit of the policy was that it was geopolitically realistic, setting Palestine in its regional context as a whole. The real gravamen of the indictment against British rule is that for the last six months of the Mandate all attempts at a peacekeeping role were given up, which meant that Jewish territorial expansion at the expense of Arab interests could take place. The institutional infrastructure of the successor state also owed more to British administration before 1936 than they cared to admit, for the British were absolutely not trying to be the facilitators of Israel.

So what made the emergence of the state of Israel possible? Fundamentally there were three favourable factors. One of them was demographic,

---

[157] E. Monroe, 'Mr Bevin's "Arab policy" ', *St Antony's Papers*, no. 11 (1961), pp. 35–6, and *Britain's moment in the Middle East, 1914–1971* (2nd edn, 1981), pp. 166–7.

[158] Bullock, *Ernest Bevin*, vol. III, p. 450.

[159] W. R. Louis, 'British imperialism and the end of the Palestine Mandate', in W. R. Louis and R. W. Stookey, eds., *The end of the Palestine Mandate* (Austin, Texas, 1986), pp. 1–31, anticipates this argument. When put to Sir Harold Wilson, he replied: 'I very much respect the arguments you have deployed based on papers which were not available to me' when writing *The Chariot of Israel* (1981). He did not accept that he had been unfair to Attlee, but added, 'I should say that Arthur Bottomley, who was Under-Secretary in the Commonwealth Office at the time and saw a little of what was going on, had a word with me the other day and used arguments rather similar to yours' (to the author, 2 March 1978). Bottomley was in the CRO from July to October 1947.   [160] Jones, *Failure in Palestine*, p. 285.

and it was crucial: the non-Arab population of Palestine rose from a tenth to a third between 1917 and 1948.[161] In 1936 alone over 60,000 immigrants had arrived, and the Jews were far healthier and better educated than the Arabs. The second was the power of international support and publicity, professional, dynamic, well-funded, operating on post-Holocaust sympathetic audiences world-wide, and above all American-supported.[162] The third factor was that anti-Zionism was made to seem anti-semitic, and Zionism fused with a virulent global anti-colonialism against the British empire and all its works; this certainly helps to explain the tacit alliance of the United States and the Soviet Union in favour of the Jews.[163]

The British minister at Cairo, 1947–51, Sir Edward Chapman-Andrews, provided an epitaph to Britain's Mandate, expressing the prevailing feeling of the Foreign Office experts on the Middle East about Israel: what had emerged was 'an enigma if not a Frankenstein'.[164]

4. Economic problems and geopolitical imperatives

Almost before the Labour administration was fully formed, the prime minister had on his desk a secret memorandum from Lord Keynes warning that Britain faced 'a financial Dunkirk'. The war had been fought with complete disregard for the financial consequences, and, wrote Keynes, Britain was 'virtually bankrupt': 'We have not a hope of escaping what might be described without exaggeration, and without implying that we should not eventually recover from it, a financial Dunkirk.' This, said Keynes, must either lead to an enforced and humiliating withdrawal from overseas obligations, or a reduced standard of living at home, with an even greater austerity than in wartime. The conclusion, argued Keynes, was inescapable. Britain would have to ask the United States for money.[165] In the event, the Americans drove a hard bargain. Keynes negotiated a loan, $3,750 million (£930 million), less than hoped for, with some disagreeable strings attached. It was, for example, proposed to abolish preferences (which were British) but only to reduce tariffs (which were American). Ministers complained that these terms amounted to a savage attack on British empire trade.[166] They resented this hard treatment of themselves

---

[161] J. L. Abu-Lughod, *The tranformation of Palestine: essays on the origin and development of Arab–Israeli conflict* (Evanston, Ill., 1971), pp. 144 ff.

[162] *PD, Commons*, vol. 445, cc. 1394–5, 12 December 1947: Bevin declared that Hitler's persecution 'multiplied many times' British difficulties, and destroyed the 'evolutionary character of the National Home'.   [163] Louis, *Middle East*, p. 395.

[164] *BDEEP*, pt 2, p. 381, despatch, 17 September 1951 (no. 163).

[165] CAB 129/1, CP(45)112, 13 August 1945; *BDEEP*, pt 2, pp. 1–5 (no. 74).

[166] CAB 129/4, CP(45)295, memo by Lord Addison (Dominions Office), 22 November 1945.

as an ally. The loan-negotiations felt as if a rich uncle was dealing with an erring nephew. The 'convertibility' string – removal of free exchange of sterling for the dollar – led to the crisis of 1947 (because the pound was weak and the dollar strong).

It was in this context, partly, that thoughts turned to African development as a means of freeing Britain from dependence on the American dollar. Bevin's reaction shows the mood:

If we only pushed on and developed Africa, we could have [the] United States dependent on us, and eating out of our hand, in four or five years. Two great mountains of manganese ore in Sierra Leone, etc. [The] U.S. is very barren of essential minerals, and in Africa we have them all.[167]

Bevin recognised that Britain could not build her economic recovery solely out of increased export of manufactured goods, because the world was becoming more industrialised. Britain also needed to get its hands on raw materials with which to buy food and other requirements, and that meant looking to the empire. Among Bevin's pet projects were selling manganese ore from Sierra Leone to the United States, and sending coal from Wankie to Argentina in return for beef. Always tempted by cosmoplastic dreams, he also talked about a new triangular oceanic trade between East Africa, India and Australia, and (like some Raffles *redivivus*), building up Singapore as a focal entrepot for the Far East.[168]

The Cabinet decided in 1947 that every effort should be made to obtain food from all possible empire sources.[169] Britain was in the throes of a fundamental economic crisis. A secret and alarming Treasury paper (July 1947) contemplated the introduction of 'a "famine" food programme' and the government direction of labour into agriculture 'as a specific national service (like military conscription)'.[170] In this desperate situation, ministers believed 'the colonial empire could make a major contribution towards the solution of our present economic difficulties'. Defence cuts were agreed, even beyond the acknowledged safety margin. Aneurin Bevan said the situation was so serious that he would 'contemplate the most drastic action, such as the withdrawal of British forces from Palestine or the complete exclusion of American films' from British cinemas.[171] Even Sir Stafford Cripps wanted to 'force the pace' of African development in order to close the dollar gap.[172] Creech Jones sent a

---

[167] Dalton Papers (London School of Economics), section I, Diary, vol. 36, p. 42 (15 October 1948); Gupta, *Imperialism and the British Labour movement*, p. 306.

[168] Bevin Papers, FO 800/435, no. 116; FO 800/444, no.29; Dalton Papers, I/34, p. 13 (Diary, 22 March 1946); and, for Wankie scheme, DO 35/3737, no. 39.

[169] CAB 128/10, CM 67(47)2, 1 August 1947, and CM 69(47)2, 5 August 1947.

[170] P. Hennessy, *Never again: Britain, 1945–1951* (1992), pp. 299–302.

[171] CAB 128/10, CM 65(47)2, 29 July 1947.

[172] CO 847/36/2, no. 24, 12 November 1947.

directive to 'the peoples of the Colonies', indicating how 'they can help us and themselves'. He wanted to export more primary colonial products to America, rubber especially, but also cocoa and sisal and minerals. And so the edicts went forth. All colonial governments were repeatedly urged to do all they could to increase food supplies for local use and export. Schemes under consideration included generally linseed, soya bean and timber; in Borneo rice, manila hemp, coal; in Sierra Leone rice and manganese ore; in Southern Rhodesia jute-substitute and tobacco; in Nigeria coal; in west Africa generally, groundnuts; in the Cameroons bananas. Rehabilitation grants were made to Malaya, Mauritius and Trinidad. It was felt more lead-ore ought to come out of Tanganyika. The large-scale cultivation of linseed and fertilisers was investigated in several colonies.[173] The Colonial Development Corporation was set up in 1948, dedicated to realising this sort of scheme. Among its projects were egg-farming in the Gambia, timber and gold-dredging in Guiana, sealing in the Falklands, and fishing in Nyasaland (Lake Malawi). The CDC's fatal flaw – nowhere more painfully illustrated than by groundnuts production in Tanganyika – was its addiction to grandiose mechanisation with high capital costs and too many operational problems.[174] Peasant production was not taken seriously enough, in the drive to make African possessions an asset, 'and not a liability as they largely now are' (Strachey).[175]

However, good quiet work was done in terms of tackling disease in man and beast, in focusing on agricultural, forestry and fisheries improvement, in promoting awareness of the need to control venereal disease and to begin game conservation, in dealing with the menace of tstetse and locust, and above all in encouraging education. Considerable efforts were made to collaborate with other African powers in these policies, especially the French, but without much positive result.[176]

Among the most serious bars to African development were the intractable problems of improving railway links, such as the enormous survey, development and operational costs, the shortage of steel and other supplies, the awkward involvement of foreign governments in unifying railway gauges, and so forth. These problems are illustrated by the failure of the most favoured project, a rail-link between Rhodesia and Kenya

[173] CAB 129/19, CP(47)177, 8 June 1947, and CAB 129/20, CP(47)242, 23 August 1947; *BDEEP*, pt 2, pp. 47–52 (nos. 82 and 83).
[174] D. J. Morgan, *The official history of colonial development*, vol. II, *Developing British colonial resources, 1945–1951* (1980), p. 350; M. Havinden and D. Meredith, *Colonialism and development: Britain and its tropical colonies, 1850–1960* (1993), pp. 281–316.
[175] CAB 129/16, CP(47)10, memo by Strachey, 4 January 1947; *BDEEP*, pt 2, pp. 243–4 (no. 116).
[176] J. Kent, 'Anglo-French colonial co-operation, 1939–1949', *JICH*, vol. 17 (1988), pp. 55–82.

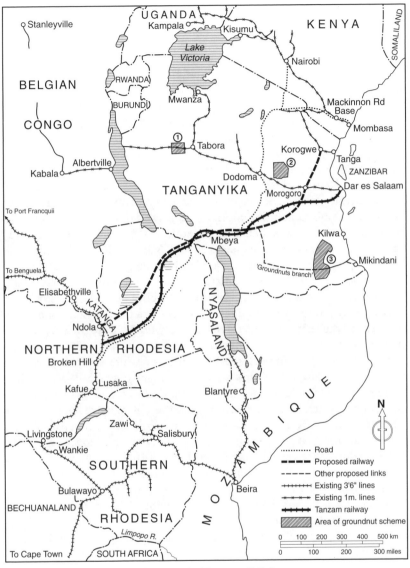

Map 2.3 Proposed Rhodesia–Kenya rail-link.
The Tanzam Railway as completed in 1975 ran from Dar es Salaam to
Kapiri Mposhi. The three main areas of the Groundnuts Scheme are
shown as numbered diagonally shaded areas.
Source: CO 537/1231, no. 102, COS(46)271, report on the development
of African communications, 13 December 1946.

from Ndola to Korogwe. It would mean unifying the gauges (which ministers thought strategically valuable), by converting 3,520 miles of East African railways from metre to 3'6" – a five-year task. Tanganyikan authorities naively put their costs at £870,000, while Kenya (with more track and rolling stock) estimated their conversion at £16 million. The new 1,125-mile link itself might be built for £11 million. However, even a 3'6" railway could not carry oversize loads such as big tanks, and would have to be duplicated by a much-improved road capable of carrying 70-ton weights, since only a route able to carry heavy equipment would provide any appreciable saving over the shipping routes. Cohen strongly favoured the 'great advantage of having an all-British railway link from the Cape to Kenya', possibly with a branch-line to Kilwa or Mikindani to evacuate groundnuts. The project lapsed, however, and for three reasons. There were doubts about the enormous costs and its economic profitability. (Creech Jones was decidedly sceptical – haunted no doubt by Labouchere's famous diatribe against the Uganda railway: 'What it will carry there's none can define; . . . It clearly is naught but a lunatic line.') Then there was the growing difficulty of being seen to co-operate with South Africa, who ran Rhodesian railways. Above all, the Chiefs of Staff decided they did not wish to develop Kenya as a major operational base after all, because it was too far from the Middle East theatre, it had insufficient industrial back-up, and it was impracticable (for racial and political reasons) to import the quantities of white or Indian labour required. The Ndola rail-link was accordingly downgraded to being 'strategically desirable but not essential', and at all events not sufficiently important to warrant a contribution from the UK defence vote. The old 'Cape-to-Cairo' dream was as far off as ever.[177] The collapse of this attempt at imperial reassertion was not, however, the end of the line. Although further rejected by the World Bank in 1963, the United Nations in 1964 and an Anglo-Canadian Consortium in 1966, the railway was completed in 1975 as the Tan-Zam railway (now the Tazara railway). Ironically it was financed by China in 1970 with a $401 million loan. The engineer in charge was a Chinese woman.[178]

The other spectacular failure was the groundnuts (peanuts) scheme in Tanganyika.[179] In 1947 the world oils and fats trade was down 40 per cent

---

[177] CAB 131/2, DO(46)48, COS report, 2 April 1946; CAB 131/4, DO(47)27, memo by A. V. Alexander, 17 March 1947, and DO(47)9/4, 26 March 1947; CO 537/1230; CO 537/1231, no. 102, COS(46)271; DO 35/2373, JP(48)122, and COS(49)6; FO 371/73042, and 73043; CO 167/58; *BDEEP*, pt 2, pp. 246–51, 275–8 (nos. 118, 130).

[178] G. T. Yu, *China's African policy: a study of Tanzania* (New York, 1975), pp. 130–1.

[179] Morgan, *Official history*, vol. II: *Developing British colonial resources*, pp. 226–307.

on pre-war levels, with a shortfall predicted for ten or twenty years. Without some massive attempt to get new supplies it was forecast in 1945 that by 1950 either the British would have an even lower margarine ration than during the war, or they would have to spend so many precious dollars on buying it that there would be no dollars left for other indispensable imports.[180] Challenged by the fact that only 60 per cent of rationed requirement came from the empire, and relishing the memory of what tanks had done in the desert war,[181] the minister of food, John Strachey, turned to a mechanised project in southern Tanganyika, where very marginal land would be rescued by military methods. If it was not to be a government scheme, the alternative was to hand Unilever a blank cheque to do what they liked. That did not appeal to Labour's social engineers. The scheme was conceived in the grand manner, but quickly ran into dire trouble. The major miscalculation was over the initial clearance of the bush, which cost ten times more than estimated. The schedules proceeded with painful slowness. Seven-eighths of the entire budget was spent on clearing only 46,000 acres of the projected total area of 3,210,000 acres.[182] There were dead jackals and some stunningly recalcitrant roots embedded in the hard red earth, which could only be shifted by bulldozers. Second-hand tractors and other machines were commandeered from all over the place, from Canada to the Philippines. They kept breaking down. Often they would not start owing to a shortage of acid for batteries. The workers disliked every aspect of their job and conditions; the result was frequent strikes and a rapid turn-over of labour. Local Africans resented the cutting down of the big baobab trees in which their rain-gods lived; some Conservative MPs wickedly asked if they had been paid compensation for eviction.[183] (The rain-gods took their revenge, and there was not enough rain for the crop.) By the end of 1950 the costs were £38,870,000. The dysfunctional project was almost certainly set up too quickly, without waiting for a pilot scheme. For this ministers must take much of the blame. They overruled their advisers in the Treasury and CO, who had almost uncannily predicted the problems. The flaws were fundamental. Ecologically and mechanically, financially and administratively, the scheme was simply no good. Although this rapidly became apparent, complete abandonment was almost unthinkable. Besotted with the whole thing, the blow to prestige and the discouragement to enterprise, were too great for ministers to contemplate. 'Groundnuts' had become a symbol of

---

[180] CAB 129/16, CP(45)4 and 10, memo by Strachey, 4 January 1947.
[181] CAB 93/6, CM 93(46)6, 31 October 1946.
[182] CAB 128/16, CM 66(49), 14 November 1949.
[183] H. Thomas, *John Strachey* (1973), p. 251.

socialist management.[184] The Cabinet wrestled with salvaging something from the wreckage.[185]

The fate of the railway and the groundnuts fiasco made the whole problem of removing obstacles to economic growth in Africa seem more intractable than ever. Inadequate transport was perhaps at the heart of the overall problem, but quite apart from the maddening frustrations of trying to get essential products out of Africa on an exiguous, congested and war-exhausted railway system, there were other severe structural defects: poor soil, inadequate water-supplies, traditional and often highly complex land-tenure systems, and dangerous dependence on monoculture. There was a severe shortage of consumer goods, such as bicycles and clothing, to provide incentives for Africans to work harder, while nutritional problems and debilitating diseases such as trypanosomiasis reduced their efficiency. Africa was not an El Dorado.[186] Social systems could only be modified slowly; planners had to work within the limits of tolerable social change and with ecological caution ('we must not create a dustbowl in Africa').[187] Moreover, the Economic Policy Committee agreed with Creech Jones that however desirable, a more positive control of African economic development was not possible, as it would be contrary to the fundamental policy of gradually transferring real political power.[188] Nor must they be open to the damaging charge of exploiting Africa, whose people already laboured under such exceptional poverty and deprivation.[189]

In addition to its economic concerns, there were other and probably even more powerful pressures driving the Labour government into a deeper commitment to empire, especially African empire, and these arose out of the cold war. By the end of 1947 resistance to communist expansion had become a central consideration, just when economic weakness and dependence on America were more apparent than ever. Attlee and Bevin wanted to hold a new deep line of defence across Africa from Lagos to Mombasa, with a major new strategic base in Kenya, at

---

[184] Morgan, *Official history*, vol. II: *1945–1951*, p. 248; J. Iliffe, *A modern history of Tanganyika* (Cambridge, 1979), p. 441.

[185] CAB 129/37/2 CP(49)231 and 232, memoranda by Strachey, 11 November 1949; CAB 128/16, CM 66(49), 14 November 1949; *BDEEP*, pt 2, pp. 282–96 (nos. 132–7).

[186] DO 35/2380, no. 3, memo by Creech Jones, 6 January 1948; *BDEEP*, pt 2, pp. 196–201 (no. 106).

[187] CO 537/3030, draft paper by S. Caine on organisation for colonial development, 27 February 1948.

[188] CO 852/1003/3, minute by Caine, 24 April 1946; *BDEEP*, pt 2, pp. 232–5 (no. 113).

[189] M. Havinden and D. Meredith, *Colonialism and development* p. 307; PREM 8/923, minute by Sir N. Brook to Attlee, 14 Jan 1948; *BDEEP*, pt 2, p. 257 (no. 121).

Mackinnon Road.[190] Attlee thought they might need to rely more on African manpower, though the Chiefs of Staff were sceptical.[191] More generally, from the CO, Griffiths warned in 1950 that they 'had to face an ideological battle in the world, especially in the Colonies'.[192] Bevin feared the Russians would sooner or later 'make a major drive against our position in Africa', so plans had to be made which would comprehensively 'organise the middle of the planet' against the 'baleful tenets' of communism. At the Cabinet in January 1948 there was general support for Bevin's proposition that positive steps should be taken to consolidate against the threat of Russian infiltration the 'physical and spiritual' forces of Western countries 'and their African and South-East Asian primary-producing possessions'.[193] His scheme for 'Western Union' was not for a formal alliance and was deliberately left vague. He was not concerned with a federal Europe. The real objective was to attract American interest in defending the West.[194] When asked if Portugal (not Britain's favourite ally) should be included, Bevin replied that this was indeed most important because of Portuguese colonial possessions in Africa. A 'Western European democratic system' should be organised, comprising if possible Scandinavia, the Low Countries, France, Italy, Greece and Portugal, with Germany and Spain added as soon as circumstances permitted: 'We must also organise and consolidate the ethical and spiritual forces inherent in this Western civilisation of which we are the chief protagonists.' (This is almost the exact language of Palmerston in 1848!)[195] Eventually Bevin hoped to involve 'every country outside the Soviet group'. All the great religions would also be mobilised, including Buddhism and Islam, in defence of the freedom of the individual against communism. In this noble, crazy, cosmoplastically hallucinatory scheme – one of the few attempts to create an ideologically comprehensive view of Britain's world role – the colonies were a vital element:

it should be possible to develop our own power and influence equal to that of the United States of America and the USSR. We have the material resources in the

---

[190] CAB 129/1, CP(45)144, memo by Attlee, 1 September 1945; *BDEEP*, pt 3, pp. 207–8 (no. 273).
[191] *BDEEP*, pt 3, 'Use of colonial manpower in the cold war', COS paper, 2 January 1951, pp. 406–10 (no. 337).   [192] CO 537/5699, no. 89A, 16 June 1950.
[193] CAB 129/23, CP(48)6 and 7; CAB 128/12, CM 2(48)5, 8 January 1948; *BDEEP*, pt 2, pp. 317–28 (nos. 142–4).
[194] Bullock, *Ernest Bevin*, vol. III, pp. 520–1. There is an incisive discussion of Bevin's more fanciful ideas in A. W. B. Simpson, *Human rights and the end of empire: Britain and the genesis of the European Convention* (Oxford, 2001, 2004), pp. 870–84.
[195] CAB 129/23/1, CP(48)6, 4 January 1948, memo by Bevin, 'The first aim of British foreign policy'; *BDEEP*, pt 2, pp. 317–18 (no. 142).

Colonial Empire, if we develop them, and by giving a spiritual lead now, we should be able to carry out our task in a way which will show clearly that we are not subservient to the United States of America or to the Soviet Union.[196]

The alternative was 'to acquiesce in continued Russian infiltration and helplessly to witness the piecemeal collapse of one Western bastion after another'.[197]

By May 1950 the emphasis had significantly shifted. In order to combat 'the great concentration of power now stretching from China to the Oder', Bevin believed they had to begin to substitute for the original concept of Western Union the wider conception of the Atlantic community.[198] The onset of the cold war had almost eliminated American 'anti-imperialism', as leading US government agencies began to see the value of the British empire in resisting communism. For the Americans, communism was now a much greater danger than residual colonialism. Outside Malaya and Cyprus, definitive communist threats in the colonies were as yet hard to pin down, but nearly all colonies had small groups of professed communist sympathisers who might stir up discontent. Hong Kong, Gibraltar, Kenya and Guiana all needed a watchful eye in this respect. Alarm was also greater in South-East Asia than Africa, with fears that communists might one day be able to dominate the entire 'rice-bowl'. The danger of communism was thought to lie not in its political theory, nor even in its anti-capitalism, but in its critique of 'colonialism'. Accordingly, the antidote was reckoned to be the removal of the economic and social conditions in which it might thrive, ensuring fair wages and improving colonial living standards. Free and democratic colonial trades unions also seemed a high priority.[199]

In the Far East, the 1949 communist take-over in China sparked off a double ministerial debate. The first aspect was whether or not to recognise the new regime. This gave anxious pause for thought, expressed in a whole batch of memoranda. Despite American refusal to recognise the People's Republic, Bevin was quite clear that there 'was a fundamental political reason' for Britain to do so: to prevent the strengthening of ties between Moscow and Peking. Any hostility towards China would only further worsen the British position and prestige in the Far East and South-East Asia: 'if we are not to drive Communist China into the arms of Moscow, we must do our utmost to maintain Western contacts'.[200] The

---

[196] CAB 129/25, CP(48)72, 3 March 1948, memo by Bevin, 'The threat to Western civilisation'; *BDEEP*, pt 2, pp. 328–30 (no. 145); FO 800/460, pp. 79–80, note for the record by F. K. Roberts, 5 March 1948.   [197] CAB 129/23/1, CP(48)6, 4 January 1948.
[198] CAB 128/17, CM 29(50)3, 8 May 1950; *BDEEP*, pt 2, p. 357 (no. 156).
[199] Hyam, intro to *BDEEP*, pt 1, pp. lii–liii.
[200] CAB 129/39, CP(50)73, memo by Bevin, 20 April 1950; R. Ovendale, 'Britain, the United States and the recognition of Communist China, *Historical Journal*, vol. 26

second aspect of the debate reflected anxiety over Hong Kong. How should they react if China chose to attack it? Some ministers were anxious about defending 'a relic of colonialism'; Cripps thought Hong Kong should be abandoned. Attlee received some sage advice from the Cabinet secretary. Sir Norman Brook thought it would be best to keep a low profile in order to avoid such an attack; it would be wrong to project Hong Kong as 'the Berlin of the East' or even as 'an outpost of Western democracy', because it would be the more humiliating if withdrawal were subsequently forced on Britain before 1997. Equally, however, the government should avoid the language of 'scuttle' or any hint of withdrawal. The prime minister insisted they had to show their determination and ability to defend the security of Hong Kong, otherwise British prestige would be seriously damaged and the whole common front against communism was likely to crumble. Some modest reinforcements were sent to Hong Kong, but the response to requests for Commonwealth assistance was disappointingly meagre. So the Cabinet stuck more or less to Brook's line. Abandonment to the Chinese was not an option because this might cause the dominoes to fall: Malaya, Thailand, Burma, and then putting India at risk. On the other hand it was no good loudly proclaiming longer-term commitments which could not be fulfilled; holding on quietly and trying to raise living standards so as to make life under the British flag seem more attractive was the best that could be done. There was no demand within Hong Kong for political progress, and certainly not for an end to the British connection. Much of the credit for stabilising relations with China must go to the long-serving governor, Sir Alexander Grantham (1947–57), combining firmness with restraint. The Communist regime was recognised, Hong Kong was not to be turned into an independent city-state, or an international free port like Trieste; and its ultimate reversion to China was to be respected, unless some other accommodation could one day be reached with a friendly and stable government of a unified China.[201]

5. The new African policy

By 1946 the Colonial Office planners were acutely aware of the need for a clear policy based on the political advancement of Africans. There were

(1983), pp. 139–58. S. R. Ashton, G. Bennett and K. Hamilton, eds., *Britain and China, 1945–1950* (Documents on British Policy Overseas, series I, vol. VIII (2002)).

[201] CAB 128/16, CM 54(49)2, 29 August 1949; PREM 8/840; Hyam, intro. to *BDEEP*, pt 1, pp. liii–liv. The essential study of Hong Kong in the 1940s is W. R. Louis – in expansive mood – 'Hong Kong: the critical phase, 1945–1949', *American Historical Review*, vol. 102 (1997), pp. 1052–84.

perhaps five main reasons for this.[202] First, African political consciousness had been stimulated by the war, and the white man's prestige
destroyed as an instrument of government, particularly in the eyes (it was
thought) of returning black servicemen. Secondly, to carry out the new
social welfare and economic development programmes, a new political
instrument was required, namely African participation. Thirdly, Colonial
Service attitudes had to be reconstructed in any case: morale was not
always good, the nostrums of Lugard and Cameron were moribund, and
officers felt frustrated by newly emerging African criticisms. The men on
the spot needed a renewed sense of 'mission', a revitalisation and extension of MacDonald's constructive vision on the eve of war. Fourthly, it
seemed Britain had to retain a positive initiative in the formulation of
African policy, otherwise control would pass to 'settler' regimes (South
African, Rhodesian and Portuguese), to whom it was a matter of life and
death. This would imperil British trusteeship policies; indeed, after the
adoption of apartheid in South Africa from 1948, an actual policy-
conflict with South African expansionist tendencies existed. Finally, and
probably most important of all, there was a massive contextual shift:
international pressures from the United Nations, American and 'world
opinion' were, as Creech Jones recognised, uncomfortably directing 'the
play of a fierce searchlight' over Africa. These outside influences were
expected to stimulate the demand for self-government. 'Prejudiced, ignorant and hostile' criticism and interference from the anti-colonial bloc
(communist and Latin American countries, together with India, and, for
a time, most vocal adversary of all, the Philippines) would be grounded
not in trying to reform imperial systems but in abolishing them entirely
and instantly as anachronistic. Officials regarded this as a recipe for widespread post-imperial disintegration, as it took no account of fitness for
self-government 'in conditions in which they really can stand on their
own' without the risk of falling under foreign domination or internal
tyranny. Britain aimed at establishing stable, effective and representative
political systems. This was a delicate operation in which the officials felt
they must not be distracted and dictated to by '58 back-seat drivers
without responsibility'. These reasons, then, internal and international,
demanded a new approach to policy in Africa.

Andrew Cohen set about formulating a practical programme and
broad objectives. The first fruit of his initiative was the famous 'local government despatch' of February 1947, which enjoined the promotion of
efficient, local, representative government as a priority, giving a firm base

[202] R. Hyam, 'Africa and the Labour government, 1945–1951', *JICH*, vol.16 (1988),
pp. 148–72, repr. in A. Porter and A. J. Stockwell, eds., *Theory and practice in the history of
European expansion overseas: essays in honour of Ronald Robinson* (1988).

for the construction of a political pyramid leading up eventually to central government.[203] This was quickly followed by a Colonial Office report dated May 1947 which has long been recognised as the centre-piece of Labour government African policy. It was prepared by the agenda committee for the African governors' conference planned for November 1947.[204] It is often referred to as the 'Caine–Cohen' report, though if reports should be named after chairmen, it should be known just as the Caine report (Sir Sydney Caine was the deputy under-secretary of the CO). However, the crucial paper on constitutional development was mainly drafted by Cohen. Even in the most advanced territory, the Gold Coast, he wrote, 'internal self-government is unlikely to be achieved in much less than a generation'; elsewhere 'the progress is likely to be considerably slower'. Accordingly, there must be a long-term plan, 'for 20 or 30 years or indeed longer' for ordered development under continuing British responsibility. African readiness for internal self-government (i.e., the stage attained by Southern Rhodesian whites in 1923), was still 'a long way off'; 'independence' (i.e., control of external affairs, with freedom to secede from the Commonwealth) was not even mentioned. Caine himself merely assumed that 'perhaps within a generation many of the principal territories of the Colonial Empire will have attained or be within sight of the goal of full responsibility for *local affairs*' (my italics). Friendly association would replace 'benevolent domination', but Caine did not see this as relinquishing the power to control the pace and 'influence the main line of policy'. These are hardly revolutionary propositions. The exact plan being laid down was hazy and no definite timetable was indicated. But some advance was essential to meet what Cohen referred to as 'constant criticism and interference from outside opinion', forcing them to work against a background of international disapproval.[205]

The assertion in the *Cambridge history of Africa* that what was envisaged in 1946 for the Gold Coast was 'independence – perhaps in fifteen years' time', is thus culpably false (quite apart from the wrong date).[206] Nor is it

---

[203] CO 847/35/6, no. 15, 25 February 1947, circular to African governors; *BDEEP*, pt 1, pp. 119–29 (no. 44)

[204] CO 847/36/1, no. 9, 22 May 1947, 'Report of the committee on the conference of African governors', *BDEEP*, pt 1, pp. 190–251 (no. 59).

[205] Report of the Committee, appendix III, 'Constitutional development' (by Cohen), para. 2, *BDEEP*, pp. 203–4; appendix II, 'General political development' (by Caine), *BDEEP*, p. 199.

[206] David Williams, in M. Crowder, ed., *Cambridge history of Africa*, vol. VIII: *1940–1975* (Cambridge, 1984), p. 341. The distinction between 'responsible self-government' and 'independence' is fundamental. Some historians need to remember what Jim Hacker learned from Sir Humphrey Appleby, 'I *must* be clear on my African terminology, or else I could do irreparable damage' (J. Lynn and A. Jay, *The complete 'Yes, Minister': the diaries of a cabinet minister, by the Rt Hon James Hacker, MP* (1984), p. 35). It should also be

possible to harden Labour policy into one of a 'real and conscious strategy of decolonisation from 1947', or to accept that in Nigeria changes from 1948 'objectively constituted decolonisation' (Pearce).[207] There may indeed have been one official who came close to somesuch outlook, John Bennett, but his radical ideas were not influential, and he was not involved in the agenda-committee report on which Pearce is relying.[208]

In fact, one has only to rehearse the kind of things Labour ministers said to or about Africans to realise the inherent implausibility of describing them as involved in the definite planning of decolonisation. Attlee told black Rhodesians they had 'a long way to go', and, even more tartly, 'politics couldn't be learned from a book'. Morrison had notoriously said that self-government for many dependent territories would be like giving a child of ten 'a latch-key, a bank account and a shot-gun'.[209] Creech Jones had some harsh things to say about the 'irresponsibility' of nationalists in East Africa, and rode roughshod over Ghanaian desires for their own university, saying dismissively they simply did not understand the issues involved. Dalton refused to become his successor in 1950: 'I had a horrid vision of pullulating, poverty-stricken, diseased nigger communities, for whom one can do nothing in the short run, and now, the more one tries to help them, are querulous and ungrateful; . . . of white settlers, as reactionary and as troublesome in their own way as nigger.'[210] A junior minister at the CO, Rees-Williams, believed Africans had a 'mendicant mentality',[211] regarding government, childlike, as 'a gigantic Father Christmas'. Field-Marshal Montgomery, Chief of the Imperial General Staff, toured much of Africa at the end of 1947 (including Gambia, Gold Coast, Nigeria, Southern Rhodesia, Kenya, Ethiopia, Sudan, Egypt, and the Union of South Africa). Though his most derisive strictures were reserved for Ethiopia (its 'pathetic Emperor', 'Gilbertian army', 'Addis in Wonderland', and an elite of 'Hollywoodian ostenstation'), and while he roundly condemned settler communities, he made no secret of his opinion that the African was 'a complete savage' who must not stand in the way of his ruthless master-plan for shaking the whole continent into

---

Footnote 206 (*cont.*)

noted that J. W. Cell, 'On the eve of decolonisation: the Colonial Office's plans for the transfer of power in Africa, 1947', *JICH*, vol.8 (1980), pp. 235–57, is also unreliable, with views misrepresented, documents misdated and mis-attributed, and with file reference-numbers predating finalisation in The National Archives (PRO).

[207] R. D. Pearce, 'The Colonial Office and planned decolonisation in Africa', *African Affairs*, vol. 83 (1984), pp. 77–93, and 'Governors, nationalists and constitutions in Nigeria, 1935–1951', *JICH*, vol. 9 (1981), pp. 289–307.

[208] CO 537/2057, no. 48; *BDEEP*, pt 2, pp. 409–21 (no. 174), 30 April 1947.

[209] Morrison in January 1943, quoted in Louis, *Imperialism at bay*, p. 14.

[210] Gupta, *Imperialism and the British Labour movement*, p. 336; Dalton diary, vol. 38, p. 12 (28 February 1950).   [211] Hyam, intro. to *BDEEP*, pt 1, p. xxxv.

action. He was taken more seriously than he should have been, but that tells us something about contemporary attitudes.[212]

So what was Labour's 'new policy' for Africa? Essentially it was one of *political advancement*, setting suitable countries on the road towards self-government. 'Political advancement' was the slogan, the guideline, the leitmotif – and it cannot be too strongly urged that the correct, the one and only, quintessential label for Labour policy is political advancement. If, to widen it a little, British policy had been articulated into a Chinese formula, it would have been 'political advancement and community development'. It is not easy to define 'community development'. It grew out of ideas of 'mass education' into a programme of mass adult stimulation in practical skills at the village level. A great deal of thought and energy was expended on trying to make Africans want self-improvement. 'Self-help', that most Victorian of values, was the magic formula. There was even a Cambridge Summer School for administrators on 'how to stimulate Africans into taking the initiative' in improving their own local communities, adopting a betterment policy of community education and development. It was not notably successful. To the cynic it looks somewhat like the spiritual equivalent of the groundnuts scheme.

Ultimate self-government was certainly the long-term Labour policy, but very much as a controlled process, carefully prepared by the British government itself. The idea was to lead colonies as rapidly as possible towards this goal, but this was not expected to be fast, and it would have to be underpinned by the necessary economic progress, and with such political guidance as would ensure that newly independent territories remained in the Commonwealth; in that respect there must be 'more Ceylons and no more Burmas' (Burma had left in 1948). The Colonial Office officials certainly believed themselves to be engaged on something important. Dusting down the early-nineteenth-century theories of Macaulay and Fowell Buxton, they issued a paper declaring:

We are engaged on a world-wide experiment in nation-building. Our aim is to create independence – independence within the Commonwealth – not to supress it. No virtue is seen in permanent dependence. A vigorous, adult and willing partner is clearly more to be desired than one dependent, adolescent and unwilling.[213]

At least one official, H. T. Bourdillon, was even more euphoric: theirs was a 'gigantic experiment', the 'boldest stroke of political idealism

---

[212] DO 35/2380, no. 1, 'Tour in Africa, Nov–Dec. 1947', 19 December 1947; *BDEEP*, pt 2, pp. 188–93 (no. 104).
[213] CO 537/5698, no. 69, May 1950, 'The Colonial Empire today: survey of our main problems and policies': *BDEEP*, pt 1, no. 72, para. 2.

which the world has yet witnessed, and on by far the grandest scale', a great experiment 'surpassing in importance any of the much publicised political experiments indulged in by the Soviet Russians or anybody else'.[214]

For these reasons it would be unwise to accept the argument of Richard Crook, writing on the Gold Coast policy: that all we see in Labour government policy is merely a series of colonial reforms of a traditional pattern, quite different – 'qualitatively different' – from decolonisation in ultimate intent.[215] The trouble with this interpretation (refreshing as it is, and to that extent important), is that it makes too sharp a distinction and drains out the more positive, longer-term elements in Labour policy. If that policy was less than decolonisation (which it was), it was also more than just a scheme of local government reform. What it was, can be located somewhere between the two, that is to say, a policy of political advancement. Crook suggests that the late 1940s were a period in which nationalism was not yet fully formed, but only in a phase of 'proto-nationalism'. This may very well be the case. And by extension one would argue that it was not yet the period of decolonisation either, but one of proto-decolonisation, in which there was 'no intention to abandon responsibilities prematurely'.[216]

The case of the Gold Coast and the collapse of the Caine–Cohen timetable there will be discussed in more detail below. For the moment, what needs to be noticed is the general point that advance in one country invariably had knock-on effects. The Gold Coast benefited from the example of India and Sudan, while the decision in 1948 to quicken the constitutional tempo in Nigeria followed more or less unavoidably in the wake of progress in the Gold Coast.[217] Andrew Cohen sent Governor Macpherson in Nigeria an advance copy of the Watson report (which proposed major changes in the Gold Coast). Macpherson agreed it was desirable to pre-empt nationalist calls for similar reforms in Nigeria:

I do not expect such a course will kill extremists but it would, I believe, convince more responsible opinion in all parts of the country that the Government is anxious to encourage constitutional advance in the way the people wish as fast as can reasonably be expected. At the same time, it would be plain to the more moderate political leaders who can speak for the bulk of the people and would regard a

[214] CO 886/49, no. 1, 'Reflections on Colonial Office organisation', 10 May 1948; *BDEEP*, pt 1, pp. 320–6 (no. 70).

[215] R. Crook, 'Decolonisation, the colonial state and chieftaincy in the Gold Coast', *African Affairs*, vol. 85 (1986), pp. 75–105.

[216] 'The Colonial Empire today', para. 2, *BDEEP*, pt 1, pp. 334–5.

[217] R. D. Pearce, 'Governors, nationalists and constitutions in Nigeria, 1939–1951', *JICH*, vol. 9 (1981), pp. 289–304.

hasty shifting of power at the centre in the present circumstances as a disaster, that no precipitate change is intended.[218]

The Macpherson constitution of 1951 led to semi-responsible government and marked the definitive end of the old Indirect Rule system. Macpherson reflected that Nigeria had obtained a constitution 'in advance of its true capacity', but 'we could not put a ring-fence around Nigeria, and we had to take the initiative, and not wait to be overtaken by events, because of what was happening, and is continuing to happen, in the Gold Coast, the Sudan, Libya, etc.'[219]

Scepticism about the fitness of Nigeria for independence was growing even before the Labour government left office. Gold Coast and Nigeria looked set to remain exceptions for a while longer. Sierra Leone and Gambia would have to be satisfied with much more limited constitutional progress for a considerable time to come.

In East-Central Africa progress was hampered by the presence of white settlers, who could not simply be repudiated. Bevin did not think that settler enterprise could or should be bottled up. That, he said, was how Britain lost the American colonies, and he was not going to play George III.[220] Attlee was also keen for some years to see supposedly 'waste spaces' taken up by Europeans, and he wanted to expand white settlement in the interests of economic development.[221] When Labour Party supporters urged the de-restriction of the White Highlands of Kenya, Creech Jones made the fateful decision: 'The Kenya question cannot be solved at this stage by this dramatic gesture.' Cohen elaborated upon this:

It would play straight into the hands of the extremists among the settlers. It would unite the settlers and a vast majority of the white population of Kenya into the most violent antagonism against the Government. It would be the end of all the efforts which are now being made by the Kenya government and by many of the Europeans in Kenya to bring on the African, politically, economically and socially . . . I cannot see that it would lead to any useful result in the long run.[222]

The Kenya settlers must not be driven into the arms of South Africa, he added.

---

[218] CO 583/287, no. 4, Cohen to Macpherson, 2 June 1948; CO 583/286, Macpherson to Cohen, 28 June 1948; M. Lynn, ed., *Nigeria* (BDEEP, 2001), pt 1, pp. 150–3 (no. 49).
[219] CO 554/298, no. 13, Macpherson to Sir T. Lloyd, 18 January 1952; D. Goldsworthy, ed., *The Conservative government and the end of empire, 1951–1957* (BDEEP, 1994), pp. 182–4 (no. 263).   [220] FO 371/69153, no. 5392, minute, 3 August 1948.
[221] CAB 21/2277, M 373/46, minute to Creech Jones, 29 October 1946; *BDEEP*, pt 2, p. 243 (no. 115).
[222] CO 533/534/11, no. 39; CO 533/556/7, pp. 2–4, minute, 18 March 1947; D. W. Throup, *Economic and social origins of Mau Mau, 1945–1953* (1987), stresses the importance of the decision in driving settlers and Kikuyu further apart.

In Central Africa, the government succumbed to settler pressure and its own civil servants and began planning a Central African Federation. The underlying rationale to this was the containment of South African expansion, checking the spread of apartheid. Gordon Walker wrote:

One of our prime aims must be to *contain* South Africa . . . prevent the spread of its influence and territorial sovereignty northwards . . . This should be a policy of equal weight and importance in our eyes with the political advancement of the Africans in our Central and East African territories.

Thus no account of Britain's slow approach to decolonisation can possibly ignore the salience of this South African factor. Colonial secretary Griffiths – regarding apartheid as 'totally repugnant' – joined with Gordon Walker in laying the foundations of the federal barrier across the 'great grey-green greasy Limpopo river'.[223]

6. The Gold Coast

The Gold Coast had a thriving African-led economy based on cocoa, and the best Western-educated population in British Africa. In this sense it was the most 'advanced' colony, but it was also politically 'difficult': there was a long history of strikes on the railways, in the mines and in the cocoa industry. In 1943 the Colonial Office view was that it might take even several generations to reach self-government. By May 1947 this had been revised to be perhaps one generation away, twenty to thirty years. In 1946 the Burns Constitution (after Sir Alan Burns, governor, 1941–7) had set up the first legislative council in British Africa with an elected African majority. The Colonial Office drew Burns's attention to a Sudan directive, which resulted in a circular drafted by Burns, and strongly approved of by the CO hierarchy, suggesting that any 'die-hards' who thought government policy was moving too fast with giving greater political power to Africans and promoting Africanisation of the civil service, 'should consider seriously whether they can conscientiously continue to serve a Government with whose policy they are in fundamental disagreement', for this policy was clear 'and there is no prospect of it being changed except in the direction of still faster progress'.[224]

The Accra Riots of 28 February to 16 March 1948 resulted in 29 people killed and 237 injured. By the standards of Indian communal

---

[223] CAB 129/45, CP(51)109, memo by Gordon Walker after a visit to South Africa, Southern Rhodesia, and the High Commission Territories, 16 April 1951; *BDEEP*, pt 4, pp. 298–315 (no. 433), esp, section iv, pp. 310–11.

[224] CO 554/152/1, minutes by Burns, Cohen, Lloyd, Ivor Thomas and Creech Jones, February 1947, and circular despatch by Burns, 14 March 1947 (no. 6); *BDEEP* pt 4, pp. 8–11 (no. 347); R. Rathbone, ed., *Ghana* (BDEEP, 1992), pt 1: *1941–1952*, pp. 37–47 (no. 17).

riots – let alone Indonesian ones – these were relatively small-scale, but they were nevertheless a profound shock to the British authorities. They were not obviously inspired by direct nationalist pressure,[225] and were certainly not communist-inspired, as initial assessments by the governor implied; Creech Jones was never convinced by this.[226] They arose out of economic grievances and might have been headed off by a stronger governor – Sir Gerald Creasy was a CO desk-official with no field experience, who had only been in post for a fortnight. There were 50,000 demobbed soldiers floating about, and the American air-staging base in Accra was closed. The price of food was forced up after two years of lower-than-average rainfall. So there was inflation and a shortage of retail goods, together with commercial dissatisfaction that Africans had little share in the importing and distribution trades. Beyond this, there was general irritation with government, which seemed slow to implement development plans and meet political grievances. The report of the Elliott Commission of early 1946 was also deeply resented, because Creech Jones acted on the *minority* report in blocking the establishment of a university in the Gold Coast, accepting the contention that one university was enough for the whole of West Africa and this should be at Ibadan in Nigeria.[227] Finally there was an alarming disease of cocoa-trees called 'swollen shoot'. Compensation was inadequate, and it was alleged that the government was in league with the unpopular United Africa Company (Unilever) to ruin the Gold Coast industry and replant in Latin America and Malaya. The Company's offices and shops were set on fire. When the government wanted to appoint as chairman of an inquiry Sir W. Fitzgerald (former chief justice of Palestine), he could not be appointed because he happened to have the same name as the local boss of the company.[228]

Perhaps it was providential, for the man who did conduct the inquiry, Aiken Watson, a junior judge, was of Fabian persuasion, very much in the mould of Creech Jones and Cohen. But even they were surprised by the stinging conclusion of his report, that the fledging Burns Constitution was 'outmoded at birth', and gave Africans insufficient political power. Watson questioned the gradualist timetable, and the competence of Governor Creasy, and recommended that Africans should play a larger part in the proceedings of the Executive Council. Although generally in

---

[225] R. Rathbone, 'The government of the Gold Coast after the Second World War', *African Affairs*, vol. 67 (1968), and 'Businessmen in politics: party struggle in Ghana, 1949–1957', *Journal of Development Studies*, vol. 9 (1973), pp. 391–401; D. Austin, *Politics in Ghana, 1946–1960* (1964), pp. 11–77.

[226] CO 537/3558, no. 122, to Sir G. Creasy, 18 March 1948; *BDEEP*, pt 3, pp. 38–9 (no. 212).

[227] CO 554/134/12, no. 35; 7 January 1946; *BDEEP*, pt 4, pp. 50–1 (nos. 361–2).

[228] *BDEEP*, pt 3, pp. 39–40 (no. 213).

line with Labour policy, the Watson Report, by exceeding its brief, is one of the most significant documents of the end of empire.[229] It led to the appointment of an all-African – but 'moderate' – committee under Mr Justice Coussey to recommend constitutional changes, which were expected to be extensive. The committee proposed (October 1949) an entirely elected legislature. The CO was grateful for a clear report.[230]

By this time, Creech Jones had appointed a new governor. Obviously he had to have the best available man in order to regain control.[231] Sir Charles Arden-Clarke had a reputation for toughness, and had come to prominence by way of Basutoland and Sarawak. He was as English as they come: clergyman's son, ex-army officer, and dog-lover. He looked like the very archetype of the good colonial governor, reassuringly tall, sun-tanned and twinkly-eyed. He set about recapturing the initiative with the injunctions 'batons not bullets', 'bloody coconuts but not bodies'.[232]

Arden-Clarke's antagonist was Dr Kwame Nkrumah. After nine years in America (where he studied theology at the Negro University of Lincoln), and two years in London studying philosophy, he was recruited by Dr J. B. Danquah to be the organising secretary of the newly-formed United Gold Coast Convention in 1947. Nkrumah drew inspiration from India and Gandhi as well as Marcus Garvey, and soon grew tired of this small elitist group of intellectuals and professionals. He formed his own Convention Peoples Party (CPP), appealing to those vigorous elements with only elementary-school education (January 1949). He quickly landed himself in jail (January 1950) for organising illegal strikes and sedition – 'positive action' – with the slogan 'Self-government now.'[233]

Nkrumah continued to direct the movement from jail, smuggling out directives on government-issue toilet-paper. Arden-Clarke decided to release him from jail after his victory in the election of 1951. They met for the first time: 'The meeting was redolent with mutual suspicion and mistrust. We were like two dogs meeting for the first time, sniffing at each other with hackles half raised trying to decide whether to bite or wag our tails.'[234] He hit upon the brilliant idea of giving Nkrumah a dog as a present, a libidinous bitch called 'Topsy', whose love-affairs gave

[229] Rathbone, *Ghana*, intro., p. xliv.   [230] CO 96/800/1, minutes, September 1949.

[231] According to R. Salloway, after the riots the government 'had virtually no effective support among the people and the forces of law and order were utterly inadequate to control the situation': quoted by F. Furedi, 'Creating a breathing-space: the political management of colonial emergencies', *JICH*, vol. 21 (1993), p. 93.

[232] D. Rooney, *Sir Charles Arden-Clarke* (1982).

[233] *The autobiography of Kwame Nkrumah* (1957, 1964); R. Rathbone, 'Nkrumah, Kwame', *ODNB* vol. XL, pp. 941–3.   [234] B. Lapping, *End of empire* (1985), p. 378.

Illustration 2.2 Sir Charles Arden-Clarke, governor of the Gold Coast, 1949–57.
A formal portrait of the man who steered Ghana to independence, after previous postings as resident commissioner in Bechuanaland, and in Basutoland, and as the first governor of Sarawak (1946–49). Sir Charles Arden-Clarke died in 1962, aged sixty-four.

them a talking-point which broke the ice. Such are the mechanisms upon which the fate of nations and empires depend. Privately, Arden-Clarke's initial impressions were decidedly unfavourable. In family letters more than once he referred to 'our little local Hitler and his *putsch*'.[235] Fairly soon, however, Nkrumah became perceived as a 'moderate', even if a mildly Marxist one. He was intelligent, idealistic, prepared to be co-operative and to listen to advice.[236] Two reasons in particular underlined the necessity of a working collaboration with him. The first was the problem of 'swollen shoot'. Radical cutting-out measures were required to preserve the cocoa industry, one of the empire's main dollar-earners. The measures were too drastic for suspicious farmers to act on at the behest of the British (the equivalent of culling to eradicate rinderpest in pastoral societies).[237] Hence, if the disease were not to get out of hand, Nkrumah's power and authority must be strengthened so as to enable him to issue the necessary directives, and 'so to prevent the economic collapse of the country'. The second reason was that Nkrumah, now apparently a former communist (and certainly deleted in Moscow from the list of useful contacts), would provide the best defence against communism.

By May 1951 Arden-Clarke was convinced there was no alternative to Nkrumah and his CPP. It could only be replaced by a similar potential government, or one of even more extreme nationalist tendencies. True to form, he expressed his conclusion to Cohen in a dog analogy:

> We have only one dog in our kennel and the whole question is whether the tail [i.e., Nkrumah's supporters] will wag the dog or the dog the tail. It has a very big tail and not much guts. All we can do is to build it up and feed it vitamins and cod liver oil; and, as soon as the opportunity offers, some of that tail must be docked.[238]

7. Cyprus and 'Enosis'

Cyprus, although not yet much in the public eye, was nevertheless vexing the policy-makers sorely in this period. It occupies a central position in the history of Labour government policy, illuminating problems of general interest. Ministers (except for Bevin) were anxious to relaunch Cyprus on a constitutional path. As their chosen governor, Lord ('Rex') Winster (the former minister for civil aviation) was specially commissioned with this task. However, he was not a success and no political

---

[235] Rooney, *Sir Charles Arden-Clarke*, pp. 105, 122.
[236] CO 537/7181, no. 3, to Cohen, 5 March 1951; *BDEEP*, pt 3, pp. 65–9 (no. 224).
[237] CO 554/298, minute by T. B. Williamson, 31 December 1951.
[238] CO 537/7181, no. 5, 12 May 1951; Rathbone, *Ghana*, pt 1, pp. 322–6 (no. 99); see also Rooney, *Sir Charles Arden-Clarke*, p. 203.

advance was achieved. This was certainly not from any lack of will on the part of the Mediterranean desk in the CO, where J. S. Bennett was a consistent advocate of promoting internal self-government, continually challenging the argument that Cypriots were 'unfit' for it and repeatedly criticising the 'lofty disapproval' of successive governors. He warned of the danger that without progress to self-government Cyprus would be left stranded as an anachronism. 'Both geographically and politically Cyprus is in the front line as a test of the sincerity of HMG's declared policy of political development in the Colonies', and thus a 'vulnerable salient in the present world ideological struggle'. It was all very well for the Chiefs of Staff to contend that it would be a strategic necessity in a 'hot' war, but meanwhile it was an embarrassment in the cold war. This was because it could be used to upset relations between necessary allies (Britain, the USA, Greece and Turkey), and because Russia could use it to discredit Britain as a colonial power. The only possible justification for holding on was the strategic argument – an argument which could not be used in public, because it would be a gift to Russian propaganda. Bennett's critique was in line with that put forward by FO pundits, who favoured a policy of timely concession (before the agitation turned to terrorism), bringing Cyprus into line with policy in India, Burma, Cyrenaica, and the withdrawals from Egypt, Palestine and Greece.[239] These analogies were of course the nub of the case put by the Cypriot leaders themselves. It was, they complained, bad enough that they were denied the measure of self-determination or independence allowed to Indians, Burmans, Newfoundlanders, Jews, Lebanese, Syrians, Iraqis, Egyptians and even Indonesians; but they were surely entitled to treatment at least equal to that which was being proposed for Libyans, Somalis and Sudanese. To the Cypriot Ethnarchy, British rule was 'enslavement under a foreign yoke'. They were increasingly prepared to say so loudly to the whole world.[240]

Enosis – union with Greece – was ruled out. That was perhaps the one consistently clear negative element in British policy, where almost every course of possible action seemed wrong. Cession would be bad for British prestige, especially with the Arab world; and it would constitute a dangerous precedent for the Falklands, Hong Kong and Gibraltar. Almost nobody in British government had a good word to say of Enosis. Governor Winster called it 'the Cyprus measles', a disease of political infancy. Comparisons along the lines of 'undulant fever' or 'children's make-believe' abounded. Mary Fisher (on the Mediterranean desk in the

---

[239] CO 537/2486, 4035, 4970 and 4978: minutes and memoranda, 1947–50: *BDEEP*, pt 3, pp. 84–90, 97–9, 105–9.   [240] CO 67/361/1.

CO) employed the whole gamut of derogatory metaphor from nail-biting to hereditary syphilis. Attlee himself, who usually had a sure instinct in discerning ephemeral nationalism from the real thing, 'froth not tide', regarded Enosis as a delusion. The danger of Enosis was that Greece was so unstable that it might become hostile to Britain overnight, with or without going communist. This was the crux: the high-minded analogy from India broke down because of Enosis. On the other hand, it was clear to the CO that British rule could not be allowed to go on unchanged. Attitudes in Government House, Nicosia, were so unimaginative and small-minded that school children were even forbidden to have blue pencils lest they should draw the Greek flag. Officials there treated educated Greeks – and, most ill-advisedly, even visiting British civil servants – as their inferiors.[241]

At the end of 1947, AKEL, the Cypriot Communist Party, petitioned for the type of constitution being reinstituted in Malta, providing internal self-government. The CO responded with a comparatively liberal constitution which would give limited home rule, with 'proper safeguards' for British strategic interests (the importance of which the Chiefs of Staff reaffirmed in April 1947). It would provide for the active participation of Cypriots in their internal affairs, while the governor retained wide powers. Also proposed was the possibility of considering responsible government in five years. To the deep consternation of officials, the Commonwealth Affairs Committee in January 1948 rejected this timetable, largely as a result of Attlee's magisterial intervention, in which he argued from Indian experience (going back to the Simon Commission) that dyarchy and 'interim' constitutions were unworkable. The Cabinet itself decided to proceed cautiously. It wanted more emphasis on local government, and was not attracted by the alternative (to a 'transitional' constitution) of immediate responsible government.[242] In April proposals were approved by ministers for an elected legislature and an advisory executive council responsible to the governor, together with two-way links between these bodies; Britain would remain in control of foreign and defence affairs.[243] This constitution was ill-received. Only the Turkish Cypriots supported the offer. It was rejected by the Enotists and disapproved of by AKEL, several of whose representatives walked out of the Consultative Assembly. There was a General Strike in August 1948, and the Assembly was dissolved. As a result of this stalemate, the British government had to decide whether to go ahead and impose the constitution or put it into cold storage. The Commonwealth

---

[241] FO 371/67083 and FO 371/72296, no. 10104, minutes by A. Watson, 1947–8.
[242] CAB 134/54, December 1947; CO 537/4035, no. 13, December 1947–January 1948; *BDEEP*, pt 3, pp. 92–100 (nos. 236–8).
[243] CAB 128/12, CM 30 (48) 9, 29 April 1948; *BDEEP*, pt 3, pp. 104–5 (no. 240).

Affairs Committee was against imposing it, though CO officials felt imposition would hardly worsen the situation. Rather against CO instincts the constitution was shelved in August 1948. It was not withdrawn. The ball was left in the Cypriot court. If 'responsible leaders' came forward to ask for its re-examination or implementation they would be welcomed. After the developments in the Gold Coast by 1951 it became unlikely that the Cypriots would accept anything less than a further advance towards a ministerial system. But already the British position was worsening from 1949. The constitutional impasse and loss of British initiative in Cyprus became more serious as a result of several developments favouring Enosis: (i) AKEL embraced it, (ii) the Greek government revived its campaign for it, and (iii) the Cypriot Ethnarchy held a plebiscite which voted 96.4 per cent for it.

The appointment of a new governor, Sir Arthur Wright, seemed to provide the opportunity to break the deadlock. But Wright was an old Cyprus hand, with twenty years' service there from 1923 to 1943, and his return proved to be a Bourbon restoration. To the despair of the officials he was an antedeluvian, unregenerate hard-liner who advocated a policy of firmness and repression, coercion and censorship. Bennett was scornful about the 'folly and impracticability' of Wright's policy. Lord Listowel (minister of state for colonial affairs) agreed with Bennett; the governor's proposed policy of coercion was 'contrary to our experience in India, Ireland and Palestine'. Predictably Creech Jones was less sure, while the FO felt the powers the governor wanted could be justified. Wright got most of what he wanted.[244]

Cyprus policy thus seemed to some officials to be in a confused state. The Chiefs of Staff were asked to provide some clarification. This they did in June 1950 with (to the CO) the unwelcome though hardly unexpected reply that the retention of Cyprus was most emphatically a strategic necessity. From Cyprus a significant proportion of targets in southern Russia, especially the oilfields, were in range of bomber-aircraft. As Britain's one firm piece of ground in the Middle East it must not fall under communist control, while the importance of Turkish co-operation against Russia was emerging ever more strongly. It was thus increasingly necessary to take seriously the Turkish government and Turkish Cypriot minority viewpoint.[245] The CO thus resigned itself to remaining 'an occupying power'; they accepted that the Chiefs of Staff's

[244] CO 537/6228, CO minutes, January–October 1950; *BDEEP*, pt 3, pp. 108–12 (no. 244); R. Holland, 'Never, never land: British colonial policy and the roots of violence in Cyprus, 1950–1954', *JICH*, vol. 21 (1993), pp. 148–76.

[245] FO 371/87224, no. 1081, letter by Marshal of the RAF, Lord Tedder, 2 October 1950; *BDEEP* pt 3, pp. 117–19 (no. 246).

opinion was definitive, and so there could be no question of reopening the issue for several years. Denied the possibility of positive policies, the CO concentrated on trying to keep the Cyprus problem out of the newspapers and the United Nations. Leading officials regretted that Wright could not be replaced by a governor with the Mountbatten touch, for they believed the slow use of local government here was not going to work.[246] But the office was quickly brought back to the recurring inability to find a solution: an imposed constitution, Griffiths pointed out, would not satisfy the United Nations. At the same time he was worried about the danger of 'drifting into another Palestine'.[247] Officials needed no reminder. Bennett for one had long understood the fragility of the situation and its parallels: so far there had been no effective rebellion or mobilisation of international opinion, but he doubted whether this would remain true in the 1950s; nor had the Cypriots as yet shown much fighting spirit, but if that should ever change the position would be gloomy indeed. And so it proved to be.[248]

8. The Islamic world

Bevin was at his most Curzonian in his understanding that the British empire ruled more than half the Muslim peoples of the world and that Britain needed to widen its vision of itself as an Islamic power. (Indeed, the empire did much to shape the state-system of the modern Muslim territories.)[249] Bevin told the American ambassador that an essential aim was to ensure peace from Morocco to Indonesia, and not to alienate the Muslim world which ran round the middle of the planet. He picked up on the assertion of the Chief of Air Staff, Lord Tedder, that if a holy war (jihad) were aroused, the dangers would be insuperable.[250] The situation in Palestine meant they had to be careful to guard against 'the dangers of aligning the whole of Islam against us'. Bevin saw the main threat to this strategically vital area as one of backwardness leading to disintegration, thus opening up opportunities for communist penetration; if the Middle East fell into hostile hands, it was doubtful whether South and South-East Asia could be held. The improvement of the economic and social conditions of the region was an essential part of his grand strategy. It would also

[246] CO 537/7453, CO minutes, 31 January–1 February 1951, by J. S. Bennett and Miss M. L. S. Fisher; *BDEEP*, pt 3, pp. 119–22 (no. 247).

[247] CO 537/7453, no. 18, 20 July 1951.

[248] CO 537/4978, no 62, minutes by Bennett, 13 December 1949; *BDEEP*, pt 3, p. 106 (no. 242).

[249] F. Robinson, 'The British empire and the Muslim world', in Brown and Louis, eds., *Oxford History of the British empire*, vol. IV: *The twentieth century* (1999), pp. 398–420.

[250] FO 800/487, pp. 175–83, 25 May 1948.

help the British economy. The Commonwealth might be a useful agency.[251] The Tennessee Valley Authority might be the model. What Bevin envisaged was a new framework of conciliatory relations in the Middle East, treating its peoples as equals.[252] He wanted joint co-operation, a partnership on a common basis, a mutual interest in 'a great design' for security and prosperity, fighting communism by raising living standards for the common people and *fellahin* through the whole core-area from Turkey to Pakistan. Further afield, he understood the necessity of meeting nationalist stirrings in Indonesia (see above p. 104).[253] As early as 1946 he promoted self-government for the Sudan, saying 'I have to face certain modern tendencies in regard to colonial or quasi-colonial problems.' He was anxious that Britain should not be seen to side with India in the horrendous dispute with Pakistan over Kashmir. He was determined North African colonies would not be returned to Italy (though Somaliland was another matter), but believed Britain should hold on to strategic bases in Libya in order to have the means of 'acting on the soft-underbelly of Europe from the Mediterranean' – a Churchillian phrase he used more than once. At the same time he promoted the achievement of independence by Libya under UN auspices (achieved in 1951).[254]

Bevin's grandiose social-partnership plans came to nothing. Many historians have had a field-day pouring contempt upon them, and they do look like mid-Victorian expansionist blueprints married to twentieth-century socialist good intentions towards the underprivileged. What the Arabs wanted, however, was not partnership with, but the disappearance of, Europeans and their enclaves. On the other hand, he called for more emphasis on 'peasants not pashas', less reliance on the 'personality of princes', which was surely a step in the right direction. Even if he had not the resources to elevate the poor of the third world, at least he helped to keep the Middle East reasonably steady, and the oil flowing, for most of the post-war decade.[255] Maybe he was right that after the 'abandonment of India and Burma, a retreat from the Middle East would appear to the world as the abdication of our position as a world power and encourage India to gravitate towards Russia'.[256]

[251] CAB 129/43, CP(50)264, 8 November 1950, 'Economic and social development of the Middle East.'
[252] Louis, *The British empire in the Middle East, 1945–1951*, is a magisterial account.
[253] Bullock, *Bevin*, vol. III, pp. 114–15, 138–55, 287, 672.
[254] PREM 8/1388/1, to Lord Stansgate, 31 August 1946 (on Sudan); CAB 131/2, DO(46)40, memo, 13 March 1946; CAB 129/9, CP(46)165, 18 April 1946; *BDEEP*, pt 3, pp. 216, 247 (nos. 227, 290); CAB 129/24, CP(48)43, 4 February 1948, 'The future of the ex-Italian colonies in Africa'.
[255] PREM 8/627/1, October 1945; Bullock, *Bevin*, vol. III, pp. 841–2.
[256] FO 800/476, 9 January 1947.

As far as Egypt was concerned, Bevin urged the view that in practice Britain would be dependent on Egyptian goodwill, and a friendly government might give Britain more facilities than could be got by treaty or bayonets.[257] His colleagues were minded to agree that the question was not what they would like in a new treaty but what they could persuade the Egyptians to accept. They could not expect independent Egypt to accept obligations not undertaken by British dominions. Attlee, summing up a major Cabinet discussion in 1946, articulated the essential point brilliantly. Despite the Chiefs of Staffs' preference, Britain could not remain 'forcibly on the ground':

> There was no more justification for this than for our claiming that our neighbours on the Continent of Europe should grant us bases for our defence. Our oil interests in the Middle East were indeed important, but our ability to defend them would only be impaired if we insisted on remaining in Egypt against the will of the Egyptian people, and so worsened our relations with the remainder of the Arab world.[258]

The government planned an evacuation of the Suez Canal Zone. However, treaty negotiations collapsed, partly because the Egyptians insisted on linking them to their claims of sovereignty over the Sudan. Bevin, driving a hard bargain on the evacuation timetable and refusing absolutely to 'sell the Sudanese into Egyptian slavery', saw all his hopes of a fresh but favourable treaty dashed. Negotiations remained deadlocked. Attlee and Bevin were unable to deliver Britain out its Egyptian bondage.

The Muslim elite in Northern Nigeria was treated respectfully and sympathetically. But there were two crises in the Muslim British world: the Malayan insurgency and the Persian oil crisis.

(1) Malaya

The government had drawn lessons from the mess the Dutch got into in Indonesia, and tried to build the foundations for self-government in Malaya as rapidly as circumstances would allow. This policy was described as one of *political advancement*, and, as in Africa, it was coupled with 'community development', probably seen at its most ambitious in Malaya.[259] Progress to self-government was to be orderly. The timetable was to be determined by Britain's own 'enlightened' programme, and not

---

[257] CAB 129/10, CP(46)229, memo, 5 June 1946.

[258] CAB 128/5, CM 58(46), 7 June 1946; *BDEEP*, pt 1, p. 17 (no. 8); J. Kent, ed., *Egypt and the defence of the Middle East* (BDEEP, 1998), pt 1, pp. 143–6 (no. 55).

[259] T. N. Harper, *The end of empire and the making of Malaya* (Cambridge, 1999) is the leading account of all this.

by seeming to yield to nationalist pressure, although the Malayo-Muslim nationalism the British encountered was, if anything, pressing for a delay in political advancement until Malays were in a position to contain the communist challenge from Chinese rebels, which became serious from the middle of 1948 and led to the declaration of a state of emergency (in effect a state of war). At all events, it was understood that Britain must come to terms with a genuine young Malay nationalist movement, promote improved living standards and assist the development of a Malayan community capable of resisting communism.[260]

Almost immediately after his arrival in South-East Asia as governor-general, Malcolm MacDonald[261] put his influential weight behind the need for policies which would 'retain full trust in British leadership in this region which is the main base of the British position in the Far East'. They should aim at the acceptance of British leadership by local people and avoid 'being at each stage [a] bit behind local political opinions (such as has been so unfortunate in the history of the Indian problem)'. There were plenty of nationalists ready to exploit any weakening in the British position. It would be most unfortunate if Malay political consciousness got into 'extremist and anti-British channels' or swept into Indonesian anti-European currents. His argument about the necessary conciliation of UMNO (United Malays National Organisation) was persuasive, and constitutional negotiations were undertaken which led to the setting up of the Federation of Malaya in 1948 (instead of a union).[262] By 1950 MacDonald believed the process of self-government 'would inevitably be

---

[260] CAB 128/17, CM 37(50)1, 19 June 1950; *BDEEP*, pt 3, pp. 188–91 (no. 270); A. J. Stockwell, ed., *Malaya* (BDEEP, 1995), pt 2: *The communist insurrection, 1948–1953*, pp. 239–42 (no. 221), and *British policy and Malay politics during the Malayan Union experiment, 1942–1948* (Kuala Lumpur, 1979), and 'British imperial policy and decolonization in Malaya, 1942–52', *JICH*, vol. 13 (1984), pp. 68–87.

[261] During his years in South-East Asia (1946–1955), MacDonald was 'a frequent visitor to an Iban long-house' (R. H. W. Reece, 'A "suitable population": Charles Brooke and race-mixing in Sarawak', *Itinerario*, vol. 9 (Leiden, 1985), pp. 67–112). MacDonald's reminiscences do not conceal his delight in Iban young women. There are lyrical descriptions of 'maidens with fresh, delicious, beguiling prettiness' and figures with 'the grace of a Greek statue'. He was especially fond of a chief's daughter who repeatedly acted as 'hostess', Segura, with 'a dark, magical bewitching beauty' and 'adorable grace', aged about thirteen when he first saw her (*Borneo people*, 1956, esp. ch. 7; 'Life in a long-house', pp, 95–115, and ch. 11 'Segura', pp. 184–98). In November 1954 a photo appeared in the *Straits Times* of MacDonald greeted at a long-house by two bare-breasted girls. Conservative MPs and right-wing newspapers such as the *Daily Telegraph* demanded his removal from office, but MacDonald denied any 'sexual relations' with them. See Clyde Sanger, *Malcolm MacDonald: bringing an end to empire* (1995), pp. 326–30 ('Segura'), and photo on p. xxviii (Siah and Sani).

[262] A. J. Stockwell, ed., *Malaya*, pt 1: *The Malayan Union experiment, 1942–1948*, pp. 236–9 (no. 92) MacDonald to CO, 25 May 1946, and pp. 252–5 (no. 96) 21/22 June 1946.

Illustration 2.3 Commissioner-General Malcolm MacDonald performing a traditional welcoming ceremony for the new governor of
Sarawak, 4 April 1950.

MacDonald was governor-general of the British territories in South-
East Asia, 1946–48, and commissioner-general, 1948–55. This Dayak
ceremony was performed at the Astana in Kuching. The new governor,
Sir Anthony Abell, is sitting far left; he had previously been Resident of
Oyo, Nigeria, and succeeded the former governor, Douglas Stewart,
who was assassinated in December 1949, shortly after arrival, by
Sarawak Malays as a protest against imperial rule from 1946.

accelerated by factors over which we shall have little or no control', such
as a new generation of younger leaders coming forward, and 'the pressure
of Asian opinion and also world opinion as expressed through UNO will
be irresistible upon Asian leaders in Malaya'. The British government, he
added, 'must be mentally prepared, therefore, to accept a quickening of
the pace'. If they lost the support of the politically conscious they would at
the same time 'get world opinion against us'. It was vital to make sure
there was no discernible difference of view on which the latter 'can take
sides against us'. Secretary of state James Griffiths agreed: twenty-five
years would be a sound assumption in a normal, peaceful world, but it
would be 'unrealistic, unsafe, and perhaps disastrous' to work on the old
assumption that they had as long as this to prepare. The transition period
would have to be shorter rather than longer: 'in the conditions as they are
today and especially in view of the control of China by the communists,

the tempo would have to be increased'. The primary dynamics of decolonisation could hardly have been more clearly stated.[263]

Getting the support of world opinion was more than ever necessary after the onset of the communist insurgency in Malaya had led to the declaration of the state of emergency. The British did not see this as a struggle against nationalism, but against communist *anti*-nationalism. The insurgency served to sharpen British perceptions of the wider international significance of South-East Asia to the general government aims of raising dollars and containing communism. Malay was recognised as the cornerstone of the whole British position in the Far East, while Singapore was the bastion of strategic power and planning in a wide area. Considerable amounts of money and manpower were drafted in to secure Britain's 'weak rear' in the cold war, although ministers were well aware of the danger of Malaya's 'devolving into a bottomless pit, devouring all our resources, and playing straight into Russian hands'.[264] By the end of 1950, with fears that Malaya was becoming 'a second Palestine', Strachey believed they 'needed a Mountbatten'.[265]

Strachey argued that the Malayan situation must be seen in a wider context:

And in South-East Asia as a whole the absolute condition of success appears to me to be that each Western nation must come to terms with the genuine local nationalist movement, even if this means the granting of full independence prematurely. The genuine nationalist movement in Malaya is only just starting: but it is starting and we must come to terms with it.

He continued: an understanding of this nationalism and 'a real desire to come to terms with it' could be combined with 'the greatest severity' in dealing with the emergency, but military necessity should not be allowed to interfere with political advancement and social development any more than it had to. The secretary of state for the colonies agreed.[266] And indeed Griffiths applied the fundamental insight generated by India, Burma and Ceylon: 'post-war events had shown that the danger lies in too slow rather than in too rapid progress' towards self-government.[267]

Though alien-Chinese led the rebels, with the Chinese making up almost two-fifths of the total population of just over five million, the

---

[263] Stockwell, *Malaya*, pt 2, pp. 223–30 (no. 218), 7 June 1950, conference at Bukit Serene.
[264] PREM 8/1406/2, 21 April 1950, MAL(C)(50)6.
[265] PREM 8/1406/2, 11 December 1950, minute to Attlee; *BDEEP*, pt 3, p. 204 (no. 272); Stockwell, *Malaya*, pt 2, pp. 272–5 (no. 230).
[266] Stockwell, *Malaya*, pt 2, pp. 234–42 (nos. 220–1) memo, 17 June 1950, and Cabinet minutes, 19 June 1950 (CAB 128/17, CM 37(50)1).
[267] PREM 8/1406/2, DO(50)94, 15 November 1950; *BDEEP*, pt 3, pp. 192–201 (no. 271).

British government would have preferred a multi-racial state in Malaya rather than the entrenchment of a permanent Malayo-Muslim supremacy, but the need for Malay co-operation during the emergency forced the government to compromise their commitment to genuine multi-racial integration. Municipal elections were arranged for 1951 as the first step in 'steady democratic progress towards self-government within the Commonwealth'.[268]

(2) Persia

Response to the Persian (Iranian) oil crisis of 1951, which dominated the last months of the life of the Labour government, completed in fact the emerging pattern of a consistent policy in dealing with nationalist challenges.[269] The context was formed by a revolutionary change in the Middle East, whereby in December 1950 the Americans in the Aramco-Saudi agreement had made a concession which set the limits of future possibility in oil extraction, namely, a profit-sharing scheme on a 50:50 basis. This was far more favourable to indigenous interests than anything known before, and, with its 'aura of fairness', almost inevitably sparked off a reaction in Persia.[270]

The Anglo-Iranian Oil Company was half-owned by the British government and it controlled the largest part of Iranian national revenue. The country had the biggest oil reserves anywhere under British control, and the AIOC was Britain's most profitable overseas investment. The oil refineries at Abadan were the largest in the world. So the shock was great when the AIOC was nationalised by the prime minister appointed in April 1951, Dr Mussadeq. He had immediately reduced all problems to the ejection of the company, skilfully mobilising public and Islamic discontent against the British. Mussadeq appeared to be a 'fanatical nationalist', a 70-year-old dressed in what to westerners looked like pyjamas – perhaps even two pairs of pyjamas of contrasting colours – who seemed to use fainting and weeping much as Gandhi had used fasting and silence, as unfair negotiating weapons. Even Attlee felt Mussadeq might be 'on the lunatic fringe'.[271] Appearances were deceptive. Mussadeq was far from stupid, and indeed had studied political science at the University of Neuchâtel, Switzerland.[272]

---

[268] 'The Colonial Empire today' (May, 1950), paras. 21–30, *BDEEP*, pt 1, p. 342 (no. 72).
[269] Louis, *British empire in the Middle East*, pp. 632–89 is the best treatment of the crisis.
[270] *Ibid.*, p. 647; G. McGhee, *Envoy to the Middle World: adventures in diplomacy* (New York, 1983) supplies a valuable American perspective, see esp. pp. 318–44, 388–404.
[271] Louis, *British empire in the Middle East*, p. 662.
[272] McGhee, *Envoy to the Middle World*, p. 388.

The British objected not so much to the principle of nationalisation but to the manner of it. Mussadeq unilaterally denounced the existing agreement without negotiation. And in September 1951 the remaining British staff at Abadan were given seven days' notice to quit. There was considerable Cabinet debate about what to do, and not a little dithering at first by Attlee and vacillation even by the Chiefs of Staff. Two men, however, consistently held to a hawkish position, Shinwell at the Ministry of Defence, and Morrison as the inexperienced foreign secretary. Morrison had to be restrained by the Cabinet from embarking on a military operation to occupy the oil installations and hold Abadan by force – he had already sent four destroyers to reinforce the three frigates in the Persian Gulf. Although he could neither pronounce foreign place-names properly nor find them on the map, and was preoccupied with his pet project, the 'Festival of Britain', this crisis was the one bit of foreign policy to claim his full attention, but he was all too determined to avoid 'scuttle and surrender'.[273] Critical colleagues wrote him off as 'a poor man's Palmerston', over-compensating for having been a conscientious objector in the First World War; 'bloody little fool Morrison', wrote Dalton in his diary. Morrison argued that they should try to 'stiffen the Americans' and use force to improve British prestige and prevent other nations from getting stroppy – Israel, Iraq and especially Egypt.[274] Other ministers took the view that force might actually strengthen Mussadeq's domestic position, and alienate the Americans and most of the Commonwealth, particularly India and Pakistan. Attlee was required to decide between conflicting ministerial advice. And it was indeed thanks to his sagacity, working in tune with American diplomacy, that a disastrous piece of pseudo-Palmerstonian gunboat-diplomacy or a proto-Suez fiasco was averted. He realised that the nationalisation had to be dealt with in much the same way as an independence-demand in a colonial territory.[275]

As Attlee ruminated on the situation, the conclusions for policy seemed to emerge clearly. Big powers should not use force against small countries. Britain could not revert to using force to protect British commercial interests, which might not in any case succeed in its purpose. Rejecting earlier assessments of Iranian nationalism as emotional and inauthentic, he decided that it was genuine, and genuine nationalist feeling in Persia and elsewhere must not be alienated by clinging to the old techniques.[276] Britain could no longer 'go about the world in a kind of Palmerstonian fashion': 'We are working under an entirely different code', determined by

[273] Louis, British empire in the Middle East, p. 686; Williams, The diary of Hugh Gaitskell, pp. 259–65.   [274] Donoughue and Jones, Herbert Morrison, pp. 496–505.
[275] Louis, British empire in the Middle East, p. 662.
[276] CAB 128/20, CM 51(51)2, 12 July 1951; BDEEP, pt 1, p. 89 (no. 36).

the UN and the rule of law. Concessionaires must now take account of the feelings and self-respect of local people. The Anglo-Iranian Oil Company had been inexcusably insensitive. He regretted that the government had not forced them to make changes in good time. It was no doubt troublesome and inconvenient to bring in the local people, but it was 'essential if Western capital and technology is to remain in the less-developed parts of the world'.[277] The right policy was 'to work for some kind of working agreement or partnership in which we supply the knowledge, the know-how and all the rest of it and the Persians manage this thing in the interests of all'.[278] Once again the historian can only applaud Attlee's magisterial incisiveness.

9. Labour's legacy

In 1948 the Colonial Office (under the guidance of Creech Jones and Andrew Cohen) formulated policies which were certainly high-minded: 'The central purpose of British colonial policy is simple. It is to guide the colonial territories to responsible self-government within the Commonwealth in conditions that ensure to the people concerned both a fair standard of living and freedom from oppression from any quarter.'[279] And for Africa specifically:

> The fundamental objectives in Africa are to further the emergence of large-scale societies, integrated for self-improvement but with effective and democratic political and economic institutions, both national and local, inspired by a common faith in progress and Western values and equipped with efficient techniques of production and betterment.[280]

The African continent, however, both politically and economically, was recalcitrant material for such aims, despite increased expenditure on Colonial Development and Welfare, and careful grooming of key nationalist leaders. On the other hand, the foundations of a multi-racial Commonwealth were laid, very much one of Attlee's achievements.

The Labour government superintended almost the last flourish of imperial idealism, hoping to convert the old 'imperialism' into something more like an ethical colonial policy. This desire to help the wretched of the earth was in part driven by the central group of ministers of working-class origin – many of them from mining communities – who had not arrived in highest office without a sense that power was there to be used to do good. There was 'an acute awareness of moral purpose' (Roger Louis).[281] It was,

---

[277] Attlee, *As it happened*, pp. 175–6.
[278] *PD, Commons*, vol. 491, cc. 1063–72, 30 July 1951, debate on foreign affairs, Middle East.
[279] CO 875/24, no. 8, circular 'Notes on British colonial policy', *BDEEP*, pt 1, p. 327 (no. 71).
[280] CO 852/1053/1, no. 8, Cambridge Summer School paper CSC(48)4, August 1948.
[281] Louis, *British empire in the Middle East*, captures this spirit in his introduction, pp. 3–50.

of course, never an aspiration uncomplicated by a multiplicity of cross-currents. At one level there was also a determination that Britain should remain a great power, and find a definite contribution to make in world leadership; above all, ministers did not want to be charged with scuttling out of imperial responsibilities. At another level, they had a prime minister who made classical allusions in parliament, thought the ancient Greek city-state might be made a model for a Gibraltar constitution, and carefully totted up the number of public schools represented in his ministerial team. The vision was marred by delusions of grandeur and residual racial and class snobberies. It also fractured on the constraints and realities of the situation, by the contradictions and intractability of many of the issues which arose; and by insufficient resources and by economic crises; by the impossibility of full co-operation with South Africa as a leading continental power, and by the difficulty of mobilising India as an ally in the Asian sector; by anti-colonial pressures in the United Nations; and by the Korean War and consequent rearmament.

The Korean War broke out in June 1950 with the invasion of South Korea by the communist North. Labour ministers had a ghastly fear that this was only a diversion, and that the Soviet Union would launch a sudden aggression against the West in either Germany or Iran; at any rate they decided that 'the danger of a general war had increased'. The Cabinet now adopted a massive rearmament programme, and did so as an act of national self-preservation in an almost apocalyptic atmosphere.[282] National Service was extended to two years. Defence estimates almost doubled from £740 million in December 1949 to £1,555 million in 1951 (in each case spread over three years). This was hopelessly over-ambitious. As a result, a balance of payments surplus of £307 million in 1950 turned into a deficit of £369 million in 1951. Some of the cost was to be met by the abolition of free spectacles and false teeth. This led to a Cabinet crisis and the resignation of Aneurin Bevan (mastermind behind Labour's greatest achievement, the National Health Service), supported by Harold Wilson and John Freeman. The Bevanites, as they were called, were right about the long-term need to cut overseas commitments, but they were wrong to ignore the immediate danger of abandoning them prematurely, and by so doing giving encouragement to Soviet expansionism. Perhaps the Cabinet over-reacted to the Korean War, but no government could ignore the chilling War Office warning that a major war was 'possible in 1951 and probable in 1952'.[283] An heroic

[282] CAB 128/18, CM 52(50)4, 1 August 1950 and CM 53(50), 11 August 1950.
[283] CAB 128/19, CM 3(51), 15 January 1951, CM 7(51)4, 25 January 1951, and CM 22(51)1, 22 March 1951 ('Social services') and CM 25(51)3, 9 April 1951; Hennessy, *Never again*, pp. 406–16; P. Williams, *Gaitskell*, pp. 278–83.

left-wing administration thus foundered in a miserable fashion, recorded in full minutes by a palpably saddened Cabinet secretary.

Attlee's Cabinet imploded with the internal incompatibilities and disagreements of an ill-assorted team (the like of which Britain will never see again). The hopes of continuing to be a great power were overwhelmed by a recognition of the ever-increasing dependence on the United States. The more ambitious military concepts could not be implemented. But although many specific objectives were unrealistic or not realised, in broad outline a remarkably coherent set of policy-guidelines for the future had emerged, a pragmatic set of indicators, at least.

The particular conundrum of relations with South Africa was analysed by Gordon Walker in September 1950 in a way which determined the fundamentals of British policy for the next thirty years, or more, and through several changes of government.[284] His 'four reasons' for trying to co-operate with South Africa, despite apartheid and embarrassing difficulties, were endorsed by the Cabinet. South Africa was important both strategically and economically: (1) geopolitically its support was vital in the struggle against communism; (2) economic links, especially in trade, were close and of mutual benefit; (3) Britain had obligations not only to the 40 per cent of the white population of British descent, but also (4) pre-eminently to the 2 million Africans in the three High Commission Territories, who were so vulnerable to South African economic pressure and expansionist aims.[285] Those who would break with South Africa and ostracise the Afrikaner nationalist regime, said Gordon Walker, 'completely fail to understand the realities of the situation'. The policy must be to contain the expansion of its apartheid doctrines beyond its borders, but otherwise to do nothing to 'unite and inflame' white opinion behind Dr Malan and his National Party.[286]

It was essentially this policy which led to the controversial decision to suspend Seretse Khama from the chieftainship of the Bangwato in Bechuanaland after his marriage to a white woman in London. There was public outrage about the government's decision, as it seemed to align British policy with South African racist attitudes. The truth was much more complicated. The threat to the High Commission Territories from

[284] R. Ovendale, 'The South African policy of the British Labour government, 1947–1951', *International Affairs*, vol. 59 (1983), pp. 41–58.

[285] CAB 129/42, CP(50)214, 25 September 1950, memo by Gordon Walker, 'Relations with the Union of South Africa'; CAB 128/18, CM 62(50)4, 28 September 1950; *BDEEP*, pt 4, pp. 284–91, 294–6 (nos. 429 and 431).

[286] CAB 129/45, CP(51)109, 16 April 1951, memo by Gordon Walker reporting his visit to South Africa, Southern Rhodesia and the High Commission Territories, January–February 1951, paras. 35–55; *BDEEP*, pt 4, pp. 312–15 (no. 433); see also Hyam and Henshaw, *The lion and the springbok*, pp. 208–10.

South Africa was a real one, and for this reason the non-recognition of Seretse can be broadly vindicated as in the best interests of Africans generally in southern Africa.[287]

It was also fear of Afrikaner expansion which led Labour into promotion of a possible Central African Federation. This piece of geopolitical engineering was part of a more general fascination with and resort to a phenomenon which I have called 'the federal panacea': the ideal – the delusion, very often – that a large federal structure can resolve problems of competing contenders for power, create consolidated post-independence units which are more viable, and have superior defence capability to ward off international competitors. Self-government seemed unrealistic for small populations. The idea had been around a long time (see above, p. 9).[288] The 1939–45 war gave a boost to these geopolitical themes. MacDonald pondered the issue of re-grouping African, West Indian, and South-East Asian colonies. Smuts declared that the time for 'pygmy units' was over: Hitler had proved that. Conservative secretary of state Lord Cranborne in 1943 had said 'the present litter of territories is entirely out of keeping with the modern world'.[289] Federations are, however, extravagant, expensive and complicated structures, requiring a number of propitious circumstances and therefore difficult to bring into being and sustain: in particular there are invariably too many fears of domination by one of the constituent elements. Nevertheless, the Labour government gave vigorous encouragement from 1948 to a federation of the West Indies, and in the same year set up the Malayan federation, and an East Africa High Commission as the first step in a possible federation of the East African territories. Then came the Central African Federation.[290] The Labour government thus gave its commitment to the federal panacea, bequeathing a number of problems to its successor. The West Indies, Southern Arabian, and Central African constructs failed.

---

[287] *The lion and the springbok*, pp. 168–97. Seretse's biographers and most other historians have been singularly reluctant to recognise the complexities of the situation as it presented itself to the British government. Almost alone in doing so are R. D. Pearce, ed., *Patrick Gordon Walker: political diaries 1937–1971* (1991), pp. 23–7, and Peter Fawcus, *Botswana: the road to independence* (Gaborone, 2000), pp. 211–12, where there is generous acknowledgement of my research, and attempts to set the record straight.

[288] Hyam, *The failure of South African expansion*, p. 2. For federalism in general, see K. C. Wheare, *Federal government* (1963).

[289] S. R. Ashton and S. E. Stockwell, eds., *Imperial policy and colonial practice, 1925–1945* (BDEEP, 1996), pt 1, p. 352, Cranborne to Attlee, 22 July 1943; Louis, *Imperialism at bay*, pp. 318–26.

[290] R. L. Watts, *New federations: experiments in the Commonwealth* (1966); Hyam and Henshaw, *The lion and the springbok*, ch. 9, 'Containing Afrikanerdom: the geopolitical origins of the Central African Federation'; P. V. Murphy, ed., *Central Africa* (BDEEP, 2005).

East Africa never got off the ground.[291] Federal Nigeria had a terrible civil war. Malaysia survived only two years in its original form, before Singapore became an independent state.

More generally, the experience of the Labour government in dealing with Asian and Arab (and to a lesser extent African) nationalism between 1945 and 1951 pointed to the necessity of recognising the limitations imposed on the exercise of continuing power by Britain, with its limited economic resources, overstretched defence requirements, and over-riding geopolitical need to win the cold war – fighting the new Russian imperialism by rooting out the vulnerable vestiges of the 'old colonial-ism'; of recognising the impossibility of holding on to territories and facilities without popular goodwill and local collaboration, and the difficulty of withholding equal concessions to similar states (especially if neighbours); of recognising the counter-productiveness of coercive methods, and the need to maintain policies of political advancement even while defeating rebels. Experience also suggested the necessity of recognising the importance of keeping the initiative, being one jump ahead of the nationalists, making timely and graceful concessions from a position of relative control, showing willingness to modify ideal time-tables in response to circumstances, being prepared to go faster rather than slower, avoiding giving too little and too late; of recognising the fun-damental good sense of deciding who the moderates were, then backing them and outmanoeuvring the 'extremists', and finding ways of turning nationalism to constructive account. Finally, it had become clear that all this was the only sure way to preserve the long-term friendship and good-will of former colonies on which future trading and strategic facilities and continuing membership of a multi-racial Commonwealth (and thus of the Western alliance) would ultimately depend.

Although these pragmatic policies operated over a wide spectrum of colonial problems, there was nothing in the way of an overall 'strategic plan' for the 'end of empire'. The nearest approach was J. S. Bennett's memorandum of 30 April 1947, written mainly under the influence of the economic crisis and impending independence for India.[292] He envisaged

---

[291] N. J. Westcott, 'Closer union and the future of East Africa, 1939–1948: a case-study in the "official mind of imperialism"', *JICH*, vol. 10 (1981), pp. 67–88; J. H. Proctor, 'The effort to federate East Africa', *Political Quarterly*, vol. 37 (1966), pp. 46–99; R. I. Rotberg, 'The federal movement in East and Central Africa, 1889–1953', *Journal of Commonwealth Political Studies*, vol. 2 (1964), pp. 141–60.

[292] CO 537/2057, no. 48, 30 April 1947, 'International aspects of colonial policy', *BDEEP*, pt 2, pp. 409–21 (no. 174); Kent, *British imperial strategy and the origins of the Cold War*, pp. 132–9, has a valuable discussion of Bennett's 'radical critique'; he has also discov-ered another like-minded civil servant, Edward Playfair in the Treasury (1934–56), who wrote, only three weeks after Bennett (18 May 1947), as follows: 'My basic thesis . . . is

winding up as rapidly as possible British commitments in the Middle East, North Africa, and South-East Asia, and then concentrating on African advancement as the core of British future activity – with American help. Bennett's memorandum was pigeonholed. The bureaucracy was ill-equipped to deal with such large issues.[293] But Bennett's outlook shows that there was indeed in theory an alternative and faster way of approaching decolonisation. Alternative, that is, to Labour's caution, a gradualism made essential because the government was determined to maintain as far as possible the structure of British global interests in the fight against communism. Labour ministers may well have been involved in a 'controlled colonial revolution', but their emphasis was distinctly on the control of the process.[294]

that any foreign policy of a great-power type is at present a very doubtful luxury for the UK . . . Strategic responsibilities should be off-loaded onto the US, or where this cannot be done re-examined to make sure they are really necessary . . . Assertion of political predominance seems positively dangerous' (p. 139). In retirement, at the time of the Falklands War, Bennett's private comment was, 'If only Attlee had had time to decolonise the Falklands, while nobody would have noticed!' (to the author, 20 June 1982).

[293] Partly for this reason, I have some reservations about the argument of W. R. Louis and R. E. Robinson, 'The imperialism of decolonisation', *JICH*, vol. 22 (1994), pp. 462–511, that the post-war British empire was 'transformed as part of the Anglo-American coalition . . . a once-British-empire modulated strategically into an Anglo-American field of influence . . . regenerated on American wealth and power'. The argument underestimates the extent to which the cold war was also a central concern for the British as well as the Americans (the British being said to be more concerned with perpetuating the empire in terms of the old 'Great Game').

[294] FO 371/107032, no. 1, Sir Gladwyn Jebb to FO, 12 January 1953.

3 'Rugged and tangled difficulties': the Churchill and Eden governments and the end of empire, 1951–56

A paradox confronts us. Although replete with major incident – the suppression of revolt in Malaya, Kenya, and Cyprus, suspension of the constitution in British Guiana, deportations of a Greek Cypriot archbishop and the kabaka of Buganda, self-government for the Sudan and Gold Coast, withdrawal from the Suez Canal Zone and Simon's Town naval base, and the climacteric disaster of the Suez Crisis – the Conservative governments led by Churchill and Eden have usually been seen as a period of quiescence in colonial policy-making,[1] and frequently criticised for failure to grapple with issues of international decline.[2] Churchill was seventy-seven years old and in uncertain health, his grip on business patchy. He abolished a number of useful cabinet committees, and wanted everything analysed on a single sheet of paper; his administration produced no major surveys of imperial problems. One historian has described his government as 'a farce of sometimes tragic

---

[1] D. Goldsworthy, '"Keeping change within bounds": aspects of colonial policy during the Churchill and Eden governments, 1951–1957', *JICH*, vol. 18 (1990), pp. 81–108. This influential article needs to be read in conjunction with Goldsworthy's edited volume in three parts, *The Conservative government and the end of empire, 1951–1957* (BDEEP, 1994). There were restrictions on the size of this volume, which were unfortunate, for there is not enough space to give the fuller treatment which the Suez Crisis and the problem of Cyprus both deserve, and the effect is to skew the emphasis away from these two predominant areas of concern. A good general account of this period is now available in F. Heinlein, *British government policy and decolonisation, 1945–1963: scrutinising the official mind* (2002), pp. 87–158. Heinlein's work is well researched (though it is not always easy to tell how far this is based on BDEEP documents rather than the original sources), and shows sound judgment. The recent volume of essays edited by the late Martin Lynn, *The British empire in the 1950s: retreat or revival?* (2006), takes its starting-point from the editor's assertion that 'the imperial policy of the Conservative governments of 1951–7 was even more positive and ambitious than suggested by Goldsworthy's celebrated description . . . a determined attempt at imperial reassertion' (p. 7). Overall, the volume does not seem to succeed in providing sustained support for this interpretation: the evidence for assertive 'revival' is patchy and ambiguous. I'd prefer to pitch my camp somewhere between Goldsworthy and Lynn.

[2] A. Adamthwaite, 'Overstretched and overstrung: Eden, the Foreign Office and the making of policy, 1951–1955', *International Affairs*, vol. 64 (1988), pp. 241–59, repr. in J. W. Young, ed., *The foreign policy of Churchill's peacetime administration, 1951–1955* (1988).

dimensions' followed by the 'fatal errors' of Eden's.[3] The dominant historical paradigm for colonial policy in these years is 'keeping change within bounds'; taking his cue from Goldsworthy's well-known phrase, L. J. Butler speaks of 'limiting change where this was feasible, rather than actively promoting it'.[4] Holland, too, discerns 'a mounting desire to try to rein in political advancement', with too much policy conducted in 'this surly spirit'.[5] Iain Macleod himself once wrote – though he is hardly a disinterested witness – that the years from 1955 were 'the locust years' when the government should have applied earlier in East and Central Africa the lessons from West Africa.[6] Nevertheless, colonial policy, under a succession of 'strong' secretaries of state, has also been described as one of the more successful aspects of Churchill's 'Indian summer' administration.[7]

It is true that there was an undertow of ministerial grumbling and even sceptical comment about colonial policy as recorded in the Cabinet minutes, anonymous in all but the case of the prime minister, but almost certainly orchestrated by Lord Salisbury (lord president of the Council, 1952–7). Other key ministers also have the reputation of being old-fashioned defenders of empire: Swinton, Lyttelton, Lennox-Boyd, and Anthony Head (War Office). It is, however, important to get this into perspective. Grumbling is quite different from policy-formation, and it was 'surly' precisely because it was not prevailing in decision-making. What stands out, in fact, is a high degree of ministerial pragmatism, and fundamental continuity of policy. In this regard, parallel to undue historical stress on the negative aspects of the Churchill and Eden governments, is an excessive overestimate of the Labour government's commitment to decolonisation. For whatever may have been the case in the transfer of power to India, Ceylon and Burma, Labour's policy elsewhere and especially in Africa was far more cautious. As we have seen, Labour ministers were essentially gradualists, who sought above all to remain in control of the process of granting self-government, a gradualism which was essential

---

[3] D. Reynolds, 'Eden the diplomatist, 1931–1956: Suezide of a statesman?' *History*, vol. 74 (1989), p. 72.

[4] L. J. Butler, *Britain and empire: adjusting to a post-imperial world* (2002), ch. 4, 'Change and control under Churchill and Eden, 1951–1957', pp. 113–14.

[5] R. Holland, review of D. Goldsworthy, ed., *The Conservative government and the end of empire, 1951–1957*, in *JICH* vol. 23 (1995), p. 544.

[6] Iain Macleod, 'Blundell's Kenya: review of "So rough a wind"', *The Spectator* (20 March 1964), review, p. 366.

[7] A. Seldon, *Churchill's Indian Summer: the Conservative government, 1951–1955* (1981), p. 372: a helpful volume. Sir Martin Gilbert's official biography of Churchill is useless on overseas policy for this period: Gilbert has little interest in the world outside Europe (defined – as by the Eurovision Song Contest – to include Israel) and America.

because they were determined to maintain as far as possible the structure of British global interests in the fight against communism.[8] Moreover, their chief official adviser on African affairs, the redoubtable Andrew Cohen, insisted on the importance of retaining the initiative against 'extremists' and of controlling nationalist movements, 'an orderly process in political advance'.[9]

Cohen told the new Conservative secretary of state, Oliver Lyttelton, that he thought it very desirable to have a formal government statement to the effect that colonial constitutional policy on the general lines of the Coalition and Labour governments would be continued; though it was primarily to reassure West Africa, it should not be confined to West Africa. Lyttelton accepted this as a good idea. He also agreed that a private telegram should go to the governor of the Gold Coast, Sir Charles Arden-Clarke, saying he had watched the political development there with sympathy and was anxious to establish friendly relations with Nkrumah. Lyttelton told Churchill he intended to allay fears about the continuity of colonial policy by saying the broad lines were above party and would not be changed; the Conservatives would aim at self-government within the Commonwealth, building up the required institutions as readily as circumstances would allow, with economic and social development to keep pace with political development; and this would apply in the less advanced as well as the more advanced colonies. The statement was made on 14 November 1951. Privately, Lyttelton believed it was necessary because 'we do not have the force to govern without the consent of the governed', and because 'with modern communications, that consent has to be engaged by open and candid discussion of policy' – consent is 'a plain necessity in the 1950s in multi-racial societies'.[10]

Continuity was tested first in the Sudan, which became the pioneer beneficiary of the transfer of power in British Africa. The change of government 'had no appreciable impact on the direction of Britain's Sudan policy', despite Churchill's attempts to slow down the pace of self-government. By 1956 Sudan was an independent republic.[11]

[8] R. Hyam, 'Africa and the Labour government, 1945–1951', *JICH*, vol.16 (1988), pp. 169 and 172, n. 54; repr. in A. N. Porter and R. Holland, eds., *Theory and practice in the history of European expansion overseas: essays in honour of R. E. Robinson* (1988).
[9] A. Cohen, *British policy in changing Africa* (1959), p. 37.
[10] CO 537/6696, no. 12, Lyttelton to prime minister, 7 November 1951, with minute by Cohen, 31 October 1951; Goldsworthy, *Conservative government*, pt 2, pp. 1–2 (nos. 173 and 174); [O. Lyttelton], *The memoirs of Lord Chandos* (1962), p. 352.
[11] D. H. Johnson, ed., *Sudan* (BDEEP, 1998), pt 1, intro., p. lxvii; W. R. Louis, 'The coming of independence in the Sudan', *JICH*, vol. 19 (1991), pp. 137–58; Goldsworthy, ed., *Conservative government*, pt 2, pp. 167–79 (nos. 254–61).

1. Personalities and other constraints

Churchill 'noted' rather than personally accepted Lyttelton's 'continuity' statement. He hoped the public would understand that they were forced to make constitutional concessions in the Gold Coast as 'the consequence of what was done before we became responsible'.[12] But as Roy Jenkins has observed, 'Churchill fulminated at the fringes of the legacy of the Labour government . . . but left the core of its work inviolate.'[13] Out of office he had denounced the banishment of Seretse Khama from the Bangwato chieftainship as 'a very disreputable transaction'; as prime minister he minuted, 'I do not see what else can be done'.[14] As distinct from Egyptian questions, he had little influence on colonial policy, though he kept an eye on South Africa. Above all, despite his historical baggage, there was no obstruction, no atavistic reassertion of imperiousness. During the anti-Mau Mau operations, Michael Blundell was surprised to find him keen to promote a conciliatory settlement. The prime minister objected to a proposal to make the possession of 'incendiary materials' punishable by up to fourteen years' imprisonment. ('Fourteen years for possession of a box of matches would not go down well'.)[15] There must be nothing like mass executions by the Kenyan courts, Churchill warned the Cabinet, because British public opinion would criticise anything resembling that.[16] His last recorded utterance in Cabinet on colonial problems showed him in pragmatic mode, and belies his reputation (unjustified) as a 'malignant racist' (see above pp. 40–2).[17] Concern had been expressed about the tensions caused throughout the Commonwealth by Indian communities, and by Indian government encouragement of opposition to colonial rule in multi-racial societies. Churchill, however, advised against any drastic action which might offend India, because they needed India's moderating influence and help with major international problems in Asia. Nor, he suggested, should it be assumed that Indian immigrant communities would prove an embarrassment: they might in some cases be 'a balancing factor'. Thus he steered the Cabinet to the conclusion that they should watch the problems

---

[12] PREM 11/1367, minute, 12 February 1952.
[13] R. Jenkins, 'Churchill; the government of 1951–1955', in R. Blake and W. R. Louis, eds., *Churchill* (Oxford, 1993), p. 499; see also R. Hyam, 'Churchill and the British empire', *ibid.*, pp. 167–86.   [14] PREM 11/1182, minute, 27 March 1952.
[15] M. Blundell, *So rough a wind: the Kenya memoirs* (1964), pp. 183–4; PREM 11/1424, f 166, Churchill to Lennox-Boyd, 5 December 1954.
[16] CAB 128/26/1, CC 33(53)1, 25 May 1953.
[17] The phrase is C. Thorne's in *Allies of a kind: The United States, Britain and the war against Japan, 1941–1945* (1978), p. 725. For an attempted refutation of this adverse opinion, see the discussion on 'racism', pp. 40–2 above.

carefully but avoid any precipitate action. Precisely the same policy was adopted with respect to West Indian immigration into Britain.[18]

This impression of Churchill as a conciliator of balanced judgment will surprise some readers. When we think of Churchill, we envisage perhaps a larger-than-life figure, with 'a dimension of depth',[19] but a man inherently combative, essentially journalistic, feasting on recycled phrases,[20] planning unsuccessful strategies by making sweeping movements with a cigar over misleading maps; a creature of moods, with an almost manic personality, prone to 'black dog' depression and exalted moments when he said he felt like Joan of Arc breathing spirit into other people; a man of dazzling extremes and dualities, reflected in the ease with which he could wear an old-fashioned Victorian frock-coat or his own ultra-modern version of the boiler-suit; the man who kept up the nation's morale during the war and defiantly proclaimed that he had not become the king's first minister in order to preside over the liquidation of the British empire. The truth is, though, that he was not all that interested in the empire, aside from its rhetorical potentialities, and as distinct from what he regarded as the larger and more portentous issues of international relations. Moreover, his official decisions about colonial issues were invariably geared towards compromise, reconciliation, and even-handed justice, however paternalistic the presentation might be. He was essentially a pragmatist who always asked what was feasible, and understood when to keep his private prejudices in check.

Anthony Eden was Churchill's heir-apparent. On coming into office as foreign secretary, Eden admitted he knew little of West Africa, but wondered whether things were 'moving at a pretty dangerous political gallop there lately'. Apart from this he left little record about his ideas on empire, but he was more progressive than some of his colleagues.[21] He had been dominions secretary for eight months in 1939–40, and if this did nothing else it at least gave him a healthy suspicion of Afrikaner politicians. He had then made a strong stand against the seductive magnetism of Smuts and his expansionist programme; and in 1956 he resented Strijdom's 'insulting' protests over the admission of Ghana to the Commonwealth: the South African prime minister was an 'obstinate, rude, purblind'

---

[18] CAB 128/28, CC 15(55)1, 17 February 1955.
[19] Isaiah Berlin, *Mr Churchill in 1940* (1949), p. 25.
[20] R. Hyam, 'Winston Churchill before 1914', *Historical Journal*, vol. 12, pp. 164–73; M. Weidhorn, 'Churchill the phrase-forger', *Quarterly Journal of Speech*, vol. 58 (1972), pp. 161–73.
[21] Goldsworthy, ed., *Conservative government*, pt 2, pp. xlvii and 2–3 (doc. no. 175, 23 December 1951); W. R. Louis, 'The dissolution of the British empire', in J. M. Brown and W. R. Louis, eds., *Oxford History of the British empire*, vol. IV: *The twentieth century* (Oxford, 1999), pp. 341–2.

bully.[22] He was critical of the Colonial Office's handling of the Cyprus problem. His chief contribution, along with Macmillan, was to 'internationalise' it, perhaps unavoidably, but this probably made it worse.

According to Churchill, Oliver Lyttelton's time as colonial secretary was 'a period of rugged and tangled difficulties', of 'grim and grave affairs' handled decisively.[23] By his own account, Lyttelton did not believe such issues could be untangled 'by any truckling to force, riots or clatter', but by being 'inflexible about law and order, and liberal and imaginative in giving these people a sense that we are going to play fair with them about self-government'.[24] In Hugh Fraser's judgment, Lyttelton's 'colonial theme' was simple: 'effective government and the orderly, gradual, but necessary progress towards self-government within the Commonwealth'.[25] Lyttelton set forth many of his major principles in a speech to the Imperial Defence College in January 1953.[26] Attempts to rule by force outraged specifically twentieth-century ideals, he said, and were very expensive and probably impossible. In any case, 'power perhaps no longer exists in our hands'. If these seemed platitudinous propositions, he continued, there were 'still some who have not observed in their preoccupations the march of time, and who are still to the right of Rudyard Kipling and Waldron Smithers,[27] who could not see that dominion over pine and palm had given way to new axioms of government by consent and grant of increased responsibility'. One of his favourite phrases was 'tempo is everything'. Perhaps Britain should have gone faster in the past, but equally perhaps in some, perhaps many, cases, they had now gone too far and too fast. The dilemma was clear: 'go too slow and you frustrate the beneficent forces. Go too quick and you bring Government into disrepute.' So – as he put it in retrospect – 'my whole mentality was that we must go as slow as we possibly could', all the time 'promising a bit and not letting pressure build up'. The difficulty was 'not to give the impression of being reactionary, when all we are trying to do is to be reasonably patient while the

[22] R. Hyam, *The failure of South African expansion, 1908–1948* (1972), pp. 167–71; R. Hyam and P. Henshaw, *The lion and the springbok: Britain and South Africa since the Boer War* (Cambridge, 2003), p. 257.
[23] Churchill Archives Centre: CHAN II/4/5, no. 46, Churchill to Lyttelton, 28 July 1954.
[24] CHAN II/4/10, p. 3, Lyttelton to Julian Amery, 10 August 1954.
[25] Hugh Fraser (parliamentary under-secretary of state at the CO, 1960–62) in *Dictionary of national biography, 1971–1980*, pp. 523–4.
[26] CHAN/II/4/17/12, no. 446, speeches, 23 January 1953; see also no. 495, 19 October 1953.
[27] Sir Waldron Smithers (1880–1954), MP for thirty years, representing Chislehurst, and then Orpington; knighted 1934. According to Macmillan, he 'fondly believed himself to be a good Tory', but was stuck in the mid-nineteenth century, a man 'for whom time does not merely stand still but if anything, runs backwards' (H. Macmillan, *Memoirs*, vol. III: *Tides of fortune, 1945–1955* (1969), pp. 303, 306).

political institutions and political classes are laboriously built up'. If these did not develop properly, Africans and others might be worse off under the evils of indigenous corruption than they had ever been under the tutelary power. It could not all be done 'by Tuesday week', especially in places where much the greater part of the population was illiterate. Whether you thought these experiments could succeed, 'depends largely on whether you slept well and have had a good dinner, or whether you have just come from luncheon in the House of Commons and are sloshing about the streets looking for a taxi'.[28]

Lyttelton came from, and in 1954 returned to, the world of business. He was an elite member of the Conservative 'magic circle', the son of a former secretary of state for the colonies, and a dominating figure with a crushing wit.[29] Lyttelton could be very tart with cloistered civil servants.[30] He freely admitted that he never knew where he was with Africans, and was more at ease with 'money-making Chinese'. Although he had enjoyed the job, his successor, Alan Lennox-Boyd, was, he conceded, more inter- ested in colonial politics than he had been.[31]

Lennox-Boyd had in fact specialised in colonial problems. Despite a basically right-wing position, he accepted that 'there is of course no stop- ping the process of devolution on which we are now well set' (1957).[32] But his classic gradualism ran up against testing challenges. He would prove to be pro-Eden and a die-hard in the Suez Crisis: 'I remain convinced that if Nasser wins, or even appears to win, we might as well as a government (and indeed as a country) go out of business.' Agreeing with Eden that it was a 'matter of life and death', he was ready to use 'any arguments from the Colonial angle which would be of any help'.[33] However, as Philip Murphy's biography shows, the conventional view of Lennox-Boyd as a negative influence and brake on colonial progress is wrong. He was remarkably pragmatic and well ahead of some of his colleagues in seeing the strength of colonial nationalism.[34] Even so, Lennox-Boyd suspected

[28] CHAN/II/4/16/3, ff 7–9, interview for records project, 27 Feb 1970; and 15/2, p. 48, 15 October 1959, letter to Iain Macleod.

[29] See generally S. J. Ball, *The guardsmen: Harold Macmillan, three friends, and the world they made* (2004).

[30] When Gorell Barnes drafted an apology after Lyttelton had divulged 'confidential' infor- mation, Lyttelton minuted, 'Dear, dear. Life is tougher than this and abject apologies of this kind should not be peppered about. At the worst this will be a 48-hour wonder and I really think we should be a trifle more robust' (CO 1015/107, no. 93, July 1952).

[31] CHAN II/4/16/3, interview, 27 February 1970, p. 35.

[32] R. Hyam and W. R. Louis, eds., *The Conservative government and the end of empire, 1957–1964* (BDEEP, 2000), pp. xlviii and 235 (no. 54, 28 May 1957).

[33] PREM 11/1152, 24 August 1956.

[34] P. V. Murphy, *Alan Lennox-Boyd: a biography* (1999), pp. viii–ix, 102–11; Hyam and Louis, *Conservative government*, pt 1, p. li.

Macmillan was relieved to replace him with Macleod, 'who did not share my preference for a gradual approach'.[35] Macmillan privately thought him 'nothing compared with Lyttelton', 'a great overgrown schoolboy, without judgment or profoundity'.[36] Knowledgeable rather than analytical, he had a vigorous, masterful manner, which stood him in good stead in his dealings with all kinds of people, from colonial governors to rent-boys.[37]

The third in this trio of tough guardians of imperial interests was Lord Swinton, the main holder in this period of the office of secretary of state for Commonwealth relations. As Philip Cunliffe-Lister, he had been colonial secretary from 1931 to 1935. Macmillan admired him greatly: 'the only really *efficient* and *experienced* politician in the government' (1952).[38] Very senior, clever, and versatile, he was forceful to the point of brutality. As far as policy was concerned, he accepted that even the 'lesser countries would continue in their progress towards "independence" (though I would hope at a less rapid rate than under the Socialist Government), however little they are really fitted for independence' (1953).[39] One of his recurring themes in speeches was that 'a united Commonwealth has a tremendous part to play – in partnership with America, in co-operation with Europe'.[40] Swinton greatly disliked

---

[35] A. H. M. Kirk-Greene, ed., *The transfer of power: the colonial administrator in the age of decolonisation: Proceedings of a symposium, March 1978* (Oxford, 1979), p. 8 (Lord Boyd of Merton).

[36] P. Catterall, ed., *The Macmillan diaries: the Cabinet years, 1951–1957* (2003), p. 310 (28 April 1954) and p. 410 (13 April 1955).

[37] Although married with three sons, Lennox-Boyd maintained a highly active homosexual lifestyle. He had a long-term partner in Major Alex Beattie of the Coldstream Guards (bodyguard to Churchill); he played the London rent-boy scene comprehensively, and miraculously escaped media exposure; and he had a dubious friendship with Feisal, an Iraqi boy-prince, making at least a couple of visits to Crown Prince Abdallah's home, and entertaining Prince Feisal in Europe. A photograph of the pretty boy, with Lennox-Boyd's inscription 'Here is the damsel I told you about', fell into the hands of a German journalist after the murder of the Iraqi royal family in the revolution of 1958, together with apparently 'incriminating correspondence' showing that he had supplied girls for the boy-prince. Incredibly, the journalist read 'damsel' literally, so it was in fact easy enough for Lennox-Boyd's lawyers to deflect the allegations: he was *not* having an affair with an Iraqi *princess!* The story did not reach the British press, but it was a close call, a scandal which could have eclipsed that of John Profumo. (CO 967/339, 'Allegations against Mr Lennox-Boyd in the German press, 1958'; Murphy, *Lennox-Boyd*, pp. 57, 81–2, 195 n. 3, 196 n. 23). There are explicit references to Lennox-Boyd and his careless behaviour in the diaries of James Lees-Milne: *Holy dread* (2001), pp. 78–9, 87–8, and in *Ancestral voices* (1975) as 'XB' – see *Beneath a waning moon* (2003). Finally, it should be noted that, in November 1958, Ian Harvey, under-secretary at the FO, was discovered in the act of sodomy with a guardsman in St James's Park; Macmillan was 'greatly distressed' by his fall from grace, 'a terrible thing' (Ball, *The guardsmen*, p. 340).

[38] Catterall, *Macmillan diaries*, p. 186 (27 September 1952), and p. 413 (5 April 1955: 'still . . . a very good and useful colleague').   [39] CAB 129/64, C(53)122, 8 April 1953.

[40] Churchill Archives Centre, SWIN II/6/19, speech at Harrogate, 25 June 1953.

Eden and predicted he would be the worst prime minister since Lord North.[41]

When we come to consider the constraints on policy-making, these were really of four kinds: the problems posed by relative decline, financial weakness, colonial nationalism, and international criticism.

First: from the outset, the chancellor of the Exchequer, R. A. Butler, was anxious about the economic situation. He called for an analysis of overseas interests to see where cuts and reductions might be made. Eden's response from the Foreign Office was a memorandum on 'British overseas obligations' (June 1952).[42] This bore a striking similarity to the survey conducted two years earlier for the Labour government.[43] It acknowledged that existing responsibilities were 'placing a burden on the country's economy which it is beyond the resources of this country to meet', but found 'strong arguments' against the abandonment of any major overseas commitments. It argued that the Russians would fill any vacuum thus created, and the balance of power would in consequence shift against the West; international status would damaged, and Britain's value as a partner and ally would diminish, and thus the special relations with the United States and the cohesion of the Commonwealth would both be undermined. Concurrent financial and economic benefits – perhaps even vital advantages – would be lost, and there would be the general but incalculable effect of the loss of prestige: 'once the prestige of a country has started to slide there is no knowing where it will stop', for the loss of prestige 'is wholly out of proportion to financial saving and might precipitate a scramble of claims'. Intriguingly, the single off-loading Eden was prepared to contemplate would be the Falkland Island Dependencies, but he stopped short of actually recommending this 'very minor relief'.[44] The Chiefs of Staff agreed: there was no possibility of reducing overseas commitments.[45] The only hope was to persuade the Americans to assume the real burdens in the Middle East and South-East Asia, 'while retaining for ourselves as much political control – and some prestige and world influence – as we can'.

[41] J. A. Cross, *Lord Swinton* (1982), p. 284; K. Robbins, 'Lister, Philip Cunliffe-, Earl of Swinton', *ODNB*, vol XXXIII, pp. 988–92.

[42] CAB 129/53, C(52)202, 18 June 1952; Goldsworthy, *Conservative government*, pt 1, pp. 4–12 (no. 3).

[43] Quoted in Heinlein, *British government policy and decolonisation, 1945–1963*, pp. 20–2.

[44] As prime minister, Eden continued to show signs of the 'what we have we hold' mentality: in a Cabinet discussion about the future of the New Hebrides Condominium, he raised a question of 'general importance': 'we might now have a changing interest in retaining direct control over some of the more isolated and unpopulated islands which might be required for purposes of scientific or military experiment . . . it would therefore be unwise to divest ourselves of direct control of all these remote and potentially useful places' (CAB 128/29, CM 38(55)5, 27 October 1955).

[45] CAB 129/55, C(52)316, 30 October 1952.

All post-war British governments, of course, had to grapple with the fact of declining power, but were reluctant to be driven into a policy of 'surrender'. Indeed, as defined by Sir Pierson Dixon (deputy under-secretary of state at the Foreign Office, 1950–54), 'the basic and funda-mental aim of British policy is to build upon lost power'. He was well aware that prestige was involved in this, 'what the rest of the world thinks of us'. But there was a dilemma: 'we are not physically strong enough to carry out policies needed if we are to retain our position in the world; if we show weakness, our position in the world diminishes with repercussions on our world-wide position'. The conclusion he was driven to was there-fore 'that we ought to make every conceivable effort to avoid a policy of surrender or near surrender' – and should persuade the Americans of the disaster which such a policy would entail for them as well as for Britain.[46]

None of this would have mattered quite so much as it did but for the cold war. Pivotal to the desire to remain a leading military power and maintain British influence in the world was the decision to produce the H-bomb. It would have a deterrent effect, but was also intended to ensure that Britain had enough influence on the USA to prevent the Americans plunging the world into war, 'either through a misguided intervention in Asia or in order to forestall an attack by Russia'.[47] The cold war also had a particular sphere. The Ministry of Defence advised at the end of 1954 that in the next few years 'our Colonial Empire in its varying stages of develop-ment is likely to be a vital "cold war" battleground'.[48] By the middle of 1956 some CO officials believed a communist subversion of Black Africa was 'now visibly preparing' in an area of 'great potential danger'.[49]

In 1956 Macmillan (chancellor of the Exchequer) and Monckton (minister of defence) took the initiative in calling for a high-level reap-praisal of defence policy. An officials' paper prepared for the Policy Review Committee then set up noted that 'the United Kingdom has ceased to be a first-class Power in material terms'; it had tried to do too much and should now concentrate on essentials such as maintaining the cohesion of the Commonwealth and getting the USA to shoulder more of the burden. The Middle East was identified as the most critical theatre politically, and 'non-military methods' should be developed for exerting and extending influence: Britain should rely on friendly

[46] FO 371/96920, no. 77, 23 January 1952; J. Kent, ed., *Egypt and the defence of the Middle East* (BDEEP, 1998), pt 2, *1949–1953*, pp. 320–1 (no. 263).

[47] CAB 128/27/2, CC 46(54)1 and 5, 6 July 1954; CC 48(54)2, 8 July, and CC 53(54)3, 26 July 1954.

[48] CAB 129/72, C(54)402, memo by Macmillan, 29 December 1954; Goldsworthy, *Conservative government*, pt 1, p. 58 (no. 18).

[49] Note by J. H. A. Watson, 15 May 1956, Goldsworthy, *Conservative government*, pt 1, p. 238 (no. 93).

co-operation rather than physical strength for the flow of oil. Eden himself noted on this submission: 'The main threat to our position and influence in the world is now political and economic rather than military . . . We must cut our coat according to our cloth. There is not much cloth . . .'.[50] The review fell victim to the Suez Crisis and was not completed.[51]

Secondly, Britain's ambitions were of course constrained by financial limitations. The Labour government had under the impact of the Korean War jacked up defence estimates to unsustainable levels. Butler warned: 'to remain a great power we must first of all have economic strength' and they were trying 'to do far more than our resources permit'.[52] That was in theory at any rate well understood. Nevertheless there was a severe shock in 1956 when the lack of funds was starkly revealed. A take-over bid for the Trinidad Oil Company from a Texas oil company had to be approved by the Cabinet because the government could not afford to buy it at £30 million and no British company would take it over. 'A new horror', Macmillan wrote in his diary, a 'major political crisis': 'I am accused of "selling out the empire" to the Yankees'.[53]

'Finance', observes Goldsworthy, 'was in some ways the greatest of all the contextual constraints on policy.'[54] Although Lyttelton had initially tried to get more money for colonial economic development by insisting that 'serious political consequences would flow if we cannot go further than we have been able to do so far',[55] there was little hope of realising this in practice. There were formidable problems in raising the level of the Colonial Development and Welfare allocations, let alone continuing metropolitan funding after independence. No other leading government department would support Colonial Office and Commonwealth Relations Office claims. The Treasury denied that its opposition to new expenditure was based on 'old maidish caution or on the love of obstructiveness for its own sake', but stemmed from 'the very critical position in which we now stand' (1956).[56] A fierce battle developed with Macmillan at the Exchequer. He warned Lennox-Boyd to expect a slowing down of

[50] CAB 134/1315, Colonial Policy Committee, memo 1 June, and minute 15 June 1956; Goldsworthy, *Conservative government*, pt 1, pp. 61–78, 91 (nos. 20, 21, and 25).
[51] The review-study was however renewed in 1957 on the initiative of Sir Norman Brook: Hyam and Louis, *Conservative government, 1957–1964*, pt 1, pp. 36–51 (nos. 4 and 5), the report on 'The position of the United Kingdom in world affairs' being published on 9 June 1958 (CAB 130/153, GEN 624/10).
[52] CAB 129/55, C(52)320, 3 October 1952; CAB 129/56, C(52)393, 5 November 1952; Goldsworthy, *Conservative government*, pt 1, pp. 31–6, 39–41 (nos. 9 and 11).
[53] Catterall, *Macmillan diaries*, pp. 563–5, June 1956.
[54] Goldsworthy, *Conservative government*, pt 1, p. xlvii, and pt 3, *Economic and social policies*, generally.   [55] CAB 129/48, C(51)22, 19 November 1951.
[56] Goldsworthy, *Conservative government*, pt 3, p. 96, to Lloyd (no. 384).

development expenditure. Lennox-Boyd protested that this would be 'a very serious step indeed', but Macmillan insisted that, serious or not, 'in our present economic situation serious and unpalatable steps may have to be taken', and he could not accept that the Colonial Office 'should in all circumstances be exempt from review' – an attitude which provides one of the roots of Macmillan's famous call in 1957 for a cost–benefit analysis of the colonies.[57] Meanwhile Lennox-Boyd got cross with Treasury attempts to by-pass the Colonial Policy Committee, as a means of pushing its cause on the new Overseas Civil Service scheme. He wrote an unusual minute: 'my answer to that is ROUND OBJECTS'. He won his point.[58]

The third constraint was colonial nationalism. 'The problem of nationalism' was the title of an important Foreign Office study-paper in 1952.[59] It acknowledged that economic weakness had led to a marked decline in British ability to influence other governments, at the same time as there had been a dynamic upsurge of nationalism, so British prestige and world power was being sapped. The use of force, it urged, to hold a large colony against its wishes was now inconceivable, and any intervention to protect British interests had practical limits set by world opinion and international law. Hence: 'in our highly vulnerable position our aim must be to minimise loss to ourselves and to establish new and fruitful relationships at all stages'. Encouraging a 'healthy nationalism' with which they could hope to deal was 'essential to our efforts to safeguard our position as a world Power and to the maintenance of a firm front against communist infiltration'. The most pertinent comment on this paper came from Trafford Smith in the Colonial Office. Force was out of date as a whole and not merely in the colonies, he wrote:

After what happened in Persia, and in present world conditions, does anyone really think that either occupation or intervention will ever be applied . . . our military and economic power will no longer stretch to meet our responsibilities, as would quickly be shown in the event of another world war. This leads to the conclusion that the important ways in which we should deal with nationalism, both inside and outside the Colonial sphere, are those which depend on publicity and propaganda, especially in the United States and the United Nations, and not by thinking in Edwardian terms of the use of military and economic power which we no longer possess.[60]

[57] Goldsworthy, pt 3, pp. 239–41 (nos. 432–4), 26 March–10 May 1956; pp. 244–5 (no. 437). For Macmillan see Hyam and Louis, *Conservative government 1957–1964*, pt 1, pp. 1–3 (no. 1, 28 January 1957).
[58] Minute 6 May 1956, Goldsworthy, *Conservative government*, pt 2, p. 134 (no. 240).
[59] CO 936/217; Goldsworthy, *ibid.*, pt 1, pp. 13–19 (no. 4).
[60] CO 936/217, minute by Trafford Smith, 22 July 1952; see also Goldsworthy *Conservative government*, pt 1, pp. 22–4 (no. 6), letter from Sir T. Lloyd to Sir W. Strang, 9 September 1952.

Just how significant nationalism was in promoting political advancement was disputed. Cohen believed that all experience, including Indian, had shown that 'self-government comes when the political pressure for it is so strong that it would be unwise to resist . . . the pace is determined far more by public pressure than by our own opinions of the stage when self-government should be granted'.[61] Successful co-operation with nationalists was a high priority, for not only was it the 'smoothest way of helping a country to self-government', but also the best bulwark against communism. Cohen hoped by 'skilful anticipation' to guide nationalist energies into 'constructive channels'; 'the most vital thing' in British African policy was 'to work in co-operation with Africans'.[62] Lyttelton was more sceptical about the centrality of nationalism: 'I do not, frankly, believe in the picture of an African nationalism spreading by contagion across the frontiers. Nationalism is a slow-growing plant, when there has never been as yet a nation.'[63]

The Afro-Asian Conference in Bandung in April 1955 brought together the representatives of twenty-nine countries, many of them only recently independent, and meeting for the first time, proclaiming their 'non-alignment'. This was a decisive event in the world context within which individual nationalist movements operated, a boost to their confidence. It focused attention on their potential, and it put colonial powers much more on the defensive.[64]

Finally, policy-making was constrained by the UN. British officials regarded the United Nations as a theatre for nationalist posturing. Much of this was thought to be retrogressive, a 'moral alibi' for pursuing selfish agendas. India seemed a particularly dangerous anti-colonial leader because so often reasonable and courteous. Cuba and the Philippines and several Latin American countries were equally vocal.[65] The great debate in Whitehall for many years was about how aggressive Britain should be at the United Nations. Some felt British achievements were not being publicised in case the anti-colonial camp seized on this as an implied admission of 'accountability'. The disadvantage was that of perpetuating 'the myth of colonialism' by encouraging the belief that there was something to hide, and obscuring 'the soundness and progressiveness being pursued uniformly, allowing for circumstances': the erosion of the British position directly served communist interests by militating against the emergence of

[61] CO 822/892, no. 8, to Lloyd, 12 January 1954; Goldsworthy, *Conservative government*, pt 2, p. 255 (no. 295).   [62] Cohen, *British policy in changing Africa*, pp. 60–2.

[63] Goldsworthy, *Conservative government*, pt 2, p. 235 n [1952].

[64] For the effect of Bandung in West Africa, see I. Wallerstein, *The road to independence: Ghana and the Ivory Coast* (Paris and The Hague, 1964), pp. 75–7.

[65] CO 936/56, no. 6 (1951).

stable and strong independent states. The Colonial Office became persuaded to be more forthcoming, as the Foreign Office and the Americans wanted. The Suez Crisis prevented immediate implementation of the new policy, because the atmosphere in the General Assembly was so hostile that anything said by Britain would only provoke a furious onslaught.[66] The issue was deferred for resolution under Macmillan's government.[67]

Gladwyn Jebb (the UK permanent representative at the United Nations) felt that the UN did more harm than good in the colonial sphere. Most members, he argued, were more interested in abolishing the whole colonial system than trying to improve it. They wanted instant revolution 'not a safety valve', pushing for interventions which would result in violent disintegration rather than furthering the British aim of 'a controlled revolution'.[68] Within the Colonial Office, the theory was, by 1954:

that the antipathy towards 'colonialism' among influential governments in the world is such that it is a concrete and important factor affecting HMG's ability to maintain satisfactory foreign relations and to achieve the objectives of UK foreign policy . . . . Anti-colonial opinion is so strong in international affairs that it has created a climate in which it is no longer possible for the CO and Colonial governments to pursue political, economic and social policies in the territories, without taking account of the repercussions of those policies on international opinion, since to do so may well, and often does, stimulate criticism and dissension which is fed back into the minds and attitudes of indigenous politicians and thus reacts on our ability to carry the policies themselves through.[69]

The truth of this analysis was to be increasingly demonstrated in the years to come, until there was a real fear of international criticism, the avoidance of which became almost the primary reason for speeding up transfers of power.[70]

---

[66] Goldsworthy, *Conservative government*, pt 1, p. 289 (no. 109) and pp. 408–13 (nos. 169–72), especially H. T. Bourdillon to I. T. M. Pink, 24 September 1956. See also D. Goldsworthy, 'Britain and the international critics of British colonialism, 1951–1956', *Journal of Commonwealth and Comparative Politics*, vol. 29 (1991), pp. 1–24.

[67] Hyam and Louis, *Conservative government, 1957–1964*, pt 1, pp. lxx–lxxii.

[68] FO 371/107032, no. 1, 12 January 1953.

[69] Minute by W. G. Wilson (International Relations Dept, CO), 6 October 1954, Goldsworthy, *Conservative government*, pt 1, p. 336 (no. 136).

[70] R. Hyam, 'The primacy of geopolitics: the dynamics of British imperial policy, 1763–1963', *JICH*, vol. 27 (1999), pp. 45–7, repr. in R. D. King and R. W. Kilson, eds., *The statecraft of British imperialism: essays in honour of Wm Roger Louis* (1999). J. Darwin in *Britain and decolonisation: the retreat from empire in the post-war world* (1988) and *The end of the British empire: the historical debate* (1991) gives full and judicious weight to international factors, as does Heinlein in *British government policy and decolonisation*. However, not all historians agree. Consider the following passage by Anthony Low: 'It has lately been suggested that international pressures and domestic constraints were at least as important as colonial pressures in propelling the West's former imperial powers to decolonise. This scarcely now seems tenable. For a start the reality of international pressures can be seriously overdrawn . . . International pressures upon colonial powers could be irritants.

2. The African colonies

(1) The Gold Coast

Political advancement in the Gold Coast was driven by a remarkable governor, Sir Charles Arden-Clarke. Privately, he was well aware that Conservative ministers thought he was going too far and too fast, 'but as no-one has been able to put forward an alternative policy that has the remotest prospect of working, I am being allowed to have my way'. The rate of political advance in Africa could not, he believed, be slowed down; 'you cannot slow down a flood – the best you can hope to do is to keep the torrent within its proper channel'.[71] After the nationalist leader Kwame Nkrumah had won 34 out of 38 seats in the election of February 1951, he was released from prison and became 'leader of government business'. Arden-Clarke decided that the dominant feature of the situation was the absence of any alternative to a Convention Peoples Party government – 'we have only one dog in our kennel' and that was Nkrumah. In Cohen's view too, Nkrumah was now more reliable than any alternative leader, and 'we may be forced, if we are to keep on good terms with the more responsible political leaders such as Mr Nkrumah and his immediate colleagues and not to force the Gold Coast government into the hands of extremists, to move more rapidly than ideally we

---

Footnote 70 (*cont.*)

But the ease with which for so long the Portuguese and Smith regimes brushed them aside seems to underline their ineffectiveness' ('The end of the British empire in Africa', in P. Gifford and W. R. Louis, eds., *Decolonisation and African independence* (Yale, 1988), pp. 33–72, repr. in Low, *Eclipse of empire: Commonwealth and decolonisation* (1993)). For Low, fundamentally, nationalist pressures were the primary determinant. But: (1) whatever may have been true of Asia before 1947, international pressures had developed into something more than 'mere irritants' in Africa after 1947, especially after international pressure propelled Libya into independence; (2) long-term and short-term considerations should not be confused – domestic constraints (the economy) were long-term factors, which cannot be treated as if they were just the short-term factors (those which might actually have *triggered* decisions); (3) it is also necessary to distinguish between intransigent powers or regimes (Portugal and Smith's Rhodesia) and the more liberal and persuadable (Britain and de Gaulle's France); (4) surely if Portugal and Smith held out for so long, does not this line of argument equally invalidate the supposed effectiveness of freedom fighters – what took them so long?; (5) there was no 'deep-seated desire to stay' in Africa. Low returned to the charge in his review of *The Oxford history of the British Empire*, criticising its contributors for 'missing' the importance of key nationalist struggles, 'downplaying of the nationalist thrust', which was in his opinion 'about 180 degrees mistaken', since these 'one-sided accounts' misrepresented decolonisation, which was a set of '*two-way* struggles': D. A. Low, 'Rule Britannia: subjects and empire in "The Oxford History of the British Empire"', *Modern Asian Studies*, vol. 36 (2002), pp. 498–9. If Low is right, one wonders how so many others have got it wrong!

[71] D. Rooney, *Sir Charles Arden-Clarke* (1982), letter to his mother, 19 April 1953, pp. 131–2.

should wish'. Should Nkrumah ask to become 'prime minister' it would be fatal to forfeit their goodwill 'by holding back excessively'.[72] The Labour secretary of state, James Griffiths, had accepted this advice. Then, in a crucial Cabinet paper in Febrary 1952, Lyttelton argued that further constitutional changes were inescapable. Nkrumah must be designated 'prime minister' for two main reasons. The first was that his Labour predecessor had pledged it, and this was morally binding. The second was that it was the clear advice of Arden-Clarke, and they could not reject the advice of 'so resolute, experienced and sagacious governor', who had handled Gold Coast constitutional development 'in a masterly fashion'. If this 'titular concession' were not made, it was doubtful if demands for full self-government and dominion status could now be held back, but making it gave a chance that a policy of 'ordered progress by successive stages' could be successfully pursued.[73] Aware that many ministers regarded the change of title as of more than symbolic significance – Nkrumah would, after all, become the first black African prime minister in the Commonwealth – in arguing the case at the Cabinet, Lyttelton said that 'though he could not welcome them, he was satisfied that, as things had gone so far, there was a definite balance of advantage in accepting' the governor's proposals. With only minor quibbling recorded, ministers approved the policy.[74]

A year later, Sir Charles Jeffries (joint deputy under-secretary of state) had little doubt that 'we can and should concede to the territory what can reasonably be described as "self-government"; indeed, it virtually exists already'.[75] So it was no great surprise when Arden-Clarke proposed an all-African cabinet, with wide responsibility for internal affairs, and over which the prime minister would normally preside. External affairs and defence remained reserved to Britain. In a Cabinet memorandum, Lyttelton once again repeated his mantra that these were the minimum concessions if they were to 'secure peaceful and orderly progress by successive stages'.[76] Elaborating this policy after the summer recess, he asked how were they to respond to the request for a declaration of readiness to grant full self-government within the Commonwealth? This was not itself 'repugnant to our general colonial policy', and Gold Coast ministers were steadily gaining in experience and offering enough evidence – 'at least

---

[72] CO 537/7181, minute 11 June 1951; R. Hyam, ed., *The Labour government and the end of empire, 1945–1951* (BDEEP, 1992), pt 3, pp. 73–4 (no. 226).

[73] CAB 129/49, C(52)28, 9 February 1952; R. Rathbone, ed., *Ghana* (BDEEP, 1992), pt 1, *1941–1952*, pp. 372–3 (no. 115).

[74] CAB 128/24, CC 16(52)6, 12 February 1952; Goldsworthy, *Conservative government*, pt 2, pp. 185–8 (nos. 265 and 266).

[75] CO 554/254, minute 9 February 1953; Goldsworthy, *Conservative government*, pt 2, pp. 188–9 (no. 267).   [76] CAB 129/60, C(53)154, 13 May 1953.

superficially' – of their ability to manage their own affairs.[77] It might be a far-reaching step, but no timetable was attached, and despite the possible objections, Lyttelton convinced the Cabinet that 'on balance we'd be well advised to meet this request'. The declaration would probably be made early in 1954 before the elections. Such changes were inescapable if there was to be continued settled government by consent, and they were not to forfeit the goodwill and African desire to retain the British connection.[78]

Nkrumah gained 72 out of 104 seats in June 1954, with 55 per cent of the vote. By October Lennox-Boyd was satisfied the African ministers had done well in many fields. They wanted independence by December 1956. Again, the line for the Cabinet was that by delaying unnecessarily 'we may forfeit the great goodwill which now exists and drive the Gold Coast out of the Commonwealth'.[79] This conclusion was based on Arden-Clarke's opinion that the political leaders had been emboldened by the pace of events in Sudan and Nigeria, and it was not worth trying to delay independence for a further year beyond August 1956, as any benefits 'would in no way compensate for the restiveness and the questioning attitude towards British motives which would inevitably develop'.[80] Once again, the officials felt it was not really possible to question his argument. The Colonial Office assessment was that despite doubts about the ability of the Gold Coast to make the grade as an independent country, it had been recognised for a long time 'that its possible administrative and political weaknesses are not likely by themselves to be the determining factor in any decision about independence'. Refusal might create worse conditions than its acceptance. But the implications were certainly wide: a healthy and stable independent Gold Coast 'would do much to strengthen the belief of other Colonial peoples and the rest of the world in our good faith and leadership', while a foundering Gold Coast 'would be a grievous set-back to our whole Colonial policy'.[81]

As the decolonisation process proceeded, however, an anti-Nkrumah party, the National Liberation Movement, developed from 1954, based on the kingdom of Ashanti. This had the effect of slowing down constitutional progress, by forcing the British government into demanding a third general election in 1956 as proof of the CPP's 'national legitimacy'.

---

[77] CAB 129/62, C(53)244, 3 September 1953; Goldsworthy, *Conservative government*, pt 2, pp. 202–4 (no. 275).
[78] CAB 128/26/2, CC 52(53)3, 16 September 1953; Rathbone, *Ghana*, pt 2, *1952–1957*, pp. 68–70, 72 (nos. 141 and 143).
[79] CAB 129/71, C(54)306, 4 October 1954; Rathbone, *Ghana*, pt 2, p. 97 (no. 154).
[80] CO 554/805, no. 1, to Gorell Barnes, 2 September 1954.
[81] CO 554/805, no. 4, minute by R. J. Vile, 23 September 1954 (Goldsworthy, *Conservative government*, pt 2, pp. 204–5, no. 276); and no. 5, Lloyd to Arden-Clarke, 1 October 1954.

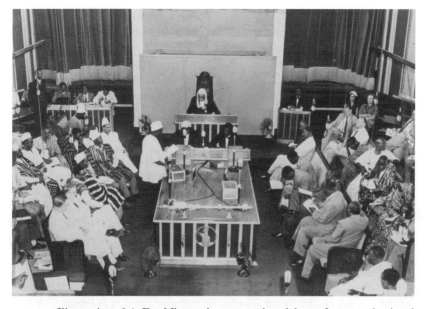

Illustration 3.1 Dr Nkrumah opens the debate for constitutional reforms, Gold Coast Legislative Assembly, 1953.
Kwame Nkrumah had recently become the first prime minister of the Gold Coast. The Speaker, Emmanuel Quist, OBE, presided over the debate; note the British parliamentary-style mace on the table. Proposals were submitted to the British government, and a new constitution was introduced in 1954 with an all-African Cabinet, and an enlarged legislature of 104 elected members. This was the constitution in force up to the date of independence in March 1957.

Nkrumah sought the help of Arden-Clarke in countering these intransigent forces in Ashanti and the Northern Territories, where, as a consequence, the governor became known as the 'CPP propaganda secretary'. In the election of July 1956 the CPP won 71 out of 104 seats, with 57 per cent of the vote, on a mere 50 per cent turnout. Nkrumah could thus demonstrate that he had a good working majority – it was in that sense a clear-cut result – rather than mass popular electoral support.[82]

As the deadline for independence approached in 1956, Arden-Clarke continued to urge the need for a 'cool head, but not cold feet'. Lennox-Boyd seemed to be 'doing a wobble and wanting to defer announcing a firm date for independence'.[83] The governor kept the pressure up until

[82] Rathbone, *Ghana*, pt 2, p. 107 (no. 160), Arden-Clarke to Lennox-Boyd, 22 December 1954, para. 6, and p. 291 (no. 240), 21 July 1956.
[83] Rooney, *Sir Charles Arden-Clarke*, p. 197 (September 1956).

Lennox-Boyd felt he had been left with no alternative. The announcement was made on 18 September, and on 6 March 1957 Ghana attained complete independence as a fully self-governing member of the Commonwealth. However, some dispiriting and pessimistic observations were received in the CRO about Arden-Clarke's 'short-sightedness', Nkrumah's 'double-facedness', and the 'immaturity and venality' of his lieutenants.[84]

(2) Nigeria

Developments in Nigeria to begin with followed those in the Gold Coast, 'the ever-increasing repercussions', as Governor Macpherson put it, of the 'persistent canker' of the political advance – 'actual or bogus' – of its neighbour.[85] Macpherson had 'gloomy forebodings' about the effect of establishing a 'prime minister' in the Gold Coast: it might be 'catastrophic', as similar changes might be demanded by the Action Group in the West and the NCNC (National Council of Nigeria and the Cameroons) in the East, thus sharpening the cleavage between the South and the more conservative Muslim North, imperilling all their carefully constructed hopes for a strong and united Nigeria, with moderate politicians working on 'reasonable, co-operative, albeit progressive lines'. He was sceptical that the speed of advance in the Gold Coast would actually work. He pleaded that, at the least, 'in weighing up the Gold Coast situation full thought will be given to the effects here . . . a slide in the Gold Coast will stack the dice against us in an almost impossible way'.[86]

Lyttelton was not persuaded. There was no alternative to advance in the Gold Coast. This might not make a difficult situation in Nigeria any easier, 'but by and large Nigeria's future will, I think, be settled by events in Nigeria'.[87] In March 1953 the southerners demanded 'dominion status' for Nigeria as a whole within three years. The northerners, however, would not support this, fearing that such rapid self-government would threaten their interests. An acute crisis ensued. This crisis forced a fundamentally new approach on the CO: a much faster timetable and a greater emphasis on regionalism. Lyttelton would agree to regional, but not federal, self-government by 1956. Both Macpherson and Lyttelton

[84] Rathbone, Ghana, pt 2, pp. 291–6, F. E. Cumming-Bruce to Sir G. Laithwaite (CRO), 21 July 1956.
[85] M. Lynn, ed., Nigeria (BDEEP, 2001), pt 1, Managing political reform, 1943–1953, Macpherson to Lloyd, 16 March 1953, pp. 520–2 (no. 182); Goldsworthy, pt 2, p. 191 (no. 269).
[86] CO 967/173, to Lloyd, 8 January 1952; Lynn, Nigeria, pt 1, pp. 432–5 (no. 152); Goldsworthy, pt 2, pp. 182–4 (no. 263).
[87] CAB 129/60, C(53)154, 13 May 1953; Lynn, Nigeria, pt 1, pp. 579–80 (no. 202).

were determined not 'to let the North down'; they feared its secession, a fear which has been highlighted by Lynn as 'the central determinant of British policy towards Nigeria after 1953'. A constitutional conference was held in London. Lyttelton secured a formula that HMG was 'not prepared to fix a definite date for self-government for Nigeria as a whole, the more so as the Northern delegation, representing over half the population of Nigeria, was unable to depart from its policy of self-government as soon as practicable'. Instead, self-government would be granted to those regions which desired it in 1956. There would be no self-government for Nigeria as a whole 'so long as any substantial part of it did not consider the time opportune'.[88] In August 1953 delegates from all Nigerian parties met in London to consider the problems of a new constitution, replacing Macpherson's of only two years before, which it was clear needed to be radically recast. When they reconvened in Lagos in January 1954, Lyttelton felt good progress was being made and the atmosphere had changed markedly in a few months. Indeed, it was, as he reported to Churchill, 'almost fabulous, and going ahead by leaps and bounds', the proof being, apparently, that they 'knock one another about much more than they knock us'. He was satisfied that the proposals meant 'we retain all the control over the subjects that matter to us' – police, judiciary and civil service were all effectively safeguarded; while more regional autonomy met the immediate aspirations of the politicians. He hoped the success of the conference would ensure political stabilisation for the next two-and-a-half years.[89] The new constitution came into being on 1 October 1954. It recognised to a limited extent the regional autonomy of regional governments for their internal administration and affairs. It carried regionalisation a stage further by declaring Nigeria a federation, with no right of secession. It also gave responsibilities to Nigerian ministers for the formulation and execution of policy. This reform checked the disarray into which the constituent parts of the country seemed to be falling. It was reckoned to be one of Lyttelton's best achievements.[90] Unity of Nigeria was the key aim; gaining time was the immediate objective, but the historical verdict can be that it was 'in no way a policy of scuttle'.[91]

---

[88] CAB 134/1551, CPC(57)27, May 1957, pt I, paras. 15–17; Hyam and Louis, eds, *Conservative government*, pt 1, pp. 5–6 (no. 2); M. Lynn, ' "We cannot let the North down": British policy and Nigeria in the 1950s', in M. Lynn, ed., *The British empire in the 1950s: retreat or revival?* (2006), pp. 144–63 – a valuable essay.

[89] PREM 11/1367, no. 305, Lyttelton to Churchill, 24 January 1954, and no. 303, telegram, 29 January 1954; Lynn, *Nigeria*, pt 2, pp. 93 and 95 (nos. 262 and 265).

[90] Hugh Fraser in *Dictionary of national biography, 1971–1980*, p. 524.

[91] Lynn, *Nigeria*, pt 1, intro. pp. lxi, lxviii, lxx.

(3) Kenya

The Mau Mau emergency persisted for most of the 1950s. Mainly confined to the Kikuyu, it was a multi-faceted, extremely complex movement, which passed through various phases, and affected different geographical areas differently. A strict definition may even be impossible.[92] It was an anti-colonial revolt, certainly, aiming to recover good land alienated to European settlers, and bringing together all manner of grievances, old and new, from missionary injunctions against clitoridectomy to government agrarian edicts about terracing. But far more Africans were killed – about 13,500 – than Europeans. In fact only thirty-two whites were murdered, fewer than those who died in traffic accidents in Nairobi between 1952 and 1956.[93] It is now usual to describe Mau Mau as in the main a Kikuyu civil war, a peasants' or squatters' revolt against the Kikuyu landed establishment, the have-nots against the haves, the young 'wild boys' against the moderate elders, 'loyalists' against dissidents. 'Regionally distinct and socially varied, they recruited squatters, townsmen, farmers and traders' (Lonsdale). The essential linkage fuelling the revolt was the alliance formed between rural radicals and the urban activists, the lawless youthful militants of 'outcast Nairobi'. Among the welter of clashing economic and material interests may also be discerned attempts to evoke alternative moralities and ways of thinking, the desire to rebuild the social order, a mythic Kikuyu communality.[94]

By the end of 1953 the British government was not unaware of the complexities, especially after a visit by Hugh Fraser (later a junior minister at the CO), who distinguished between the Kiambu-based political elite (the radical conservatives), the 'priestly hierarchy', and the Nairobi

---

[92] The historiography of Mau Mau is incomparably richer than for any other issue (Suez apart) covered by this chapter. Essential background includes D. W. Throup, *Economic and social origins of Mau Mau, 1945–1953* (1987), and 'The origins of Mau Mau', *African Affairs*, vol. 84 (1985), pp. 399–433; J. M. Lonsdale, 'Mau Maus of the mind: the making of Mau Mau and the remaking of Kenya', *Journal of African History* vol. 31 (1990), pp. 393–421 (together with a revised paper, 'Mau Maus of the mind revisited', 1993); 'The moral economy of Mau Mau', in B. Berman and J. Lonsdale, *Unhappy Valley: conflict in Kenya and Africa*, book 2: *Violence, and ethnicity* (Nairobi, Athens, Ohio, 1992), chs. 11 and 12, pp. 265–504, esp. pp. 402–5; E. S. Atieno Odhiambo and J. Lonsdale, ed., *Mau Mau and nationhood* (Nairobi, Athens, Ohio, 2003), esp. ch. 3: 'Authority, gender and violence', pp. 45–75, by Lonsdale. As to the meaning of 'Mau Mau', Lonsdale now favours the explication 'the greedy eaters', implying a protection racket (p. 60). For a recent assessment of the historiography, see M. Chege, 'Review article: Mau Mau rebellion fifty years on', *African Affairs*, vol. 103 (2004), pp. 123–36.   [93] B. Lapping, *End of empire* (1985), p. 425.

[94] F. Cooper, 'Mau Mau and the discourses of decolonisation', *Journal of African History*, vol. 29 (1988), pp. 313–20; D. Peterson in Atieno Odhiambo and J. Lonsdale, eds., *Mau Mau and nationhood*, pp. 85–6.

gangsters.[95] Sinister intelligence was also produced about Asian communists stirring the pot, or at least organising Nairobi taxi-drivers into useful logistical roles.[96] Mau Mau, the Europeans believed, was uniquely depraved, a psychotic, atavistic reversion to primitivism, and at best, nasty hooliganism – something in need of psychiatric interpretation,[97] and eventually of purgative 'rehabilitation'. Much of this perception was based on revulsion at its oathing ceremonies. Historiographical reassessment, however, which began with Nottingham and Rosberg, depicted it as an 'integral part of an ongoing, rationally conceived nationalist movement', using traditional oathing as a 'rationally conceived strategy'.[98] Since then, many historians have similarly played down the peculiar pathology of Mau Mau, but to say merely that in the forests, illiterate squatters 'developed a frontier culture',[99] is to indulge in an unusually massive obfuscation. Equally misleading is the notion of one army captain that this was just masturbatory pre-school stuff, 'no more than the antics of naughty schoolboys'.[100] In truth, Lyttelton was not so far off the mark when he described the Mau Mau oath as 'the most bestial, filthy and nauseating incantation which perverted minds can ever have brewed . . . I can recall no instance when I have felt the forces of evil to be so near and so strong.'[101] Oathing ceremonies took place deep in forest clearings by flickering bonfire-light, underneath arches of banana stems studded with sheep's eyes: all was naked, hypnotic, orgasmic. The *kaberichia* cocktail was drunk for the third oath (for there were several): a mixture of sacrificial sheep's blood, blood from a menstruating woman, and fresh semen, sometimes first ejaculated into the vagina of a dead sheep and then sucked out.[102] When husband and wife were sworn, they were bound together naked with the intestines of a goat. Single men might have intercourse with a sheep. There was a whole hierarchy of oaths, which related to rank and function, the most depraved being intended to gear men up for killing with *pangas* (heavy kitchen knives). From the fourth oath

---

[95] PREM 11/472, Lyttelton to Churchill, 9 October 1953.
[96] CO 822/447, weekly reports of the commissioner of police, 1952–3.
[97] J. C. Carothers, *The psychology of Mau Mau* (Nairobi, 1954).
[98] C. G. Rosberg and J. Nottingham, *The myth of 'Mau Mau': nationalism in Kenya* (New York, 1966), pp. xvii, 352.
[99] F. Furedi, *The Mau Mau war in perspective* (Nairobi and Ohio, 1989) p. 62. For a corrective, see D. L. Barnett and Karari Njama, *Mau Mau from within: autobiography and analysis of Kenya's peasant revolt* (1966), esp. pp. 122–6.
[100] Captain (later General Sir) Frank Kitson, quoted by John Lonsdale, 'Mau Maus of the mind: the making of Mau Mau and the remaking of Kenya', *Journal of African History*, vol. 31 (1990), p. 414.   [101] *Memoirs of Lord Chandos*, pp. 386, 394–7.
[101] *Memoirs of Lord Chandos*, pp. 386, 394–7.
[102] F. D. Corfield, Report: *Historical survey of the origins and growth of Mau Mau* (Cmnd 1030, 1960), pp. 84–5, 163–7.

onwards, British intelligence believed that naked women, usually prostitutes, were involved in the ceremony, often with a ram's penis or donkey's testicles placed in their vagina or anus, and then eased out by the candidate. From the fifth oath onwards putrified flesh, including human brains, was reportedly eaten. Drinking menstrual blood was supposed to characterise the sixth, mixed with urine for the eighth.[103]

The British regime in Kenya had been slow to grasp the seriousness of the stirrings, or perhaps it would be fairer to say that Governor Sir Philip Mitchell was over-complacent. At any rate, his successor, Sir Evelyn Baring, was quick to see how formidable Mau Mau was, and recommended the declaration of a state of emergency and the arrest of Jomo Kenyatta. These crucial recommendations were dated 9 and 10 October 1952. He was anxious to get control before 'bitter memories of bloodshed will bedevil all race relations', in the way that he had seen them do in South Africa. Lyttelton accepted this advice.[104] Mau Mau, he realised had 'gone both wider and deeper' than previously thought, and they must not relax until 'we are sure that the poison has been drawn off from the bloodstream of Kenya's life', not least by bringing 'a little discipline into the youth of Kenya, which they lack'.[105] Ironically the emergency and the arrest of Kenyatta only accelerated the momentum and forced many illiterate Kikuyu into their secret forest war. It was an anxious business. Lyttelton paid three visits to Kenya, Lennox-Boyd two.

Kenyatta was probably the most misunderstood nationalist leader in the history of British Africa. The governors and politicians were mistaken in identifying him as the evil and communist planner master-minding Mau Mau, the leader 'to darkness and death', in Sir Patrick Renison's notorious denunciation of 1960. It was a silly case of he '*must be*' its architect, because of his 'commanding personality',[106] even though Special Branch pointed out that there was no direct evidence to prove Kenyatta was behind it,[107] while a Colonial Office official admitted, 'I doubt if we shall ever know just how far Kenyatta is in close control of it.'[108] At the simplest level, the government was confusing the *symbol* of revolt with its

---

[103] CO 822/800, Special Branch reports, 1954. It should be noted that Professor Lonsdale is sceptical as to whether menstrual blood really could have been used, as that would associate oaths with sorcery.

[104] CO 822/444, nos. 1 and 4, Baring to Lyttelton, 9 and 10 October 1952; CAB 129/55, C(52)332, 13 October 1952; C. Douglas-Home, *Evelyn Baring: the last proconsul* (1978), pp. 227–9; Goldsworthy, *Conservative government*, pt 2, pp. 234–8 (no. 286).

[105] CAB 129/57, C(52)407, 14 November 1952.

[106] Corfield Report, *Historical survey*, pp. 51 and 219. Pending John Lonsdale's biographical study of Kenyatta, for a reliable assessment, see B. Berman, 'Kenyatta, Jomo', *ODNB*, vol. XXXI, pp. 338–41.   [107] CO 822/438, no. 48 (April 1952).

[108] CO 822/444, minute by P. Rogers, 3 October 1952.

architect – just as it had done with Dinuzulu in the Natal uprising of 1906. Historians now believe that Kenyatta had long ago lost control of developing Kikuyu militancy, and was even in some sense the *victim* of Mau Mau. He was in many ways compromised as a possible revolutionary leader by his life-style, which could be seen as too westernised. If he had regularly and unequivocally denounced the violence, his own life could have been in danger.[109]

Kenyatta was put on trial in a remote northern agricultural station at Kapenguria, quite deliberately chosen in order to reduce publicity and the likelihood of big demonstrations. A retired colonial judge, Ransley Thacker, QC, was appointed as presiding magistrate; he was regarded by the settlers as one of their own. A large ex-gratia payment was arranged for him by Baring so as to assist his re-location after the trial. Even more blatantly, the major prosecution witness, Rawson Macharia, was bribed with the promise of a safe conduct to the UK, with funding for a university course and the prospect of government employment on return. Thus did the British abet perjury. More honourably – in retrospect – the defending counsel, D. N. Pritt, QC, argued that there was no case to answer: 'It is the most childishly weak case made against any man in any important trial in the history of the British empire.' Kenyatta was cross-examined for ten days, and was careful not to incriminate his fellow-defendants, though Fred Kubai and Bildad Kaggia were genuinely involved in the organisation of Mau Mau. Thacker found all the defendants guilty, and pronounced the maximum sentence of seven years' hard labour. Remarkably, the Judicial Committee of the Privy Council refused leave to appeal – which seems a scandalous miscarriage of justice.[110]

By the end of the last week of 1954, there were 18,920 Africans held in custody in 176 different institutions. Eventually, at least 80,000 were detained – probably many more. Confessions were remorselessly

---

[109] Lapping, *End of empire*, p. 441, testimony of Fred Kubai, one of the 'real' (urban) leaders of Mau Mau.

[110] *Ibid.*, pp. 414–19. Lapping expresses surprise that Baring had not learnt more from his father Lord Cromer's experience in Egypt, where twenty years of patiently constructive effort had been undermined by the 'brutal mismanagement' of justice during the Dinshawai incident of 1906. A group of uniformed British officers had gone pigeon-shooting, without permission, trampling over village lands in the Nile delta. Angry at interference with their food supply, and after a woman had been accidentally shot, infuriated villagers made a concerted assault on the officers. The British reaction was hysterical, and the courts ordered several villagers to be flogged and four to be hanged. The public executions were perhaps carelessly carried out. Flora Shaw made a lonely protest in *The Times* about 'disgraceful . . . panic-stricken sentences', carried out with unseemly swiftness in order to minimise protest. The Dinshawai incident destroyed any possibility of a nationalist co-operation with British administration and entered deeply into Egyptian national mythology (P. J. Vatikiotis, *The modern history of Egypt* (1969), pp. 194–5).

pursued. Beatings and forced labour took place in detention camps. An extraordinary list of offences attracted the death penalty, including administering or freely taking the Mau Mau oath, possessing arms, ammunition, and explosives, or harbouring anyone likely to carry out acts 'prejudicial to public order'. The number of state executions exceeded the number ordered by the French in Algeria: in Kenya 1,090 Africans were hanged. Behind all this, the colonial power was in collusion with private feuding and score-settling, and involved in brutal malpractices and collective punishment of villages by police, troops, and 'loyalist' Kikuyu home-guards. There were repeated unfair verdicts in court, and an almost complete disregard for human rights,[111] although over a hundred policemen were prosecuted for abuses.

The overall plan of the government was to defeat terrorism[112] and simultaneously to defuse revolutionary potential by tackling some of its agrarian causes.[113] Throughout the emergency there was a concurrent programme of land reform, into which the government injected £5.7 million. This strategy of searching for the means of military victory while promoting economic and political reforms was applied from the lessons of defeating the communist insurgency in Malaya. On the political side, the key event was the 'Lyttelton constitution' of 1954, a notable achievement which finally ruled out self-government for the European community alone, giving one African and two Asians ministerial posts. By and large the objectives the government set itself were achieved. The revolt did not significantly spread to other African peoples, the settlers' political power was pruned back, and the Africans were given more representation in government – all as a result of the massive infusion of metropolitan power required to defeat Mau Mau.

[111] D. Anderson, *Histories of the hanged: Britain's dirty war in Kenya and the end of empire* (2004), and Caroline Elkins, *Britain's Gulag: the brutal end of empire in Kenya* (2005); see also S. Carruthers, 'Being beastly to Mau Mau', *Twentieth Century British History*, vol. 16, (2005), pp. 489–96. It is vitally important that these abuses are known and recorded, but I am uneasy about the abuse of language involved in describing Kenya as Britain's 'Gulag', and Elkins's repeated comparisons with Nazi concentration camps; Anderson is less strident, but even he labels a home-guard post as 'Kenya's Belsen'. In the mid-1950s, the real Gulag contained more than *2.5 million* enslaved prisoners, more than *thirty times* the number detained in Kenya, and much higher mortality rates. We need to make sure we have language left to denounce the worst evils of all, which is why we should try not to appropriate terms like Gulag, Belsen, Holocaust and Apartheid to describe anything but their transcendently dreadful originals.

[112] Churchill favoured the sort of aerial intimidation he had used in Iraq in 1921: CAB 131/13, D 4(53)4, Defence Committee meeting, 6 March 1953. It *was* used, in a very limited way.

[113] D. F. Gordon, 'Mau Mau and decolonisation', in W. R. Ochieng' and K. K. Janmohamed, eds., *Some perspectives on the Mau Mau movement*, special issue of *Kenya Historical Review*, vol. 5, no. 2 (1977), pp. 333–41.

(4) Uganda

An extraordinary crisis erupted here in 1953, centred on the kabaka of Buganda, Mutesa II.[114] He was alarmed by rumours of a possible East African federation. In any case he sought separate independence for Buganda with a fixed timetable. This was in direct conflict with the British objective of a self-governing unitary Uganda, in which Buganda was geographically the keystone: its secession it would be a bit like taking England out of the United Kingdom. The kabaka feared the down-grading of Buganda's special position. The government were worried that he might stir up the other three 'traditional' rulers. If he expressed these 'extreme nationalist' ideas publicly it seemed likely that this would lead to riots and bloodshed 'on such a scale that suppression would require substantial forces'. Lyttelton wondered if he should make a 'personal attempt' to 'bring him to his senses', for this was not the loyal co-operation with HMG legally enjoined by the Uganda Agreement of 1900.[115] As governor, Sir Andrew Cohen decided stern measures were required, nothing less than the deposition and deportation of the kabaka. According to Cohen, Mutesa was out to make trouble, and was 'in such an unreasonable frame of mind that he is prepared to embark on a trial of strength with the Protectorate Government . . . I am sure that he is a hopeless case'.[116] Few of the field officers supported Cohen on this. The Resident in Buganda, R. E. Stone, for example, was much more sympathetic to the kabaka, feeling that he was pulled in two directions at once by conflicting loyalties, and managing a difficult situation well.[117] Lyttelton had a hard decision to make. In effect he had to choose between sacking the kabaka and sacking the governor. It was always a drastic step to dismiss a governor, as it seemed to undermine imperial authority; there was the added complication that Cohen was the darling of the Labour Party establishment.[118] So although he had the gravest doubts, Lyttelton represented the kabaka to his colleagues

---

[114] J. Iliffe, *Honour in African history* (Cambridge, 2005), pp. 319–21 Older and longer accounts include D. E. Apter, *The political kingdom in Uganda: a study in bureaucratic nationalism* (Princeton, NJ, 1961), pp. 271–300; D. A. Low, *Buganda in modern history* (1971), pp. 107–30; D. A. Low and R. C. Pratt, *Buganda and British overrule, 1900–1955: two studies* (Oxford, 1960), appendix I to pt 2, 'The crisis of 1953–1955', pp. 322–33; Seldon, *Churchill's Indian summer*, pp. 365–8 is also useful.

[115] CAB 129/64, C(53)324, 18 November 1953; Goldsworthy, *Conservative government*, pt 2, pp. 250–4 (nos. 293–4).

[116] CO 822/598, no. 8, Cohen to Lyttelton, 7 November 1953.

[117] Kirk-Greene, *The transfer of power: the colonial administrator*, pp. 111–23; see also Lord Boyd's remarks at p. 57.

[118] CHAN II/4/16/3, interview 27 February 1970, f. 50; *Memoirs of Lord Chandos*, pp. 418–21.

Illustration 3.2 E. F. Mutesa II, kabaka of Buganda.
The kabaka studied at Magdalene College, Cambridge, from 1945 to 1948, and is shown here wearing his college tie. He was popularly known as 'King Freddie', which neatly sums up his ambivalent position poised between tradition and modernity, acting both as the debonnaire perfect English gentleman and as the inflexible upholder of African monarchy and court rituals. After acting as President of Uganda, he died in exile in 1969, aged only forty-five.

as an intransigent weakling, in defiance of HMG, who should be removed.[119]

There was uproar in Buganda. A state of emergency was declared. Mutesa's official sister died of shock. Even Mau Mau took up the kabaka's complaint. The legality of the action was tested in court. Professor Keith Hancock led an independent inquiry, retaining his credibility despite the fact of being known as 'Wancocko' (meaning 'chicken' in Luganda, which has no 'H'). A year passed. Cohen changed his mind. After a visit, Lennox-Boyd felt the balance of arguments for relenting, 'always close, had definitely shifted to allowing the kabaka's return', on strict conditions which would ensure his 'constitutionality'. There were obvious dangers of damaging British prestige, compromising the exclusion of Seretse in Bechuanaland, of seeming to be weak, and of encouraging 'the worst elements'. But ironically the court ruling was that despite the kabaka's having been indeed 'disloyal', and his deposition therefore justified, it was HMG who had technically acted in breach of the 1900 Agreement. This ruling the government decided to accept. It was politically important not to prolong the uncertainty by an appeal, and of course it enabled them to reinstate the kabaka without seeming to bow to political pressure. Ministers therefore agreed to present this new decision as a consequence of a legal judgment, not as a reversal of policy ('no change of policy, but a change of situation').[120]

Nevertheless, by underestimating the strength of Bagandan national pride, traditional loyalties and sense of honour, and by deporting the kabaka in 1953 only to restore him a year later, Cohen was strongly criticised, even though prepared to be apologetic.[121] It seemed uncharacteristically naive. Perhaps he was right to insist on challenging Buganda separatism. But equally it could be argued that Mutesa showed just as much courage in bringing his obstreperous people back into the fold. Without him this might have been impossible.

Essentially this controversy, between British prestige and Ganda honour, boiled down to a matter of personalities. Although politically solid in their loyalty, the Baganda did not regard Mutesa as an entirely popular figure, on account of his personal life, his 'impossible private life' as Cohen called it. Lyttelton believed him to be a 'rascal of the first order', who had practised 'every perversity' from incest with his sister to homosexuality,

---

[119] CAB 128/26/2, CC 68(53)7, 19 November 1953; Goldsworthy, *Conservative government*, pt 2, pp. 253–4 (no. 294).

[120] CAB 129/70, C(54)287, 9 September 1954; CAB 129/71, C(54)317, 20 October 1954, and C(54)336, 9 November 1954; CAB 128/27/2, CC 69(54)4, 22 October 1954, and CC 74(54)6, 10 November 1954.

[121] R. E. Robinson in *Dictionary of National Biography, 1961–1970*, pp. 227–9.

and every indulgence from drink to drugs. Mutesa was also monumentally stubborn and opinionated.[122] His personal relations with Cohen as governor were made more difficult because Cohen was a left-winger who regarded the kabakaship as a precious kind of royalty with no special virtue apart from a dubious tradition. He wanted the kabaka side-lined and Uganda 'modernised'. Cohen had no real sympathy for Mutesa's predicament, which involved having to prove to his people that he was not a British agent, or even a traitor, or at least to keep abreast of popular discontent. For his part, Mutesa felt Cohen constantly berated him and was behaving liked an upstart emperor to his undoubted regality (he was the thirty-fifth kabaka), and yet an ursine figure, sloppily dressed, both preposterous and ill-mannered ('it is bad manners and I'm not having it').

There was a little-known but considerable back-history to their relationship. Cohen had superintended Mutesa's Cambridge education. He had chosen Magdalene College for him, partly because when at Trinity College one of his closest friends had been there, and both of them admired it, and partly because one of the most influential tutors was the brother of George Turner, the principal of Makerere College where Mutesa had his secondary education. Cohen smoothed the path for an *ad hominem* Cambridge course, mostly in History (one of his supervisors was the fledgling African historian, J. D. Fage); he negotiated for him an honorary captaincy in the Grenadier Guards (of which Mutesa was very proud); he exercised considerable control over his vacation activities and travels. Generally Mutesa was under close scrutiny, protection, and control from the Colonial Office. Officials felt things had gone well for him as a student, though there was some headshaking about his extravagance.[123] In the light of this, and only five years later, Cohen had, no doubt rather stupidly, expected as governor to exercise a similar paternalistic control. Hell, it seems, hath no fury like a mentor scorned. Although he had welcomed Cohen's appointment, Mutesa found that 'any stored-up cordiality from the past ran out swiftly . . . our relationship deteriorated fairly rapidly from mild friendship through polite restraint to open enmity . . . good fellowship drained away'. On the other hand, the kabaka continued to get on well both with Lyttelton and Lennox-Boyd.[124]

[122] CHAN II/4/16/3, ff. 23–4. Iain Macleod thought nobody else he ever had to deal with 'came anywhere near the Kabaka for sheer blind, pig-headed obstinacy': R. Shepherd, *Iain Macleod* (1994), pp. 245–6.

[123] There are several Colonial Office files on the education of the kabaka: CO 537/2110, 1507, 3595, 3596, and 3597. There is further relevant material in Magdalene College Archives, F/OMP/IV/9/i. This material is summarised in Sean Cooper, 'Educating the Kabaka: Magdalene, Buganda and the empire, 1945–1948', *Magdalene College Magazine*, no. 34 (1989–90), pp. 39–44.

[124] The Kabaka of Buganda, *The desecration of my kingdom* (1967), pp. 113–26, 135.

(5) Tanganyika

Sir Edward Twining was a decidedly old-style governor, so it was a surprise ('a very strange change of view', commented Lennox-Boyd) when, towards the end of 1956, after nearly seven years in office, he proposed a reorientation of policy. This he based on an assessment that European settler leadership (never as strong in Tanganyika as in Kenya) was hopeless, politically bankrupt, and on its way out. There were, argued Twining caustically, too many Germans and Greeks, and recently the government had not been able to recruit any decent British farmers, only 'BBC violinists, bar-tenders and hairdressers'. The Asians were also useless. Government therefore should move towards a transition to African leadership, and attempt to 'capture' Julius Nyerere – if he was 'available' – since he seemed to be more sensible and reasonable than West African leaders. At any rate, it would be a fatal mistake, he concluded, to let Nyerere become a disruptive dissident. Now: to shift away from the concept of a multi-racial society with an enduring core of European leadership, to an African state with the European prop gradually removed, would be a big step, as officials in London were well aware. They pondered the issue for several weeks before passing it up to Lennox-Boyd, who decided to leave his consideration of it until he was relaxed and had plenty of time. And so he came to write his minute about it ten days later, on 25 December 1956. On the internal evidence of its shaky and near-illiterate scrawl, we may conclude that it was written after a good Christmas dinner. He agreed that the governor should in principle be authorised to attempt to 'gather Nyerere into the fold', though he had some queries about it. His officials were not entirely of one mind about possible public recognition of Tanganyika's future as an African state, but agreed it would be sensible to select the right sort of 'moderate' Africans for grooming. Among the officials, Bourdillon was the most enthusiastic: 'We must not of course allow the UN tail to wag the Tanganyika dog, but unless we keep the Trusteeship Council reasonably sweet during the difficult years ahead it may be able to cause quite a lot of trouble which will adversely affect orderly progress in Tanganyika.' From this point of view he felt it was most important 'that we should be able, while resisting pressure for "government by timetable", to give evidence of steady and systematic constitutional advance'. It would, he added, 'be fatal if Mr Nyerere is allowed to become a dissident and disruptive voice speaking with the support of the UN'.[125]

---

[125] CO 822/912, no. 26, Twining to Gorell Barnes, 12 November 1956, with minutes by Gorell Barnes, Mathieson, Sir John Macpherson, 29 November–11 December, by Bourdillon, 12 December 1956, and Lennox-Boyd, 25 December 1956. The reply (no. 30) was sent from Mathieson to the governor, 28 December 1956; Goldsworthy, *Conservative government*, pt 2, pp. 264–78 (nos. 298–9).

Nothing very dramatic emerged from this initiative. Twining did not really know how to handle Nyerere, and was too easily upset by his attitudes and opinions. Nyerere did not warm to Twining. However, the old idea of an equal three-way split between Europeans, Africans, and Asians, regardless of the actual population proportions, was soon abandoned. In 1957 the official members of the Executive Council were redesignated ministers, and assistant ministers – four Africans, one European, and one Asian – were appointed to the Legislative Council.[126]

3. Other territories

(1) Malaya and Singapore

One of Lyttelton's first decisions on taking office was to give priority to visiting Malaya, seeking a stronger direction of the campaign to restore law and order, without raising the costs of the military commitment. Churchill agreed.[127] Malaya was perceived not just as a local problem, but as only one part of a world-wide struggle against communism.[128] Lyttelton's chief contribution was the appointment of General Templer, a strong, energetic but highly controversial figure. Templer had a central and dynamic role in breaking the deadlock and turning the tide in Britain's favour by his parallel strategy of 'the shooting side' and a civilian campaign to win 'hearts and minds', a refrain with which he is associated, though he did not invent it. Intelligence-gathering significantly improved. Almost equally important was Lyttelton's choice of a second-in-command, the brilliant Donald MacGillivray.[129] Malaya was rescued from potentially terminal disarray. However, despite these appointments, the change of government, and the changes in the war on terror, 'the underlying political objectives remained unchanged' (Harper). Early in 1952 the directive to Templer clearly set out the objective of a fully self-governing country, 'in due course' (which perhaps meant 1960),

[126] J. Iliffe, *A modern history of Tanganyika* (Cambridge, 1979), and 'TANU and the Colonial Office', *Tanzania Zamani: a Journal of Historical Research and Writing*, vol. 3, no. 2 (1997, Historical Association of Tanzania, Dar es Salaam), pp. 1–62; D. Bates, *A gust of plumes: a biography of Lord Twining of Godalming and Tanganyika* (1972), pp. 276–9.

[127] PREM 11/122, Lyttelton to Churchill, 30 October 1951, and CAB/128 23, CC 5(51)3, 8 November, and CC 10(51), 22 November 1951; A. J. Stockwell, ed., *Malaya* (BDEEP, 1995), pt 2; *The communist insurrection, 1948–1953*, pp. 315–16 (nos. 248 and 253); Goldsworthy, *Conservative government*, pt 2, pp. 373–4 (no. 342).

[128] CAB 128/24, CC 7(52)2, 25 January 1952.

[129] Simon C. Smith, 'General Templer and counter-insurgency in Malaya: hearts and minds, intelligence and propaganda', *Intelligence and National Security*, vol. 16 (2001), pp. 60–78; Ball, *The guardsmen*, pp. 297–300.

'a united Malayan nation' with a 'broader citizenship'.[130] By the end of
1953 the communist insurgency was in retreat militarily. From 1954,
Tunku Abdul Rahman presided over an Alliance made up of UMNO, the
Malayan Chinese Association, and the Malayan Indian Congress, and
was demanding *merdeka* (independence), partly motivated by the
Ghanaian example. By mid-1955 the pressure for a rapid advance
towards self-government had mounted. Lennox-Boyd was anxious that
'we must keep the initiative' and negotiate before nationalism gained
further momentum.[131] In August 1955 the Cabinet decided it should not
be induced by fear of adverse world opinion to move more rapidly
towards the grant of full internal self-government 'than was in the interests of the people themselves'. But so long as responsibility for defence,
internal security and foreign relations remained in British hands, 'it was
not to our advantage to delay transfer of full responsibility in other
matters'.[132] The Alliance won a landslide election victory, gaining fifty-
one out of fifty-two seats.

The Tunku as chief minister showed himself to be a shrewd consensus politician. He was determined now to end the Emergency, going
into the forest to meet the communist leader Chin Peng at Baling, a
village in northern Kedah, in December 1955. The British were nervous
about these talks, but the Tunku proved himself capable of handling
Chin Peng firmly, refusing to compromise with him, and insisting on
surrender without any discussion of terms, making it clear that there
would be no division of Malaya like Korea or Vietnam. The Baling talks
completed the Tunku's transformation 'from agitator to statesman'.
The British government felt much easier about the Alliance demand for
independence. Its new-found confidence in the Tunku was crucial to
the acceleration of decolonisation which ensued.[133] Lennox-Boyd
argued in favour of far-reaching concessions, going 'a very long way', in
order to establish goodwill and strengthen the commitment of the
politicians to fight communism. To wait any longer might even be
dangerous:

Sooner rather than later we should have to concede in the most unhappy circumstances what we could earlier have granted with an air of generosity, the

---

[130] T. N. Harper, *The end of empire and the making of Malaya* (Cambridge, 1999) p. 310; A. J.
Stockwell, 'British imperial policy and decolonisation in Malaya, 1942–1952', *JICH*,
vol. 13 (1984). pp. 82–3, and Stockwell, *Malaya*, pt 2, pp. 372–3 (no. 268), 2 February
1952.

[131] CAB 129/76, CP(55)81, 20 July 1955; Stockwell, ed, *Malaya*, pt 3: *The Alliance route to
independence, 1953–1957*, pp. 133–6 (no. 356).

[132] CAB 128/29, CM 28(55)3, 15 August 1955.

[133] A. J. Stockwell, 'Abdul Rahman', *ODNB*, vol. I, pp. 53–4; *Malaya*, pt 1, p. lxxvi and pt 3,
p. 226.

support of world opinion, and the promise of loyal co-operation. The tide is still flowing in our direction, and we can still ride it; but the ebb is close at hand and if we do not make this our moment of decision we shall have lost the power to decide. Not far off the French have shown us what can happen if such a tide is missed.

Accordingly, they must 'recognise the inevitability of the advance to full self-government before very long'.[134] Attlee himself could not have put it better.

MacDonald as commissioner-general presented similar arguments to an audience of business leaders, the Singapore Rotary Club, urging them to support an orderly transfer of power as a check to 'violent Communism':

This is a revolutionary time in Asia. Right across the continent an upsurge of Nationalist feeling, like a tidal wave, has been sweeping away foreign governments . . . If the government did not advocate [self-government and at a later date independence] the support of the people would pass to the forces of violence, of destruction and of chaos in these territories . . . Making themselves the champions of these legitimate aspirations of the people . . . is the best assurance that the process of change in Malaya shall continue to be peaceful and constitutional as well as radical, causing the least possible upset to the economy and security of the country.[135]

The Cabinet debated whether they should seek formal 'appropriate' guarantees to safeguard economic interests. The line was, if Malays aim at self-government they must pay their own way, but if, as seemed more likely, Britain had to give financial assistance, then the government should try to safeguard its commercial interests, because 'our financial stake in the Federation was one of the buttresses of the sterling area'.[136] However, the British business community was not asking for binding undertakings, so simple assurances were accepted.[137]

Early in 1956 a conference in London laid out the basis for independence in 1957. What the British government had done between 1948 and 1957 was to forge a unified economic and political administration, an impressive infrastructure, and a strong authoritarian state-system, all of which proved vital to the successor regime. Britain defeated the insurgents by a massive effort, and kept communal ideological cleavages under

---

[134] Stockwell, *Malaya*, pt 3, pp. 233–41 (no. 394), memo by Lennox-Boyd, 7 January 1956.
[135] N. J. White, *Decolonisation: the British experience since 1945* (1999), pp. 35, and 115.
[136] CAB 128/29, CM 25(55)8, 21 July 1955; Stockwell, *Malaya*, pt 3, pp. 138–9 (no. 358); Goldsworthy, ed., *Conservative government*, pt 2, pp. 383–4 (no. 349).
[137] CAB 128/30/1, CM 4(56)3, 17 January and CM 9(56)7, 8 February 1956; Stockwell, *Malaya*, pt 3, pp. 252–3 and 259–60 (nos, 400 and 401); Goldsworthy, *Conservative government*, pt 2, pp. 389–91 (nos. 353 and 354); N. White, 'Government and business divided: Malaya, 1945–1957' *JICH*, vol. 22 (1994), pp. 251–74.

control. This was a major contribution of the colonial state to future independent state-building.[138]

Singapore was treated in a way which contrasted sharply with Malaya. The 'city of the lion' ('*Singa pura*', Sanskrit) was a fortress colony, and control of the base and the dockyard was considered vital to Far Eastern strategy, to the defence of Malaya, Australia, New Zealand, and Fiji, and the provision of reinforcements for Hong Kong; it was also thought to be helping to discourage Indonesian aggression. There were 32,000 troops stationed in Singapore and no obvious alternative location in the region. After liberation in 1945 Singapore was detached constitutionally from the mainland. Limited internal self-government was introduced in February 1955, with David Marshall (a local-born Jewish lawyer who led the Labour Front) as the first 'chief minister', heading a weak coalition. He was supported by the British government, fearful that a pro-communist government would otherwise take over. In January 1955 Lennox-Boyd decided Singapore could not go to full self-government at the same time as Malaya, because Britain must remain in complete control of internal security (as well as external). Marshall asked for more, and Governor Sir R. B. Black was sympathetic.[139] However, in March–April 1956 Lennox-Boyd asserted categorically to his Cabinet colleagues, after consultation with the Chiefs of Staff, in two hard-hitting memoranda, that Britain could not concede full independence to Singapore: it was 'a delusion', and Singapore could not be a viable state on its own. The over-riding consideration was to see that it did not become prey to the serious threat of communist subversion, and that its port and 'incomparable naval facilities' remained available for the free world, as a vital part of its defence system. (The Chiefs of Staff declared the naval base to be increasing in value.) Singapore must not become 'an independent Chinese outpost at the strategic heart of South-East Asia'. Lennox-Boyd recognised that 'over the last ten years Asian nationalism has created such pressures that it would be idle to think we could control them at will', and Singapore was as politically conscious as anywhere in Asia: 'All political parties are caught up in the flood-tide of Asian nationalism and anti-colonialism' and were demanding *merdeka* (independence). This was 'common form in the mid-twentieth century' and part of 'an inevitable historical process'. But what made things difficult in Singapore was the precarious

---

[138] Wang Gundwu, review of Harper, *The end of empire and the making of Malaya*, in *Modern Asian Studies*, vol. 37 (2003), pp. 765–8; W. R. Louis, 'The dissolution of the British empire in the era of Vietnam', *American Historical Review*, vol. 107 (2002), pp. 6–10.

[139] James Low, 'Kept in position: the Labour Front-Alliance government of chief minister David Marshall in Singapore, April 1955–June 1956', *Journal of Southeast Asian Studies*, vol. 35 (2004), pp. 41–64.

balance of political parties, coupled with 'the levantine approach and almost psychopathic personality' of Marshall. Nevertheless, if refusal of independence led to his resignation, and then to the suspension of the constitution, they must ensure that the British case 'before the world is as solidly based as possible'. A row could not be avoided, but it ought to be 'so contrived that it does the least damage to our cause with world opinion generally, with middle-of-the-road opinion in this country and in particular opinion in Asian countries'. For good measure Lennox-Boyd added that 'Singapore has all the elements of another "Cyprus" and a refusal could quickly lead to a "Saigon" situation', with strikes, sabotage, and having to live behind barbed-wire. It was therefore of 'supreme importance' that something short of independence must be offered. Like Malta, Singapore had special characteristics which called for special, unique and imaginative treatment. It might possibly get its freedom through federation with Malaya. But at all events the Conservative government was determined to retain control of the internal security arrangements. The government proposed these should remain (in effect) with the high commissioner.[140] Marshall rejected this as 'Christmas pudding with arsenic sauce', and resigned.

(2) Cyprus

In June 1953, coronation celebrations were treated to displays of organised contempt by Greek Cypriot schoolboys, who had been indoctrinated by Archbishop Makarios to regard themselves as 'athletes of the noble Cyprus struggle', striving 'to get in the wind of much desired freedom through our rulers' doors'. In Nicosia, schoolboys spat on shop windows with royal decorations; in Paphos, 800 boys stoned the police in order to remove union jacks from the stadium; in Larnaca, a stock of 500 coronation mugs was smashed.[141] As late as September 1954 a junior minister, Lord Carrington (parliamentary secretary to the Ministry of Defence), favoured 'polite inattention' to the Ethnarchy's activities: 'if it was not for UNO, I do not think there would be any need for deep anxiety in the future'.[142] At this stage, a lot of the trouble was indeed caused by schoolboys, whipped up by the Greek Orthodox Church and its civil arm, the Ethnarchy. Many British officials regarded the campaign for Enosis

---

[140] CAB 129/80, CP(56)85, 23 March 1956, and CP(56)97, 14 April 1956, memos by Lennox-Boyd; CAB 128/30/1, CM 29(56)5, 17 April 1956; Goldsworthy, *Conservative government*, pt 2, pp 391–404 (nos. 355–7).

[141] CO 926/10, no 7, report of archbishop's speech, and no. 44, Governor Sir A. Wright to Lyttelton, 8 June 1953.

[142] CAB 134/801, Cyprus Committee, CS(54) 7th meeting, 7 September 1954.

(union with Greece) as fundamentally artificial, as well as non-negotiable, and a bit of a joke. It was all about to get much more serious. On 1 April 1955 the Greek Cypriot underground organisation, EOKA, now inspired by a mysterious, ruthless leader named Grivas, launched a bombing campaign in support of the demand for Enosis.[143] Cyprus became second only to Egypt as a leading problem for the British government.

The Colonial Office lacked a free hand in determining Cyprus policy. It had to reckon not only with the strategic imperatives of the Chiefs of Staff but also the international concerns of the Foreign Office. The former it could reluctantly accept as an absolute, incontestable block on advance to self-government, removable only by a revised strategic evaluation; the latter was an inter-departmental source of mutual irritation and tension. The strategic argument was that aircraft from Cyprus bases could strike deep into the Soviet Union and this was one of the few places from which this could be done. Without a major base here, the defence of the Middle East might be impracticable, and Turkey would be isolated and exposed. To the Turks, Cyprus was an offshore island, only forty miles away.[144] Both the Turks and the British worried about an independent Cyprus in union with a Greece perceived as politically unstable and tempted by communism, which must be contained globally; 'we must avoid the risk of another British Guiana in a much more vital area'[145] (see below, pp. 210–11). And of course loss of prestige would be involved if any ex-colonial territory fell under another country.

Colonial Office officials did not want the strategic argument explicitly used in public as a justification for the retention of sovereignty, as it might change and was not the sole reason. The new Conservative departmental ministers were persuaded to accept this orthodoxy.[146] It was much less easy to control what issued from the Foreign Office. Despite the value attached to Greek friendship, the Greeks were told by the FO in late 1951 that there was no hope of modifying the British opposition to Enosis. Eden then made things much worse, doing lasting harm to Anglo-Greek relations, by angrily telling the Greek prime minister, Field-Marshal Papagos, in 1953 that he would not even discuss it. There could be no change of

---

[143] On Cyprus generally, see Hyam, *Labour government*, pt 1, intro, pp. xxxix–xlii; Goldsworthy, *Conservative government*, pt 2, pp. 328–57 (nos. 321–33); R. Holland, 'Never, never land: British colonial policy and the roots of violence in Cyprus, 1950–1954', *JICH*, vol. 21 (1993), pp. 148–76, and *Britain and the revolt in Cyprus, 1954–1959* (1998); Murphy, *Lennox-Boyd*, pp. 113–23.

[144] Hyam, *Labour government*, pt 3, pp. 117–19 (no. 246, October 1950).

[145] FO 371/112848, nos. 179 and 183 (July 1954); CAB 134/801, Cyprus Committee memo, COS(54)303, 13 September 1954.

[146] CO 537/7464, minutes 3–6 November 1951.

sovereignty because the Cyprus question 'did not exist', nor could it ever arise in future, he said, adding gratuitously that there was a considerable Greek population in New York, larger than in Cyprus, but he did not suppose the Greek government was demanding Enosis for them. 'He told me *never*', complained a stunned Papagos. Eden was utterly inflexible and later withdrew the invitation to a further proposed meeting.[147]

It is against this background that we should read a second and far more devastating and notorious 'never'. Henry Hopkinson (minister of state at the CO) on 28 July 1954, answering a supplementary question after a Commons statement on Cyprus, inadvertently let slip that 'it has always been understood and agreed that there are certain territories in the Commonwealth [*sic*] which, owing to their particular circumstances can never expect to be fully independent'.[148] It sounded as if the Conservative government was about to retreat from the bipartisan policy of leading territories to self-government. Although the Foreign Office was prepared to defend this gaffe as unfortunate but justified, the Colonial Office could not, since it conflicted with its assumption that strategic circumstances might change, and as far as it was concerned, the safest line was merely to declare that there was 'no change of policy'.[149]

But the damage had been done. Hopkinson's 'never' not only destroyed his ministerial career, and introduced a permanent chill into the Cyprus conflict, but reverberated throughout the world's anti-colonial fraternity, thus entering the mythology of the end of empire. Three weeks later, Greece applied to put the right of Cyprus to self-determination on the agenda at the UN. Most foreign countries sympathised with the Greek case. There were 30 votes for inscription, 19 against, and 11 abstentions. To the dismay of the British government, the Americans did nothing to prevent inscription, the Canadians abstained at the General Assembly, and even Australian support was distinctly wobbly.[150]

Not surprisingly, by the end of 1954 Churchill was demanding 'a firm and realistic policy'.[151] Here at least Eden agreed with him, arguing that a 'tougher and more energetic' course was needed, 'otherwise we shall drift from one set-back to another, like the French!':

---

[147] FO 371/107499, no. 3, note of meeting, 22 September 1953; FO 371/107502, no. 56, Ambassador Sir C. Peake to FO, telegram, 14 November 1953.

[148] A. N. Porter and A. J. Stockwell, eds., *British imperial policy and decolonisation*, vol. II pp. 319–25 (no. 44).

[149] FO 371/112850, nos. 232, 233, 239; CO 926/12, no. 12A, minute by Sir J. Martin, 28 March 1952.

[150] Holland, *Britain and the revolt in Cyprus*, p. 42; S. Mayes, *Makarios: a biography* (1981), p. 55.

[151] FO 371/112883, no. 1247, M 239/54, prime minister to colonial secretary, 15 December 1954.

I fear that many people here do not yet realise the seriousness of trouble we are creating for ourselves over Cyprus – I am convinced that Turks will never – I mean never – agree to its return to Greece. If we do not stand up for our rights and fight back – as we should do – Turks will conclude we are on the way out and demand Cyprus *from us*. We shall then really be in trouble, as well as have destroyed Greeko [*sic*]-Turkish friendship.[152]

Following this through, Anthony Nutting, the newly-appointed minister of state at the Foreign Office, initialled a paper arguing that there was 'a considerable case for a policy of firmness in the present combined with reasonableness and open-mindedness for the future'. This pointed to a public statement accepting the principle of self-determination as an ultimate goal, the main object being to strengthen the British position at the UN by enabling the USA to support Britain, and by taking the edge off the opposition of the anti-colonials – for if the Americans voted for the Greeks at the next UN session, the Greeks would win, thus making British efforts to handle the stalemate in Cyprus increasingly difficult. Nutting commented: 'I would not set so much store by the UN aspect if I didn't feel that discussions there and the passage of adverse resolutions would be bound to have repercussions on the situation in Cyprus itself.' Britain must surely avoid being put 'in the same position as France, whose Moroccan, Tunisian and Algerian record is raked over year by year by the mischief-makers in the Assembly with seeming adverse repercussions upon law and order in North Africa'.[153]

Eden, however, totally pulled to pieces Nutting's initiative. Such a course, he believed, would be widely regarded as a surrender (that dread word!), and he was not convinced the Greeks could keep up their fight. He vented his frustration on file:

We have recently announced a Constitution. Not enough people want to work it, so we run around and look for another. We never allow our medicine time to work. We should keep up pressure, and make life as uncomfortable for them as possible, and let no glimmer of weakness on our side emerge. Meanwhile, of course, we should strengthen police in Cyprus, improve our broadcasting, etc. I had hoped we should have done this long ago. Nothing ever seems to be done in Cyprus, only moans issue from time to time.[154]

Nevertheless, Eden accepted Lennox-Boyd's recommendation to make an improved constitutional offer. The official and nominated majority offered in July 1954 would be replaced by an elected majority, a step

---

[152] FO 371/112871, no. 886, minute 19 October 1954; FO 371/112881, no. 1198, minutes 9 and 11 December 1954.
[153] FO 371/117622, no. 53, 18 January 1955; FO 371/117624, nos. 96 and 97, minutes 25 January and 8 February 1955; FO 371/117625, no. 110, 14 February 1955.
[154] FO 371/117625, no. 107, 9 February 1955.

eventually leading to full internal self-government. This still fell short of the 1948 proposal of an almost fully elected legislature, because 'there would be too many risks yet, with a people untrained in politics and with the Communists the best organised party'.[155] Eden accepted that the change would have a useful impact on American opinion. The Turks had better be reassured, he added, that the proposals would not lead to their being stampeded out and that the British government contemplated no change in sovereignty for the foreseeable future, and indeed intended to stay as long as the world situation made it necessary.[156] The Cabinet's Cyprus Committee recognised that the situation would deteriorate if nothing was done, so it recommended offering a constitution leading to full internal self-government in a comparatively short period of years. Realising that such a route-map was likely to lead to self-determination in the long run, and that there might be unacceptable defence implications, the Committee decided no assurances would be given for the moment. A tripartite conference would be arranged between governments, as Macmillan wanted.[157] But in September 1955 the Cabinet refused to let the foreign secretary give any undertakings implying willingness to concede self-determination. Prime Minister Eden defined Cyprus as 'not merely a question whether a country should be allowed to govern itself but an international issue of the most explosive character . . . It was essential to avoid leaning so far towards the Greeks, as to risk alienating the Turks.' Macmillan feared that there would be difficult times ahead, in which 'Cyprus would have to be handled as a joint political and military operation aimed at getting the moderate people on our side and at isolating the extremists'.[158]

As foreign secretary (April to December 1955) Macmillan took a close interest in the Cyprus question. 'My impression', he wrote, 'is that there is a growing understanding that this is not and never has been a "colonial" question. If it were that, it would be easily solved on the lines of the advances we are making in our colonies elsewhere.'[159] What it was, he thought, was 'the conflict between age-old pressures in the Eastern Mediterranean dating back to almost the earliest periods of civilised history'. The Greeks had 'sown the wind and are now reaping the whirlwind'. Let the medicine work. The 'modern doctrine of

[155] CAB 129/74, C(55)92, memo 6 April 1955 by Lennox-Boyd.
[156] CAB 129/74, C(55)93, memo 5 April 1955 by Eden.
[157] CAB 130/109, GEN 497, no. 2, 21 July 1955; Diana Weston Markides, 'Britain's "New look" policy for Cyprus and the Makarios–Harding talks, January 1955–March 1956', *JICH*, vol. 23(1995), pp. 479–502.
[158] CAB 128/27, CM 30(55)1, minutes of meeting, 5 September 1955.
[159] FO 800/667, Macmillan to Sir R. Scott, 9 September 1955.

self-determination has great merits. But it is certainly not of universal application.'[160] There were indeed deep polarities in this conflict, and Macmillan was right about that.

The Turks rejected the proposals, frightened off by implied eventual self-determination. British efforts now turned to lobbying at the UN to prevent the Cyprus question being inscribed again. Macmillan appealed to US secretary of state Dulles: if they could act in harmony it would 'prevent further discussion of this vexed problem in an atmosphere which is full of such explosive possibilities'.[161] Attitudes were sounded out from India to Venezuela, Iceland to Ethiopia, Lebanon to Liberia, Uruguay to Afghanistan, Guatemala to Pakistan, Siam to Brazil, Hayti to Iraq. The diplomatic hard work paid off, and the Cyprus item was defeated.

Field-Marshal Harding (lately Chief of the Imperial General Staff) was now sent in as governor to restore law and order, in the hope that 'conciliation can gain a foothold'.[162] Harding was a no-nonsense soldier, not too imaginative in his sympathies, and ill-equipped to deal with Archbishop Makarios, subtle, enigmatic, and vigorously magnetic. The deportation of the archbishop soon followed (March 1956). He had refused cooperation, but the detention without trial of an archbishop was a serious step. Worse, Eden – apparently now entering a vindictive phase – insisted on deportation to the Seychelles, tiny, tropical, remote islands without air links. Macmillan thought this was inappropriately harsh, but was not prepared to argue the toss with the prime minister over this. Eden sought a 'new formula' around (in effect) self-determination. Macmillan was not happy with this either, but there was strong pressure from other ministers. Macmillan became increasingly sarcastic in his minutes: 'of course in this already metaphysical realm of argument about self-determination restatements often have valuable results' – and of a redfraft, 'This is the PM's *new formula*.' The Foreign Office files on Cyprus reveal Macmillan as a strong minister who knew what he wanted said and done – or not, as the case may be.[163]

Makarios had finally declined to accept government statements of policy as a basis on which he could promise co-operation. Should some fresh initiative now be taken? asked Eden at the end of May.[164] The governor attended a Cabinet meeting in June 1956, stating his conviction

[160] FO 371/117654, no. 950, telegram to Mr Lambert (Athens), 7 September 1955.
[161] FO 371/117658, no. 1040, telegram 19 September 1955.
[162] FO 371/117667, no. 1341, Macmillan to Dulles, 21 October 1955.
[163] FO 371/117665, no. 1277, minutes by Macmillan, 12 and 13 October; FO 371/117666, no. 1310 (to prime minister, 20 October 1955), and no. 1326.
[164] Minutes of Cabinet meetings: CAB 128/30/1, CM 18(66)1, 5 March 1956, and CM 38(56)3, 29 May 1956.

that Cypriots would not co-operate unless they were assured that the right of self-determination would at some future stage be conceded; HMG would have to say it accepted the principle and was seeking practical means of applying it, but that the question must not be raised for the time being. The central problem remained that there was little prospect of Turkish agreement to any solution which gave a definite date for the application of self-determination.[165] Macmillan lamented into his diary: Cyprus was still as intractable as ever, 'a running sore' which couldn't be resolved 'by verbal formulae however cleverly devised'.[166] At the last Cabinet discussions of Cyprus in 1956, the possibility of partition was ventilated.[167]

The government was now definitely on the slippery slope, pushed along by the pro-Turk Foreign Office. Harding was in favour of partition. But not the constitutional commissioner appointed in April 1956, Lord Radcliffe. With his Indian experience, he regarded it as a counsel of despair. Lennox-Boyd was decidedly wary, but thought it might be a useful way of excluding Enosis. And so in a crucial statement – quite possibly ill-advised – he announced that partition could be an eventual option after a British withdrawal. 'Double self-determination' was at once rejected by the Greeks, and in no time at all the situation was again deadlocked, especially as studies revealed that partition would be impossible without forcible removal of communities. The British government was now dangerously close to falling into the trap some had forecast: alienating the Turks (holding out for equal representation) whilst still fighting the Greeks.[168]

(3) Malta

Although a community of only 300,000 people, Malta was among the most difficult of colonial problems, because, as Lyttelton put it, 'the Maltese aspire to political independence and to financial dependence', without advice or control from the British provider. There was much political friction in Malta, especially between the Catholic Church and the Labour Party led by Dom Mintoff, and obstruction 'of a medieval complexity'. Union with Italy was talked about, but Lyttelton thought

---

[165] CAB 128/30/1, CM 41(56)6, minutes of meeting, 12 June, and CM 44(56)5, minutes, 19 June 1956.

[166] CAB 128/30/2, CM 99(56)2, minutes, 12 December, and CM 102(56)1, minutes, 17 December 1956.

[167] Catterall, *Macmillan diaries*, p. 567 (19 June 1956) and p. 576 (21 July 1956).

[168] Holland, *Britain and the revolt in Cyprus, 1954–1959*, pp. 155–171; Evanthis Hatzivassiliou, 'Blocking "Enosis": Britain and the Cyprus question, March–December 1956', *JICH*, vol. 19 (1991), pp. 247–63.

this would do neither of them any favours.[169] Borg Olivier and his party (closely allied to the Catholic Church) wanted greater constitutional freedom than under internal self-government; Dom Mintoff – who took over as prime minister in February 1955 – wanted closer integration with the United Kingdom, an arrangement which would include parliamentary representation (perhaps three MPs). A viable economy seemed unlikely, given its tiny size and lack of resources and dependence on the British naval presence. Defence and garrison administration provided jobs for over a quarter of the labour force. Despite the doubts, the Conservative government was reluctant to turn down the principle of integration, lest Mintoff demand independence with a defence treaty and substantial aid. The Cabinet debated whether or not representation in the House of Commons could be contemplated, because the consequences of immediate outright rejection might be serious.[170] Matters came to a head in June and July 1955, and a Round Table Conference on the 1930s Indian model was set up to examine all the implications. There was considerable ministerial support for 'an imaginative gesture': 'Faced as they were with constitutional difficulties in various parts of the Colonial Empire, the Government could ill afford to risk a serious constitutional crisis in Malta.' Moreover, 'when awkward negotiations were to be opened about Cyprus and criticism might be expected at the forthcoming transfer of the naval base at Simonstown, it would seem anomalous that the Government should reject a request by a Colonial people for a form of closer association with this country'. Were they to quarrel with the Cypriots because 'they wanted to leave us and with the Maltese because they wanted to draw closer to us?'. It was an awkwardly powerful argument, and discussion returned to it again and again.[171]

Surprising as it now seems, the Round Table Conference recommended representation at Westminster if this was the clear wish of the Maltese. Ministers remained divided as to its wisdom and feasibility, and so they kept the discussion going.[172] They were worried about strong Tory back-bench opposition. Macmillan wrote in his diary in the spring of 1956: the Cabinet were 'getting all tied up about Malta – with the usual shilly-shallying'. He thought they should take a firmer lead, for if they were not careful, the question of the integration of Malta would

[169] *Memoirs of Lord Chandos*, p. 426.
[170] CAB 129/67, C(54)141, 14 April 1954; Goldsworthy, *Conservative government*, pt 2, pp. 312–17 (no. 314); CAB 129/76, CP(55)53, 27 June 1955.
[171] Minutes of Cabinet meetings: CAB 128/29, CM 19(55)10, 30 June 1955, and CM 20(55)5, 5 July 1955.
[172] CAB 128/30/1, CM 2(56)4, minutes, 4 January 1956, and CM 22(56)9, minutes, 13 March 1956.

'end up like that of the abolition of Hanging – a matter for individual conscience'.[173]

As a romantic scheme in the grand 'visionary idealist' tradition, integration had great appeal for Lennox-Boyd, and he devoted a lot of time to it. He was shocked and angered when Mintoff without consultation suddenly announced he would hold a referendum, to which Lennox-Boyd was opposed. As he feared it might, the referendum in February 1956 proved both divisive and indecisive: 74 per cent voted 'yes' to representation at Westminster, but the turn-out was only 59 per cent, so those in favour accounted for only 44 per cent of the qualified electorate. Abstentions – primarily at the instigation of the Church – were very high.[174] Lennox-Boyd was deeply disillusioned, and blamed Mintoff. In 1957 the Maltese government rejected proposals for integration-without-representation. Negotiations broke down in the following year, with both Mintoff and Olivier demanding independence. Agreement on this was eventually reached in July 1964.[175]

(4) British Guiana

By comparison with the Mediterranean colonies, British Guiana was only a minor trouble-spot, a faraway country of which little was known, but an anxiety to the government none the less. A new constitution with universal suffrage, a two-chamber legislature, and a ministerial system was introduced in April 1953. Less than six months later the constitution was suspended, to prevent 'the subversion of government' by the majority party, the People's Progressive Party, led by Dr Cheddi Jagan, and appealing mainly to the East Indian community who made up over half the population. The PPP was filled with deepest bitterness and distrust of British government and businesses and of white society. Jagan, a qualified dentist, had been brought up on a sugar estate, typical in its dreadful housing and social conditions. Jagan was inspired by Nehru's autobiography. His rival Forbes Burnham was a lawyer, who had twice been abused publicly overseas for being black. He led the People's National Congress. Both of them made no secret of their desire to rule in the interests of 'the working class'. Jagan was accused of being a communist. Ministers were alleged to have incited strikes for political purposes, seeking a totalitarian dominance by penetrating trades unions and schools, and to have neglected their

[173] Catterall, *Macmillan diaries*, p. 545.
[174] D. Austin, *Malta and the end of empire* (1971), pp. 30–5; Murphy, *Alan Lennox-Boyd*, pp. 123–8.
[175] Hyam and Louis, eds., *Conservative government 1957–1964*, pt 1, pp. 693–718 (nos. 242–55).

administrative duties. It was even alleged that there was a plot to burn down the capital Georgetown, largely built of wood. There were official fears that the PPP was aiming at a communist republic completely independent of the UK, perhaps acting as a centre of communist organisation for the whole of the British West Indies and Central America – which would be a grave danger, and a serious embarrassment in relations with the USA. It seemed clear to Whitehall that 'extremists' were in control.

By September 1953 Lyttelton decided that the Guyanan ministers had abused the chance given them to act responsibly: 'a halt must now be called . . . the constitution had been perverted'.[176] Or, as Churchill put it, suspension was abundantly justified because ministers had demonstrated that their mismanagement could only lead to the ruin of the colony.[177] It may not have been quite so simple. Objections to radical economic reforms came from adversely affected foreign sugar and bauxite companies.[178] And although Jagan was a self-styled Marxist, and his American-born wife had been a member of the Young Communist League in Chicago, it was hardly proven that either were 'proper' communists, or that communist bloc countries (or even Castro in Cuba) were interested in them; but they undoubtedly had communist and fellow-travelling contacts outside Guiana.

Suspension continued until 1957. Full internal self-government came into effect in 1961. The British successfully cultivated Burnham as an alternative to Jagan. It was Burnham who led the country to independence in 1966.

(5) The Caribbean colonies

The new constitution in British Honduras in 1953 was based on the recommendations of an independent committee appointed in 1947. The leading People's Party was not actually known to be affiliated to international communist organisations, so the Cabinet was satisfied that 'the dangers of deferring its introduction were certainly greater than those involved in allowing it to go forward in accordance with existing plans'. Delays would mean the Conservative government would be suspected of having changed their liberal policy towards colonial constitutional advance. However, the more right-wing ministers pressed their view that

---

[176] S.R. Ashton and D. Killingray, eds., *The West Indies* (BDEEP, 1999), pp 49–58 (nos. 13–15), CO letters and minutes, 13–24 September 1953.

[177] CAB 128/26/2, CC 54(53)2, 2 October, and CC 56(53)1, 8 October 1953; Goldsworthy, *Conservative government*, pt 2, pp. 363–4 (no. 337); *Memoirs of Lord Chandos*, pp. 427–9.

[178] H. Johnson, 'The British Caribbean from demobilization to constitutional decolonization', in Brown and Louis, *Oxford history of the British empire*, vol. IV, pp. 617–18, and 'Jagan, Cheddi B', in *ODNB*, vol. XXIX, pp. 583–5.

this consideration 'should not prevent the Government from exercising due caution in guiding the evolution of colonial territories towards independence or from exercising a restraining influence when circumstances warranted it'. They lost the argument. The Cabinet ruled that there should be no modification in this case.[179]

Both British Guiana and British Honduras decided not to join the West Indies Federation, plans for which had been on the drawing-board since 1947. The Conservatives did not interrupt the slow-moving process. Lyttelton himself accepted that regular air services had fundamentally changed the situation and removed one of the major obstacles: 'regional co-operation has become physically possible just when the need for it has been most strongly felt', by which he meant 'the secular trend' indicating that small territories might be better off together both economically and politically. He explicitly stated that changes of government in Britain involved 'no change of attitude or policy towards the question of West Indies federation'.[180] In the course of the next few years, commissions were set up and reports received on various issues: fiscal, civil service, judicial, migration, trade and tariffs. By February 1956 the government was ready to hold a conference in London with the aim of getting agreement to establish the federation: 'the whole political future of the West Indies was at stake', according to Lennox-Boyd. Financial assistance from the UK was a key issue. The existing level of assistance for several territories was in Lennox-Boyd's view 'required on a scale which is incompatible with the reality of political independence', and he was anxious that the West Indians must understand 'they cannot have both extensive financial assistance and complete independence'. Economic growth would be essential.[181] Planning continued, turning after the conference mainly towards the powers of the federal government and the site of the capital. The appointment of a governor-general was announced in April 1957, and the federation finally came into being on the first day of January 1958.

4. Commonwealth issues

(1) Smaller colonial territories and the future of the Commonwealth

One of the main areas in which diehard Conservative ministers fought a rearguard action concerned the future size and shape of the Commonwealth. But it is also one of the most striking demonstrations of

[179] CAB 128/26/2, CC 70(53)6, 24 November 1953; Goldsworthy, pt 2, p. 364 (no. 338).
[180] CO 1027/38, no. 13, address to conference, 13 April 1953.
[181] Ashton and Killingray, *The West Indies*, pp. 116–17 (no. 38), and 138–9 (no. 47), minutes from Lennox-Boyd to Sir H. Foot, 6 January and 23 June 1956.

the ineluctable pressures towards continuity, and of the way in which officials persuaded ministers into pragmatic changes of view. The first issue was the admission of Ghana as an equal, which happened despite the protests of the South African prime minister, Dr Malan. There really was little alternative, given the membership of republican India. The next issue was the protracted consideration of a possible 'two-tier' system of Commonwealth membership which would preserve the old 'white club' as an inner circle against the proliferation of 'black' states. A committee of officials investigated this. Over the years it consistently recognised the difficulty of trying to predict and classify types of members. Countries they might list for retention of colonial status were liable to get 'overrun by progressive nationalism'.[182] Another committee on Commonwealth membership under Sir Norman Brook (the cabinet secretary) concluded that solving the problem by formal differentiation of status was impracticable and unrealistic. Any hint of second-class status would probably lead newly-independent states to secede, and this 'would be tantamount to adopting a policy of deliberately weakening our own strength and authority in world councils by a series of self-inflicted wounds'. The committee's report provided a very clear statement of where they saw 'decolonisation' had got to by the end of 1954. Helping countries to manage their own affairs was, it said, a process which

cannot now be halted or reversed, and it is only to a limited extent that its pace can be controlled by the UK government. Sometimes it may be possible to secure acceptance of beneficial delay in order to ensure a more orderly transition. But, in the main, the pace of constitutional change will be determined by the strength of nationalist feeling and the development of political consciousness within the territory concerned.

Colonial politicians expected to reach independence in their own lifetime, which was natural enough, and:

if they cannot satisfy their followers that satisfactory progress is being maintained towards that goal, their influence may be usurped by less responsible elements. Any attempt to retard by artificial delays the progress of Colonial peoples towards independence would produce disastrous results. It would, in particular, be likely to have the consequence that, when power had eventually to be transferred, it would be handed over to a local leadership predisposed towards an anti-British policy.[183]

Brook took the precaution of writing personally to Churchill about this, explaining that there could not be an intermediate status of

---

[182] DO 35/2218, no. 7A, meeting, 2 January 1952.
[183] DO 35/5057, no. 143; CAB 129/71, C(54)307, 11 October 1954; Goldsworthy, pt 2, p. 36 (no. 192).

Commonwealth membership. He knew this would be unpalatable to the prime minister, but 'I am convinced that this is the only policy which can preserve the strength and influence of the Commonwealth in the world of the future.' For if territories passed out of the Commonwealth this would 'spell for the future a Commonwealth of dwindling power – it would condemn the Empire to "death by a thousand cuts" '. We have, Brook concluded, 'to live in the present and plan for the future'.[184]

The matter came before the Cabinet early in December 1954. Several ministers greatly regretted the course of Commonwealth development envisaged in the report, and found it difficult to believe it would be possible to extend to the wider circle of Asians and the Gold Coast the old close, intimate co-operation: 'It was unfortunate that the policy of assisting dependent peoples to attain self-government had been carried forward so fast and so far.' Could formal equality be elided into something nominal? Perhaps they could devise informal methods of consultation 'which would permit free and close co-operation between those members which actually exercised an influence in world affairs'? In the end, however, there was 'general agreement' that a two-tier system was not going to happen.[185] But first the prime ministers of Canada, Australia, and New Zealand were to be given a chance to express their views. (They accepted the new situation, with some apprehensions.)[186]

Brook had emphasised that 'the vital thing was to encourage members to think alike on most major international problems'. This appealed to Eden, who praised 'an excellent report': 'I agree with every word of it. An encouraging and important feature is that Commonwealth countries are beginning to talk to each other much more than they did even a few years ago.'[187] Swinton had for some time in his own mind capitulated, and sadly accepted that they must be 'driven to the conclusion' that the two-tier idea would not work. Arguments against second-class membership were decisive: the Gold Coast would secede rather than accept it, and if that happened there would be no hope of keeping any African state in the Commonwealth. Britain might be faced 'with a choice between South Africa and the Gold Coast'.[188] Sir Charles Jeffries no doubt reflected the view of many officials when he wrote that if it came to it, they must face the loss of South Africa.[189] Lord Salisbury of course saw it differently; he

---

[184] Goldsworthy, *Conservative government*, pt 2, p. 43 (no. 193), Brook to Churchill, 1 December 1954.

[185] CAB 128/27/2, CC 83(54), minutes of meeting, 7 December 1954.

[186] DO 35/5060.

[187] DO 35/5057, no. 108, minute by Eden, [nd], and no. 140, minute by Brook, 26 January 1955.   [188] DO 35/5057, no. 109, minute by Swinton, 16 May 1954.

[189] CO 1032/10, 21 November 1952; Goldsworthy, *Conservative government*, pt 2, p. 174 (no. 259).

would choose the older dominions 'even including South Africa' in preference to 'these immature countries', small places inhabited 'by primitive peoples'.[190]

(2) Anglo-South African relations

Three major pieces of unfinished business confronted the incoming Conservatives in October 1951: what to do with Seretse Khama, whether or not to set up the Central African Federation, and how to settle the future of Simon's Town naval base near Cape Town. Elements of continuity were strongly in evidence in all of these. They decided to make the exclusion of Seretse from the Bangwato chieftainship permanent (1952). They determined to bring into being the Federation of Rhodesia and Nyasaland (established on 1 August 1953). They concluded a surprisingly favourable agreement over Simon's Town (1955).[191] Meanwhile, too, they held firm in defence of the High Commission Territories (Basutoland, Bechuanaland, and Swaziland) against the South African expansionist desire to incorporate them. Churchill – who claimed to have 'thought a great deal about South Africa since 1899' – was opposed to any idea of transferring the Territories to South Africa, since they would be administered 'in accordance with very old-fashioned ideas'.[192] In April 1954 he made in the Commons a statement, the strongest and most uncompromising rejection of South African overtures yet made by a British government: 'we could not fall in with their views without failing in our trust'. There are pre-echoes here of Macmillan's 'wind of change speech'. When Malan refused to accept this rebuff he was simply ignored.[193]

These Conservative policies were all logical developments from those of the Labour government, though this is not to say that a re-elected Labour Party would have done exactly the same. The problem of Seretse and the question of federation were dealt with in ways which give striking evidence of how ambitious civil servants could utilise changes of government to seize the initiative and push through their own preferred solutions. Lord Ismay, briefly the secretary of state for Commonwealth relations, was inexperienced and particularly vulnerable to suggestion. By educating their new masters in the subtle realities of Anglo–South African relations of which they were not previously aware, officials

---

[190] Goldsworthy, *ibid.*, pt 2, p 5, minute February 1953 (no. 177).
[191] Hyam and Henshaw, *The lion and the springbok*, esp. pp. 190–3, 216–23, and 255–8.
[192] PREM 4/44/1, note by Churchill, 7 October 1941.
[193] Hyam and Henshaw, *The lion and the springbok*, pp. 257–8. Despite the policy differences between the two governments, Sir John Le Rougetel as high commissioner had 'most friendly' personal relations with Dr Malan (letter to the author, 15 January 1972).

Illustration 3.3 Conference in London to discuss Central African Federation: Oliver Lyttelton with ministers and governors, January 1953. Left to right: the Marquess of Salisbury (Lord Privy Seal), Sir Gilbert Rennie (governor of Northern Rhodesia), Viscount Swinton (secretary of state for Commonwealth relations), Sir Godfrey Huggins (prime minister of Southern Rhodesia), Sir Geoffrey Colby (governor of Nyasland), Mr Lyttelton (secretary of state for the colonies), Mr. H.L. d'A. Hopkinson (minister of state for colonial affairs). Throughout 1952 the issue was regarded as in the balance, and a final constitutional conference was therefore postponed from October 1952 to January 1953 in order to give the Federation of Rhodesia and Nyasaland a fairer wind. Hopkinson had visited the region in August 1952 to try to calm African fears. The principal significance of the January conference held in London at Carlton House lay in the British government's agreement to further weakening of safeguards for Africans. After a Southern Rhodesian referendum in its favour in April, the Central African Federation came into being on 1 August 1953.

ensured that ministers were forced to adopt in power a policy on Seretse which they had attacked in Opposition. Playing on the natural desire of politicians fresh to office to appear efficient and decisive, officials emphasised the messiness of the 'temporary exclusion' of Seretse from the chieftainship ('a bad compromise giving everyone the worst of all worlds', 'a classic example of procrastination'). They also harped upon 'the failure of the late Government to take a more definite line', to 'give a lead to opinion' in favour of federation in Central Africa. The officials had fully worked-out plans to lay before ministers as to how these issues could be tackled best. Though he will not have realised it, Salisbury issued a memorandum prepared for him by the CRO in 1952 which followed precisely the reasons laid down in Gordon Walker's memorandum of September 1950 for trying to preserve good relations with South Africa (see above, p. 164).[194] Andrew Cohen and G. H. Baxter, the principal proponents, virtually the architects, of the federal solution for Central Africa, exerted an influence which went far beyond the normal boundaries of civil service advice. The Conservative government was thus able to announce major decisions both on Seretse and on federation within one month of taking office.[195] Simon's Town was approached more slowly.

A good deal of ill-thought-out idealism was invested in the federal project. Although to some extent in the initial stages London's hand was forced by the determined pressure of the settlers (threatening to withdraw economic co-operation in such matters as the copper supply), the fundamental dynamic behind it was the containment of South African expansion, particularly Afrikaner immigration into the Rhodesias.[196] 'Fear of South Africa was Number One for me', Lyttelton admitted privately (though not in public or in his *Memoirs*). Although he never made a speech denouncing apartheid – the official doctrine was that this was an internal matter for South Africa – he regarded it as 'an absolutely fatal policy in the long run and absolutely against our ideas'. He came to believe Southern Rhodesia was 'poisoned by the South African virus'.[197] In December 1952 Lyttelton, Swinton, and Salisbury joined forces to persuade the Cabinet to go ahead with federation despite African opposition. Salisbury argued that abandonment of the scheme in the face of black African protest would mean that

---

[194] CAB 129/55, C(52)306, memo 24 September 1952; Goldsworthy, *Conservative government*, pt 1, pp. 350–5 (no. 141); for Gordon Walker's memo, see Hyam, *Labour government*, pt 4, pp. 284–90 (no. 429), 25 September 1950, and *The lion and the springbok*, p. 17.

[195] These processes can be followed in DO 35/3600 and DO 35/4135; see also important observations in Seldon, *Churchill's Indian Summer*, pp. 361 and 432.

[196] Hyam and Henshaw, *The lion and the springbok*, ch. 9, 'Containing Afrikanerdom', esp. pp. 225–9 on Afrikaner immigration. Philip Murphy has shown how skilfully the settlers' leaders, Welensky and Huggins, played upon these fears (which not all officials shared) to prepare the ground for their federal proposals: P. Murphy, ed., *Central Africa 1945–1965* (BDEEP, 2005), pt 1, intro., pp. xliv–xlvi, and 'Government by blackmail: the origins of the Central African Federation reconsidered', in M. Lynn, ed., *The British empire in the 1950s: retreat or revival?* (2006), pp. 53–76.

[197] CHAN II/14/15/1, ff. 52–3, to R. A. Butler, 6 December 1971; CHAN II/14/16/3, f. 29, interview, 27 February 1970.

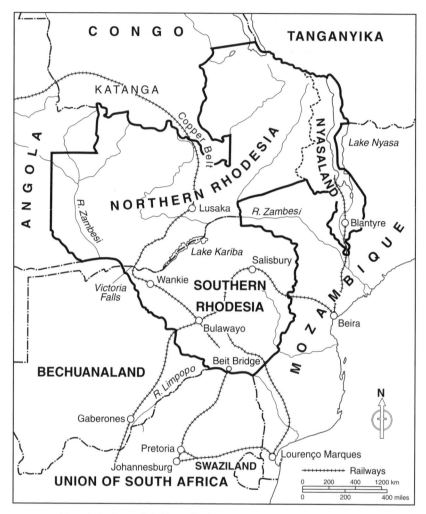

Map 3.1 Central African Federation: the Federation of Rhodesia and Nyasaland 1953–63, is marked with a heavy boundary line.

'moderate African resistance to extremists would collapse', the extremists would become more uncompromising, racial tensions would get worse, and the British government would lose prestige.[198] More positively, Swinton advocated federation as 'a unique opportunity for mixed community', potentially 'a light far beyond its borders',[199] or,

---

[198] CAB 129/57, C(52)445, memo 16 December 1952; DO 121/146, to Sir J. Kennedy, 24 September 1952.   [199] SWIN II/6/20, speech, 20 July 1953.

as he said in Cabinet, 'possibly the last opportunity for adopting in Africa a progressive policy based on the ideal of co-operation between races'. His sobering argument, that without it Southern Rhodesia would probably join the Union, proved decisive with his colleagues.[200] Safeguards for African interests were whittled away under settler pressure.

The new federation was destined to fail. There was a continuing anxiety about what the Rhodesian settlers might do. CO officials first considered the possibility of a 'Boston Tea-Party' in October 1956, almost ten years before the actual declaration of unilateral independence by Southern Rhodesia (UDI).[201]

By contrast, the Simon's Town agreement was a matter for quiet relief and much less controversy.[202] Churchill came into office determined to maintain British interests in the naval base as an effective link in the imperial line of communications to Australasia. Negotiations over its future had begun under the Labour government but ran into stalemate. Determined that South Africa's strategic ports – 'more important to the British Commonwealth of Nations than Gibraltar or Malta' – should not 'go down the drain like Southern Ireland', Churchill held out for the best possible terms, despite the need for economies in the defence estimates. In this respect he maintained continuity of policy with the tough bargaining stance of Attlee and Shinwell, and expressly rejected the advice of Ismay and the attempt of the CRO not only to re-open negotiations but to do so on a more conciliatory footing. Following Churchill's lead, the Defence Committee accordingly agreed in March 1952 not to take any fresh initiative.[203] By the summer of 1954, however, the South African government was again pressing, and pressing hard, for the transfer of Simon's Town. Why? asked Churchill suspiciously. Was it because Malan was working towards the final severance of South Africa from Britain? If so, the surrender of Simon's Town would be taken as a symbol of British decline and fall. In his last extended minute on South Africa, nearly fifty years after the first (in 1906 on the Transvaal constitution), he wrote:

No weakening of our rights over Simonstown should be tolerated . . . I do not think we should be lured into bringing NATO into Simonstown. The Americans

---

[200] CAB 128/25, CC 107(52)4, 22 December 1952.
[201] Murphy, *Central Africa*, pt 1, p. 423 (no. 162), CO minutes October–November 1958; Goldsworthy, pt 2, pp. 307–10 (no. 312), CO minutes, October 1956.
[202] Hyam and Henshaw, *The lion and the springbok*, ch. 10, 'Strategy and the transfer of Simon's Town, 1948–1957', pp. 241–9.
[203] CAB 131/12, D 1(52)1, Defence Committee meeting, 12 March 1952.

are getting a footing in many parts of what was once our Empire, but I do not think our weakness has yet become so pronounced as to require American protection to preserve our rights in Simonstown in any period which we need to consider at the moment.[204]

In Cabinet, although admitting that the significance of Simon's Town was becoming largely symbolic, Churchill was 'reluctant to contemplate any transaction which would be represented as yet another surrender of the political rights and responsibilities of the United Kingdom'. Nor did he want to do anything which might discourage the 'loyalist elements in South Africa'.[205]

In December 1954, however, Churchill resigned himself to approving a further round of talks, since these seemed likely to produce a satisfactory agreement. Swinton was anxious to avoid further delays: within Britain's grasp was 'a new partnership which is not only vital to the Commonwealth defence and communications but may hold the Union fast with the Empire in spite of apartheid and all that'.[206] As he told Macmillan, it was right to come to a settlement: 'if we miss the chance, it won't come again'. Macmillan felt they had made 'a real advance with South African concessions'.[207] The hard bargaining was strongly kept up, too, by Eden and the Defence Committee after Eden became prime minister in April 1955. It was Eden himself who made a most important contribution, being determined to improve the position of 'Coloured' workers at the base, if only to forestall left-wing criticism. It seemed an over-ambitious objective, but the government pulled it off: a late victory for trusteeship. The South African government made an astonishing concession: 'Coloured' recruitment to the base would be exempt from the colour bar.[208]

And so in 1955 Britain obtained agreements on Simon's Town which were unexpectedly favourable. Availability was granted to Britain in any war (whether or not South Africa was involved) and naval collaboration would continue. Whilst not actually congratulating him, Churchill assured Eden he did not see what else he could have done: 'we live in days when neither South Africa nor Naval defence stand on their foundations of a few years ago'.[209]

---

[204] PREM 11/1765, minutes 30 August and 6 September 1954.
[205] CAB 128/27/2, CC 57(54)4, 27 August, and CC 58(54)2, 1 September 1954.
[206] *The lion and the springbok*, p. 246: Swinton to first lord of the Admiralty, 22 December 1954.   [207] Catterall, *Macmillan diaries*, p.383 (21 January 1955).
[208] CAB 131/16, DC 3(55)1, Defence Committee meeting, 10 June 1955.
[209] PREM 11/1765, Churchill to Eden, 4 July 1955.

5. Egypt: decline and fall

(1) The evacuation of the Canal Zone

The Suez Canal Base was a huge muddled mass of installations, work-shops and railways covering an area as big as Wales. It was regulated by a treaty of 1936, due to expire in 1956. The Labour government, however, decided it was necessary to start discussions in 1946 about a new arrangement. The elements in the problem were five in number. (1) Egypt was seen as essential to Western defence, the geopolitical pivot of the Middle East and North Africa, the shield of Africa against Russian expansion, the cross-roads of Commonwealth communications, and the channel for oil. (2) Rising Arab nationalism objected increasingly to Western presence on such a provocative scale on Egyptian soil; the risk of disorders in and around the base was ever present, partly because it looked temptingly like a vast wholesale supermarket tantalisingly full of consumer goods. (3) The base could not be moved; every alternative examined – Cyrenaica, Cyprus, Jordan, Israel (Gaza), and Kenya – all proved one thing, that Egypt fulfilled the strategic and logistical requirements to near-perfection. (4) It seemed impossible to reduce Egyptian objections by allowing the locals more participation in its running as a live organisation, since the 'wogs' were neither trusted nor thought to have the technical expertise needed. (5) On the other hand, friendly co-operation with Egypt was desirable; otherwise there would be permanent alienation, which would probably drive Egypt into the communist camp.

The Labour government wrestled with this problem without finding a solution. Negotiations were fatally compromised by Egyptian insistence on linking a settlement to recognition of the Sudan as part of Egypt under King Farouk as 'king of the Sudan' (see above p. 156). At the very least, recognition of Farouk's claim would provoke widespread disturbances which government might not be able to control.[210] But then in January 1952 the king was toppled in an army coup, amid anti-foreign riots. Egypt's new army rulers were solidly hostile to British influence as it had been exercised for the past seventy years. From now on and for the next four years the problem of Egypt dominated the external policy of the Conservative administration.[211]

When Eden as foreign secretary presented the problem to the Conservative Cabinet he stressed the need to take account of the rising tide of nationalism in the Middle East. Early 1952 seemed a favourable

---

[210] Hyam, *Labour government*, pt 1, pp. 80–7 (nos. 32–5).
[211] M. Mason, ' "The decisive volley": the battle of Ismailia and the decline of British influence in Egypt, January to July 1952', *JICH*, vol. 19 (1991), pp. 45–64.

moment to try to reach agreement. If they could not, 'the best to which we can look forward is a recrudescence of anti-British activities in Egypt, the virtual liquidation of our commercial interests there, and renewed attacks on our position in the Canal Zone on such a scale that our base there would once again be rendered inoperative as a wartime base'.[212] Eden was convinced that the operational value of a base in a hostile country was very small. Concessions would be unavoidable in the end. Despite Churchill's misgivings, it was agreed to open negotiations accepting the principle of a progressive, phased withdrawal of British combatant troops, with provision for immediate use in war, on condition that the Egyptian government would agree to participate in a collective defence organisation for the Middle East. In this way, withdrawal could be presented as 'redeployment', as part of a new, general, imaginative defence policy for the region.[213]

Later in 1952 the Chiefs of Staff reported in the Global Strategy Review that the base would be vulnerable in future to nuclear attack. Britain, they said, should have the nuclear deterrent, and should reduce the size of the base; the Far East was 'far more important' in the cold war.[214] Meanwhile, Eden became concerned about the lack of progess and did not want to be confronted with a situation in which the only alternatives would be military occupation of Egypt or an evacuation with no safeguards in place.[215] Eden issued a significant memorandum in February 1953:

I have been giving continuous thought to our Egyptian conundrum . . . In the second half of the twentieth century we cannot hope to maintain our position in the Middle East by the methods of the last century. However little we like it, we must face the fact that commercial concessions whose local benefit appears to redound mainly to the Shahs and Pashas no longer serve in the same way to strengthen our influence in these countries, and they come increasingly under attack by local nationalist opinion. Military occupation could be maintained by force, but in the case of Egypt the base upon which it depends is of little use if there is no local labour to man it. We have learned the first lesson in Persia: we are learning the second in Egypt.

[212] CAB 129/49, C(52)32, memo, 11 February 1952, and CAB 128/24, CC 17(52)4, meeting, 14 February 1952; J. Kent, *Egypt and the defence of the Middle East* (BDEEP, 1998), pt 2, *1949–1953*, pp. 326–30, 335–6 (nos. 267 and 270).

[213] CAB 129/50, C(52)63, memo 5 March 1952, and CAB 128/24, CC 29(52)7, meeting 12 March 1952: Kent, *Egypt and the defence of the Middle East*, pt 2, pp. 351–4, 358–9 (nos. 281 and 285); PREM 11/392, Eden to Churchill, 7 November 1952.

[214] Kent, *Egypt and the defence of the Middle East*, pt 2, pp. 398–429 (no. 308). See also J. Kent, 'The Egyptian base and the defence of the Middle East, 1945–1954', in R. Holland, ed., *Emergencies and disorder in the European empires after 1945*, special issue of *JICH*, vol. 21 (1993), pp. 45–65.

[215] CAB 129/58, C(53)17, memo 14 January 1953; Kent, *Egypt*, pt 2, pp. 536–48; FO 371/102795, no. 17.

The 'tide of nationalism was rising fast', his memorandum continued. 'If we are to maintain our influence in this area, future policy must be designed to harness these movements rather than to struggle against them.' Anything which looked to local nationalism like military occupation by foreign troops would be counter-productive. If British soldiers were left in the Canal Zone in defiance of the Egyptians they would be wholly absorbed in coping with the situation which their very presence created.[216] This was the authentic voice of Ernest Bevin.

Eden was now having to face up to the problem of the apprehensions of the far-right Conservatives, who were complaining of 'defeatism and flabbiness'. He wrote to Lord Hankey, a director of the Suez Canal Company whose mind was filled with apocalyptic forebodings, as follows:

In the middle of the twentieth century we must deal with Egypt as an independent nation in her own right . . . I am anxious that you should know that what we are trying to do in Egypt is not to run away from a régime which often says crude and hostile things, but rather to lay the foundations of security in the Middle East in the new and changed circumstances that now prevail there. By this I mean of course not so much the new régime in Egypt, as the change in our own position in the world. It is a case of 'new times, new methods.'

Just so. No hint here – it can be said emphatically – of the Suez adventure to come.[217]

In the Foreign Office, Eden's principal adviser on Egypt was Roger Allen (assistant under-secretary of state, 1953–4). An agreement with Egypt, he wrote, 'presupposes a new conception of Anglo-Egyptian relations, namely co-operation with Egypt instead of maintenance of our position by force. It very likely will not work, and it almost certainly will not work smoothly, but in the absence of sufficient force, there seems no alternative.' A policy of 'masterly inactivity' would simply drive the Egyptians to attack, 'and the situation would then get completely out of control'. So it would be more logical and more dignified to pull out. Any disturbances would threaten British lives, which could only lead to occupying Cairo, and eventually all of Egypt to protect the Canal Zone: 'The truth of the matter is that we are at present keeping 80,000 men in the Canal Zone for no purpose except to maintain themselves.' Staying put and letting British troops be shot at would only damage all Britain's

[216] CAB 129/59, C(53)65, memo 16 February 1953; Kent, *Egypt*, pp. 563–4 (no. 361); Goldsworthy, *Conservative government*, pt 1, pp. 125–6 (no. 38).
[217] PREM 11 /635, Eden to Maurice Hankey, 25 February 1953; Churchill Archives Centre, HNKY 14/25, Hankey to Amery, Vansittart and Killearn, 28 February 1953; Kent, *Egypt*, pt 3: *1953–1956*, p. 11 (no. 372).

interests in the Middle East.[218] Allen believed American help was vital: 'If the Americans are not with us, they will certainly influence Egyptians against our proposals outside conference room, and strengthen the Egyptian position by offering arms and economic assistance not in conjunction with us.' In other words, 'they will give the Egyptians the bait out of the package proposals while we are struggling to force a naked hook down the Egyptian throat'. The attitude of Americans to the Middle East he described as twenty years behind their attitude to other parts of the world.[219]

In Cabinet, Churchill said in February 1953 that the 'first need' seemed to be to assure themselves of the full sympathy and support of the United States government in the approach they were proposing to make.[220] Accordingly, both Churchill and Eden appealed to President Eisenhower for his help in bringing about a peaceful solution. Britain, they said, was not going to be 'knocked about with impunity'; on the other hand maintaining 80,000 troops there indefinitely at immense expense was not in the British interest, as there were 'lots of places where they could be used better or the money saved'. Eisenhower was not at all responsive. By the end of 1953 Churchill resorted to some exceptionally plain speaking with him; 'we do not think you ought to give them moral and material support while they threaten and assault our troops and conduct a campaign of hatred against us'. No doubt Egypt seemed a petty problem to the president, but it could cause a deep and disastrous setback in Anglo-American relations: if they were on opposite sides it would 'gird on every enemy we have in common throughout the world'.[221]

For most of 1953 the tactic was to stand firm and not show undue interest in a settlement. Indefinite stalling was not of course possible or envisaged, but what Churchill had earlier called the 'patient sulky pig' posture seemed to be having a good effect.[222] Churchill was above all concerned with international prestige, with the primary importance of avoiding any appearance of being kicked out, 'a prolonged humiliating scuttle

---

[218] FO 371/102812, no. 391, minute by R. Allen, 30 June 1953; FO 371/102765, no. 121, minute 26 May 1953, and no 124; FO 371/102796, no. 18, minute 14 February 1953; FO 371/102813, no. 422, minute 5 May 1953; Kent, *Egypt*, pt 3, pp. 71–2 (no. 408, 30 June), and pp. 559–60 (no. 359, 14 February).

[219] FO 371/102798, no. 53, minute 9 March 1953; FO 371/102811, no. 374, minute 30 June 1953.

[220] CAB 128/26/1, OC 12(53)1 and 2, meeting 17 February 1953; Kent, *Egypt*, pt 2, pp. 566–8 (no. 364). See also the valuable essay by W. R. Louis, 'Churchill and Egypt, 1946–1956', in Blake and Louis, eds., *Churchill*, pp. 473–90.

[221] PREM 11/704, Churchill to Eisenhower, 25 February 1953 (PM 32); PREM 11/484, telegram 22 December 1953 (T 315/53); also PREM 11/699; Kent, *Egypt*, pt 3, pp. 12, 164–5 (nos. 373 and 461).

[222] FO 371/102820, no. 590, 29 October 1953; FO 371/102810, no. 351, 5 June 1953.

before all the world'.[223] ('Scuttle' was a foundational word in the Churchillian lexicon.) British troops who remained behind should be uniformed and armed.[224] He was adamant about this, but it was much debated. Churchill was still not fully committed to working for a settlement, and continued to dictate letters and notes to Eden of a high-handed nature.[225] His behaviour at Cabinet Eden might well have reasonably considered to be improper and exasperating in a chairman. Eden kept reiterating as best he could that agreement would be more advantageous than breakdown, which would be 'more of a scuttle', a fight 'which we can ill afford and from which we should emerge, though victorious in arms, without a friend left in the Middle East'.[226]

In order to retain the initiative, the drift had to be stopped. Things came to the boil in mid-March 1954. Eden's memorandum for the Cabinet stated there was no alternative to an agreement, without the risk of an even more serious and burdensome commitment and the virtual certainly of, in the end, humiliating withdrawal. The idea of a reduced number of soldier-technicians remaining behind was now seen as giving 'hostages to fortune'; they would have no military value. Better to have civilian contract labour (including Americans) and concentrate negotiations on the right of re-entry in an emergency.[227] At a Cabinet meeting, Churchill vented his feelings of 'great anxiety' about these proposals, 'both on merits and because of political criticism'. Too much would depend on the Egyptians keeping their promises. After a further Cabinet meeting, he agreed the plan could go ahead, though he would have preferred a definite rupture of negotiations and taking a stand on the 1936 Treaty.[228] In June 1954, while he accepted the military argument for redeployment, 'he continued to be impressed by the political disadvantages of abandoning the position we had held in Egypt since 1882'. In the end, though, he accepted that the 'radical result' of developments in nuclear technology of itself required a review, so withdrawal could be represented as based on a strategic reassessment. 'Obsolescence' was a word Churchill had always adored, and it won him over.[229]

---

[223] PREM 11/700, Churchill to Eden, 11 December 1953, quoted in H. V. Brasted, C. Bridge and J. Kent, 'Cold War, informal empire and the transfer of power: some "paradoxes" of decolonisation resolved?', in M. Dockrill, ed., *Europe within the global system, 1938–1960: Great Britain, France, Italy and Germany, from great powers to regional powers* (Arbeitskreis Deutsche England-Forschung, vol. 30, Bochum, 1995), pp. 11–30.

[224] CAB 128/26/1, CC 26(53)1, 14 April 1953; Kent, *Egypt*, pt 3, p. 44 (no. 388).

[225] PREM 11/484, 28 December 1953; PREM 11/700, 11 December 1953; Kent, *Egypt*, pt 3, pp. 158–9, 166–7 (nos. 456 and 464).   [226] FO 371/108413, no. 8.

[227] CAB 129/66, C(54)99, memo 13 March 1954; Kent, *Egypt*, pt 3, pp. 236–8 (no. 503).

[228] CAB 128/27/1, CC 18(54)1, 15 March 1954, and CC 21(54)2, 15 and 22 March 1954; Kent, *Egypt*, pp. 238–43 (nos. 504 and 505).

[229] CAB 128/27/1, CC 43(54)1, 22 June 1954; Kent, pt 3, pp. 275–8 (no. 525).

Agreement on the evacuation of the Canal Zone was reached in July 1954 because there were important advantages. Smaller bases, redeployment, and dispersal of troops was not only more efficient, but saved money, and gave better safety as well as strategic flexibility. The agreement was for seven years. It included Egyptian promises of free navigation in the Suez Canal, and, it was hoped, would lead to an improvement in Britain's relations with the Arab world.[230] It followed almost entirely the lines of the Labour government's plan seven years earlier. All this patient effort proved to be wasted, as the agreement was an immediate casualty of the Suez invasion in the autumn of 1956.[231]

(2) The Suez Crisis

Nothing so far in our analysis of the Conservative government enables us to predict what happened next. Ministers in general, and Eden in particular, had invariably shown every sign of pragmatically pursuing rational, fairly progressive extra-European policies. In the late summer and autumn of 1956 all this seemed to change – hardly more than a year after Eden had at last taken over as prime minister.[232]

This was because of Colonel Gamel Abdel Nasser, prime minister of Egypt from 1954 and president from 1956. Son of a post-office worker, he had master-minded the Egyptian army coup of 1952. To Arabs he was a charismatic figure, but a hate-figure in the West, far more than he deserved to be, for, although determined to evict British influence, he was fundamentally an honest man of modest life-style.[233]

Early in March 1956, Glubb Pasha (Lieutenant-General Sir John Glubb) was dismissed from his long-held post (as Chief of General Staff, Arab Legion, in Amman) by the king of Jordan. This action cast doubt on Jordan's reliability as an ally, and Eden blamed it on Nasser (wrongly).

[230] CAB 129/69, C(54)248, memo 23 July 1954; Kent, pt 3, p. 298 (no. 539); Goldsworthy, *Conservative government*, pt 1, pp. 131–2 (no. 42).

[231] W. R. Louis, 'The tragedy of the Anglo-Eyptian settlement', in W. R. Louis and R. Owen, eds., *Suez, 1956: the crisis and its consequences* (Oxford, 1989), pp. 44–71 (ch. 3).

[232] The best introduction to the Suez Crisis is probably still D. Carlton, *Britain and the Suez Crisis* (Oxford, 1988). Keith Kyle, *Suez* (1991) is certainly authoritative, but a long and complex narrative; something of his views may be gleaned from his essay, 'To Suez with tears', in W. R. Louis, ed., *Still more adventures with Britannia: personalities, politics, and culture in Britain* (Austin, Texas and New York, 2003), pp. 265–84. Of the memoirs, the most illuminating is Selwyn Lloyd, *Suez, 1956: a personal account* (1978), though of course it is an apologia. An excellent account is provided by J. Pearson, *Sir Anthony Eden and the Suez Crisis: reluctant gamble* (2003): concisely written, it is as strong on the chronological narrative as on historiographical comment: see esp. pp. 1–19 and 169–80. The clear nature of Eisenhower's advice is confirmed in Peter G. Boyle, ed., *The Eden–Eisenhower correspondence, 1955–1957* (North Carolina, 2005).

[233] P. J. Vatikiotis, *Nasser and his generation* (1978); A. Nutting, *Nasser* (1972).

Reacting violently, he told Nutting that he wanted Nasser not just isolated and removed, but murdered, and 'didn't give a damn' if the result was anarchy and chaos in Egypt.[234] A few months earlier it had been revealed that the Egyptian government was buying arms from the Soviet bloc. It seemed that despite the evacuation of British troops from the Canal Zone, Nasser was determined to continue being unfriendly towards Britain. For his part, Nasser was annoyed at the Baghdad Pact concluded in February 1955 by Britain with Iraq and Turkey.[235] This curious construct seemed to Nasser a rebuff and a challenge, and he had refused to join it after the one and only – and, as it proved, fateful – meeting between Eden and Nasser, when Eden was patronising. Nasser felt that Eden lectured him as if he were a junior official, behaving 'like a prince dealing with vagabonds'.[236] Then, early in July 1956, Dulles, the American secretary of state, withdrew the promise of US funding for the Aswan High Dam, consequentially followed by Britain and the World Bank also pulling out.

On 16 July 1956 Nasser nationalised – strictly, de-internationalised – the Suez Canal Company, in which the British government held about 44 per cent (17.7/40ths, since 1875) of the shares. At the Cabinet on 27 July the discussion revealed a feeling that 'failure to hold the Suez Canal would lead inevitably to the loss one by one of all our interests and assets in the Middle East, and, even if we had to act alone, we could not stop short of using force to protect our position if all other methods of protecting it proved unavailing'. There were three decisions: (1) the Egyptians 'must be subjected to the maximum political pressure' to reverse their decision to nationalise the Suez Canal Company, 'and, in the last resort, this political pressure must be backed by the threat – and, if need be, the use – of force'; (2) the opportunity should be taken to find 'a lasting settlement of this problem', which was 'not a legal issue but must be treated as a matter of the widest international importance'; (3) the Chiefs of Staff should be authorised to plan preparations for military action 'should they prove unavoidable'.[237] The formula of 'the last

---

[234] Lapping, *End of empire*, p. 262, modifies the account in A. Nutting, *No end of a lesson: the story of Suez* (1967), p. 25 (which has 'destroyed' not 'murdered'). March 1956 may indeed represent a turning-point: at the Cabinet on 21 March Eden secured a definite decision for 'a realignment of policy in the Middle East' and 'a new policy towards Egypt' (e.g., possibly withdrawing Aswan dam finance), based on the belief that Nasser would not be co-operative or friendly (CAB 128/30/1, CM 24(56)5).

[235] Matthew Elliot, 'Defeat and revival: Britain in the Middle East', in W. Kaiser and G. Staerck, eds., *British foreign policy, 1955–1964: contracting options* (2000), pp. 239–56.

[236] D. Carlton, *Anthony Eden a biography* (1981), p. 365.

[237] CAB 128/30/2, CM 54(56), 27 July 1956; Goldsworthy, *Conservative government*, pt 1, pp. 165–9 (no. 54). The Cabinet discussions and decisions are usefully summarised in R. Rhodes James, *Anthony Eden* (1986), and in Carlton, *Britain and the Suez Crisis*, pp. 132–55 (appendix II).

resort' was adopted as a means of preserving consensus. At the meeting on 14 August the Cabinet noted that the use of force 'would be unlikely to obtain general support without some further cause being provided by the Egyptian government'. In other words, there should be some further provocative act by Nasser.[238] One of the main concerns of the Egypt Committee (which really took charge) was how to 'bring matters to a head'. They sought a means of 'provoking an incident with Egypt', which was difficult, because the Egyptians had been meticulous in observing the agreement and had not interfered with the removal of stores. As far as the hawks of the Egypt Committee were concerned, their hidden agenda and main aim was the downfall of Nasser and his unhelpful government; 'a direct approach' to this was difficult, so they would use the issue of navigation in the canal, getting it under international control.[239]

Sir Walter Monckton, minister of defence, began to emerge as the principal doubter. In committee on 24 August colleagues were shocked by an extraordinary outburst.[240] Which he repeated more soberly at the Cabinet on 28 August: military action would be 'condemned by a substantial body of public opinion in countries overseas, including several independent countries of the Commonwealth'. With opinion in the UK itself also divided, Monckton added, 'our vital interests in other parts of the world would also be affected; we must, in particular, expect sabotage against oil installations in other Arab countries'. So, he concluded, 'first exhaust all other means of curbing Colonel Nasser's ambitions, and let no opportunity pass of settling by agreement'. Even Salisbury urged caution, and 'doing our utmost to secure our objective by peaceful means', and if force ultimately had to be used, 'we should seek the maximum international support for its use', going first to the United Nations. However, it was also argued that were Nasser to succeed, 'our whole position in the Middle East would be undermined, our oil supplies would be in jeopardy, and the stability of our national economy would be gravely threatened'. Summing up, Eden said the Cabinet was evidently united in believing 'the frustration of Colonel Nasser's policy was a vital British interest which must be secured, in the last resort by the use of force'. He recognised that 'every practicable attempt should be made to secure a satisfactory settlement by peaceful means', but exploring these 'should not be allowed to weaken our resolution or reduce the weight of our pressure on

---

[238] CAB 128/30/2, CM 59(56)3, 14 August 1956: PREM 11/1152, Sir N. Brook to Eden, 25 August 1956.

[239] PREM 11/1140, p. 281; CAB 134/1216, p. 87, EC 11(56)1, 7 August 1956.

[240] PREM 11 /1152, letters to 'Anthony' [Eden], from 'Alec' [Lord Home], 'Bobbety' [Lord Salisbury] and 'Alan' [Lennox-Boyd], all 24 August 1956.

the Egyptian government'. As Carlton comments, Eden's policy had now assumed 'an essentially schizophrenic character'.[241]

On 6 September ministers agreed to refer the matter to the Security Council, because Selwyn Lloyd, as foreign secretary, emphasised the desirabilility of being seen to make the fullest possible use of all available international machinery in the search for a peaceful settlement. But other voices stressed the danger of delay, of a 'slow economic strangulation as Egypt extended her control over the Arab world and the oil-producing countries'.[242] At the Cabinet on 11 September, with the news that Egypt had rejected proposals for international control of the canal, Macmillan thought it unlikely it could now be secured without the use of force, and they should 'bring the issue to a head'. This provoked Monckton into declaring that 'any premature recourse to force especially without the support and approval of the United States, was likely to precipitate disorder throughout the Middle East and to alienate a substantial body of opinion in this country and elsewhere throughout the world'. But the Cabinet approved the prime minister's summing up: 'if peaceful means fail, we should be justified in the last resort in using force to restore the situation'; it would, however, be a difficult exercise of judgment to decide if the point had been reached 'when recourse must be had to forceful measures'; meanwhile, opinion in America and France should be weighed.[243]

So far, the historian might feel, so fairly good. Selwyn Lloyd's negotiations in New York were going quite well. Eden was not yet finally committed to abandoning peace-talks, and he had indeed put his finger on the crucial point but not foreclosed it: how were they to decide when 'the last resort' had been reached, and they could 'push the button'? A dangerous shift was however apparent at the Cabinet on 24 October. According to the minutes: if the government went for a negotiated settlement they would have to recognise that 'their second objective of reducing Colonel Nasser's influence throughout the Middle East' would have to be abandoned; 'discussions' with the French government were 'proceeding'.[244] The focus now tightened. (Up to this point, the Suez issue was still only one item among the heterogeneous mix on the agenda: housing, war pensions, House of Lords reform, capital punishment, the price of sugar, rent restrictions, legislative plans, agricultural policy, finding economies, and the major issue of the European Free Trade Area and general relationship to Europe.) The crucial turning-point came on 24 and 25 October. The prime minister proposed Anglo-French military action 'to safeguard the

---

[241] CAB 128/30/2, CM 62(56)2, 28 August 1956; Carlton, *Britain and the Suez Crisis*, p. 51.   [242] CAB 128/30/2, CM 63(56), 6 September 1956.
[243] CAB 128/30/2, CM 64(56), 11 September 1956.
[244] CAB 128/30/2, CM 73(56)7, 24 October 1956.

canal'. Israel was planning to attack Egypt, and 'we should never have a better pretext for intervention'. Arguments were put forward in support, such as Lloyd's that 'our influence throughout the Middle East was gravely threatened', but powerful doubts were also raised which should have given Eden pause: action without the specific authority of the United Nations 'might do lasting damage to Anglo-American relations. There was no prospect of securing the support or approval of the United States Government.' Facing the risk 'that we should be accused of collusion with Israel', ministers decided upon intervention and the issue of an ultimatum to Egypt. But this was most definitely not a united decision, even despite the fact that the Cabinet was not properly informed of exactly what was being secretly agreed with the French.[245]

The Anglo-French forces went into action on 31 October. On 2 November Britain was roundly condemned by the UN, and the Cabinet may have received royal representations (the minutes are withheld until 2007 at least). The Egyptians blocked the Canal on 4 November. At midnight on 6 November a ceasefire was ordered. The next day Eden lamented that the United States government had not understood how dangerous was the situation in the Middle East, with the threat of Russian interference.[246] A memorandum for the Egypt Committee on 8 November records that the ceasefire had been forced upon Britain by: (a) United Nations pressure, the grave risk of its imposing oil sanctions on Britain; (b) the possibility of an anti-British Russian intervention, which would demand re-alignment with the estranged US government; and (c) the political climate in the United Kingdom. Fears of 'a run on the pound' were not listed, and perhaps these were largely confined to Macmillan.[247] Treasury papers had been laid before the Cabinet towards the end of August stressing the importance of avoiding a crisis, since it was easy to predict that the canal would be blocked in retaliation and oil supplies thus endangered.[248] Macmillan produced his own personal paper, which, being Macmillan, he wanted to entitle 'The economic consequences of Colonel Nasser'; this came to a clear conclusion that

---

[245] CAB 128/30/2, CM 73(56)7, 24 October 1956, and CM 74(56)1, 25 October 1956. See also W. Scott Lucas, *Divided we stand: Britain, the US and the Suez Crisis* (1991), p. 223; I find it hard to recommend this book – the author is an American with anti-British views and a belief that the Americans were blameless; the impression is one of striving for a new interpretation, which takes the form of emphasising the role of MI6, but it is notoriously difficult to rely on 'speculations' about the role of intelligence. For further criticisms of Lucas's work, see a review by M. Elliot in *Contemporary British History*, vol. 11 (1997), pp. 168–70, of his edited volume *Britain and Suez: the lion's last roar* (1996).

[246] CAB 128/30/2, CM 81(56), 7 November 1956.

[247] CAB 134/1217, p. 298, EC(56)67, memo, 8 November 1956. But see also D. B. Kunz, 'Economic diplomacy in the Suez Crisis', in Louis and Owen, *Suez, 1956*, pp. 215–32.

[248] CAB 128/30/2, CM 62(56)2, 28 August 1956.

'without oil, both the UK and Western Europe are lost'. But there was no hint of worry about 'a run on the pound'.[249]

The Suez Crisis was a counter-productive, catastrophic fiasco, marked by deception, hypocrisy, myopia, and confusion, and ending in humiliating failure. Its central feature was obsessive, almost apocalyptic paranoia about Nasser. This was not confined to Eden. Selwyn Lloyd – unkindly but not inaccurately described as monkey to the prime minister's organ-grinder – said 'the salient point is that Nasser was an enemy of this country . . . a public enemy', both menacing and dangerous. Looking back, he was quite certain 'we were right in assessing Nasser as a potential Hitler, another megalomaniac dictator, who would do infinite damage to Western interests.[250] Eden himself preferred the analogy of a 'Moslem Mussolini'. Suez is a striking example both of 'sexing up the dossier' (using suspect intelligence) and of the dangers of choosing the wrong historical analogy for guidance, especially Hitler (even if this particular absurdity is understandable in men of their generation). The correct analogue for Nasser was Urabi Pasha, leader of the Egyptian army revolt in 1882 – a historical parallel of which Nasser was strongly conscious. Nasser's intellectual inspiration was not *Mein Kampf*, but the writings of Ahmed Hussein, theorist of 'Young Egypt'.[251] But in any case, as President Eisenhower pertinently warned Eden, Nasser's support was 'shaky in many important quarters', and it was most improbable that he would emerge as 'the acknowledged leader of Islam': 'you are making of Nasser a much more important figure than he is . . . a picture too dark and severely distorted'.[252]

It is hard to believe that things would have gone quite so badly awry but for Eden's temperament and ill-health, and the severe decline which had set in by October.[253] Some historians, however, have tried to rationalise it all and not make a drama out of a crisis. There was, they say, 'more to the Suez Crisis than Eden's liver' – it is too easy to see it as a freak lapse into adventurism – and then even more surprisingly add that they see it as a carefully calculated plan to restore British global influence.[254] Unfortunately, this

---

[249] PREM 11/1152, 24 August 1956.

[250] Selwyn Lloyd, *Suez, 1956*, pp. 193, 247–8 and 260.

[251] T. Little, *Egypt* (1958), pp. 210–11: 'Nasser was remaking the Arabi rebellion all over again in more appropriate circumstances'; P. J. Vatikiotis, *Nasser and his generation* (1978), pp. 52–9.

[252] PREM 11/1177, p. 48, 'Ike' to 'Anthony', 9 September 1956; PREM 11/1100, p. 190, message, 3 September 1956.

[253] Pearson, *Sir Anthony Eden and the Suez Crisis*: 'he was not the same man in October as he had been in July', p. 173.

[254] J. Darwin, 'British decolonisation since 1945: a pattern or puzzle?', *JICH*, vol. 12 (1984), p. 201; R. Holland, 'The imperial factor in British strategies from Attlee to Macmillan', 1945–1963', *ibid.*, p. 178.

interpretation is not based on any close reading of the documents. The records demonstrate beyond all doubt that the episode was an aberration, something which simply did not evolve naturally out of government policy as settled and agreed. Eden's own entirely rational policies hitherto were based on recognition of the need to come to terms with nationalism and abandon all thoughts of Palmerstonian gunboat-diplomacy as out-of-date and impracticable, 'from which we should emerge . . . without a friend in the Middle East' (above, p. 225). But when in April 1956 Eden began to depart from this understanding, and Brook (as Cabinet secretary) fired a warning shot across his bows, reminding him of his memorandum of 1953 (above, pp. 222–3), Eden was furious and would not listen.[255]

There are four main reasons for regarding Suez as an aberration. First, Eden acted out of character. Second, the law officers pronounced the use of force to be illegal. Third, the normal processes of government were suspended. And fourth, the American reaction was disastrously miscalculated. As to the first: Evelyn Shuckburgh (FO assistant under-secretary) began to notice early in 1956 that Eden was 'greatly deteriorated'. Then, a few weeks later, 'he seems to be completely disintegrated', petulant, provocative, yet weak and unable to focus on the important things.[256] Anthony Nutting was even prepared to put a definite date on the change. From 1 March 1956, when Glubb Pasha was dismissed, 'he began to behave like an enraged elephant, completely losing his touch'.[257] Nor were such observations restricted to Eden's inner circle. The Opposition leader Hugh Gaitskell wrote in his diary (9 March 1956), 'everybody was saying that he couldn't last much longer'.[258] Of course deterioration was not a linear process, and Eden's moods and performance fluctuated, but as the summer wore on, several officials were telling their wives that Eden had gone 'mad', 'bananas' or 'potty'.

Secondly, his law officers told Eden bluntly that the use of force in retaliation for Nasser's nationalisation would be illegal. They advised him that the climate of world opinion had dramatically changed, and justifications which would have been accepted without question fifty or even twenty-five years ago would now be completely rejected. Sir Reginald Manningham-Buller, the attorney-general, and Sir Harry Hylton-Foster, the solicitor-general, made this absolutely clear: if the lord chancellor, Lord Kilmuir, said force was not illegal under the charter of the UN, then

---

[255] PREM 11/1457, minute by Brook, 14 April 1956; minute by F. A. Bishop, 15 August 1956.

[256] E. Shuckburgh, *Descent to Suez: diaries, 1951–1956* (1986), ed. J. Charmley, pp. 330–1 and 345.   [257] Nutting, *No end of a lesson*, pp. 25–9.

[258] Philip M. Williams, ed., *The diary of Hugh Gaitskell, 1945–1956* (1983), p. 452 (9 March 1956).

he was wrong; and if the government attempted to claim legality in public, or if they themselves were questioned in parliament, they would resign.[259] The Foreign Office legal adviser, Sir Gerald Fitzmaurice, said the lord chancellor used 'a lot of dubious arguments and half-truths'; Fitzmaurice's department insisted it had 'from the beginning and at all times strongly opposed the use of force as having no legal justification in any of the circumstances that had or have arisen hitherto'.[260]

Thirdly, it was not just the law officers who were ignored. Part of the 'aberration' was that Eden began refusing advice from all but one or two close colleagues in the Egypt Committee (which had the executive role), officials like his private secretary (Freddie Bishop) and Sir Ivone Kirkpatrick (permanent under-secretary at the Foreign Office, who only encouraged his misguided resolve).[261] Unfortunately, Roger Allen – who had given him such good Egyptian briefings in 1953 and 1954 – was now pursuing his diplomatic career (shortly becoming ambassador to Greece). Even the relevant ambassadors were cut out of the loop. Sir Humphrey Trevelyan in Cairo, sceptical of Nasser's chances of realising his wider aims, was kept in the dark, and had to look on aghast: 'All that I had been trying to build was in ruins. It was, I confess, difficult at that time not to come to tears, not of self-pity, but of vexation and despair.'[262] Sir Gladwyn Jebb in Paris was excluded from the discussions with the French government, complaining that it was 'novel' for matters of the highest importance to be conducted without officials present or notes being taken. (Eden disputed this.)[263] Normally Cabinet government proceeds by the discussion of memoranda prepared by officials. There were almost none during the Suez Crisis. Nor were ministers kept properly informed. Furthermore, Eden ordered the destruction of the minutes of the Egypt Committee for 17 October through to 1 November, and even insisted Macmillan must destroy his personal diary for the last three

---

[259] PREM 11/1129, Manningham-Buller to Eden, 1 and 13 November 1956.

[260] FO 800/748, minute by Fitzmaurice, 1 November 1956; G. Marston, 'Armed intervention in the 1956 Suez Canal Crisis: the legal advice tendered to the British government', *International and Comparative Law Quarterly* vol. 37 (1988), pp. 773–817, draws on many archival records, but Marston did not see FO 800/748, a file carefully compiled to make sure the legal department's unequivocal stance was on record.

[261] Kirkpatrick 'comes across in the [official] papers as hysterical and at times just silly'; no doubt he was under great pressure in this episode, but his performance 'fell below the better traditions of the British civil service. Like Eden his attitudes had been formed in relation to the rise of Hitler': A. W. B Simpson, *Human rights and the end of empire: Britain and the genesis of the European Convention* (Oxford, 2001, 2004), pp. 894–5 and n. 62.

[262] Humphrey Trevelyan, *The Middle East in revolution* (1970), p. 130; review of Selwyn Lloyd, *Suez, 1956* in *The Times*, 6 July 1978, p. 4.

[263] PREM 11/1126, Gladwyn Jebb to foreign secretary, 17 October 1956.

months of 1956.[264] Eden's attempts also to cover his tracks by destroying copies of the Sèvres Protocol – the infamous 'collusion' document – were frustrated by the survival of a single copy in the Israeli prime minister's hands.

Eden had plenty of good advice available. Even Lord Home – prepared to agree that 'we are finished if the Middle East goes, and Russia and India and China rule from Africa to the Pacific' – warned Eden that some colleagues felt the use of force 'would divide country, Party and Commonwealth so deeply that we should never recover'.[265] Brook made a powerful protest that 'it would be a mistake to put the Cabinet at the final fence too soon', doubting that the 'last resort' had come, and warning that at least half-a-dozen ministers were unhappy and three more were waverers.[266] In fact Monckton did resign as minister of defence (though not from the Cabinet, in order not to rock the boat unduly). Nutting resigned from his Foreign Office post. Admiral of the Fleet, Lord Mountbatten, tried to get the expedition called off and to resign, but was ordered to stay at his post by Lord Hailsham.[267] The effect of such widespread suspension of normal processes and pursuing such an aberrant course – seizing the helm and driving the ship onto the rocks – was an unprecedentedly large number of protests and contemplated resignations among junior ministers and civil servants. The tally of actual resignations would have been higher if the expedition had gone on for more than its six days and eighteen hours. An historical investigation into the civil service response to Suez has concluded that the significant specific failure of the government machine was the basic inability of officials to get ministers, especially Eden, to listen to the long list of their sensible arguments against a highly questionable policy and preconceived prejudices, and get Eden to reconsider his approach instead of ignoring them.[268]

[264] A. Thurston, ed., *Sources for colonial studies in the Public Record Office*, vol II: *Records of the Cabinet, Foreign Office, Treasury and other records* (BDEEP, 1998), p. 164 – the minute numbers were reallocated to cover the tracks; Catterall, *Macmillan diaries*, p. 607, n. 68.   [265] PREM 11/1152, Home to Eden, 24 August 1956.

[266] PREM 11/1152, Brook to Eden, 25 August 1956; see also M. D. Kandiah, 'British domestic politics, the Conservative Party and foreign policy-making', in Kaiser and Staerck, *British foreign policy*, pp. 67–8.

[267] PREM 11/1090, 'Dickie' Mountbatten to Eden, 2 November, and to Lord Hailsham, 4 November; minutes by Hailsham and Eden, 5 November 1956.

[268] J. W. Young, 'Conclusion', in S. Kelly and A. Gorst, eds., *Whitehall and the Suez Crisis* (2000), pp. 221–3, and L. Johnman, 'Sir Gerald Fitzmaurice, senior legal adviser to the Foreign Office', pp. 46–63; C. Brady, 'The Cabinet system and management of the Suez Crisis', *Contemporary British History*, vol. 11 (1997), pp. 65–93; A. Adamthwaite, 'Suez revisited', *International Affairs*, vol. 64 (1988), pp. 449–64, repr. in M. Dockrill and J. W. Young, eds., *British foreign policy, 1945–1956* (1989), pp. 225–45 (ch. 10); Kyle, *Suez*, pp. 166, 381, and 397.

Leaders of Commonwealth governments were also not consulted, with the exception of all-too-like-minded Menzies of Australia. Most members were shocked by the unprincipled action, and resented the lack of consultation. This was true of Canada, though there perhaps more in sorrow than in anger: as Lester Pearson put it, it was 'like hearing a beloved uncle had been had up for rape'. India and Ceylon were fiercely and publicly opposed, with Nehru siding openly with Nasser. Even the prime minister of New Zealand wavered. In the famous words of Lester Pearson, Suez brought the Commonwealth 'to the verge of dissolution'.[269]

Finally, if Commonwealth governments were disappointed and upset, the American administration was downright angry. This was perhaps the most aberrant feature of all, since if there had been one cardinal rule followed by all British policy-makers since 1945 it was to keep on the right side of the USA.[270] The 'Suez' chapter in Macmillan's memoirs is entitled 'The Anglo-American schism'. Lloyd's retrospective apologia suggests that misjudgments were not about British power but about the American reaction. Ministers, he wrote, did not foresee Eisenhower's opposition; not to have the Americans at least winking and benevolently neutral was unthinkable.[271] Eden and Macmillan assumed they could rely on their friendship with Eisenhower, and failed to check – a mistake, it has to be said, that Attlee did not make over Persia, nor would Callaghan in Cyprus, or Thatcher on the Falklands. In fact Eden did not even listen to what was being said, and said plainly and repeatedly. Eisenhower warned him, 'the use of force would . . . vastly increase the area of jeopardy'; he urged the 'unwisdom of even contemplating force at the moment' until every peaceful means had been 'thoroughly explored and exhausted' (1 August 1956). He telegraphed his 'deep concern' on 30 October, and on 4 November telephoned, 'what the hell is going on?'[272] As far as Eisenhower was concerned, 'how could we possibly support Britain and France, if in doing so we lose the whole Arab world?' – Britain and France were setting the clock back fifty years and would unite the whole world from Dakar to the Philippines against the West.[273] Dulles had said 'a way had

---

[269] DO 35/6338, no. 64, minute by A. W. Snelling, 26 November 1956; PREM 11/1096; DO 35/ 6334 (Canada), 6336 (Australia), 6337 (New Zealand), 6338 (South Africa), 6339 (India), 6340 (Pakistan), and 6341 (Ceylon); J. Eayrs, ed., *The Commonwealth and Suez: a documentary survey* (Oxford, 1964); P. Lyon, 'The Commonwealth and the Suez Crisis', in Louis and Owen, eds., *Suez, 1956*, ch. 13.

[270] W. R. Louis, 'American anti-colonialism and the dissolution of the British Empire', *International Affairs*, vol. 61 (1985), pp. 395–420.

[271] Lloyd, *Suez, 1956*, pp. 36–7, 252, 260.   [272] PREM 11/1177, nos. 26, 28, 48 and 68.

[273] Quoted in G. Warner, 'The United States and the Suez Crisis', *International Affairs*, vol. 67 (1989), pp. 303–17.

to be found to make Nasser disgorge what he was attempting to swallow'. Eden quoted this in a Cabinet memorandum – as indeed have almost all historians since – without the vital qualifying phrase which immediately followed: 'force was the last method to be tried to accomplish this . . . if all other methods failed'. No wonder, then, that Eden's colleagues misread the signals from America.[274] And when the prime minister was told that Dulles thought a large section of British public opinion would probably think it a UN matter, Eden's pencilled comment was 'Mind his own business.'[275] Dulles had, however, judged British reaction better than the prime minister. Undoubtedly Eden had for quite a long time been fed up with playing second fiddle to the Americans. With hindsight, his statement to the Cabinet a year before acquires a degree of ominousness: 'Our interests in the Middle East were greater than those of the United States because of our dependence on oil, and our experience in the area was greater than theirs. We should not therefore allow ourselves to be restricted over-much by reluctance to act without full American concurrence and support.'[276] It was his most serious error of judgment.

What are we to conclude? Why had it all gone wrong? It might be argued that Eden was seduced by the French government, who had concerns about Nasser surpassing those of the British, and offered Eden an artificially induced way of 'bringing matters to a head', of getting to 'the last resort'. At a more fundamental level, the truth is that Eden should never have become prime minister. Perhaps he would not have done had more of his generation survived the First World War. He had a complete lack of political flair. He was humourless. He was trapped in clichés, and Churchill was always correcting his spelling. He had an innate volatility of temperament, and could fly into violent rages, especially with subordinates. During the height of the crisis, several observers reported him to be in a state of histrionic, manic exaltation, sweeping Cabinet doubters and service chiefs along, brushing aside all counter-argument.[277] His wife, Clarissa Churchill, complained that she felt as if the Suez Canal were flowing through their drawing room, but did nothing to calm him down. (She was thought of as 'Lady Macbeth of Suez' by Gladwyn Jebb's wife.)[278]

---

[274] PREM 11/1098, CM(56)56.   [275] PREM 11/1100, p. 227 (30 August 1956).
[276] CAB 128/29, CM 34(55)8, 4 October 1955.
[277] J. Colville, *The fringes of power: Downing Street diaries, 1939–1956* (1985), pp. 722–4.
[278] William Clark, *From three worlds: memoirs* (1986), pp. 146–56; Lady Cynthia Gladwyn, *Diaries of Cynthia Gladwyn* (ed. Miles Jebb, 1995), p. 191: Ivone Kirkpatrick complains that Clarissa Eden tells AE not to weaken, and that she interferes – 'how dangerous all this sounds. Is it really a case of "infirm of purpose, give me the dagger"? It's said to be "Clarissa's War".'

And what about Eden's liver? He suffered from a severed bile duct and recurrent fevers as the result of a botched operation. He was certainly on benzedrine, and occasionally when the pain was bad, pethedine. Drugs and stimulants were stepped up from July 1956. His press secretary resigned, deciding that he was 'literally mad', and 'went so that day his temperature rose to 105°F'. This was on 5/6 October, when Eden admitted to Eisenhower in a dictated telegram, 'I have been struck down by a tiresome virus with a high temperature but I hope to be about again in a day or two.'[279] What he did not admit to was undergoing a surgical procedure. The Boston Clinic specialist who saw him in April 1957 said his judgment could well have been impaired by his condition for the last six months. It is indeed known that chronic liver disease can lead to intermittent neuropsychiatric disorders such as mood swings and intellectual malfunction.[280]

None of this helped. But essentially the Suez venture was, paradoxically, a logical outcome of the agreement to evacuate the Canal Zone. Eden had fought hard to achieve this against the constant sniping of Churchill and the virulent protests of the die-hards. He became angered by Nasser's refusal to deliver better Anglo-Egyptian relations, after all the efforts Eden had made and the confidence vested in his regime.[281] Sir Evelyn Shuckburgh came to as good a judgment as it seems possible to get. In answer to the question 'did Eden go potty?' he wrote:

Eden was a most intelligent, sensitive and experienced man, but weak and constantly concerned to show that he was strong . . . The fact that Britain was now broke, morally exhausted and wildly over-stretched was *understood* by Eden perfectly well but not perhaps sufficiently well absorbed into his consciousness to offset his pride at becoming, at long last, its spokesman. He had been long subjected to the continuous pressure of his party to show himself more strong, more Churchillian. If anyone was potty it was the Suez Group of Tories, the Churchill entourage, the Amerys, etc.: who for years had been jeering at Eden as a scuttler.

All through his time as foregin secretary (Shuckburgh continued), he had wanted to co-operate with Egypt, including Nasser, in the search for a settlement with Israel (Plan Alpha), knowing that Egypt was the one Arab

---

[279] PREM 11/1102, p. 185; CAB 134/1217, EC(56)167; Goldsworthy, *Conservative government*, pt 1, pp. 171–3 (no. 56); Carlton, *Britain and the Suez Crisis*, pp. 156–8 (appendix III). After the immediate crisis was over, Eden was in such a bad state that he left (23 November) for recuperation at the retreat in Jamaica where Ian Fleming wrote his 'James Bond' novels.

[280] Clark, *From three worlds*, pp. 208–9; Rhodes James, *Eden*, pp. 523 and 597; W. H. J. Summerskill, et al., 'Neuropsychiatric syndrome associated with Hepatic Cirrhosis and an extensive portal collateral circulation', *Quarterly Journal of Medicine*, ns, vol. 25 (1956), pp. 245–65, quoted by Hugh Thomas, *The Suez affair* (1966), p. 217.

[281] Colville, *The fringes of power*, p. 721.

country which would have the power, if it had the will, to do anything at all about it; but he allowed Nasser and indeed Dulles to get under his skin, which was too thin:

He was driven off this course by the stronger winds which blew around him when he got to No. 10 and for which, if truth be told, he was not suitably rigged, and he certainly seems to have been emotionally over-excited. I thought I knew him quite well at the time and I could hardly believe that he would commit such follies . . . But I do not think he was mad. He was a tragic figure.[282]

Eden's latest biographer is not too far wide of the mark in saying that the Suez Crisis unfolded with the 'inexorable momentum of a Greek tragedy'.[283]

Even before the Suez Crisis was entirely over, and before Eden had formally resigned – though now out of the fray – the remaining Conservative ministers set about restoring normality. The top priority was to mend their fences with the Americans. At the last Cabinet before Macmillan took over as prime minister, they reminded themselves that 'the Anglo-American alliance was vital to the security of the free world: but the Suez Crisis had made it plain that there must be some change in the basis of Anglo-American relations'. Fearing that Britain's 'special position' would not continue, the best way of recovering their standing with the USA might be closer political and military association with the European Economic Community, 'short of federation'. The ministerial cry now was for rallying their dispirited Conservative supporters by 'new themes . . . and positive policies'.[284] Thus was British policy restored to Eden's sensible insight in 1953, 'new times, new methods'.

In this connection, one crucial fact is not generally realised: that major discussions in Cabinet on whether Britain could associate more closely with Europe – outside the community 'Six' – through EFTA (European Free Trade Association) took place concurrently with the Suez Crisis: on 14 and 18 September, 3 October and 13 November.[285] The central issue was how the Commonwealth would react to a greater British involvement – Macmillan said 'much will depend' on the attitude of Commonwealth countries. The effect of Commonwealth disillusionment over Suez, and the lack of consultation about it, was to make members much more indifferent to the European outcome. They scarcely both-

---

[282] Letter from Sir Evelyn Shuckburgh to the author, 29 March 1953. The press has some responsibility for the pressures on Eden: notoriously, the *Daily Telegraph* had called for 'the smack of firm government' (3 January 1956).

[283] Thorpe, 'Eden, Anthony', *ODNB*, vol. 17, p. 678.

[284] CAB 128/30/2, CM 3(57), 8 January 1957; Goldsworthy, *Conservative government*, pt 1, pp. 107–10 (no. 29); Porter and Stockwell, eds, *British imperial policy and decolonisation*, vol. II, pp. 445–50 (no. 69).

[285] CAB 128/30/2, CM 65(56)2, CM 68(56)10, and CM 83(56)1.

ered to protest. Thus Suez unfroze the way forward over Europe in a way that could not have been predicted in August 1956. In mid-November Macmillan reported to the Cabinet a 'surprising and encouraging degree' of Commonwealth support, and this convinced previously doubtful ministers.

Can we go further with the consequences of Suez? Was Suez the beginning of decolonisation? Historiographically the battle-lines are drawn between those who make a high estimate of the effects, and those who feel they can be exaggerated. Anthony Low believes that it is always local nationalist pressure which forces transfers of power, and Suez is therefore 'irrelevant'.[286] By contrast, Roger Louis takes the view that 'if there is any single event that marks the turning-point in the dissolution of the African empires, it is the Suez Crisis of 1956'.[287] This, to my mind, is a significantly stronger position, because: (1) Suez broke both the British imperial grip and the French cultural grip on the crucial area of the Middle East;[288] (2) it forced a reconsideration of military deployments, which improved the prospects of Malta and Cyprus for self-government, and enabled Ceylon to get rid of British bases; (3) it had a psychological impact on Macmillan's colonial policy, even if he could not act immediately; and (4) it made Britain 'Public Enemy Number One' at the United Nations for the next dozen years or so, with major implications for decolonisation.[289]

One final observation may be made. Suez was the most divisive political event of the last half-century in Britain, hugely more electrifying to public opinion than Thatcher's action in the Falklands or Blair's in Iraq. It was a moment of blinding revelation for many British people that the days of empire were numbered. It completely shattered the automatic trust and confidence of younger generations – and some older ones as well – in the good faith and honesty of their governments.[290] Politicians

---

[286] *Contemporary Record*, vol. 1 (1987–8), pp. 31–3, debate between D. A. Low and B. Lapping, 'Did Suez hasten the end of empire?' See pp. 181–2 (n. 70) for a comment.

[287] W. R. Louis, *Ends of British imperialism: the scramble for Suez, and decolonization* (2006), intro. 'Suez and decolonization: scrambling out of Africa and Asia'. P. Gifford and W. R. Louis, eds., *Decolonisation and African independence: the transfer of power, 1960–1980* (Yale, 1988), p. xlv. See also Morgan, *The official history of colonial development* vol. V (1980), p. 343, who sees a 'post-Suez revaluation' leading to 'an acceleration of colonial change from 1957'. Eden's press secretary, William Clark, believed that 'within six months the process of decolonisation in Africa began' (*From three worlds*, p. 215).

[288] A. Hourani, 'Conclusion', in Louis and Owen, *Suez, 1956: the crisis and its consequences*, pp. 406–8.

[289] W. R. Louis, 'Public enemy Number One: the British empire in the dock at the United Nations, 1957–1971', in M. Lynn, ed., *The British empire in the 1950s: retreat or revival?* (2006), pp. 186–213.

[290] According to Ian Winchester, then a junior official on the Egyptian desk at the FO (and later an assistant under-secretary of state, FCO), diplomats had been reassuring alarmed enquirers that 'HMG could be relied upon to play a straight bat', and felt let

would no longer get the benefit of the doubt. No subsequent generation would be as unquestioning as the last cohorts of national servicemen. Suez was for many a source of irreversible enlightenment, not least when evaluated in conjunction with John Osborne's seminal play at the Royal Court Theatre, *Look back in anger* (May 1956; television November 1956; film 1958), which seemed to validate a subversive outlook on life and politics. From this point onwards, deference to the Establishment, and indeed all establishments and hierarchies, would wither away. There was a new generation of protest, with criticism of foreign, imperial and nuclear arms policies better organised and more widespread than ever before. Press outrage was kept alive after Suez by a series of shameful incidents in Africa in the next few years. The anti-apartheid movement reached by the late 1950s what was probably the peak of its popular support. Of all this, Macmillan, succeeding Eden as prime minister, was acutely aware. Public opinion had never been able effectively to lead governments where they did not want to go in overseas policy, and this did not change. Nevertheless, the new critical awareness of the public, and its willingness to take an ethical stand, was an important development.[291]

Footnote 290 (*cont.*)

   down when this proved not to be the case (I. S. Winchester in conversation with the author, July 1960). For the reaction of the doyen of Commonwealth studies, Professor Mansergh, see R. Hyam, 'Mansergh, Nicholas', *ODNB*, vol. XXXVI, p. 543 ('I shall never vote Conservative again').

[291] Nicholas Owen, 'Critics of empire in Britain', in *The Oxford History of the British Empire*, vol. IV, *The twentieth century*, pp. 203–10; D. Sandbrook, *Never had it so good: a history of Britain from Suez to the Beatles* (2005), pp. 177–83 on 'Look back in anger'.

4 'The wind of change is blowing': the Macmillan and Douglas-Home governments and the end of empire, 1957–1964

Once, changing trains at Baker Street, Attlee had been asked by a woman, 'have you ever been told you look just like Mr Attlee?' 'Frequently', he replied, laconically in character.[1] Such a thing could never have happened to Harold Macmillan. 'SuperMac', having been a head-turningly handsome schoolboy, developed an unmistakably old-world patrician presence blended with the media-consciousness of a consummate stage-actor. He had style, he had wit, and he had them in abdundance – though this is not to say he entirely avoided resort to banality, bluff, and bad history. The important thing was that he had learned how to command attention. As a minister, he had frequently demonstrated panache, and a mastery of the Cabinet memorandum as a minor art-form, incisive, witty and jaundiced at the same time.[2] No-one but Macmillan would have dared to quote Stanley Holloway's comic monologue 'Albert and the lion' in a paper about the traitors Burgess and Maclean ('Sum one 'ad got to be summoned, so that was decided upon'). When chairing Cabinet meetings, it amused him to use analogies from the shooting-field which he knew nine-tenths of ministers would not understand.[3] Unlike Eden, his abilities – wide knowledge of affairs and insight, professionalism, and administrative capacity – genuinely marked him out as a politician worthy

---

[1] R. C. Whiting, 'Attlee, Clement R.', *ODNB* vol. II, pp. 875–84.

[2] For example, see pp. 230–1 above, and his memorandum, 'The great debate: financial and economic policy', the final heading of which was a Churchillian 'Action this day' (CAB 129/53, C(52)226, 4 July 1952); and 'Smog' – 'Today everybody expects the Government to solve every problem. It is a symptom of the Welfare State. Governments are judged by their apparent ability to take the initiative in matters like 'smog'. Ridiculous as it appears at first sight, I would suggest that we form a Committee. Committees are the oriflamme of democracy . . . We cannot do very much but we can seem to be very busy – that is half the battle nowadays' (CAB 129/64, C(53)322, 18 Nov. 1953). Macmillan also could be playful with the record. When the ambassador reported on the 'Confrontation' riots at the British embassy in Djakarta, 'The charred corpse of my poor old Princess is causing an elegant traffic-jam', Macmillan minuted cryptically, 'I hope the historian will not misunderstand this paragraph' (PREM/11/4310, September 1963; – the Princess van der Plas was in fact a Triumph-model motor-car).

[3] CAB 129/78, CP(55)161, 19 October 1955; Lord Home, *The way the wind blows: an autobiography* (1976), p. 191.

of the top job. Underneath the 'unflappable' image, however, Macmillan was an agitated worrier, a specialist in worst-case scenarios. Also, he could be ridiculously pompous. And, true, he had behaved appallingly badly during the Suez Crisis ('first in, first out'), showing neither judgment nor loyalty, nor his usual diplomatic skill and political competence. But then he was not the only incoming prime minister against whom black marks could be entered; historians are apt to forgive such lapses provided not too many serious mistakes are made in No. 10 – Churchill springs to mind, does he not?[4]

With Macmillan, this study moves to its climax. It was he who presided over a voluntary decolonisation, not wholly unorchestrated, a decisive period of British self-reappraisal as a world power. One historian has called him 'the great decolonizer of the British empire in Africa'.[5] Another has bravely but authoritatively accredited Macmillan with 'the grand reorientation of British policy which was to be his chief achievement . . . [a] series of decisions and initiatives of profound importance for Britain's place in the world'.[6]

1. Policy-making: ministers, officials, and governors

Macmillan is of course famous for his proclaimed awareness of the need to come to terms with the nationalist 'wind of change' in Africa. His speech in Cape Town on 3 February 1960 was not just an official declaration (though it was that), nor did it represent a sudden personal conversion. In June 1955 we find him writing to the ambassador in Paris: 'The tide of the world is set in the direction of national . . . autonomy and identity . . . Time is not on the side of France, and she will not be able to swim

---

[4] The two-volume official biography by Alistair Home, *Macmillan*, vol. I: *1894–1956* (1988), is particularly good on the Suez Crisis (pp. 393–447). Otherwise, the best books on Macmillan are S. J. Ball, *The Guardsmen: Harold Macmillan, three friends, and the world they made* (2004), esp. pp. 319–27 and 399–401, and John Turner, *Macmillan* (1994), esp. ch. 8 'Imperial retreat', pp. 176–211. See also L. Siedentop, 'Mr Macmillan and the Edwardian style', in V. Bogdanor and R. Skidelsky, eds., *The age of affluence, 1951–1964* (1970), pp. 17–54. R. P. T. Davenport-Hines, *The Macmillans* (1993), pp. 162–349 is worth reading on his private life. Macmillan's marriage was a humiliating mess. Robert Boothby, MP, was Lady Dorothy's over for many years, and fathered one of her daughters. Macmillan was a man of innocence and sexual detachment. This left him ill-equipped to deal not only with his wife's adultery but with the Profumo affair (involving colleagues and prostitutes), which blighted the twilight of his premiership and mystified him: 'I had no idea of this strange underworld . . . all this kind of thing was not only distasteful but unthinkable' (*Memoirs*, vol. VI, pp. 437–44).

[5] D. Birmingham, *The decolonization of Africa* (1995), p. 13. Until 1958 Macmillan occasionally wrote and spoke about not intending to preside over the liquidation of the empire, but such remarks were only playful echoes of Churchill, and should not be taken seriously.

[6] H. C. G. Matthew, 'Macmillan, (Maurice) Harold', *ODNB*, vol. XXXV, pp. 879–96.

against the tide of nationalism in North Africa any more than we have been able to do elsewhere in the world.'[7] Again, as early as July 1957 Macmillan made a speech describing nationalism 'as a tidal wave surging from Asia across the ocean to the shores of Africa', powerful, swift and elemental: 'it can be led, but it cannot be driven back'.[8] Macmillan regarded this tide of colonial nationalism as one of the two biggest developments in the world since 1945. The other was the ideological struggle against communism 'which really dominates everything . . . really holds the front of the stage'.[9] It was within these parameters that he approached the higher level of decision-making upon colonial problems. It was very much the essence of his policy to find ways of harnessing colonial nationalism so as to prevent the spread of communism. This indeed was the theme at the heart of the Cape Town speech.

It is perhaps hard to see that Macmillan had any deep conviction which would predispose him to favour the continuation of formal colonial rule. He came to the highest office with a particular set of previous conditioning experiences. He probably knew as much about the French empire as the British, after his three-year involvement with North Africa during the war, which had shown him how much damage imperial pretensions could do to a great power and how tiresome settler communities could be.[10] Even before this, briefly at the CO in 1942 as parliamentary undersecretary, he had proposed an extraordinarily bold scheme for 'buying out' the European farmers of the Kenya 'white highlands' and repatriating most of them (see above, p. 89).[11] Then, as chancellor of the Exchequer in the last months of the Eden government, he had taken the initiative for a reappraisal of overseas defence commitments ('The future of the UK in world affairs').[12] Reviewing government expenditure as a whole, he took the line that if available resources were too small to go

---

[7] FO 371/113803, letter to Sir Gladwyn Jebb, 10 June 1955.

[8] Quoted in D. Horowitz, 'Attitudes of British Conservatives towards decolonisation in Africa', *African Affairs*, vol. 69 (1970), p. 16.

[9] R. Hyam and W. R. Louis, eds., *The Conservative government and the end of empire, 1957–1964* (BDEEP, 2000 – hereafter cited as *CGEE*) pt 2, pp. 662–3 (no. 541), to Sir R. Menzies, 8 February 1962. C. Waters, 'Macmillan, Menzies, history and empire', *Australian Historical Studies*, vol. 33 (2002), pp. 93–107.

[10] Ball, *The Guardsmen*, p. 321; and S. J. Ball, 'Harold Macmillan, the Second World War and the empire', in R. Aldous and S. Lee, eds., *Harold Macmillan: aspects of a poltical life* (1999); and 'Banquo's ghost: Lord Salisbury, Harold Macmillan, and the "high politics" of decolonisation, 1957–1963', *Twentieth-Century British History*, vol. 16 (2005), pp. 74–102, in which Ball suggests that Macmillan's rejection of a continuing 'Greater Britain' was in part a reaction to Salisbury's intransigent position.

[11] S. R. Ashton and S. E. Stockwell, eds., *Imperial policy and colonial practice, 1925–1945* (BDEEP, 1996), pt 1, pp. 337–40 (no. 66).

[12] D. Goldsworthy, ed., *The Conservative government and the end of empire, 1951–1957*, pt 1, pp. 61–3 (nos. 20 and 21).

round, colonial development might have to be slowed down. The impact could, he admitted, be serious, but 'in our present economic situation, serious and unpalatable steps may have to be taken', and he would not exempt colonial development from review. (See above, pp. 178–9). Lennox-Boyd concluded that Macmillan 'wasn't really an Empire man'. Nor was Macmillan entirely happy about the level of the financial settlement made as Ghana approached independence.[13]

When Macmillan became prime minister in January 1957, he wanted the entire colonial position reassessed as one of the first acts of his administration. As D. J. Morgan comments dryly, 'whether he would have felt so had he moved directly from the Foreign Office rather than the Treasury is an interesting matter for speculation'.[14] What is beyond doubt, however, is the rebuff given by officials to his call for 'something like a profit and loss account' and an assessment of which colonies would be likely to become 'ripe for independence over the next few years'.[15] As a result, any hopes Macmillan might have had of speeding up transfers of power in the colonies were – other than Cyprus – put on the back-burner for the next two years. His position was then enormously strengthened by an unexpectedly solid electoral victory in October 1959, after which the colonial empire unravelled instantly and without remission. In part that process was facilitated by the way he had actively encouraged further preparatory policy studies. In this sense, the two intervening years were not wasted years.

Macmillan's chosen instrument for speeding up decolonisation from October 1959 was Iain Macleod, who, although aged only forty-six and without directly relevant experience, seemed to have the right kind of qualities for a task likely to be both difficult and controversial: 'it would need a Minister of great imagination, even genius'.[16] He believed Macleod shared his own brand of 'Disraelian Tory radicalism'. So did Lord Hailsham, the other possible candidate for the CO, but Macmillan disapproved of his unfortunate marital circumstances, even though Hailsham was not the 'guilty partner'. It may also be noted in passing than he did not promote his son-in-law, Julian Amery, already in post as parliamentary under-secretary at the CO since November 1958, and this

[13] Goldsworthy, *Conservative government, 1951–1957*, pt 3, pp. 239–41; D. J. Morgan, *The official history of colonial development* (1980), vol. V. *Guidance towards self-government in British colonies, 1941–1971* pp. 89–90. My thanks to Philip Murphy for drawing my attention to Lennox-Boyd's opinion of Macmillan, given in an interview with Gillian Peele, 21 February 1975.   [14] Morgan, *Guidance towards self-government*, p. 93.

[15] *CGEE*, pt 1, pp. 1–2 (no 1), 28 January 1957.

[16] H. Macmillan, *Memoirs*, vol. V *Pointing the way, 1959–1961* (1972), pp. 18–19, There are three particularly good essays on Macleod: D. Goldsworthy, 'Macleod, Iain', *ODNB* vol. XXXV, pp. 810–18; A. Howard, 'Iain Macleod: the "dark horse" at the back of the Tory field', *The Listener* (9 October 1980), pp. 457–8; Edward Pearce, 'Iain Norman Macleod', in *The lost leaders* (1997), pp. 244–354.

despite the fact that nepotism held no terrors for Macmillan. He thought Amery a skilful negotiator, having an 'exceptional combination of patience and determination'. Amery was, however, a right-wing diehard upholder of his father L. S. Amery's vision of the geopolitical verities of empire and its need for fortress colonies. Clearly this was not the kind of outlook Macmillan wished to see directing the CO. Instead, it is possible that he had earmarked Macleod for the post as early as May 1959. At least one MP noticed that from about this time Macleod began attending parliamentary debates on colonial and Commonwealth matters.[17]

There were in all four secretaries of state for the colonies during the Macmillan years: Alan Lennox-Boyd (July 1954 to October 1959), Iain Macleod (October 1959 to October 1961), Reginald Maudling (October 1961 to July 1962) and Duncan Sandys (July 1962 to October 1964). There were two secretaries of state for Commonwealth relations: Lord Home (April 1955 to July 1960) and Sandys (July 1960 to October 1964). Any ranking of these five key ministers would probably put Maudling at the bottom, despite his important contribution to independence for Kenya and Northern Rhodesia, simply because he occupied his office for a mere nine months. By contrast, Home spent five years at the CRO before taking over the FO in 1960 for three years, followed by one year as prime minister: a total of more than nine years – the nine crucial years, it may be argued – at the centre of policy-making during the 'end of empire'. He was also a close and continuous confidant of Macmillan in a way none of the others ever was. The only other leading 'overseas' minister, in the later years at least, was R. A. Butler (home secretary, 1957–1962), put in charge of a Central Africa Office for eighteen months (March 1962 to October 1963), and then foreign secretary. Among the junior ministers, an especially active role was played by Lord Perth as minister of state at the CO for over five years, under three successive secretaries of state. Although he emerged from and returned to political obscurity, Perth made himself useful in these years by providing an element of informed continuity. Julian Amery during his two years at the CO made a distinctive if sometimes unsettling contribution, specialising on colonies where defence issues were involved.

<hr>

[17] Lord Alport, *The sudden assignment . . . the Federation of Rhodesia and Nyasaland, 1961–1963* (1965), p. 28. There may have been a party-political calculation in Macleod's appointment. In discussions in May 1959 Macleod impressed Macmillan by clearly identifying 'black African policy' as a most difficult problem, severely criticised by 'the vital middle voters', and the only subject upon which the government was regularly defeated in university debates (PREM 11 /2583, Macleod to Macmillan, 25 May 1959; *CGEE*, pt 1, pp. 160–1 (no. 29)); Macmillan almost quoted this letter five months later – see below p. 257.

All the five principal ministers of the inner group were strong characters. Lennox-Boyd was perceived as a dominant, exuberant, and quixotic personality, a right-winger, who hated racial prejudice and got on well with colonial governors, not least because he tended to back their judgment.[18] Macleod also had plenty of confidence. He was a legendary bridge-player, a fine orator and debater, quick, well-organised, and sometimes ingenious in decision-making, but many found him hard, tense, abrasive, and even rude. (He was often in pain, caused by arthritis and ankylosing spondylitis.) Lord Salisbury's jibe in March 1961 that he was 'too clever by half' proved to be damaging to Macleod's reputation. Complex he certainly was. By contrast, Maudling was more genial but much less good at public speaking. He was reckoned to be a centre-right Conservative. Despite a keen intellect, he was an unfocused bon viveur and perhaps too relaxed.[19] Sandys was less clever, more ponderous, and more to the right politically than these two, but methodical, a tough and patient negotiator, forceful, and (as his permanent under-secretary admitted), 'if necessary, brutal'. Some senior advisers, including the Chiefs of Staff, found him unnecessarily inconsiderate, while Nehru remarked that Sandys reminded him of the sort of Englishman who used to put him in jail. Sandys was perhaps deliberately brought in to counterbalance Macleod's liberal instincts, even maybe to be a brake to Macleod's accelerator.[20]

Home was naturally possessed of a gracious, unpompous, easy self-confidence, 'capable without being clever'. He was a shrewd and competent administrator, who generally came to sound official conclusions by rational processes whatever his private prejudices. He was well-read in Victorian political biography, but joked about using matchsticks to help with statistics. There was undoubtedly serious temperamental incompatibility between Home and Macleod. Home regarded Macleod as lacking in judgment to an alarming degree ('he clearly believed Lumumba was the greatest man in Africa'), and thought he should have stuck to domestic politics. For his part, Macleod regarded Home as an unregenerate traditionalist. As far as decolonisation was concerned, Home accepted Macmillan's 'wind of change' diagnosis as correct, although he was not satisfied that 'freedom is everything and the rest nothing'. As Prime Minister Sir Alec Douglas-Home (having renounced his peerage) from

---

[18] P. Murphy, 'Boyd, Alan Lennox-', *ODNB*, vol. VII, pp. 23–5; and *Alan Lennox-Boyd: a biography* (1999), which is essential reading. See also pp. 174–5 above.
[19] R. Shepherd, 'Maudling, Reginald', *ODNB*, vol. XXXVII, pp. 402–6.
[20] N. Piers Ludlow, 'Sandys, Duncan', *ODNB*, vol. XLVIII, pp. 911–14; J. S. Garner, *The Commonwealth Office, 1925–1968* (1978), pp. 357–9; K. O. Morgan, *Callaghan: a life* (1997), p. 410.

October 1963, he was less 'presidential' – and less agitated and emotional – than Macmillan. He and Australia's Robert Menzies once fixed a Commonwealth Prime Ministers' Meeting to coincide with a test match at Lords: fortunately Macmillan did not seem to realise this. He conducted Cabinet meetings crisply. He was a calm navigator, and Douglas Hurd's assessment of his performance as prime minister is a fair one: 'he scaled no heights; his vessel hit no rocks'.[21]

All these ministers in the last or penultimate phase of dismantling the empire had to work extremely hard. It was not uncommon for more than one constitutional conference to be taking place simultaneously. Sir Kennedy Trevaskis of Aden provided striking vignettes of Macleod and Sandys at work. He found Macleod preoccupied with the West Indies, Northern Rhodesia, East Africa, Mauritius and Gambia. Trevaskis eventually got ten minutes with him to talk about Aden's serious problems. Macleod was eating a sandwich, glancing at newspapers, and issuing instructions to his secretary on points in them: 'he was like one of those international chess champions who think nothing of taking on a couple of dozen opponents at once. It was admirable, but seemed an odd way to wind up an empire.' Of Sandys, Trevaskis recalled that his appointments book 'read like an imperial gazeteer' and he 'looked wan with fatigue . . . but not as wan as his red-eyed officials. He was beset by a host of crises – a revolt in Zanzibar, mutinies in Kenya, Tanganyika and Uganda, near war in Cyprus . . . Rhodesia'.[22]

Macmillan became disillusioned with both his chosen CO lieutenants. Macleod revealed 'many faults', threatened resignation too often, was too proud, too emotional, too ambitious, too unpopular. And then, to Macmillan's astonishment, Maudling, replacing him (in order to restore some Party consensus, after the most difficult decisions had been taken), did not produce a 'steadier' atmosphere but proved to be 'plus noir que les nègres, more difficult and intransigent than his predecessor'. The truth is that Maudling's tenure was a measure of Macleod's success as – in one historical assessment – 'the principal architect of African decolonisation'.[23]

On the eve of his departure for his African tour, Macmillan told the Cabinet secretary, Sir Norman Brook: 'Africans are not the problem in

---

[21] Douglas Hurd, 'Home, Alex F. Douglas-', *ODNB*, vol. XXVII, pp. 861–7; Lord Home, *The way the wind blows*, p. 186; Ball, *The guardsmen*, p. 334; D. R. Thorpe, *Alec Douglas-Home* (1996). Iain Macleod and Enoch Powell refused to serve in his ministry, but Powell's remark that his views on Africa were 'positively Portuguese' is ludicrous.

[22] Kennedy Trevaskis, *Shades of amber: a South Arabian episode* (1968) pp. 164, 194 and 205.

[23] Macmillan, *Pointing the way*, pp. 18 and 174; *Memoirs*, vol. VI, *At the end of the day, 1961–1963* (1973), pp. 313–14; Horne, *Macmillan*, vol. II, p. 408; Goldsworthy, 'Macleod', *ODNB*.

Africa, it is the Europeans who are the problem.'[24] Meeting settlers at first
hand impressed upon Macmillan the strength of their views. The Africans
could not, he thought, be dominated permanently, but 'nor can the
Europeans be abandoned' (see below, page 283). As decolonisation gathered momentum, Macmillan began to feel the settlers were being lost
sight of: 'no-one seems to worry very much about the Europeans'.[25] More
than once he reminded his ministers of Britain's 'moral obligation' to the
settlers. Macleod had to ease him along and persuade him that there was
no such thing as a safe colonial policy. In retrospect, Macleod showed
considerable understanding of the prime minister's mind:

I think the difficulty with Harold Macmillan in relation to Africa was that he had
all the right instincts, as his 'Winds [sic] of Change' speech showed quite clearly.
He was more than prepared for a rapid move to independence – as his appointment of myself showed. But from time to time he wanted, as I daresay we all do,
the best of both worlds, he didn't want to fall out with his good friends either at
home or in Central or East Africa as the case may be. Whereas, I took the brutal,
but I think practical view that this was an omelette you couldn't make without
breaking eggs and one couldn't be friends with everybody however much one
wanted to do it, while one was pursuing such a policy.[26]

This astute interpretation receives support from an American insight into
Macmillan's government (April 1963): 'From a narrow national interest
point of view they would probably prefer to get out [of Southern
Rhodesia] as quickly as possible. However, as in the case of other dependent territories, they are showing a marked sense of responsibility and
making persistent endeavours to work out pragmatically arrangements
acceptable to the various elements concerned'.[27]

Of the civil servants, Norman Brook, as secretary of the Cabinet, and,
by 1957, with ten years' experience behind him, was already an Olympian
figure. The most powerful man in Whitehall, he was able to offer the
prime minister much appreciated magisterial advice until the very end of
1962, when he was succeeded by his deputy, Burke Trend, from January
1963.[28] Brook was closely involved in the production of many of the
major reports and surveys. Trend ran the Africa Committee. Both were
keenly involved in organising Commonwealth conferences. In the CO,
the permanent under-secretaryship in this period was divided (at August
1959) between Sir John Macpherson and Sir Hilton Poynton, while

[24] *CGEE*, pt 2, p. 550 (no 497), minute, 28 December 1959.
[25] CAB 21/4772, f. 62, M 182/63, to J. Boyd-Carpenter, 7 May 1963; *CGEE*, pt 1, p. 405 n
2 (no 124), minute, 5 January 1961.   [26] R. Shepherd, *Iain Macleod* (1994), p. 199.
[27] *Foreign relations of the United States, 1961–1963* (hereafter cited as *FRUS*), vol. XXI *Africa*
(Washington, 1995), p. 529 (no. 338), 16 April 1963, State Dept paper.
[28] 'Brook, Norman', *ODNB*, vol. VII, pp. 859–62 (by K. Theakston).

Sir John Martin was deputy under-secretary of state throughout, jointly with Sir William Gorell Barnes between 1959 and 1963. Macpherson had returned to the CO after being governor (and governor-general) of Nigeria, from 1948 to 1955, an experience which gave a hard-edged practicality to his recommendations. Poynton was clever, but did not get on with Macleod and was perceived as a patrician civil servant of the old school; so was Martin in many ways, but perhaps more balanced and open-minded about decolonisation. Among the assistant under-secretaries, Leslie Monson became especially prominent, in charge of East and Central Africa from 1959. By contrast, one of the radical high-flyers of the period before 1951, John Bennett, was in effect side-lined, being shuffled around a rapid succession of the less active CO departments and then denied all further promotion for the last twenty-five years of his career.[29]

The governors who superintended the transfer of power on the spot had an enhanced role in this period, rather like plants which put on their finest display as a herald of death. Mostly they conformed to a generic type. Invariably their biographers and memorialists describe them as tall, fine-looking and well-built, with a rugged, pipe-smoking virility, often sporty but also good at local languages, diligent as well as intelligent, jovial, entertaining and charming.[30] They were a touch old-fashioned ('preserving a number of nineteenth-century British qualities in prime condition, as if under glass'), perhaps even a bit too good to be true.[31] There was a fundamental paradox built into their job-specification. They were expected to be respectful of their charges, patient and graceful in diplomatic negotiation, but also to be firm and decisive in action. 'To exercise the dualism of authority and accommodation constituted the ultimate skill in the art of decolonisation' (Kirk-Greene).[32]

The governors who loomed largest in the Whitehall limelight were those who took a radical stance: Hugh Foot and Richard Turnbull. Foot was a left-winger of Quaker education, who as governor of Cyprus (1957–60) helped to achieve a settlement there, though he felt he disagreed with Lennox-Boyd about almost everything. As the British permanent representative to the UN, Foot had an even more fundamental disagreement

---

[29] *ODNB*: Sir H. Poynton (by S. R. Ashton), vol. LV, pp. 191–3; J. J. S Garner (by Alex May), vol. XXI, pp. 482–3; W. B. Leslie Monson (by L. Allinson), vol. XXXVIII, pp. 678–9.

[30] *ODNB*: see esp. entries by A. H. M. Kirk-Greene: on C. Arden-Clarke, vol. XI, pp. 856–7; Maurice Dorman, vol. XVI, pp. 572–3; J. S. Macpherson, vol. XXXV, pp. 996–7; J. W. Robertson, vol. LVII, pp. 242–3; together with J. M. Redcliffe Maud (by R. Armstrong), vol. XXXVII, pp. 390–2, and G. K. N. Trevaskis (by A. d'Avray), vol. LV, pp. 351–2.

[31] C. H. Johnston, *The view from Steamer Point: being an account of three years in Aden* (1964), p. 183.   [32] A. H. M. Kirk-Greene, 'Turnbull, Richard G', *ODNB*, vol. LV, pp. 593–4.

with Poynton, and increasingly found Conservative government policy on Rhodesia unacceptable. He resigned in October 1962 (see below, page 306). He came into his own again under the Labour government of 1964.[33] Turnbull in Tanganyika was widely recognised as a powerful and robust figure, performing for East African decolonisation a role comparable with that of Sir Charles Arden-Clarke ten years earlier for West Africa. Tanganyika seemed a model of how to transfer power: swift, smooth, peaceful, and apparently amicable. Like Foot, Turnbull was a rowing fanatic. Unlike him, he had an earthy streak, which showed itself, for example, in teaching his beloved parrot to swear roundly before reciting the Lord's Prayer. Turnbull provides a notable case of a governor who seized the initiative and who was able decisively to speed up the timetable.

The post of high commissioner in South Africa was the most demanding of the 'ambassadorial' appointments, combining relations with the Afrikaner government and responsibility for the three High Commission Territories, Basutoland, Bechuanaland and Swaziland. It was filled with great panache by a former academic town-planning expert, Sir John Maud, for four years (January 1959 to December 1962). His despatches were among the best received from what historians like to call the 'periphery' during the Macmillan premiership, full of caustic insight into the evils of the apartheid regime.[34]

2. Planning: surveys and statements

The Macmillan government is notable for the large number of policy studies it produced, most of them initiated by the prime minister himself, starting with 'Future constitutional development in the colonies', 1957. Barely two weeks after taking office, Macmillan called for an analysis of progress towards independence, and 'something like a profit and loss account' for each colony; he wanted to know whether Britain stood to lose or gain by its departure.[35] It is probable that he saw the exercise as moving in tandem with the defence review entrusted to Sandys. (The prime minister asked for a 'Chequers weekend' discussion in late February to take account at least of the strategic aspects of colonial constitutional development; the CO refused to co-operate, since the information by then available would be incomplete.) In the event the assembling of the analysis was so complex that the process could not be finalised within the time-scale

[33] L. M. Jeger, 'Foot, Hugh', *ODNB*, vol. XX, pp. 242–3.
[34] R. Armstrong, 'Maud, J. M. Redcliffe', *ODNB* vol. XXXVII; *CGEE* pt 2, pp. 455–62 (no 462), 14 May 1963 (CAB 129/114, C(63)102), and pp. 503–4 (no. 479).
[35] *CGEE*, pt 1, pp. 1–2 (no 1), 28 January 1957, minute to Lord Salisbury, (CAB 134/1555, CPC(57)6).

Macmillan had envisaged, with Cabinet consideration perhaps in June 1957.[36] The main CO paper, co-ordinated by Ian Watt (an assistant secretary) was ready in May. CO ministers praised it highly: 'this is a stupendous job – splendidly done' (Lord Perth), 'a magnificent achievement on which all who have worked so hard in the Department deserve the highest possible praise' (Lennox-Boyd). The secretary of state thought it both comprehensive and realistic, and said later that he constantly referred to it.[37] Governors were not consulted, the permanent under-secretary taking the view that it was 'best not to alarm them by the knowledge that this exercise is being conducted'.[38] Moreover, Brook, in a remarkable piece of bureaucratic obfuscation, began to argue that the whole purpose of the reappraisal was simply information-gathering; the prime minister was *not* concerned to evaluate or write off colonies in order to save money. Officials like Watt himself and Sir Frank Lee of the Treasury dismissed this tendentious briefing with a pinch of salt.[39] Brook further played down the exercise by advising the prime minister that Cabinet discussion was not required after all, since any policy decision would require special consideration in the light of each local situation. Macmillan – perhaps disappointed that the result was not more supportive of his presuppositions – agreed that circulating the reports would suffice.[40]

The thrust of the officials' argument was that withdrawing from colonies might produce some modest financial saving but would be discreditable where it was not dangerous, and not only for strategic reasons. They advanced four reservations. The first was a worry about withdrawal of British authority from multi-racial communities, especially Kenya, Fiji, and Mauritius, where the presence of Indian immigrants was, after all, entirely Britain's responsibility. The second was a warning that withdrawal

---

[36] There were three interlocking papers in response to the prime minister's directive: they should be seen as *complementary* (dealing with different aspects), and not as a *sequence* modifying or qualifying each other – a mistake made by A. G. Hopkins, 'Macmillan's audit of empire, 1957', in P. Clarke and C. Trebilcock, eds., *Understanding decline: perceptions and realities of British economic performance* (1997), pp. 234–60. No particular significance attaches to the order in which they were written, nor do they show an 'increasing' importance of the economic dimension. Hopkins also exaggerates the supposed 'major change in Conservative policy' involved (see Murphy, *Alan Lennox-Boyd*, p. 169), and the extent to which Macmillan got what he wanted. In short, it is not a reliable essay, and illustrates the dangers of interpretation based on only a limited number of files.

[37] *CGEE*, pt 1, pp. 4–28 (no. 22), May 1957, 'Future constitutional development in the colonies' (CAB 134/1551, CPC(57)27); CO 1032/144, no. 9, minutes, 20 February 1957; CO 1032/146, minutes, 23 and 25 May 1957; CO 1032/147, no. 161, Lennox-Boyd to R. A. Butler, 14 February 1958.

[38] CO 1032/144, no. 12, Macpherson to Brook, 5 March 1957.

[39] CO 1032/146, minute by I. Watt, 11 June 1957. As we shall see below, Macmillan definitely sought 'to reduce the burdens' in South-East Asia and the Pacific Islands (p. 315).

[40] PREM 11/2617, minute, 4 August 1957.

might lead to a vacuum into which other powers would move: France into Gambia and Sierra Leone, Yemen into Aden, Greece, Turkey or even Egypt into Cyprus, Indonesia into Borneo, the United States into Guiana, Guatemala into Honduras, and Argentina into the Falklands. British prestige would be damaged, and the risk of communism would then be increased. The third reservation was concern that trusteeship obligations would be repudiated. Where international reputation, strategic requirements or global prestige could not be said to be at stake, the officials raised the objection of 'moral abdication'. This was held to operate for Seychelles, Mauritius, the Solomons, and Gilbert and Ellice Islands; the last two indeed could be expected to 'revert to a primitive mode' of chaos and barbarism. Finally there was a risk that an expanding South Africa might use the opportunity of British withdrawals to take over the High Commission Territories, the two Rhodesias, and even Tristan da Cunha, all of which would be equally bad for the inhabitants and for British prestige and moral standing. (Fear of the spread of apartheid seems to have been as great as fear of communism.) In short, massive, not to say fanciful, objections were raised to reducing British colonial commitments. Indeed, the response was even more negative than a similar exercise (though on a much smaller scale) undertaken by the FO in 1952, when at least the Falkland Island Dependencies were identified as a possible sacrifice (see above, p. 176). Now the Falklands were clearly marked out for retention (because abandonment of the British population to the fate of Argentinian rule 'would be discreditable and severely damaging to prestige'); while the Falkland Island Dependencies were said to be an important base for Antarctic research, the loss of which would contribute to damaging British prestige and influence, 'especially in scientific circles'.

However, what is significant here is that no economic or strategic objections were advanced as a general bar to constitutional progress. Even in territories where the strategic requirements were reckoned to be large, it was forecast that the government might for political reasons be forced to reduce their military expectations. Officials recognised that much would depend on policies pursued after independence, because the economic and financial implications of the grant of independence did not flow from the grant itself; the maintenance of goodwill and friendship was therefore the vital thing. The conclusion of the whole matter was, then, as far as economic factors were concerned, that the officials pronounced a *nihil obstat*. And accordingly they highlighted the salience of political considerations and prestige calculations.[41]

---

[41] *CGEE*, pt 1, pp. 28–37, memo by Brook, 6 September 1957, 'Future constitutional development in the colonies'.

As to the other main issue, progress towards independence, two themes emerged strongly. One was scepticism about the speed of advance in Nigeria. The Gold Coast had 'set a pace too fast' for Nigeria, and the prospects for the latter's future under self-government seemed doubtful. But there could be no turning back. The other theme was the identification of East Africa as the pivotal area for future constitutional planning, caught as it was – or so the officials argued – between Islamic instability and Soviet expansion moving potentially southwards, with South African expansion and apartheid moving potentially northwards, and possibly even Indian expansion moving potentially westwards. Local internal nationalism would be growing all the time.

Macmillan's desire for a defence policy combining maximum effectiveness with minimum cost was speedily delivered by Sandys as minister of defence. The 1957 Defence White Paper[42] was a rigorous reappraisal which arose directly out of Macmillan's cogitations as chancellor of the Exchequer and before that as minister of defence himself. He commissioned Sandys to secure substantial savings in costs and manpower. In the last five years defence had been absorbing ten per cent per annum of GNP, and the aim was to get it down to seven per cent by 1962. The priority given to the nuclear deterrent was upgraded (perhaps reflecting disillusionment over the reliability of the United States in the Suez Crisis). Consequent upon this, the end of National Service (conscription) was decreed for 1962, together with reductions in the size of the Navy and RAF Fighter Command. For the remaining all-volunteer (regular) conventional forces, mobility was to be the key doctrine. Presented to the Cabinet as a five-year plan amounting to 'a fundamental revolution in our defence policy', the new policy stopped short of questioning the need for a global role. The government believed it was important to remain a nuclear power, in order to have the maximum influence on world affairs. The cuts, however, were deep, and the huge reduction in manpower (to 375,000) was bound to make sustained counterinsurgency operations problematic. British army strength in the colonies was slashed by almost two-thirds. A settlement in Cyprus was now urgently required. To the extent that calculations about the feasibility of continuing to hold on to colonies by force were integral to decisions to transfer power, the new defence policy can be said to have contributed to decolonisation.

[42] A. N. Porter and A. J. Stockwell, eds., *British imperial policy and decolonisation*, vol. II *1951–1964* (1989), pp. 452–64 (no. 77); S. J. Ball, 'Harold Macmillan and the politics of defence: the market for strategic ideas during the 'Sandys era' revisited', *Twentieth-Century British History*, vol. 6 (1995), pp. 78–100; L. W. Martin, 'The market for strategic ideas in Britain: the "Sandys era"', *American Political Science Review*, vol. 56 (1962), pp. 23–41.

In the summer of 1958 another major officials' report emerged, 'The position of the United Kingdom in world affairs', in which Brook completed an initiative for which Macmillan had been mainly responsible before he became prime minister (see above p. 177). Although there were several departmental submissions, the FO draft by Peter Ramsbotham of the Planning Section formed the core of it. The CO insisted (once again) that its obligations should not be abandoned ('to do this anywhere would undermine confidence and imperil our policy everywhere'), and Brook was (once again) sympathetic; he also played up the Commonwealth. The CO were pleased with the final report: 'an excellent and well thought out paper', which suited them nicely. Lennox-Boyd found it a 'worthwhile document'. On the other hand, the Treasury did not like the prospect of 'some immediate but limited expenditure in support of colonial and Commonwealth commitments'. The report concluded that there was no scope for reducing overseas commitments on the scale required, nor could further major defence cuts be contemplated.[43]

In receiving this report, Macmillan decided he wanted officials to look further ahead, over the next ten years, and to make a comprehensive study of total resources in relation to total overseas commitments. Thus the 'Future policy study, 1960–1970' was designed as a large-scale planning exercise which might become a blueprint for whichever government took office after the general election in October 1959. Sir Patrick Dean (deputy under-secretary of state at the FO) was put in charge. Lennox-Boyd supported it: 'I am strongly in favour of this and think that such a wide-ranging study will be of great value to the members of a new administration.' Into it were fed not only the 'position of the UK' report, but despatches from Malcolm MacDonald on India, and correspondence about the South-West Pacific. The CRO submitted a major new survey of the Commonwealth, the Treasury an analysis of 'economic strength', and the FO a paper on Anglo-American relations. Of these the most contentious was the Commonwealth paper, even in its revised form. The CO and the FO considered that claims for the value of the Commonwealth had been over-pitched by the CRO. Surely the Americans did not listen to Britain *because* of the Commonwealth? Surely Britain was not a spokesman for the Commonwealth? And if it was economically 'good business', surely this did not depend on its cohesion as a political entity?[44]

The basic premise of the report was gloomy: that during the 1960s Britain's relative power would certainly decline. Its fundamental

[43] *CGEE*, pt 1, pp. 43–51 (no. 5), 9 June 1958, officials' report, 'The position of the United Kingdom in world affairs' (CAB 130/153, GEN 624/10).

[44] *CGEE*, pt 1, pp. 87–107 (no. 17), 24 February 1960, Cabinet report, 'Future policy study: 1960–1970'.

conclusion was therefore that the preservation of the Atlantic alliance was 'the core of our foreign policy' and 'in the last resort, the most basic of our interests'. The study was emphatic that the first, the ultimate, aim of British policy in the 1960s would be to check the growing power of the Sino-Soviet bloc. The implications of this conclusion were perceived with succinct clarity by Ramsbotham: 'United Kingdom power will thus be founded on United States partnership, buttressed by Western European solidarity (we hope), and usable through the instrument of the Commonwealth.'[45]

Integration with Europe was certainly seen as a possible alternative to the Atlantic alliance; but no more than that. As Dean put it: 'I am concerned that we should not lightly consider throwing away the bird-in-the-hand of the Anglo-United States interdependence and special relationship for the as yet bird-in-the-bush plan for much closer association, leading perhaps to integration, with Western Europe.' The British ambassador to France, Sir Gladwyn Jebb, could not persuade him that it was 'later than you think' and not too soon for the European option to be more fully thought out.[46]

The CO felt this important and inevitably complicated exercise had been handled very efficiently by Dean and the permanent under-secretaries. They thought 'a *fascinating* set of papers' had been assembled; they were especially impressed by the Treasury paper, which was unexpectedly sympathetic to increasing the amount of aid. Carstairs (one of the assistant under-secretaries of state, who had a philosophical turn of mind) contributed two criticisms of the draft report: successfully urging that a clearer statement of fundamental objectives was needed,[47] but less successfully trying to inject some traditional trusteeship doctrines.

Not included in the 'Future policy study' was a report on 'Democracy in backward countries', which Macmillan wanted kept separate. This examination of the validity of the Westminster model of government was organised by Brook, relying chiefly on FO advice. Unfortunately the FO took two years to produce its paper, and when it did so, neither the CRO nor the CO liked it. Meanwhile, the CO was conducting its own investigation into the reasons for the apparent failure of democratic parliamentary institutions. This whole debate resonated within the cold war context, validating the idea that post-independence deviations from the Westminster model should be viewed tolerantly. Stable and popular government was what mattered, and it was probably at least as important to

[45] FO 371/143707, no. 72, minute, 22 September 1959.
[46] *CGEE*, pt 1, p. 108 (no. 18), 23 March 1960.
[47] *CGEE*, pt 1, pp. 82–7 (nos. 15 and 16).

make 'these countries less backward as to make them democratic'. In any case, whatever doubts there were about the Westminster model, theorising seemed to CO officials to be largely irrelevant. It would be quite impracticable to offer an alternative, since this would be resented by emerging nations themselves.[48]

'Africa in the next ten years' was a report prepared early in 1959 by officials of the Africa Committee working under its chairman Burke Trend of the Cabinet Office. It provided an interdepartmental view as well as a basis for ministerial talks with, and persuasion of, the Americans and Canadians (November 1959), and the French (December 1959). Its central thesis was as follows:

> If Western governments appear to be reluctant to concede independence to their dependent territories, they may alienate African opinion and turn it towards the Soviet Union; if on the other hand they move too fast they run the risk of leaving large areas of Africa ripe for Communist exploitation.

By thus starkly demonstrating how policy was impaled on the horns of a dilemma, the paper undoubtedly sent a very clear cautionary message to ministers. When officials discussed their draft report, they felt the emphasis on defence might seem rather heavy, but in the last resort it was difficult to define British interests in Africa in other than strategic terms, which seemed likely to remain strong for the next decade. They had in mind particularly the need for over-flying rights to ensure communications to the Persian Gulf and South-East Asia. They also addressed the South African problem. Although they felt that on balance South Africa would probably still be in the Commonwealth through the 1960s, it was fundamentally important not to be thought identifying with its policies.[49]

The US State Department received the paper as 'a very fine intelligence document', 'remarkably perceptive'. The Americans did not wish to dissent from it, although they could have wished for something more specific on future policy. The French also found it 'excellent and comprehensive', if rather too optimistic in tone: perhaps a more catastrophic view should be taken in the light of the Congo?[50] The prime minister's personal advisers were much less indulgent. Tim Bligh (principal private secretary) thought it only quite good, but not very original and not very profound about many of the fundamental questions. De Zulueta (the foreign affairs

---

[48] *Ibid.*, pp. 146–59, 383.

[49] *Ibid.*, pp. 113–33 (no. 20), June 1959, officials' report, 'Africa in the next ten years'; CAB 134/1353, AF 8(59)3, 7 April 1959. See also R. Ovendale, 'Macmillan and the wind of change in Africa, 1957–1960', *Historical Journal*, vol. 38 (1995), pp. 455–77.

[50] FO 371/137970, nos. 5 and 12; FO 371/137973, no. 31; FO 371/146505 no. 4; FO 371/146502, no. 16. The Congo problem is discussed below, pp. 306–8.

private secretary) was unimpressed. Unfortunately, perhaps, he secured Macmillan's signature to his critique, which was neither well-informed (his views on Indirect Rule and on the kabaka of Buganda were obviously out of date) nor realistic (Africa was 'one of the few parts of the world in which European powers still have direct influence'). In reply, Lennox-Boyd attempted politely to put the prime minister straight. But the prime minister's request for further investigation was readily conceded. Moreover, Macmillan in March 1960 authorised a South-East Asian counterpart, modelled upon it, as an off-shoot of the 'Future policy study'. A committee chaired by Sir R. Scott (formerly commissioner-general for South-East Asia) reported in October 1960: 'Future development and policy in South-East Asia'.[51]

The 'wind of change' speech takes its place in the sequence of key state-papers and policy declarations.[52] The idea of an African tour was entirely Macmillan's own, one which came to him after the 1959 election victory. Africa, he explained to Brook, seemed to be the biggest problem 'looming up for us here at home':

> We just succeeded at the General Election in 'getting by' on this. But young people of all Parties are uneasy and uncertain of our moral basis. Something must be done to lift Africa on to a more national plane as a problem to the solution of which we must all contribute, not out of spite – like the *Observer* and *New Statesman* – and not out of complacency – but by some really imaginative effort.

Undertaking a journey immediately after Christmas would bring this African problem 'into the centre of affairs'. Brook was to be sure to tell him if this was a bad idea, 'but I have the feeling that it might be a good idea and just get something moving in what seems [to be a] log-jam of ideas'. Macmillan's original plan was to start the tour in the Union, and of course if the South African government would not receive him then the whole thing would probably be called off.[53] In fact Verwoerd was not averse to the visit, but the sequence had to be reversed, with the Union coming last. This was mainly because South African MPs would not reconvene until mid-January. Macmillan himself had not intended to visit the High Commission Territories, but Maud persuaded him that this would be a mistake, since it would be interpreted as lack of interest in them.

---

[51] *CGEE*, pt 1, pp. 133–7 (no. 21); FO 371/173550, no. 4.
[52] *CGEE*, pt 1, pp. 167–74 (no. 32), 3 February 1960, address to the South African parliament; M. Makin, 'Britain, South Africa, and the Commonwealth in 1960: the "winds of change" reassessed', *Historia (Historiese Genootskap van Suid-Afrika/Historical Association of South Africa)*, vol. 41 (Pretoria, 1996), pp. 74–88.
[53] CAB 21/3155, Macmillan to Brook, 1 November 1959.

The general preparation of the speeches for the tour[54] was begun by Bligh, who set out some suggested themes which were then considered by various CO departments, who submitted drafts to the prime minister's office for co-ordination and refinement. The Ghana draft, forwarded by Poynton, was largely the work of High Commissioner Arthur Snelling and, in the CO, of O. H. Morris and J. H. Robertson. C. G. Eastwood (an assistant under-secretary of state) revised the collective CO advice that the prime minister should be 'a man in a hurry' in Africa into an exhortation to 'remember the pace of change in Africa'. (The CRO brief made a similar plea: 'in the face of the rising flood of African nationalism the pace at which we have to move becomes very delicate'.) Gorell Barnes (deputy under-secretary of state) counselled the prime minister against referring to a time-table: 'we are not on the run, with our dependencies pace-making; we are discharging our obligations in a conscientious and orderly manner'. The Nyasaland speech was drafted in the high commissioner's office at Salisbury and, unsurprisingly, was badly received in the CO. It seemed too supportive of Sir Roy Welensky (federal prime minister) and the Federation, too committed to a limited franchise and slower African progress. As Perth complained, such an emphasis could only spread 'alarm and despondency' in Northern Rhodesia and Nyasaland. Radical redrafting was therefore undertaken, by Perth himself.

The preparation of the crucial keynote speech to the South African parliament in Cape Town was entrusted to Maud, since he seemed to have mastered the knack of speaking forcefully to Afrikaners without mortally offending them. Macmillan's directive to Maud was that he 'must philosophise but not attack'. In two discussions with Maud on 14 December 1959, when they planned the outlines of the speech, Macmillan said he believed 'there was a very strong demand' in Britain that he should 'indicate that the vast majority of people in this country did not agree with the Union government's policy on apartheid . . . he must really try to find some phrase which indicated a critical approach'. It would be fruitless to tell them that we did not approve of apartheid, but criticism could be expressed in terms of how Britain dealt with not dissimilar problems; South Africa was not the only state grappling with racial diversity. Maud agreed this would be an excellent approach; necessary courtesies must be observed, but they were after all dealing, in Maud's view, with a police-state run by Transvaal thugs; the main objective would be to get them to be less ostrich-like, and look at themselves against the background of the world as a whole. Maud emphasised the

---

[54] For the preparation of the speech, see CO 1027/143, nos. 1, 2 and 40; CAB 21/3156 and 3157.

theme that 'the stage was still being set in Africa as to whether the forces of nationalism would be harnessed for or against Communism'. This theme was built into the speech, and the records also show clearly that the sentence which came at its climax was a revision worded by Maud. This was the unequivocal statement that there were some aspects of South African policies which made it impossible to support them 'without being false to our own deep convictions about the political destinies of free men, to which in our own territories we are trying to give effect'.

Meanwhile, Home had asked the former high commissioner in South Africa, Sir Evelyn Baring, to think of themes which would help to create a more emollient atmosphere. Baring helpfully suggested references to Scotland, the Afrikaans language, pioneers, and accomplishments in farming and industry. Maud consulted his deputy, Jack Johnston, despite having to produce a first draft at speed. This went to the CRO, then back to the prime minister's secretaries and to Brook. The CO was simply shown the resultant draft at the end of December. The reaction there was decidedly favourable: 'this is a clever speech' (O. H. Morris); 'very good and courageous, if possibly a little long' (Eastwood); 'goes further than might have been expected in the direction that we in the CO would wish it to take' (J. H. Robertson). Robertson reported to Bligh how relieved the CO was that a good deal would be said about the Afro-Asian Commonwealth and the way in which South Africa was an embarrassment to Britain: 'I have been asked to say to you that if the prime minister had not felt able to take this sort of line when he was in South Africa, we think the repercussions in many colonial territories might have been serious.' Indeed, the underlying sub-text of the speech as a whole was that South Africa was a liability to the West in the geopolitical context of the all-important 'struggle for the minds of men', whether 'the uncommitted peoples of Asia and Africa would swing to the East or to the West', the battle against communism. This battle required coming to terms with the rising tide of African national consciousness: 'the wind of change is blowing through this continent'. If they did not came to terms with it, 'we may imperil the precarious balance between East and West on which the peace of the would depends'.

The famous phrase occurred only about a third of the way into the speech. It was first used on 9 January in the Ghana speech, following a reference to states which had recently achieved independence, and those who were about to do so, Togoland, Somaliland and Mali: 'the wind of change is blowing through British East and Central Africa and through the Belgian Congo'. It attracted little attention, but someone in Macmillan's entourage thought it worth repeating, and inserted it at the last moment into the Cape Town speech. Who this was is not entirely certain. Two members of the party, John Wyndham (one of the private secretaries) and Tim Bligh, both later disclaimed any knowledge of the phrase's genesis (which might be thought *almost* to prove neither of them was responsible). On the other hand, the CRO's D. W. S. Hunt (later Sir David) did claim to be the 'author'. It may well be that Hunt made the insertion into the Cape Town speech, but the phrase itself belongs to a section of the Ghana speech apparently written by J. H. Robertson before 15 December. Robertson was allowed to accompany the prime minister in order specifically to help with the finalisation of his speeches.[55]

The address was received by the South African parliament in silence, with only a mild titter where laughter was expected. The Opposition and the Africans were, however, jubilant, and no-one could deny its impact. From the British point of view it was a triumph. Maud commented privately and at once that 'the whole thing will have done untold good out here'. His considered judgment was that it made the visit 'probably the most important event in South Africa since 1948', for, as Hunt declared, the speech was the visit. Back in Whitehall, a planned declaration on British colonial policy was finally abandoned, Sir Alexander Clutterbuck explaining to the CRO: 'we now have the Cape Town speech as our *locus classicus*, and no-one can say that our broad policy is not known to the world'. In the CO, it was seized upon by John Bennett (who had long urged the need for a faster and more radical approach to decolonisation) as 'an important speech . . . one of the most noteworthy statements of United Kingdom policy about Africa and the developing Commonwealth which has been made in recent years'. At his insistence copies were transmitted to all governors, thus underlining the status of the speech as a definitive guide to government thinking.[56] Brook reported to the Cabinet that the prime minister was generally thought to have been both courteous and courageous.

Within weeks the phrase 'wind of change' entered the discourse of decolonisation, quoted and appealed to by ministers, proconsuls and

---

[55] CAB 21/3155; PREM 11/4937, Bligh to Egremont, 26 May 1964; Lord Egremont, *Wyndham and children first* (1968), p. 182; David Hunt, *On the spot: an ambassador remembers* (1975), p. 53; see also C. Baker, *State of emergency: crisis in Central Africa, Nyasaland, 1959–1960* (1997), pp. 185–90. The intriguing thing is that almost all previous metaphors (including those by Macmillan himself) had spoken of tides and floods, not winds – an exception was Archbishop Makarios, who had used the word 'wind': see p. 202 above).

[56] *CGEE*, pt 2, pp. 394–8 (no. 444), D. W. S. Hunt to CRO, 8 February 1960; CO 859/1477, minute by J. S. Bennett, 8 March 1960. The speech was also highly influential among African leaders, e.g., Sobhuza of Swaziland (see below, p. 377) and Nelson Mandela, who in 1994 recalled the encouragement it had given to his cause, repeating his admiration for it in the moving speech he gave in Westminster Hall during his state visit to Britain in July 1996.

officials alike. Macleod invoked it. Home referred to it (p. 284 below). Macmillan mournfully quoted it against himself when South Africa left the Commonwealth ('the wind of change has blown us away': see below, p. 325).

In order to establish the exact significance of the speech in the evolution of British policy towards its own colonies, we may observe that nowhere did it employ the old well-worn slogans about multi-racialism and partnership (in the idiomatic Central African sense). Instead, it endorsed the term 'non-racial' which had been used by the foreign secretary, Selwyn Lloyd, at the UN General Assembly on 17 September 1959, 'our policy is non-racial'. The term seems rather suddenly to have come into use during 1959, Maud using it in connection with Swaziland in February; it was also applied to Basutoland (December 1958), Kenya, Tanganyika and Zanzibar. Macmillan's speech gave it greater prominence.

Importantly too, the speech meshed in with the new clarity of thought which Macleod brought to colonial policy from October 1959. For Macleod, the 'real problem' at the heart of all his challenges, was East-Central Africa, especially Kenya. 'The final test of our policies' would come in Kenya, Nyasaland and Northern Rhodesia. The basic difficulty was 'to achieve an orderly transfer of power to the Africans without losing the confidence of the Europeans'. The overriding consideration was to make sure East Africa did not become sympathetic to the Sino-Soviet cause. The speed of advance was driven by events, 'above all in the Congo'. Macleod's Cabinet memorandum of 3 January 1961 contains his well-known statement that he had tried to 'define the pace of British colonial policy in Africa as "not as fast as the Congo and not as slow as Algeria"'. He invited his colleagues to recognise that 'pressure from the United Nations, now that Belgium and France are dropping out as colonial powers, will increasingly concentrate on us'.[57]

An officials' interdepartmental paper in August 1961 firmly returned the focus to the cold war context. Africa was a 'target in the east-west struggle' and policy-makers must always remember the need to keep it out of the communist camp. Over-flying rights still seemed essential for the maintenance of the British position in the world. But much the most effective policy was 'to disengage, to leave the Africans alone, to advise and help only when our advice and help is asked for'.

The main policy surveys of the early 1960s were concerned with the expansion of the Commonwealth and the future of the smaller colonial

[57] *CGEE*, pt 1, pp. 164–7, 178–87 (nos. 31, 35–7) minutes and memoranda, 29 December 1959 to 31 May 1960, and pp. 510–11 (no. 160), 8 February 1960 (PREM 11/2586, 3030, & 3240; CAB 134/1560).

territories, those too small to aspire to realistic independence. A most important CO survey produced in September 1963 showed that although there were still forty British dependent territories, independence was the proclaimed goal for twenty-four of them. These were expected to get it by 1965, though no date could as yet be given for the High Commission Territories. This left sixteen small territories, most of which could probably find their future within a UN category of 'free association' with Britain, allowing them internal autonomy. The CO pondered whether a 'general act of decolonisation' could be made by 1965. Everyone seemed to agree this was neither possible nor wise, and that no general solution could be proposed for colonies whose status was so diverse. The CO believed, however, that these sixteen colonies could all make significant political advances. The survey was tested on other departments and no substantial modifications resulted, so the paper held the field for the remainder of the life of the Conservative government.

As prime minister, Sir Alec Douglas-Home (as he now was) in Canada in February 1964 proclaimed 'the virtual end of the process of decolonisation', making a ritual reference to its beginnings in the Durham Report of 1839. 'Colonialism is nearly at an end' and it was time to take up the challenge of other problems. And Duncan Sandys announced to the Commonwealth Prime Ministers' Meeting on 8 July 1964, 'we have no desire to prolong our colonial obligations for a day longer than is necessary'. These pronouncements were as near as the Conservative government came to a formal declaration of the 'end of empire'.[58]

3. Political developments

In the midst of these high-minded cogitations about policy, it is easy to lose sight of the messier realities on the ground, the nastier, more brutal underside of decolonisation. During the Macmillan government there were riots, strikes or boycotts, often violent, in Sierra Leone, Uganda, Nyasaland, Zanzibar, British Guiana, and Brunei. Over a longer period there was a continuous history of violent crack-downs against strikers, right through from the West Indies and the Copper Belt in the 1930s to the Gold Coast in the 1940s and Swaziland in the 1960s. Abuses by soldiers and police officers regularly resurfaced: in Ireland in 1917 to 1922, and later in Palestine, Cyprus, Kenya, Malaya, and Aden, especially when 'emergency regulations' could be used for revenge attacks and as a cloak

[58] *CGEE*, pt 1, pp. 211–20 (no. 46), 'The future of British colonial territories', September 1963; pp. 231–2 (no. 52), statement by Sandys, 8 July 1964 (CAB 148/2, f. 221), and pt 2, pp. 268–73 (no. 389), speech by Sir A. Douglas-Home, 11 February 1964 (PREM 11/4794, ff. 25–9).

for murkier actions. Control of news-media and information was a top priority for those involved in controlling awkward situations.[59] Even so, it is surprising how little ministers and officials in London seem to have known – or wanted to know – about discreditable incidents, from the time of the suppression of the Arab revolt in Palestine in the late thirties onwards (see above pp. 57–8). My impression is that they knew far less about misbehaviour overseas than their predecessors had done, for example about sexual exploitation in the colonies before the First World War.[60] It would seem that increases in the number of expatriate personnel and in bureaucratic systems simply left more interstices and files in which to hide. But when serious abuses did get into the public domain, all hell was liable to break loose.

On the morning of 3 March 1959, the president of the Nyasaland Congress Party, Dr Hastings Banda, was arrested at his house in Limbe, and bundled off into a truck, still wearing only his pyjamas, to be flown to Southern Rhodesia together with seventy-two other detainees – there was a rumoured ANC murder-plot against Europeans. At Nkata Bay twenty Africans, demonstrating against the arrests, were shot dead (and others followed in the days to come). On the same day, 1,200 miles to the north, eleven Africans were killed at a remote 'rehabilitation' camp for hard-core Mau Mau detainees (not convicted criminals), as a result of beatings administered to force them to work on an irrigation scheme. About twenty others were seriously injured at Hola Camp in the same incident. If one had to choose a single fateful date which signalled the moral end of the British empire in Africa it would thus be 3 March 1959. Macmillan told his Cabinet colleagues that the system which led to the Hola deaths had 'undoubtedly been wrong'. Macleod later recalled his sense of outrage: 'this was the decisive moment when it became clear to me that we could no longer continue with the old methods of government in Africa, and that meant inexorably a move towards African independence'. Macleod believed that the same was true for Macmillan.[61]

In July 1959 the report of Sir Patrick Devlin (a high court judge) into the Nyasaland disturbances was published, stating on the first page that 'Nyasaland has become, doubtless only temporarily, a police state.' The

[59] D. M. Anderson and D. Killingray, eds., *Policing and decolonisation: politics, nationalism and the police, 1917–1965* (Manchester, 1992), esp. pp. 1–21, 'An orderly retreat? Policing and the end of empire'; F. Furedi, 'Creating a breathing-space: the political management of colonial emergencies', in R. Holland, ed., *Emergencies and disorder in the European empires after 1945*, special issue of *JICH*, vol. 21 (1993), pp. 89–106.

[60] R. Hyam, *Empire and sexuality: the British experience* (1990, 1991, 1998) pp. 157–81, 'Chastity and the Colonial Service'.

[61] Shepherd, *Iain Macleod*, pp. 159–61. There is a good account of the Hola crisis in Murphy, *Lennox-Boyd*, pp. 208–16.

report as a whole was a merciless condemnation of the government, and the fact that a senior British judge could speak of a 'police state', and couple it with such an acid parenthesis, had a profound effect on British opinion. This was a phrase more electric to contemporaries than the rather tame 'wind of change' which followed it half a year later. Macmillan now dismissed Devlin privately as an embittered hunch-back Irish lapsed Roman Catholic. Whatever flaws there were in the Devlin Report, the Cabinet was patently being misled in an invitation to make a comparison between the Nyasaland disturbances and Mau Mau 'and possibly with the Indian Mutiny'.[62]

Southern Rhodesia had also declared a state of emergency early in 1959, in the course of which some five hundred people were detained without trial, among them Guy Clutton-Brock. He was an ANC member, a missionary farmer, reported by the native commissioner of Rusape, H B Masterson, as an 'odious and harmful influence', a 'subversive' – because he let natives eat with him at his own table, even sleep at his house, and did not teach them to rise to their feet if a European entered the room. The Cabinet was compelled to consider the case of Clutton-Brock after Barbara Castle in the House of Commons had described the Rhodesian government's action against him as 'absolutely fantastic'. The Cabinet decided that it was 'ill-advised' of the Rhodesian authorities to victimise so prominent and distinguished a European, and even though it was contrary to established practice to interfere on behalf of British nationals with dual citizenship, pressed the Federal government to release him. When he died in 1995 he was proclaimed 'a hero of Zimbabwe'.[63]

Even before it knew of the Hola massacres, though aware that two newspapers in Kenya had been banned (which seemed bad enough), the CO was alarmed that the government would be seen as declaring war on African nationalist aspirations. Accordingly, the CO permanent under-secretary drafted for Lennox-Boyd a public statement reaffirming his commitment to preparing for self-government in Africa as quickly as possible. In the course of the early summer of 1959, during the crisis over Hola Camp and the Devlin Report, Lennox-Boyd offered his resignation twice over.

All these unfortunate episodes, and the bad attendant publicity, in the long run played into the hands of Macmillan and Macleod by reducing opposition to their plans for constitutional advancement. If these events, and especially Hola, made them more determined, and improved the

---

[62] *CGEE*, pt 2, p. 541 (no. 494), 20 July 1959, Cabinet discussion of Lord Devlin's report (CAB 128/33, CC 43(59)1; *Report of the Nyasaland Commission of Inquiry* (Cmnd 814, 1959); Ball, *The Guardsmen*, p. 347.

[63] CAB 128/33, CC 18(59)5; DO 35/7711; obituary in *The Times*, 2 February 1995.

chances of Conservative Party acquiescence, the electoral victory of October 1959 delivered them the necessary power to act.

At around the same time, there were vital facilitating influences coming from outside as well. Independence was to be granted by the UN to Somalia in 1960 consequent upon the surrender of the Italian trustee-ship. Accelerated political progress there would inevitably lead to a demand for equivalent advancement in British Somaliland and in neigh-bouring territories, especially Aden and Kenya, whose peoples were more advanced than the Somalis. As Gorell Barnes put it: Britain 'was com-pelled to move with the tide'. The governors of East Africa realised that an independent and united Somalia would 'increase the difficulty of con-trolling the pace of constitutional development' in their own territories, but this was preferable to the emergence of a hostile Somalia.[64]

In the middle of 1958, de Gaulle had challenged francophone Africans to choose between a continuing relationship with a revamped French Community or independence out in the cold. Sékou Touré's supporters in Guinea voted 95 per cent (in the referendum held in September 1958) against the new Community constitution. Suddenly de Gaulle was urging Macmillan to see that France and Britain must decide jointly whether to stay in Africa or go. The writing on the wall could not have been plainer. As Macmillan's official biographer understood, de Gaulle's African policy had a profound influence on Macmillan.[65] Lennox-Boyd also pon-dered the implications of French policy:

I have been considering the effect on British territories of the recent referendum in French Africa and the possibility of the French action having some lessons for us. We have yet to see how things will settle down; but we should take stock of our own position in the light of these dramatic developments on the French side . . . My provisional conclusions are that some results of French policy are bound to have repercussions, possibly unfavourable, in British territories, especially in Sierra Leone; that it would be wrong for us to try to follow the French example in any general way; but that the French action, taken as a whole, is likely on balance to be a good thing for us and the West.[66]

De Gaulle was gradually driven into an unequivocal offer of 'self determination' in September 1959. The Belgians in January 1959 announced far-reaching plans for constitutional advancement in the Congo, which by the end of the year had telescoped into independence by June 1960. These developments, British officials recognised, were 'bound to have major repercussions in British East Africa'. Together the French and Belgians were putting Britain into the position where the period of

---

[64] *CGEE*, pt 1, p. 549 (no. 183) and p. 551 (note to no. 184), December 1958.
[65] Horne, *Macmillan*, vol. II, p. 177.
[66] CO 967/337, PM(58)52, to Macmillan, 16 October 1958.

British leadership in the transfer of power in Africa would appear to be coming to an end. The possibility was unfolding that Britain might be 'classed with the Portuguese as the obstacle to further advance'.[67] This was not an appealing prospect to either Macmillan or Macleod.

Almost all officials and politicians felt that a pace of political advancement faster than they would have preferred had been unexpectedly forced upon them. Sir James Robertson, governor-general of Nigeria, may be quoted here:

> The trouble is that we have not been allowed enough time: partly this is because we are not strong enough now as a result of two world wars to insist on having longer to build up democratic forms of government; partly because of American opposition to our idea of colonialism by the gradual training of people in the course of generations to run their own show; partly because of dangers from our enemies, the Communists, we have had to move faster than we should have wished.[68]

And Joe Garner, permanent under-secretary of the CRO:

> with the wind of change in Africa and throughout the world, the impact of nationalism and pressures in the United Nations, the pace of constitutional development has been forced in recent years. The result is that a number of countries have now been included as Commonwealth members before they can be regarded as fully mature and responsible, and fully capable of standing on their own feet.[69]

From a Colonial Service perspective, Robertson advised Macmillan that although Africans would not be ready for independence for fifteen to twenty years, they should have it at once, otherwise all the most capable would be in prison and learn nothing about administration.[70]

The underlying dynamics of the accelerated pace appear to be centred around calculations about the feasibility of holding on to colonial territories demanding change, and the pressures of external and especially neighbouring example. The CO understood well that the emergence of strong personalities such as Kwame Nkrumah (in the Gold Coast) and Julius Nyerere (in Tanganyika) was a vital factor in progress to independence, and – with the exception of South Arabia – they had no desire to exclude such leaders by backing, or artificially creating, authoritarian puppet regimes (based on traditional chiefs or feudal rulers), which could only lead 'to the creation of a revolutionary force against the set-up that we had created'.[71] As to feasibility, the

---

[67] *CGEE*, pt 1, p. 125 (no. 20) para. 84, 'Africa in the next ten years'.
[68] CO 936/572, to Eastwood, 26 June 1959.   [69] DO 161/95, no. 12, note, 30 April 1962.
[70] Macmillan, *Pointing the way*, p. 119.
[71] CO 936/572, no. 92, minutes of a meeting in CO, 20 May 1959; see also Eastwood's remarks on 7 April 1959 (CAB 134/1353, AF 8(59)3), and Sir L. Monson's recollections in A. H. M. Kirk-Greene, ed., *The transfer of power: the colonial administrator in the age of decolonisation* (1979), p. 29.

dilemma was well expressed in Lennox-Boyd's memorandum on Nigeria in May 1957: 'either to give independence too soon and risk disintegration and breakdown of administration; or to hang on too long, risk ill-feeling and disturbances, and eventually to leave bitterness behind'.[72] The British meanwhile faced almost insoluble administrative problems in coping with a discontented and possibly rebellious Nigerian population. Also, conventional wisdom was already well established generally that the 'risks of going too slow were probably greater than the risks of going too fast'.[73] As to neighbouring examples: Ghana had set a dangerous but unavoidable precedent, so Nigeria had to be given what Ghana had. Chain reactions were operating. Sierra Leone moved forward under the impact events in Ghana and Nigeria and the French territories, especially Guinea, so that 'anything less than a real measure of advance would cause trouble'. What happened in West Africa must eventually be repeated in East Africa. Kenya's political advancement was speeded up as a result of Somaliland's impending independence; Tanganyika profited especially from the example of the Congo. Nyasaland was the beneficiary of the acceleration of the timetable in Kenya; Northern Rhodesia in its turn followed Nyasaland. So did Zanzibar, where the feasibility of getting troops into it was in doubt after the independence of Kenya. Further afield, even the Solomon Islands began to move forward after Australia announced plans to introduce universal suffrage in Papua New Guinea from 1964.

The question must thus arise as to whether the influence of ministers in London made much difference. Clearly there were elements of continuity between each of the Conservative secretaries of state for the colonies and an underlying support by at least some of their advisers for policies of constitutional progress. As Macleod recognised in respect of Kenya, solid disagreement from his officials 'might have halted me in my tracks'. As to continuity, it was his predecessor Lennox-Boyd who had said, 'there is of course no stopping the process of devolution on which we are now well set'.[74] However, judgments about timing were crucial. Macleod's own assessment of his role seems a fair one:

The change of policy that I introduced in October 1959 was, on the surface, merely a change of timing. In reality, of course it was a true change of policy, but I telescoped events rather than created new ones.

---

[72] *CGEE*, pt 1, p. 341 (no. 100), memo by Lennox-Boyd on Nigeria, 7 May 1957 (CAB 134/1555, para. 16).
[73] *CGEE*, pt 1, p. 9 (no. 2), 'Future constitutional development in the colonies', May 1957, para. 52.   [74] *Ibid.*, p. 235 (no. 54), minute by Lennox-Boyd, 28 May 1957, para. 2.

He published his definitive apologia in the *Spectator* in 1964, defending the deliberate decision to speed up the movement towards independence:

And in my view any other policy would have led to terrible bloodshed in Africa. This is the heart of the argument . . . Were the countries fully ready for Independence? Of course not. Nor was India, and the bloodshed that followed the grant of Independence there was incomparably worse than anything that has happened since to any country. Yet the decision of the Attlee Government was the only realistic one. Equally we could not possibly have held by force to our territories in Africa. We could not, with an enormous force engaged, even continue to hold the small island of Cyprus. General de Gaulle could not contain Algeria. The march of men towards their freedom can be guided, but not halted. Of course there were risks in moving quickly. But the risks of moving slowly were far greater.[75]

Here was a British Conservative minister, whether consciously or unconsciously, echoing one of the earliest colonial nationalists, the Irish leader C. S. Parnell ('No man has a right to fix the boundary to the march of a nation', 1886). It is a measure of the fundamental changes afoot.

It would be a work of supererogation to summarise here all the political developments and constitutional advances in each of the British colonies. What follows is therefore a selection of some of the more significant cases: Cyprus, Nigeria, Tanganyika, Kenya, Nyasaland and Northern Rhodesia, Aden, Malaysia, and the West Indies Federation. But a preliminary observation should be made. Even apart from the obvious question-marks hanging over territories claimed by other powers – Hong Kong (by China), Gibraltar (by Spain), the Falkland Islands (by Argentina), and Honduras (by Guatemala) – almost every colony had puzzling and unique problems of its own. In Uganda progress was bedevilled by the relationship of its four kingdoms, especially Buganda, to the centre: a complex, confused, and according to Macleod even 'somewhat Gilbertian' situation. The governor of Uganda, Sir Frederick Crawford, despaired of 'our problem children', roundly denouncing 'these bumptious, beer-swilling, bible-punching, bullying, braggart Baganda'.[76] Secession was ruled out. In geographically anomalous Gambia, and tiny St Helena, the problem was one of viability. In Malta too – 'a small but terribly difficult problem' (Home) – the worry was how 320,000 'not very industrious people living on a relatively barren island group' would manage without high

---

[75] Macleod, 'Trouble in Africa', *Spectator*, no. 7075, p. 127, 23 January 1964, repr. in Porter and Stockwell, eds., *British imperial policy*, vol. II pp. 570–1 (no. 82); Shepherd, *Iain Macleod*, pp. 168 and 181.

[76] *CGEE*, pt 1, p. 182 (no. 36), memo by Macleod, 'Colonial problems in 1961', 3 January 1961 (CAB 134/1560, CPC(61)1); CO 822/1450, no. 249, Crawford to Turnbull, 25 July 1959.

employment in the naval dockyard.[77] In Fiji, the peculiarity was the unwillingness of the Fijians to contemplate any form of independence, locked as they were in ethnic rivalry with a powerful immigrant Indian community. In Guiana the communist leanings of Dr Jagan bred hesitancy, assiduously played upon by the Americans, fearing that independence would result in another Cuba or Congo. In Southern Rhodesia the problem was the intransigence of the 250,000 Europeans, most of them bent on blocking progress to African majority rule.

(1) Cyprus

The following magisterial passage by Professor Nicholas Mansergh can hardly be bettered:

[W]hen confronted with a demand for self-determination which had the backing of the Orthodox Church and the leadership of the Archbishop, the British imperial authorities . . . resorted to the cruder device of episcopal and archiepiscopal deportation in a vain endeavour to bring to an end a prolonged and painful struggle for which psychologically they were ill equipped and the character of which, in conjunction with earlier experience in Ireland, and contrary to the fashionable assumptions of the time, suggested that similarities in race and colour, not differences, served most to intensify the bitterness of national revolt against the imperial power.[78]

A conflict of this character had long been feared both by the CO and FO as anomalous, dangerous, and embarrassing.

One of the earliest acts of the Macmillan government was to release Archbishop Makarios from his 'archiepiscopal deportation' to the Seychelles, of which Macmillan had never approved. It was hoped that this would clear a path towards a settlement. Macmillan was prepared to give priority to Cyprus in part because the problem was familiar to him from his time as foreign secretary in 1955. The baffling deadlock encountered then persisted into 1957.[79] The problem was essentially a strategic one, with two elements. The first was that the Chiefs of Staff had declared that Britain needed a secure command of Cyprus as a whole. The second was that the British government feared an independent Cyprus would implement Enosis, union with Greece, and Greece might become communist. In any case, good relations with a strong Turkey as a NATO ally

---

[77] *CGEE*, pt 1, pp. 693–718 for Malta; see also D. Austin, *Malta and the end of empire* (1971).

[78] N. Mansergh, ed., *Documents and speeches on Commonwealth affairs, 1952–1962* (1963) intro, p. 3. Mansergh's observation also applies to negotiations with Malta's Dom Mintoff, which were far less amicable than many independence struggles.

[79] FO 371/117665, minute, 13 October 1955; CAB 129/75, CP(55)33, memo, 11 June 1955; FO 371/117635–117667.

on its eastern flank were essential. And Turkey was vehemently opposed to Enosis. To Turkey, Cyprus was an off-shore island only forty miles away, and one-fifth of the Cypriot population was Turkish. Thus for Britain the wishes of Turkey increasingly became more important than those of Greece: 'to keep in with the Turks – both in Turkey and in the island', as Julian Amery rather bluntly expressed it.[80]

The Colonial Policy Committee agreed in June 1957 that they needed 'release from the odium and expense which we carried at present'.[81] Governor Sir John Harding told the committee that without a political settlement, 10,000 troops would be required indefinitely, plus 6,000 reinforcements – which was impossible. Ministers dreaded 'a second Palestine'. In December hard-line Harding was replaced by the more flexible Hugh Foot, who carried credibility with the Labour Party. It was hoped he would get to grips more closely with the colonial politicians and buy time. Foot produced a plan for qualified internal self-government, leading to self-determination after a period of up to seven years – apparently basing his hopes on a sort of compulsory co-operation across the ethnic divide. Ministers felt this would commit Britain to continuing close involvement, which 'could not be reconciled with the policy of progressive reduction in the strength of the Army'. They could not go on indefinitely 'bearing the burdens and costs' of sole responsibility for administration, with the risk of renewed large-scale violence. Instead of Foot's plan, Macmillan preferred a 'tri-dominium' solution, which would bring in representatives of the Greek and Turkish governments as resident advisers. At Zürich in February 1959 the foreign ministers of Greece and Turkey announced (to general surprise) that they had after months of negotiation agreed that Cyprus should be independent, more or less under the Macmillan Plan. Macmillan regarded the settlement, confirmed at the London conference of February 1959, as one based on a parity of sacrifice. The British ended the Emergency and agreed to abandon sovereignty, except over ninety-nine square miles of base-enclaves. The Greeks agreed not to press for Enosis. The Turks agreed not to pursue their preferred outcome of partition. The new state would have a Greek Cypriot president (Makarios was the first), a Turkish Cypriot vice-president (both with a veto in certain matters), and a cabinet of seven Greek Cypriots and three Turkish Cypriots. This 7:3 proportion was repeated right down the administrative ladder; in other words, Turkish Cypriots were entitled to 30 per cent of posts even though they had less than 20 per cent of the population. The constitution of July 1960

---

[80] *CGEE* pt 1, p. 688 (no. 237), minute, 8 June 1959.
[81] *CGEE* pt 1, pp. 652–3, 20 June 1957 (CAB 134/1555, CPC 10(57)).

was not exactly a popular solution, nor did it last for long. Cyprus became an independent republic on 16 August 1960. In December 1963 fighting broke out again, barely three-and-a-half years into independence. Britain invoked the help of the United Nations, who policed a 'green line' demarcation between the two sides. In 1974 Turkey invaded Cyprus and consolidated *de facto* partition.

Partition was of course the one thing the British had steadfastly hoped not to be responsible for. In Macmillan's words, it would be a 'confession of failure'. It would be immensely difficult to carry out, internal 'bitterness and bloodshed' being matched by the damage it would do to British prestige and international reputation. No-one in the CO believed partition had any attractions except as a last resort. Lennox-Boyd minuted: 'A "Palestinian solution" is distasteful to me.' The Chiefs of Staff, and constitutional adviser Lord Radcliffe, were against it.[82] The FO, however, with their special pro-Turkish concerns, always seemed to hanker after it, and as prime minister, Douglas-Home (a former foreign secretary) did not flinch from it as the probable 'final solution'.[83]

Cyprus gained independence because of British strategic revaluation and a need to cut costs. In 1954 a government spokesman had implied that Cyprus would 'never' be independent. (See p. 204.) Although that should probably have read 'not yet', the strategic objections then were formidable. Cyprus, however, was a principal beneficiary of the post-Suez shake-up. It had proved to be of limited use in that operation, and once it was clear the military planners did not need to hold the entire island as a base for major military purposes, the strategic requirements could be reduced to the retention of airfields. The prospect – which Foot warned about repeatedly – of 'civil war in Cyprus, possibly leading to war between Greece and Turkey', also increased the pressure for a peaceful disengagement.[84]

Decolonisation in Cyprus was a messy and mangled affair, less well-managed than elsewhere. The British were essentially mystified by the whole idea of a political-prelate. To them, 'Black Mac' was a Rasputin figure. They misjudged the extent of Makarios's control, as they had of Kenyatta's, which led to the archbishop's controversial deportation. In Cyprus, however, 'only' nine executions took place during the insurgency. Nevertheless, these actions, together with allegations of atrocities, resulted in 1956 in the Greek government's bringing the first inter-state case under the European Convention of Human Rights (1953) against

---

[82] CO 926/704 and 1053, minutes, 1957–1958; *CGEE*, pt 1, pp. 653–5 (no. 219), memo by Macmillan, 9 July 1957.
[83] *CGEE*, pt 1, pp. 692–3 (no. 241), minute by Douglas-Home, 27 December 1963.
[84] *CGEE*, pt 1, pp. 676–7 (no. 231) letter from Foot to Lennox-Boyd.

the very country which had done so much to bring it into being. Although the British government came out of the Cyprus cases in the Strasbourg Court pretty well, these had been damaging to prestige and authority.

Perhaps there were simply too many conflicting responsibilities for Britain in Cyprus, in a situation where power had gone, and where too many other interests also had other differing responsibilities. To conclude, here is another masterly passage, this time by Robert Holland:

Archbishop Makarios had a responsibility to his Church and its vision of a 'faithful' and redeemed Cyprus. Grivas had a responsibility to a national heroism in which his own exiguous personality was sublimated. The Greek Government had a responsibility to a certain conception of Hellenism, albeit one in which Cyprus was far from possessing the most powerful resonances. The Turkish government had a responsibility to take whatever opportunities came its way to help its co-religionists and protégés, and to recover some echo of its own imperial past. Even the [British] Cyprus Government, the most hollowed out of all these actors, had a responsibility common to all autocracies – to keep its head above water for as long as strength permitted. It was because of the clash of all these responsibilities that, amongst the various nationalities and creeds involved in the passing of colonial Cyprus, some had died, some grieved, many were hurt in some way, whilst most people were left hoping – to echo the battered but partially resurrected vision of Governor Foot – for whatever Promised Land they had been looking for.[85]

(2) Nigeria

With a population approaching 50 million, Nigeria was the biggest colony in the empire. Its political development was dominated by the choreography of adjusting the interests of four ethnic groups: Hausa-Fulani (in the Northern Region), the Yoruba (in the Western Region), the Ibo (in the Eastern Region), and the minorities scattered in each region amounting to about a third of the total in each case. All participants in constitutional conferences tried to create states to their own specification and limit the powers of their fellow-Nigerians. The Northern Peoples' Congress was a rigorously conservative Muslim party; the Action Group under Chief Awolowo expressed a distinctively Yoruba nationalism; while only Azikiwi's NCNC (National Council of Nigeria and the Cameroons), based in the East, as the first country-wide mass party, showed much commitment to a new Nigerian nationality.[86]

[85] R. F. Holland, *Britain and the revolt in Cyprus, 1954–1959* (1998), p. 329. This is an outstanding study, but there is also another important account embedded in A. W. B. Simpson's magisterial *Human rights and the end of empire: Britain and the genesis of the European Convention* (2001, 2004), pp. 884–1052.

[86] R. L. Sklar, *Nigerian political parties* (Princeton, NJ, 1963); Ashley Jackson, 'Azikiwe, Nnamdi', *ODNB*, vol. III, pp. 66–7.

Illustration 4.1 Nigerian constitutional conference: Mr Lennox-Boyd
greets the delegates, September 1958.
Left to right: Chief Obafemi Awolowo (premier, Northern Region),
Alhaji Abubakar Tafawa Balewa (federal prime minister), Ahmadu
Bello the Sardauna of Sokoto (premier of the Northern Region),
Dr Nnamdi Azikiwe (premier of the Eastern Region). At this
meeting in London, the British government agreed to grant independence to the Federation of Nigeria as from 1 October 1960, and decided
to incorporate provisions for fundamental human rights in the constitution.

Internal self-government was granted to the Eastern and Western
Regions in the summer of 1957, and to Northern Nigeria in the
spring of 1959. Pivotally between these two events came the critical
ministerial decisions in October 1958. Lennox-Boyd told the Cabinet
he would 'certainly not like to assert that self-government will in
Nigeria be good government', but there seemed to be nothing to be
gained by postponing a decision to accept demands for 1960 as the
date for independence, since any attempt to 'continue to govern a
discontented and possibly rebellious Nigeria would present well-nigh
insuperable administrative problems', because much effective power
had already been transferred. The Cabinet agreed that no useful
purpose would be served by delay, thus forfeiting Nigerian goodwill, so

'the balance of advantage' lay with going ahead with the 1960 target-date.[87]

Lennox-Boyd was adamant that they could not meet the fears of minority groups by creating additional states for them. This was because of concern that reconstructing the state-framework would cause unacceptable delay. Macmillan sent out his old school-chum, lifelong friend and favourite trouble-shooter, Harry Willink (commercial lawyer, former Conservative minister of health, and a vice-chancellor of the University of Cambridge), to make a reassuring report. The terms of reference to the commission were tightly enough drawn to make sure they did not seriously consider additional state-formation as an option. The Willink Commission's report did not deny that minorities had genuine cause for alarm; it noted that the imbalance in the relative weight of the three constituent parts was 'unusual'; and admitted that there were 'intangible qualities which induced people to want separate states'. As against these considerations, it concluded that separate states would not in fact provide remedies for the fears expressed, while it would be worryingly difficult to create 'clean' boundaries which did not create fresh minorities:

> But there is also a general consideration of the first importance . . . With the approach of independence the tendency has been [to] . . . a sharp recrudescence of tribal feeling. But it does not necessarily follow that this will continue . . . It would be a pity if separate states had been created which enshrined tribal separation in a political form that was designed to be permanent.[88]

Even to set up a separate state for the Mid-West 'would accentuate and underline tribal divisions which a wise statesmanship would seek gradually to obliterate'. Instead, influenced by Christian pressure-groups, the Commission sought to allay minority fears by constitutional entrenchment of virtually all the clauses of the European Human Rights Convention. These sixteen clauses might not have been of much practical benefit to Nigeria, but the Commission (secretly guided by the CO) thought it important to provide a signal, and a 'standard to which appeal may be made by those whose rights are infringed'. Nigeria thus became the first African country with a constitution embodying fundamental rights, and this became an almost mandatory precedent. In moving the Second Reading of the Nigerian Independence Bill in July 1960,

---

[87] *CGEE*, pt 1, pp. 354–6 (no. 105), memo by Lennox-Boyd, 20 October 1958 (CAB 129/95, C(58)213); M. Lynn, ed., *Nigeria* (BDEEP, 2001), pp. 563–6 (no. 458).

[88] H. U. Willink, *Nigeria: report of the Commission appointed to inquire into the fears of the minorities and the means of allaying them* (Cmnd 505, 1958) esp. pp. 33, 97–103; Simpson, *Human rights and the end of empire*, pp. 862–70; J. D. Hargreaves, 'From strangers to minorities in West Africa', *Transactions of the Royal Historical Society*, 5 ser., vol. 31 (1981), pp. 95–114.

Macleod went out of his way to praise the inclusion of this code of human rights.[89]

Nevertheless, the British determination to preserve the integrity of a Nigeria as the single unit which they had created, in fact bequeathed an inherently unstable structure, which failed even to survive in the short-term. Nigeria became an independent federation on 1 October 1960 with three regions, and a federal republic three years later – with four regions. In 1967 the regions were replaced with twelve states, increased to nineteen in 1976, with Nigeria moving towards a system of government on the US pattern. It was of course the discovery and exploitation of oil which made it possible to throw off Willink's well-intentioned straight-jacket, by providing the necessary revenues. (Ironically, the British 'colonial state' had abandoned the search for oil in Nigeria in 1913 after oil was discovered in Persia.)[90]

Despite the all-too-real doubts of officials about 'disruptive and parochial' politics, 'personalities at sixes and sevens', British policy-makers were anxious to meet the wishes of Nigeria's leaders, many of whom were admired as dignified, gentlemanly and non-confrontational. A graduate of American universities, Nnamdi Azikiwe ('Zik') seemed to be a man they could do business with; while everyone liked the northerner Abubakar Tafawa Balewa, knighted as the first federal prime minister in 1960. As the most populous state in Africa by far, and geopolitically at a nodal point of Commonwealth communications, Britain needed Nigerian continuing friendship quite badly for strategic as well as economic reasons. The essential parameters had in any case been set by Ghana, though a friendly Ghana was not so important.[91] As a result, Nigeria's was not an heroic nationalist struggle, and the whole civilised narrative and discourse of Nigerian decolonisation was all about timing. If the timing was for a while dictated by Northern Nigerian politicians, with their conservatism and distrust of Christian-educated southerners, that consideration was resolved by increasing realism in the North.[92]

(3) Tanganyika

In 1957 the official members of the Executive Council were redesignated ministers, and assistant ministers (four Africans, one European and one

[89] *PD, Commons*, vol. 626, cc. 1793–4, 15 July 1960.
[90] *Yearbook of the Commonwealth, 1980* (1980), p. 278; J. M. Carland, *The Colonial Office and Nigeria, 1898–1914* (1985).
[91] *CGEE*, pt 1, pp. 347–52 (no. 103), CRO minutes, August–September 1958.
[92] J. E. Flint, review of Lynn, *Nigeria* (BDEEP), in *JICH*, vol. 32 (2004), pp. 166–9.

Asian) were appointed to the Legislative Council.[93] The old idea of an equal three-way split between Europeans, Africans and Asians, regardless of the actual population proportions, was abandoned. A general election was held in 1958, preparatory to the establishment of a council of ministers. Lennox-Boyd defined a policy of gradualness, a controlled, step-by-step, middle-of-the-road constitutional advance in order to prevent 'frustration and bitterness',[94] and by January 1959 he expected independence in perhaps 1970.

In May 1959 Governor Sir Richard Turnbull presented radical proposals for stepping up the speed of political advancement in Tanganyika.[95] Turnbull thought Nyerere had real potential: a Roman Catholic graduate of Edinburgh University, he was an unassuming scholarly man, who translated two of Shakespeare's plays into Swahili. In his turn, Nyerere appreciated Turnbull's speaking Swahili with him. For the CO, Turnbull's thesis was that there had been 'a great upsurge of nationalism in the Belgian Congo which had not been foreseen'. A similar turmoil in Nyasaland and Ruanda-Urundi had erupted. And it 'could not be expected that Tanganyika would remain immune from the trend of events elsewhere in Africa'. Accordingly his plan was to 'tame Nyerere', using him to rob those he called 'the wild men' on the lunatic fringe of their glamour. To do this, reasonableness and co-operation with Britain on Nyerere's part must be shown to be a paying proposition. Therefore, Britain should introduce immediately an unofficial majority, smack 'the wild men' down, and encourage the moderates. Although Turnbull did not think Tanganyika was really ready for independence for twenty years yet, without this kind of political progress, he forecast a chillingly apocalyptic scenario, predicting two major insurrections in Tanganyika. The first would come in 1960 or 1961. The second would arrive, apparently, in 1970, and it would be a 'combination of Mau Mau and the Maji-Maji rebellion, with the support of modern techniques of guerrilla warfare and fifth-column activities'. The forces available to put such uprisings down would be wholly inadequate. Turnbull's advice was that holding to 'ordered progress to self-government' would depend primarily on Nyerere's not being supplanted by an 'extremist', but also on Britain's

---

[93] The most illuminating work on Tanganyika is by John Iliffe: *A modern history of Tanganyika* (1979), pp. 561–4, and 'TANU and the Colonial Office', *Tanzania Zamani: a Journal of Historical Writing and Research*, vol. 3, no. 2 (Dar es Salaam, 1997), pp. 1–62. See also R. C. Pratt, *The critical phase in Tanganyika, 1945–1968: Nyerere and the emergence of a socialist strategy* (1978).

[94] *CGEE*, pt 1, pp. 371–83 (nos. 116 and 117), memo by Lennox-Boyd, and minutes of Colonial Policy Committee meeting, 10 and 17 August 1959.

[95] *CGEE*, pt 1, pp. 450–83 (nos. 140–6), January–November 1959; CO 822/1449, no. 227, and CO 822/1450, no. 254, Turnbull to CO, May–August 1959.

finding enough money to spend between 1960 and 1970 on education and training in order to sugar the pill of political gradualism. Basically what he envisaged was chopping about four years off the timetable, that is to say, reaching an unofficial majority in the Council of Ministers by late 1960 instead of early 1965.

Lennox-Boyd and his officials were flummoxed by this extraordinary initiative, which contradicted a policy agreed at Chequers only five months previously. For the remainder of his time in office, Lennox-Boyd prevaricated, some plausibility being lent to this by the impending general election in Britain. However, Turnbull met Macleod on 16 November 1959, only weeks after Macleod had taken over, and Macleod was persuaded. Lest we attach too much importance to Macleod's enabling role, it is worth noting that his predecessor was probably beginning to accept Turnbull's line.[96] But we are entitled to take the view that Macleod was more genuinely sympathetic, and considerably better at getting Turnbull's policy through the Colonial Policy Committee than Lennox-Boyd would have been. Macleod sold the policy to his colleagues by telling them that he believed the governor's argument was sound: if the government did not concede the unofficial majority, 'we may be faced with serious disturbances and may lose the opportunity of some years of constructive effort' in the vital matter of economic and social development. Macleod also emphasised the inability of the police to cope with any serious trouble, especially in circumstances where Britain could expect little support either inside or outside Tanganyika. Indeed, they would face active UN criticism for failure to ensure peace by a positive response to a claim for self-government requested in a reasonable and constitutional manner. Rejection could only lead to non-co-operation and administrative breakdown. Finally, the Cabinet in November accepted that it was necessary to advance the timetable in order to maintain peaceful development, and confidence in Britain. And so in December 1959 a second general election was announced, with constitutional changes which would bring in an elected majority on both the Executive and Legislative Councils in August 1960. Of the seventy-one seats, fifty were open to contest by all races. In the event Nyerere's TANU party won seventy seats. Just before the election Macleod argued that 'the wind of change has been gathering force since last November, so the thinking of all of us has been speeded up'; the government could now contemplate Tanganyikan independence by July 1962 instead of 1968.[97] In fact independence was reached in December 1961.

[96] CO 822/1450, minutes by Monson, 2 November 1959.
[97] *CGEE*, pt 1, pp. 482–3 (no. 146), Colonial Policy Committee meeting, 20 November 1959 (CAB 134/1558, CPC 6(59)1); pp. 483–6 (no. 147), CO minutes, 3–18 July 1960.

What were the dynamics behind the dramatic speeding up of the transfer of power in Tanganyika? First, there had been the collapse of faith in its European settlers, well under way even by 1957. Then there was the near inevitability of promoting a personable, moderate, collaborative nationalist leader, of co-opting Nyerere as the best available African, for whom there seemed to be no acceptable alternative: the policy which Arden-Clarke had called (with respect to Nkrumah) backing 'the one dog in our kennel' (see above, p. 150). Calculations about governability also came to the fore: here, Turnbull's scare tactics performed an historic function. The 'wind of change' was evoked to telling effect, in combination with the influence of what was happening in neighbouring states, particularly in the Congo. Finally, there was a recognition of the importance of keeping on the right side of world opinion and heading off the pretensions of the UN to assert itself.

(4) Kenya

Where Tanganyika led, Kenya was bound to follow, profiting from Turnbull's 'no immunity from neighbouring trends' argument. The first African elections were held in Kenya in March 1957, but deadlock ensued. A new constitution equalised the communal representation of Africans and Europeans and a common roll was introduced (the Lennox-Boyd constitution). Fresh elections were held in March 1958. By June 1959 Macmillan was looking for 'perceptible movement': heading off African disturbances without driving the settlers into trying to join the Union of South Africa.[98] At the Lancaster House Conference in January 1960 Macleod devised a complex new constitution, under which the Africans (on a greatly extended common roll) could expect to secure thirty-three out of sixty-five elected seats in the Leg Co. Macleod had in effect been able to concede the principle of majority rule and was well pleased with the way things had moved forward. Crucial to this was the emergence of the New Kenya Group, mainly Europeans, led by Michael Blundell, who could be persuaded to think nationally for Kenya as a whole; one of their number was Macleod's youngest brother, Rhoddy Macleod.[99] The question from then on was the timing of

[98] *CGEE*, pt 1, p. 161 (no. 29), note, 1 June 1959.
[99] On the background: M. Blundell, *So rough a wind: the Kenya memoirs of Sir Michael Blundell* (1964), and review by Iain Macleod, *Spectator* (20 March 1964), p. 366 ('Blundell's Kenya'); K. Kyle, *The politics of the independence of Kenya* (1999); G. Bennett and C. G. Rosberg, *The Kenyatta election: Kenya, 1960–1961* (1961). Michael Blundell was minister of agriculture (1955–9, 1961–3); he wrote a book on the wild flowers of Kenya.

Illustration 4.2 Mr Macleod with Mr Nyerere, announcing agreement
on the constitutional development of Tanganyika, March 1961.
Mr Macleod as secretary of state for the colonies visited Tanganyika to
chair this conference, and is shown on the verandah of Government
House, Dar es Salaam, with Julius Nyerere, and Sir Richard Turnbull
the governor, indicating agreement on internal self-government for
Tanganyika from 1 May 1961, and full independence from 28
December 1961 (later amended to 9 December 1961). On 1 May 1961
Nyerere, formerly chief minister, became the country's first prime min-
ister. (Tanganyika Information Service.)

independence, which as Macleod saw it was 'to go as slowly as possible, but not as slow as Alec Home [now foreign secretary] would like', because that would lead to 'a Cyprus on our hands again'.[100] But Macleod absolutely rejected the idea being floated that it would be possible in practice 'to maintain our position in Kenya by consent for anything like eight years', as some ministers were suggesting. He pointed to 'the growing pressure in the United Nations to bring Colonial territories to independence'. He reminded them of the success of their policy in Tanganyika, which was 'largely due to our willingness to consider a progressive and early transfer of power to the Africans'. The Colonial Policy Committee accepted that if, as seemed possible, Tanganyika, Uganda and Zanzibar were likely to move fairly quickly towards independence, 'it would be impossible to justify to the Kenya Africans the maintenance of United Kingdom rule in Kenya merely on account of the presence of significant numbers of Europeans'.[101] Macleod's successor, Maudling, reinforced the same message in November 1961: 'arithmetic and African nationalism' had destroyed European political power, and it was impossible to continue to rule Kenya for some years to come, because this would require the use of force, which could only lead to 'another outbreak of Mau Mau' and great disorder, 'possibly reaching even Congo proportions'.[102] However distasteful it was, they had to face the fact that Jomo Kenyatta would end up as prime minister, since he was the leader the Africans acknowledged.

Full internal self-government was introduced, following an unhelpful London conference early in 1962, but Kenya remained 'an extremely intractable problem' (Macmillan). The issues anxiously discussed by the Cabinet over the next two years included: safeguards and compensation for over 3,000 European farmers, the threat of economic and financial collapse (which a European exodus would exacerbate), the maintenance of law and order between the Kikuyu and their rivals, whether or not to retain a military base, whether or not to allow the Somali-majority Northern Frontier District to join the Somali Republic. (The integration of the NFD into a 'Greater Somalia' might forestall a frontier civil war, another Congo or Kashmir, but it would upset Ethiopia – 'the emperor

[100] *CGEE*, pt 1, pp. 407–8 (no. 125) 6 January 1961, Macleod to Macmillan.
[101] CAB 134/1560, CPC 1(62)2, Minutes of Colonial Policy Committee, 6 January 1961.
[102] *CGEE*, pt 1, pp. 523–6 (no. 169), Minutes of Colonial Policy Committee, 15 November 1961; pp. 529–30 (no. 172), memo by Maudling, 30 January 1962. Macmillan juxtaposed the analogies slightly differently in a highly characteristic diary entry, bemoaning the balance of evils: 'If we have to give independence to Kenya, it may well prove another Congo. If we hold on, it will mean a long and cruel campaign: Mau Mau and all that' (*Memoirs*, vol. VI, *At the end of the day*, p. 291).

Illustration 4.3 Governor Malcolm MacDonald speaking at the inauguration of responsible government in Kenya, 1 June 1963, with Jomo Kenyatta and other ministers.
From left to right: Jomo Kenyatta, Oginga Odinga, Tom Mboya, James Gichuru, Clyde Sanger. Responsible government was conceded after KANU (the Kenya African National Union) had won the election. This was the occasion when Kenyatta gave the national slogan *Harambee* (let's all pull together) instead of *Uhuru* (freedom). Independence followed on 12 December 1963.

would get very excited', said Macmillan.)[103] In the face of such problems, it is perhaps hardly surprising that ministers turned once again to 'the federal panacea'. Macleod thought an East African federation would be 'a wonderful prize'. Malcolm MacDonald (now governor of Kenya) regarded it as 'a dream answer'.[104] The prospects were repeatedly reviewed, it being always understood that the initiative would have to be left to local politicians. Despite an initial interest in the idea, especially by Nyerere, they eventually got cold feet.

[103] PREM 11/4511, note of a meeting with Nyerere, 13 December 1963; CAB 134/1561, CPC 5(62)1, 2 March 1962, minutes of Colonial Policy Committee.
[104] *CGEE*, pt 1, pp. 490–1 (no. 150), minute by Macleod to Macmillan, 22 November 1960; pp. 538–40, MacDonald to Sandys, 7 June 1963.

Thus in speeding up the timetable for decolonisation in Kenya, the same fundamental imperatives were at work as they had been for Tanganyika: fears of the country dissolving into chaos, worries about the whole situation going sour on them, the ineluctable impact of what was happening in neighbouring territories (especially the negative example of the Congo), the desirability of pre-empting the growth of Russian and Chinese influences and the necessity of submitting to the overriding dictates of cold war considerations. Kenyatta duly became president of Kenya in 1964, after a year as prime minister, and proved to be much less extreme than the white settlers had feared.

(5) Nyasaland and Northern Rhodesia

Here, there were astonishing underlying tensions and contortions in the ministerial handling of the future of the Central African Federation (established in 1953).[105] Macleod twice threatened resignation, Maudling once. For Macmillan it 'haunted, not to say poisoned' the last years of his premiership.[106] He personally did not believe they had the right to break up something which had a chance of working, though his condescending attitude to critics reflects his distinctly Augustinian attitude – as if to say, 'make us sinless with regard to empire, O Lord, but not just yet'. Ministers struggled to keep the doomed Federation afloat, because it represented their commitment to stability and multi-racialism in Central Africa. Nevertheless Macmillan thought it laughable that the settlers could play a leading part in 'partnership'. They were to him the scum of Europe. He had no intention of being beaten by Welensky ('it is the Europeans who are the problem').[107] At the same time, the government did not want to fall out irretrievably with the white Rhodesians who were the chief beneficiaries of Federation, lest they were driven into the arms of South Africa (regional military alliance was more likely than political integration), or refuse Britain the over-flying rights which were essential for the protection of the High Commission Territories. In June 1959 Home advised buying time by appointing a commission of inquiry into discontent: 'properly managed it would carry us on for nine months'.[108] In asking Walter Monckton (the retired former Conservative

---

[105] P. Murphy, ed., *Central Africa* (BDEEP, 2005). For background, see J. Darwin, 'Central African Emergency, 1959', *JICH*, vol. 21 (1993), pp. 217–34; C. A. Baker, *State of emergency: crisis in Central Africa, Nyasaland, 1959–1960* (1997), and *Retreat from empire: Sir Robert Armitage in Africa and Cyprus* (1998). See also R. I. Rotberg, *The rise of nationalism in Central Africa: the making of Malawi and Zambia, 1873–1964* (Harvard, 1966).   [106] Macmillan, *At the end of the day*, p. 295.
[107] Ball, *The guardsmen*, p. 346.
[108] PREM 11/2588, M 38/59, to Macmillan, 1 June 1959.

Cabinet minister and lawyer) to chair this commission, indeed to avert 'a maelstrom of trouble', Macmillan set out his own views crisply:

> The cruder concepts, whether of the left or the right, are clearly wrong. Africans cannot be dominated permanently (as they are trying to do in South Africa) without any proper opportunity for their development and ultimate self-government. Nor can the Europeans be abandoned. It would be wrong for us to do so, and fatal for the African interests.[109]

When a few months later Macleod took office, the new secretary of state quickly concluded that the resentments building up in the Federation 'will be our most difficult single problem to solve'. He agreed with Macmillan (towards the end of 1960) that 'the crux of the matter' was that they 'did not want an Algeria' in Central Africa, even if on a smaller scale.[110]

Macleod's first task was to calm things down in Nyasaland, where there was an extraordinary leader, Dr Hastings Banda, who had returned in July 1958 after forty-three years away. He had worked in the Rand mines, studied in the USA, and ended up in Britain. Loaded with American degrees in arts and medicine, he became a respected GP in North London, and an elder of the Church of Scotland. At one level he was precisely the type to whom power should be transferred, but Banda led an implacable campaign against the Federation, and this had landed him in prison (see above, p. 263). Towards the end of 1959 Macleod had come to the conclusion that continuing detentions under the emergency would be indefensible before the Human Rights Commission. Early in December he raised the question of Banda's release, preferably before the arrival of the Monckton Commission. 'There are no more moderate leaders likely to emerge than Banda himself', he wrote to the prime minister, and 'an imaginative offer on constitutional advance at a fairly early date' was the best and perhaps the only hope of holding the position.[111] However, the CO officials were dubious about releasing Banda, since the governor had assessed the risks of doing so as dangerous. But neither

---

[109] Lord Birkenhead, *Walter Monckton: the life of Viscount Monckton of Brenchley* (1969), p. 341, letter to Monckton, 22 August 1959.

[110] *CGEE*, pt 1, p. 166 (no. 31), 29 December 1959, minute, 'Reflections on policy', to Macmillan (PREM 11/2586, PM(59)65); PREM 11/3080, note by Wyndham, 13 November 1960; Horne, *Macmillan*, vol. II, *1957–1986*, p. 211.

[111] *CGEE*, pt 2, pp. 543–5 (no. 495), minute by Macleod to Macmillan, 3 December 1959. Philip Murphy has uncovered evidence that months before the general election of 1959, a serious discussion had been taking place in the CO (initiated by Lord Perth) about the release of Hastings Banda from detention, which has implications for 'continuity of policy' between the pre- and post-Macleod phases: 'Censorship, declassification and the history of the end of empire in Central Africa', *African Research and Documentation*, no. 92 (2003), pp. 17–18.

Illustration 4.4 Mr R. A. Butler reaches agreement with Dr Hastings
Banda at the Nyasaland constitutional conference, 23 November 1962.
Mr Butler was minister in charge of the Central African Office from July
1962. Dr H. Kamuzu Banda's Malawi Congress Party won the elections
of August 1961, and the conference in Marlborough House, London,
led to the introduction of a new constitution on 1 February 1963 under
which internal self-government was achieved in the spring of 1963 with
Dr Banda as first prime minister.

Macmillan nor Macleod fully trusted Governor Sir Robert Armitage; he
was 'not giving a real lead', when a 'positive policy' was needed, and he
had been rude to Macmillan when they met in January 1960. Home by
then was also convinced that 'the wind of change' was blowing strongly,
that the political log-jam must be broken, and that it would be dangerous
to stand still in Nyasaland politically. He accepted that Banda could be
used 'to further our constitutional plans'.[112] Macleod's timing for the
release was, however, deeply controversial. He threatened to resign, but a
compromise solution was found, since Macmillan could not afford to lose
him after only four months in office. So Banda was released on 1 April
1960, shortly before the Monckton Commission completed its work in

[112] *CGEE*, pt 2, pp. 552–4 (no. 499), 22 March 1960, Lord Home to Sir W. Monckton.

Nyasaland, and he was thus able to give evidence as a free man.[113] This was the decisive step. Macleod was proved right when it did not lead to an escalation of violence. The Commission's report vigorously sounded the death-knell of the Federation, as Macmillan had no doubt intended.[114] A new constitution was agreed in July 1960. Elections in August 1961 resulted in a majority for Banda's Malawi Congress Party. Internal self-government was achieved in the spring of 1963.

But it was Northern Rhodesia, not Nyasaland, which was 'the true problem' of the region, Macleod believed. His decision to speed up change there arose out of two favourable developments by the autumn of 1960: agreement on the Nyasaland constitution, and the Monckton Report's recommendation of an African majority on the Northern Rhodesia Leg Co, in the context of its general conclusion that the Federation could not be maintained in its present form. The nationalist leader Kenneth Kaunda had restrained his followers. Macleod realised that Kaunda ought to be able to show that his moderate policy was producing results; violence could break out if there was no move soon. Welensky (the settlers' leader) was firmly told 'we cannot hold the position by a Canute-like process of ordering the tides to return . . . move we must'.[115] Macleod tried to find a solution 'somewhere around parity' in the Leg Co, a token African majority amongst the elected members, which would swiftly resolve into an actual majority. At the February 1961 conference, Kaunda demanded an immediate African majority. Macleod persuaded him that although what was on offer fell short of what Tanganyika, Kenya and Nyasaland had got, it was safely and definitely on the right lines for the future.[116] The settlement was, however, saddled with a new voting system of almost incomprehensibly labyrinthine psephological complexity, and there followed months of ministerial wrangling, back-bench dissent, pressure from Welensky, devious discussions and back-trackings, as various formulae – 'transient phantoms in an unreal dream', Macmillan described them[117] – were produced and examined and discarded. Successive Cabinets wrestled with technicalities they ought never to have got involved in. By June 1961 there seemed to be an agreed solution, but after widespread African protest and disorder, in September 1961 Macleod sought to reopen the policy-decision to make it more favourable to the Africans.

---

[113] *CGEE*, pt 2, pp. 550–4 (no. 498), 23 February 1960 (CAB 128/34, CC 12(60)4).

[114] Ball, *The guardsmen*, p. 349.

[115] *CGEE*, pt 1, p. 180 n. 10 (no. 35); PREM 11/3078, PM(60)56, minute to Macmillan, 15 September 1960; CO 1015/2274, no. 61, 30 May 1960.

[116] *CGEE*, pt 2, pp. 557–9 (no. 502) 20 February 1961, minutes of Cabinet meeting (CAB 128/35/1, CC 8(61)).   [117] Macmillan, *At the end of the day*, p. 316.

Not long afterwards Macmillan removed him from the CO. His successor Maudling decided that Macleod was indeed right: there must be a constitution acceptable to Africans, giving them a chance of winning at least a small majority, otherwise there would be civil disobedience and rioting, and 'the situation would get out of hand'.[118] He too threatened resignation, and in all probability Macleod (now leader of the House of Commons) and Perth would have resigned in sympathy. The new constitution came into force in September 1962. As Macmillan later admitted, 'the delay between December 1960 and February 1962 achieved nothing'. It is hard not to agree with Richard Lamb: 'The only verdict can be that it antagonised the Africans without pacifying the Europeans'.[119]

In March 1962, Butler took over ministerial responsibility for Central Africa. With inscrutable cunning and finesse he managed to gain the confidence of all sides. In Zomba the Africans honoured him with the name 'Large Elephant'. He got on well with Banda and retained Welensky as a friend. Macmillan was naturally thankful to transfer matters to his 'wise and experienced hands'. Butler achieved the orderly dissolution of the Federation on terms which the settler lobby of the Conservative Party had to accept. The crucial issue was Banda's demand for secession. Banda was acting co-operatively, taking 'a moderate and constructive line', according to Macmillan, so concessions to him could be contemplated, just as they had been to Nyerere and Kaunda.[120] Butler decided that the importance of retaining Banda's goodwill outweighed the danger of worsening relations with Welensky, and did so in the main because they could not cope with a serious security situation in Nyasaland. In any case, 'against the pace elsewhere in Africa, the extent to which we can hope to apply the brake . . . is extremely limited'. Sandys was in full agreement: to fight Nyasaland on secession would lead to 'another Cyprus'.[121] It was also pointed out that recent precedents from the West Indies would make it difficult to refuse to agree to secession. Ministers, however, did not wish to give any encouragement to Banda to secede, partly because of the economic implications (almost certainly making increased aid from Britain necessary), and partly because Northern Rhodesia would almost automatically follow suit. For seven months Butler spun out the time on secession, but by October 1962 he could no longer continue to do so without a show of force: 'this would not only be inherently mistaken but was also impracticable'. In the long run, he argued, it would be more expensive

[118] *CGEE*, pt 2, pp. 570–4 (no. 506), 26 February 1962 (CAB 128/36/1, CC 16(62)).
[119] R. Lamb, *The Macmillan years, 1957–63: the emerging truth* (1995), p. 272.
[120] *CGEE*, pt 2, p. 587 (nos. 512 and 513), 20 November and 12 December 1962.
[121] *Ibid.*, pp. 578 (no. 509) and pp. 582–5 (no. 511), Cabinet discussion, 8 November 1962 (CAB 128/36/2, CC 67(62)2).

Illustration 4.5 Kenneth Kaunda makes the closing speech of thanks at the conference arranging independence for Zambia, 19 May 1964.
Mr Kaunda as prime minister for Northern Rhodesia, standing on the right, facing Mr Duncan Sandys (secretary of state for Commonwealth relations) on the opposite side of the table (fourth from the left) at Marlborough House, London. Northern Rhodesia became independent as the Republic of Zambia on 24 October 1964.

financially than the consequences of secession, and extremely costly in terms of international reputation. Though secession would inevitably mean in time the dissolution of the Federation, 'there was really no alternative'.[122]

---

[122] CAB 130/189, GEN 775, no. 1, minutes of meeting, 24 October 1962; *CGEE* pt 2, p. 580 (no. 510), Cabinet minutes, 29 October 1962 (CAB 128/36/2, CC 64(62)2). The Central African question increasingly 'weighed very heavily on my mind', wrote Butler. As an issue with serious party divisions, it reminded him of the struggle for the India Bill in the early 1930s. He described himself as 'particularly obsessed with the difficulty of winding up the Federation without consent . . . There is no wonder that a great heaviness hangs upon me, especially as the weeks go by with no development. I think the only sure guide is to undertake no action which is not morally defensible' (Murphy, *Central Africa* pt 2, pp. 361–2 (no. 347), minute, 6 March 1963, and pp. 373–4 (no. 354), minute, 14 May 1963).

Home in particular clung to the notion that some sort of Northern and Southern Rhodesian association could be maintained. This continued to be explored. The Cabinet reluctantly accepted Northern Rhodesian secession on 28 March 1963. A decision on the long-term future of an unregenerate Southern Rhodesia was, on Macmillan's advice, deferred as long as possible, since it could only be 'profoundly damaging' and probably 'a fatal blow to the Commonwealth' to accept the whites' demand for immediate independence.[123] The Federation was dissolved on 31 December 1963. Nyasaland became independent as Malawi on 6 July 1964. Northern Rhodesia became independent as Zambia on 24 October 1964. Southern Rhodesia became independent as Zimbabwe on 18 April 1980.

(6) Aden

The first acquisition of Victoria's empire (1838), Aden 120 years later was fast becoming the last imperial frontier.[124] It had an excellent natural harbour, and had developed as an important coaling station on the route to India and the east. This had unlovely results: Kipling's 'unlit barrick-stove'; 'the cinder-heap of the world'. From the later 1950s its value was increasing as other bases and footholds came under threat: not only was it a staging-post 'East-of-Suez', but the citadel of oil-bunkering, the protector of Middle East oil interests, especially in Kuwait, and the base from which military commitments in the Persian Gulf and East Africa could be discharged. Thus it was not totally surprising when a government minister declared in 1956 that Aden could not expect to aspire to more than internal self-government 'for the foreseeable future'.[125] In 1960 it became the headquarters of Middle East Command, and by 1964 there were 8,000 troops stationed there.

Aden was a particularly intractable case for decolonisation. At its heart was the port of Aden Colony. But it was surrounded by successive 'layers' of unfavourable circumstance which made it hard to manage. The tiny Colony itself was, according to Macleod, 'a very politically conscious place',[126] penetrated by militant trades unions, the ATUC being led by the pro-Nasserite al-Asnag, and composed largely of Yemeni migrant workers staffing the expanding BP oil refinery opened in 1954

[123] *CGEE*, pt 2, p. 594 (no. 518), Cabinet minutes, 28 March 1963 (CAB 128/37, CC 20(63)2), and p. 598, n. 2 (no. 520), 4 April 1963.

[124] Two of the three governors in this period wrote historical memoirs: C. H. Johnston, *Steamer Point*, and G. Kennedy N. Trevaskis, *Shades of amber: a South Arabian episode* (1968) which are essential reading. See also R. Gavin, *Aden under British rule, 1839–1967* (1975).   [125] *CGEE*, pt 1, p. 17 (no. 2) para. 134.

[126] *CGEE*, pt 1, p. 413 (no. 127) memo, 11 April 1961.

in the aftermath of the Iranian oil crisis of 1951. There were eighty-four strikes in 1959 alone. By then the colony had a population of 37,000 Adenis, but 48,000 Yemenis, in effect a fifth column whose task was to spearhead the incorporation of Aden into Yemen. The immediate surrounding 'layer' was the turbulent and murderously unstable hinterland of South Arabia, a protectorate which the British had almost entirely ignored, leaving it to its traditional princes, tribal rulers and warring factions. Because it was claimed by Yemen, the protectorate could not stand by itself and the rulers sought to 'put their paws' on Aden and bring its international port within their ambit. If Aden developed constitutionally on its own, this would seem disastrous to the Yemenophobic princes of the hinterland, who were friendly to Britain. In February 1959 a somewhat chaotic Federation of the states of the Western Protectorate was formed. Then, in the outer layer came the hostile neighbour itself, Yemen, ruled by 'a gloomy medieval imam' until 1962, when he was overthrown by a republican coup dominated by Nasserites. In British eyes, Yemen became a virtual Egyptian puppet-state, with 70,000 Egyptian troops stationed there. British government departments were divided on according recognition, the FO in favour, the CO and MoD against. Macmillan could see attractions in recognition: it was 'repugnant to political equity and prudence alike that we should so often appear to be supporting out-of-date despotic regimes and to be opposing the growth of modern and more democratic forms of government'.[127] Moreover, recognition might embarrass Nasser, whom Macmillan persisted in regarding as 'another Hitler'. And in the background beyond Egypt there was the UN, where the international witch-hunt against 'colonialism' was in full cry, and British policy in South-West Arabia was routinely denounced as 'the engine of oppression'.

The new governor towards the end of 1956 was Sir William Luce, fresh from acting as constitutional adviser to the governor-general of the Sudan during its run-up to independence. With this background, Luce had no difficulty in recognising that to deny self-government to Aden beyond about 1967 would involve 'a head-on collision with Aden Arabs'. The decline of British power, the policy of moving from dependence to independence, Arab nationalism, and Russian expansion – all these impinged on Aden, and, he concluded, pointed to a gradual disengagement leading to the 'termination of British control' within the decade. Macmillan seems to have been sceptical. There was general agreement in the CO that Luce's idea of a federation in the hinterland need not be discouraged,

---

[127] CAB 130/189, GEN 776, no. 3, 5 February 1963, minutes of a meeting on the Yemen.

but they were less sure about letting go of sovereignty in Aden. Amery fought for a rejection of Luce's radical policy, and for sticking with the hard line of 1956. Aden, he argued, was a vital fortress colony, controlling a key position globally, which it was geopolitically advantageous to retain.[128] In May 1959 – a year after Luce's proposals were received – Lennox-Boyd was still stalling: 'the wisest course will be to play for time and to avoid defining our policy too clearly'.[129] Before leaving his post, Luce developed his idea of bringing together the friendly princes of the hinterland and the friendly moderates of the Colony. His procedural suggestions for engineering this constitutional merger did not convince the CO, and gave them 'much to think about'. The Defence Committee confirmed that the retention of the base was still essential. Macleod wanted the views of the new governor, Sir Charles Johnston, before deciding anything. In March 1961 Johnston confirmed that merger would be the right solution, preceded by self-government in Aden Colony, the aim being the creation of an 'independent and prosperous Arab state in relations of friendly partnership with ourselves'.[130] After going to Aden to see for himself, Macleod decided to support this plan. He admitted that the princes would not like an election in Aden under a self-governing constitution, and neither would the British government if the moderates did not win (in which case direct rule would have to be resumed), but, applying his trusty doctrine of 'lesser risk', Macleod believed it would be 'less dangerous to our interests than would be the certain dangers involved in our refusing the moderates their wish for constitutional advance'. Accordingly he would tell the hinterland rulers that although they could have their merger, 'we could not exclude Aden Colony from the general aims of our overall colonial policy', and must give due weight to the principles of consent.[131]

After some grumbling by the minister of defence, Harold Watkinson, and by Amery, the Cabinet accepted that merger should be encouraged if the parties could agree upon it. The policy was seen as a means of securing defence facilities for as long as possible. Sovereignty over Aden would continue for the moment. The CO was still aiming to 'pay out the rope as slowly as we decently can', regarding the merger as a way of buying time, although recognising that even the moderates were 'susceptible to the

---

[128] *CGEE*, pt 1, pp. 557–69 (nos. 188 and 189), letters from Sir W. Luce to W. L. Gorell Barnes, 27–28 March 1958, and reply, 14 April 1958; pp. 575–80 (nos. 193 and 194), minutes by J. Amery, 10 March and 27 April 1959.
[129] *CGEE*, pt 1, pp. 580–4 (nos. 195 and 196), 13 May and 14 August 1959.
[130] *Ibid.*, pp. 598–602 (no. 199), despatch, 3 March 1961; C. H. Johnston, *Steamer Point*, pp. 36–40.
[131] *CGEE*, pt 1, pp. 606–11 (no. 200), memo, 3 May 1961 (CAB 134/1560, CPC(61)10).

wind of change' and sensitive to charges from Cairo that they were 'British stooges'.[132]

In September 1962 the Aden Leg Co. voted for merger, and the Federation of South Arabia came into being on 18 January 1963. The status of Aden was again considered towards the end of the year, with Trevaskis as high commissioner proposing its advance to full internal self-government. A decision in favour was temporarily thrown off course by an assassination attempt against him (December 1963), but by the end of February 1964 ministerial opinion was beginning to crystallise around the doctrine of timely concession: 'if we ignored the pressure for constitutional advance there would be serious political trouble, in the face of which we should eventually have to give way'.[133] At a constitutional conference in London in June 1964 it was agreed that the federal constitution should be reformed on a democratic basis with a view to independence no later than 1968; also that Britain would renounce sovereignty over Aden as soon as practicable, at a date to be agreed after a general election in October, and with a defence agreement covering the retention of the British base. It had taken more than six tortuous years to reach these not very remarkable conclusions, which were then put back into the melting-pot by the Labour government. Towards the end of 1967 Aden and the Protectorates were finally abandoned to the Yemen-based National Liberation Front, who established a Soviet-Marxist successor government.

(7) Malaysia

On 31 August 1957 the British formally transferred power to a Malayan elite headed by the fairly anglophile Tunku Abdul Rahman; any possible alternative government, they believed, would certainly be less well-disposed to them.[134] The subsequent transformation of the Federation of Malaya into the Federation of Malaysia in September 1963 represented a major reconstruction of the map of South-East Asia, accompanied by

---

[132] *Ibid.*, pp. 616–23 (no. 203), October 1961; PREM 11 /4173, minute, 15 March 1963.

[133] *CGEE*, pt 1, pp. 637–9, minutes of Defence and Oversea Policy Committee, 26 February 1964.

[134] On Malaya and Malaysia: A. J. Stockwell, ed., *Malaya* (BDEEP, 1995), pt 3: *1953–1957*, nos. 439–67 (February–August 1957), and *Malaysia* (BDEEP, 2004); and 'Malaysia: the making of a neo-colony?', *JICH*, vol. 26 (1998), pp. 138–56, repr. in P. Burroughs and A. J. Stockwell eds., *Managing the business of empire: essays in honour of David Fieldhouse* (1998); Harper, *The end of empire*; Matthew Jones, 'Creating Malaysia: Singapore security, the Borneo territories, and the contours of British policy, 1961–1963', *JICH*, vol. 28 (2000), pp. 85–109, and *Conflict and Confrontation in South-East Asia, 1961–1965; Britain, the United States and the creation of Malaysia* (2002).

Illustration 4.6 Mr Macmillan signs the document establishing the Federation of Malaysia, 9 July 1963.

Agreement was reached at 11.30 p.m. on 8 July 1963, after lengthy discussions between the representatives of the states to be federated: Malaya, Singapore, and the colonies of North Borneo (Sabah) and Sarawak. The Malaysia agreement document was signed on 9 July to bring into effect the Federation. It was a project to which Mr Macmillan was particularly committed. A Malaysia Act passed the British parliament in July 1963, and Malaysia eventually came into being on 16 September 1963.

accusations that it was a 'neo-colonialist plot'. Paradoxically, however, if Britain had given a blank refusal to this project, the accusation would have been one of 'preventing the natural development' of the Malay world. In Singapore, the first prime minister under internal self-government, Lee Kuan Yew, needed the merger with Malaya in order to 'finish off colonialism' as a political issue there. Tunku Abdul Rahman had an expansionist desire to double Malaya's territory and get access to the oil revenues of Brunei; negatively, the incorporation of Singapore was designed to head-off the possibility of an independent communist state's establishing itself on Malaya's doorstep. For he had come to realise that he would not for much longer be able to rely on a positive and effective British presence in Singapore. Its incorporation alone would upset the racial balance of Malaya by adding 1.5 million Chinese, so the Borneo territories were a necessary way of redressing the balance and sweetening the pill.

From the British government point of view, 'Greater Malaysia' seemed to offer the resolution of several problems. First, it would be 'an ultimate solution' for Singapore, 'the best and possibly the only hope for longer-term stability', neutralising communist tendencies and, after re-negotiation of defence facilities, reducing the prospect of increasing hostility to the base. Secondly, it might provide a viable future for the three Borneo territories, which would otherwise be vulnerable to Indonesian encroachment. Thirdly, it might forward the purposes of decolonisation, including retrenchment, in an area where Britain was from 1954 the last colonial power. Lastly, a Greater Malaysia might form a stable bloc of anti-communist territory in geopolitically significant South-East Asia. As commissioner-general, Malcolm MacDonald had for many years (and perhaps as far back as 1947, though even then he was not the first to propose a consolidation) propounded some such theory, calling it 'the grand design'. In February 1958 he publicly committed himself to a Borneo federation, the ultimate objective being a confederation of five territories. But clearly the British could not take the initiative in its consummation. Hence the decisive importance of the Tunku's public conversion to the scheme on 27 May 1961.[135]

There was, however, considerable opposition in Borneo and from its neighbours in Indonesia and, to a lesser extent, the Philippines. The Sultan of Brunei, recently oil-rich and apprehensive of Chinese influence, stood aside at the last minute. Merger was a divisive issue in Sarawak, where communism was making extensive inroads into its large Chinese

[135] Stockwell, *Malaysia*, pp. 227–30 (no. 74), and *CGEE* pt 1, pp. 738–41 (nos. 264 and 265), Defence Committee minutes, 25 October 1961, and Cabinet minutes, 16 November 1961, on 'Greater Malaysia'; Stockwell, *Malaya*, pt 3, p. 111 (no. 346), MacDonald to CO, 2 April 1955.

population. Local opinion was canvassed by a commission led by Lord Cobbold (recently retired governor of the Bank of England). The results were construed as sufficiently reassuring for the scheme to go ahead.[136]

The Greater Malaysia project was of close personal concern to Macmillan, and to a remarkable extent. He was looking for 'significant economies' in defence expenditure in South-East Asia: 'our limited resources and our growing commitments elsewhere make it essential that we should gradually reduce our military and colonial responsibilities in South-East Asia'. He described himself as 'extremely anxious that it should come off'. However, he was conscious of the practical difficulties, and was not going to superintend either the creation of a 'partial power vacuum' or a shot-gun wedding. At the end of 1961 he warned Lord Selkirk (commissioner-general, South-East Asia) that 'Merdeka Day', independence, could not realistically be achieved as early as August 1962: 'it might well be fatal to the whole project if we appeared to be rushing our fences, particularly in relation to the Borneo territories'.[137] Equally, though, he took a firm line with the faint-hearts. The governor of North Borneo (Sabah), Sir William Goode, was suspicious both of federations in general and of the Tunku's intentions, clearly reluctant to 'hand over' to him, complaining darkly that Borneo had already once been 'steam-rollered', by the Japanese. Unless the Tunku seemed more co-operative and prepared to give some real help to its people, 'Malaysia must be off', so a tougher line should be taken with him. Macmillan picked up the two telegrams in which these views were advanced and he reacted crossly to what he thought was the governor's lack of understanding of the realities of the situation:

I am rather shocked by [this] and the attitude it reveals. Does he realise (a) our weakness in Singapore, and (b) our urgent need to hand over the security problem there? The whole mood is based on a false assessment of our power. If this is the Colonial Office point of view, we shall fail.

This confidential note was meant for Brook, but by accident a copy of it was sent by the Cabinet Office to the secretary of state for the colonies. Both Maudling and the CO staff were angered by it, Maudling replying to Brook that the governor was 'fully aware' of the importance of Malaysia.[138]

[136] V. I. Porritt, *British colonial rule in Sarawak, 1946–1963* (Kuala Lumpur, 1997).

[137] *CGEE*, pt 1, pp. 744–5 (no. 269), letter to Lord Selkirk, 5 August 1963; PREM 11/4188, Macmillan to Selkirk, 12 March 1962; CAB 21/4626, M 86/62, to Sandys, 26 March 1962, and to Selkrik, 19 December 1961.

[138] Stockwell, *Malaysia*, pp. 314–15 (no. 117), and CAB 21/4847, M 161/62, minute to Brook, 21 June 1962. The transcription in *CGEE*, pt 1, intro., p. lix, inaccurately gives 'assumption of our power' instead of the correct transcription, which is 'assessment of our power'. The editor apologises for this error; Macmillan's handwriting is difficult.

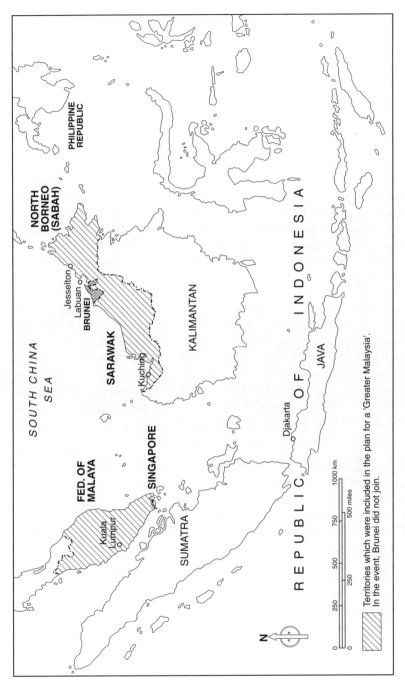

SOUTH CHINA
SEA

PHILIPPINE
REPUBLIC

NORTH
BORNEO
(SABAH)

Jesselton

Labuan
BRUNEI

SARAWAK

Kuching

KALIMANTAN

FED. OF
MALAYA

Kuala
Lumpur

SINGAPORE

SUMATRA

REPUBLIC OF INDONESIA

Djakarta

JAVA

N

| 0 | 250 | 500 | 750 | 1000 km |
| 0 | 250 | 500 | 500 miles |

Territories which were included in the plan for a 'Greater Malaysia'.
In the event, Brunei did not join.

Map 4.1 Greater Malaysia.

As in the case of Cyprus, Malaysia was bedevilled by the conflicting interests and responsibilities and the contrary objectives involved. These did not, however, include pressure from business concerns, as the economic value of Malaya was waning. But there were worrying differences between Whitehall departments, the CRO wanting to press ahead, the CO advocating delay in the name of trusteeship until the Borneo territories were more advanced – which led Sandys to complain 'we couldn't allow the susceptibilities of headhunters to wreck the project'. (This was a serious snag, partly because delay might increase instability in Singapore.)[139] There were further similarities with the Central African Federation. Both were set up for essentially geopolitical reasons, and both provoked inter-racial resentments and unrest, with a dominant territory (Malaya/Southern Rhodesia), and a small backward one (the Brunei revolt having its parallel in the Nyasaland emergency). Malaysia was only brought into being with much faltering along the way. The Tunku wavered, three times threatening to pull out of the project, while the Sultan of Brunei actually did so.

Indonesia officially declared its opposition to Malaysia on 13 February 1963, launching *Konfrontasi* ('Confrontation') some weeks later. There was an armed incursion on the Kalimantan border on 12 April 1963, and British and Commonwealth troops were sent into Borneo, an expense which could ill be afforded. Eventually, President Sukarno withdrew his exhausted Indonesian troops in 1966, after a portentous struggle, leaving Malaysia the victor of Confrontation. Meanwhile, Singapore had seceded in 1965, thus destroying one of Britain's main objectives in promoting the project in the first place.

(8) The West Indies Federation

Few federations failed faster than the West Indies, which lasted only from January 1958 to February 1962.[140] Though its antecedents extended back many years, its formal creation got off to a bad start. In Britain, the Treasury, trying to save money, quibbled about the exact date when the

---

[139] Stockwell, *Malaysia*, intro., pp. li–lviii.

[140] The most comprehensive study of the West Indies Federation is the intro. to S. R. Ashton and D Killingray, eds., *The West Indies* (BDEEP, 1999) by S. R. Ashton, but there is also a useful narrative in Morgan, *The official history of colonial development*, vol. V, pp. 144–78. For selected documents see *CGEE* pt 1, pp. 749–93 (nos. 272–88). Secondary studies include: D. Lowenthal, ed., *The West Indies Federation: perspectives* (New York, 1961); E. Wallace, *The British Caribbean from the decline of colonialism to the end of Federation* (Toronto, 1977); J. Mordecai, *The West Indies: the federal negotiations* (1968); G. K. Lewis, *The growth of the modern West Indies* (1968); S. J. Hurwitz, 'The Federation of the West Indies: a study in nationalisms', *Journal of British Studies*, vol. 6 (1966), pp. 139–68.

Federation was to come into legal existence, but backed down. In the West Indies, at the federal government's first press conference, its Barbadian prime minister, Sir Grantley Adams, shocked everyone by personal attacks on his political rivals and by threatening retroactive taxation. There was also a tricky problem over the site for the capital. The Chaguaramas peninsula in Trinidad had been identified as suitable. Although the Americans had a base there since 1941 it did not seem to be much used. However, the American Defense Department would not release it, because it was the terminal station of a secret anti-submarine monitoring system. Macmillan appealed personally to Eisenhower, apparently adding to the FO draft a final cheeky sentence, 'All this "liquidation of colonialism" is going so well that I would be sorry if there was any hitch, especially one in the Caribbean.' In fact the British gave in, a decision which Lennox-Boyd announced rather too quickly, causing resentment in the West Indies, especially with Dr Eric Williams, prime minister of Trinidad, who led an anti-American campaign. Port-of-Spain in Trinidad was selected instead of Chaguaramas as the capital.[141]

The Federation had never been envisaged as 'an end in itself', but rather as a device to enhance the prospects of West Indians for independence, and so achieve political disengagement by Britain. These prospects were reviewed in the CO in May 1959. Doubts were expressed as to their readiness, while Home at the CRO was anxious about the impact of early moves to independence on his Central African problem. But even Julian Amery admitted 'our power of putting on the brake . . . is now very limited . . . we have to be very careful how we use it. The Federation is still a delicate plant'.[142] A federal intergovernmental conference of constitutional review, held in September 1959, was not exactly a success – indeed Philip Rogers (an assistant under-secretary at the CO), who attended it, described it as 'disastrous'. It settled little and in fact presaged the collapse of the Federation. Governor-general Lord Hailes was determined to be optimistic, but this did not impress the CO or dent its gloominess. The CO would have preferred a more active attempt to promote the fragile Federation. Macleod was 'not sure how I read the tea-leaves'.[143] In December 1959 Grantley Adams caused consternation by calling for dominion status within months. Macleod paid a visit in June 1960 and said he would do all he could to speed the advance to independence. Macmillan toured the islands in March

---

[141] PREM 11/2280, f. 76, Macmillan to Eisenhower, 19 July 1957: Ashton and Killingray, *The West Indies*, pp. 174–6 (no. 63) and intro., pp. lx–lxii.

[142] Ashton and Killingray, *The West Indies*, p. 280 (no. 104), minute by J. Amery to Lord Home, 27 August 1959; *CGEE* pt 1, p. 747 (no. 278).

[143] *CGEE*, pt 1, p. 781 (no. 281), 31 December 1959.

and April 1961; most of the concerns put to him were financial. The Lancaster House Conference in May and June 1961 quickly ran into trouble, causing Macleod considerable alarm. If the Federation failed, it would mean 'balkanisation', leaving behind a gaggle of indigent islands and a very anxious American neighbour. His colleagues would not allow him to divert funds from Africa – a clear demonstration of the low priority accorded to the West Indies.[144] Agreement was, however, reached to strengthen the Federation and work for independence by 31 May 1962. Everything was then overtaken by a referendum in Jamaica (19 September 1961) which voted 54.1 per cent to withdraw from the Federation. The British government decided it could neither stop the dissolution of the Federation, nor refuse Jamaica's request for independence on its own. Macleod was saddened, but with the examples of Cyprus and Sierra Leone before him, felt he could not resist.[145] Dr Eric Williams, the historian-prime minister of Trinidad, declared a new arithmetical proposition – '1 from 10 equals 0' – and withdrew his country too, which also had to be granted independence. A possible reconstruction into a federation of the remaining eight came to nothing. In 1967 St Lucia, St Kitts-Nevis-Anguilla, St Vincent, Dominica, and Grenada entered into 'associated statehood' with Britain.

Why did the Federation fail? On the face of it, the British West Indies should have been eminently suited to co-operate in a single government. They had a common language, a common heritage, and a common devotion to cricket and calypso and (mostly) to Christianity. Air travel was beginning to reduce the distances between them. The total population (three million) was about the same as Canada's at the time of Confederation in 1867, but with the advantage of not being afflicted with a communal problem like Quebec. The most immediate explanation for failure offered at the time was that 'the leadership was awful'. There is no denying this. The bickering leaders were variously assessed in the CO as irresponsible, immature, impatient and inefficient. Adams was 'not big enough for the job', unimaginative, tactless, rude, vain and lazy, quite apart from his failing health and mental powers. Hailes reported that it was being predicted that Adams would become 'a West Indian Mussadiq', retiring to bed whenever things looked dangerous. Rogers complained of Sir Grantley's 'appalling inadequacy'. But as Rogers had also recognised from the outset, if Norman Manley (chief minister of Jamaica since 1955) did not 'go to the Federation' and become its prime minister, 'it will be so weak that its survival is doubtful'. The leading

[144] *Ibid.*, pp. 782–5 (no. 283), minute from Macleod to Macmillan, 7 June 1961.
[145] *Ibid.*, pp. 785–6, minutes of Cabinet meeting, 28 September 1961 (CAB 128/35/2, CC 52(61)4; PREM 11/4074, PM(61)73, minute to Macmillan, 22 September 1961.

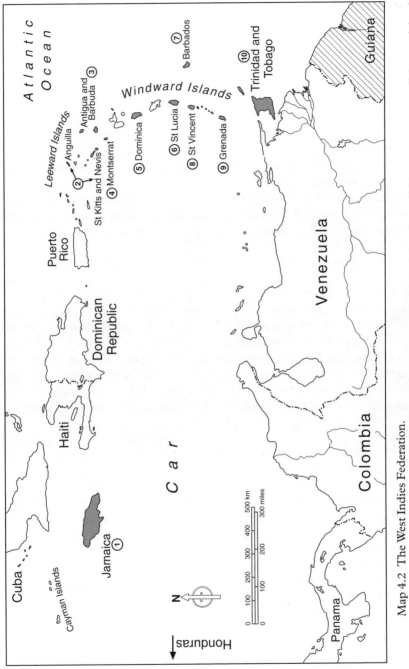

Map 4.2 The West Indies Federation.
The member-units are dark-shaded and numbered. Guiana and Honduras (just off the map, west-centrally) never joined.

politicians put 'the second eleven' into bat, and then unsportingly refused even to give any encouraging shouts from the boundary.[146]

The failure of all worthy institutions and projects is, however, invariably ascribed to 'poor leadership', and as a historical explanation it does not take us very far. Did the fault lie rather with the compromising looseness of the federal structure? The West Indies undoubtedly had one of the weakest federal systems ever called into existence. There was no common currency or customs union. There were restrictions on inter-island migration. The only responsibilities of the central power were for external relations, communications between the islands, a university college, and a regiment, the last two together pre-empting half the federal budget. That budget was tiny, only one-tenth of the revenue of either Trinidad or Jamaica. No direct taxation was ever raised, no common postage stamp ever issued. Many federal powers were left dormant. But this structural laxity was an effect of the weakness of commitment to the Federation rather than its cause.

The roots of failure were in fact to be found in the fundamental unsuitability of the units for federation, their congenital incompatibility, the result of 'centuries of isolation, mistrust and mutual ignorance' and jealous 'local particularism'.[147] The ten were unequal in weight: Jamaica had over half the total population, Trinidad a quarter; both were far ahead of the others in economic development, nervous of having to bail them out. Once the large mainland colonies of Guiana and Honduras stood aside, the rest were mainly competitive and not complementary in their economies. Only 5 per cent of exports were between the islands. The smaller ones were highly disparate. Barbados, with a unique constitution, had been self-governing since 1639. St Lucia, a coaling station, had been disputed between Britain and France, and although British since 1814, it still relied on the Quebec civil code and Roman Catholic schools; its population mostly spoke 'a queer patois of antique French warped by a rustic kind of English'.[148] St Vincent was dependent on arrowroot. Montserrat was minuscule (only thirty-two square miles), dominated by a sinister mountain and, Hailes thought, 'a strange kind of Irishness'; Nevis he described as 'almost sullenly poor'. The Cayman Islands, some 200 miles west of Jamaica, preoccupied mainly with tourism and turtle-fishing, were neither wholly in nor wholly out. Technically members of the Federation, they were not represented in the federal legislature nor did they contribute anything financially.

[146] CGEE, pt 1, p. 750 (no. 272), 25 September 1957, minute by P. Rogers; p. 763 (no. 276), 12 June 1959, minute by G. W. Jamieson.
[147] Ashton and Stockwell, Imperial policy and colonial practice, intro., pp. xlv and lvii.
[148] J. Morris, Pax Britannica: the climax of an empire (1968), p. 160.

4. Problems: the international context

(1) Foreign policy

The problems to be discussed in this section are relationships with foreign countries concerning colonial questions, mainly America, Europe, and in the United Nations. All of these occupied important positions in British policy-making: the United States by providing financial underpinning and strategic cover, together with supportive advice and unwelcome irritation in about equal measure; Europe by acting as, in effect, a potential alternative to the Commonwealth; the United Nations by forcing the pace of decolonisation.[149]

The post-war world was at once profoundly anti-imperial and in the West anti-communist. Fortunately for Britain, the Americans came to believe that communism was a more serious threat than 'colonialism', but anti-colonialism was a world-wide movement, exploited not just by communists, but also affecting countries which had never been colonies, and often led by those Asian and African states to whom Britain had given independence sooner rather than later. Thus even Hilton Poynton of the CO realised that the international climate had become 'a more decisive factor' to be taken into account in the formulation of British policy.[150] Contextualising Africa in cold war terms became almost an obsession, to the point where by 1961 Sir Andrew Cohen was worried that 'killing communism' seemed to be the chief objective of African policy, rather than the desirability of preparing stable and viable regimes for independence.[151] Analysis of Soviet expansion, its aims, methods and success-rate, was repeatedly undertaken, together, where appropriate, with those of Chinese communism. In particular, the situation in Africa was subject to close and regular scrutiny. More specifically, Ghana was the object of concern and intense interest. The high commissioner, Sir Arthur Snelling, quite clearly identified Ghana as 'a key battleground in the cold war'. The dilemma was: if Britain did not help Ghana a clear field would be left for the Russians to appear her only true friend; but helping the corrupt ministers surrounding Nkrumah, such as K. A. Gbedemah and

---

[149] Two collections of essays are useful here: R. Aldous and S. Lee, eds., *Harold Macmillan and Britain's world role* (1996), and W. Kaiser and G. Staerck, eds., *British foreign policy, 1955–1964: contracting options* (2000); together with W. R. Louis and R. E. Robinson, 'The imperialism of decolonisation', *JICH*, vol. 22 (1994), pp. 462–511. Frank Heinlein, *British government policy and decolonisation, 1945–1963: scrutinising the official mind* (2002), keeps international factors strongly in focus.

[150] *CGEE*, pt 2, pp. 307–11 (no. 405), circular from Sir H. Poynton to governors, 29 September 1960.

[151] *Ibid.*, p. 247 (no. 382), 16 March 1961, Cohen's statement to a meeting of officials.

K.Botsio, might well back-fire. Snelling's valedictory despatch raised the sombre possibility of Ghana's leaving the Commonwealth and leading a pan-African, anti-British movement.[152]

Macmillan attempted a global over-view in a memorandum he called 'The grand design' produced over the Christmas holidays, dated 3 January 1961.[153] It was a typically elegant but theoretical essay calling for co-operation between the United States, Britain and France, because 'the Communist danger – in its various forms – is so great and so powerfully directed that it cannot be met without the maximum achievable unity of purpose and direction'. In a sentence which resembled one of Ernest Bevin's, he called for 'the great forces of the free world' to organise themselves 'economically, politically and militarily in a coherent effort to withstand the Communist tide all over the world', and in particular to use their economic power more efficiently. It is perhaps a little surprising that only three years later his successor, in a notable speech in Canada, was able to identify a double 'sea-change' in world affairs: 'colonialism', declared Sir Alec Douglas-Home, 'is nearly at an end' and 'positive co-existence' had emerged, signalling a foreseeable end to the cold war. It was therefore time to move on and tackle the 'problem of problems', the disparity between rich and poor nations.[154] Reports of the death of the cold war proved to be an exaggeration.

Of all Britain's international relationships, none was more vital than that with the United States. In the aftermath of what Macmillan revealingly referred to as 'the Anglo-American schism', the Suez Crisis of 1956,[155] rebuilding the American relationship was a top priority. One obstacle to this was what was regarded in Whitehall as the negative, unreconstructed and prejudiced attitude of the Americans (in at least some quarters of Washington) towards British 'colonialism'. The CO urged the prime minister not to flinch from tackling this as soon as possible. The Bermuda Conference in March 1957 offered a good opportunity. The State Department and the British Embassy in Washington collaborated in presenting a paper on 'Means of combating Communist influence in tropical Africa'. In it, they agreed that 'the best counter to Soviet aims is to pursue resolutely and systematically the constructive policy of leading dependencies as rapidly as is practicable toward stable self-government or independence in such a way that these governments are willing and able to preserve their political and economic ties with the West'. At one of the

---

[152] *Ibid.*, pp. 256–60 (no. 384), 5 December 1961, Sir A. Snelling to CRO.
[153] PREM 11/3325, extensively reproduced in Macmillan, *Pointing the way*, pp. 323–6.
[154] *CGEE*, pt 2, pp. 268–73 (no. 389), speech to the Empire Club of Canada, at Toronto, 11 February 1964.
[155] H. Macmillan, *Memoirs*, vol. IV: *Riding the storm, 1956–1959* (1971), pp. 89–179.

meetings, the foreign secretary Selwyn Lloyd suggested that Africa was 'likely to be the great battle of the next ten years. The battle of the Middle East had caught us unawares; we must be ready for the battle of Africa.' The meeting agreed that the communists did indeed aim to dominate Africa; and the Americans accepted that the British 'evolutionary' approach to decolonisation was right.[156] The British felt all this represented a considerable advance towards a better understanding between the two nations. By October 1957, Lloyd claimed that the 'special relationship' was restored. Macmillan believed with satisfaction that the two had agreed on their 'interdependence'.[157] What this meant in practice never became entirely clear.

The Americans were increasingly interested in Africa, especially once Kennedy became president. Being more interested made them better informed, and this in turn meant, the British believed, that the US government was more understanding of and less ready to criticise British policy. They did not put pressure on Britain to proceed any faster with decolonisation. Even over Central Africa, where a legitimate critique could have been forcefully developed, they seemed to become more sympathetic and patient, perhaps because they had concluded that there was no immediate threat of communist infiltration.[158]

The contrast between this relaxed indulgence over Rhodesia, and the truculent pressure the Americans tried to exert over Guiana shows just how far they evaluated British performance in cold war terms. Guiana posed a serious strategic risk to the Americans, since it would be as ideal a location for Russian missiles as Cuba, and because it could prove to be the thin end of the wedge for communism in Latin America. The British wanted to be rid of responsibility for aid and move towards independence. Home had a sharp exchange with Dean Rusk (the long-serving US secretary of state), and dealt firmly with the American attempt to retard independence in Guiana and instigate a CIA operation against Dr Jagan. Macmillan was incredulous, and wrote ruefully in his diary, 'The Americans are the first to squeal when "decolonisation" takes place uncomfortably near to them.'[159] In June 1963 Kennedy again insisted on pursuing his Guiana concerns with Macmillan, but the British had no

---

[156] FO 371/125292; *FRUS, 1955–1957*, vol. 27, p. 795; *CGEE*, pt 2, pp. 230–3 (no. 376), circular from Selwyn Lloyd to FO representatives in Africa, 10 April 1957.

[157] *CGEE*, pt 2, p. 238 (no. 378), 28 October 1957, to Cabinet (CAB 128/31/2, CC76(57)2).

[158] L. J. Butler, 'Britain, the United States and the demise of the Central African Federation, 1959–1963', *JICH*, vol. 28 (2000), pp. 131–51; *CGEE*, pt 2, pp. 241–3 (no. 380), 10 July 1958, despatch from Lord Hood to Selwyn Lloyd.

[159] *CGEE* pt 1, p 808 (no. 295), minute by Macmillan, 21 February 1962; Ashton and Killingray, *The West Indies*, pp. 486–9 (nos. 180–2), February–March 1962.

profound interest in the territory and were only anxious to be rid of it. In any case, as Home pointed out, they could not possibly revert to direct rule without destroying Britain's image as a decolonising power. Sandys, however, was not altogether unmoved, slowed things up a bit and made two visits; the voting procedure was changed to proportional represent-ation – something the CO had hitherto opposed.[160] As a result, Jagan held only twenty-two seats as against twenty-nine by his opponents (December 1964), and on this basis independence was eventually granted in April 1966.

Apart from this one exception, relations with the United States in the colonial field had become fairly smooth. Even so, the Anglo-American relationship as a whole in 1964 needed almost as much careful nurturing as it had in 1959.

Problems with the United Nations consumed immense quantities of time, energy and paper. One over-arching theme dominated British rela-tions with the UN in this period: whether or not (in the mid-1950s) to resign from it, or one of its agencies, or (in the early 1960s) to withdraw from its specialist Committee of Seventeen (later Twenty-Four) which was charged with overseeing the termination of 'colonialism'. In general terms, it was desirable that the UN should function as an effective guar-antor of world peace, and so leaving it would be dangerous, 'an abdication of responsibility'.[161] On the other hand, the hostility to British colonial policy displayed therein was objected to. The arguments were finely bal-anced, and there was no agreed British position. As permanent British representative on the Trusteeship Council (1957–61), Cohen wanted a modification of the previous rigid line. He recommended remaining forthright and firm, but also being forthcoming and flexible. Poynton dis-agreed ('I have always been, and unashamedly remain, on the extreme right wing over this'), regarding Cohen's approach as 'extremely distaste-ful'. Macleod said he shared Poynton's anxieties, but felt it would be wise to follow Cohen's advice.[162]

Then in December 1960 came the epoch-making Resolution 1514 (XV), demanding 'a speedy and unconditional end to colonialism', sponsored by forty-three Afro-Asian nations, Britain and the United States abstaining. The Resolution maintained that unpreparedness must not be made a pretext for delaying independence, and target dates should be set. The Committee of Seventeen was established to imple-ment the Resolution, or at least to monitor progress (November 1961).

---

[160] *Ibid.*, pp. 811–12 (no. 298), 28 May 1963, minutes of Oversea Policy Committee; Lamb, *The Macmillan years*, pp. 364–8.

[161] *Ibid.*, pt 2; pp. 305–7 (404), FO memo by I. T. M. Pink, 7 February 1957.

[162] CO 936/679, minutes, 7 and 11 February 1966.

However, in the General Assembly 1961 debate on colonialism, a Soviet-inspired resolution for an early and general target date (the end of 1962) was killed off. Even Krishna Menon of India opposed this, saying that immediate independence for South-West Africa and the High Commission Territories could only condemn them to indefinite South African domination. A Nigerian resolution for a date of 1970 – which the British government could have accepted – was withdrawn. Similarly, in the 1962 Assembly, a target-date proposal was again defeated, failing to secure a two-thirds majority. An earlier motion by Guinea and the communist bloc for setting 24 October 1963 as the date encountered considerable opposition, including Nigeria's. The upshot was that the Committee was merely instructed to report on all colonial territories the following year – so far it had concentrated on Africa. These were helpful 'modifications' of the Resolution 1514 from the British view-point, making it easier to remain in what had now become the Committee of Twenty-Four. Nevertheless, a chain of developments had been started which Britain could not ignore: if some territories at least were not 'speeded up' it would look as if no notice at all was being taken of Resolution 1514.[163]

Much of the internal debate was focused in the early months of 1962. It was triggered by Sir Hugh Foot's memorandum of 22 December 1961, arguing that although Britain could not tolerate interference in the administration of colonies, total non-co-operation must only be a last resort. This point had not yet been reached. In a Churchillian metaphor, he proclaimed his battle-plan: 'We should fight on the resolutions. We should fight in the corridors. We should fight in the Committees. We should never abstain'.[164] The CRO welcomed this, and wondered whether the initiative might not be taken by making a declaration of intent about colonial policy. Sandys himself drafted a possible declaration or resolution, committing Britain to a completion of the transfer of power by 1970. Both Macmillan and Home (who paid close attention to all UN matters) liked the idea. But Maudling did not, apparently influenced by Poynton, who reiterated that the only real choice was between co-operation or withdrawal. A declaration, it was also pointed out, might be dangerous ('what would happen to the Falklands if they became independent?'), as well as self-congratulatory. The Africa Committee was asked to consider. It was unhelpful about the prime minister's angle on this, perhaps being unwilling to give him an outright rebuff. The CO and FO

---

[163] *CGEE*, pt 2, pp. 656–7 (no. 538), 29 June 1961, C. J. Eastwood (CO) to L. J. D. Wakely (CRO).
[164] *Ibid.*, pp. 319–22 (no. 409), 27 December 1961, memo by Sir H. Foot, 'Colonial questions at the United Nations'.

were more blatantly dismissive. Maudling continued to press for a firm line against the Committee of Seventeen.[165]

Foot had talks in London in March 1962 and found himself depressed by Poynton's attitude. Maudling and Home had talks to try to resolve their differences. The only way forward was to present an agreed general analysis and let the pros and cons be argued out at Cabinet. The Cabinet in effect decided against Maudling's more intransigent line.[166] The possibility of a formal declaration of policy was discussed again in June 1962, but the CO reacted against it, thinking it would be counter-productive and seen as a hypocritical attempt to divert attention from Southern Rhodesia, on which Britain would be attacked by India, Tanganyika, and Ghana, all arguing it was the most important example of 'colonialism'. Southern Rhodesia was certainly the principal reason for Britain's difficulties, 'an absolute liability'. In August 1962 Foot expressed his concern that Britain was perceived as the friend of Welensky, Salazar (the Portuguese dictator), Verwoerd, and Tshombe. In October 1962 he resigned, warning that the government was drifting to disaster over Southern Rhodesia. He thought Britain spoke with the petulance of a retired governess, 'conservative' in the worst sense, 'negative, defensive, cowardly, sterile'.[167]

After Foot's resignation, Sir Patrick Dean remained as Britain's principal representative at the UN but his views were similar: the Committee was not a serious threat, so it would be more sensible to remain on it and act as a tormenting gad-fly, rather than behaving like an early Christian facing the lions. There was a major discussion on tactics again in July and August 1963, with the familiar array of arguments. The CO officials believed it was damaging to be exposed to such vehement attacks, and too much goodwill was being used up in trying to mobilise the support of friends. Opinion within the office was, however, divided between the options.[168] The FO supported Dean, believing the communists would like Britain to 'run away'; to leave would only make the Committee more extremist and tarnish Britain's image as a modern, sympathetic, reasonable nation. In short, the conclusion of this latest round of exhaustive discussions was once again that the balance of advantage was in favour of 'soldiering on'.

The Congo was the scene of the UN's most high-profiled involvement during the early 1960s.[169] In 1959, the Belgian government, faced with

[165] *Ibid.*, pp. 322–5 (no. 410), 5 January 1962, letter from Maudling to Home.
[166] *Ibid.*, pp. 350–1 (no. 422), 7 June 1962 (CAB 128/36/1, CC 40(62)4).
[167] H. Foot, *A start in freedom* (1964), pp. 227–31.
[168] CO 936/877, no. 1, circular from Sir J. Martin to governors, 5 February 1963.
[169] Alan James, *Britain and the Congo crisis, 1960–1963* (1996). See also J. Turner, *Macmillan*, pp. 191–8, 'The Congo and the limits of power'.

riots and revolts, offered self-government on a progressively telescoping time-table. Diverse political parties emerged. Their leaders – Lumumba, Kasavubu, Tshombe, Mobuto, Gizenga, Bomboko – all had utterly different intentions for the Congo's future, and established competing power-bases ('more like the Crazy Gang than anything I can remember': Macmillan, diary, September 1960). Lumumba came to seem dangerous because he appealed for Soviet aid. Eisenhower and Macmillan agreed it would be good if he could 'fall into a river full of crocodiles'.[170] By contrast, Tshombe, who led the secession of the mining province of Katanga in July 1960, seemed much more congenial, able, and friendly to the West, and he kept fair order in his prosperous province. However tempting it may have been, the British government consistently refused to recognise his regime. African states would have regarded recognition of Katanga as a 'colonialist' attack on the unity of the Congo; but there was a thousand-mile border with Northern Rhodesia, and what if Northern Rhodesia broke with the Central African Federation and joined Katanga?

Both Macmillan and Home were apprehensive of 'another Korea', and, in Home's case, 'another Spanish Civil War', if the Russians supported the rest of the Congo against Katanga. 'Russia was the whole problem', or so Macmillan told Kennedy in 1962.[171] Thus, from the beginning, the Cabinet supported a UN presence as the best hope of stabilising the Congo and preventing armed communist intervention and Soviet domination. To this extent the UN presence (opposed by the Russians) was a convenient instrument for the Western powers to fill the vacuum. Britain agreed the UN could use a degree of force to maintain law and order, but not to impose a political solution (which might well fail). Katanga must be returned to the fold by negotiated settlement, Tshombe coaxed into co-operation with the central government, perhaps in a federal arrangement. A Foreign Office minister, Lord Lansdowne, had reported in September 1961 that any idea of an independent Katanga's peacefully existing alongside a truncated Congo was a fantasy. The British government was opposed to the use of sanctions.

Led by India and Nigeria, a number of Commonwealth countries were unhappy about British Congo policy. Malaya, Ghana and even Canada thought Britain guilty of equivocation. They were suspicious of pressure from the Central African Federation, sensitive about any supposed lack of

---

[170] Macmillan, *Pointing the way*, p. 269 (the Crazy Gang were a group of five or six music-hall comedians – originally three double-acts, Flanagan and Allen, Nervo and Knox, Naughton and Gold – popular on the London stage in the 1950s); *FRUS, 1958–1960*, vol. 14, p. 495.

[171] *CGEE*, pt 2, p. 289 (no. 394), minute by Home, 14 September 1960; PREM 11/3630; *FRUS, 1961–1963*, vol. 20, p. 761, 19 December 1962.

co-operation with the UN. Home appealed to the United States for closer co-ordination of their policies, and, since stalemate persisted, Macmillan repeated the appeal directly to Kennedy in May 1962. By this time, Home and Macmillan favoured a package of financial aid and technical assistance, to which Britain would contribute, organised by the UN and channelled to a federal state. Both sides were to be offered economic aid for reconstruction as an inducement to co-operate in a negotiated settlement.[172] Home claimed Britain was genuinely keen to see Katanga reincorporated: 'we are not dragging our feet simply with a view to delaying the application of the "wind of change" to our own territories'.[173] Britain remained opposed to sanctions, but the UN held to a different view, wanting to expedite the ending of the Katanga secession by increasing the economic pressure on Tshombe. The Cabinet agreed not to participate actively in an international embargo on purchases of Katangan copper or in measures designed to prevent by physical means the passage of exports from Katanga, because this would probably fail. Attempts at reconciliation of Tshombe came to nothing. The final UN campaign against him was relatively bloodless. The dire consequences feared by Britain did not materialise. Tshombe capitulated in the middle of January 1963. The Cabinet decided against British intervention or attempting to rescue Tshombe from the predicament he had got himself into, despite the support he had among some Conservative MPs. Sanctions would not be actively opposed.

The main concern of the government throughout the Congo crisis was to try to stabilise the situation. According to Home – who had a dim view of Africans in this part of the world – 'unless we are very careful we could get a belt of chaos from Angola, through the Congo, Ruanda-Urundi to Kenya. That would be a dreadful prospect'. The limits of British influence were, however, painfully obvious in that although the Russians were kept out, the crisis was resolved in ways largely outside British control. What happened in the Congo was a cautionary tale in several senses; governors were asked for their opinions about the lessons to be learned.[174]

It is not possible within the confines of this analysis to do justice to Britain's first application to join the European Economic Community (EEC).[175] Of the leading Cabinet deliberations, the most important were

---

[172] *CGEE*, pt 2, pp. 297–99 (no. 400), 20 August 1962, Cabinet memo by Home (CAB 129/110, C(62)132).

[173] *CGEE*, pt 1, pp. 199–200 (no. 40), 6 March 1962, Lord Home to Ambassador J. H. A. Watson.

[174] Home, *The way the wind blows*, p. 129; *CGEE*, pt 2, pp. 307–11 (no. 405), 29 September 1960, CO circular letter to various governors.

[175] The classic account of British policy towards Europe is Miriam Camps, *Britain and the European Community, 1955–1963*, (1964). Essential reading on the first application now includes: J. W. Young, *Britain and European unity, 1945–1992* (1993), ch. 3;

on 13 July 1960, and on 18 June 1961, when the formal decision was taken. The arguments were thought to be strong each way. In favour of joining these were: (1) 'If we remained outside it, our political influence in Europe and in the rest of the world was likely to decline'; and (2) 'we should not only avoid tariff discrimination by its members against our exports, but should also be able to participate in a large and rapidly expanding market'. As against this: (1) 'we should be surrendering independent control of our commercial policies to a European *bloc*, when our trading interests were world wide; we should have to abandon our special economic relationship with the Commonwealth'; and (2) control of agricultural and horticultural policies would also be lost, 'thus increasing the cost of living'. There were perhaps three underlying factors which tipped the decision in favour of an application to join. One was that this was what the Americans, by and large (for cold war geopolitical reasons), wanted Britain to do. Another was that Macmillan saw it as in line with his 'grand design' by contributing to an anti-communist consolidation. And thirdly there was some hope of savings on the British contribution to NATO defence.[176] However, the Cabinet was divided, in part because of Commonwealth considerations. Much attention was paid to reconciling possible membership with the interests of Commonwealth countries, especially those of Australia, New Zealand and Canada, all of which had serious worries about the consequences, not merely for their own trading relationships with Britain but also for the impact on the strength of the Commonwealth should British links with it unravel. African states indicated concern that the Community might perpetuate, through arrangements of 'association', their inferior relationship with their former colonial masters. In July 1961 – following the precedent of 1949 when ministers were sent to Commonwealth countries to sound out opinion on the continuation of India's membership as a republic – Sandys was dispatched to Australia, New Zealand and Canada, Thorneycroft to India,

J. R. V. Ellison, 'Accepting the inevitable: Britain and European integration', in W. Kaiser and G. Staerck, eds., *British foreign policy, 1955–1964: contracting options* (2000), pp. 171–89; Alex May, ed., *Britain, the Commonwealth and Europe: the Commonwealth and Britain's applications to join the European Communities* (2001), pp. 53–131 (chs. 5–7 by George Wilkes, Alex May, M. D. Kandiah, and G. Staerck); L. J. Butler, 'The winds of change: Britain, Europe and the Commonwealth, 1959–1961', in B. Brivati and H. Jones, eds., *From reconstruction to integration: Britain and Europe since 1945* (1993) pp. 157–65; N. Piers Ludlow, 'A mismanaged application: Britain and EEC membership, 1961–1963', in A. Deighton and A. S. Milward, eds., *Accelerating, deepening and enlarging: the European Economic Community, 1957–1963* (2000).

[176] *CGEE*, pt 2, p. 191 (no. 363), 13 July 1960 (CAB 128/34, CC 41(60)), and pp. 199–204 (no. 365), 18 June 1961, minutes of an *ad hoc* ministerial meeting held at Chequers on 'Europe and the Commonwealth'.

Pakistan, Ceylon, Singapore and Malaya, Perth to the West Indies, Edward Heath to Cyprus, and John Hare to Nigeria, Ghana, Sierra Leone and Gambia. The results of this consultation were given to the Cabinet on 18 July 1961.[177] At the Commonwealth Prime Ministers' Meeting in September 1962 Macmillan, who had been prepared for 'grumbling acquiescence', was shaken by the vehemence of the doubts expressed. Nevertheless, an unusually full and informative communiqué recorded agreement that the application would go ahead. The government's answer to Commonwealth criticisms was that initial shocks and adjustments could be overcome, and that in the long run British political and economic strength would decline outside the European Community, eventually leading to a permanent weakening of the whole Commonwealth. Consultations continued right through the period of negotiation until de Gaulle delivered his veto on 14 January 1963.

(2) The Commonwealth

When Canada's Lester Pearson said the Suez Crisis 'brought the Commonwealth to the verge of dissolution',[178] this was not just because most of the other members were upset by the lack of consultation, but because they were shocked, and disapproved of the whole venture. In marked contrast to his exertions to restore the Anglo-American relationship, Macmillan did little to mend fences with the Commonwealth. His reflections at the time of the Commonwealth Prime Ministers' Meeting in July 1957 were decidedly languid and rhetorical. What was to be the future of the Commonwealth? – Clearly it was entering a new phase, an 'inescapable evolution': 'the stream of gradual change was now to be augmented into a fast-flowing river, which might soon break its banks through its torrential force'. How could the mystique which kept the old organisation together be maintained? Well, he would have to try at least 'to guide these disparate forces into a common faith'. In practice he did not do much. His tour of India, Pakistan, Australia and New Zealand in 1958 was undertaken more to restore a show of governmental vitality 'when things were at a low ebb' than to strengthen the Commonwealth chain.[179] He retained a sentimental attachment to his old Commonwealth relationships and was aware of the Commonwealth as a useful psychological cushion for the end of empire. Moreover, it was an increasingly valuable instrument to

---

[177] *Ibid.*, pp. 211–14 (no. 368), 21 July 1961, Cabinet minutes (CAB 128/35/2, CC 42(61)).

[178] J. Eayrs, ed., *The Commonwealth and Suez: a documentary survey* (1964), p. 194.

[179] Macmillan, *Riding the storm*, pp. 350 and 378: CAB 21/3155, Macmillan to Sir N. Brook, 1 November 1959.

keep communism at bay. Its unity was therefore important, and one of his main efforts as prime minister centred on the attempt to keep South Africa in the Commonwealth, thus running the risk of cutting himself off from the only element of 'common faith' which had any real potential, commitment to a multi-racial future. Of course the trouble was that Macmillan did not like the changes brought by Afro-Asian membership. In characteristically Edwardian metaphors, he complained privately that it was no longer like gaining admission to Brooks's but joining the RAC (Royal Automobile Club). It had changed from a 'small and pleasant country-house party' into a 'sort of miniature United Nations'.[180] Selwyn Lloyd was convinced that Macmillan and Macleod, for all their rhetoric, did not really care about the Commonwealth, and he urged Home upon becoming prime minister to effect a 'change of emphasis' and set about fostering Commonwealth links, despite the difficulties.[181] Home was not unresponsive.

Those difficulties were of course formidable. As Lloyd himself wrote, the facts were 'that the Africans are opposed to us over Southern Rhodesia, that Mr Nehru has never really liked us, that Australia does not buy our aircraft, that Canada discriminates against us, that there are wide differences over attitudes towards Communism'. Sir Patrick Dean deplored the lack of cohesion between Commonwealth members at the United Nations, where the attacks they led on Britain were a public demonstration that the Commonwealth concept was, he believed, 'empty of political content'.[182] The ambassador in Addis Ababa, John Russell, reported that the Commonwealth delegates to the conference of thirty-two heads of independent African states in May 1963 were disunited; most of them avoided his embassy like the plague; 'in Africa the expression of Commonwealth is about dead'.[183] Sir Norman Brook thought the only common link with any continuing relevance was speaking the English language, which at least might carry 'a constructive promise' of openness to the same ideas.[184]

It was against this background that officials wrestled to find a renewed role for the Commonwealth. Plainly it could not be made into a self-sustaining economic unit; it was not significant in power terms; but in theory at any rate it ought to give Britain enhanced standing in the world,

---

[180] CO 926/1196, recalled by Sir J. Martin, minute, 11 January 1960 (on other occasions Macmillan referred to Boodle's rather than Brooks's); *CGEE*, pt 2, p. 664 (no. 541), Macmillan to Sir R Menzies, 18 February 1962.

[181] *CGEE*, pt 2, pp. 697–8 (no. 549), Selwyn Lloyd to Sir A Douglas-Home, 7 November 1963.   [182] *Ibid.*, pp. 692–6 (no. 548), 25 September 1963, memo to Home.

[183] FO 371/167141, no. 162.

[184] *CGEE*, pt 2, pp. 669–71 (no. 544), 24 April 1962, Brook to Macmillan.

and it could have a valuable function in keeping developing countries out of the Soviet bloc. It ought to be able to form a bridge between advanced and developing nations. It had roots in every part of the world except, marginally, Latin America. Its very existence might be a good answer to charges of 'colonialism'. In a more visionary interpretation, its diversities might even be made constructively complementary. An officials' investigation into the 'intangible links' in 1960 concluded that it was 'a very vigorous social organism', promoting useful contacts between professional people, students, and sportsmen, although too many of these relationships were only bilateral with Britain.[185]

On the other side of the balance-sheet, the Commonwealth was threatened by the weakening of sterling, by the unreconcilable opinions and 'unreliable behaviour' of some the new independent leaders, and by intra-Commonwealth disputes, notably the 'grim hostility' between India and Pakistan over Kashmir. Above all there were the three problems of the increasing size of the club, of immigration into Britain, and of the European Common Market negotiations. The probable impact of British entry into Europe was disturbing because so incalculable, but it certainly seemed from the periphery as if the government might be prepared to go in on any terms, regardless of Commonwealth interests. As to its growth, by 1962 the Commonwealth was ceasing to be a relatively small group of relatively large countries: decolonisation had created the problem that the tail was now uncomfortably wagging the dog.

What could be done to make the expanding Commonwealth function more effectively? A declaration of principles was rejected. A Commonwealth court of appeal never got off the ground. The possibility of a Commonwealth Youth Trust came to little, though the government did agree to build 5,000 new hostel places for overseas students. It was decided in 1958 that Empire Day must be renamed Commonwealth Day. Much the most useful achievements, however, were those of the Montreal Trade and Economic Conference in 1958, which pioneered the way for a better deal on aid for newly independent countries, and took a significant initiative in the field of education. The British team, led by Home, put forward a plan which, according to him, 'was received with acclamation and has proved itself of very considerable value'. The Conference proposed a scheme of studentships and fellowships (target: one thousand) to be funded by Commonwealth governments, in the hope that the Commonwealth would 'increasingly furnish new opportunities for its young people'. The other

---

[185] *Ibid.*, pp. 643–52 (no. 535), 9 August 1960, CRO survey of the Commonwealth, 'The British legacy'.

recommendation was to encourage co-operation in education generally, especially the supply and training of teachers. A Commonwealth Educational Conference was held at Oxford in July 1959 to give effect these recommendations, followed by a conference held in New Delhi in January 1962 to review progress.[186]

'Islands', Macmillan once remarked, 'can become rather a bore, whether in the Mediterranean or in the Pacific'.[187] What was known as the 'Smaller Colonial Territories' problem was undeniably intractable. At issue was the question of whether they could be members of the Commonwealth, or even independent at all. Two-tier membership was rejected by the Cabinet in 1954–5 (see above, p. 214), but the idea refused to die; indeed, as the Commonwealth got bigger, the scheme revived, it being argued that it might be more acceptable once larger numbers of smaller units were to be excluded from the first tier. A concept of 'statehood' (self-government in domestic affairs, but dependence on Britain for defence and external affairs) had been put forward in 1955 for the small fry who would fall short of Commonwealth membership. At the end of 1958 the CRO suggested that Brook's committee on the subject should take another look at 'statehood', in the context of the rapid growth of nationalism and a possible agreement on Cyprus. The prime minister approved, and serious work started in March 1959, a report being completed by June of that year. The committee preferred the CO's title of 'Commonwealth state' to the CRO's recommended 'associated state' as the designation for a 'comfortable half-way house' between self-government and independence. Such states would not attend Prime Ministers' Meetings. There was, however, by this time no question of any independent states being relegated to a second tier: such possible future members as the West Indies Federation, Kenya, Uganda and Tanganyika. The report was never considered by ministers because of the impending autumn election, but in April 1960 Macmillan proposed that a group of Commonwealth (not merely British) officials should reopen investigations under Brook's chairmanship. Brook's study group concluded in July 1960 that within the next decade membership of the Commonwealth would probably rise from seventeen to twenty-four and could well double. Such an increase might not be unmanageable, and it was certainly desirable in principle to grant only full membership to all.[188] Cohen offered a critique suggesting that the timetable envisaged was too long

---

[186] Home, *The way the wind blows*, p. 117; Mansergh, *Documents and speeches*, pp. 700–2.
[187] Foreign secretary's Private Office papers, FO 800/667, Macmillan to Sir R Scott, 9 September 1955.
[188] *CGEE*, pt 2, pp. 636–43 (no. 534), 23 July 1960, officials' report on 'The constitutional development of the Commonwealth' (Brook report).

drawn out and would make for 'a rather hard road in front of us at the UN':

We must not of course give way to international pressure which is irresponsible, but this kind of international interest will inevitably grow . . . [and] seems likely to have its effect on opinion, in a number even of those small territories which have so far shown no signs of aspirations to independence.

For 'international reasons' therefore, finding a practical means of terminating colonial status would be a good idea, although a single 'managed solution' was impossible, Cohen thought, because of the policy of decentralisation, the special circumstances of 'fortress colonies', and the difficulty of concurrent international claims (he listed Aden, Honduras, Falklands and Basutoland).[189]

The estimates of July 1960 were, as Cohen had foreseen, quickly overtaken. Mauritius and Zanzibar were moving up the queue. In April 1962 the Chadwick Report revised the forecast to thirty or perhaps thirty-five Commonwealth members by 1970. This important document, 'The evolution of the Commonwealth', grappling with 'a serious and immediate problem', once again rejected all restrictions on membership. For the smaller territories, 'free association' was now the preferred term, because this could be aligned with a UN definition, and Western Samoa was now available as a model.[190] Western Samoa became independent in January 1962 in a special agency relationship with New Zealand, approved by the UN. Elsewhere, attacks might be pre-empted by removing the Smaller Colonial Territories as soon as possible from the purview of the UN.[191]

As luck would have it, the United Nations had itself provided a way out. Under Resolution 1541 (XV) of December 1960 – not to be confused with the more general Resolution 1514 (XV) – a non-self-governing territory could become self-governing by (i) sovereign independence, (ii) 'free association' with an independent state, or (iii) integration with an independent state. Integration with the United Kingdom as a solution scarcely survived its failure to be adopted for Malta. The conditions of 'free association' were the consent of the state, ability to determine its own internal constitution, and to change its status at any time. These criteria did not seem too difficult to comply with, and 'free association' thus appeared to be a distinctly possible relationship for a number of British territories, among them the Falklands, St Helena, Pitcairn, Gibraltar, and

---

[189] CO 1032/225, no. 99, letter to CO, 17 January 1961.
[190] *CGEE*, pt 2, pp. 672–88 (no. 545), 24 April 1962, officials' report on 'The evolution of the Commonwealth' (Chadwick report: John Chadwick was an assistant undersecretary in the CRO).
[191] W. D. McIntyre, 'The admission of small states to the Commonwealth', *JICH*, vol. 24 (1996), pp. 244–77.

the Gilbert and Ellice Islands.[192] Although the UN General Assembly debate in 1963 showed increasing concern over Smaller Colonial Territories, there was also a clear understanding that sovereign independence was not possible for all, and nothing was said which seemed to interfere unduly with the plans the British government were now working on. But there was a degree of urgency: the conditions of 'association' might be made harder to accept in future.[193]

One disappointment for Macmillan was that it proved impossible to arrange for Australia and New Zealand to take over responsibility for preparing some of the Pacific islands for decolonisation. It seemed to him an obvious way of reducing the colonial burden for Britain. In 1958, not only the prime minister, but Brook, the CRO, and the Official Committee on Colonial Policy – to say nothing of the duke of Edinburgh – all hoped a 'rationalisation' of this kind could be achieved.[194] But the CO opposed it and the Cabinet upheld the CO. An open battle developed between the CO and the CRO, the CO sticking to its traditional ethical concept of trusteeship, its duty to promote 'political and economic advancement' in the interests of the inhabitants, and arguing strongly that a transfer to Australia, with its 'white Australia' programme, would be dangerous.[195] Nor were the Australians keen to acquire fresh responsibilities.[196] It was decided in 1964 that the status quo would be preserved in the New Hebrides. (They became independent in 1980.)

The Commonwealth Immigrants Act of 1962 removed the right of all British subjects, irrespective of colour or country of origin, to enter freely into the United Kingdom. For the first time a legal framework of restriction on immigration was enacted. Asian and black immigration had perhaps never been welcomed by British government, but for many years it was unwilling to check it by legislation. Between 1950 and 1961 'coloured immigration' was discussed by the Cabinet on thirty-seven separate occasions, but the number of immigrants involved never seemed significant enough to justify taking such a problematic step.[197]

---

[192] *CGEE*, pt 1, pp. 211–20 (no. 46) [27] September 1963, CO memo, 'The future of British colonial territories'.

[193] Morgan, *Official history of colonial development*, vol. V, pp. 202–5, summarising despatch from Sir P. Dean to R. A. Butler, 27 January 1964.

[194] *CGEE*, pt 2, pp. 709–10 (no. 554), 15 December 1958, minutes of Colonial Policy Committee; pt 1, pp. 58–61 (nos. 9 and 10), minute by Macmillan (16 June 1959), and minutes of a Cabinet committee meeting (9 July 1959).

[195] *Ibid.*, pt 2, pp. 710–11 (no. 555), 29 June 1959; pp. 715–21 (no. 559), October-November 1959, CO memo and minutes.

[196] R. C. Thompson, 'Conflict or co-operation? Britain and Australia in the South Pacific, 1950–1960', *JICH*, vol. 23 (1995), pp. 301–16.

[197] I. R. G. Spencer, *British immigration policy since 1939: the making of multi-racial Britain* (1997), p 50; Randall Hansen, *Citizenship and immigration in post-war Britain* (2000).

Although not finally able to determine immigration policy, the CO monitored the issue carefully, mainly from a West Indian perspective. Junior minister John Profumo acted as its representative on the Committee on Colonial Immigrants, which kept the general situation under regular review. Lennox-Boyd and Home had both played a crucial part in opposing a bill in 1955, and they were equally determined in 1958 that a similar bill – precipitated by a sudden increase in Indian and Pakistani immigration – should also fail.[198] The Cabinet agreed once again in July 1958 that 'legislation to control immigration from the Commonwealth was not yet required'. Disturbances in Nottingham and Notting Hill (23 August to 2 September 1958) led to a reconsideration of this decision,[199] but in fact the riots made it harder to make any major pronouncement about control. The CO worked hard to head off legislation by persuading West Indian governments to take administrative action as a means of reducing the flow at source. Norman Manley agreed various ways could be found to produce a marked falling off from Jamaica. This administrative action was not ineffective, and there was a temporary drop in numbers. Although the Cabinet at around the turn of 1960 and 1961 found the position 'disquieting', it was still reluctant to grasp the nettle.[200]

A brief prepared in the CO early in 1961 took the line that a stark choice lay ahead. Restrictions would create severe difficulties for West Indian governments and weaken the respect paid to Britain as the centre of the Commonwealth; but to leave things as they were could mean unacceptable and deteriorating social consequences at home. The issue was kept off the agenda of the Commonwealth Prime Ministers' Meeting in March 1961, but immediately afterwards Macmillan toured the West Indies, where Dr Eric Williams warned him legislation would result in 'social revolution and a Castro situation'.[201] In May 1961 Macleod successfully secured a delay in announcing legislation in order not to prejudice the results of the Jamaica referendum on its continued membership of the Federation. (Jamaica nevertheless voted to withdraw.) Macleod minuted in September 1961: 'I have no doubt that the Cabinet will go ahead with this sort of a Bill. Sad indeed, but for myself I have thought it inevitable since the spring of this year.' And again, five days later: 'I detest the Bill and am painfully aware of its imperfections. But it is wiser to do

---

[198] *CGEE*, pt 2, pp. 756–64 (nos. 569 and 570), CO minutes, February–June 1958.

[199] *Ibid.*, pp. 764–5 (nos. 571 and 572), Cabinet minutes, 1 July and 8 September 1958 (CAB 128/32/2, CC 51(58)6 and CC 69(58)3).

[200] *Ibid.*, pp. 771–4 (nos. 577 and 578), Cabinet minutes, 16 February and 30 May 1961 (CAB 128/35/1, CC 7(61)2, and CC 29(61)7).

[201] PREM 11/3236, record of meeting on 25 March 1961.

it now than to wait.' Poynton agreed with him in 'disliking this intensely'.[202] The Cabinet decision was taken on 10 October 1961,[203] on the basis of a memorandum by R. A. Butler, arguing that controls should be accepted as 'a sad necessity' because of the need to deal with the strain on housing resources and the danger of social tension created by large unassimilated communities. (The Treasury had expressly said there was no justification on economic grounds for restriction.) According to Butler, the bill was 'not inherently discriminatory': 'it purports to regulate flexible employment, but it will inescapably be seen as operating almost exclusively on coloured people'.[204] The deciding factor was the rise in numbers: from 21,000 in 1959 to an estimate of more than 100,000 for 1961. In subsequent Cabinets, the resulting Irish anomaly was dealt with; Macmillan – who found the whole policy 'hard and disagreeable' – was searching for the best way 'in *common sense*' out of a dangerous political position.[205] The controversial Commonwealth Immigrants Act (opposed by the Labour Opposition) did not solve the problem it was meant to tackle. This was apparent even before the Conservative government left office.

(3) South Africa's departure from the Commonwealth

Not many parts of the empire or Commonwealth saw such a catalogue of unexpected dramas as Southern Africa in the first half of the 1960s. Arriving as high commissioner in January 1959, Sir John Maud had no idea that within little more than a year a British prime minister would tell the South African parliament for the first time, and once and for all, that its policies were objectionable; that in just over two years South Africa would leave the Commonwealth; and perhaps most remarkable of all, that by the time his term ended in 1963, independence for the three High Commission Territories, Basutoland, Bechuanaland and Swaziland, would have become a live issue.[206] During the decade of the 1960s historic objectives were achieved. For South Africa a republic, for Britain disengagement without too much dishonour, and for the Basotho, Swazi and Tswana peoples a fresh chance to live their own lives in their own way. Seretse Khama and Sobhuza II both emerged, against the odds, as

[202] CO 1032/306, no. 322, minutes by Macleod, 29 September and 4 October 1961; CO 1032/307, minute by Sir H. Poynton, 8 November 1961.

[203] *CGEE*, pt 2, pp. 775–7 (no. 580), 10 October 1961, Cabinet minutes (CAB 128/35/2, CC 55(61)3); Ashton and Killingray, eds, *The West Indies*, pp. 453–4 (no. 164).

[204] CAB 129/107, C(61)153, memo on 'Commonwealth immigration', 6 October 1961.

[205] PREM 11/3238, minute, [25] November 1961.

[206] J. Redcliffe-Maud, *Experiences of an optimist: memoirs* (1981), p. 4.

national leaders, though in sharply contrasting modes, and did so at about the same time Nelson Mandela began his long imprisonment.

British policy towards South Africa always walked a tightrope between co-operation and containment, between the demands of national interests and the necessities of international reputation. Any apparent condoning of apartheid put in jeopardy British relations with Afro-Asian states; but there were plausible reasons for maintaining mutually beneficial economic and defence connections with South Africa, and above all for not provoking any South African hostile move against the High Commission Territories. The continuation of over-flying rights was also vital (and quietly confirmed after departure from the Commonwealth). By the end of 1959, South Africa's patience was about to be tested by a combination of steps which would be extremely unpalatable: a multiracial constitution for Bechuanaland, purposeful economic development for Swaziland, and the withdrawal of Britain's 'support' in the international arena.[207]

The substantive point of policy embedded in the 'wind of change' speech was a warning that South Africa could no longer expect British support at the United Nations. Cohen, as British representative on the Trusteeship Council, had wanted to put more distance between the British and South African positions. By November 1959 it was clear to officials that the balance between maintaining good relations with the Union and improving the British reputation at the UN needed correcting; but the CRO was anxious not to push South Africa to the 'parting of the ways' by handling this in the wrong way. Macmillan's visit provided exactly the right opportunity for engineering the change of policy. A draft Cabinet memorandum was now turned by Home into a personal minute to Macmillan. It is the pivotal document of Anglo-South African relations in the ten years before 1961. Its most striking propositions were an admission that the Commonwealth would 'undoubtedly be happier and closer-knit were the ugly duckling out of the nest', and an argument that South Africa was 'a liability to the West' in the cold war.[208] Several senior ministers were asked to comment. All of them were supportive.[209]

The test of the new policy was not long in coming. When in April 1960 the UN General Assembly passed a resolution condemning the Sharpeville

---

[207] Hyam and Henshaw, *The lion and the springbok*, pp. 254–72, 'The parting of the ways: the departure of South Africa from the Commonwealth, 1951–1961', repr. from *JICH*, vol. 26 (1988), pp. 157–75.

[208] *CGEE*, pt 2, pp. 384–7 (no. 439), 17 December 1959, minute by Home to Macmillan, 'Policy towards South Africa: the United Nations items'.

[209] *Ibid.*, pp. 387–91, 399–402 (nos. 440–2, 445, 446), minutes by Selwyn Lloyd, Macleod, D. Heathcoat Amory, and Treasury officials, January–March 1960.

shootings in March, Britain voted for it. At the Commonwealth Prime Ministers' Meeting in May 1960 Eric Louw (the South African foreign minister) raised the question of whether South Africa would be welcome as a member after becoming a republic.[210] This was regarded as premature and ham-fisted, but the signs were not encouraging. Alarm-bells began ringing for Macmillan: 'If we do *nothing*, the Commonwealth will seem to have no faith and purpose. If we *do too much*, South Africa will secede and this may mean the beginning of a general break up.'[211] In the months before the next meeting he wrote letters to Diefenbaker of Canada and Nehru of India, urging them at least to come to it uncommitted on this serious issue, for 'there is a real danger to the whole Commonwealth structure and the beginning of a break-up now'.[212] Meanwhile, officials had been at work for some time assessing the probable effects of a South African departure. Maud's advice was to try to keep South Africa in (as the best way of helping the Africans);[213] while CRO officials briefed the prime minister to argue tactically to the last in favour of South Africa's remaining, but, if it came to it, to follow majority opinion and acquiesce in departure, though 'still with every show of reluctance'.[214]

At the crucial Commonwealth Prime Ministers' Meeting in March 1961, the general mood initially was that South Africa might be given one more chance.[215] Nehru and Diefenbaker made the opening statements, affirming the necessity of a truly multi-racial Commonwealth and a policy of non-discrimination. They were later supported by the newcomer to the circle, Nigeria's Abubakar Tafawa Balewa. Ayub Khan of Pakistan and Mrs S. R. D. Bandaranaike of Ceylon stressed the danger of emerging nations falling prey to communism if these principles were not upheld. Menzies for Australia and Holyoake for New Zealand sounded caution-ary notes about not taking 'irrevocable steps'. Even Nkrumah seemed uncertain whether racial equality had to be formally declared. Mrs Bandaranaike weighed in on the theme of the 'battle for African minds'; she commented that the danger of a split in the Commonwealth was just as great if South Africa remained in or was expelled. Verwoerd then made a long defence of the theory and practice of apartheid. Next, Nkrumah took the initiative in declaring that this did not help the discussion, since

[210] J. D. B. Miller, *Survey of Commonwealth affairs: problems of expansion and attrition, 1953–1969* (Oxford, 1974), pp. 142–9; O. Geyser, *Watershed for South Africa: London, 1961* (Durban, 1983), pp. 54–100.

[211] Diary entry quoted by Horne, *Macmillan*, vol. II, p. 204.

[212] *CGEE*, pt 2, pp. 412–14 (no. 452) Macmillan to J. Diefenbaker, 18 November 1960; PREM 11/3393, Macmillan to Nehru, 6 January 1961 (T8/61).

[213] *CGEE*, pt 2, pp. 410–11 (no. 451), Sir J. Maud to CRO, 13 August 1960.

[214] *Ibid.*, pp. 414–18 (no. 453), CRO briefing to prime minister, 22 February 1961.

[215] Hyam and Henshaw, *The lion and the springbok*, pp. 264–70.

(a)

Illustration 4.7 Commonwealth Prime Ministers' Meeting, March 1961. This was the meeting which discussed South Africa's future membership of the Commonwealth as a republic.

(a) Mr Macmillan with Mr Nehru, followed by Lord Home, on the staircase of Lancaster House, London, before the opening of the conference.

(b) Mr Sandys (secretary of the state for Commonwealth relations) with Mr Diefenbaker (prime minister of Canada) and Alhaji Sir Abubakar Tafawa Balewa (federal prime minister of Nigeria) at Lancaster House, before the meeting.

(c) Dr Verwoerd (prime minister of South Africa) leaves Lancaster House after announcing that South Africa would leave the Commonwealth, looking not at all despondent, 15 March 1961.

(b)

(c)

'the real issue was the whole future character of the Commonwealth'. Abubakar agreed that if members could not subscribe publicly to the principle of racial equality, 'their association was meaningless'. At this point Macmillan offered an interim summing-up, hoping for a compromise formula which would accept South Africa's continuing membership as a republic (in itself constitutionally not really a problem), but also reaffirming the feeling of all other members against racial discrimination. This was plainly the moment for someone to sharpen the issue and it was Nehru who did so: 'the eyes of the world were on this meeting and the Commonwealth prime ministers should make it absolutely clear where they stood'.

So ended the first day. The outcome was uncertain. Only Mrs Bandaranaike had so far used language which appeared to commit her to refusing consent to South Africa's continuing membership. Overnight, Macmillan tried hard to persuade Verwoerd to make some conciliatory gesture. Verwoerd refused. The second day was taken up with Macmillan's attempts to draft a communiqué reflecting both sides of the argument. He said that he recognised all the prime ministers were subject to the pressure of public opinion on racial equality, and 'it was of great importance to make clear to the peoples of the Commonwealth and of the world where we stood on this issue'. Verwoerd jibbed at this – hardly unexpectedly. Further redrafting was played around with, but as Nehru observed, the more they talked the more obvious was the difference of opinion. The second day ended with a powerful statement from Mrs Bandaranaike, which reflected the hardening of attitudes. Dr Verwoerd, she said, was obviously not intending to change his policy, and the prime ministers were unable to compromise on the issue of human rights; Mr Macmillan's drafts had failed to bring out the salient point of their discussions, since 'the real question was whether South Africa could be permitted to remain within the Commonwealth while her racial policy remained unchanged'.

Nevertheless, even at this stage, if Verwoerd had accepted the right of other members to record their detestation of apartheid and their commitment to non-discrimination as basic to the multi-racial Commonwealth – even if he could not subscribe to it himself – South Africa's membership could probably have been continued. He considered his position overnight. Next morning he seemed ready to swallow this unpalatable pill, provided he could as part of the same communiqué set out a justification for his government's policy. Both Nehru and Diefenbaker considered that the draft gave too much emphasis to Verwoerd's views. It was Abubakar who focused the crux of the debate: South Africa was not going to change, and he would have to consider whether Nigeria should remain a member if South Africa stayed in. Nehru seized on this leverage to give notice that even if South Africa now remained, India would at the earliest opportunity raise the question again. Nkrumah joined in with what proved to be a hammer-blow: Ghana would have to reconsider its own membership at a later stage if South Africa were not expelled. 'Strong, if not angry words began to be used'.[216]

. Verwoerd took exception to these remarks; South Africa should not, he complained, have to be threatened or made to feel unwelcome. He would have to 'reconsider his position'. Presumably there was then a moment of climactic silence, eventually broken by Macmillan, who said they would all have to reconsider their positions. A tea-break served to confirm the inevitable. Verwoerd formally withdrew his request for South Africa to remain a member after 31 May 1961 as a republic. There was no further discussion. Macmillan quickly produced a brief communiqué for immediate release. It was just three sentences long, little more than a simple statement that the prime minister of South Africa had withdrawn his application 'in the light of the views expressed on behalf of other member-governments and the indication of their future intentions regarding the racial policy of the Union government'.

Later that evening, a highly despondent Macmillan chewed over the results and how the tactics had evolved. He felt the decisive factor had been the position of Abubakar, who might not politically have survived putting his name to a document agreeing to South Africa's continuing membership.[217]

Lord Home sent Macmillan a consoling note: Macmillan had done all that was humanly possible to keep South Africa in, but he did not see 'how with emotion overcoming reason it was possible to get a different result'. It had become clear to Home that morning, after a conversation with Ayub Khan, 'that the only alternative was the break-away of the Asian and African members. That could not be faced.'[218]

Macmillan's memoirs deployed emotive adjectives in describing the departure of South Africa from the Commonwealth: unhappy, painful, very sad, tragic, disastrous. It affronted his sense of history that he had presided over the departure of a 'founder member' of the Commonwealth. It disgusted him as a politician that problems could not be sensibly

---

[216] Harold Evans, *Downing Street diary: the Macmillan years, 1957–1963* (1981), p. 213.

[217] *CGEE*, pt 2, pp. 451–2 (no. 458), note for the record, 15 March 1961 (PREM 11/3535). Although Macmillan never found it easy to forgive Diefenbaker (that 'woolly tub-thumper') for his 'holier than thou' attitude, Diefenbaker was not the prime mover in South Africa's departure, *pace* F. Hayes, 'South Africa's departure from the Commonwealth, 1960–1961', *International History Review*, vol. 2 (1980), pp. 453–84.

[218] *CGEE*, pt 2, p. 452 (no. 459), Home to Macmillan, 15 March 1961.

Illustration 4.8 Commonwealth Prime Ministers' Meeting: dinner with the Her Majesty the Queen, 16 March 1961.

This gathering in Buckingham Palace was not a well-posed photograph. Left to right: Abubakar Tafawa Balewa (Nigeria), Dr Nkrumah (Ghana), Mr Diefenbaker (Canada), Mr Nehru (India), Field-Marshal Ayub Khan (Pakistan), HM the Queen, Sir Roy Welensky (Federation of Rhodesia and Nyasaland), Mrs Sirimavo Bandaranaike (Ceylon), Mr Macmillan, Mr. Menzies (Australia), Archbishop Makarios III (president of Cyprus), Mr Holyoake (New Zealand), Tunku Abdul Rahman (Malaya). Mrs Bandaranaike was the widow of S. W. R. D. Bandaranaike (assassinated in 1959); she became leader of the Sri Lanka Freedom Party, and the world's first woman prime minister (1960–5).

resolved: was every problem to be met with such rigidity, incomprehension, and lack of compromise as Verwoerd had displayed? He confided to Sir John Maud, 'the wind of change has blown us away'.[219]

With remarkable speed the spin-doctors were at work. Duncan Sandys told high commissioners ten days later: 'the removal of any doubt about the acceptance of the principle of multi-racialism should enhance the prestige of the Commonwealth in the world as well as its own solidarity'.[220]

The departure of South Africa did not solve the central problems of Anglo-South African relations. South Africa could not be treated as if nothing had changed, and, in Brook's words, they had to avoid any suspicion that South Africa 'having jumped out of the Commonwealth window, is being let in again by the back-door'.[221] Nevertheless, the old imperatives to keep on terms as good as possible with South Africa, despite apartheid, in a reasonable working relationship, remained.[222] The British government had to continue to treat South Africa as half-ally and half-untouchable at the same time, uneasily balancing on the tightrope between provocation and conciliation. Always, it had to be remembered that, in the long run, there would almost certainly be a black government in Pretoria. If British policy seemed to the Africans too unsympathetic they might turn to the communist bloc: 'if an eventual explosion in South Africa (assisted no doubt by outside forces) led to the installation of a pro-Communist Black Government, this would be a crowning disaster'.[223] Hard decisions had to be taken about voting on UN resolutions about sanctions. In June 1964 the government voted for a resolution in the Security Council condemning apartheid, but remained opposed to economic sanctions, mainly because it believed they would hurt Africans, and do 'irreparable damage to Basutoland, and serious damage to Swaziland and Bechuanaland'. On arms sales, a distinction was drawn by the Cabinet between weapons which might be used for internal repression and those required for external defence.[224]

The future of the High Commission Territories had for so long been considered in terms of their vulnerability to South African expansionist pressure and in the face of repeated South African demands to take them

---

[219] Macmillan, *Pointing the way*, pp. 285–305, esp. p. 302 (diary, 21 March 1961).

[220] CAB 129/104, C(61)40, 27 March 1961, to high commissioners.

[221] *CGEE*, pt 2, pp. 453–4 (no. 461), Cabinet minutes, 3 August 1961 (CAB 128/35/2, CC 47(61)2); PREM 11/3994, Sir N. Brook to Macmillan, 20 March 1961. A committee of officials on future relations with South Africa met 26 times under the chairmanship of Sir A. Clutterbuck, 28 March–24 November 1961 (CAB 134/2493).

[222] *CGEE*, pt 2, pp. 462–8 (no. 463) 28 June 1963, briefing despatch for the new high commissioner, Sir H. Stephenson (CAB 129/114, C(63)109).

[223] *Ibid.*, pp. 481–2 (no. 469), FO minutes, 13–17 September 1963.

[224] *Ibid.*, pp. 486–8 (no. 474), FO briefing for prime minister, 29 June 1964.

over, that it proved hard for all sides to adjust their policies to any other framework, even after the departure of South Africa from the Commonwealth put a formal end to the possibility of a transfer of administration. As late as May 1963 Maud saw the future of the three territories as 'inextricably bound up with that of the Republic', and self-determination as therefore probably 'the most difficult of all our dilemmas in Southern Africa'.[225] Geographically and economically, Basutoland was particularly problematic: could it ever aspire to real independence? Nevertheless, with the encouragement of its constitutional adviser, Professor D. V. Cowen, and its resident commissioner, A. G. T. Chaplin, this is what by 1962 it did aspire to. Modern political parties were founded in all three countries between 1959 and 1962, mainly in response to announcements of constitutional reform. Bechuanaland and Basutoland had Legislative Councils by 1961, Swaziland by 1963. Further advances were agreed in 1964 for Bechuanaland and Basutoland, though not without nervousness as to the South African reaction. The decisions were momentous, but South Africa kept quiet, and their progress was relatively smooth, leading to independence in 1966, with Swaziland following in 1968.

The five-year period between the elections of October 1959 and October 1964 had seen a remarkable set of changes to the empire and Commonwealth, as the 'wind of change' became gale-force. The momentum affected the thinking of Conservative ministers across the board, from Macleod with his doctrine of 'the lesser risk' of concessions made sooner rather than later, to Rab Butler's realisation that shows of force were not only 'inherently mistaken' but impracticable; even Julian Amery came to recognise that Britain's power of putting on the brake 'is now very limited'. Technically, in terms of a dynamic colonial policy, the quinquennium of Conservative management compares favourably with what the Liberals achieved between 1905 and 1910, and the Labour government between 1945 and 1951. As a Labour victory in the autumn of 1964 brought to a close thirteen years of Tory rule, there was a natural excitement about the prospect of fresh ways of doing things, but as far as the empire–Commonwealth was concerned, there was little scope for immediate dramatic new developments. Britain had in fact already entered the phase of residual decolonisation. This did not mean, however, that the Labour government was to be free of bad headaches in the colonial field.

[225] *CGEE*, pt 2, p. 461 (no. 462), despatch to Home, 14 May 1963.

5   'We could no longer afford to honour our pledges': the Wilson government and the end of empire, 1964–1968

'Great Britain has lost an empire and has not yet found a role'; a role based on the Commonwealth 'is about played out'.[1] These blunt and undiplomatic words of Dean Acheson, the respected retired American secretary of state (1949–53), in 1962 were received mournfully and by some officials as simply untrue. Empire might be having an euthanasian death, but, as if by way of compensation, Britain was in fact trying to make the Commonwealth work and giving its continuing international role a blood transfusion, clinging desperately to the remnants of its great-power status. Just as in the 1930s a declining position in the Far East had led to a fixation with the Singapore naval base, so now in the 1960s the loss of formal empire led psychologically to the obstinate promotion of an Indian Ocean role and a reluctance to let go of 'informal empire' East-of-Suez. As a result, defence and decolonisation in the mid-1960s were in a dysfunctional relationship. Defence arrangements were escalating and not co-ordinated with the time-tables and consequences of decolonisation. Defence plans were also increasingly out of step with what could be afforded. The underlying problem, as always, was the mismatch between actual resources and supposed requirements. Christopher Mayhew, resigning as minister for the navy, in 1966 likened British defence to a Hindu cow: it was neither fed properly nor put out of its misery.[2] This had come about as much through defects of perception as poor economic performance. Harold Wilson had a Kiplingesque notion that 'our frontiers are on the Himalayas', promising to maintain by all necessary means India's 'political and geographical integrity'.[3] There

---

[1] *The Times*, 6 December 1962; D. Brinkley, 'Dean Acheson and the "Special Relationship": the West Point speech of December 1962', *Historical Journal* (1990), vol. 33, p. 603. When Acheson subsequently spoke – during the Rhodesian crisis – of 'the stupid policy of a bewildered country under a third-rate prime minister', Wilson neatly dismissed Acheson as having 'lost a State Department and not yet found a role' (*ibid.*, p. 618).

[2] L. W. Martin, *British defence policy: the long recessional* (Adelphi Papers no. 61, 1969), p. 6.

[3] The statement was made at the opening of the Nehru Memorial Exhibition in New Delhi in June 1965. It is often quoted, without a reference, but one is given by Neville Brown, *Arms without empire: British defence role in the modern world* (1967), p. 55, quoting *The Guardian*, 11 June 1965 (see J. Darwin, *Britain and decolonisation* (1998), p. 291).

were echoes of 'the Great Game' here, but it was surely by now a geopolitical fantasy. (Indians were definitely not impressed by this unsolicited
revival of the Pax Britannica). However, though the retreat from Aden and
Southern Arabia might be characterised as an abject abdication, elsewhere
– and again, as if by way of some compensation – the Labour government
had no intention of simply liquidating all its remaining responsibilities.[4]
Wilson continued to produce his grandiloquent incantations, 'we are a
world power and a world influence or we are nothing'. Macmillan had also
sometimes talked in this way. The difference was that Wilson actually
seemed to believe his own rhetoric.[5]

Dean Acheson's remarks were resented in part because British policy-
makers did not think themselves too slow to respond imaginatively
to changed circumstances. British governments actively sought a new
role through membership of the EEC. The first application was by
Macmillan's government in 1962, the second by Wilson's in the middle of
1967. Both applications failed, with de Gaulle delivering his second veto
in November 1967 ('for the British Isles really to moor themselves alongside the Continent, a very vast and very deep transformation is still
required').[6] It could be argued that Britain was not missing any buses realistically available, and that the applications were far-sighted but essentially premature. True, these approaches were inspired at least in part by
imperial and economic decline. Nevertheless, the Commonwealth should
not be seen as obsolescent in Acheson's sense, or as it so often has been
seen by historians, as a fatal impediment or distraction. Rather, the
Commonwealth was then still at the core of British 'official mind' cosmology, and of external activity, throwing up nasty problems requiring urgent
attention in a way that Europe did not. Indeed, it was precisely this continuing concatenation of intractable problems (especially the financially
crippling East-of-Suez role, a sterling crisis, and the political consequences of Rhodesian UDI in 1965) which created the pressure for the
second application. The Commonwealth thus provided an unavoidable
context, and determined the mindset within which most of the debate
about the European option took place and the terms of entry were discussed. No less than Macmillan and the Conservatives, Wilson and his
team still broadly hoped to use the EEC as a prop to the Commonwealth
rather than as a replacement. There need not, they hoped, be a conflict of
interest. If Europe could be an 'outward-looking' community, and

[4] S. R. Ashton and W. R. Louis, eds., *East of Suez and the Commonwealth, 1964–1971* (in
three parts, BDEEP, 2004: hereafter cited as *ESC*).
[5] J. Frankel, *British foreign policy, 1945–1973* (1975), p. 85.
[6] *ESC*, pt 2, p. 42 (no. 144).

enhance existing British policies in the world by 'exerting a more powerful and effective influence', then that would fit their objectives quite well. Britain would add 'the strength and the balance to play the role in the world which the importance of Europe warrants'. But de Gaulle would have none of it.[7] (See further below, pp. 340–3.)

The government remained determined to join Europe. This was from 1968 linked in parallel with withdrawal East-of-Suez, concentrating on the defence of Europe in partnership with the USA as part of an overall geopolitical reappraisal which would 'make Europe the centre of policy'.[8] With unrelenting pressure from financial imperatives, recall of the legions in January 1968 enabled commitments belatedly to be brought into line with capabilities.

Although in a technical sense the empire was not entirely finished by 1968, its rulers were thereafter only playing out a coda. The Conservative government after 1970 stalled on East-of-Suez withdrawal, but all troops were finally out by 1976, pretty much as envisaged by their predecessors in 1967. If one examined the runes, the ultimate destinies of Rhodesia and Hong Kong could hardly be in doubt, however hard it would be to get to 1980 in the case of the former, or however long it took to get to 1997 for the latter. If a Falklands War (1982) could not have been seriously predicted, that in itself is indicative, and it was in truth only a bizarre footnote to empire, a marginal atavistic gesture, however blustery and costly. British adjustment to the end of empire is an important subject in its own right, but outside the scope of this study.[9] And so 1968 forms the natural terminus for this account, the year not only marking the demise of the CRO and the end of imperial pretensions of East-of-Suez, but the year in which Swaziland gained its independence, the last in the main linked sequence of British African colonies. It did so almost without anybody noticing, and in an extraordinary mode contrary to everything a Labour government can have believed in. The government was hardly able to determine the future in monarchical Swaziland any more than it had been able to for Marxist Aden (South Yemen).

---

[7] *ESC*, pt 2, pp. 13–14 (no. 139), joint Cabinet memo by Wilson and Brown, 16 March 1967. There is a most important essay by P. R. Alexander, 'The Labour government, Commonwealth policy and the second application to join the EEC, 1964–1967', in Alex May, ed., *Britain, the Commonwealth and Britain's application to join the European Communities* (2001), ch. 8, pp. 132–55.

[8] CAB 129/136, C(68)42, memo by Brown, 23 February 1968.

[9] For an early and still unsurpassed (and probably unsurpassable) analysis of the pathology of Thatcherism in the context of the end of empire, see Nicholas Boyle, 'Understanding Thatcherism', in *Who are we now? Christian humanism and the global market from Hegel to Heaney* (Notre Dame, Indiana, 1998), pp. 13–34, first published in *New Blackfriars*, vol. 69, no. 818 (1988) pp. 307–24.

Which reminds us that the performance of the Labour government over a range of colonial and Commonwealth issues was surprising to most people and disappointing to many. It seldom lived up to expectations. As one historian has written, 'it appeared to compromise, to vacillate, and sometimes to be less than honest and honourable'. Even apart from the mess in Rhodesia after UDI, its response to the tragic Nigerian civil war (1967–1970) 'seemed cynical where it was not uncertain'.[10] Not only did it not repeal the restrictive Commonwealth Immigrants Act (1962), but tightened it yet further. Callaghan restricted the right of Kenyan Asians who had retained British citizenship to enter the UK. Imposed human resettlement in order to build an Anglo-American military facility in Diego Garcia was a shock, while the use of proportional representation and suspect co-operation with the Americans in order to keep Dr Jagan out of power in British Guiana also dismayed left-wing opinion. The government was criticised for falling short of its proclaimed desire to promote aid and development and to tackle Third World poverty. There was a new ministerial mantra now: 'we can no longer afford . . .'. Principles seemed to be sacrificed all along the line, or to get submerged in the interests of tough, 'realistic', traditional policies which seemed barely distinguishable from Conservative ones.[11] Contradictory pressures between acting on moral principles or the dictates of pragmatism make the debates of the Wilson Cabinet of special interest. High-minded opposition to racism emerged as a salient characteristic of this government, a government almost excessively alive to its potential dangers, but agreement on principles fractured here too, not only on political and economic considerations with respect to South Africa and Rhodesia, but in Britain itself as immigration became more of a problem. Bipartisan continuity of policy continued to register many victories, leaving a sense of Labour strategies muddled in execution.[12]

---

[10] D, Judd, *Empire: the British imperial experience from 1765 to the present* (1996), ch.23, 'Rhodesia's Unilateral Declaration of Independence, November 1965: variable winds of change and Wilson's Labour government, 1964 to 1970', pp. 372–400, is an interesting short introduction. See also L. J. Butler, *Britain and Empire: adjusting to a post-imperial world* (2002), ch.6, 'Imperial aftermath', pp. 171–88. For an analysis of expectations on taking office, see P. Catterall, 'Foreign and Commonwealth policy in Opposition: the Labour Party', in W. Kaiser and G. Staerck, eds., *British foreign policy, 1955–1964: contracting options* (2000), pp. 61–88

[11] C. Wrigley, '"Now you see it, now you don't": Harold Wilson's foreign policy, 1964–1970', in R. Coopey, S. Fielding, and N. Tiratsoo, eds., *The Wilson governments, 1964–1970* (1993), pp.123–35.

[12] J. W. Young, *The Labour governments, 1964–1970*, vol. II, *International policy* (2003); this is a particularly fine study, with clear discussion of conflicting viewpoints, and solidly based on the archives.

1. Mentalities and priorities

After Macmillan's retirement, Harold Wilson was the dominant political figure in British politics from 1963 until 1976. He was Britain's first grammar-school prime minister, brought up as a Congregationalist in religion. He remained a man of much personal kindness and natural modesty. He projected a northern lower-middle-class homeliness, his pipe as much a trade-mark as it had been for Baldwin, or as ever a cigar had been for Winston Churchill.[13] Wilson began his career as an economics don, then became a wartime Whitehall technocrat, before becoming an MP in 1945 and a Cabinet minister at the age of thirty-one in 1947, as president of the Board of Trade. Brilliant with statistics, his mind was nimble but narrow in range and interests (he loved railway timetables). He was hard-working and well-informed, but obsessed with tactics. A bouncy resilience made him seem an inconsistent and zigzagging opportunist, who did not like forward-thinking.[14] Instant problem-solving was what he liked, but he was notoriously devoid of political principles: 'light ideological baggage', in Roy Jenkins's caustic phrase, 'almost excessively lacking in dogma and doctrine'. However, Wilson did have two commitments, one greater, one lesser. The greater loyalty was a passionate belief in Israel, about which he wrote 'one of the most strongly Zionist tracts ever written by a non-Jew' (Jenkins again), *The chariot of Israel* (1981).[15] His government was committed to Israel in a way far removed from that of Attlee and Bevin. The lesser commitment was to the Commonwealth, which he believed had a continuing economic potential, and for which he showed a genuine fondness. Indeed, he has been called 'an Old Commonwealth sentimentalist'.[16] This was partly because he loved New Zealand lamb, partly because he disliked racialism, partly because he was proud to be able to claim forty-three close relations living in Australia, where he spent six months as a schoolboy in 1927. Wilson came into office with a greater enthusiasm for the Commonwealth than Macmillan and Douglas-Home seemed to have. In May 1963 he had as leader of the Opposition suggested a ten-point programme for the Commonwealth, with an emphasis on developing trade and economic relationships. In

---

[13] John Vincent, review of Austen Morgan, *Harold Wilson* (1992), in *Sunday Telegraph*, 7 June 1992, p. xi.

[14] P. Hennessy, *The prime minister: the office and its holders since 1945* (2000), pp. 323–4.

[15] R. Jenkins, 'Wilson, (James) Harold', *ODNB*, vol. LIX, pp. 544–55. This is more helpful than J. P. Macintosh's essay in *British prime ministers in the 20th century*, vol. II, (1978), pp. 171–215, which is almost entirely about domestic policy.

[16] B. Donoughue, 'Harold Wilson and the renegotiation of the EEC terms of membership, 1974–1975' in B. Brivati and H. Jones, eds., *From reconstruction to integration: Britain and Europe since 1945* (Leicester, 1993), p. 204.

February 1965 he issued a directive to examine reversing the trend towards a falling proportion of British trade with the Commonwealth. On both occasions officials were dismissive of his ideas.[17] Paradoxically, in comparison with Macmillan and Home, he had only a superficial grasp of imperial affairs.

His high hopes for the Commonwealth were smashed by bitter experience. Initially he enjoyed the apparent togetherness of the prime ministers' club and his contacts with Afro-Asians, but severe disenchantment set in, especially after the acrimonious Prime Ministers' Meeting in September 1966, at which he was subjected to a barrage of gross and vicious abuse over failure to resolve the Rhodesian problem. Though Wilson himself at this meeting remained cool and quietly patient, gone was the restrained atmosphere even of 1961 when South Africa's departure was discussed.[18]

Wilson believed in a beneficent British imperial and global role, as a unique and distinctive function, 'an influence', as he put it, 'for good and an influence for peace'.[19] Shortly after his first official visit to the USA, in a speech on foreign affairs to the Commons (16 December 1964), he emphasised how 'all our Commonwealth history and connections mean that Britain can provide for the Alliances and for the world peacekeeping role a contribution which no other country, not excluding America, can provide'. He went on to attack those who disagreed, 'defeatists in this country and some cynics abroad', and then tied in the moral aspects of the deployment of power: 'We cannot maintain a world role by military strength alone . . . acceptance of the British role depends on the image we present in our relations with foreign and Commonwealth countries', which should show them loyally 'that we are at one with them in the things that matter to them – in fighting oppression and racialism'. These were, he continued, issues of 'transcendent importance' at a time of great international fluidity (more than once he referred to the recent Chinese detonation of a nuclear device). The government's conclusion 'from the first, long cool look at this whole problem' was that the triple contribution to NATO, Europe, and 'East-of-Suez' was in danger of fatally weakening the economy, 'and correspondingly weakening our real defences'. 'The plain fact is we have been trying to do too much', with defence expenditure running at 7.1 per cent of GNP. Yet, as commentators have often pointed out, there was an unresolved tension between this and the rhetoric that 'no-one in this House or indeed in the country, will wish to give up or call

---

[17] *ESC*, pt 3, pp. 444–5 (no.396), 7 April 1965; R.G. Casey, *The future of the Commonwealth* (1963), stresses the lack of Conservative interest, pp. 10–11.

[18] *ESC*, pt 2, p. 364 (no. 254), MacDonald's despatch, 9 December 1966.

[19] P. Darby, *British defence policy East of Suez, 1947–1968* (Oxford, 1973), p. 283.

in question' Britain's world role. Least of all was that tension moderated by the hint that it might be necessary 'in certain respects to develop our strength', although in a 'cost-effective way'. There could be no abdication from 'our duty to the Commonwealth and to world peace'.[20]

The new prime minister went out of his way to declare that the political emancipation of colonies had been 'inevitable and desirable', but like Attlee before him Wilson was anxious to avoid charges of 'scuttle'. Clearly, too he cared deeply about retaining as much as possible of Britain's world-power status and the prestige it might convey. 'Put brutally, this meant that he wanted to be head-prefect to Lyndon B. Johnson's headmaster', only too willing to meet American urgings to maintain the parity of sterling and an East-of-Suez role.[21] This role was in many ways a function of giving priority to the supposedly 'special relationship' with the USA, a proof of the claim to have a 'seat at the top table'. Thus in key respects, fundamental continuities through changes of British government were once again well to the fore.

Wilson's team in foreign and colonial affairs was meant to be headed by the well-qualified if somewhat dowdy and tactless Patrick Gordon Walker. In the event, grim electoral fiascos relieved him of office after three months, though he seems to have continued to offer advice on overseas policy. (He returned to the Cabinet in January 1967 as minister without portfolio.) He was succeeded at the Foreign Office by the solid and uncharismatic Michael Stewart, the proverbial 'safe pair of hands', if ever there was one, at least from a civil service perspective, though his austere schoolmasterly manner and right-wing *real-politik* made him unpopular with the left. Stewart was replaced for a while (August 1966 to March 1968) by George Brown, a maverick and controversial figure, imaginative but oafish, a working-class South Londoner who spectacularly rejected the temperance ethic commonly expected of Labour politicians of his provenance. Brown admired Bevin, naturally, and perhaps more ominously, Palmerston. His relations with his officials were volatile, and he was always complaining about 'the old protocol-ridden regime' at the FO. Brown was strongly pro-European, sceptical of the relationship with the USA, and not much concerned about the Commonwealth. He was also pro-Arab, pro-Egyptian and anti-Israel, which to some extent circumscribed Wilson's deep commitment to a pro-Israeli position.[22]

[20] *PD, Commons* vol.704, cc. 424–6, 16 December, foreign affairs debate.

[21] Jenkins, *ODNB*, vol. LIX, p. 551.

[22] See *ODNB* for entries on Gordon Walker (by R. D. Pearce), vol. LVI, pp. 880–3; Stewart (by Tam Dalyell), vol. LII, pp. 734–5; Brown (by K. Whitton), vol. VIII, pp. 36–40; Bottomley (by D.Goldsworthy), vol. VI, pp. 764–5; Greenwood (by K. O. Morgan), vol. XXIII, pp. 620–1.

The first of the secretaries of state at the CO was 'Tony' Greenwood, the privileged son of a former Labour Party deputy leader and Cabinet minister. As a young man Greenwood had supported Indian independence, Zionism, and a ban on hunting. As a minister, he was preoccupied by Aden. Despite his travels to trouble-spots, it quickly became apparent that he lacked grip and assertiveness. He was demoted to the Ministry of Overseas Development in December 1965. Greenwood's opposite number at the CRO, Arthur Bottomley, was another Wilson henchman. Bottomley was one of the last of the old-style Labour trades-unionist politicians with little formal education. A schoolboy protégé of Attlee's in Walthamstow, he started out as an office-boy and railway-carriage cleaner; in 1946 Attlee made him under-secretary of state for the dominions. Bottomley became really interested in overseas problems; in opposition he travelled to Kenya, Ghana and Cyprus. At the CRO he had the misfortune to have to deal mainly with the Rhodesian problem. His open and straightforward nature, simplicity even, was not an asset in dealing with the doggedly devious Ian Smith. He was succeeded by Henry Bowden, and finally by Gorge Thomson, the most effective of the three, until his office was merged with the Foreign Office in October 1968.

Two other ministers were to be influential upon colonial policy, the left-winger Oxford graduate Barbara Castle at the newly created Ministry of Overseas Development, and James Callaghan at the Treasury. Callaghan had a good knowledge of overseas problems; he had served in Asia during the war with the navy, and for five years (1956–61) had been Opposition spokesman on colonial affairs, travelling to almost all parts of the Commonwealth and establishing a range of contacts with nationalist leaders. His outlook was similar to Macleod's, and he was no great enthusiast for Europe.[23]

Ministerial views were of course moulded to an extraordinary extent – extraordinary to them, that is – by their civil servants. They came into office not entirely naive, but nevertheless amazed by the influence of officials, not least in determining and recording the terms of Cabinet debate and decision.[24] Barbara Castle recalled, 'I had not realised how completely the civil service was in control', and how determined to keep it that way through 'departmental brainwashing', successfully talking

---

[23] K. O. Morgan, *Callaghan: a life* (1997), esp. pp. 136–43, 165, 180; and 'Imperialists at bay: the British Labour Party and decolonisation', *JICH*, vol. 27 (1999), pp. 233–54, repr. in R. D. King and R. W. Kilson, eds., *The statecraft of British imperialism: essays in honour of Wm Roger Louis* (1999).

[24] A. Howard, ed., *The Crossman diaries: selections from the diaries of a Cabinet minister, 1964–1970* (1979), pp. 84–7 (18 April 1965).

ministers into upholding the 'departmental interest'.[25] The anti-empire animus of some ministers – in such sharp contrast to Attlee's team – was thus held in check.

Among the proconsuls, some veterans were brought back, such as Humphrey Trevelyan to Aden and Hugh Foot at the United Nations. Foot was elevated to the peerage as Lord Caradon and given the status of minister of state at the FO, in order, as Wilson put it, 'to act as it were as a conscience, as a goad, to persuade us to reconsider our policies'.[26] The term 'Caradonian' came to signify total commitment to the UN, to peace and decolonisation.[27] Malcolm MacDonald was an elder statesman of the most useful kind – apart, perhaps, from the prolixity of his reports. He was now established as the most literate 'empire' minister and proconsul of his generation. He had been in charge of the Dominions Office from 1935 to 1938, and of the Colonial Office from 1938 to 1940, and left his mark on policy (see above, pp. 85–7). After nine years serving in South-East Asia, where he had become almost the 'fourth white raja' of Sarawak, his historical importance as a central figure in the progress of decolonisation was apparent.[28] He was then the last governor of Kenya, from 1963 to 1964, bringing his genius to bear on winning the trust of Kenyatta and Mboya. Wilson appointed him as roving ambassador in Africa, from 1967 to 1969, where his friendly sympathies (and casual dress) were effectively deployed, especially with any leaders he could interest in ornithology. Nevertheless he found the assignment difficult and uncomfortable. 'It is quite a job', he wrote to his wife, 'trying to cope with the affairs of a dozen different countries in different parts of eventful Africa.' Privately, too, he was never entirely convinced that the Wilson government's good intentions for emerging nations matched his own.[29] Africans might be making appalling mistakes, but should, he thought, be treated patiently, and their 'grand elemental human qualities' recognised, such as their natural friendliness and the fact that they had little innate sense of racial discrimination and were generally much less wedded to theories and ideologies than Asians (or even many Europeans).[30]

---

[25] Barbara Castle, *Fighting all the way* (1993), pp. 340–1. J. Lynn and A. Jay, *The complete 'Yes, Minister': the diaries of a Cabinet minister, by James Hacker* (revd edn, 1984) draws particular inspiration from the Wilson years, via Marcia Falkender and Bernard Donoughue (P. Riddell, review of B. Donoughue, *Downing Street diary: with Harold Wilson in No. 10* (2005), in *Times Literary Supplement*, no. 5337, 15 July 2005, p. 8).

[26] Harold Wilson, *The Labour government. 1964–1970: a personal record* (1971), p. 11.

[27] W. R. Louis, 'Public enemy Number One: the British empire in the dock at the United Nations, 1957–1971', in M. Lynn, ed., *The British empire in the 1950s: retreat or revival?* (2006), p. 197.

[28] Clyde Sanger, *Malcolm MacDonald: bringing an end to empire* (Liverpool, 1995), p. 322.

[29] P. Lyon, 'MacDonald, Malcolm', *ODNB*, vol. XXXV, pp. 260–3.

[30] *ESC*, pt 2, p. 254 (no. 215), to CRO, 17 January 1966.

When all is said and done, the dominant mentality of Wilson's government was the inability to shake off the delusions of grandeur and desire to play the international stage. From the perspective of a self-confessed 'fanatical Little Englander', Richard Crossman (minister of housing and local government until 1966 when he became lord president of the Council) consistently stood for an alternative world view, a policy of 'England the offshore island' against Wilson's 'futile attempts to keep Great Britain great'. Crossman felt Wilson was encouraged in this by George Brown particularly, but also by the Cabinet secretary, Burke Trend. 'They all seem unaware that they are figures of fun as long as Britain is on the edge of economic ruin.'[31]

Turning now to the priorities of the Labour ministers, two issues in particular raised big questions of moral position and allegiance: arms sales to South Africa, and possible entry into Europe.

(1) Arms sales to South Africa

After the Sharpeville shootings of 1960 and the departure of South Africa from the Commonwealth in 1961, British opinion turned even more sharply against the Afrikaner regime and its apartheid policies.[32] Wilson came into office with a promise to end all arms sales to South Africa. Implementation of this clear commitment was far from straightforward.[33] The previous government had agreed in 1962 to a deal (worth about £25 million) to allow the sale of sixteen Buccaneer naval strike aircraft to the South African navy (not on the face of it suitable for use in internal repression). Within a day or two of taking office Wilson issued an instruction 'that all shipments of arms to South Africa should cease forthwith'. Brown and Gordon Walker immediately complained – quite rightly – that this was over-hasty.[34] Gordon Walker pointed out the danger of South African retaliation against the vulnerable High Commission Territories. Over-flying rights across South Africa were essential for access to the Territories, as indeed was recognised by the Cabinet. Moreover, there were economic arguments, put by Callaghan and Brown, that Britain could not afford to lose either the Buccaneer contract for aircraft already built, or the South African market in general. There were strategic arguments that Simon's Town was essential to the performance of an

---

[31] Howard, ed., *The Crossman diaries: selections*, pp. 238 (22 October 1966), 358 (9 November 1967), 372 (26 November 1967), 411 (17 March 1968).
[32] R. Hyam and P. J. Henshaw, *The lion and the springbok: Britain and South Africa since the Boer War* (2003), pp. 319–23.
[33] J. W. Young, 'The Wilson government and the debate over arms to South Africa in 1964', *Contemporary British History*, vol.12 (1998), pp. 62–86.
[34] PREM 13/92, 17–19 October 1964.

East-of-Suez role, and Verwoerd seemed to be muttering threateningly about the Simon's Town agreements, on which the effectiveness of the Cape route to the east depended.[35]

The sale of the Buccaneers went through. Apart from this, and with perhaps something of the purity and daring open only to an incoming government in the first flush of victory and office, ideological principles prevailed. The export trade would have to forgo a potential boost. The prime minister made a statement in the Commons on 17 November 1964 to the effect that 'from today' there would be no new contracts and all outstanding defence-procurement licences with South Africa would be revoked, except where known to relate directly to current contracts with the South African government. This was, he said, in order to fulfil Britain's obligations to the United Nations and to bring policy into line with UN resolutions. In answer to a question he further declared that his government would base itself on 'international morality'.[36]

There are parallels here with the termination of further contracts for Chinese Labour on the Witwatersrand by the incoming Liberal government of December 1905. In both cases the debate was fierce and contentious, moral issues colliding with pressures towards continuity of policy and honouring the commitments of predecessor governments. Concessions to practical realities had to be made.[37] Just as the Liberals in 1906 had let existing contracts run their course, so the Labour government allowed Buccaneer sales to go ahead. Wilson tried hard to fulfil his pledges, exploring thoroughly the possibilities of alternative foreign purchasers, but no such alternative could be found.

A major challenge to the 'ethical policy' of 1964 was mounted in the autumn of 1967 and it proved to be highly divisive.[38] The South African government submitted a list of equipment it was likely to need in order to play its role under the Simon's Town agreements. The three main departments concerned with the issue of selling arms to South Africa (the FO, CRO, and MoD) were by September 1967 all in agreement that 'a major switch' in this policy was essential. They persuaded their ministers to re-open the question in Cabinet and seek a repudiation of the statement of November 1964. Was a blanket ban serving geopolitical and cold war interests? Denis Healey (minister of defence, 1964–1970) wanted a more

---

[35] CAB 128/39, CC 10(64), Cabinet minutes, 24 November 1964.

[36] *PD, Commons* vol. 702, cc. 199–207, 17 November 1964.

[37] R. Hyam, *Elgin and Churchill at the Colonial Office, 1905–1908* (1968), pp. 59–78.

[38] T. Bale, 'A "deplorable episode"? South African arms sales and the statecraft of British Social Democracy', *Labour History Review*, vol. 62 (1997), pp. 22–40 – not based on archives, but insightful. For the archives, see *ESC*, pt 3, pp. 328–9, 341–8, 377–84.

'realistic' policy which would revive the Conservative distinction between weapons for internal use in suppressing the blacks and those of external value to Commonwealth concerns. This distinction, Stewart pointed out, was a very tricky one to operate. Brown was preoccupied with the economic situation after devaluation in July 1967. Thomson recognised that 'it is the domestic political opposition to any change of policy that must be weighed against the economic damage'.[39] Brown and Healey submitted a joint memorandum. This argued that refusal of the South African request for naval equipment would adversely affect Anglo-South African relations as a whole, with the possible loss of staging, storage and overflying facilities, communications and surveillance, thus impairing operational flexibility and generally weakening any influence on South Africa; and all this apart from the valuable orders involved and the possible adverse effect on the trading position, which could lead to severe and 'probably irretrievable' commercial and economic losses. As against these arguments they acknowledged Lord Caradon's insistence that a reversal of the ban would put Britain 'in the doghouse' indefinitely, since the attitude on arms for South Africa was fundamental to the whole British situation at the UN. Brown and Healey conceded that there were thus 'clear and serious disadvantages' either way; but argued that the political disadvantages could be retrieved with time, and therefore 'the consequences of a refusal of the South African request are thus likely to be more lasting and damaging for our real interests'.[40]

Wilson, however, proclaimed himself 'irrevocably opposed' to the sale of arms. If economic concerns were to be raised 'regardless of wider overseas policy issues, regardless of moral issues', then they must at least be subjected to wide and rigorous examination and justification on merit.[41] Moreover, he believed that it would lead to the resignation of at least six (junior) members of the government, and it would alienate Labour supporters to a point where the government with its slender majority might not survive. Wilson was strongly supported by Stewart: 'the greatest issue in world politics in the future was race', and 'we were opting out of that great issue if we accepted George [Brown]'s proposal and submitted ourselves to the politics of pure expediency and opportunism'.[42] The resumption of arms sales would, he thought, destroy any vestige of the multi-racial Commonwealth. He was probably the minister who said that supplying the equipment would put Britain against 'the overwhelming majority of the United Nations', and who later warned the Defence and

[39] *ESC*, pt 3, pp. 328–9, minute, 5 March 1967 (no.369).
[40] *ESC*, pt 3, pp. 342–8 (no.375), memo, 11 September 1967.
[41] Wilson, *Labour government*, pp. 470–9.
[42] *Crossman diaries*, pp. 330–1, 14 September 1967.

Oversea Policy Committee that 'the moral issue involved was so important and our commitment to it so deep' that Britain must not supply arms.[43]

The embargo remained under serious attack from a powerful group of ministers. Callaghan attacked it as inhibiting measures which would right the stricken balance of payments. Brown declared that although he recognised the moral case and shared the general repugnance for apartheid, contracts worth as much as £300 million were at stake. Other ministers, too, agreed that 'in our present economic circumstances we could no longer afford to act as the world's conscience' and supplying arms did not mean condoning apartheid. As against that, it was pointed out that the ban had not so far noticeably damaged trade, and the change of policy was a big one, which would set Britain against the overwhelming majority at the UN. Wilson insisted that 'not only the government's political and economic credibility were at issue but also its moral credibility'; to agree would be contrary to the principles the government stood for, and if they acted to carry economic credibility with industry they would risk being pushed into other policies advocated by the Opposition and thus lose all political credibility.[44]

Rumours of a Cabinet row leaked out, and alarm spread in the Parliamentary Party. A major revolt seemed in prospect if there was a change of policy. This emotive crisis came to the boil just before Christmas 1967. Wilson's style of government got tangled up with it, partly because he was thought to have back-tracked and misled Brown as to his opinion. Wilson became angry. Not just because he thought those who opposed him so wrong, but because of inaccurate, tendentious and prejudiced reports that he had been defeated in Cabinet. Opinion was in fact fairly evenly divided. The 'junta of right-wing heavyweights' – Brown, Healey, Callaghan, and Gordon Walker – wanted change. Stewart, Castle, Gardiner, Greenwood, and Benn supported the prime minister's stand on existing policy. The tense Cabinet meeting on 15 December 1967 was variously described as 'sulphurous' (Gordon Walker), 'the most unpleasant meeting I have ever attended' (Healey), and one in which 'the knives were really out' (Castle). Crossman and Jenkins would have preferred a compromise delaying-tactic.[45] However, Wilson played the press and the moralism of the Party

---

[43] CAB 148/30, OPD 39(67)4, 8 December 1967.
[44] *ESC*, pt 3, pp. 377–81 (no.378), Cabinet minutes, 15 December 1967.
[45] *Crossman diaries*, pp. 374–82, 13–18 December 1967; R. D. Pearce, ed., *Patrick Gordon Walker: political diaries, 1932–1971* (1991), pp. 317–18, 23 December 1967; D. Healey, *The time of my life* (1989), p. 338; Barbara Castle, *The Castle diaries, 1964–1970* (1984), p. 339.

skilfully, and persuaded the Cabinet that his authority – and theirs – required the settlement of the issue forthwith. According to the minutes: 'It was generally recognised that in the present situation no other decision was politically possible . . . Delay would merely provide further opportunity for public opinion to be mobilised against the Government.'[46] In the end only Brown and Healey were still objecting. On 18 December Wilson announced that there would be no change. Next day, Stewart made an impassioned speech in the Commons. They were dealing with 'some of the very greatest issues of world politics and of human affairs'. Although not explicitly pillorying South Africa, he argued that 'tyrannies based on race are at this time particularly dangerous'. After two centuries of racial exploitation and two world wars using black soldiers in 'white men's quarrels', they could not expect 'the world to be the same again. That is why the whole question ferments so intensely'. People must understand 'how great, how terrible, and, if things go ill, how deadly, an issue this could be.' What they had to do now was to work for reconciliation between the white and coloured races. In this context, 'one's attitude towards *apartheid* is crucial', because its peculiarity was making white and black live separately and do so permanently, which could only lead to disaster. And so, Stewart concluded, 'on every issue, morality, ultimate wisdom, and the truest expediency in the long run for this country – our policy was right three years ago and is right now'.[47]

The incoming Conservative government in June 1970 took a different view, and announced its intention to renew (limited) arms sales.[48]

(2) Entry into Europe?

By contrast with the South African issue, Wilson's mind on Europe was notoriously elusive and evasive. His principal private secretary, Oliver Wright, advised him in January 1966 about Europe in the context of foreign policy as a whole. Although Wright felt the moment was not right for joining Europe, that moment might come in the future. One possible scenario was failure to resolve the Rhodesian problem, in which case, 'public opinion in this country would undergo a revulsion from

---

[46] *ESC*, pt 3, 381–4 (no. 379), meeting, 18 December 1967.

[47] *PD, Commons*, vol. 756, cc.1152–8, 19 December 1967.

[48] *ESC*, pt 3, pp. 399–404 (no.384), 17 August 1970, despatch from the ambassador, Sir A. Snelling. If Heath had gone ahead with large sales of arms to South Africa, 'he would have done even more damage to Britain's standing and influence in the world than Anthony Eden did through the invasion of Suez, 1956': Arnold Smith (with C. Sanger), *Stitches in time: the Commonwealth in world politics* (1981), p. 205 – that, from the Commonwealth secretary-general, is a measure of the seriousness of the issue.

[Commonwealth] responsibilities and would seek refuge in a form of Euro-chauvinism'.[49]

This does indeed seem to be what happened in Wilson's own mind. If Britain got enmeshed in an economic war of attrition with Rhodesia, EEC membership might become essential for maintaining the British financial position and restoring international confidence in the economy. Barbara Castle's comment was, 'It was knowledge of the appalling dangers which faced us in Rhodesia that prevented any serious opposition to the new approach' over Europe.[50] Crisis meetings were held in mid-July 1966. With the financial position so gloomy, several ministers now made a strategic switch from Commonwealth to Europe. Sir Con O'Neill from the FO perspective assumed that ministers were mainly interested in joining the EEC 'as an effort to strengthen the base from which we exert world influence', and that membership was intended to 'reverse the inward looking and third force tendencies' in the EEC. O'Neill seems to have reflected directly the approach of Michael Stewart.[51]

According to Hugh Cudlipp, editor of the *Daily Mirror*, 'Wilson's discovery of Europe was a gigantic red herring "to distract attention from Rhodesia and the economic mess at home"'.[52] Retrospectively, Oliver Wright came to a not dissimilar conclusion: 'I think he took to the Common Market *faute de mieux*, a matter of the head rather than the heart'; Rhodesia had made Wilson realise that 'the Commonwealth could no longer be regarded as a source of power'. Certainly, for Wilson, never an idealistic pro-European, and anxious not to wreck Commonwealth trade, 'the economic arguments for joining seemed finely balanced'. He was well aware, too of how the question linked to the East-of-Suez defence cuts. It was hoped that these cuts could renew confidence in sterling and undermine the French government's argument that Britain had too many extra-European commitments to be suited to membership. However, it may well be the case that Wilson did not overcome his misgivings about the impact of the EEC on the Commonwealth and the balance of payments, but instead gave priority to the unity of the Cabinet and the management of the Party, by allowing the application to proceed, knowing it was likely to fail.[53]

---

[49] PREM 13/905, Wright to prime minister, 28 January 1966.
[50] CAB 128/41/3, CC 55(66)1, Cabinet meeting, 9 November 1966; *The Castle diaries, 1964–1970*, p. 183, 9 November 1966; see also Douglas Jay, *Change and fortune; a political record* (1980), p. 368: Europe became a useful distraction from Rhodesia and the economy.   [51] CAB 148/69, OPD(0) (66)24, 29 July 1966.
[52] Cecil King, *The Cecil King diary, 1965–1970* (1972), p. 95, 10 November 1966.
[53] I rely here heavily on P. R. Alexander, 'The Commonwealth and European integration: competing commitments for Britain, 1956–1967: (unpublished Cambridge PhD dissertation, 2000), pp. 253–73, and appendix 2, p. ii (J. O. Wright to dissertation

There was, however, never a clear majority of the Cabinet strongly in favour of joining the EEC, and much of the case was vaguely presented. The running was made mainly by the FO, where officials increasingly maintained that exclusively British interests should take priority when policy issues had to be decided; the moral case for overseas responsibilities and aid did not impress them.[54]

The crucial Cabinet decision was on 30 April 1967. Signalling its historical importance, the minutes are unusually long, though with the exception of the foreign secretary, opinions recorded were not attributed. Brown outlined the options, and stressed that he believed membership of the Community 'would give us far greater opportunities in foreign policy in relation to Western Europe, to Europe as a whole, and to the rest of the world'. The addition of a European connection to existing links with the USA and the Commonwealth 'would give us opportunities for political leadership which would not exist if we remained in isolation'. The minutes recorded nine arguments against an immediate application, and six in favour; 'The balance of opinion in the Cabinet proved however to be substantially in favour of making an immediate application for entry unaccompanied by conditions.' If the economic consequences of joining proved to be no more than evenly balanced, 'the political advantages of joining were decisive':

If we continued in our present position we must recognise that in international politics our influence had markedly declined. For example, we had been obliged to adopt United States policies in a number of fields and even in relation to a former dependency, Guyana; the Soviet Union had been the effective mediator between India and Pakistan during the recent conflict in Kashmir; and we have been unable to discharge fully our obligations in respect of Rhodesia.

Some ministers thought British policy was becoming too closely dependent on the United States, which a large number of government supporters disliked. Others thought not joining would lead to estrangement from the USA. Most seemed to agree that 'joining the Community was essential if we were to avoid finding ourselves increasingly isolated and powerless in world affairs'. The idea was that as a member Britain could be influential in persuading the others to be more liberal and less inward-looking: 'we

Footnote 53 (cont.)
    author, 14 April 1999); and P. R. Alexander, 'The Labour government, Commonwealth policy and the second application to join the EEC, 1964–1967', in May, ed., *Britain, the Commonwealth and Britain's application to join the European Communities* ch. 8, pp. 132–55. For a different view, see H. Parr, 'A question of leadership: July 1966 and Harold Wilson's European decision', *Contemporary British History*, vol. 19 (2005) pp. 437–58. See also Jay, *Change and fortune*, pp. 384–9, 426–8.
[54] *ESC*, pt 1, intro. by S. R. Ashton, p. xxxii.

could hope to gain a new role of political leadership which would provide the political stimulus formerly given by our imperial role'. It was even suggested that entry into Europe should be regarded 'as a first step towards the ultimate ideal of world government'. The argument about safeguarding Commonwealth interests had now been subordinated to the view that Commonwealth countries were making no attempt 'to look beyond their narrow national interests'. The policies of Australia and New Zealand were cited as evidence.[55]

2. Generalities

(1) International pressures

As my analysis of decolonisation moves into its final phase, the role of international elements seems to increase, especially in their UN aspects. In 1967 a major Cabinet-level planning-paper on Africa recognised that 'our colonial policy has for long had decolonisation as its aim, and the pace of decolonisation has been strongly influenced by the increasing insistence of world opinion on the right of peoples to govern themselves'. Accordingly, Britain had been willing to break up the Central African Federation after a brief existence, and accept all the disadvantages to British interests in seeking to ensure progress towards majority rule in Rhodesia. But not all places, the paper concluded, were amenable to decolonisation, however much international opinion might think so.[56] In principle, a Labour government would want to be committed to making the UN the corner-stone of its foreign policy, promoting its prestige and effectiveness. In practice, the UN displayed such 'an impossible bias' towards independence as a cure-all for colonial problems in defiance of awkward facts, that the UN became part of Britain's problem with the residual territories. Nowhere, it seemed, was too small or insignificant to attract the attention of the United Nations. Argentina took its dispute over the Falkland Islands to it in 1964 (see below pp. 360–4). A handful of rather disreputable rebels in tiny Anguilla appealed to it in their search for disassociation with St Christopher and Nevis in 1969.[57] And so it went on.

As early as 1947 a Colonial Office official had described the situation in the UN as becoming one of 'open war', the colonial powers versus the rest. The Suez venture made matters much worse, destroying

---

[55] *ESC*, pt 2, pp. 24–37 (no. 142), Cabinet minutes, 30 April 1967.
[56] *ESC*, pt 3, pp. 348–67, 16 October 1967, 'Future policy in Africa', memo of African sub-committee of Defence and Oversea Policy Committee.
[57] *ESC*, pt 1, intro, p xciv, and pt 3, p. 109 (no. 309), note.

any reputation Britain had for 'wisdom, honesty, fair-dealing and restraint'.[58] Thereafter Britain was under suspicious scrutiny. Attacks on Britain's colonial record were humiliating, attempts by the UN to extend its influence into colonies were seen as an unmitigated nuisance. The degree of gratuitous interference could sometimes be farcical. A nice example occurred in the Cameroons, where one of the *fons* (or kings) was reported to the Trusteeship Council by the Daughters of the American Revolution for maintaining one hundred wives. Action was demanded. The British government was then severely taken to task for allowing such a thing, in other words for not being 'colonial' and paternalistic enough. The *fon* himself could not see what all the fuss was about, since he was 102 years of age. Anyhow, he complied with the UN demand to sack his wives, only to remarry some younger new women instead.[59]

More seriously, in December 1960 came the notorious Resolution 1514(XV), demanding a 'speedy and unconditional end to colonialism', and requiring target-dates to be set (see above, p. 304). Soon the FO's files exceeded 500 a year on United Nations issues alone. Tremendous effort was required behind the scenes to 'square' more than fifty delegations in line with any British position. In September 1962 all British governors were sent a government circular explaining that 'mainly for international reasons', the sooner 'we can change our public posture the better', since UN pressure was 'likely to bedevil our international position for so long as we continue to be regarded as a colonial power'. One official indeed now described the whole notion of colonial status as 'a horrible embarrassment'. The official mind-set was definitely moving 'toward a final solution' of the colonial problem.

By the time the Labour government look office the Committee of 24 (the Special Committee on Colonialism, the UN's colonial ginger-group set up to monitor progress on the 1960 resolution) was beginning to get agitated about Southern Africa, but it discussed not only the High Commission Territories and the Central African countries, but Aden, Malta, Fiji, Kenya, Zanzibar, Gambia and British Guiana. They demanded visiting missions to Aden, Fiji and British Guiana, all of which had explosively difficult problems. These visits struck chill into official hearts. It was now obvious to the CO that the Committee had 'become

---

[58] Hyam and Louis, *The Conservative government and the end of empire, 1957–1964*, pt 2, p. 404 (no. 404 [*sic*]), I. T. M. Pink (CO), 7 February 1957.

[59] Draft transcript of Witness Seminar on 'Decolonisation and the Colonial Office', at the Institute of Contemporary History, 1989, contributions by Aaron Emanuel and Sir H. Poynton, *not* printed in N. Owen, ed., in *Contemporary British History*, vol. 6 (1992). Somehow the Daughters of the American Revolution managed not to catch up with Sobhuza of Swaziland (see below, p. 380).

a political factor of importance in all delicate situations' (Jerrom). By 1965 Sir David Hunt as high commissioner to Uganda reflected 'on the spot' anxieties when he wrote that the disproportionate representation of Africa at the UN, totalling 35 votes now, was of huge significance. Hunt explained his fear of communist meddling, which could lead African countries to become 'outrageous' in their treatment of Western interests, and make life intolerable at the UN, quite apart from its local African implications. His despatch was widely circulated to high commissioners.[60] By 1965 Caradon was reporting, 'We are no doubt in for a very rough time in the United Nations this year since we shall not be able to move in the directions which the Afro-Asians wish on Southern Africa, questions on which they feel intensely.'[61]

By 1966 a full-blown crisis was in train. Sir Paul Gore-Booth, permanent under-secretary at the FO, decided 'the time for quiet reasonableness has passed': Britain should either walk out of the Committee or become more aggressive. It was the old, old dilemma. Caradon, however, would not support withdrawal. To him (as also to another minister of state, Eirene White, daughter of Thomas Jones, Lloyd George's aide), this would be an unacceptable reversal of policy signalling a symbolic reversion to the days of the Suez Crisis, re-establishing Britain as a reactionary power. 'I do not believe in walking out or running away', he declared, but preferred to fight the issues 'even with the wildest men amongst the Afro-Asians', those with what Gore-Booth called their 'unfair, destructive nonsense'.[62] Thomson at the CO again put the case for withdrawal:

We have now come practically to the end of our programme of decolonisation and we shall soon be left with territories too small and unviable to achieve independence and with a limited number of extremely difficult and delicate questions – the disputed territories of Gibraltar, Falklands, British Honduras, Fiji with its deep racial problem, Hong Kong and New Hebrides . . .

Our continued presence in the Committee of 24 erodes our authority and confuses responsibilities.

Brown, however, was advised clearly by Goronwy Roberts, minister of state in the FCO, that he should not associate himself 'with a retreat by Britain from full United Nations participation – for this is how it would look and how it would be regarded in this country and abroad'. Brown accepted the unpalatable fact that 'our difference on these questions is not just with the Committee but with the majority at the United

[60] *ESC*, pt 1, intro., p. cvi, and pt 3, pp. 297–301 (no. 359), 9 February 1965.
[61] Louis, 'Public enemy Number One', pp. 199–200.
[62] FO 371/189811, 15 February 1966 (Gore-Booth); *ESC*, pt 2, pp. 59–61 (no. 148), 11 December 1967 (Lord Caradon).

Nations'.[63] The counter-attack was mounted more boldly, but it was not until January 1971 that Britain finally broke with the Committee of 24, thus ending almost twenty years of official debate.

Apart from the UN, there was one other and entirely new supranational agency which had an effect on the emerging pressures for decolonisation, and this was the Strasbourg Court of Human Rights, operating from 1953, and before which Britain had already been hauled between 1956 and 1959 for alleged atrocities in suppressing the Cyprus revolt.[64] (See above, pp. 271–2.)

It will therefore be apparent in this account, that of the historians' trinity of forces (domestic constraints, colonial politics and international pressures), as far as the decolonisation of the formal empire is concerned, international factors were the most important. However, in the 'informal' sphere of Britain's world role it was financial weakness which proved fatal. A firm date can be ascribed to the latter (16 January 1968) but not to the former. Why? The following pages attempt an answer.

(2) Decolonisation

The colonies which became independent under the Labour government to the end of 1968 were Zambia (1964), the Gambia (1965), Guyana, Botswana, Lesotho, and Barbados (1966), Aden (1967), Mauritius and Swaziland (1968). The CO had, before Labour took office, promised or expected independence for all of these, and only in the case of Swaziland did much actual constitutional decision-making actually take place under the Labour government. To his colleagues on taking office in October 1964 Wilson decreed a policy of positive decolonisation of the formal empire. He told Greenwood he was to work himself out of a job as quickly as possible.[65] Greenwood and his under-secretary visited more than half of the remaining 31 dependent territories in the first seven months. Greenwood went to Aden and South Arabia, British Guiana, eight West Indian islands, and Mauritius, while Mrs Eirene White went to Gibraltar, the three High Commission Territories, and Fiji. Greenwood laid out his policy to the Defence and Oversea Policy Committee in May 1965. 'At this stage in our colonial history our main task must be to liquidate colonialism', giving independence to every territory which wanted it and was

---

[63] *ESC*, pt 2, pp. 64–6 (no. 149), 8 February 1968, and pp. 66–7 (no. 150), 9 February 1968 (Brown to Thomson).

[64] A. W. B. Simpson, *Human rights and the end of empire: Britain and the genesis of the European Convention* (2001, 2004), pp. 835, 1057.

[65] D. J. Morgan, *The official history of colonial development*, vol. V, *Guidance towards self-government in British colonies, 1941–1971* (1980), pp. 218, 343; *ESC*, pt 3, p. 10 (no. 283).

capable of sustaining it. Although each territory would probably need a tailor-made solution, 'nevertheless we should formulate a general policy, both to give coherence and pace to our efforts and to win understanding and support from world opinion and people in the territories themselves'.[66] However, no public declaration about the 'end of empire' was made. This is surprising, because it would have at the same time maintained, and provided the defence of, the principles of continuity (since the Conservatives had *almost* made such a declaration), as well as making a grand historical gesture.

Greenwood's main concern was to 'resist any temptation to drift', with *ad hoc* solutions for the remaining territories which all presented special difficulties. It was essential to carry international opinion, which is why he was keen to involve the UN in South Arabia, the High Commission Territories, and the Pacific islands. There might then be a fair chance of escaping criticism in the UN. To prevent a multiplicity of acts of parliament, Greenwood proposed a general enabling bill which would publicise the policy and streamline the process, and 'serve to show that we really mean business'.[67] Accordingly, the CO was at work on a paper to bring the UK 'in sight of a final liquidation of our colonial empire'. This was a development of the paper they had shown to new ministers in October 1964.[68] The draft completed in August 1965, stated the intention of bringing independence to as many as desired it and were capable of it. A strong indication was given that 'free association' as defined by the UN would be considered for most if not all of the remainder – in other words, a large measure of internal self-government, then voluntary association with an independent state. Greenwood's hope was that his paper would 'modernise the relationship between this country and its remaining dependencies' and explain to parliament 'our general colonial policy', which was based on the belief that 'the colonial relationship is intrinsically undesirable'. A way must be found to deflect international criticism from which even France, Holland, New Zealand, and the United States were free, by removing the 'stigma of colonialism'.[69]

The FO was worried that 'decolonisation' was becoming too automatic and habitual. Britain must not deprive itself of islands deliberately acquired (not in a 'fit of absence of mind'), pieces of 'real estate of potential strategic value'. Nor should they create a 'rash of tiny independent islands' in the Caribbean. They must be careful not to abdicate at the wrong moment, like the Belgians had done in the Congo, or let

---

[66] *ESC*, pt 3, pp. 1–10 (no. 282), 31 May 1965.
[67] *ESC*, pt 3, pp. 30–5 (no. 285), circular, 18 August 1965.
[68] *Conservative government, 1957–1964*, pt 1, pp. 211–25 (nos. 46 and 49).
[69] *ESC*, pt 3, pp. 41–7 (no. 287), 14 September 1965, memo by Greenwood.

themselves be confronted 'by grab tactics' from Argentina over the Falklands or Spain over Gibraltar. The FO believed that a dramatic new policy such as Greenwood proposed would be extremely difficult to put through. It would need to be a bipartisan policy, but it would be hard to persuade all parties 'on the issue of what would be seen as a daunting number of blank cheques'.[70]

Greenwood's paper was by now in deep trouble. Arguments against it were powerfully and indeed fatally marshalled against it in the FO, where the deputy under-secretary of state, Sir John Nicholls, described the counterblast as 'quite superb, a model of its kind for clarity, cogency and conclusiveness'. The FO objections were: (a) the advantage at the UN would be only short-term, and in any case they did not want to reactivate its interest by taking the initiative; (b) it would stimulate claims by Argentina, Venezuela, Guatemala, South Yemen and Cyprus; while the exclusion of Hong Kong, Gibraltar and maybe the Falklands would all seem provocative; (c) what would happen if HMG could not agree a territory was capable of sustaining independence? – in practice Britain would always be over-ruled, because 'free association' could be used as a stepping-stone; and this would lead to a succession of UDIs; (d) the prospect of territories being able to demand independence in this manner would gravely endanger the strategic interests of Britain and its allies in important islands, notably British Indian Ocean Island territories established in November 1965; Australia, New Zealand and the USA would be alarmed if these Pacific islands became independent, thus opening the area to possible hostile penetration; and there were also strategic dangers for the Caribbean.

The third and fourth arguments had been neglected since accelerated decolonisation had been adopted from 1959. Their reassertion now led the FO to the conclusion that the only satisfactory way of safeguarding foreign policy interests was to avoid making any promises of independence or free association. Greenwood accepted that the difficulties outweighed the advantages of issuing the general declaration.[71]

The 'decolonisation' decisions which had to be taken for individual territories in the next few years were rather low-key affairs, excepting only in Aden. Despite racial tensions in Mauritius and Fiji, both proceeded to independence without attracting much interest in the UK. In Fiji, the Fijians and Indians were highly distinct communities, living largely apart, and there were European settlers too, the Indians approaching 50 per cent of the total population, while the Fijians were about 44 per cent. The

---

[70] *ESC*, pt 3, p. 28 (no. 284), 6 July 1965, FO memo.
[71] Morgan, *Official history of colonial development*, vol. V, pp. 236 (Nicholls), 229–32, 27 August 1965; *ESC*, pt 3, pp. 35–47 (nos. 286 and 287).

Fijians pressed for protection against the economic enterprise and political ambitions of the Indians. The British government did not want ethnic divisions to hold up internal self-government: total harmony in multiracial communities (from the time of Canadian confederation onwards) had never been thought an essential pre-requisite. But while London prodded, the Fijians were active in procrastination. Progress stalled. When independence was reached in 1970 the governor could hardly conceal his amazement, commenting that differences were potentially dangerous, but at least there seemed to be frank acknowledgement that 'only by playing it cool can Fiji avoid following Malaysia to the very edge of the pit'.[72] The CO and the Indians had both wanted to move away from racial voting, but it was the Fijian and European advocacy of communal representation which won the day. The system of separate electorates for Fijians and Indians carried its own problems. In 1987 Fiji was expelled – as it proved – for ten years from the Commonwealth because of its treatment of Indians.

(3) The multi-racial Commonwealth

The potential potency of racial issues on politics hit the Labour government right at the outset. Gordon Walker suffered a double humiliation at the hands of the electors of Smethwick (October 1964) and Leyton (January 1965), and consequently he had to resign as foreign secretary. In a malign inversion of the attacks he had suffered during the Seretse Khama affair in 1950–1, in the Midlands constituency he was now slandered, not as racially prejudiced, but as a nigger-lover, with votes seeping away on the cry that you stood to lose your job and get a black neighbour if you voted Labour. Such scare-tactics had been more characteristic of the Afrikaner rural back-veldt than Midlands England, and were thus deeply shocking to the soul of British Labour. The salience of race was sharpened with Enoch Powell's notorious speech in Birmingham on immigration three years later, when he denounced the 'dangerous and divisive' tendency of immigrant communities to seek domination instead of integration; this filled him with foreboding ('like the Roman, I seem to see "the River Tiber foaming with much blood"').[73]

Just a month before Powell's outburst, the prime minister had spoken in the Commons of 'the world now dominated, as the Commonwealth is, by problems of race and colour'. Sir John Nicholls, who left the FO in

---

[72] ESC, pt 3, p. 266 (no. 353), 8 October 1970.
[73] ESC, pt 3, pp. 592–3 (no. 448), 20 April 1968.

1966 to become the ambassador in Cape Town, commented that 'we can no more afford to ignore these problems than could the governments of the sixteenth century afford to overlook religious problems'. They would have to be central 'to any foreign policy which we seek to establish in the coming years', because racial strife was tearing the United States apart, upsetting British domestic unity, and threatening (through the intractable problem of Rhodesia) the continued existence of the Commonwealth. Nicholls thought the government's attitude towards South Africa was dangerously equivocal: apartheid was diametrically opposed to British racial policies, but economic interests required the closest possible co-operation. The attempt to remain friendly with South Africa but to assert impeccable racial credentials with the Afro-Asian world was an awkward compromise which 'smacks of appeasement in the Munich sense', and Britain could end up incurring the hostility of both sides.[74] (Malcolm MacDonald pointed to a similar analogy: the African states regarded apartheid as 'as totally abhorrent as Hitler's policy of Jewish suppression', and it must be realised that the issue of sale of arms touched vitally on their quarrel with South Africa.)[75]

The Labour government dealt with this dilemma entirely within the basic parameters originally devised by Gordon Walker in 1950–1 (see above p. 164) the essence of which was that there were good reasons, including those of material self-interest, to remain friendly with South Africa despite apartheid, and that those who would ostracise South Africa and have nothing to do with it 'completely fail to understand the realities of the situation'.[76] South Africa had, if anything, been increasing in economic importance to Britain in the intervening fourteen years. It was now the third largest market, especially valuable in fairly sophisticated export goods.[77] The British government would not support apartheid (for example, by supplying arms) but it would oppose sanctions. It was a delicate and 'gruelling tight-rope' to have to walk. Morally the Afrikaner 'racial tyranny is detestable' but it was not going to collapse in the foreseeable future, for it seemed impervious to broad historical forces ('the wind of change').[78] British policy was grounded in the assumption that the fundamental theories and aims of the existing Afrikaner regime could not be changed by external pressure, but its methods might be softened if contact

[74] *ESC*, pt 3, pp. 593–6 (no. 449), 22 April 1963, letter to Sir D. Allen.
[75] *ESC*, pt 3, pp. 417–19 (no. 387), 6 December 1970, FCO note.
[76] Hyam and Henshaw, *The lion and the springbok*, p. 35. See above, p. 164.
[77] An FCO assessment reckoned that in the scale of priorities for British interests, South Africa ranked eleventh out of 131 countries, just behind Australia and India, and ahead of New Zealand and Ireland: *ESC*, pt 2, p. 101 (no. 157), 30 October 1968.
[78] *ESC*, pt 3, pp. 326–8 (no. 368), 29 November 1966, FO planning paper.

was maintained; at any rate 'ostracism would simply consolidate the South African hard-liners' (Thomson).[79] This policy was criticised by Commonwealth and international leaders as not robust enough and too favourable to South Africa. Caradon suggested that this policy, coupled with Rhodesia, could damage British interests and split the Commonwealth, 'and all the goodwill we have earned by our liberal policies of colonial emancipation will be thrown away'. Caradon thought it might help, though, if the government saw the South African problem in a less defeatist fashion, and in the context that in the long run a system 'built on the domination of one race by another by force cannot survive'.[80] Sir John Maud had given similar advice to the previous government.[81]

All of this led officials to report to the Defence and Oversea Policy Committee in 1967 that within the next ten years racial problems in southern Africa might become 'a major world issue, perhaps intensified by parallel racial problems in the United States, and possibly also in the United Kingdom'.[82]

Fundamental decisions about immigration were indeed required. The Labour government found itself involved in a staggering reversal. In opposition, the Party had emasculated the Conservative's Commonwealth Immigration Act, so that the rate of entry was continuing to rise alarmingly. According to Crossman, Sir Frank Soskice as home secretary had to be 'gradually dragged out of his purely liberalistic attitude' and made to tell Wilson that 'public opinion will become exasperated' without tighter immigration controls, since resentment was strong in the areas where coloured immigrants were concentrated.[83] Soskice proposed to combine more effective controls with measures to improve racial integration. This was the origin of the Race Relations Board. Another tactic was to send Lord Mountbatten on a mission to try to enlist the co-operation of a number of Commonwealth governments in restricting immigration to Britain. He visited Malta, India, Nigeria, Canada, Jamaica, Trinidad, and Cyprus; Pakistan, with memories of 1947, denied him entry, and generally he did not make much progress. He reported lamely that a breathing-space would be useful.[84]

It was already clear, as Crossman put it, that 'immigration can be the greatest potential vote-loser' if they allowed a flood to come in. It was 'the

---

[79] *ESC*, pt 3, pt 3, pp. 328–9 (no. 369), 5 March 1967 (minute by Thomson); pp. 331–3 (no. 371) 21 March 1967 (memo by Brown).

[80] *ESC*, pt 3, pp. 320–2 (no. 365), 14 July 1965.

[81] *The lion and the springbok*, pp. 263–4.

[82] *ESC*, pt 3, p. 353 (no. 376), memo, 16 October 1967, para. 20.

[83] *Crossman diaries*, p. 67, 5 February 1965.

[84] *ESC*, pt 3, pp. 547–52 (no. 436), 4 January 1965 (memo to prime minister); p. 553, n.4.

hottest potato in politics', and politically fear of it was 'the most powerful undertow today'.[85] An unexpected and worrying complication emerged by 1968, when the Africanisation policy of the Kenyan government meant that perhaps 150,000 Kenyan Asians might enter Britain within the year. Callaghan as home secretary proposed to extend controls to overseas citizens of the UK without obvious direct connections. There were about 400,000 persons who had the right to come and live permanently in Britain, perhaps half of them from East Africa. Asian immigrants were arriving from Kenya at the rate of 200 to 300 a day. Such a large influx, said Callaghan, 'was more than we could absorb', and unless it could be greatly reduced, 'there was a very real risk that our efforts to create a multi-racial society in this country would fail'. His forthcoming Race Relations Bill – which would make illegal racial discrimination in housing, employment and the provision of goods and services – could be jeopardised. Thomson disagreed forcibly with Callaghan's restrictive legislation. It would 'be wrong in principle, clearly discriminatory on grounds of colour, and contrary to everything that we stood for'. Opinion in Cabinet – as so often – was divided. 'Reasons of moral principle' suggested it would be going back on solemn pledges given as recently as 1963 (as part of the independence process for Kenya), and that it would be criticised internationally as creating a new class of refugees. On the other hand, it was argued that in the present economic situation and with great pressure on social services, especially education ('some schools might soon be used wholly by immigrant children'), 'we could no longer afford to honour our pledges'.[86]

At a further Cabinet discussion a week later, Callaghan reported that the governments of Kenya, India, and Pakistan were all unhelpful about providing some mitigation of the problem. Thomson fought a losing battle with the moral case. As frequently happened, this foundered in the face of perceived pragmatism. Moral arguments were outweighed by the practical implications for race relations and social services (especially housing, it was now said) if restrictive legislation was not introduced. It was expected that this would keep the total annual entry to a manageable 7,000.[87] According to Crossman, Callaghan got distinctly carried away, dismissing anyone who opposed the legislation as 'a sentimental jackass'; he was going to stop the nonsense of this 'bloody liberalism', as indeed public opinion demanded.[88]

[85] R. Crossman, *The diaries of a Cabinet minister*, vol. I *1964–1966* (ed. J. Morgan, 1975), pp. 149–50; or *Crossman diaries*, pp. 67–8, and 120 (5 February and 2 August 1969).

[86] *ESC*, pt 3, pp. 571–6 (no. 444), minutes of Cabinet meeting, 15 February 1968.

[87] CAB 128/43, CC 14(68)2, minutes, 22 February 1968.

[88] Crossman, *Diaries of a Cabinet minister*, vol. II *1966–1968* (1976), p. 679.

Despite immigration, the Commonwealth continued to have its high-minded advocates. Malcolm MacDonald thought that the almost comprehensively multi-racial Commonwealth could be an asset in solving the baffling problems of inter-racial disparities and rivalries, 'some of the most critical and potentially dangerous problems' now facing humanity. 'If we continue to foster, guide and lead it', he wrote, the Commonwealth 'may yet prove to be the British people's finest contribution to a happier human civilisation.'[89] Among ministers, Stewart was as receptive as any to talk of this kind. He clearly hated racialism and hoped the Commonwealth 'could help the world by establishing some standards in this respect'.[90] Bowden also agreed, and put his name to a Cabinet memorandum drawing attention to the Commonwealth's special 'and perhaps critical significance in relation to what may well be the most explosive problem in the world over the next half-century'. According to this paper, the complex of links in trade, commerce, and education, the technical and professional assistance which the Commonwealth could provide, and the shared use of the English language, gave Britain considerable opportunities for exercising an influence in the world, 'out of proportion to her comparative economic and military strength', opportunities which it would be wrong not to maximise. But there was a down-side. The disadvantages of the Commonwealth were that it focused increasing pressure on British policy-making, and it was unpopular with public opinion, mainly because of immigration from the new Commonwealth.[91]

Bowden's successor Thomson was equally susceptible to the idea that 'the Commonwealth exactly corresponds with the needs and problems that are going to dominate the next hundred years of history'. In an address delivered to the Royal Commonwealth Society to celebrate its centenary in 1968, Thomson took up the theme of the 'unique inventory of experience, skill and wisdom' which the British might contribute to contemporary progress: 'here is a world role for us to play that looks to the future and not to the past'. He connected this with the progressive nature of withdrawal from East-of-Suez. In a particularly striking passage discussing the need think realistically about the painful problems of the moment, he said that other Commonwealth countries had to adjust as much as Britain. Those Africans who wanted them to use force to bring about a Rhodesian solution 'are still living as much in the age of Imperial

[89] *ESC*, pt 2, pp. 369–70 (no. 254), 9 December 1966, despatch.
[90] *ESC*, pt 2, p. 446 (no. 275), 15 January 1969.
[91] CAB 129/129 [*sic*], C(67)59, 24 April 1967; *ESC*, pt 2, pp. 418–29 (no. 268). This report was not discussed by the Cabinet, and no decision resulted, but it was an important statement of official assessments of the Commonwealth in the later 1960s.

gunboat diplomacy as those Britons who feel that somehow Britain must be able to impose peace in the tragic civil war in Nigeria'.[92]

All surveys by officials noted that the Commonwealth must now be involved in the problems of rich and poor, haves and have-nots. These found their practical application in the politics of aid. Commonwealth countries were the main recipients. Africa received 42 per cent of all British aid in 1966 (£60 million out of £63 million to Commonwealth African countries). The Labour government for the first time provided a Cabinet minister for this work. In 1965 Mrs Castle set out the policy of the new Ministry of Overseas Development. It took over the old CO objectives of helping developing countries to raise their living standards and promote social and economic progess and development, but added hopes of improving the lot and the happiness of ordinary people: 'the basis of the aid programme is therefore a moral one'.[93] But here too moral objectives in pursuit of a vague concept of 'African development' were challenged by the voices of pragmatic realism. Increasingly from 1968 the FCO and the Board of Trade were able to push their contrary view that the purpose of aid was not simply development for its own sake, but to promote British interests, political as well as economic, even to use aid as a 'sprat to catch a mackerel', the more general improvement of political and trading conditions for Britain. Aid decisions were constantly confused by questions of whether recipients were politically deserving, and consequently decisions were not always well-founded, even in the context of preventing the extension of communist influence. The old project of a Tanzania–Zambian rail-link was rejected once again as 'not a sound economic proposition', while press reports that the Chinese would take it on were dismissed out of hand – quite wrongly, as it turned out (see above, p. 134).[94]

For all the rhetoric, not much was actually achieved in Commonwealth development in these years. The one notable new departure owed little to the government. The Commonwealth Secretariat was established in the summer of 1965, but the initiative had come a year earlier from Nkrumah and others, who criticised the routine concentration on cold war issues at Prime Ministers' Meetings, when the main question of the day ought to be relations between rich and poor countries. Nkrumah called for a 'central clearing-house' in London to co-ordinate and circulate information about plans for trade, economic and technical development and aid. The Commonwealth prime ministers accepted the

[92] *ESC*, pt 2, pp. 434–9 (no. 271), 29 February 1968.
[93] *ESC*, pt 1, intro., pp. cvii, cxviii.
[94] CAB 148/20, OPD(65)65, 30 March 1965; *ESC*, pt 3, pp. 437–43 (no. 395).

possibility that this might become a 'symbol of co-operation'. The British government was willing to support it, provided the secretariat did not develop in any way into a policy-making body or deal with defence questions.[95]

3. Particularities

(1) Aden

A federation of princely states friendly to Britain was set up in 1959 in the western part of the hinterland of Aden, and the intention was to include Aden within it. This structure was further evidence of the British resort to the 'federal panacea' so characteristic of the 1950s and early 1960s, the belief that small states would be vulnerable and unviable as independent countries, and that fragmentation would reflect poorly on the imperial legacy. It looked as if the awkward nationalists of industrialised Aden would be delivered into the hands of old-fashioned feudal rulers. Such a merger – which came about in 1962 – was described by the governor of the day, Sir Charles Johnston, as 'like bringing modern Glasgow into a federation with the 18th-century Highlands of Scotland'.[96] As if this were not difficult enough, the plan was further complicated by the Yemeni revolution which brought Nasser's Egypt into the frame. Nevertheless, the federation of South Arabia was in 1964 promised by the Conservative government independence no later than 1968.[97]

In this trouble-spot, bipartisanship held few attractions for Labour ministers. Greenwood came into office at the CO determined to reverse Conservative policy by ditching the feudal rulers who had become allies. Instead, and rejecting the advice of his officials, he wanted to involve the UN, and decided to negotiate with the radical nationalist, al-Asnag, prison-graduate and the mastermind behind the influential Aden TUC. He persuaded Greenwood that he was the true representative of majority opinion, a popular and peace-loving nationalist leader, and that relying on the federal sultans was backing the wrong horse. Governor Trevaskis, closely identified with Conservative policy, and sceptical of treating with al-Asnag, was recalled only two months into the Labour government. He

---

[95] CAB 148/17, OPD(64)12, 11 December 1964, memo by Bottomley; *ESC* pt 2, pp. 325–33 (no. 244); W. D. McIntyre, 'Britain and the evolution of the Commonwealth Secretariat', *JICH*, vol. 28 (2000), pp. 135–58. For some thoughtful reflections on the Commonwealth in 1966, see N. Mansergh, 'The Commonwealth and the future' *International Studies*, vol. 9 (New Delhi, 1966), repr. in Diana Mansergh, ed., *Independence years: the selected Indian and Commonwealth papers of Nicholas Mansergh* (New Delhi, 1999), pp. 181–94.   [96] *ESC*, pt 1, p. 235 (no. 65), letter to FO, 11 April 1967.
[97] *CGEE, 1957–1964*, pt 1, pp. 641–6 (nos. 213–15), April–May 1964.

was replaced by Sir Richard Turnbull, who had so successfully brought Tanganyika to independence. Greenwood wanted to switch to a unitary state, which he thought offered an escape from the constitutional impasse in which irreconcilable interests contended, by allowing, he hoped, progressive forces to develop and a stable liberal settlement to emerge. He wanted the base abandoned, because it was expensive, vulnerable, and criticised in the UN, but this was not acceptable to the Chiefs of Staff.[98] Greenwood had only just concluded his first talks with al-Asnag about creating a new unitary state, when in December 1964 attacks began on British servicemen in Aden, whose numbers had been inflated to 8,000, four times the strength of the traditional garrison. The NLF (National Liberation Front) was a recently-founded Yemeni organisation dedicated to driving the British out. Its activities led to al-Asnag's setting up his own military force with Egyptian backing, FLOSY (the deceptively cosy acronym for the Front for the Liberation of South Yemen). In effect, Aden was soon in the grip of civil war, and Greenwood's attempt to win Adeni support revealed as a fantasy. Neither the NLF nor FLOSY would recognise the other as representing the nationalist cause. The UN was up in arms, perversely refusing to accept the good faith of any British initiative for Aden. Into this maelstrom Turnbull was pitched, bearing high hopes that he could bring order out of chaos. But within months urban terrorism and guerilla operations in the hinterland were worse than ever, the superintendent of police had been killed (August 1965), and so too had the Speaker of the Legislative Assembly (September 1965). Finding that the chief minister, Abd al-Qawi Makkawi, supported the NLF and would not denounce terrorism, and that members of the Assembly refused even to condemn the murder of their head, and with he himself – like his luckless predecessor – the target of an assassination attempt, Turnbull concluded it was essential to suspend the constitution and reimpose direct rule. His decision was in no sense taken lightly, and Turnbull expected full government backing. However, the Labour ministers were fumblingly confused, and terrified of UN disapproval.[99] Greenwood's opposition to direct rule (it would 'merely strengthen the terrorists' and cause serious embarrassment at the UN) was overruled by Healey and the Defence and Oversea Policy Committee.[100] A state of emergency was declared, and Makkawi

---

[98] K. Pieragostini, *Britain, Aden and South Arabia: abandoning empire* (1991), pp. 168, 195; CAB 148/17, OPD(64)16, 30 December 1964; PREM 13/113 ff. 201–3; *ESC*, pt 1, pp. 158–9 (no. 36) and 174–5 (no. 42).

[99] D. Ledger, *Shifting sands: the British in South Arabia* (1984), pp. 59–64. However, Kennedy Trevaskis disapproved of Turnbull's policy as a politically grotesque action: 'resort to a blunderbuss, picked up from the racks of an imperial museum' (*Shades of amber: a South Arabian episode* (1968), p. 236).

[100] CAB 148/18, OPD 41(65)1, 23 September 1965.

was sacked, but Turnbull was refused the necessary powers to deal with terrorism – powers which the government later granted to his successor. Turnbull was convinced ministers were simply too concerned about UN reactions. The situation thus inevitably deteriorated further. Turnbull seemed to wear his frustrations lightly, relaxing by taking mammoth walks over Aden's dreary dark satanic hills.[101]

By the beginning of 1966, FO officials were reconsidering whether the UN might best be able to find some kind of post-colonial stability for this treacherous region. Opinion was divided, with some seeing the benefits of a successor regime which was not both ramshackle and regarded as a British puppet-state. But others had grave misgivings about involving the UN, as it would look like 'an ignominious scuttle', something with 'a nasty whiff of the Palestinian scuttle' about it.[102] Additionally, it did not seem probable that the UN would have a change of heart and inaugurate 'a kind of idyllic period of peace and co-operation instead of vituperation and trouble-making'. The CO was strongly against it, but although the idea was dropped, it formed the sympathetic background to agreeing to let in a visiting mission from the dreaded Committee of 24.[103]

Turnbull knew he must try his best with the mission, but was concerned that if it decided it would have 'no truck with the "unrepresentative Federal Government" it can cause nothing but the greatest damage'.[104] It turned out that the mission did indeed refuse to deal with the British colonial state. The mission was led by a Venezuelan friendly with Nasser. His two colleagues came from Afghanistan and Mali. They stayed only a few wretched days, displaying a singular lack of backbone. They arrived amid what seemed an ill-omen, unprecedented storms which burst open the graves in cemeteries and made 10,000 people homeless. A general strike was launched in protest at their presence. Both the NLF and FLOSY refused to make contact, regarding them as tools of the British oppressors – such were the complexities and perversities of Aden! This left the envoys with almost nobody to talk to, except Turnbull, whom they elected to find deeply unco-operative. He himself was distinctly unimpressed by them. In a typical bit of Turnbullian rhetorical jocularity he described his encounter as 'a sad record of ineffective flattery, futile sucking-up and quite unproductive self-abasement'.[105]

---

[101] A. H. M. Kirk-Greene, 'Turnbull, Richard G', ODNB, vol. LV, pp. 593–4.
[102] Louis, original draft of 'Public enemy Number One', minutes by S. Falle and R. Allen (14 and 17 January 1966); minute by D Greenhill (18 January 1966) – my thanks to Professor Louis for these references.
[103] ESC, pt 1, pp. 182–4 (nos. 46 and 47), January–June 1966.
[104] FO 961/33, Turnbull to Caradon, 12 January 1967.
[105] Louis, original draft of 'Public enemy Number One', Turnbull to D, McCarthy, 11 April 1967–my thanks to Professor Louis for this quotation.

Most informed observers thought Turnbull was coping well with his exceptionally difficult task. But some Labour ministers felt he must carry much of the blame for the failure of the UN mission. Lord Shackleton (temporarily minister for South Arabia) in particular seems to have lost confidence in him, and in Turnbull's tough insistence that this was a struggle to be met with decisive action.[106] Turnbull's competence began to be questioned; was he unable to demonstrate any new thinking in devising a solution? Was he now 'a tired man'?[107] It may be conceded that Turnbull with his Africanist background had not understood the inwardness of Muslim politics nor the subtleties – some might say eccentricities – of Arab politicians; his acceptance of a 'resignation' was greatly resented. He found them tiresome, none as amenable as 'dear Julius' (Nyerere). Nevertheless he certainly did not deserve to be sacked by his employers, barely two years after they had summarily dismissed his predecessor and solicited his help. Well, sacking people is what desperate governments tend to do, since it looks like taking decisive control; as Thomson put it, 'to reassure opinion here and in Aden that we were acting to maintain control of events.[108] Although Turnbull accepted his fate with dignity, such was the indignation, anger even, in Whitehall, that on his arrival back at London airport he was met by nearly all the heads of department and the service chiefs.[109] They all knew what an impossible assignment it had been. His successor described it as like 'fencing with a vacuum'.[110]

What seems to have happened is that George Brown at the FO – worried that the situation in Aden 'is bad and getting worse' – [111] was also determined to restore diplomatic relations with Egypt (broken off in 1965 over Rhodesia), and especially to mend fences with President Nasser. This might provide a good 'exit-strategy' from Aden, as Nasser controlled FLOSY and had the leaders of NLF in Cairo under his influence. A British–Egyptian deal might put a stop to terrorism and pave the way for an acceptable successor regime.[112] However, Brown's policy required a high commissioner who was respected and trusted by Nasser, and there was only one man who fitted the bill – once the inevitable suggestion of Lord Mountbatten had been rejected – Sir Humphrey Trevelyan.

---

[106] Pieragostini, *Britain, Aden and South Arabia*, pp. 193–4; G. Balfour-Paul, *The end of empire in the Middle East: Britain's relinquishment of power in her last three Arab dependencies* (1991), p. 87.

[107] *ESC*, pt 1, pp. 233–4 (no. 64), 10 April 1967, a savage minute by Gordon Walker; and p. 246 (no. 69).

[108] *ESC*, pt 1, pp. 208–9 (no. 58), minute by Thomson, 3 March 1967.

[109] Ledger, *Shifting sands*, p. 120.

[110] H. Trevelyan, *The Middle East in revolution* (1970), p. 264.

[111] *ESC*, pt 1, p. 209 (no. 59), memo, 8 March 1967.

[112] B. Lapping, *End of empire* (1985), pp. 302–3.

Illustration 5.1 Sir Richard Turnbull leaves Aden, inspecting the Federal Camel Corps, 16 May 1967.
After his controversial dismissal as high commissioner, Turnbull was accorded full honours by the Camel Corps of the Federal Regular Army at Steamer Point, Aden before his departure, to be replaced by Sir Humphrey Trevelyan. (Associated Press, London.)

Although Trevelyan was retired, Brown would 'not take no for an answer'.[113]

Departure from the military base had already been announced for 31 December 1968 in February 1966 as part of the defence review. Roads and schools were still being built, the new married quarters for servicemen still unfinished, part of the biggest military building scheme ever undertaken by the British government.[114] The shaky federation would be left to its fate, which would almost certainly mean its collapse. The feasibility of continuing British rule was hopelessly compromised by the assassination of some half-a-dozen Special Branch officers and by a mutiny in the federal army and police in July 1967, taking control of Crater district; 27 British soldiers were killed. In September 1967 Trevelyan secured

[113] M. T. Thornhill, 'Trevelyan, Humphrey', *ODNB*, vol. LV, pp. 338–40; *Middle East in revolution*, p. 220; Trevelyan had been ambassador to Egypt, from 1955 to 1956, but was kept in the dark about Eden's intentions; he was ambassador to Iraq, 1958–61.

[114] R. Gavin, *Aden under British rule, 1839–1967* (1975), pp. 347–50; Darby, *British defence policy East of Suez*, pp. 206–10.

ministerial approval for fixing a date for departure, whatever the internal situation. Brown justified the advance of date as necessary to meet a deteriorating situation caused by revolutionary upheaval. 'There is no evidence that we could achieve anything useful, to Arabs or ourselves, by staying longer'; and now the Egyptians had left Yemen the problem 'is no longer one in which outside powers should remain to play a part'. So – 'we should as soon as possible leave the Arabs to sort out their own problems without the complication of our military presence'.[115] Crossman's diary records how George Brown apologised to the Defence and Oversea Policy Committee towards the end of October 1967, 'for having to tell us that we'll be out by November instead of January. The rest of the Committee couldn't be more pleased. Really we've been miraculously lucky in Aden – cancelling all our obligations . . .'.[116] Lord Shackleton in the Lords did not sound so buoyant: 'We consider we are not in a position to help South Arabia any more by our presence. We still hope that there will be a government there, but if there is no government to hand over to, we can't hand over to a government'.[117]

In fact the NLF, having seen off FLOSY, emerged victorious. The People's Democratic Republic of Yemen, uniquely in the annals of British decolonisation, turned to Soviet Marxism, the only such regime throughout the Middle East. A poor result. It was to Wilson's government what Palestine had been to Attlee's – only worse. The difference is that Aden is now largely forgotten.

The Labour government made a mess of Aden, not least in the context of the cold war. Their Conservative predecessors had dithered and procrastinated and bequeathed an unworkable federation. Labour ministers chipped away at the federation with a mixture of cravenness and clumsiness without constructing anything to put in place of the federal clients who were being cynically ditched, leading to a humiliating withdrawal and a vicious successor regime dedicated to everything they found repugnant.[118]

If in the mid-1960s the governorship of Aden must have seemed the worst job in the empire, the governorship of the Falkland Islands must have seemed the least demanding. But here too was another colony heading for disaster, though much more slowly.

(2) The Falkland Islands

What have we acquired? What, but a bleak and gloomy solitude, an island thrown aside from human use, stormy in winter, and barren in

---

[115] *ESC*, pt 1, pp. 270–2 (no. 84), memo by Brown, 26 October 1967 (CAB 129/133/2, C(67)169).   [116] *Crossman diaries*, pp. 347–8.
[117] Lapping, *End of empire*, pp. 307–8.   [118] Trevaskis, *Shades of amber*, p. 242.

summer; an island which not the southern savages have dignified with habitation; where a garrison must be kept in a state that contemplates with envy the exiles of Siberia; of which the expense will be perpetual, and the use only occasional.

Works of Samuel Johnson: Political writings, vol. X, ed. D. J. Greene (Yale, 1977), *Thoughts on the late transactions respecting Falkland's Islands* (1771), p. 369.

'The job of the Governor of the Falkland Islands is rather like a mixture of old-fashioned squire and chairman of a rural district council.' So wrote the official who knew most about them.[119] In other words, the Falklands were of no importance to Britain as an imperial power. Unfortunately they were claimed with passion as the 'Malvinas' by the government of Argentina.[120] The question was raised by the Argentinians at the United Nations in 1964, and a General Assembly resolution (1 December 1965) urged both parties to negotiate a solution to the dispute.

British officials were totally baffled by the impatient and bombastic Latin American mentality. They would have agreed with Carlyle, who in 1843 sneered at 'all South America raging and ravening like one huge dog-kennel gone rabid'.[121] At the end of 1966 they suggested what they thought a dignified transitional period for the Falklands, a 'freeze of sovereignty', to last forty years. The British government's offer was contemptuously rejected by the government of Argentina. But by March 1967 the British government really was for the first time actively contemplating a policy of ceding sovereignty, provided the conditions were acceptable to the Islanders, whose wishes, it was decided, must be respected.[122] Ministers agreed it was in British interests to achieve an amicable settlement of a

[119] J. S. Bennett, CO minute, 25 May 1967, quoted by Ashton, *ESC* intro., p. cxxx, n. 72.

[120] A British garrison was established in West Falkland in 1765, when Lord Egmont (first lord of the Admiralty) described the Falklands as 'the key to the whole Pacific Ocean' (this was of course before the opening of the Panama Canal). The British were driven out by Spaniards from East Falkland in 1770, which had had a Spanish settlement since 1767. The Spanish handed it back in 1771, but the British abandoned it in 1774, leaving the flag flying 'as a mark of possession'. The Spanish also pulled out in 1811, but the Buenos Aires government re-opened a settlement in 1828, which was destroyed by the Americans in 1831. The British occupation was resumed in 1833; this was accepted by the Americans as continuing the earlier settlement, and thus not in breach of the Monroe Doctrine. Only in the 1880s did Argentina begin to assert its mystical and emotional myth of the 'Malvinas' as theirs. Apart perhaps from geography, the Argentinian claim appeared weak, as there was no explicit transfer of the islands by Spain when recognising the independence of Argentina (J. Goebel, *The struggle for the Falkland Islands* (1927; 2nd edn, 1982, ed. J. C. J. Metford)).

[121] Quoted by V. G. Kiernan, *The lords of human kind: European attitudes towards the outside world in the imperial age* (1969), p. 304.

[122] Lord Franks, *Falkland Islands review: Report of a Committee of Privy Counsellors* (Cmnd 8787, 1983), pp. 4–7 (cited hereafter as the *Franks report*). This can now be read in conjunction with L. Freedman, *The official history of the Falklands Campaign*, 2 vols. (2005).

dispute exposing Britain to UN criticism and upsetting relations with Argentina, its most important Latin American trading partner. In July 1967 Judith Hart (minister of state, CRO) admitted to the Argentinian ambassador that it was important to keep 'the United Nations happy while Britain and the Argentine worked out a solution together'.[123] The Argentinian case received overwhelming support at the UN, where the views of a tiny white British population cut little ice with the Afro-Asians and the communist bloc. They were seen as selfish 'white settlers' trying to thwart 'legitimate nationalist aspirations'.[124] George Brown spoke with the Argentinian foreign minister, Dr Costa Mendez, in New York and told him that if the proposals for transfer of sovereignty to Argentina were acceptable to Islanders there would be no difficulty; Argentina should show it had begun to get the Islanders' acquiescence – when this had started 'the problem would begin to solve itself'.[125]

The government was anxious to restore the travel and communications facilities which the Argentine government had suspended. A 'memorandum of understanding' was proposed as a means of defusing the dispute and buying time. This would commit the British to considering transfer of sovereignty on conditions; it would be coupled with a statement that they must be satisfied the population was ready to accept Argentinian safeguards and guarantees. Stewart and Thomson submitted that this was 'a reasonable position to defend in Parliament'.[126] In November 1968 Lord Chalfont (minister of state, FO, 1964–70) visited the Falklands. In his report, he concluded that 'our policy is sound in principle: if it were acceptable to the Islanders, then we should be prepared to transfer sovereignty to Argentina'. Wool sales were declining, young people were drifting away, and the economic advantages of close association with Argentina would become slowly more apparent, as Britain tried to get the Islanders 'to face the underlying realities of their and our situations'. Argentina should be asked to be patient, since things would lead 'gradually but inexorably to the acceptance of Argentine sovereignty'. Chalfont predicted serious parliamentary opposition, but recommended the government to press ahead 'with a policy that is logical, far-seeing and intellectually defensible'.[127]

Actually, parliamentary opposition proved to be too fierce to proceed. Nevertheless, what was done by the Labour government was absolutely crucial to the future unfolding of the dispute. The issues were clearly

---

[123] *ESC*, pt 3, pp. 143–5 (no. 319), 24 July 1967, 'Anglo-Argentine discussions'.
[124] *ESC*, pt 3, p. 170 (no. 329), FO notes, November 1968.
[125] *ESC*, pt 3, pp. 150–1 (no. 322), 21 September 1967.
[126] *ESC* pt 3, pp. 161–8 (no. 327), 20 September 1968, joint Cabinet memo (FCO 42/52, no. 529).
[127] *ESC*, pt 3, pp. 171–82 (no. 330), 5 December 1968, report to Stewart.

exposed. A Foreign Office memorandum (1965), on 'international and strategic aspects' of the remaining territories, offered a sensible perspective. If Britain opposed the Argentine claim simply because the Falkland Islanders did not want to be governed from Buenos Aires, 'we should perhaps calculate how much it would cost us to bribe all 3,000 [*sic*: an over-estimate] Falkland Islanders to emigrate to New Zealand (or to accept Argentine sovereignty on the basis of special guarantees and privileges) as against what it could cost us in military expenditure and the loss of economic interests if we were to have a really serious quarrel with the Argentine'.[128] Believing that Argentina did not really 'care twopence about actually administering the Islands, and simply wants to paint them her colour on the map', J. S. Bennett proposed a separation of the issues of administration and sovereignty, through 'leaseback', that is, in return for Britain's ceding sovereignty, Argentina would grant the UK a long lease with the exclusive right of administration. This would in theory give Argentina what it most wanted, a title-deed, and provide Britain with 'a transitional generation during which the practical status quo remains but everybody knows that it is coming to an end when the old people are dead'.[129] This compromise proved to be immensely significant, in fact the basis of the British negotiating position right through to 1982.[130] It seemed ingenious, but a shrewd historian has offered a deadly commentary on this proposal, as a curious example 'of the policy-making process stuck in a cul-de-sac': 'Decolonisation offered an elegant way of abdicating burdens. Lease-back would invert this, combining unwelcome responsibility with uncertain control. Argentina would eventually allege some violation of the lease and evict the administration in circumstances just as humiliating as 1982 but without the possibility of redress.'[131]

The importance of the Labour government's contribution does not end with lease-back, however. A major feature of the problem by the early 1980s was that British governments had boxed themselves into a corner by their fundamental insistence that the wishes of the Islanders must be paramount, and presumably therefore regardless of cost. Acceptance of the validity of this veto left almost no room for manoeuvre.[132] It was the Labour government which laid down this fatal proposition, despite knowing the risks it entailed, and in bizarre contrast to its ruthless

---

[128] *ESC*, pt 3, p. 24 (no. 284), FO memo, 6 July 1965.

[129] FCO 42/45, no. 154, minute, 13 July 1967: *ESC*, pt 3, p. 143 (318), note 2. Bennett was for many years the official in charge of the Falkland Islands, in the CO, CRO and FCO.   [130] *Franks Report*, paras 33, 61, 70, 73, 80–4, 96 and 282.

[131] Ged Martin, review of Freedman, *The official history of the Falklands Campaign*, in *Round Table*, vol. 95 (January 2006), pp. 153–7.

[132] *Franks report*, p. 77 (para. 282) and p. 89 (para. 338).

removal of the population of Diego Garcia (see below, p. 391). The population of the Falklands was a mere 2,100 and falling. By 1978 it was down to 1,867. As an official pointed out, the situation could become 'more and more unreal'. If the population fell to 1,000 or fewer, would they still be able to abide by the proviso of 'acceptability'?[133] The FO thought London should decide finally whether a settlement was in accordance with the Islanders' wishes and interests. As against this, other officials understood that it was probably completely impossible for any British minister to stand in the House of Commons and state that the government was ceding British territory contrary to the wishes of the inhabitants.[134] What increasingly came into play, therefore, was a curious variation on the theme of 'domestic constraints': not this time the usual economic lack of resources so much as the metropolitan political constraints provided by a parliamentary lobby, which seemed to rule out putting any pressure on the Islanders by way of an education campaign about 'the realities'. This was a rare case of a lobby exercising a prohibitive power, and the unfortunate result in the long run was an unnecessary war in 1982.[135]

Education in the realities was something also required, more immediately and on a much bigger scale, for the settlers in Central Africa.

(3) Rhodesia

The Central African Federation collapsed in 1963 for three main reasons: a fundamental lack of clarity as to its nature, purpose, and organisation; a drastic structural imbalance constitutionally and economically between its constituent parts; and black opposition to it as an evolving symbol of white domination and oppression. The ambivalence implicit in yoking together Southern Rhodesia (which had internal self-government since 1923) and two underdeveloped black units precluded a decisive lead being given to the progressive development of the Federation.[136] As Macmillan wrote later, had he realised 'the almost revolutionary way in which the situation would develop and the rapid growth of African nationalism through the whole African continent', he would probably have opposed putting together three countries 'so opposite in their character and so different in their history'.[137] The inequalities between them

---

[133] ESC, pt 3, p. 142 (no. 318), minute by Trafford Smith, 9 June 1967.

[134] ESC, pt 3, p. 150 (no. 321), FO minute by H. A. F. Hohler, 10 August 1967; Franks report, p. 28 (para. 99).

[135] The Argentinian writer Jorge Luis Borges seemed to say it all when he dismissed the war as a contest between two bald men fighting over a comb.

[136] J. S. Garner, The Commonwealth Office, 1925–1968 (1978), p. 384.

[137] H. Macmillan, Memoirs, vol. V: Pointing the way, 1959–1961 (1972), p. 133; and vol. VI: At the end of the day, 1961–1963 (1973), p. 323.

and the smallness of the overall pool of experienced people to run a federal as well as three territorial governments (drawn almost entirely from the 300,000 European settlers, mostly in Southern Rhodesia) had indeed been forcefully identified in the Labour cabinet in 1951 as objections to going ahead with setting it up.

The federal prime minister was Roy Welensky. Rumbustious 'Roy-boy' was the thirteenth son of a Lithuanian Jewish father and an Afrikaner mother. He was a former train-driver, boxing champion, and trade unionist.[138] He was less well-educated than his African opponents; if he had been an African his educational attainments would not have been sufficient to entitle him to vote. His nicknames included 'the Napoleon of Broken Hill' and the 'Wellington of Wankie' (an unfortunate transliteration of Hwange). The other prominent figure was Dr G. M. Huggins, a worthy but rather dull bourgeois figure, who, on elevation to the peerage took the name of his old public school, Malvern (the school so hated and reviled by C. S. Lewis).[139] The policies of Welensky and Huggins towards the black communities proved to be disastrous. The distribution of economic benefits was unfair. For example, the federal government was able to spend more on the education of Europeans than the three state governments together had available for Africans. The much vaunted policy of 'partnership' quickly degenerated into a fraud. While something was grudgingly done for Africans, in terms of removing some 'petty apartheid', nothing was genuinely done with them. Public swimming-pools were de-segregated, but this should not have been too much of a hardship, since Salisbury (now Harare) had an exceptionally high proportion of private pools. Even so, multi-racial bathing was to whites the second most unpopular reform after mixed lavatories, and seen as a threat 'to the dignity, chastity and health of the community's young, and above all its daughters'. It was reversed in 1967. Either way, blacks were unimpressed. What mattered was that African political advance was frozen.[140]

White Rhodesians were not generally admired by British politicians – certainly not by Macmillan, or Macleod, who referred to the 'bottomless stupidity' of the right-wing United Federal Party. The Liberal leader Jeremy Thorpe memorably characterised the settlers as 'the failures of Surbiton'. Harold Wilson described Rhodesia after rebellion in 1965 as 'a police state run by racial supremacists'.[141] There had been a long-standing official concern they they might take the law into their own

---

[138] Roy Welensky, *Welensky's 4,000 days: the life and death of the Federation of Rhodesia and Nyasaland* (1964).

[139] L. H. Gann and M. Gelfand, *Huggins of Rhodesia* (1964), pp. 256–72.

[140] C. Rogers and C. Frantz, *Racial themes in Southern Rhodesia* (1962), pp. 92–4.

[141] *ESC*, pt 2, p. 215 (no. 204), Wilson to President Kaunda, 13 December 1965.

hands in one way or another' in order to escape British disapproval. This might take the form of a 'Boston tea-party' – a unilateral declaration of independence (UDI), or creating a new state by the incorporation of break-away Katanga and the Copper Belt of Northern Rhodesia, or seeking to throw in their lot with the Union of South Africa as a fifth province (South African acceptance was not thought in Whitehall to be very likely but could not be ruled out), or forming an alliance with South Africa (and perhaps Angola). This last possibility was something which had been identified in 1962 as an 'extremely grave threat', likely to destroy 'all hope of good race relations' in British Africa. It was actually more worrying than UDI, which, because it would be illegal, would wrong-foot the Rhodesian whites.[142]

In the event the Europeans did opt for UDI and rebellion, which they declared on 11 November 1965 – it seemed shameless, but Armistice Day had not been originally intended – amid a flurry of nauseating rhetoric wrenched out of an archaic colonial tradition and of a distinctly eschatological kind about the defence of civilisation and freedom.[143] Ian Smith, the slippery and single-minded prime minister, believed that white-controlled independence was a 'precondition of the survival of Southern Rhodesia as a worthwhile country'. If the act was anti-British, then Britain itself had already gone to the dogs. If it was treason, then that was better than the 'gradual extinction of civilised life in this country'.[144] In truth, as Wilson recognised, 'they were determined men utterly resolved on one proposition, and that was that we should not seek majority rule in Rhodesia in their life-time. It was as simple as that.'[145] In other words, UDI was a device for (un)constitutional regression.[146] The settlers' imperative was to control African nationalism, still relatively quiescent. The rebels calculated that black opposition was containable (as it proved to be until 1971), and that South Africa would provide covert support with 'business as usual'.[147] The settler regime had emerged militarily strong after the collapse of the Federation, inheriting virtually the whole of the armed forces, with an efficient Air Force. The rebels were also

---

[142] *Conservative government, 1957–1964*, pt 2, p. 581 (no. 510), 29 October 1962, Cabinet meeting.

[143] J. Barber, 'The impact of the Rhodesian crisis on the Commonwealth', *Journal of Commonwealth Political Studies*, vol. 7 (1969), pp. 83–94; J. Barber, *Rhodesia: the road to rebellion* (1967), pp. 30, 226; an indispensable account is J. D. B. Miller, *Survey of Commonwealth affairs: problems of expansion and attrition, 1953–1969* (1974), pp. 197–246.

[144] *CGEE, 1957–1964*, pt 2, p. 618 (note to no. 527), 8 September 1964.

[145] 26 December 1965, quoted in R. C. Good, *UDI: the international politics of the Rhodesian rebellion* (1973), p. 51.   [146] R. Blake, *A history of Rhodesia* (1977), pp. 381–4.

[147] J. Day, 'The creation of political myths: African nationalism in Southern Rhodesia', *Journal of Southern African Studies*, vol. 2 (1975), pp. 52–65.

enormously helped by Wilson's disavowal of military response. There were good reasons why the British government would hesitate to send in troops: uncertainty as to the public reaction, and the loyalty and morale of British soldiers fighting 'kith and kin', the Chiefs of Staffs' anxiety about the logistics of getting into landlocked Rhodesia, and the dangers of a protracted commitment (like the French in Algeria). All this had been thoroughly foreseen by the planners. But the one effective weapon was uncertainty, the threat that Britain might use force. There is reason to believe Smith might have backed down in the face of this threat, knowing that he could not expect to defeat British forces. As it was, he felt he had been given the green light.[148]

Wilson irrevocably and fatefully threw away this weapon despite private advice from the archbishop of Canterbury that morality demanded the use of force if all else failed, and provided it could be restricted to a police action. The Most Reverend Michael Ramsey went further and declared publicly that if the government thought it practicable to use force to protect the rights of the majority of the Rhodesian people, Christians 'would have to say that it would be right to use force to that end'. An explosion of horror greeted the archbishop's pronouncement: nothing so controversial had been uttered from the See of Canterbury since 1688; one peer cursed him in the corridors of Westminster as a 'bloody bugger'. But Ramsey had received plenty of clerical reports from Africa and knew far more about the real nature of the white Rhodesian regime than most people in government – ministers were not well-informed about the situation on the ground. He was also not without political instincts; as a young man he had been hailed by Asquith as a future Liberal prime minister.[149] No doubt it was right for various reasons to rule out the use of an invasion-force, but it was a catastrophic error for Wilson to announce in a broadcast in Rhodesia, even before UDI, that it would not be used ('this thunderbolt will not be coming', 30 October 1965). It is perhaps possible that Wilson's intention, in part at least, was to reinforce the message he had already given to Joshua Nkomo, that African leaders should reduce what were seen as unrealistic and unreasonable nationalist expectations of the British

---

[148] P. Murphy, ed., *Central Africa* (BDEEP, 2005), pt 1, *Closer association, 1945–1958*, intro., pp. lxxxv–lxxxvii ('A decision had effectively been reached in 1961 that armed intervention in Central Africa in the face of opposition from local European troops was not politically feasible'); pp. 423–31 (no. 162), CO minutes, October–November 1958; pt 2: *Crisis and dissolution, 1959–1965*, pp. 439–45 (no. 384), report by the Defence Planning Staff of the Chiefs of Staff Committee, 19 June 1964: having to fight the Southern Rhodesian Regular Army and the Royal Rhodesian Air Force 'would not only place an unacceptable strain on the loyalty of British troops but would also prove militarily impracticable'.   [149] O. Chadwick, *Michael Ramsey: a life* (1990), pp. 241–50.

government, such as that they would introduce immediate majority rule, if necessary imposed by UK armed forces. 'This was clearly impossible', the lord chancellor, Lord Gardiner, advised his colleagues, 'and the Nationalist leaders were at present quite unqualified to govern'.[150]

Wilson made extraordinary efforts to prevent UDI, flying to Rhodesia, perhaps convincing himself that he could prevent it. Sceptical colleagues noted that he called it 'his Cuba', the test of his strength and ability to handle a really difficult situation as successfully as President Kennedy. But once UDI was declared he seemed to have little idea how to deal with it. 'Nothing more conventional, prim and proper', commented Crossman, 'could be conceived than this government's reaction to what they describe as rebellion in Rhodesia'; even covert operations or systematic propaganda seem not to have been considered. Only Judith Hart (minister of state, CRO, 1966–7) was prepared to 'think the unthinkable', a non-violent use of force against key economic targets by pin-point bombing after prolonged public warning.[151]

Farce it was, and farce it remained. 'The whole of this polite revolution has all the properties of a play, a film-fight, in which each party carefully plays a part, with the blows being delivered in slow-motion at the time, but appearing more dramatic later when speeded up on the screen of history'.[152] Not that there was no potential for a disaster. Lord Caradon warned Harold Wilson:

For long past I have feared a division in the world on racial issues with all the Africans and all the Asians and the Russians (and the Communist Chinese too) on one side and the Western powers on the other, with the break-up of the multiracial Commonwealth and a race conflict in Africa. It seems to me that the grant of independence to a white minority government in Rhodesia would set off such a train of terrible events.[153]

That much agreed, the Labour government did not treat this issue with burning passion, perhaps because no-one in Whitehall believed the rebellion could succeed. Despite his initial feeling that it was 'fundamentally a moral problem' about 'race and colour',[154] Wilson was much concerned with his electoral prospects, and therefore did not want to

---

[150]   Murphy, ed., *Central Africa*, pt 1, intro., pp. civ–cvi, and pt 2, p. 524 (no. 419), Cabinet committee meeting, 25 March 1965, statement by Lord Gardiner.

[151]   *Crossman diaries*, pp. 141–2; (14 November 1965); *ESC*, pt 2, p. 270 (no. 219) [November 1966].

[152]   R. W. M. Dias, '[Rhodesia:] Legal politics: norms behind the *Grundnorm*', *Cambridge Law Journal*, vol. 26 (1968), p. 259.

[153]   (Robert) Michael Stewart Papers, Churchill Archives Centre, STWT 9/5/4, Caradon to Wilson, 3 June 1966 (copy).

[154]   *ESC*, pt 2, p. 221 (no. 207), to Commonwealth prime ministers, 11 January 1966.

appear excessively harsh towards Rhodesian 'kith and kin'. Nor did
ministers want outright confrontation with South Africa, for sanctions
would have to involve measures against South Africa to stand any
chance of working, and that could react on the High Commission
Territories and indeed on the stability of the whole region. They
were also worried about the economic backlash of sanctions on
Britain itself, especially if supplies of popular Rhodesian tobacco, and
Zambian copper for British industry, were interrupted. This could
produce, it was said, a disastrous dislocation of British industry and the
frustration of economic plans, even leading to devaluation and bankruptcy.[155] The purpose of sanctions changed over the years. Initially
sanctions were designed to try and produce a 'loyalist' reaction, but
instead of strengthening the moderates, they merely alienated them.
Sanctions were then revised in order to force concessions. This did not
work either.[156] Wilson found the UN and infuriated Afro-Asian
members of the Commonwealth on his back, calling for some real
action. Tanzania broke off diplomatic relations with Britain (so did
Ghana, more briefly), and there was a Zambian jibe about 'a toothless
bulldog'.

The facing this illegal purported independence was the governor from
1959 to 1969, Sir Humphrey Gibbs, a patrician Old Etonian, a
Rhodesian dairy-farmer, perhaps even a rare example of the almost
mythical 'gentlemanly capitalist', trying to uphold the decent values of
a paternalistic ethical empire, personally concerned to ensure that
gentlemen of whatever race, provided they had the right schooling,
should run things.[157] He was not of the stature that would enable a comparison to be made with the great Lord Elgin in Canada confronted
with the Montreal rebels in 1849, when the Queen's representative
was pelted by the mob with stones the size of cobbles and bricks, and
never gave in.

The secretary of state for Commonwealth relations defined five principles as conditions for recognition of Rhodesian independence:

First, the principle and intention of unimpeded progress to majority rule, already
enshrined in the 1961 Constitution, would have to be maintained and guaranteed. There would also have to be guarantees against retrogressive amendment of
the Constitution. There would have to be immediate improvement in the political
status of the African population. There would have to be progress towards the

---

[155] Morgan, *Callaghan*, p. 250; *ESC*, pt 2, p. 192 (no. 197).
[156] Garner, *The Commonwealth Office*, pp. 392–3.
[157] P. Henshaw, review of Alan Megahey, *Humphrey Gibbs, the beleaguered governor: Southern
Rhodesia, 1929–1969* (1998) in *Canadian Journal of African Studies*, vol. 32 (1998),
pp. 636–8.

ending of racial discrimination. The British Government would need to be satisfied that any basis proposed for independence was acceptable to the people of Rhodesia as a whole.[158]

A sixth principle was added in January 1966: no oppression of the majority by the minority, or of the minority by the majority. These principles remained the basic negotiating position for successive British governments.

The initial practical problems of UDI arose out of the consequences for Zambia. Kaunda asked for British troops to defend the Kariba hydro-electric-power complex. Wilson had to pacify Kaunda, but held to the policy of not using force in Rhodesia: 'we do not want to take a sledge-hammer to this when a pair of nutcrackers will do'.[159] Rhodesia imposed heavy duties on the export of coal and coke from Wankie, and then in retaliation for oil sanctions, cut supplies of oil to Zambia passing through Rhodesia. An international rescue was mounted by air, rail and lake to get essential oil supplies to Zambia.

Wilson felt he had to take personal charge of the Rhodesian problem. It became an obsession. It did his reputation no good. Foolishly, in January 1966 he told Commonwealth leaders that sanctions would end UDI in 'weeks not months'.[160] Aiming above all to return Rhodesia to a legal relationship with Britain, and believing Smith might be split from the hardliners, he decided upon negotiations, meeting Smith on board the naval cruiser HMS *Tiger* in December 1966, just off Gibraltar. Not quite cloak-and-dagger stuff, but dramatic enough; Smith had to take sea-sickness pills. Although Wilson did his best to sound tough and principled, he offered Smith a remarkable number of concessions for a new constitution.[161] When Barbara Castle –Wilson's fiercest critic on Rhodesia – complained in Cabinet that in a choice between evils the prime minister had chosen the greater evil, since the terms amounted to a sell-out, Wilson told her: 'Let's not forget we aren't like General MacArthur on the battleship *Appotomax*, accepting the unconditional surrender of the Japanese . . . This is a British government which has failed to reach its objectives painfully accepting the best agreed terms they could get for the voluntary winding-up of the rebellion by the rebels themselves, and since that is the case we can't quite expect the terms we would have imposed if we'd

---

[158] CRO to prime minister of Southern Rhodesia, 21 September 1965: F. Madden, ed., *Imperial constitutional documents, 1765–1965: a supplement* (1966), pp. 111–12; E. Windrich, ed., *Rhodesian problem: a documentary record, 1923–1973* (1975), p. 205.

[159] *ESC*, pt 2, p. 214 (no. 204), Wilson to 'My dear Kenneth', 13 December 1965.

[160] B. Pimlott, *Harold Wilson* (1992), pp. 366–81, 449–58.

[161] *ESC*, pt 2, pp. 271–4 (no. 220), 3 December 1966.

won' – this said in a clear and measured way.[162] Even so, Smith and his
supporters, ever suspicious, turned these terms down, major concessions
and all. Crossman thought Wilson swung egotistically from 'extreme
appeasement' to an almost hypocritically indignant stand on 'a great
moral issue' when Smith refused.[163]

Shortly after the *Tiger* talks, the UN Security Council finally approved
selective mandatory sanctions, and a ban on oil exports to Rhodesia from
any country, so the government had to withdraw all previous offers from
Smith and announce that their policy was now, as the Commonwealth
prime ministers had wanted, 'Nibmar' (No independence before majority rule). Nevertheless, Wilson's main concern was to keep channels
of communication with Smith open, in the hope of reaching a settlement,
a policy which international agitation, whether in the UN or the
Commonwealth, only inhibited. Desperately wanting to believe that there
was a good prospect of success and that Smith might finally come to heel,
Wilson arranged further talks which were eventually held on HMS
Fearless in October 1968. The terms on offer were not much different
from those discussed on *Tiger*. Mrs Castle was furious once again; 49
Labour MPs voted against the government and 100 abstained in a debate
on the proposals – and Smith again rejected them. Their thirty hours of
debate afloat Wilson said was the most exhausting experience of his life.
He was surprised by Smith's sharpness and drive.[164]

Shortly after this, Smith decided to declare a republic. This decision
was both a momentous way of deepening the rebellion and a studied
insult to Wilson's willingness to contemplate a deal. In July 1969 the
small, mainly white, electorate in a referendum voted for a new republican constitution. The impasse was now complete. It was deeply embarrassing. Governor Gibbs finally abandoned his enclave at Government
House. It was to stand empty for ten years.

Could the Rhodesian problem have been handled differently? Or
perhaps it was a truly intractable issue? Certainly neither conciliation nor
coercion was possible. Sanctions were a two-edged weapon and could not
be pressed to the point where they inflicted economic damage on Britain
itself. This meant Smith was not really put under sustained pressure.
Force, as we have seen, continued to be ruled out as too dangerous and
impracticable. The result of ruling out that option was farcical, but at
least it was not tragedy, given that war on the settlers could have stimulated turmoil in Britain, for anti-war sceptics could never have been

---

[162] Crossman, *The diaries of a Cabinet minister*, vol. II: *1966–8* (ed. J. Morgan), pp. 147–9
(4 December 1966); *Crossman diaries* (ed. Howard), pp. 249–54 (6–8 December 1966).
[163] *Crossman diaries*, pp. 253–4.   [164] *Ibid.*, pp. 473–4 (8–15 October 1968).

won round grudgingly as they were mostly to be when fighting the Argentinians in the Falklands in 1982; there was also the danger of widening the area of conflict in Africa, 'setting Africa ablaze'. Abdication was not a serious option either. It would offend the Commonwealth as a surrender to an illegal regime; it would be 'a great blow to our national prestige and difficult to reconcile with our desire to maintain a world role'.[165] Declaring it to be a problem of proven intractability and impossible to solve, and handing over to the United Nations, would have smacked of a previous Labour government's unhappy withdrawal from Palestine in 1948. The UN indeed was seen as part of the problem, since it served as the agency whereby militant African states could co-ordinate their pressure on Britain.[166]

The Defence and Oversea Policy Committee reviewed the position in March 1968. Sanctions had been tried at 'considerable economic and moral cost to ourselves'. Having to buy alternative (American) tobacco supplies – then considered vital for national contentment – had an adverse effect on the balance of payments. An argument in favour of pulling out arose from disengagement from the Far East, 'and there was even more reason to do so in Africa, which in world terms was much less important'. On the other hand, ministers doubted whether there was any escaping profound responsibilities: 'the question of race relations was the most vital issue of this century; and in the present tide of opinion a policy of secret disengagement was impossible'. The prime minister summed up saying it was clear they faced a long haul. Long-term policy was unclear, 'although it remained a firm objective to avoid action which would lead to economic confrontation with South Africa'. Meaningless gestures should be avoided. A negotiated settlement seemed impossible as long as 'the extremists of the present regime remained in power', but the door should not be closed on the possibility. In the UN, the tactics should be to retain control of the situation and avoid developments there which would be against British interests and limit their freedom of action.[167]

One reason why the Rhodesian crisis was so worrying was the impact it might have on the High Commission Territories, dangerously sandwiched between Rhodesian instability and predatory South Africa. The FO wanted the UN brought in to provide economic assistance for development and then gradually to assume political responsibility. This of course was never going to get ministerial approval. Wilson then put forward in 1968 a proposal for a Southern African development plan, for the benefit of the previously federated Central African territories and

[165] ESC, pt 2, pp. 255–60 (no. 216), 28 July 1966, J. O. Wright to prime minister.
[166] Miller, Survey of Commonwealth affairs, pp. 244–6.
[167] ESC, pt 2, pp. 286–91 (no. 228), minutes of committee meeting, 8 March 1968.

Basutoland, Bechuanaland, and Swaziland. He asked for it to be given priority investigation, seeing it as a means by which the neighbouring countries might be persuaded to accept a Rhodesian settlement falling short of Nibmar. Sums of the order of £50 million for each of ten years might be raised from various sources, and all this would be additional to aid they would receive. Officials in the main Whitehall departments were quick to question the plan, on the grounds that Britain could not afford it (£10 million would have to come from Britain), and that other countries would not participate. The Ministry of Overseas Development thought it 'thoroughly unsound in terms of aid'. The idea was not pursued.[168]

(4) Swaziland

Swaziland became independent in 1968, the last of the British African territories to do so, with the peculiar exception of Zimbabwe. It will be particularly instructive to examine this fag-end of British decolonisation at some length, for it has some surprising things to tell us.[169]

The first thing to notice is that Swaziland was a notable example of intensive economic improvement under 'the late colonial state', which showed just what could be achieved, given the chance. The post-independence prosperity of Swaziland was almost entirely due to the measures taken from about 1950. Before the 1950s very little had been done, apart from setting up an asbestos export industry in 1938 at Havelock, which became one of the five largest asbestos mines in the world. Within a period of ten years, however, by the end of 1964 a trans-territorial highway and railway line to Mozambique, connecting Swaziland to the port of Lourenço Marques (Maputo), had been completed; a central power-scheme, a new iron-ore mine at Ngwenya, and a coal-mine at Mpaka had all been opened; and an industrial estate at Matsapa (with Swaziland's first cotton ginnery) was almost fully operational. The Ngwenya mine supplied high-grade iron ore to Japan. In 1950 a government-run cattle-holding area at Impala Ranch (25,000 acres) was established for cattle culled from over-stocked herds. The timber resources of 80,000 acres of forest in northern Swaziland were

---

[168] P. J. Henshaw, ed., *Southern Africa* (BDEEP, forthcoming), minute by prime minister, 30 August 1968; *ESC*, pt 3, pp. 394–6 (no. 382).

[169] The key analyses are by C. P. Potholm: 'Changing political configurations in Swaziland', *Journal of Modern African Studies* vol. 4 (1966), pp. 313–22; *Swaziland: the dynamics of political modernisation* (Berkeley, CA, 1972); 'Swaziland under Sobhuza II: the future of an African monarchy', *Round Table: the Commonwealth Journal of International Affairs*, vol. 64, no. 254 (1974), pp. 219–27; and, for the relationship with South Africa, 'Swaziland', in C. P. Potholm and R. Dale, eds., *Southern Africa in perspective* (New York, 1972), pp. 141–53.

exploited from 1955. In 1959 the Usutu Pulp Company was formed to process the timber of a 107,000-acre estate of pine (and some eucalyptus), the largest man-made forest in Africa. Several irrigation schemes were completed, the biggest at Malkerns, over 6,000 acres, with a diversified output, notably rice and citrus fruits; there was also a large irrigated dairy-farming area in the north, and, a little to the south of it, the Vuvulane sugar-producing scheme. By 1962 sugar had become Swaziland's major export. Nearly all of these were Colonial Development Corporation projects, and among its few unequivocal successes. Central to all these developments was the completion of the freight railway operated by the Caminhos de Ferro de Mozambique. The track followed a route first surveyed eighty years earlier, along the Usushwane river valley out of the mountainous highveld, and it linked many of the new industrial enterprises: 139.5 miles in all. It gave Swaziland an outlet to the sea independent of South Africa. The progress of the railway project was monitored at the highest ministerial level, with Macmillan taking a particular interest.[170]

Politically, each of the three High Commission Territories show how political progress sometimes only followed metropolitan constitutional initiatives. Modern political parties were founded in all three only from 1959, mainly in response to announcements of constitutional reform. British stewardship was adversely criticised in the UN General Assembly in 1962. Basutoland and Bechuanaland achieved independence in 1966 relatively smoothly. Swaziland was a bit more problematic and dropped a little behind. It provides a fascinating exception to the classic pattern of fruitful co-operation between British proconsul and national leader in the transfer of power – Mountbatten and Nehru, Arden-Clarke and Nkrumah, Maurice Dorman and Milton Margai, Turnbull and Nyerere, MacDonald and Kenyatta, Glyn Jones and Hastings Banda, Peter Fawcus and Seretse Khama. That Brian Marwick, of all people, should fall out with Sobhuza (the royal Swazi leader) was surprising. Marwick had grown up in Swaziland, and spoke siSwati perfectly; he had spent most of his career there (apart from six years in Basutoland and three in Nigeria), and he had written the standard anthropological account of the Swazi. But his friendly relations with Sobhuza withered away in disillusionment as the latter became 'too obsessed with his personal position to act in a statesmanlike manner'.[171] The course for Swaziland had been set by High Commissioner Sir John Maud early in 1959: long-term policy was 'the

[170] H. S. Simelane, *Colonialism and economic change in Swaziland, 1940–1960* (Mbabane, Swaziland, 2003); *Conservative government and the end of empire, 1957–1964*, pt 2, pp. 34–40, 68–79 (nos. 310, 311, 323–6).
[171] DO 119/1425, no. 1, despatch, 25 April 1962.

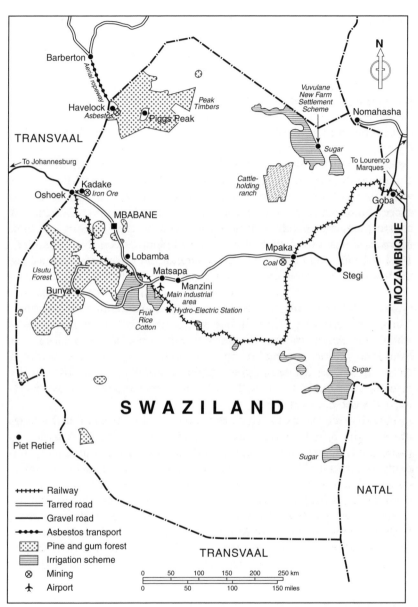

Map 5.1 Swaziland: railway and economic development to 1964

creation of a non-racial state'. Marwick also was firmly committed to 'the establishment of a non-racial democracy'.[172] Sobhuza, the Swazi National Council, and the European settler community who held ⅖ths of the land, in more or less unholy alliance, would have none of it. They preferred a multi-racial power-sharing in a Leg Co. divided 50:50 between Europeans and Swazis, and no elections on a common roll. This was completely at odds with British decolonisation policy in general, and all officials believed it would only pile up trouble for the future. There had to be scope, they believed, for meeting changes which were bound to develop rapidly in Swaziland as elsewhere, and the constitution had to commend itself to the rising generation of educated Swazi. Moreover, it was important not to fail in creating a non-racial state, if only because a successful Swazi model might have a beneficial effect on South Africa. A constitution was therefore imposed in 1963 by the secretary of state. Marwick refused to allow Sobhuza a tribal plebiscite on this. In January 1964 Sobhuza went ahead with his referendum notwithstanding, asking the Swazi to choose – in effect – between 'the lion' (himself) and the 'reindeer' (Marwick). (It should he noted that while the lion was a recognised symbol of Swazi royalty, the reindeer is an animal unfamiliar to Africans.) The exact figures are disputed, but by any standards there was an overwhelming demonstration of support for Sobhuza.[173] Marwick left Swaziland, angrily cursing 'in some quarters, an impenetrable conceit, a clutching at crutches to support limping traditions, a Canutism in the face of the rising tides of new thoughts and experiences which are flooding our Swazi backwater'.[174]

This diatribe seems to have been directed not so much at the king, more at the 8,000-strong European community, who he regarded as embittered, selfish, irresponsible and aggressively manipulative, too ready to back a traditionalist king as their protection against black majority rule. Marwick's formal farewell message in 1964 adopted the well-tried medieval English device of attacking royal advisers rather than the monarch himself. Swaziland, he said, had failed to produce political leaders capable of giving the king 'sound, objective and fearless advice', or of removing the heavy burden from him. The tribal 'Swazi Nation' administrators he thought saggingly inefficient and consumed with

---

[172] DO 119/1407, no. 27, despatch, 23 February 1959.

[173] H. Kuper, *Sobhuza II, Ngwenyama and king of Swaziland: the story of an hereditary ruler and his country* (1978). Variant figures given include: Kuper, 122,000:154; Potholm, 123,000:162; Matsebula (see note 185 below), 124,218: 162. The total votes cast were said to exceed 100 per cent by 5 per cent.

[174] J. Halpern, *South Africa's hostages: Basutoland, Bechuanaland and Swaziland* (Harmondsworth, 1965 edn), pp. 360–2.

paranoia. 'Rule the country or get out' was his final and distinctly intemperate advice to London: the Swazi state was rotten to the core and in crisis.[175]

Marwick's successor was Sir Francis Loyd, with more than twenty years' experience in Kenya. Loyd was much more indulgent towards Sobhuza, perhaps comparing him mentally with the newly statesmanlike Kenyatta, and not unfavourably.[176] Loyd chaired a commission to prepare a new constitution; it had European members but no 'modern' African politicians.

Sobhuza and the whole extended Dlamini royal family had always been regarded by the British as a useless, self-indulgent, anachronistic survival, the 'Swazi Nation' as a hollow memory of ageing traditionalist illiterates. High Commissioner Lord Harlech in 1941 had described Swaziland as 'a hopeless little country' with 'wretched people': Sobhuza he found polygamous, 'sensual, suspicious and intensely superstitious', the unsurprising target of missionary criticism.[177] But from about 1960, rather suddenly Sobhuza began to be hailed as a sort of African de Gaulle: 'he is a lovable character – shrewd, determined and conservative', with wide interests in world affairs, while 'his admiration for General de Gaulle is a revealing characteristic'.[178] The transformation was consolidated by his remarkable landmark speech on 23 April 1960 before an invited audience of 2,500 notables. Sobhuza spoke in siSwati for two hours. He was influenced by Macmillan's 'wind of change' speech, to which he referred at least three times, and by the 'worrying prospect' of the influence of developments in other parts of Africa, not least the troubles in Nyasaland and the dissolving Congo. The idea of 'one man one vote' was, he said, unsuited to Africa, or to Swaziland at any rate, where 'modern politics' could lead to civil war. He thought it unsafe for Africans to forget their customs and grasp at unfamiliar alien European ones, which all too easily led to exploitation by 'power-greedy' upstart leaders.[179]

---

[175] *Conservative government and the end of empire, 1957–1964*, pt 2, pp. 517–22 (no. 486).

[176] If Loyd really did see a comparison with Kenyatta, he was not alone – see R. J. M. Wilson to FO, 9 December 1966 (*ESC*, pt 3, p. 74 (no. 296); Wilson was in the British embassy). Kenyatta was by 1966 regarded as one of Africa's 'wise leaders', a 'true statesman' and 'mellow sage', according to Malcolm MacDonald (*ESC*, pt 2, pp. 253–5 (no. 215), to CRO, 17 June 1966, and p. 366 (no. 254) despatch to FCO, 9 December 1966).

[177] PREM 11/44 no. 1, 2 October 1941. The unfavourable view went back to an influential book by Archdeacon C. C. Watts, *Dawn in Swaziland* (1922), esp. pp. 122–3; for further evidence, see also R. Hyam, *The failure of South African expansion, 1908–1948* (1972), pp. 99–100; Kuper, *Sobhuza II*, p. 146.

[178] *Round Table, quarterly review of British Commonwealth Affairs*, vol. 53 (1963), pp. 33–6, 'The High Commission Territories: a remnant of British Africa'.

[179] Kuper, *Sobhuza II*, pp. 210–17; DO 119/1409, no. 9.

The next few years were to see an astonishing erosion of all the official British guidelines on transfers of power, and a series of unprecedented concessions by the Labour government. The issue of the ownership and control of mineral rights – previously the exclusive domain of the colonial state – was the vital hinge of decolonisation debate in Swaziland. Sobhuza knew that to have any chance of effective survival in the new era his political power must be backed by economic power. The imposed 1963 constitution had put the power of legislation over minerals into the hands of the Leg Co., and the actual granting of rights and concessions in the hands of the British Commissioner, acting after consultation. Sobhuza now planned to get back unfettered control of the minerals, within the framework of a royalist control of independence. He seized on British faint-heartedness to realise his aims, counting on a Labour government's finding it too embarrassing to reject demands for independence from an overwhelming majority of Swazi, just because they happened to be pro-monarch.[180]

Thus in the constitution of April 1967 providing for internal self-government, the Labour government conceded to a ruler widely regarded as 'reactionary' what their Conservative predecessors had steadily refused. The title of 'king' was accepted, though previously it had been insisted that Sobhuza was merely 'paramount chief'. This change acknowledged the claim made by the monarchy since 1903. The constitution vested control of the minerals in the king, acting with the advice of his cabinet, which was bound to consult a committee appointed by the king. It gave the king absolute power to block changes in constitutionally entrenched clauses, which included the establishment of the monarchy and the powers of the king.[181]

The contrast with Lesotho is instructive. Whereas the adoption of the Westminster model appeared to be a fixed condition for the independence of Lesotho in 1966 – even if it meant a minority government in charge and the reduction of the paramount chief (*morena*) to the position of a figure-head – in the emerging Swazi formula the paramount (*ngwenyama*, the lion) was allowed to be a virtual royal dictator. From 1966 the BaSotho monarch merely had the constitutional right to be informed and to appoint one-third of the Senate, even though – in striking contrast to Sobhuza – Moshoeshoe II (great-great-great-grandson of Moshoeshoe I) was a Roman Catholic educated at Ampleforth, more westernised, and of course monogamous.[182] Even more striking, the *kgosi*

[180] J. Halpern, in *Venture*, vol. 18, no. 6 (Fabian Society, 1966); R. P. Stevens, 'Swazi political development', *Journal of Modern African Studies*, vol. 1 (1963), pp. 327–50.

[181] *A yearbook of the Commonwealth for 1980* (12th edn, 1980), pp. 333–4.

[182] R. F. Weisfelder, *The BaSotho monarchy: a spent force or a dynamic political factor?* (Ohio, 1972).

of the Bangwato in Botswana, Seretse Khama, became a commoner president. Well-versed in British ways of thought, and married to an Englishwoman, Seretse was drawn to democracy as Sobhuza was not. Other hereditary Tswana chiefs decided to behave tactfully, and there was no confrontation in Bechuanaland between traditionalists and modernisers; most of the chiefs became civil servants paid by central government.[183]

The 1967 Swazi constitution was designed to take the country into independence with as few adjustments as possible. (These were agreed at Marlborough House in February 1968.) Three years earlier, Sobhuza had founded his Mbokodvo party or 'national movement' (INM: it means 'grindstone', a hard implement but able to blend, something in use in every household and a traditional symbol).[184] In the elections of 1967, Mbokodvo, led by Prince Makhosini Dlamini, got 79.4 per cent of the vote, taking, with its allies, all 24 elected seats in the assembly, a clean sweep. Of the eight parties contesting the election, six failed to win any seats at all. Because barely half the children of school-age actually went to school – Swaziland had one of the highest illiteracy rates in the world, 75 per cent – the 'ballot papers' were small woven squares like table-mats. Candidates were represented by symbols, such as a pair of spectacles, a plough, a comb, a pair of trousers (though quaintly this was drawn by the only woman candidate). Voters drove a six-inch nail through the symbol of the candidate of their choice.[185]

After continuing demonstrations of support for Sobhuza, and the bandwagon success of his own Mbokodvo movement, absorbing the European parties, the Labour government made more retrogressive concessions to him. Under the 1968 independence constitution: (a) the ngwenyama was recognised as king of Swaziland (and not just king 'of the Swazi') and head of state; (b) six out of thirty members of the House of Assembly were appointed by the king, as was the prime minister; (c) control of the country's mineral wealth was vested directly in the king, advised not by the cabinet but by a minerals committee appointed by him (so ended the saga of 'King Sobhuza's Mines'); (d) the ndlovukazi (she-elephant), or Queen Mother (actually the senior wife of the king) would act as regent when required.

---

[183] P. Fawcus (with A. Tilbury), *Botswana: the road to independence* (Gaborone, 2000), esp. pp. 208–28. Ironically, the contentious renunciation of the chieftainship in 1956 by Seretse and Tshekedi Khama proved to be 'the decisive turning-point' for Botswana (p. 53).   [184] Kuper, *Sobhuza II*, p. 250.
[185] J. S. M. Matsebula, *A history of Swaziland* (2nd edn, 1976, 1988) p. 194; Halpern, *South Africa's hostages*, p. 365.

It was a constitution without parallel in the annals of British decolonisation,[186] a striking demonstration of the way in which the British policymakers not only threw in the towel but had come to value prospects of stability above democracy in successor states. The British handed over power to in many ways a more-or-less unreconstructed Nguni-style monarch, with about 120 wives. The Swazi Queen Mother of the time was a sickly, illiterate old woman who had never worn a pair of shoes in her life.

The independence constitution lasted only five years, until 1973, when Sobhuza – alarmed by the appearance of a first official Opposition in parliament – abolished it, and dissolved all political parties, saying that elections produced only subversive politicians and other 'hyenas urinating upwind to stampede the cattle below'. By the time of his diamond jubilee in 1981 he had successfully restored and indeed strengthened the monarch's role as chief arbiter of decision-making. His nominated successor among his five hundred or so children (he had about 320 sons), the fourteen-year old Makhosetive, his son with Ntombi Laftwala (Queen Regent, 1983–6), was crowned as King Mswati II in April 1986. Mswati was educated at the Dorsetshire public school, Sherborne. In 2002 when Zena Mahlangu, a teenage schoolgirl, was abducted by royal aides to become Mswati's tenth wife, there was a challenge to royal absolutism in the High Court. In 2003, it was reported that he had picked his eleventh wife from thousands of semi-naked girls parading in the traditional 'reed dance'.[187]

How is this astonishing outcome in Swaziland to be explained? On the face of it, much of what could be said of the Swazi *ngwenyama* in about 1960 could be said of the *kabaka* of Buganda or the *morena* of Basutoland, where traditional systems had also survived. But Mutesa II and Moshoeshoe II, as independence approached, were already much weaker in their positions, and were both young and politically inexperienced enough to be outwitted. In Swaziland it was Sobhuza who did the outwitting, with his amiable wiliness and political skills locally unrivalled.[188] Throughout his rule since 1921 he had been steadily manoeuvring to recover rights and lands for the royal house and Swazi Nation tribal organisation. He is not to be dismissed as an unthinking traditionalist. Rather he was brilliant at 'invented tradition', rejuvenating and expanding the old political system to create the Swazi kingdom in the name of a tradition which had a good deal more to do with the efforts of

---

[186] *Swaziland: annual reports* (Her Majesty's Stationery Office).

[187] Bill Nasson, *Britannia's empire: making a British world* (Stroud, Glos., 2004), p. 199; *Round Table*, vol. 93, no. 373, p. 15, D. Ingram, 'Commonwealth update'.

[188] J. E. Spence, 'Sobhuza II, king of Swaziland', *ODNB* (2004), vol. LI, pp. 521–2.

an emerging royal elite to establish status and control, than it did with continuity from an imagined past.[189] The climax of this process, and the turning-point for Swaziland, was the king's decision to fight the June 1964 elections with a king's party, Mbokodvo. This eventually created a broader social and political base for the king. There was no real Swazi nationalism, merely a 'Dlamini nationalism'. The majority of chiefs or noble landlord rulers were members of Dlamini royal clan. More than two-thirds of all chiefdoms were controlled by its members. They had almost total control over rural life and agricultural development. 'Dlamini nationalism' now succeeded in neutralising opposition and gaining support in the towns, and it thus became recognised by the British as the predominant political force in the country.[190]

British policy, by 1967, had left the monarchy with an even firmer base from which to continue its work in moulding the post-colonial state, short-circuiting the drive to political modernisation. British policy had fatally rejected as an unsuitable collaborator in the transfer of power the Ngwane National Liberatory Congress (NNLC), the most promising hope of the modernisers. It was rejected because it had organised the first trade unions and initiated strikes in 1963 in the forestry, asbestos, iron-ore, and sugar industries, strikes which mobilised 8,000 workers, who turned ugly and unruly. Faced with the prospect of violence and a general strike (which Sobhuza would be unable to stop), a state of emergency was declared, and a British army battalion of Middle East Command (700 kilted Gordon Highlanders) was flown in from Kenya in June 1963.[191] A rotating battalion remained for four years, inhibiting the development of a modern politics after political leaders were put on trial. The duration and costs of these trials weakened the NNLC for several years. The situation in Swaziland itself did not require the prolonged presence of the garrison. Swaziland was simply and unfortunately the most convenient location for British military presence in southern Africa to deal quickly with any trouble in the High Commission Territories, which now seemed most likely to occur in Basutoland. This was an insurance policy against any breakdown of internal order such as would invite South African intervention. It seems to have had a deterrent and stabilising effect, and was

---

[189] Hugh Macmillan, in an unfavourable review of A. R. Booth, *Swaziland: tradition and change in an African kingdom* (Boulder, Colorado, 1983), in *Journal of African History*, vol. 26 (1985), p. 444.

[190] P.-H. Bischoff, *Swaziland's international relations and foreign policy: a study of a small African state in international relations* (European University Studies, Political Series, vol. 158, Berne, 1990), pp. 89–162 on the approach to independence. This book ranges more widely than its title suggests.

[191] J. Raitt, '"Green Belt" in Swaziland', *Journal of Royal United Service Institution*, vol. 109 (1964), pp. 40–4.

approved by Sobhuza. By the end of 1966, however, it was becoming too embarrassing for a Labour government to have 'blond Caucasians with guns' amidst a black population, and when a regional backlash was threatened against Rhodesian sanctions, Healey was determined to get them out before a denial of over-flying facilities marooned them. This created the final pressure for Swazi independence. In all three High Commission Territories independence was based on Labour's desire to be permanently rid of responsibility for defence and internal security in countries where there were no British interests.[192]

The feebleness of political opposition played straight into the hands of the king. Political leaders were hopelessly divided among themselves and they were inept. The first party formed, the African nationalist Swaziland Progressive Party (SPP, 1960), was subject to splits: first the NNLC broke away (1962), and then two further splits occurred in 1964. The SPP looked to Ghana for inspiration and funding. These wider contacts and the goals and rhetoric of the Pan-African movement were seductive though largely irrelevant. The leader of the NNLC, Dr Ambrose Zwane, as part of his campaign in the 1964 election, presented a series of torch- and candle-lit morality plays to commemorate Lumumba of the Congo, a figure only slightly better known in Swaziland than the reindeer. Zwane stood in the same constituency as the other principal politician, Dr Allen Nxumalo, leader of the 'non-racial' Swaziland Democratic Party. (Again, in 1972, when the NNLC had split into two parties, Zwane stood directly against the leader of the other faction, Samketi.) Energies were thus seriously dispersed, when they needed to be concentrated. The contrast is striking with the construction of the Alliance by the Malayan politicians of UMNO (United Malays National Organisation) and MCA (Malayan Chinese Association) in 1955, putting them in a strong negotiating position vis-à-vis Britain.

Some other factors may have militated against the development of a modern politics. Only 8 per cent of Swazi were urbanised in 1964 (13 per cent in 1970). The economy flourished under Sobhuza's stewardship. And there was no army, so often elsewhere the focus of discontent against an incumbent regime. The Swazi European community's ultra-conservative party, the United Swaziland Association (USA), decided to support Mbokodvo, and sealed its fate thereby, being swallowed up by it. Initially over-confident, the Europeans over-played their hand. The USA collapsed with unexpected rapidity, not even contesting the 1967 elections.[193]

---

[192] Henshaw, ed., *Southern Africa* (BDEEP), drawing mainly on the papers in CO 1048.

[193] Potholm, 'Changing political configurations in Swaziland', pp. 321–2; *The Times* obituary, 'King Sobhuza II', 24 August 1982.

In large measure, however, the outcome in Swaziland was the direct result of the weary complaisance of the British Labour government, deeply concerned to head off United Nations interference, which might make South Africa more unsympathetic to Swaziland. Gordon Walker as, briefly, foreign secretary, wanted to get the UN involved politically, 'otherwise we are going to be faced with extremely awkward decisions'. Serious doubts were expressed by the CO and by Ambassador Stephenson: it was risky and unnecessary. Gordon Walker thought them 'over-cautious': 'we don't want to keep these [High Commission] territories. They could be an immense embarrassment to us. If the UN is there it may make them more sensible about economic sanctions [against South Africa]. If SA takes action against the territories, with the UN there, this would not be a disaster; but I am sure they would not.'[194] Impetus for a UN political involvement lapsed with Gordon Walker's departure from the FO, leaving 'independence' as the only possible route to decolonisation.

Attachment to Sobhuza meant that ministers felt if the wishes of the Swazi people could be met in recognising him as 'king of Swaziland' progress towards independence should be smooth. But if not, 'there would be deep resentment and very possibly political unrest, which would gravely complicate the task of bringing Swaziland successfully to independence'.[195] However, either the true situation was not understood, or it was obscured. When John Stonehouse (parliamentary under-secretary of state, CRO, 1966–7) said in the Commons on 28 November 1966 that they expected the king to 'be a constitutional monarch' and 'most of the political power will be clearly in the hands of the elected Ministers at the next election', this hardly reflected the views of informed observers on the spot.[196] And no further clarification was ever offered to Parliament. In 1970 it was being confidently asserted by Sir Arthur Galsworthy (deputy under-secretary of state, CRO, 1966–8) that all the supposed difficulties about combining a king-ruler and a political party system had fallen away.[197] Just three years were required to prove how wrong he was.

Are there any possible parallels? Tonga, which became independent in June 1970, is not really comparable. The 'king of Tonga' ruled a mere 90,000 people (as opposed to 500,000 in Swaziland), under a constitution formulated in 1875; and although Tonga had great regional prestige

---

[194] *ESC*, pt 3, pp. 61–2 (no. 291), minute, 5 January 1965.
[195] *ESC*, pt 3, p. 68 (no. 294), minute to prime minister by Lord Longford, 4 February 1966.
[196] *ESC*, pt 3, p. 73 (no. 296), 9 December 1966, letter from R. J. M. Wilson to FO. Prime Minister Harold Wilson never refers to Swaziland in *The Labour government* except once in passing, to mention its first appearance at a Commonwealth Prime Ministers' meeting in 1969 (p. 592).
[197] *ESC*, pt 3, p. 264 (no. 352), 8 July 1970, Galsworthy to foreign secretary.

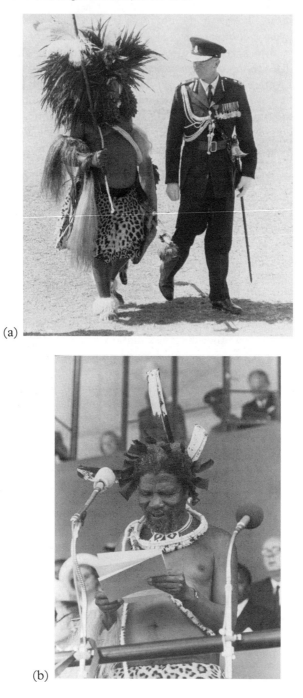

(a)

(b)

(c)

Illustration 5.2 Swaziland independence celebrations, 1968 and 1969.
(a) King Sobhuza II in traditional royal warrior's ceremonial dress, with
the Queen's last commissioner, Sir Francis Loyd.
(b) King Sobhuza II speaks to the Swazi people about independence.
(c) Princess Alexandra of Kent opens the Swaziland Parliament building in Lobamba as part of the independence anniversary celebrations,
September 1969, in the presence of King Sobhuza. The *Ndlovukazi* is
seated on the right.
(Swaziland Information Service.)

as the last of the old Polynesian kingdoms, it was by then almost wholly Christian, another feature differentiating it from Swaziland. King Taufa'ahau Tupou II was educated at the University of Sydney, and succeeded his mother Queen Salote in 1965. Perhaps a better parallel would be the Sultan of Brunei, Omar Ali Saifuddin III (1950–67), who also managed to escape democratic politics, by refusing to join Malaysia in 1963, retaining the autonomy of his kingdom (population about 85,000), to the dismay of and despite the pressure from the British government. The Sultan was criticised (rather as Sobhuza had been) as a decadent remnant of feudal society. As in Swaziland, government became a family business; the Sultan was as determined to keep control of oil revenues as Sobhuza was of the minerals.[198] Today, the Sultan of Brunei is one of the richest men in the world. Britain remained responsible for the external defence of Brunei for many years, even though other responsibilities East-of-Suez were run down from 1968.

(5) East-of-Suez

In official parlance the 'Indo-Pacific theatre' was preferred to 'East-of-Suez'. The Indian Ocean, with all its vibrant inter-connections of migrations, cultures, trade and shipping, had become a 'British lake', wherein imperial supremacy was originally maintained as a kind of overspill from the Indian raj, and interests, especially strategic interests, continued to be pursued with only a brief interruption by the Japanese in the Second World War. In the era of decolonisation the capacity to project military power throughout the region was increased.[199] Treaty base-rights remained in Ceylon until 1957 and Singapore until 1971. Military interventions took place in newly-independent countries around the Indian Ocean rim: in Malaysia (1963), Kuwait (1961), Tanzania (1964) and Mauritius (1965). Of these, much the most alarming was the *Konfrontasi*, (Confrontation) with Indonesia (a greatly superior enemy, with a population of 100 million) in Malaysia. With 8,000 troops in Borneo by the end of 1964, and 20,000 on the Malaysian mainland (with more to follow), there was real potential for this involvement to become Britain's Vietnam. The relief when Sukarno called off Confrontation in 1966 was

---

[198] *Yearbook of the Commonwealth for 1980*, pp. 346–8, for Tonga; for Brunei, see A. J. Stockwell, ed., *Malaysia* (BDEEP, 2004), pp. lxxxii–lxxxv, and 421; and 'Britain and Brunei, 1945–1963: imperial retreat and royal ascendancy', *Modern Asian Studies*, vol. 38 (2004), pp. 785–820.

[199] Ashley Jackson, 'The British empire in the Indian Ocean', in D. Rumley and S. Chaturvedi, eds., *Geopolitical orientations: regionalism and security in the Indian Ocean* (New Delhi, 2004), pp. 34–55.

enormous.[200] In 1965 a new colony was established, the British Indian Ocean Territory. For a time this included dependencies of Mauritius and the Seychelles, such as Aldabra, but the latter reverted to the Seychelles upon independence in 1976, after which the territory comprised only those islands forming the Chagos Archipelago. Due south from Bombay and the Maldives, and about equidistant from Zanzibar and Jakarta, centred on Diego Garcia, the Territory remained strategically important, not least to the Americans.[201]

Sustained American interest in Britain's East-of-Suez role dated from 1962, because the USA did not want to have to expand its own commitments in the region while fighting in Vietnam. The American administration had lost little time in impressing on Wilson the importance of Britain's East-of-Suez role, particularly since Britain would not commit troops to Vietnam. The Americans were prepared to support and subsidise the British government to continue a presence which Wilson wanted in any case to maintain. Dean Rusk (US secretary of state for most of the 1960s) said 'Don't pull out, Britain, because we cannot do the job of world policeman alone', urging that 'the UK has a multiplying effect on our own role'.[202] Gordon Walker regarded it as a fundamental principle of foreign policy that 'influence in and around the Indian Ocean' was more important than having forces in Germany or bases in the Mediterranean. In his view, Britain should remain strong enough to offer the USA a 'global partnership' or an interdependent 'co-ordination of world politics, without which our role as a world power lacks reality'.[203] These were splendid geopolitical propositions, but not all ministers agreed with them. The continuation of the eastern presence was contested by some of them from the beginning. Reaching a decision in 1968 to leave was an incremental and complex process, much complicated by ministerial equivocation and changes of opinion. It was something which

---

[200] W. R. Louis, 'The dissolution of the British empire in the era of Vietnam', *American Historical Review*, vol. 107 (2002), pp. 1–25 (Presidential address). According to an FCO memo (March 1967), the end of Confrontation in 1966 was Britain's 'greatest success' of the decade: 'the East Asian watershed is not ahead of us in Vietnam but behind us in Indonesia', *ibid*, p. 19.

[201] See the excellent map in *ESC*, pt 2, opp. p. 238 (no. 345), and the sketch-map overleaf.

[202] D.B. Kunz, ' "Somewhat mixed up together": Anglo-American defence and financial policy during the 1960s', *JICH*, vol. 27 (1999), pp. 213–32, repr. in R.D. King and R.W. Kilson, eds., *The statecraft of British imperialism: essays in honour of Wm Roger Louis*.

[203] 'Thoughts on foreign policy', August 1964, Churchill Archives Centre, GNWR 3/4, printed in R. D. Pearce, ed., *Patrick Gordon Walker: political diaries, 1932–1971*, pp. 298–302; *ESC*, pt 1, pp. 53–6 (no. 9), minute to prime minister (PREM 13/216, ff. 6–9), 23 November 1965. The partnership with and the influence upon shaping US policies was, Gordon Walker thought, 'cardinal to the conduct of our whole foreign policy' (*ESC*, pt 1, p. 300 (no. 89) memo, 19 November 1964).

divided right-wingers and left-wingers. Among key ministers, Callaghan came to an early conclusion that 'the basis of our policy should be to lessen our commitments as quickly as we can', in order to avoid the serious risk of bankruptcy.[204] Healey seems to have been ready *in principle* to reduce military commitments, and Brown was definitely sceptical about the East-of-Suez role. Both had concerns about timing and fixed dates, however, and Brown became increasingly willing that withdrawal should be gradual. Wilson and Healey wanted to keep options open, and contrived to project an image of reluctance and indecision. In addition to not unreasonable hesitations, two factors retarded a decision to pull out. The first was Indonesian *Konfrontasi*, for to withdraw would hand victory to Sukarno and quite possibly lead to the break-up of Malaysia, as well as removing the last vestiges of British influence and upsetting Australia and New Zealand. The second was equally crucial: fear of the American reaction to a precipitate withdrawal.[205]

The decision to end the East-of-Suez role was therefore the result of a lengthy, tortuous and muddled reappraisal, even if the principle had seemed sound and realistic for several years.[206] In fact, it was not a policy which had to be initiated by Labour ministers, because the officials' reassessment had begun even before the Labour government took office. It is a notable example of planners seeing the desirability of withdrawing from a region before nationalist or international opinion turned seriously against it, even if no definite timetable was set.[207]

A major reconsideration of defence requirements had taken place in the summer of 1964, leading to significant conclusions about 'future politico-strategy' in the last days of the Conservative government. Although the implications of an enforced withdrawal from Far East bases had been contemplated as early as 1960, and the value of fixed bases in general was being seriously questioned from 1961 ('nowhere did we seem to have absolute security of tenure and absolute freedom from strings'), a much more systematic analysis was under way in the late summer of 1964. Reports were commissioned from officials, covering the Middle East, the Far East, Europe, and the overall future situation. Their instructions were to assume that within the next decade

[204] FO 371/180205, no. 7, Callaghan to Gordon Walker, 1 January 1965.

[205] J. Subritzky, 'Britain, *Konfrontasi* and the end of empire in Southeast Asia, 1961–1965', *JICH*, vol. 28(2000), pp. 209–27; Louis, 'The dissolution of the British empire in the era of Vietnam', *American Historical Review*, vol. 107, pp. 13–24.

[206] P. Darby, 'East of Suez: a reassessment', in J. Baylis, ed., *British defence policy in a changing world* (1977), p. 60; this essay is almost entirely theoretical, however.

[207] J. W. Young in *The Labour governments*, vol. II: *International policy*, pp. 220–6, which provides a particularly helpful account in ch. 2, 'Economics, defence and withdrawal from East-of-Suez', pp. 31–61.

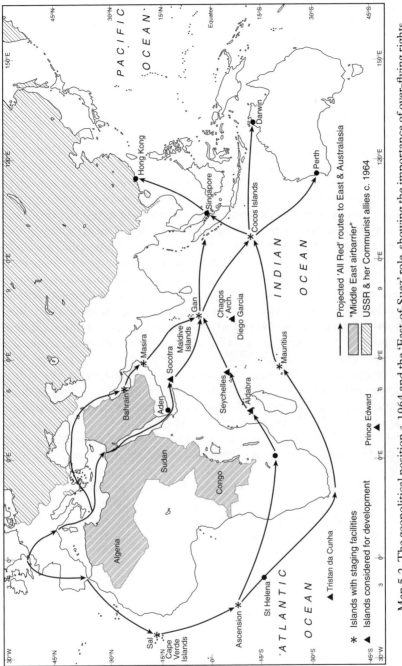

Map 5.2 The geopolitical position *c.* 1964 and the 'East-of-Suez' role, showing the importance of over-flying rights.

Singapore and Aden would be lost. These terms of reference 'represented a distinctly more radical approach than that underlying previous studies of this nature in recent years'. A sharper and more critical view could thus be taken of 'the relevance of our existing commitments to our real interests'. The long-term military value of Singapore was found to be declining, while politically the presence of so many troops was a public relations liability. It would be important to withdraw before being asked to go, and a balance had to be struck between the 'dangers of staying too long and the opposite dangers of withdrawing too fast' – the classic dilemma of decolonisation. Military presence in the Far East was found to be significantly more expensive than in the Persian Gulf, and partly for this reason the latter should have priority for continuation if it came to a choice between them. Simultaneously, a junior FO official submitted a paper recommending the dismantling of the Gulf political treaty structure, which he held was actually 'delaying progress by obscuring the need for it'. All these papers are striking evidence of at least a willingness to get rid of all forms of colonial control, whether formal or informal, even if bureaucratic inertia prevented their rapid implementation. One sentence used at this time surfaced again prominently in the reasoning behind the disengagements of 1967–1968: that global influence 'depends not only on military strength but also on our economic power and the respect (or lack of it) which the nations have for our economic performance'.[208]

Meanwhile, in developing the 'flexible mobile strategy' of the future 'island bases scheme', considerable hopes were pinned on the prospects for American help East-of-Suez. The joint development of a new defence strategy in the Indian Ocean – American support-facilities on British-owned islands for shared use – would of course solve many problems. The Aden–Gan–Singapore line of communication had recently been completed after three years spent constructing an air staging-post at Gan in the Maldives, which the inhabitants had to be coaxed to accept. This would now be reinforced by a new more southerly route to the Far East, Australia and New Zealand: Aldabra (Seychelles)–Diego Garcia (Mauritius) –Cocos/Keeling (Australia).[209] A joint survey programme with the Americans was undertaken (June to August 1964) to identify prospective sites for island staging-posts, with refuelling facilities for ships and aircraft.

So long as Britain operated militarily in the Indian Ocean area there was a strong interest in improved air, naval and communications facilities, and in seeing the Americans involved in them. Even if commitments

---

[208] *CGEE, 1957–1964*, pt 1, pp. 294–307 (nos. 79–81).
[209] *CGEE, 1957–1964*, pt 1, pp. 277–86 (nos. 73–6).

were in future reduced, there was much to be said for having the Americans already present. The USA was interested because it had no bases between the Mediterranean and the Philippines. The Americans were prepared to pay the construction costs of new developments. The British would merely have to pay compensation to local interests: compensation to Mauritius and Seychelles, buying out commercial interests, and meeting modest resettlement costs. Several islands were required together to provide the full range of communications-station, aircraft runway, naval anchorage, and fuel storage depot. Stewart and Healey regarded this as a 'strategically valuable and imaginative project', something which would give flexibility to East-of-Suez commitments at no capital cost and small recurrent outlay.

Since these isolated baselets were vulnerable to flooding, it should have been obvious that this strategy was not going to be easy to operate, even with the Americans as allies.[210] The more immediate danger was that it risked UN hostility by over-riding the interests of the inhabitants and by introducing a foreign military presence into an area previously free of fighting forces. It was proposed to deal with these objections by arguing that the UN had no competence to concern itself with a sovereign territory without an indigenous population. The inhabitants of British Indian Ocean Territory were said to be contract labourers from Mauritius and Seychelles, working on copra plantations.[211] However, this was being economical with the truth. About one-third (128 out of a population of 389 on Diego Garcia) were in fact second-generation inhabitants. Some also had dual Mauritian–UK nationality.[212] This information was withheld from the public at the time when the population of Diego Garcia was resettled in Mauritius. The announcement about the new facility was made in 1970, and the agreement formalised by an Anglo-American exchange of notes in 1972. Diego Garcia was operational by 1973. The decision was so sensitive, and the legal challenges to it so active, that documents are still withheld from the public.[213]

Ironically, the whole East-of-Suez scheme was always under threat from the need to find defence cuts. Defence capability was remorselessly

[210] Neville Brown, *Arms without empire: British defence role in the modern world* (Harmondsworth, 1967), pp. 51–7.
[211] *ESC*, pt 3, pp. 236–40 (no. 345), 7 April 1965, joint memo by Stewart and Healey, 'Defence facilities in the Indian Ocean'.
[212] *ESC*, pt 3, pp. 250–5 (no. 348), 25 July 1968, minute by Stewart to prime minister (PREM 13/2565).
[213] *ESC*, pt 1, intro., p. cxxv, n. 2; and pt 3, pp. 258–9, no. 4 (no. 350). Legal claims were contested in the courts in the mid-1970s, in 1998 and 2000, and in May 2006 a High Court judgment ruled that the government's attempts to block return of the Islanders to some of the islands was 'irrational' and 'unlawful'. (*The Times*, 12 May 2006, p. 43.)

sliced away year by year.[214] In 1965 the Treasury had delivered a fatal blow by securing the failure of the navy's bid for new carriers, so that the project had in reality already become in Crossman's eyes an untenable 'fantastic illusion'. Yet Wilson was still saying he would never allow deep cuts to deny Britain a world role, because the 'special relationship' must be kept up, and any withdrawal 'could not fail to have a profound effect on my relations with LBJ[ohnson] and the way the Americans treat us'.[215] The rhetoric about remaining East-of-Suez was now apparently out of line with actual plans. In February 1966 Healey announced a package of defence economies and a set of revised strategic principles. In future Britain would not embark on major military operations overseas unless acting with an ally; military assistance would not be made available unless the country affected could provide the necessary facilities; there would be no attempt to cling on to defence facilities in an independent country against its will. The cuts in the navy were so severe that the navy minister (Mayhew) and the First Sea Lord resigned. Although Wilson admitted to Dean Rusk in June 1966 that the Singapore base was 'much criticised at present in Britain as a symbol of the Kiplingesque quality of our Far Eastern policy',[216] Healey still wished to remain in Singapore base for as long as possible on acceptable terms, as troops there were a stabilising influence and a deterrent to local conflicts.[217]

In March 1967 Brown and Healey recommended a revised time-table for British military withdrawal from South-East Asia: we could not 'retain commitments for which our forces are inadequate'. The aim would be to reach half-way mark by 1970–1 and to be completely out by 1975–6, resulting by then in savings of up to £300 million. Bowden expressed the concerns of the CRO. Planning a total withdrawal from Singapore and Malaysia, he argued, represented a drastic reversal of policy, while the speed of the run-down could lead to a chaotic situation, because of the severe strains on local economies. These strains could be formidable in Singapore, where there was a real risk of a

---

[214] P. Darby, *British defence policy East of Suez, 1947–1968* (1973), pp. 263–5; S. Dockrill, *Britain's retreat from East of Suez: the choice between Europe and the world?* (2002); Matthew Jones, 'A decision delayed: Britain's withdrawal from South-East Asia reconsidered, 1961–1968', *English Historical Review*, vol. 117 (2002), pp. 569–95, and *Conflict and Confrontation in South-East Asia, 1961–1965* (2002), pp. 281–94. For a different but informed perspective, Lee Kuan Yew, *From third world to first: the Singapore story, 1965–2000* (New York, 2000), ch. 3, 'Britain pulls out', pp. 31–47.

[215] *Crossman diaries*, p. 189 (15 June 1966), p. 163 (14 February 1966). Wilson was well aware of the realities: 'we can't kick our creditors in the balls' (quoted by Louis, 'The dissolution of the British empire in the era of Vietnam', p. 4).

[216] *ESC*, pt 1, p. 94 (no. 17, 10 June 1966).

[217] *ESC*, pt 1, pp. 90–2 (no. 16), minutes of Defence and Oversea Policy Committee meeting, 13 May 1966.

communist take-over.[218] Notwithstanding these warnings, the Cabinet authorised the go-ahead for consultations about these proposals with the USA, Australia and New Zealand, and then with Singapore and Malaysia. As a result, the government felt it had to offer assurances about willingness to maintain some sort of continuing presence after 1975–6, though precisely what was left vague. In July 1967 the supplementary defence White Paper acknowledged that an East-of-Suez commitment would no longer be tenable, and set out the time-table for scaling part of it down. By 1971 British forces in Malaysia and Singapore would he halved (to 40,000), and withdrawn completely by 1977. It was essentially a streamlining exercise, begging several basic questions. The future of the Persian Gulf was unclear, and the Indian Ocean strategic policy was left untouched.[219]

As a result and curiously, 'East-of-Suez' could be held to be still alive. What changed everything, finally, was the long-resisted and psychologically painful devaluation of sterling, following upon a major financial crisis in July 1966. The devaluation, which was from \$2.80 to \$2.40 (14.3 per cent), took place in November 1967. It revealed to all the world the hollowness of British claims to a world role. It eroded the prime minister's credibility and perhaps his confidence too. It led to the resignation of the chancellor, Callaghan, and his replacement by Roy Jenkins. This may have made a significant shift in the balance of forces within the Cabinet, for Jenkins was highly critical of what he regarded as out-of-date imperial pretensions.[220]

There was a fraught series of meetings in and out of Cabinet in the first half of January 1968.[221] Healey, Stewart, Brown, and Callaghan held out to the end for some delay. Jenkins scathingly noted (not entirely fairly) that Brown, Healey and George Thomson (CRO) all 'defended Britain's world-wide role with an attachment to imperial commitments worthy of a conclave of Joseph Chamberlain, Kitchener of Khartoum and George Nathaniel Curzon'.[222] Jenkins told them he wanted Britain to withdraw from South-East Asia by the end of the financial year 1970–1 and from the Gulf by 1969 or even the end of 1968. Britain, he said, 'had come to the point of defeat on the economic road, and unless we took the kind of measures he was proposing' he saw no prospect of a solution for many years ahead.[223] When the issue came before the

[218] *ESC*, pt 1, pp. 105–8 (nos. 22 and 23) Cabinet memos, 31 March 1967.
[219] My unwillingness to see July 1967 as the point of no return follows Brown, *Arms without empire*, pp. 157–9 (app. 2).
[220] J. Pickering, *Britain's withdrawal from East of Suez: the politics of retrenchment* (1998), pp. 162–74.   [221] *ESC*, pt 1, pp. 120–7 (no. 28), 4 January 1968.
[222] R. Jenkins, *A life at the centre: memoirs* (1991), pp. 224–7.
[223] *ESC*, pt 1, p. 120 (note 1 to no. 28), letter to prime minister, 20 December 1967.

Cabinet, Jenkins spoke of the need 'to cut our coat according to our cloth' and reduce planned expenditure both at home and overseas. He admitted that his proposals 'represented a formidable and unpalatable programme of economies', but they were essential for economic and financial health.

Brown argued for delay by at least a year. According to his information, 60,000 people would be thrown into unemployment in Singapore, triggering unrest which could lead to a communist overthrow of Lee Kuan Yew's government. The goodwill of local administrations was becoming ever more important: 'if we aroused their distrust they had it in their power to organise against us'. Even if Britain ceased to be a world power, 'we should continue to retain world interests and to need friends and allies to defend them. We could not afford to flout international opinion in the way the French did.' Brown was supported by Thomson, but other voices challenged whether an extra year would make a significant difference, or whether unemployment would be as massive as feared, or necessarily lead to disorder:

Moreover, the question at issue was more than one of mere timing: our credibility as a nation was involved. So far our reductions in defence expenditure had always been too little and come too late. This was our opportunity to make radical final decisions and to make clear that our future defence role would be concentrated in Europe. Our experience in Aden had proved the advantages of fixing an early date for withdrawal and adhering to it. Our standing in the world depended on the soundness of our economy and not on a worldwide military presence.[224]

This sounds like the authentic voice of the prime minister. When President Johnson expressed his 'deep dismay', Wilson explained to him that the government was not acting in a 'Little England' spirit, but from 'a blend of exasperation at our inability to weather the successive economic storms of the past 20 years and determination, once and for all, to hew out a new role for Britain in the world at once commensurate with her real resources yet worthy of her past'. There was, he added, at last a nationwide realisation that this could not be done 'on borrowed time and borrowed money'.[225]

Wilson's quiet but firm conversion was the key to the decision to withdraw. He was pleased to achieve it without resignations. He made his 'great Statement' on 16 January 1968 to the Commons, presenting it as 'a major exercise restraining the growth of public expenditure'.[226] They

---

[224] *ESC*, pt 1, pp. 120–7 (no. 28), 4 January 1968, minutes of Cabinet meeting, 'Public expenditure: post-devaluation measures.'
[225] *ESC*, pt 1, p. 138 (no. 33), tel to President, 15 January 1968.
[226] *Crossman diaries*, p. 389; Wilson, *Labour government*, p. 479.

had to 'come to terms with our role in the world'. Accordingly, there would be big changes in the function, size and scope of the armed forces. There would be immediate defence cuts of more than £100 million. The island-base project at Aldabra would be axed. Singapore, Malaysia, and the Persian Gulf would now all be evacuated by the end of 1971. No special capacity for East-of-Suez operations would be maintained. No military bases in future would exist outside Europe and the Mediterranean. Instead there would be 'a general capability based in Europe' which would be available for overseas deployment, especially in Malaysia and the Gulf states. All this was 'necessary in the national interest so that we can restore the strength of the economy'. He intoned the dictum which had floated around ever since the 1930s and to which he himself had referred on 16 December 1964 (see above, p. 332); 'There is no military strength . . . except on the basis of economic strength.' Defence 'must not be asked in the name of foreign policy to undertake commitments beyond its capability . . . We have been living beyond our means'. Commitments and capabilities must 'match and balance each other'. There were risks, but 'we believe they are risks that must be accepted'.[227] All this, the historian must think, simply recognised profound and enduring truths.

The Cabinet decision had been far from uncontentious. Moreover, the USA, Australia, New Zealand, Malaysia, and Singapore were all opposed to it. There were Conservative jibes of 'scuttle'.

So what had tipped the balance? It does not seem to have signalled a clear switch to Europe from a world role.[228] Wilson in fact seemed to think it could lead to 'a new place on the world stage'. He projected the reductions as 'realistic', something which would strengthen 'our real influence and power for peace'. In anyone else this would just be a presentational spin, but Wilson always believed his own rhetoric. Financial constraints were important. Every overseas soldier increased the balance of payments deficit, and unit costs were rising all the time.[229] Or as Darby puts it, 'ultimately lack of resources rather than intellectual rejection' ensured the abandonment of the East-of-Suez role.[230] But there were necessary preconditions. Officials had long preached the outmoded character of western overseas bases, and clearly a geopolitical change of this magnitude would have to have support of the Chiefs of Staff. But one contextual point of

[227] *PD, Commons* vol. 756, cc. 1577–1607, 16 January 1968, debate on public expenditure.
[228] Dockrill, *Britain's retreat from East of Suez*, and review by A. J. Stockwell, in *JICH*, vol. 32 (2004), pp. 171–3.
[229] S. Strange, *Sterling and British policy: a political study of an international currency in decline* (1971), p. 314.   [230] Darby, *British defence policy*, p. 334.

importance must not be overlooked. An essential precondition was the unexpected ending of Indonesian *Konfrontasi*.

Similarly, the Egyptian defeat by Israel in the 1967 Six Days War and the consequent eclipse of Nasser, created a more favourable climate for leaving the Persian Gulf. This was well understood in the FO: 'The 1967 war was the turning-point . . . we would never have had a chance of making an orderly withdrawal from the Gulf nor would the Sheikhs have had a chance of survival if the revolutionary Arabs had not been completely deflated by the results of the June war.' Furthermore, the disastrous and humiliating evacuation under fire from Aden in November 1967 'marked the nadir in the popularity of the British Empire', making it a bit easier to accept further adjustment.[231] The officials (mainly FO) who prepared the defence review believed that Britain could not stay indefinitely in the Gulf after the withdrawal from Aden. In their analysis, 'by the mid-1970s we must expect a world where almost all colonial and quasi-colonial traces have disappeared and the overseas deployment of British power has contracted further than at present. If we have not gone from the Gulf, the pressures on us to go are likely to be very severe indeed.' The position could in theory be maintained to some extent:

But we would be left far too exposed not only to local subversion but also to international criticism and British domestic impatience over our clinging to a position with anachronistically imperial overtones. Experience suggests that, beyond a certain point, the cost in political and military terms of such a position outweighs the advantages which the prolongation of our stay is designed to secure; and prejudices our chances of protecting our interests in other ways after our departure.[232]

This was a good statement of the accumulated wisdom of the 'official mind' about decolonisation. The awkward problem of the smaller islands remained, so there could be no ultimately final end to empire. In May 1968 the Defence and Oversea Policy Committee considered the fate of what was left: Ascension Island, Easter Island, the Falkland Islands, the Seychelles, Gibraltar and so on. According to Crossman, 'The paper submitted went right through the list, providing us with excellent reasons for staying in each one and increasing the amounts of troops available. Not a single recommendation to wind up.'[233] Crossman lamented this, but made no attempt to challenge it, since none of his colleagues, least of all the prime minister, wanted to pull out. Wilson apparently said he was not going down in history as 'the Lord North who gave up Gibraltar'.[234]

---

[231] W. R. Louis, 'The British withdrawal from the Gulf, 1961–1971', *JICH* vol. 31 (2003), pp. 83–108.   [232] *ESC*, pt 1, p. 413 (no. 118), report, 28 September 1967.
[233] *Crossman diaries*, p. 144 (29 May 1968).
[234] Tam Dalyell, *Dick Crossman: a portrait* (1989), pp. 207–8.

But for all that, Wilson's announcement about the withdrawal East-of-Suez on 16 January 1968 was at once perceived to be of historic significance, comparable with Attlee's transfer of power in India,[235] and Macmillan's 'wind of change' speech and all that flowed from it. Certainly it was the most important decision taken by the Wilson government in imperial and international policy.[236] Here was the moment of the recall of the legions, the end of the Pax Britannica in the Indian Ocean, the removal of the last remnants of a physical British presence in the Middle East, the effective termination of the British imperial-global cosmoplastic system, 'the most momentous shift in our foreign policy for a century and a half' (Gordon Walker),[237] the break-through of what Crossman called the 'status barrier'. In his words, 'The status barrier is as difficult to break through as the sound barrier: it splits your ears and it's terribly painful when it happens', particularly (he recognised) for those ministers who had since 1964 consistently operated an opposite policy.[238] It was, in a word, Recessional. Wilson himself publicly recognised this. Hansard records the following exchange:[239]

MR MAXWELL: While congratulating my right hon. Friend and his Administration on being the first Prime Minister in 20 years to bring our legions home from the East – [*Laughter*] –

MR SPEAKER: Order. We can now leave the Romans alone . . .

THE PRIME MINISTER: I would have thought that my hon. Friend would have been sufficiently up to date to leave the Romans alone, as you have said, Mr Speaker, and at least to have gone as far as Kipling's 'Recessional', which may be more relevant.

*

The tumult and the shouting die;
The Captains and the Kings depart;
. . .
Far-called, our navies melt away;
On dune and headland sinks the fire:
Lo, all our pomp of yesterday
Is one with Nineveh and Tyre!

Recessional Hymn (1897) by Rudyard Kipling

---

[235] 'Another Labour government is writing the end of a chapter a Labour government had then begun': George Thomson (the last secretary of state for Commonwealth relations), 'Britain's plan to leave Asia', *Round Table*, vol. 58, no. 229 (1968), p. 117. [236] Young, *International policy*, p. 56

[237] P. Gordon Walker, *The Cabinet* (rev. edn 1972), p. 122.

[238] *Crossman diaries*, pp. 393–6 (7–15 January 1968).

[239] *PD, Commons* vol. 756, c. 1607. (Ian) Robert Maxwell, MC (1923–91), Labour MP for Buckingham, 1964–1970, scientific publisher, member of the Fabian Society, later revealed as a notorious swindler.

Epilogue

At the actual moment of the transfer of power to a former dependency, the mode of departure often reflected the independence process, whether friendly or not. India on 14–15 August 1947 was the first,[1] and remains the most poignant because of Nehru's mellifluous words:

> Long years ago we made a tryst with destiny, and now the time comes when we shall redeem our pledge . . . At the stroke of the midnight hour, while the world sleeps, India will awake to life and freedom. A moment comes, which comes but rarely in history, when we step out from the old to the new, when an age ends and when the soul of a nation, long suppressed, finds utterance.[2]

Delirious crowds mobbed Mountbatten's vice-regal coach. Nehru scrambled aboard. Some onlookers, nearly crushed beneath its wheels, were pulled up: an Indian woman with infants, the Polish wife of a British officer, an Indian press reporter. Next morning, the crowds unharnessed the horses and dragged the carriage themselves, cheering the British and letting off fireworks. It was just like some huge traditional Hindu *mela*, or chaotic *tamasha* (free for all); Khushwant Singh, a journalist, commented in amazement that it was as if 'this nation had become more pro-British than it had ever been since the British came'.[3] (It was much quieter in Karachi, though.)

Nine months later in Palestine, the atmosphere was grim. Law and order had disintegrated, roads and railways were in chaos, postal services had ended. The evacuating British destroyed the police-dogs, but tried to salvage most of the equipment, 'from their locomotives to the last of the paper-clips'. The departing high commissioner, Sir Alan Cunningham, made an apologetic address: 'we who are leaving have experienced great sadness in the latter tortured years . . . we have failed to find the soil in

---

[1] N. Owen, ' "More than a transfer of power": independence day ceremonies in India, 15 August 1947', *Contemporary British History*, vol. 6 (1992), pp. 415–51.

[2] N. Mansergh, ed., *Documents and speeches on British Commonwealth affairs, 1931–1952* (1953), vol. II, p. 700.

[3] P. Ziegler, *Mountbatten: the official biography* (1985), p. 425; B. Lapping, *End of empire* (1985), pp. 1–3, 90–1.

which [the seed of agreement] could germinate'.[4] Cunningham left Jerusalem in a bullet-proof car previously used by the King in the London Blitz, seen off by a hastily assembled colour-party of the Suffolk Regiment who gave the salute. The British consul described the scene: 'a few bedraggled Arabs, who happened to have gathered near the Damascus Gate, raised a feeble cheer . . . A pathetic epilogue to nigh thirty years of toil and sacrifice'. Cunningham then made the dash for the port of Haifa, suffering the indignity of having to pass through road-blocks of both Jewish and Arab irregular troops.[5] Twenty years later, at Aden, the British shot their way out on 29 November 1967. They managed to sing 'Things ain't wot they used to be', the helicopters whirring over the harbour, whisking the high commissioner to an aircraft carrier, as guerillas began looting abandoned stores and entering government house.[6] It was hardly better in Cyprus, where Sir Hugh Foot's departure was much more muted than he wished. On 10 August 1960 he said goodbye to the now President Makarios and Vice-President Dr Kucuk, then drove to Famagusta, and made a final troop inspection before boarding ship to a salute of guns. And that was it – no speeches, no sentimental songs, no member of the royal family present.[7]

Over the years, the happier ceremonies were refined into a routine, designed to give an impression of British as well as national achievement. The central moment was usually the lowering of the flag at government house for the last time, at dusk, to the accompaniment of bugle or trumpet. The union flag was neatly folded by the duty-soldier, who handed it to the sergeant-major, who handed it to the officer-in-charge, who handed it to the governor, who handed it to the sovereign's representative, who handed it to an aide-de-camp. There was normally a decorous garden-party, as well as a gathering for the populace, probably at the football stadium, with speeches and traditional dancing. When Rhodesia became Zimbabwe, on 17 April 1980, there was a final demonstration of British technical and ceremonial skills with a fly-past of jets overhead precisely at midnight.

The ceremonies were the last act in what became an official routine in getting a country ready for independence. According to Sir Colin Allan, governor of the Seychelles (1973–6) and the Solomons (1976–8). 'There

[4] T. Segev, *One Palestine, complete: Jews and Arabs under the British Mandate* (transl. by H. Watzman, 2000, 2001) p. 489; N. Shepherd, *Ploughing sand: British rule in Palestine, 1917–1948* (1999) pp. 242–3.

[5] W. R. Louis, 'Sir Alan Cunningham and the end of British rule in Palestine', in A. N. Porter and R. Holland, eds., *Theory and practice in the history of European expansion overseas: essays in honour of R. E. Robinson* (1988), p. 143, repr. from *JICH*, vol. 16 (1988).

[6] M. Thornhill, 'Trevelyan, Humphrey', in *ODNB*, vol. LV, p. 340.

[7] R. F. Holland, *Britain and the revolt in Cyprus, 1954–1959* (Oxford, 1998), p. 336.

is a check-list of about eighty points under ten main headings. They are ticked off in a bureaucratic way one by one – relevant or not – it is as simple as that. Only one or two will be so controversial as to require substantial negotiation. It has all been done, over forty times before!'[8]

Ceremonies for the transfer of power could be emotional occasions and hold a few surprises, none more curious than when Nelson Mandela was inaugurated president of the republic of 'new' South Africa in 1994, and 'Land of hope and glory', full version, was sung.[9] We know from the television pictures that on 30 June 1997 Chris Patten, the departing governor of Hong Kong, shed a tear. Assuredly he would not have been the first to have done so. At the inauguration of Malaysia in September 1963, the new governor of Sarawak, Datu Abang Haji Openg, collapsed under the strain, 'hardly an auspicious omen', said Sandys, who was present.[10] For Botswana, however, the traditional omens came good. As the wind got up during the independence ceremony in 1966, the first signs of blessed rain appeared, developing into a steady downpour over the next few days. This was one of the most trouble-free and painless transfers of power anywhere. The new regime even named a street in Gaborone after Sir Peter Fawcus, the last-but-one Queen's commissioner.[11]

Plans for the independence celebrations for Swaziland in September 1968 were severely disrupted by the sudden death of Princess Marina, mother of the duke of Kent, the Queen's cousin, who was due to represent her. The programmes had already been printed. Instead of the duke doing so, the constitutional instruments embodying *somhlolo* (independence) were presented to King Sobhuza by George Thomson, performing almost his last major public duty before the abolition of the office of secretary of state for Commonwealth relations a few weeks later. He read a message from the Queen:

On this day of your country's independence, my thoughts are with you all. You are now taking your place among the nations of the world, and it is with special pleasure that I welcome you to our Commonwealth of Nations; I send you our good wishes and I pray that God may bless and guide you through the coming years.[12]

---

[8] Colin Allan, 'Bureaucratic organisation for development in small island states', in R. T. Shand, ed., *The island states of the Pacific and Indian Oceans: the autonomy of development* (Development Studies Centre Monograph no. 23, Canberra, 1980), p. 403.

[9] P. J. Henshaw, 'Land of Hope and Glory: Mandela's New South Africa', *Queen's Quarterly: A Canadian Review*, vol. 101 (1994), p. 439.

[10] A. J. Stockwell, ed., *Malaysia* (BDEEP, 2004), p. 578 (note to no. 226), 18 September 1963.

[11] P. Fawcus (with A. Tilbury), *Botswana: the road to independence* (Gaborone, 2000), pp. lx–xii, 187, 207, 223.

[12] J. S. M. Matsebula, *A history of Swaziland* (2nd edn, 1976, 1988), p. 199.

Music was supplied by the Band of the Malawi Rifles. The Taiwanese and the Japanese sent fireworks. Children gave a display of 'massed physical training'. Sobhuza wore the traditional royal warrior's ceremonial dress, swathed in lions' manes, leopard skins, and a gigantic head-dress – a headband of otter-skin, surmounted by double plumes of the tail-feathers of the *lisakabuli* (widow bird). 'Glaring with a kind of stylized fury', he received the homage of his subjects, who knelt and even prostrated themselves before him.[13] Bonfires were ordered to be lit on beacons throughout the country. Celebrations had begun two weeks before. There was an independence exhibition in the new national *somhlolo* stadium, with a dancing contest, and a special 'dance of the virgins'. There was a horse-show, tennis championships, the football cup final, and international football matches against Lesotho and Portugal. There was a gala performance of Joe Orton's *Loot*.

In his broadcast on the eve of independence, Sobhuza said that the people 'will now once more shape their own destiny and manage fully their own internal and external affairs. This day marks our reaching the top of a hill to which the climbing has been an arduous task', a struggle in which he and the people had 'persevered to endure, since the turn of this century'. He exhorted the people to work hard and to co-operate together, since this was the 'prerequisite of self-maintenance'. One year later, he stressed that the sense of national unity had helped to overcome the difficulties of the first year, marked unfortunately by crippling drought. The duke of Kent's sister, Princess Alexandra, and her husband the Hon. Angus Ogilvy, attended the independence anniversary celebrations in September 1969, which followed the planned programme for the original ceremony. This time the associated events included a boxing tournament and athletics championships, and a gala performance of a review called *Free as air*. At the main event in the national stadium, Princess Alexandra waited patiently as 117 of the king's wives took precedence over her. She replied to an address by Sobhuza. The king was dressed minimally in a leopard-skin kaross, beads and feather tassels, both nipples exposed, and carrying a spear and shield. For the opening of the new parliament building, however, he wore English morning-dress (see pp. 384–5).[14]

The parliament building in Lobamba was to prove something of an unnecessary white elephant. The extraordinary nature of the coming of *somhlolo* to Swaziland reminds us that there is no simple way to generalise about the meaning of the transfer of power.

---

[13] J. Morris, *Farewell the trumpets: an imperial retreat* (1978), p. 521.
[14] *Independence comes to Swaziland, September 6, 1968*, programmes for *Independence celebrations* and *Independence anniversary celebrations* (Swaziland Government Information Service, 1968, 1969), author's archive.

Decolonisation in Swaziland, and elsewhere in its later phases, may be understood as the waiving of the classic pre-requisites and tests of fitness for self-rule. As these were worked out in the nineteenth century (for white communities), four requirements operated: (1) the state must be economically viable and able to defend itself; (2) there should be a friendly and reliable elite, ready to take over; (3) there should be a reasonable expectation that 'minorities' (sometimes numerical majorities) would be justly treated and protected; and (4) British strategic interests would not be endangered. Doubts over any one of these desiderata could hold up or preclude a transfer of power. 'Viability', in various guises, continued to be the crucial test into the 1960s. As a report in 1956 put it, 'a country must be able to stand on its own feet economically and financially . . . finance its own administration and be able and prepared to assume responsibility for its own defence and its own international relations'. As late as 1960 'the essential attributes of sovereignty' were still being defined in the CO in this fashion.[15] From the mid-1960s, however, less and less was heard of viability. The classic tests were effectively whittled down to one, namely, identifying a political elite willing to take over. Signs of emerging 'statesmanship' (as in Abdul Rahman, Kaunda, or Sobhuza) were seized upon gratefully.

Our understanding of decolonisation can be usefully deepened by reference to the opinions of the officials. Civil servants were uniquely well placed by their experience, access to information, and closeness to the transfers of power to grasp the dynamics of what was happening, at least in terms of the immediate reasons and context for decisions taken. As quotations in the foregoing pages show, their emphasis was generally upon timing. They assume – at least from about 1949 – that independence will in principle be given wherever possible. What fascinated them was how the process came to be speeded up. The reasons they put forward to explain this were always about external influences, usually nationalist, but also in later phases, international pressures. 'Joe' Saville Garner in the CRO believed the British empire came to an end 'because other people's empires were crumbling all around': Germany, Italy, Holland and Japan had all ceased to be imperial powers after the war, and from 1958 to 1960 there were major advances to self-rule in French West Africa and the Belgian Congo, decisive influences on timing from which the British colonies could not be insulated.[16] The gradualist ideals of the

---

[15] S. R. Ashton and D. Killingray, eds., *The West Indies* (BDEEP, 1999), p. 280 (no. 104), report of the London Conference on British Caribbean federation, CO minute, 27 August 1959; and p. 326 (no. 188), CO memo, 16 January 1960. C. W. Newbury, *The West African Commonwealth* (Duke, 1964), pp. 77–8.

[16] J. S. Garner, *The Commonwealth Office, 1925–1968* (1978), p. 344.

officials were put under pressure by nationalist demand, and to this extent the colonial situation may be regarded as causing modifications of the timetable. Liquidation was not a one-way process, neither solely driven by metropolitan policy and planning, nor by anti-colonial nationalist demand. The two elements needed to come into an effective conjunction of interest, which was not too difficult to achieve when there was mediation by a proconsul 'on the spot' trusted by both sides.[17] In the final analysis, however, we cannot conclude that both elements, centre and periphery, were equally important. The metropolitan side, with the decision-making power, was the one which holds the explanatory key, in part because British governments remained fiercely determined to retain the initiative. Colonies which demanded self-government usually got it, but we cannot say that they thereby determined the outcome. The really significant historical question to ask is how the imperial power had got psychologically to the point where it was prepared to open the door to self-rule when nationalist leaders knocked and asked. In any case, demand can be an ambiguous thing. By the mid-1950s Lennox-Boyd on a number of occasions was told privately by colonial politicians not to take their public requests too seriously; they had, they explained, to make demands for speeding up, in order to keep their local political support, but they realised that they needed more time and to be better prepared. There was even one case of an African politician who asked Lennox-Boyd to lock up certain opponents during an election.[18]

Should we understand decolonisation as a positive success-story, or as something less glamorous? Despite all the intractabilities and complexities, and palpable failure in some cases, relatively smooth and peaceful transfers of power were effected after 1959. Zanzibar and Aden were exceptions, and there were too many examples of violent suppression of local disturbances. But there was nothing quite comparable with the scale of foreign chaos, often bitter, in Algeria, Indonesia, Belgian Congo, Western Sahara or Mozambique. The Falklands War of 1982 was a

---

[17] For this model, see my essay, 'The primacy of geopolitics: the dynamics of British imperial policy, 1763–1963', in *Statecraft of British imperialism* pp. 27–52. The call for a more effective historiographical dialogue between 'metropolis' and 'colonial nationalism' was strongly made by M. Twaddle in 'Decolonisation in Africa: a new historiographical debate?' in B. Jewsiewicki and D. Newbury, eds., *African historiographies: what historiography for which Africa?* (Beverley Hills, 1986), ch. 10, pp. 123–38.

[18] D. Morgan, *The official history of colonial development*, vol. V: *Guidance towards self-government in British colonies, 1941–1971* (1980), p. 22; A. H. M. Kirk-Greene, ed., *The transfer of power: the colonial administrator in the age of decolonisation* (1979), p. 5. Compare what the Irish foreign minister Garret Fitzgerald allegedly said in 1974 when Wilson contemplated withdrawal from Ulster, Fitzgerald begging American Secretary of State Henry Kissinger to pressure the British government to stay (D. Godson in *Times Literary Supplement*, 24 April 1998, p. 15).

striking demonstration of how much worse things might have been. Some historians – and not just conservative ones – regard the management of the dissolution of the empire as deserving of praise. Noel Annan writes, 'The peaceful divestment of the Empire was the most successful political achievement of Our Age.'[19] Or again, 'The civilised acceptance of a post-imperial role was the great enduring triumph of British history since 1945' (K. O. Morgan).[20]

If we are reluctant to go that far, can we at least speak of an euthanasian end? According to the dictionary, *euthanasia* is 'a quiet and easy death'. With India independent, it could be argued that most of the British political elite fundamentally lost interest in the empire, after a flurry of Labour activity in Africa in the late 1940s. This holds true for Churchill, who knew things had to change, even if he regretted it, as well as for Attlee, who was twenty years ahead of his time. It also holds good for Macmillan and Duncan Sandys, as well as for more eccentric figures like Enoch Powell, sulking because India no longer had a viceroyalty open to him.[21] From 1948, the gradual winding up of empire was not seriously contested at the highest level of government, even if it was at times an issue for diehard Conservative right-wing supporters. But Lord Salisbury could not for long stay in Macmillan's Cabinet, and Julian Amery never reached it. There were more resignations, or threats of resignations, over the failure to follow a progressive policy at the time of the Suez Crisis than over transfers of power. These were never an election issue, and no government lost office by liquidating imperial responsibilities.

The relative ease and quiet of it all was possible because the management of decolonisation remained a preoccupation restricted to the governing elite, who presented a remarkably united front and mostly accepted the desirability of continuity of policy. It ought to be a commonplace of political and constitutional theory that public opinion, press and media attitudes, and lobbying campaigns generally, are less effective in the sphere of external policies, where 'the national interest' prevails, than in protests about domestic and localised concerns.[22] Specialist pressure groups were treated in Whitehall with disdain. Business interests had almost no discernible impact on policy-decisions about decolonisation and were not a

---

[19] N. Annan, *Our age: portrait of a generation* (1990), p. 357.

[20] K. O. Morgan, 'Imperialists at bay: British Labour Party and decolonisation', in King and Kilson, *Statecraft of British imperialism*, p. 253.

[21] P. V. Murphy, *Party politics and decolonisation: the Conservative Party and British colonial policy in tropical Africa, 1951–1964* (1995), pp. 26–31; Bernard Porter, *The absent-minded imperialists: empire, society and culture in Britain* (Oxford, 2004), pp. 3–4.

[22] J. W. Young, *The Labour governments, 1964–1970*, vol. II: *International policy* (Manchester, 2003), pp. 18–19.

serious problem.[23] Several regional studies have confirmed this.[24] This is so because although it may not invariably be the case that 'power tends to corrupt' (though it happens distressingly often), power undoubtedly changes perception and perspective. For one thing, power gives access to privileged information and expert advice which MPs and the general public do not have, and this can powerfully reinforce a ministerial sense of being *right*, in a way that lobbyists and protestors, whether parliamentary or non-parliamentary, are thought not to be and unable to be. There was, for instance, highly vocal opposition in the Labour Party to Bevin's hard-line policy towards the Soviet Union in his first two years at the FO, but it made no difference, except to make him more careful what he said in public.[25] And it is a similar story for even well-organised partisan pressure-groups, for left-wing bodies such as the Seretse Khama Fighting Committee (1950), and the Movement for Colonial Freedom (organised to oppose the establishment of the Central African Federation), or right-wing ones like the League of Empire Loyalists (1954), the Suez Group (disgusted by the evacuation of the Canal Zone), and the Monday Club (commemorating what was seen as the black day of Macmillan's 'wind of change' speech, and aiming to stop a rapid transfer of power in Africa). The existence of such groups was certainly a matter for government concern, but they achieved little more than making ministers more cautious about the presentation of policy. Presentation could be quite skilfully managed. The trick was to stress above all the duty and necessity of party loyalty, and to appeal to the civilised good sense of bipartisanship and the principle of continuity of national policy, while persuading those sceptical about the transfer of power that there were future prospects in maintaining links, commercial and otherwise, with successor regimes coaxed into grateful co-operativeness. It was also suggested that Britain could retain prestige through the Commonwealth and a continuing global influence, despite the ending of formal imperial control. Party discipline enforced by

[23] John Darwin notes the 'Olympian disregard of official policy for commercial interests in the formulation of its political and constitutional programme': *Oxford History of the British Empire*, vol. V: *Historiography* (ed., R. W. Winks, Oxford, 1999), p. 555. Sarah Stockwell concludes that from the late 1950s 'geopolitical considerations emerge as more significant [than economic interests] in determining Britain's handling of colonial nationalism' and there were no neo-colonial conspiracies ('Trade, empire, and the fiscal context of imperial business during decolonization,' *Economic History Review*, vol. 57 (2004), pp. 142–4).

[24] For example: R. L. Tignor, *Modernisation and British colonial rule in Egypt, 1882–1941* (Princeton, NJ, 1966) and *Capitalism and nationalism and the end of empire: state and business in decolonising Egypt, Nigeria and Kenya, 1945–1963* (Princeton, NJ, 1998); S. E. Stockwell, *The business of decolonisation: British statecraft in the Gold Coast* (Oxford, 2000); N. J. White, *Business, government and the end of empire: Malaya, 1942–1957* (Kuala Lumpur, 1996); A. M. Misra, *Business, race and politics in British India, c 1860–1960* (Oxford, 1999).

[25] J. Saville, *The politics of continuity: British foreign policy and the Labour government, 1945–1946* (1993), pp. 60–4.

the whips could be effective in keeping even quite large numbers of MPs in check.[26]

Although none of them wanted to be accused of 'scuttle', by 1959 few ministers wanted to prolong the life of the empire, and nobody was able to mount effective opposition to them. Was this dignified euthanasia or simply an anti-climax? George Boyce concludes his survey of decolonisation with these words: 'So complex is the picture now emerging that the expression "end of empire" might be better replaced by something like "old empires never die, they just fade away"'.[27] There was indeed not so much a failure of *will* – more a lack of interest and passionate commitment. In this sense, the British empire ended as it began, in 'a fit of absence of mind'.[28] In applying this insight of Sir John Seeley – the winding-up of the empire as a mirror-image of its acquisition – we need to remember that Seeley never meant to imply 'absent-mindedness', merely to draw attention to a lack of awareness as Britain boldly 'conquered and peopled half the world', and to the minimal impact all this had on national consciousness from the late eighteenth century onwards. And it *is* this lack of concern about what was happening – aside from a handful of incidents – which is so striking about decolonisation. If the dissolution of the empire made few people miserable or pessimistic, or had little impact on society, this was mainly because it never had much impact in the first place.[29] Paul Scott's character, the Cambridge historian Guy Perron, insists on the 'overwhelming importance' in British-Indian affairs of the 'indifference and ignorance of the English at home'.[30] This was even more true of the rest of the empire.

It may seem paradoxical to suggest an 'absence of mind', a lack of awareness, when we have given prominence to the bureaucratic 'seething of thought' in the 1940s, to the policy-studies and energetic planning of the 1960s, and so forth. Clearly there was no 'absence of mind' in the three government departments most involved. But the historian has to remember how reflective memoranda often got lost in the pressure of immediate business. Officials who came up with the most radical ideas seldom had them accepted as guides for action by their colleagues, as John Bennett learned to his cost. Generally speaking, ministers and officials found pragmatism and instinct better guides, what Attlee would have

---

[26] N. Owen, 'Decolonisation and post-war consensus', in H. Jones and M. Kandiah, eds., *Myth of consensus: new views on British history, 1945–1964* (1996), pp. 157–81.

[27] D. George Boyce, *Decolonisation and the British empire, 1775–1997* (1999), p. 270. Compare Jack Gallagher: 'At last, without convulsion, without terror, and without agony, the great ship goes down' (*Decline, revival and fall of the British empire* (1982), p. 153).   [28] J. R. Seeley, *The expansion of England* (2nd edn, 1909), pp. 10, 205.

[29] Porter, *The absent-minded imperialists*, pp. 318–19.

[30] Paul Scott, *A division of the spoils*, Raj Quartet, vol. IV, (1977 edn), p. 222.

called 'realism'.[31] The conclusion to which pragmatism consistently pointed was that continuation of colonial rule was not actually feasible in the face of determined nationalist protest, since the resources did not exist to put down serious disturbances. As the Labour chancellor of the Exchequer, Hugh Dalton, put it so memorably in 1947, 'If you are in a place where you are not wanted and have not got the force or perhaps the will to squash those who do not want you, the only thing to do is to come out' (see above, p. 109). Thus the pragmatic doctrine of 'the lesser risk' of concessions tended to prevail, especially when international interference also threatened.

Which brings us to something very significant. When former CO officials were quizzed by historians at a 'witness seminar', organised by the Institute of Contemporary British History in 1989, they all stressed strongly that action in winding-up the empire had been taken pragmatically, and not in accordance with a long-term policy; that if ministers had such a policy, they, the advisers, did not know of it; what they were aware of was simply the speeding up of timetables in individual countries, *seriatim*.[32] And it is precisely this accumulation of pragmatic responses to local circumstances that the historian mainly observes in the archival record. Quite suddenly, when CO officials sat down to assess the situation in September 1963, and as they thought, to plan the end of empire, they realised that the empire had in fact virtually been wound up already, or that intentions were already in place for political advancement in twenty-four of the remaining smaller territories.[33] Also, Foreign Office officials, at least by the middle of 1964, were already contemplating the elimination of the East-of-Suez role. It is this willingness to decolonise – all-pervasive in Whitehall by 1964 – which enables us to speak of an euthansian end. There had quietly evolved a 'culture of decolonisation.'[34]

---

[31] Owen, 'Decolonisation and post-war consensus', p. 160. It is interesting in this connection that John Bennett thought it probable that his great memorandum of April 1947, 'International aspects of colonial policy' (see above, pp. 166–7), had been destroyed (personal knowledge).

[32] N. Owen, ed. (with intro. by A. H. M. Kirk-Greene), 'Decolonisation and the Colonial Office', Witness Seminar, Conference at the Institute of Contemporary History, University of London, 1989, *Contemporary British History*, vol. 6 (1992). The principal 'witnesses' were Sir Hilton Poynton, Aaron Emanuel, John Bennett, Sir Leslie Monson, Sir Duncan Watson, Sir Alan Johnston, and Professor Kenneth Robinson.

[33] R. Hyam and W. R. Louis, eds., *The Conservative government and the end of empire, 1957–1964* (BDEEP, 2000), pt 1, pp. 211–20 (no. 46), CO memo, 'The future of British colonial territories'.

[34] For changes between 'the old guard' (Twining, Mitchell, Renison, etc.) and the 'new generation' of colonial governors (MacDonald, Arden-Clarke, Turnbull, etc.), see A. H. M. Kirk-Greene, 'On governorship and governors in British Africa', in L. H. Gann and P. Duignan, eds., *African proconsuls: European governors in Africa* (Stanford and New York, 1978), pp. 232–61.

The two politicians most responsible for it were Attlee, in the Asian phase, and Macmillan, in the African. By the time Wilson took office in October 1964, decolonisation may be said to have entered its residual phase. There were severely awkward problems for the Labour government, and little disposition actively to shuffle off remaining responsibilities. But the mantra repeatedly deployed was that 'we could no longer afford to honour our pledges', or perform trusteeship roles, or act as the world's policeman. A pragmatic sense of what was feasible with inadequate resources blocked most of the attempts by Labour ministers to have an ethical foreign policy or maintain a global role.

If pragmatism is one feature which stands out, the other is the importance attached to prestige. The perceived position of Britain as a great power, its credibility, was right at the centre of the post-war approach to coping with decline and decolonisation. The geopolitical lode-star by which colonial situations were judged was that which revealed where the *balance of advantage* lay in promoting British prestige.[35] Decisions about foreign and colonial policy – whether about withdrawing from empire, entering Europe, or about giving aid – are all in some sense calculations about prestige, how best to maintain or improve it. Prestige might be obtained by transfers of power, but equally prestige might be diminished by a premature withdrawal from colonies, which could be represented as discreditable or as detrimental to British interests. Much of the argument about post-war colonial policy hinged on the resolution of this paradox in the context of the cold war. Broadly speaking, the Labour government theory of the late 1940s was that prestige would be more likely to accrue by timely transfers of power to moderate nationalists; Attlee and his ministers accepted the Colonial Office proposition that 'the transfer of power is not a sign of weakness or of liquidation of the Empire, but is, in fact, a sign and source of strength'.[36] There was some backward slippage from this credo while a prominent Conservative theory of the 1950s emphasised the risks and the negative implications of political advancement for colonial territories. By contrast, the decisions of Macmillan, Macleod, Maudling, and eventually even Sandys and Home, rested on a

---

[35] Powerful support is lent to this argument by H. V. Brasted, C. Bridge and J. Kent, 'Cold War, informal empire and the transfer of power: some "paradoxes" of decolonisation resolved?' in M. Dockrill, ed., *Europe within the global system, 1938–1960: Great Britain, France, Italy and Germany, from great powers to regional powers* (Arbeitskreis Deutsche England-Forschung, vol. 30, Bochum, 1995), pp. 11–30, esp p. 23, n. 40. See also John Kent, 'The Egyptian base and the defence of the Middle East, 1945–1954', in R. Holland, ed., *Emergencies and disorder in the European empires after 1945*, pp. 45–65, and John Kent, ed., *Egypt and the defence of the Middle East* (BDEEP, 1998) pt 1, intro.

[36] *The Labour government and the end of empire* (BDEEP), pt 1, p. 358 (no. 72), 'The colonial empire today', para. 84 (May 1950).

fundamental and historically important calculation after 1959 that on balance 'holding on' would be more damaging to prestige than giving up, and certainly more expensive.

In any case, Britain did not want to be found in the last colonial ditch, vilified internationally along with the bad guys like the Portuguese, the 'wily, oily Portuguese' as Churchill used to call them. Britain did not take the initiative in the decolonisation of Africa, any more than Britain had spearheaded the partition. Great power rivalry led Britain into the nineteenth-century scramble for Africa, and great power rivalry – in the shape of the cold war and a competition for international respectability and support – induced the British twentieth-century scramble to get out of Africa. Britain's policy was essentially reactive, that is to say, it was one of following other powers into empire-building in Africa (in order not to be excluded), and into decolonisation (so as not to be ostracised and dictated to).[37]

The British empire rose, flourished, and declined in a particular set of international contexts. The way it operated depended not only on favourable external and geopolitical circumstances, but also on the feasibility of imperial control, in terms both of the acquiescence of peoples ruled, and of the ability to match available resources to the maintenance and defence of a far-flung system. All these preconditions were under threat in the period after 1918. Although the empire was impressively mobilised economically and militarily on behalf of the British war effort after 1939, the overall long-term trend towards an increasingly unmanageable and dysfunctional imperial system was not reversed. What happened in the international sphere after the Second World War gradually but decisively reinforced the sense that a global empire was not only beyond Britain's means, but was now also threatening its prestige and reputation, and becoming a liability.

The cold war determined the main outlines of British policy. Because of it, Britain had to satisfy the nationalists, side with the USA, strengthen the Commonwealth and square the United Nations. Because of it, the whole thrust of decolonisation was to proceed in such a way as to encourage the emergence of pro-Western nationalist states.[38] This became a major cause of the falling out with the country with which Britain should have been in a natural 'special relationship', South Africa, because its institutionalised racism became a handicap in the global struggle against

---

[37] My argument here is in line with W. R. Louis, *Ends of British imperialism: the scramble for empire, Suez, and decolonization* (2006), pp. 28–31.

[38] W. R. Louis and R. E. Robinson, 'The imperialism of decolonisation', *JICH*, vol. 22 (1994), p. 494: calculations about the strategic significance of nationalism and the non-aligned nations in the cold war 'motivated the final dismantling of formal empire'.

communism. For, as a rising Conservative star, Quintin Hogg (as Lord Hailsham, a future lord chancellor), recognised as early as 1950, 'Our long-run future depends on the confidence with which we are regarded by Africans. The future of our civilisation and religion very largely depends upon the extent to which we can carry these people with us in the fight against Communism'.[39]

What the British people really cared about in the twenty years after the end of the Second World War was not the future of the empire, but how to avert the probability of what Hugh Dalton called 'a hideous danger', the 'brooding fear of the Third World War',[40] and with it, the threat of nuclear annihilation.[41] In this context, the words of Clement Attlee have an insistent resonance, and perhaps the last word should rest with him: 'an attempt to maintain the old colonialism would I am sure have immensely aided communism'.[42]

---

[39] *PD, Commons* vol. 473, cc. 334–58 (28 March 1950), debate on Seretse Khama.
[40] LSE Library, Dalton Diary, vol. 38, p. 66 (9 December 1950).
[41] 'It was hardly surprising that many ordinary people in the fifties and sixties lay awake at night worrying about nuclear Armageddon': D. Sandbrook, *Never had it so good: a history of Britain from Suez to the Beatles* (2005), p. 236. Sandbrook tellingly juxtaposes chapters on 'The war game' and 'The end of empire' (pp. 205–59, 260–89); while Ashley Jackson makes the essential point crisply: 'In a world where the Cuban missile crisis led many people to think that nuclear destruction was about to occur, loosening the ties of empire was, in many ways, small beer indeed' (*The British Empire and the Second World War* (2006), p. 532).
[42] C. R. Attlee, *As it happened* (1954), p. 189. (See p. 96 above.)

Appendix

The achievement of independence within the Commonwealth

Date		Territory	New name	Commonwealth status
1947	14 Aug.	Pakistan		Republic 1956; outside 1971–89
	15 Aug.	India		Republic 1949
1948	4 Jan.	Burma	Myanmar 1988	Outside
	4 Feb.	Ceylon	Sri Lanka 1972	Republic 1972
1956	1 Jan.	Sudan		Outside
1957	6 Mar.	Gold Coast (+ UK Trust Territory of Togoland)	Ghana	Republic 1960
	31 Aug.	Malaya	into Malaysia 1963	
1960	26 June	British Somaliland	into Somalia	Outside
	16 Aug.	Cyprus		Republic
	1 Oct.	Nigeria		Republic 1963
1961	27 Apr.	Sierra Leone		Republic 1971
	1 June	North Cameroons	into Nigeria	
	1 Oct.	South Cameroons	into Cameroun	Outside
			North and South reunited as United Republic of Cameroon, 1972, Republic of Cameroon, 1984	Joined 1995
	9 Dec.	Tanganyika	Tanzania (with Zanzibar) 1964	Republic 1962
1962	6 Aug.	Jamaica		
	31 Aug.	Trinidad and Tobago		Republic 1976
	9 Oct.	Uganda		Republic 1967
1963	16 Sept.	Singapore	joined Federation of Malaysia	Republic 1965, as separate state, seceding
	16 Sept.	North Borneo	Sabah	
	16 Sept.	Sarawak		

Appendix (continued)

Date		Territory	New name	Commonwealth status
	10 Dec.	Zanzibar	Tanzania (with Tanganyika)	Republic 1964
	12 Dec.	Kenya		Republic 1964
1964	6 July	Nyasaland	Malawi	Republic 1966
	21 Sept.	Malta		Republic 1974
	24 Oct.	Northern Rhodesia	Zambia	Republic
1965	18 Feb	The Gambia		Republic 1970
1966	26 May	British Guiana	Guyana	Republic 1970
	30 Sept.	Bechuanaland	Botswana	Republic
	4 Oct.	Basutoland	Lesotho	Sovereign monarchy
	30 Nov.	Barbados		
1967	30 Nov.	Aden	into (South) Yemen	Outside
1968	12 Mar.	Mauritius		
	6 Sept.	Swaziland		Sovereign monarchy
1970	10 Oct.	Fiji		Outside 1987–98
1972	18 Apr.	East Pakistan	Seceding as Bangladesh	Republic
1973	10 July	Bahamas		
1974	17 Feb.	Grenada		
1976	28 June	Seychelles		Republic
1978	7 July	Solomon Islands		
	1 Oct.	Ellice Islands	Tuvalu	Special membership
	3 Nov.	Dominica		Republic
1979	22 Feb.	St Lucia		
	12 July	Gilbert Islands	Kiribati	Republic
	27 Oct.	St Vincent and Grenadines		
1980	18 Apr.	Southern Rhodesia	Zimbabwe	Republic
	30 July	New Hebrides	Vanuatu	
1981	21 Sept.	British Honduras	Belize (1973)	
	1 Nov.	Antigua and Barbuda		
1983	19 Sept.	St Christopher and Nevis	St Kitts-Nevis	

Not included: Protected States, nor former dependencies of Australia, New Zealand and South Africa; nor Hong Kong (where British rule ended in 1997 with retrocession to China).

Select Bibliography

I Unpublished records
  1 Cabinet and Prime Minister's Office
  2 Government departments
  3 Private papers
II Published primary sources
  1 Official publications
  2 Main published selections of documents
III Published secondary sources
  1 Biographies, memoirs, speeches, and diaries
  2 Biographical reference works
  3 Select list of general works
  4 Select list of journal articles and chapters in books

I *UNPUBLISHED RECORDS*

The main research on which this book is based covers the period 1945 to 1964, and the records listed below have been searched for these two decades. In addition, the following pre-1945 files have also been searched: (i) the records of Anglo-South African relations from 1905, (ii) those relating to Kenya from 1904 onwards, (iii) a range of records between February 1921 and October 1922, when Winston Churchill was secretary of state for the colonies, and (iv) the files of the Prime Minister's Office, which have been used from 1930. Changed personal circumstances prevented completion of my coal-face research for 1964 to 1968, for which period I rely on the *British Documents on the End of Empire Project* (BDEEP) published documents.

All quotations from government archives appear by permission of the Controller of H. M. Stationery Office.

1 *CABINET AND PRIME MINISTER'S OFFICE* (THE NATIONAL ARCHIVES, KEW)

Cabinet Office registered files: CAB 21
Cabinet Conclusions/Minutes: CAB 23, CAB 128
Cabinet memoranda: CAB 37, CAB 129
Cabinet committees: General: CAB 130
                        Defence: CAB 131

Africa/Colonial Policy/ Economic Policy: CAB 134
Oversea Policy: CAB 134
Defence and Oversea Policy: CAB 148
Commonwealth Prime Ministers' Meetings: CAB 133
Prime Minister's correspondence and papers: PREM 1 (1930–9),
   PREM 4 (1941–5), PREM 8 (1945–51), PREM 11 (1951–64),
   PREM 13 (from 1964)

2 GOVERNMENT DEPARTMENTS (THE NATIONAL ARCHIVES, KEW)

(a) Colonial Office: geographical classes

Aden: CO 725, CO 1055
Africa, general: CO 847
Africa, East: CO 822
Africa, West: CO 554
African Studies Branch: CO 955
Atlantic: CO 1024
Barbados: CO 28
Bermuda: CO 37
Central Africa and Aden: CO 1015
Ceylon: CO 54
Cyprus: CO 67
Eastern: CO 825
Falkland Islands: CO 78
Far East: CO 1030
Fiji: CO 83
Gambia: CO 87
Gibraltar: CO 91
Gold Coast: CO 96
Honduras, British: CO 123
Hong Kong: CO 129
Jamaica: CO 137

Kenya: CO 533
Mediterranean: CO 926
Nigeria: CO 583
Nyasaland: CO 525
Pacific: CO 1036
Rhodesia, Northern: CO 795
Sarawak: CO 938
Seychelles: CO 530
Sierra Leone: CO 267
South Africa, high commissioner:
   CO 417
Southern Africa (Basutoland,
   Bechuanaland, Swaziland):
   CO 1048
Straits Settlements (Malaya): CO 273
Tanganyika: CO 691
Trinidad: CO 295
Uganda: CO 536
West Indies: CO 318, CO 1031
Zanzibar: CO 618

(b) Colonial Office: subject classes

Appointments: CO 877
Circular despatches: CO 854
Colonies, general: CO 323, CO 1032
Colonies, general supplementary ['secret']: CO 537
Confidential print, Africa: CO 879
Confidential print, miscellaneous: CO 885
Defence: CO 968
Economic: CO 852
Establishment: CO 866
Finance: CO 1025
International relations: CO 936
Legal: CO 1026
Oversea Service: CO 1017

Private Office papers: CO 967
Public relations and information: CO 875, CO 1027
Research: CO 927
Social services: CO 859
Welfare and students: CO 876

(c) Dominions Office/Commonwealth Relations Office
General correspondence: DO 9, DO 35
Confidential print: DO 116
Supplementary ['secret'] correspondence: DO 117
South Africa, high commissioner: DO 119
Private Office papers: DO 121
South Africa, High Commission Territories: DO 157
Southern Africa: DO 180
Central Africa: DO 183

(d) Foreign Office
Correspondence, political: FO 371 (departmental files on Africa, Arabia,
Commonwealth liaison, Dominions political, Planning, South-East Asia,
Southern [Europe]/Greece [for Cyprus], United Nations, Western/general)
Ministerial Private Office papers: FO 800 (Bevin, Morrison, Eden, Macmillan)

(e) Service Chiefs and Departments
Admiralty, First Sea Lord's Papers: ADM 205
Chiefs of Staff Committee minutes: DEFE 4
Chiefs of Staff Committee memoranda: DEFE 5, CAB 80
Registered files, general: DEFE 7
Secretariat's registered files: DEFE 11

(f) Treasury
Imperial and Foreign Division: T 220
Overseas Finance Division: T 236
Commonwealth and Foreign Division: T 296

3 PRIVATE PAPERS

A. V. Alexander Papers (Churchill College, Cambridge: Churchill Archives
    Centre, AVAR)
Attlee Papers (Churchill Archives Centre, ATLE)
Sydney Buxton Papers (Newtimber Place, Hassocks, Sussex)
Dalton Papers (Library of Political and Economic Science, London School of
    Economics)
A. D. Garson, CO diaries (Magdalene College, Cambridge: Archives, F/ADG)
Gordon Walker Papers (Churchill Archives Centre, GNWR)
Hankey Papers (Churchill Archives Centre, HNKY)
Dean Inge Diary (Magdalene College, Cambridge: Archives, F/WRI)
Oliver Lyttelton Papers (Churchill Archives Centre, CHAN II)

E.F. Mutesa, Kabaka of Buganda (Magdalene College Archives, tutorial file, F/OMP/IV/9)
Noel-Baker Papers (Churchill Archives Centre, NBKR)
I. A. Richards Papers (Magdalene College Archives, F/IAR)
Smuts Papers (Cambridge University Library, microfilm)
Stewart Papers (Churchill Archives Centre, STWT)
Swinton Papers (Churchill Archives Centre, SWIN I and II)

+ Author's archive: letters from Sir Harold Wilson, Lord Listowel, Sir John Le Rougetel, Sir Evelyn Shuckburgh, and J. S. Bennett

II PUBLISHED PRIMARY SOURCES

1 OFFICIAL PUBLICATIONS

(a) Parliament
Debates, House of Commons, and *House of Lords* (1905–68)

(b) Command Papers and other government papers

Cd 9109	*Report on Indian constitutional reforms* (1918) (Montagu-Chelmsford Report)
Cmd 681	*Report of the committee appointed by the Government of India to investigate the disturbances in the Punjab, etc* (1920) (the Hunter Report on Amritsar)
Cmd 1700	*White Paper on Palestine* (1922) (Churchill)
Cmd 6607	*West Indies Royal Commission Report, 1938–1939* (1945) (Moyne Report)
Col. 231	*Report of the Commission of Inquiry into disturbances in the Gold Coast, 1948* (Watson Report)
Cmd 7913	*Bechuanaland Protectorate: the succession to the chieftainship of the Bamangwato Tribe* (1950)
Cmd 8707	*Basutoland, the Bechuanaland Protectorate and Swaziland: a history of discussions with the Union of South Africa, 1909–1939* (1952)
Carothers, J. C.	*The psychology of Mau Mau* (Government Printer, Nairobi, 1954)
Cmnd 237	*The United Kingdom's role in Commonwealth development* (1957)
Cmnd 505	*Nigeria: report of the Commission appointed to inquire into the fears of minorities and the means of allaying them* (1958) (Willink Report)
Cmnd 814	*Report of the Nyasaland Commission of Inquiry* (1959) (Devlin Report)
Cmnd 1030	*Historical survey of the origins and growth of Mau Mau* (1960) (Corfield Report)
Cmnd 8787	*Falkland Islands review: report of a committee of Privy Counsellors* (1983) (Franks Report)

(c) Departmental reports
Foreign and Commonwealth Office, *A yearbook of the Commonwealth, 1980* (12th edn, 1980)
Her Majesty's Stationery Office, *Swaziland: report for the year 1964* (1966)

2 *MAIN PUBLISHED SELECTIONS OF DOCUMENTS*

British Documents of the End of Empire Project (General Editors: S. R. Ashton and D. J. Murray):

Series A: vol. I: *Imperial policy and colonial practice, 1925–1945* (ed. S. R. Ashton and S. E. Stockwell, 2 parts, 1996)
    vol. II: *The Labour government and the end of empire, 1945–1951* (ed. R. Hyam, 4 parts, 1992)
    vol. III: *The Conservative government and the end of empire, 1951–1957* (ed. D. Goldsworthy, 3 parts, 1994)
    vol. IV: *The Conservative government and the end of empire, 1957–1964* (ed. R. Hyam and W. R. Louis, 2 parts, 2000)
    vol. V: *East of Suez and the Commonwealth, 1964–1971* (ed. S. R. Ashton and W. R. Louis, 3 parts, 2004)
Series B: vol. I: *Ghana, 1941–1957* (ed. R. Rathbone, 2 parts, 1992)
    vol. II: *Sri Lanka, 1939–1948* (ed. K. M. de Silva, 2 parts, 1997)
    vol. III: *Malaya, 1942–1957* (ed. A. J. Stockwell, 3 parts, 1995)
    vol. IV: *Egypt and the defence of the Middle East, 1945–1956* (ed. J. Kent, 3 parts, 1998)
    vol. V: *Sudan, 1942–1956* (ed. D. Johnson, 2 parts, 1998)
    vol. VI: *The West Indies* (ed. S. R. Ashton and D. Killingray, 1999)
    vol. VII: *Nigeria, 1943–1960* (ed. M. Lynn, 2 parts, 2001)
    vol. VIII: *Malaysia* (ed. A.J. Stockwell, 2004)
    vol. IX: *Central Africa, 1945–1965* (ed. P. Murphy, 2 parts, 2005)

Documents on British Policy Overseas:

R. Bullen and M. E. Pelly, eds., Series I, vols. I and III (1984, 1986), Series II, vol. I (1986)
S. R. Ashton, G. Bennett, and K. Hamilton, eds., *Britain and China, 1945–1950*, Series I, vol. VIII (2002)

Foreign Relations of the United States (Washington):

FRUS, 1955–7, vol. XVIII *Africa* (ed. J. P. Glennon and S. Shaloff, 1989)
FRUS, 1958–60, vol. XIV *Africa* (ed. H. D. Schwar and S. Shaloff, 1992)
FRUS, 1961–3, vol. XIII *Western Europe and Canada* (ed. G. W LaFantasie, 1994)
    vol. XX *Congo Crisis* (ed. H. D. Schwar, 1994)
    vol. XXI *Africa* (ed. N. D. Howland and G. W. LaFantasie, 1995)

vol. XXIII   *Southeast Asia* (ed. E. C. Keefer
and G. W. LaFantasie, 1994)

Gilbert, M., ed., *Winston S. Churchill*, vol. IV *Companion*, part 3: *Documents, April 1921 to November 1922* (1977)

Madden, F., ed., *Imperial constitutional documents 1765–1965: a supplement* (1966) *Select documents on the constitutional history of the British Empire and Commonwealth* (Westport, Conn.):

vol. VI *The Dominions and India since 1900* (with J. Darwin, 1993)

vol. VII *The dependent empire, 1900–1948: colonies, protectorates and Mandates* (with J. Darwin, 1994)

vol. VIII *The end of empire: dependencies since 1948*, part 1: *West Indies, British Honduras, Hong Kong, Fiji, Cyprus, Gibraltar, and the Falkland Islands* (2000)

Mansergh, N., ed., *Documents and speeches on Commonwealth affairs, 1931–1952* (2 vols., Oxford, 1953) and *1952–1962* (Oxford, 1963)

Mansergh, N., E. W. R. Lumby, P. Moon, *et al.* eds., *Constitutional relations between Britain and India: the transfer of power, 1942–7*, 12 vols. (1976–83)

Morgan, D. J. *The official history of colonial development* (1980):

vol. I *The origins of British aid policy, 1924–45*

vol. II *Developing British colonial resources, 1945–51*

vol. III *A reassessment of British aid policy, 1951–65*

vol. IV *Changes in British aid policy, 1951–70*

vol. V *Guidance towards self-government in British colonies, 1941–71*

Porter, A. N. and A. J. Stockwell, eds., *British imperial policy and decolonisation*, vol. I: *1938–1951* (1987), vol. II: *1951–1964* (1989)

Tinker, H., ed., *Constitutional relations between Britain and Burma: the struggle for independence, 1944–1948*, vol. I: *From military occupation to civil government, 1 January 1944–31 August 1946* (1983); vol. II: *From general strike to independence, 31 August 1946–4 January 1948* (1984)

Turner, J., ed., *Macmillan: Cabinet papers, 1957–1963, on CD-ROM* (set of three, Adam Matthew Publications, Marlborough, Wilts/Public Record Office, 1999), 'Decolonisation' intro. by P. Murphy

van der Poel, J., ed., *Selections from the Smuts Papers*, vols. V–VII: *1919–1951* (Cambridge, 1973)

Windrich, E., ed., *The Rhodesian problem: a documentary record, 1923–1973* (1975)

III PUBLISHED SECONDARY SOURCES

All books are published in London unless otherwise stated.

1 *Biographies, Memoirs, Speeches and Diaries*

Acheson, Dean. *Present at the creation: my years in the State Department* (1969)

Addison, P. *Churchill: the unexpected hero* (2005)

Alport, Lord. *The sudden assignment: being a record of service in Central Africa, during the controversial years of the Federation of Rhodesia and Nyasaland, 1961–63* (1965)

Amery, L. S. *My political life*, vol. II: *War and peace, 1914–29* (1953); vol. III: *The unforgiving years, 1929–40* (1955)

Atiyah, E. S. *An Arab tells his own story: a study in loyalties* (1946)

Attlee, Clement R. *As it happened* (1954)

Awolowo, O. *Awo: the autobiography of Chief Obafemi Awolowo* (Cambridge, 1960)

Ball, S. J. *The Guardsmen: Harold Macmillan, three friends, and the world they made* (2004)

Barnett, D. L. and Karari Njama, *Mau Mau from within: autobiography and analysis of Kenya's peasant revolt* (1966)

Bates, D. *A gust of plumes: a biography of Lord Twining of of Godalming and Tanganyika* (1972)

Birkenhead, Lord. *Walter Monckton: the life of Viscount Monckton of Brenchley* (1969)

Blake, R. and W. R. Louis, eds., *Churchill* (1993)

Blundell, M. *So rough a wind: the Kenya memoirs of Sir Michael Blundell* (1964)

Bretton, H. L. *The rise and fall of Kwame Nkrumah: a study of personal rule in Africa* (1966)

Brockway, A. Fenner. *Towards tomorrow: autobiography* (1977)

Brooke, Sylvia. *Queen of the headhunters: autobiography* (1970)

Brown, Judith M. *Nehru: a political life* (2003)

Buganda, Kabaka of. *The desecration of my kingdom* (1967)

Bullock, A. *Life and times of Ernest Bevin*, vol. I *Trade Union leader, 1881–1940* (1960), vol. II: *Minister of Labour, 1940–45* (1967), vol. III: *Foreign secretary, 1945–1951* (1983)

Burridge, T. *Clement Attlee: a political biography* (1985)

Butler, R. A. *The art of the possible: the memoirs of Lord Butler* (1971)

Carlton, D. *Anthony Eden: a biography* (1981)

Casey, R. G. *The future of the Commonwealth* (1963)

Castle, Barbara. *The Castle diaries, 1964–1970* (1984), and *Fighting all the way* (1993)

Catterall, P., ed., *The Macmillan diaries: the Cabinet years, 1951–1957* (2003)

Cell, J. W. *Hailey: a study in British imperialism, 1872–1969* (Cambridge, 1992)

Churchill, Winston S. *India: speeches and an introduction* (1931)
The Second World War (6 vols., 1948–54)

Clark, William. *From three worlds: memoirs* (1986)

Clarke, P. F. *The Cripps version: the life of Sir Stafford Cripps, 1889–1952* (2002)

Clarke, Richard, *Anglo-American economic collaboration in war and peace, 1942–49* (ed. A. Cairncross, Oxford, 1982)

Colville, J. *The fringes of power: Downing Street diaries, 1939–56* (1985)

Cross, J. A. *Sir Samuel Hoare: a political biography* (1977)
Lord Swinton (Oxford, 1982)

Crossman, Richard. *The diaries of a Cabinet minister*, vol. I: *1964–1966*, vol. II: *1966–68* (1975–1976)

Dalton, Hugh. *Memoirs*, vol. III: *High tide and after, 1945–1960* (1962)

Dalyell, Tam. *Dick Crossman: a portrait* (1989)

Davenport-Hines, R, *The Macmillans* (1992)

Dilks, D., ed., *The diaries of Sir Alexander Cadogan, 1938–1945* (1971)

Dixon, P. *Double diploma: the life of Sir Pierson Dixon, don and diplomat* (1968)

Donoughue, B. and G. W. Jones. *Herbert Morrison: portrait of a politician* (1973)

Douglas-Home, C. *Evelyn Baring: the last proconsul* (1978)

Egremont, Lord. *Wyndham and children first* (1968)

Evans, Harold. *Downing Street diary: the Macmillan years, 1957–1963* (1981)

Foot, Hugh. *A start in freedom* (1964)

Foot, M. *Aneurin Bevan: a biography*, vol. II: *1945–1960* (1973)

Furse, R. *Aucuparius: recollections of a recruiting officer* (Oxford, 1962)

Gann, L. H. and M. Gelfand, *Huggins of Rhodesia* (1964)

Gilbert, M., ed., *Winston S. Churchill*, vol. IV: *1917–1922* (1975), vol. V: *1922–1939* (1976)

   Churchill's political philosophy (1981)

Gladwyn, Lady Cynthia [Jebb]. *Diaries of Cynthia Gladwyn* (ed. Miles Jebb, 1995)

Gollin, A. M. *Proconsul in politics: a study of Lord Milner in opposition and in power* (1964)

Gopal, S. *Jawaharlal Nehru: a biography* (1975)

Griffiths, James. *Pages from memory* (1969)

Grimble, A. *Return to the islands* (1957)

Hailsham, Lord. *A sparrow's flight: memoirs* (1990)

Hancock, W. K. *Smuts*, vol. II: *The fields of force, 1919–50* (Cambridge, 1968)

Harris, K. *Attlee* (1982)

Healey, Denis, *The time of my life* (1989)

Henderson, Nicholas. *The Private Office: a personal view of five foreign secretaries and of government from the inside* (1984)

   Channels and tunnels: reflections on Britain and abroad (1987)

Home, Lord. *The way the wind blows: an autobiography* (1976)

Horne, A. *Macmillan: the official biography*, vol. I: *1894–1956* (1988), vol. II: *1957–1986* (1989)

Howard, A. *RAB: the life of R. A. Butler* (1987)

   ed., *The Crossman diaries: selections from the diaries of a Cabinet minister, 1964–1970* (1979)

Hunt, D. *On the spot: an ambassador remembers* (1975)

Hussey, C. *The life of Sir Edwin Lutyens* (1950)

Jay, Douglas. *Change and fortune: a political record* (1980)

Jeffery, K. *Field Marshal Sir Henry Wilson: a political soldier* (Oxford, 2006)

Jeffries, Charles. *Whitehall and the Colonial Service: an administrative memoir, 1939–56* (1972)

Jenkins, Roy. *Mr Attlee: an interim biography* (1948)

   Asquith (1964)

   Nine men of power (1974)

   A life at the centre: memoirs (1991)

Jones, Thomas. *Whitehall diary*, vol. II: *1926–1930* (ed. K. Middlemas, 1969)

Kaggia, Bildad. *Roots of freedom, 1921–63: the autobiography of* (Nairobi, 1975)

Kilmuir, Earl of. *Political adventure; the memoirs of* (1962)

Kirkpatrick, Ivone. *The inner circle: memoirs* (1959)

Kuper, H. *Sobhuza II, Ngwenyama and king of Swaziland: the story of an hereditary ruler and his country* (1978)

Lee Kuan Yew. *From third world to first: the Singapore story, 1965–2000* (New York, 2000)

Leith-Ross, Sylvia. *Stepping stones: memoirs of colonial Nigeria, 1907–1960* (ed. M. Crowder, 1983)

Lloyd, Selwyn. *Suez, 1956: a personal account* (1978)

Louis, W. R. *'In the name of God, go!': Leo Amery and the British empire in the age of Churchill* (1992)

Lyttelton, Oliver. *The memoirs of Lord Chandos* (1962)

MacDonald, Malcolm. *Borneo people* (1956)
People and places: random reminiscences of the Rt Hon Malcolm MacDonald (1969)
Titans and others (1972)

McGhee, G. *Envoy to the Middle world: adventures in diplomacy* (New York, 1983)

Macintosh, J. P., ed., *British prime ministers in the 20th century*, vol. I: *Balfour to Chamberlain* (1977), vol. II: *Churchill to Callaghan* (1978) (esp. R. Blake on Eden)

McLachlan, D. *In the chair: Barrington-Ward of 'The Times', 1927–1948* (1971)

Macmillan, Harold, *Memoirs*, vol. I: *Winds of change, 1914–39* (1966); vol. II: *The blast of war 1939–45* (1967); vol. III: *Tides of fortune, 1945–55* (1969); vol. IV: *Riding the storm, 1956–1959* (1971); vol. V: *Pointing the way, 1959–1961* (1972); vol. VI : *At the end of the day, 1961–1963* (1973)

Mandela, Nelson, *Long walk to freedom: the autobiography of* (1994)

Marquand, D. *Ramsay MacDonald* (1977)

Maudling, Reginald. *Memoirs* (1978)

Mayes, S. *Makarios: a biography* (1981)

Megahey, Alan. *Humphrey Gibbs, the beleaguered governor: Southern Rhodesia 1929–1969* (1998)

Moon, Penderel, ed., *Wavell: the viceroy's journal* (Oxford, 1973)

Moran, Lord. *Winston Churchill: the struggle for survival, 1940–65* (1966)

Morgan, Austen. *Harold Wilson* (1992)

Morgan, K. O. *Callaghan: a life* (Oxford, 1997)

Murphy, P. V. *Alan Lennox-Boyd: a biography* (1999)

Murray-Brown, J. *Kenyatta* (1972)

Nehru, Jawaharlal. *An autobiography* (1936, 1938)

Nkrumah, Kwame. *The autobiography of Kwame Nkrumah* (2nd edn, 1964)

Paice, E. *Lost lion of empire: the life of 'Cape-to-Cairo' Grogan* (2001)

Pearce, E. *The lost leaders* (1997) (esp, Macleod and Butler)

Pearce, R. D., ed., *Patrick Gordon Walker: political diaries, 1932–1971* (1991)

Pelling, H. M. *Winston Churchill* (1974)

Perham, Margery. *Lugard*, vol. II *The years of authority, 1898–1945* (1960)

Pimlott, B. *Hugh Dalton* (1985)
Harold Wilson (1992)

Redcliffe-Maud, John. *Experiences of an optimist: memoirs* (1981)

Rhodes James, R. *Churchill: a study in failure, 1900–1939* (1970)
Anthony Eden (1986)

Robertson, James. *Transition in Africa, from direct rule to independence: a memoir* (1974)

Rooney, D. *Sir Charles Arden-Clarke* (1982)
Kwame Nkrumah: the political kingdom in the Third World (1988)

Roskill, S. *Hankey: man of secrets*, vol. III: *1931–1963* (1974)

Sanger, C. *Malcolm MacDonald: bringing an end to empire* (Liverpool, 1995)

Sharwood Smith, B. *'But always as friends': Northern Nigeria and the Cameroons, 1921–57* (1969)

Shepherd, R. *Iain Macleod* (1994)

Shuckburgh, Evelyn. *Descent to Suez: diaries, 1951–1956*, (ed. J. Charmley, 1986)
Stephens, M. *Ernest Bevin: unskilled labourer and world statesman, 1881–1951* (1981)
Stewart, Michael. *Life and Labour* (1980)
Storrs, R. H. A. *Orientations* (1943, 1945)
Strang, Lord. *Home and abroad* (1956)
Swinton, Lord. *As I remember* [nd, ? 1949]
    Sixty years of power: some memories of the men who wielded it (with J. Margach, 1966)
Thomas, H. *John Strachey* (1973)
Thorpe, D. R. *Selwyn Lloyd* (1989)
    Alec Douglas-Home (1996)
Tlou, T., and N. Parsons and W. Henderson. *Seretse Khama, 1921–80* (Gaborone and Bramfontein, 1995)
Turner, John. *Macmillan* (1994)
Vansittart, Robert. *The mist procession: the autobiography of Lord Vansittart* (1958)
Vatikiotis, P. J. *Nasser and his generation* (1978)
Watkinson, Harold. *Turning-points: a record of our times* (1986)
Welensky, Roy. *Welensky's 4000 days: the life and death of the Federation of Rhodesia and Nyasaland* (1964)
Williams, Francis. *Ernest Bevin: portrait of a great Englishman* (1952)
    ed., *A prime minister remembers* (1960), repr. as *Twilight of empire: memoirs of Prime Minister Clement Attlee* (Connecticut, 1978)
Williams, Philip M. *Hugh Gaitskell: a political biography* (1979)
    ed., *The diary of Hugh Gaitskell, 1945–1956* (1983)
Wilson, Harold. *The Labour government, 1964–1970: a personal record* (1971)
Wood, I.S. *Churchill* (2000) (esp. ch 9, 'Churchill and the British empire', pp. 156–75)
Ziegler, P. *Mountbatten: the official biography* (1985)

2 BIOGRAPHICAL REFERENCE WORKS

The Colonial Office List (annual)

Hulugalle, H. A. J. *British governors of Ceylon* (Colombo, 1963)
Kirk-Greene, A. H. M., ed., *A biographical dictionary of the British colonial governor*, vol. I: *Africa* (1980)
    ed., *A biographical dictionary of the British Colonial Service, 1939–66* (1991)

Matthew, H. C. G. and B. Harrison, eds., *The Oxford Dictionary of National Biography* (60 vols. Oxford, 2004):

(a) Politicians
Abdul Rahman, Tunku, by A. J. Stockwell, vol. I, pp. 53–4
Amery, Leopold, by D. Lavin, vol. I, pp. 932–6
Attlee, Clement, by R. C. Whiting, vol. II, pp. 875–84
Azikiwe, Nnamdi, by A. Jackson, vol. III, pp. 66–7
Baldwin, Stanley, by S. Ball, vol. III, pp. 460–77
Balfour, Arthur, by R. Mackay and H. C. G. Matthew, vol. III, pp. 486–513
Banda, Hastings, by J. McCracken, vol. III, pp. 657–9

Bandaranaike, Solomon W. R. D., by R. C. Oberst, vol. III, pp. 660–2
Bevin, Ernest, by C. Wrigley, vol. V, pp. 604–12
Blundell, Michael, by J. Johnson, vol. VI, pp. 336–8
Bottomley, Arthur, by D. Goldsworthy, vol. VI, pp. 764–5
Brown, George, by K. Whitton, vol. VIII, pp. 36–40
Chamberlain, Neville, by A. J. Crozier, vol. X, pp. 934–55
Churchill, Winston, by P. Addison, vol. XI, pp. 652–85
Creech Jones, Arthur, by P.M. Pugh, vol. XXX, pp. 443–5
Cripps, Stafford, by P. Clarke and R. Toye, vol. XIV, pp. 200–6
Eden, Anthony, by D. R. Thorpe, vol. XVII, pp. 664–79
Gandhi, Mohandas, by J. M. Brown, vol. XXI, pp. 372–9
Gordon Walker, Patrick, by R. D. Pearce, vol. LVI, pp. 880–3
Greenwood, Anthony, by K. O. Morgan, vol. XXIII, pp. 620–1
Hoare, Samuel, Viscount Templewood, by R. J. Q. Adamson,
   vol. XXVII, pp. 364–8
Home, Alec Douglas-, by D. Hurd, vol. XXVII, pp. 861–7
Jagan, Cheddi, by H. Johnson, vol. XXIX, pp. 583–5
Kenyatta, Jomo, by B. Berman, vol. XXXI, pp. 338–41
Khama, Seretse, by Q. N. Parsons, vol. XXXI, pp. 506–7
Khama, Tshekedi, by W. Henderson, vol. XXXI, pp. 507–9
Lennox-Boyd, Alan, by P. Murphy, vol. VII, pp. 23–5
Lloyd, Selwyn, by D. R. Thorpe, vol. XXXIV, pp. 157–63
Lyttelton, Oliver, by P. Murphy, vol. XXXIV, pp. 968–70
MacDonald, Malcolm, by P. Lyon, vol. XXXV, pp. 260–3
MacDonald, Ramsay, by D. Marquand, vol. XXXV, pp. 268–83
Macleod, Iain, by D. Goldsworthy, vol. XXXV, pp. 810–18
Macmillan, Harold, by H. C. G. Matthew, vol. XXXV, pp. 879–96
Makarios III, archbishop, by C. M. Woodhouse, vol. XXXVI, pp. 257–8
Maudling, Reginald, by R. Shepherd, vol. XXXVII, pp. 402–6
Milner, Alfred, by C. W. Newbury, vol. XXXVIII, pp. 302–9
Morrison, Herbert, by D. Howell, vol. XXXIX, pp. 335–44
Mutesa II, E. F., Kabaka of Buganda, by O. Furley, vol. XL, pp. 39–40
Nehru, Jawaharlal, by S. Gopal, vol. XL, pp. 343–51
Nkrumah, Kwame, by R. Rathbone, vol. XL, pp. 941–3
Noel-Baker, Philip, by D. Howell, vol. III, pp. 397–9
Nyerere, Julius, by C. Pratt, vol. XLI, pp. 305–8
Sandys, Duncan, by N. P. Ludlow, vol. XLVIII, pp. 911–14
Senanayake, Don, by H. Moore and R. C. Oberst, vol. XLIX, pp. 751–3
Sobhuza II, King of Swaziland, by J. E. Spence, vol. LI, pp. 521–2
Stewart, Michael, by T. Dalyell, vol. LII, pp. 734–75
Swinton, Earl of, Philip Cunliffe-Lister, by K. Robbins,
   vol. XXXIII, pp. 988–92
Wilson, Harold, by R. Jenkins, vol. LIX, pp. 544–55
Wood, Edward, Lord Halifax, by D. J. Dutton, vol. LX, pp. 81–9

(b) *Civil servants and colonial governors*
Arden-Clarke, Charles, by A. H. M. Kirk-Greene, vol. XI, pp. 856–7
Baring, Evelyn, by A. Clayton, vol. III, pp. 828–9

Brook, Norman, by K. Theakston, vol. VII, pp. 859–62
Brooke, Raja Vyner, by R. H. W. Reece, vol. VII, pp. 916–17
Burns, Alan, by A. H. M. Kirk-Greene, vol VIII, pp. 970–1
Caine, Sydney, by P. M. Pugh, vol. IX, pp. 449–50
Cohen, Andrew, by R. E. Robinson, vol. XII, pp. 418–19
Dean, Patrick, by A. Campbell, vol. XV, pp. 627–9
Dorman, Maurice, by A. H. M. Kirk-Greene, vol. XVI, pp. 572–3
Foot, Hugh, by L. M. Jeger, vol. XX, pp. 242–3
Garner, Joe Saville, by A. May, vol. XXI, pp. 482–3
Gibbs, Humphrey, by D. Lowry, vol. XXII, pp. 46–7
Jeffries, Charles, by A. P. Baker, vol. XXIX, pp. 897–8
Laithwaite, Gilbert, by M. Maclagan, vol. XXXII, pp. 233–4
Liesching, Percivale, by L. Lloyd, vol. XXXIII, pp. 746–7
Lugard, Frederick, by A. H. M. Kirk-Greene, vol. XXXIV, pp. 727–32
Macpherson, John, by A. H. M. Kirk-Greene, vol. XXXV, pp. 996–7
Mansergh, Nicholas, by R. Hyam, vol. XXXVI, pp. 542–3
Maud, John Redcliffe-, by R. Armstrong, vol. XXXVII, pp. 390–2
Monson, Leslie, by L. Allinson, vol. XXXVIII, pp. 678–9
Mountbatten, Lord Louis, by P. Ziegler, vol. XXXIX, pp. 547–58
Poynton, Hilton, by S. R. Ashton, vol. XLV, pp. 191–93
Robertson, James, by A. H. M. Kirk-Greene, vol. XLVII, pp. 242–3
Robinson, R. E., by A. S. Thompson, vol. XXI, pp. 313–14 (subsumed
    under 'Gallagher, John')
Trend, Burke, by Edward Heath, vol. LV, pp. 308–9
Trevaskis, Kennedy, by A. d'Avray, vol. LV, pp. 351–2
Trevelyan, Humphrey, by M. T. Thornhill, vol. LV, pp. 338–40
Turnbull, Richard, by A. H. M. Kirk-Greene, vol. LV, pp. 593–4

3   SELECT LIST OF GENERAL WORKS

Abu-Lughod, J. L. The transformation of Palestine: essays on the origin and develop-
    ment of Arab–Israeli conflict (Evanston, Ill., 1971)
Addison, P. The road to 1945: British politics and the Second World War (1975)
Ajayi, J. F. A. and M. Crowder, eds., History of West Africa, vol. II (1974)
Aldcroft, D. H. The British economy, vol. I: The years of turmoil, 1920–1951 (1986)
Aldous, R. and S. Lee, eds., Harold Macmillan and Britain's world role (1996)
    eds, Harold Macmillan: aspects of a political life (1999)
Aldrich, R. J., ed., British intelligence, strategy and the cold war (1992)
Alford, B. W. E. British economic performance, 1945–1975 (1988)
Anderson, D. Histories of the hanged: Britain's dirty war in Kenya and the end of
    empire (2004)
    and D. Killingray, eds., Policing and decolonisation: politics, nationalism and the
    police, 1917–1965 (Manchester, 1992)
Annan, N. Our age: portrait of a generation (1990)
Apter, D. E. The political kingdom in Uganda: a study in bureaucratic nationalism
    (Princeton, NJ, 1961)
Ashby, E. Universities, British, Indian and African: a study in the ecology of higher edu-
    cation (with M. Anderson, 1966)

Atieno Odhiambo, E. S. and J. M. Lonsdale, eds., *Mau Mau and nationhood: arms, authority and narration* (Nairobi, 2003)

Austin, D. *Politics in Ghana, 1946–1960* (1964)
  Britain and South Africa (Oxford, 1966)
  Malta and the end of empire (1971)

Baker, C. A. *State of emergency: crisis in Central Africa, Nyasaland, 1959–1960* (1997)
  Retreat from empire: Sir Robert Armitage in Africa and Cyprus (1998)

Balfour-Paul, G. *The end of empire in the Middle East: Britain's relinquishment of power in her last three Arab dependencies* (Cambridge, 1991)

Ball, S. J. *The Cold War: an international history, 1947–91* (1998)

Banton, M. *The idea of race* (1977)
  Racial theories (2nd edn, 1998)

Barber, J. *Rhodesia: the road to rebellion* (1967)

Barnett, C. *The collapse of British power* (1972)

Bartlett, C. J. *The long retreat: a short history of British defence policy, 1945–70* (1972)

Bauer, Y. *From diplomacy to resistance: Jewish Palestine, 1939–1945* (1970)

Bayly, C. A. and T. N. Harper. *Forgotten armies: the fall of British Asia, 1941–1945* (2004)

Bell, M., R. Butlin and M. Heffernan, eds., *Geography and imperialism, 1820–1940* (Manchester, 1995)

Bennett, G. *Kenya; a political history: the colonial period* (Oxford, 1963)
  and C. Rosberg. *The Kenyatta election: Kenya, 1960–61* (1961)

Berlin, I. *Mr Churchill in 1940* (repr. from *Cornhill Magazine*, 1949)

Berman, B. and J. M. Lonsdale, *Unhappy Valley: conflict in Kenya and Africa*, vol. II: *Violence and ethnicity* (1992)

Berridge, G. R. *Economic power in Anglo-South African diplomacy: Simonstown, Sharpeville and after* (1981)

Bethell, N. *The Palestine triangle: the struggle between the British, the Jews and the Arabs, 1935–1948* (1979)

Birmingham, D. *The decolonization of Africa* (1995)

Bischoff, P.-H. *Swaziland's international relations and foreign policy: a study of a small African state in international relations* (European University Studies, Political Science, vol. 158; Berne, 1990)

Blake, R. *A history of Rhodesia* (1977)
  The decline of British power, 1915–64 (1985)

Boardman, R. *Britain and the People's Republic of China, 1949–74* (1976)

Boyce, D. G. *Decolonisation and the British empire, 1775–1997* (1999)

Brendon, P. *The dark valley: a panorama of the 1930s* (2000)

Breuilly, J. *Nationalism and the state* (2nd edn, 1993)

Bridge, C. *Holding India to the empire: the British Conservative Party and the 1935 constitution* (1986)

Brown, Judith M. *Gandhi's rise to power: Indian politics, 1915–22* (Cambridge, 1972)
  Gandhi and civil disobedience: the Mahatma and Indian politics, 1928–34 (Cambridge, 1977)
  Modern India: the origins of an Asian democracy (New Delhi, 1985)
  and W. R. Louis, eds., *The Oxford History of the British Empire*, vol. IV: *The twentieth century* (1999)

Brown, Neville, *Arms without empire: British defence role in the modern world* (Harmondsworth, 1967)

Burns, A. R. *Colour prejudice* (1948)

Burroughs, P. and A. J. Stockwell, eds., *Managing the business of empire: essays in honour of David Fieldhouse* (1998), repr. from *JICH* vol. 26 (1998)

Butler, L. J. *Britain and empire: adjusting to a post-imperial world* (2002)

Cain, P. J. and A. G. Hopkins, *British imperialism, 1688–2000* (2nd edn, 2001)

Cairncross, A. *The years of recovery: British economic policy, 1945–51* (1985)

Camps, M. *Britain and the European Community, 1955–1963* (Princeton and Oxford, 1964)

Cannadine, D. *Ornamentalism: how the British saw their empire* (2001, 2002)

Carlton, D. *Britain and the Suez Crisis* (Oxford, 1988)

Ceadel, M. *Pacifism in Britain, 1914–45: the defining of a faith* (Oxford, 1980)

Chan, S. *The Commonwealth in world politics: a study of international action, 1965–85* (1988)

Chanock, M. L. *Unconsummated Union: Britain, Rhodesia and South Africa, 1900–45* (Manchester, 1977)

Clarke, P. F. and R. C. Trebilcock, eds., *Understanding decline: perceptions and realities of British economic performance* (Essays in honour of Barry Supple, Cambridge, 1997)

Cohen, A. B. *British policy in changing Africa* (1959)

Cohen, M. J. *Palestine: retreat from the Mandate: the making of British policy, 1936–45* (1978)

Churchill and the Jews (1985)

Coleman, J. S. *Nigeria: background to nationalism* (Berkeley, CA, 1963)

Constantine, S. *The making of British colonial development policy, 1914–40* (1984)

Coupland, R. *The Indian problem, 1833–1935* (Oxford, 1942)

Cowling, M. *The impact of Hitler: British politics and British policy, 1933–1940* (Cambridge, 1975)

Crowder, M., ed., *Cambridge history of Africa*, vol. VIII: *From c. 1940 to c. 1975* (Cambridge, 1984)

Darby, P. *British defence policy East of Suez, 1947–1968* (Oxford, 1973)

Three faces of imperialism: British and American approaches to Asia and Africa, 1870–1970 (Yale, New Haven, 1987)

Darwin, J. *Britain, Egypt and the Middle East: imperial policy in the aftermath of war, 1918–22* (1981)

Britain and decolonisation: the retreat from empire in the post-war world (1988)

The end of the British empire: the historical debate (Oxford, 1991)

Davenport, T. R. H. *South Africa: a modern history* (5th edn, with C. Saunders, 2001)

Dewey, C. *Anglo-Indian attitudes: the mind of the Indian Civil Service* (1994)

Dilks, D., ed., *Retreat from power: studies in Britain's foreign policy of the twentieth century*, vol. I: *1906–39*, vol. II: *After 1939* (1981)

Great Britain, Commonwealth and wider world, 1939–45 (pamphlet, Hull, 1998)

Dockrill, M. and J. W. Young, eds., *British foreign policy, 1945–56* (1989)

ed., *Europe within the global system, 1938–60: Great Britain, France, Italy and Germany, from great powers to regional powers* (Arbeitskreis Deutsche England-Forschung, vol. 30, Bochum, 1995)

Dockrill, S. *Britain's retreat from East of Suez: the choice between Europe and the world?* (2002)

Drummond, I. M. *British economic policy and the empire, 1919–1939* (1972) *Imperial economic policy, 1917–1939: studies in expansion and protection* (1974)

Dumett, R.E., ed., *Gentlemanly capitalism and British imperialism: the new debate on empire* (1999)

Duus, P., ed., *Cambridge History of Japan*, vol. VI: *The twentieth century* (Cambridge, 1988)

Eatwell, R. *The 1945–51 Labour governments* (1979)

Eayrs, J., ed., *The Commonwealth and Suez: a documentary survey* (Oxford, 1964)

Edmonds, R. *Setting the mould: the United States and Britain, 1945–50* (Oxford, 1986)

Elkins, C. *Britain's Gulag: the brutal end of empire in Kenya* (2005)

Endicott, S. L. *Diplomacy and enterprise: British China policy, 1933–1937* (Manchester, 1975)

Fage, J. D. *A history of Africa* (4th edn, with W. Tordoff, 2002)

Fawcus, P. *Botswana: the road to independence* (with A. Tilbury, Gaborone, 2000)

Fieldhouse, D. K. *Black Africa, 1945–80: economic decolonisation and arrested development* (1986)

Forbes Munro, J. *Africa and the international economy, 1800–1960: an introduction* (1976)

Frankel, J. *British foreign policy, 1945–1973* (1975)

Fraser, T. G. *Partition in Ireland, India and Palestine: theory and practice* (1984)

Freedman, L. *The official history of the Falklands Campaign*, vol. I: *The origins of the Falklands War*, vol. II: *War and diplomacy* (2005)

Friedman, I. *The question of Palestine, 1914–1918: British–Jewish–Arab relations* (1973)

Furedi, F. *The Mau Mau war in perspective* (Nairobi and Ohio, 1989)

Furnivall, J. S. *Colonial policy and practice: a comparative study of Burma and Netherlands India* (Cambridge, 1948)

Fussell, P. *The Great War and modern memory* (Oxford, 1975)

Gallagher, J. *The decline, revival and fall of the British empire: The Ford Lectures and other essays* (ed. A. Seal, Cambridge, 1982)

and G. Johnson and A. Seal, eds., *Locality, province and nation: essays on Indian politics, 1870–1940* (Cambridge, 1973)

Garner, J. S. *The Commonwealth Office, 1925–1968* (1978)

Gavin, R. *Aden under British rule, 1839–1967* (1975)

Geyser, O. *Watershed for South Africa: London, 1961* (Durban, 1983)

Gibbs, N. H. *Grand strategy*, vol. I: *Rearmament policy* (History of the Second World War, UK military series, 1976)

Gifford, P. and W. R. Louis, eds., *Transfer of power in Africa: decolonisation, 1940–60* (Yale, New Haven, 1982)

eds., *Decolonisation and African independence: the transfer of power, 1960–1980* (Yale, New Haven, 1988)

Goldsworthy, D. *Colonial issues in British politics, 1945–61* (Oxford, 1971)

Good, R. C. *UDI: the international politics of the Rhodesian rebellion* (1973)

Gordon, M. R. *Conflict and consensus in Labour's foreign policy, 1914–1965* (Stanford, CA, 1969)

Gordon Walker, P. *The Commonwealth* (1975)

Gray, R. *The two nations: aspects of the development of race relations in the Rhodesias and Nyasaland* (Oxford, 1960)

Gregory, R. G. *India and East Africa: a history of race relations within the British empire, 1890–1939* (Oxford, 1971)

Gupta, P. S. *Imperialism and the British Labour movement, 1914–1964* (1975)

Haggie, P. *Britannia at bay: defence of the British empire against Japan, 1931–1941* (Oxford, 1981)

Hailey, Lord, *An African survey, revised 1956: a study of the problems arising in Africa south of the Sahara* (Oxford, 1957)

Halpern, B. *The idea of a Jewish state* (Harvard, 1961)

Halpern, J. *South Africa's hostages: Basutoland, Bechuanaland, and Swaziland* (Harmondsworth, 1965)

Hancock, W. K. *Survey of British Commonwealth affairs*: vol. I: *Problems of nationality, 1918–36* (1937): vol. II: *Problems of economic policy* (in two parts, 1942) *Argument of empire* (1943)
  The wealth of colonies (Cambridge, 1950)

Hansen, R. *Citizenship and immigration in post-war Britain* (2000)

Hardie, F. *The Abyssinian crisis* (1974)

Hargreaves, J. *The end of colonial rule in West Africa* (1979)
  Decolonization in Africa (2nd edn, 1996)

Harkness, D. W. *The restless dominion: the Irish Free State and the British Commonwealth of Nations, 1921–1931* (1969)

Harper, T. N. *The end of empire and the making of Malaya* (Cambridge, 1999)

Havinden, M. and D. Meredith. *Colonialism and development: Britain and its tropical colonies, 1850–1960* (1993)

Heinlein, F. *British government policy and decolonisation, 1945–1963: scrutinising the official mind* (2002)

Hennessy, P. *Never again: Britain, 1945–1951* (1992)
  The prime minister: the office and its holders since 1945 (2000)

Heussler, R. *Yesterday's rulers: the making of the British Colonial Service* (Syracuse, 1963)
  The British in Northern Nigeria (1968)
  British rule in Malaya: the Malayan Civil Service and its predecessors, 1867–1942 (1981)

Hicks, U. K. *Federalism: failure and success* (1978)

Higham, R. *Britain's imperial air routes, 1918 to 1939* (1960)

Hillmer, N. and P. Wrigley, eds., *The first British Commonwealth: essays in honour of Nicholas Mansergh* (1980), repr. from *JICH*, vol. 8 (1979)

Hodgson, M. G. S. *The venture of Islam: conscience and history in a world civilisation*, vol. III: *The gunpowder empires and modern times* (Chicago, 1974)

Hodson, H. V. *The great divide: Britain–India–Pakistan* (1969)

Holland, R. F. *Britain and the Commonwealth alliance, 1918–39* (1981)
  European decolonisation, 1945–61: an introductory survey (1985)
  The pursuit of greatness: Britain and the world role, 1900–70 (1991)
  Britain and the revolt in Cyprus, 1954–1959 (Oxford, 1998)
  ed., *Emergencies and disorder in the European empires after 1945* (special issue of *JICH*, vol. 21, 1993)

Hopkins, A. G. *An economic history of West Africa* (1973)

Hourani, A. *Arabic thought in the liberal age, 1798–1939* (Oxford, 1962, 1967)
  A history of the Arab peoples (1991)
Howard, M. *The continental commitment: the dilemma of British defence policy in the era of the two world wars: the Ford Lectures, 1971* (1972)
Howarth, T. E. B. *Prospect and reality: Great Britain, 1945–55* (1985)
Howe, S. *Anticolonialism in British politics: the Left and the end of empire* (Oxford, 1993)
Hunt, R. and J. Harrison, *The district officer in India, 1930–47* (1980)
Hyam, R. *Elgin and Churchill at the Colonial Office, 1905–1908* (1968)
  The failure of South African expansion, 1908–1948 (1972)
  Britain's imperial century, 1815–1914: a study of empire and expansion (3rd edn 2002)
  Empire and sexuality: the British experience (1990, 1991, 1998)
  and P. Henshaw, *The lion and the springbok: Britain and South Africa since the Boer War* (Cambridge, 2003)
Iliffe, J. *A modern history of Tanganyika* (Cambridge, 1979)
  Africans: history of a continent (Cambridge, 1995)
  Honour in African history (Cambridge, 2005)
Ingram, E. *The British empire as a world power* (2001)
Ingrams, D., ed., *Palestine papers, 1917–22: the seeds of conflict* (1972)
Jackson, A. *The British empire and the Second World War* (2006)
Jackson, W. *Withdrawal from empire: a military view* (1986)
Jalal, A. *The sole spokesman: Jinnah, the Muslim League and the demand for Pakistan* (Cambridge, 1985)
James, A. *Britain and the Congo crisis, 1960–1963* (1996)
James, L. *The rise and fall of the British empire* (1994)
Jeffery, K. *The British army and the crisis of empire, 1918–1922* (Manchester, 1984)
Jeffrey, R., ed., *Asia, the winning of independence* (1981)
Johnston, C. H. *The view from Steamer Point: being an account of three years in Aden* (1964)
Johnston, W. R. *Great Britain, great empire: an evaluation of the British imperial experience* (Queensland, 1981)
Jones, Martin, *Failure in Palestine: British and United States policy after the Second World War* (1986)
Jones, Matthew. *Conflict and Confrontation in South-East Asia: Britain, the United States, Indonesia and the creation of Malaysia, 1961–1965* (Cambridge, 2002)
Judd, D. *The British imperial experience, from 1765 to the present* (1996)
Kahler, M. *Decolonization in Britain and France: the domestic consequences of international relations* (Princeton, NJ, 1984)
Kaiser, W. and G. Staerck, eds., *British foreign policy, 1955–1964: contracting options* (2000)
Kamoche, J. G. *Imperial trusteeship and political evolution in Kenya, 1923–1963: a study of the official views and the road to decolonisation* (Washington, 1981)
Katouzian, H. *The political economy of modern Iran: despotism and pseudo-modernism, 1926–79* (1981)
Kedourie, E. *England and the Middle East: destruction of the Ottoman empire, 1914–21* (1956)

The Chatham House version and other Middle Eastern studies (1970)

Islam in the modern world (1980)

Kelly, J. B. *Arabia, the Gulf and the West* (1980)

Kelly, S. and A. Gorst, eds., *Whitehall and the Suez Crisis* (2000), repr. from special number of *Contemporary British History*, vol. 13 (1999)

Kennedy, D. *Islands of white: settler society and culture in Kenya and Southern Rhodesia, 1890–1939* (Duke, 1987)

Kennedy, P. *The rise and fall of British naval mastery* (1976)

The realities behind diplomacy: background influences on British external policy, 1865–1980 (1981)

Strategy and diplomacy, 1870–1945: eight studies (1983)

Kent, J. *The internationalization of colonialism: Britain, France and Black Africa, 1939–56* (Oxford, 1992)

British imperial strategy and the origins of the Cold War, 1944–1949 (Leicester, 1993)

Kent, M. *Oil and empire: British policy and Mesopotamian oil, 1900–20* (1976)

Kenyatta, J. *Facing Mount Kenya: the tribal life of the Gikuyu* (1938)

Kershaw, G. *Mau Mau from below* (Nairobi, 1997)

Kiernan, V. G. *The lords of human kind: European attitudes towards the outside world in the imperial age* (1969)

Killingray, D. and R. Rathbone, eds., *Africa and the Second World War* (1986)

Kilson, M. *Political change in a West African state: a study of the modernisation process in Sierra Leone* (Harvard, 1966)

King, R. D. and R. W. Kilson, eds., *The statecraft of British imperialism: essays in honour of Wm Roger Louis* (1999), repr. from *JICH* vol. 27 (1999)

Kirk-Greene, A. H. M., ed., *The transfer of power: the colonial administrator in the age of decolonisation: proceedings of a symposium, March 1978* (Oxford, 1979)

On Crown Service: a history of H. M. Colonial and Overseas Services, 1937–97 (1999)

Britain's imperial administrators, 1858–1966 (2000)

Kirkman, W. P. *Unscrambling an empire: a critique of British colonial policy, 1956–66* (1966)

Krozewski, G. *Money and the end of empire: British international economic policy and the colonies, 1947–58* (2001)

Kuniholm, B. R. *The origins of the Cold War in the Near East: great power conflict and diplomacy in Iran, Turkey and Greece* (Princeton, NJ, 1980)

Kyle, K. *Suez* (1991)

The politics of the independence of Kenya (1999)

Lamb, R. *The failure of the Eden government* (1987)

The Macmillan years, 1957–63: the emerging truth (1995)

Lapping, B. *End of empire* (based on the television series, 1985)

Leakey, L. S. B. *Mau Mau and the Kikuyu* (1952)

Ledger, D. *Shifting sands: the British in South Arabia* (1984)

Lee, B. A. *Britain and the Sino-Japanese War, 1937–39: a study in the dilemmas of British decline* (Stanford, CA, 1973)

Lee, J. M. *Colonial development and good government: a study in the ideas expressed by the British official classes in planning decolonisation, 1935–64* (Oxford, 1967)

and M. Petter, *The Colonial Office, war and development policy: the organisation and the planning of a metropolitan initiative, 1935–1945* (1982)

Leifer, M., ed., *Constraints and adjustments in British foreign policy* (1972)
Lewis, G. K. *The growth of the modern West Indies* (1968)
Lewis, J. *Empire state-building: war and warfare in Kenya, 1923–52* (Ohio, 2001)
Leys, C. *European politics in Southern Rhodesia* (Oxford, 1959)
    and C. Pratt, eds., *A new deal in Central Africa* (1960)
    and P. Robson, *Federation in East Africa: opportunities and problems* (Nairobi, 1965)
Little, T. *Egypt* (1958)
Louis, W. R. *Great Britain and Germany's lost colonies, 1914–1919* (Oxford, 1967)
    British strategy in the Far East, 1919–1939 (Oxford, 1971)
    *Imperialism at bay, 1941–45: the United States and the decolonization of the British
        empire* (Oxford, 1977)
    *The British empire in the Middle East, 1945–1951: Arab nationalism, the United
        States and post-war imperialism* (Oxford, 1984)
    Ends of British imperialism: the Scramble for empire, Suez, and decolonization
        (2006)
    and H. Bull, eds., *The 'Special Relationship': Anglo-American relations since 1945*
        (Oxford, 1986)
    and R. Owen, eds., *Suez 1956: the crisis and its consequences* (Oxford, 1989)
    and R. W. Stookey, eds., *The end of the Palestine Mandate* (Austin, Texas, 1986)
Low, D. A. *Buganda in modern history* (1971)
    Lion rampant: essays in the study of British imperialism (1973)
    The contraction of England (inaugural lecture, Cambridge, 1985)
    Eclipse of empire: Commonwealth and decolonisation (Cambridge, 1990)
    The egalitarian moment: Asia and Africa, 1950–80 (Cambridge, 1996)
    Britain and Indian nationalism: the imprint of ambiguity, 1929–42 (Cambridge,
        1997)
    ed., *Soundings in modern South Asian history* (Berkeley, CA, 1968)
    ed., *Congress and the Raj: facets of the Indian struggle, 1917–1947* (1977)
    and R. C. Pratt, *Buganda and British overrule, 1900–1955: two studies* (1960)
    and Alison Smith, eds., *History of East Africa* vol. III (Oxford, 1976)
Lowe, P. *Great Britain and the origins of the Pacific War: a study of British policy in
        East Asia, 1937–41* (Oxford, 1977)
Lowenthal, D., ed., *The West Indies Federation: perspectives on a new nation* (New
        York, 1961)
Lucas, W. Scott. *Divided we stand: Britain, the US and the Suez Crisis* (1991)
Ludowyk, E. F. C. *The modern history of Ceylon* (1966)
Lugard, F. D. *The dual mandate in tropical Africa* (1922, 1929)
Lynn, M., ed., *The British empire in the 1950s: retreat or revival?* (2006)
MacDonald, J. Ramsay. *Labour and the empire* (1907)
McGregor Ross, W. *Kenya from within: a short political history* (1927)
McIntyre, W. D. *The rise and fall of the Singapore naval base, 1919–1942* (1979)
    The significance of the Commonwealth, 1965–90 (1991)
    British decolonisation, 1946–97: when, why and how did the British empire fall?
        (1998)
McKenzie, F. *Redefining the bonds of Commonwealth, 1939–48: the politics of prefer-
        ence* (2002)
MacKenzie, J. M. *Propaganda and empire: the manipulation of British public opinion,
        1880–1960* (Manchester, 1984)

Macmillan, W. M. *The road to self-rule: a study in colonial evolution* (1959)

McTague, J. J. *British policy in Palestine, 1917–1922* (Lanham, USA, 1983)

Mansergh, N. *Survey of British Commonwealth affairs: problems of external policy, 1931–39* (1952)

Survey of British Commonwealth affairs: problems of wartime co-operation and post-war change, 1939–52 (1958)

The Commonwealth experience, vol. I: *The Durham Report to the Anglo-Irish Treaty*, vol. II: *From British to multi-racial Commonwealth* (2nd edn, 1982)

The unresolved question: the Anglo-Irish settlement and its undoing, 1912–72 (Yale, New Haven, 1991)

Independence years: the selected Indian and Commonwealth papers of Nicholas Mansergh (ed. Diana Mansergh, New Delhi, 1999)

Matsebula, J. S. M. *A history of Swaziland* (2nd edn, 1976, 1988)

Maxon, R. M. *The struggle for Kenya: the loss and reassertion of imperial initiative, 1912–1923* (1993)

May, A., ed., *Britain, the Commonwealth and Europe: the Commonwealth and Britain's applications to join the European Communities* (2001)

Miles, R. *Racism* (1989)

Miller, J. D. B. *Sir Winston Churchill and the Commonwealth of Nations* (Queensland lecture, 1966)

Survey of Commonwealth affairs: problems of expansion and attrition, 1953–1969 (Oxford, 1974)

Monroe, E. *Britain's moment in the Middle East, 1914–1971* (2nd edn, 1981)

Moore, R. J. *The crisis of Indian unity, 1917–40* (Oxford, 1974)

Churchill, Cripps and India, 1939–1945 (Oxford, 1979)

Escape from empire: the Attlee government and the Indian problem (Oxford, 1983)

Making the new Commonwealth (Oxford, 1987)

Endgames of empire: studies of Britain's Indian problem (New Delhi, 1988)

Mordecai, J. *The West Indies: the federal negotiations* (1968)

Morgan, K. O. *Labour in power, 1945–51* (Oxford, 1984)

Morris, J. *Pax Britannica: the climax of the empire* (1968)

Farewell the trumpets: an imperial retreat (1978)

Morris-Jones, W. H. and G. Fischer, eds., *Decolonisation and after: the British and French experience* (1980)

Mountbatten, Lord Louis, Earl Mountbatten of Burma, *Reflections on the transfer of power and Jawaharlal Nehru* (2nd Smuts Memorial Lecture, Cambridge, 1968)

Murphy, P. V. *Party politics and decolonisation: the Conservative Party and British colonial policy in tropical Africa, 1951–1964* (Oxford, 1995)

Nasson, Bill. *Britannia's empire: making a British world* (Stroud, Glos., 2004)

Neidpath, J. *Singapore naval base and the defence of Britain's eastern empire, 1919–1941* (Oxford, 1981)

Newbury, C. W. *The West African Commonwealth* (Duke, 1964)

Nish, I. H. *Alliance in decline: a study of Anglo-Japanese relations, 1908–1923* (1972)

Northedge, F. S. *Descent from power: British foreign policy, 1945–73* (1974)

Nutting, A. *No end of a lesson: the story of Suez* (1967)

Ogden, C. K. *Debabelization: with a survey of contemporary opinion on the problem of a universal language* (1931)

Olusanya, G. O. *The Second World War and politics in Nigeria, 1939–1953* (Lagos, 1973)

Ooi Keat Gin. *Of free trade and native interests: the economic development of Sarawak, 1841–1941* (Singapore, 1997)

Orwell, George. *The collected essays, journalism and letters of George Orwell* (ed. S. Orwell and I. Angus, 4 vols., 1968)

Ovendale, R. *'Appeasement' and the English-speaking world: Britain, the United States and the Dominions, and the policy of 'appeasement', 1937–1939* (Cardiff, 1975)
Britain, the United States and the end of the Palestine Mandate, 1942–48 (1989)
ed., *The foreign policy of the British Labour governments, 1945–1951* (Leicester, 1984)

Pandey, B. N. *The break-up of British India* (1969)

Parker, G. *Western geopolitical thought in the twentieth century* (1985)

Pearce, R. D. *The turning-point in Africa: British colonial policy, 1938–1948* (1982)
Attlee's Labour governments, 1945–1951 (1994)

Pearson, J. *Sir Anthony Eden and the Suez Crisis: reluctant gamble* (2003)

Philips, C. H. and M. D. Wainwright, eds., *The partition of India: policies and perspectives, 1935–1947* (1970)

Pickering, J. *Britain's withdrawal from East of Suez: the politics of retrenchment* (1998)

Pieragostini, K. *Britain, Aden and South Arabia: abandoning empire* (1991)

Pollard, S. *The development of the British economy, 1914–67* (2nd edn, 1969, 1973, 1976)

Porritt, V. L. *British colonial rule in Sarawak, 1946–1963* (Kuala Lumpur, 1997)

Porter, Andrew N., ed., *Atlas of British expansion overseas* (1992)
and R. Holland, eds., *Theory and practice in the history of European expansion overseas: essays in honour of R. E. Robinson* (1988), repr. from *JICH*, vol. 16 (1988)

Porter, Bernard. *The lion's share: a short history of British imperialism* (4th edn, 2004)
Britain, Europe and the world, 1850–1982: delusions of grandeur (1983)
The absent-minded imperialists: empire, society and culture in Britain (Oxford, 2004)

Potholm, C. P. *Swaziland: the dynamics of political modernisation* (Berkeley, CA, 1972)

Potter, D. C. *India's political administrators, 1919–1983* (Oxford, 1986)

Pratt, L. R. *East of Malta, West of Suez: Britain's Mediterranean crisis, 1936–1939* (1975)

Pratt, R. C. *The critical phase in Tanzania, 1945–1968: Nyerere and the emergence of a socialist strategy* (Cambridge, 1976)

Pringle, R. *Rajahs and rebels: the Ibans of Sarawak under Brooke rule, 1841–1941* (1970)

Reece, R. H. W. *The name of Brooke: the end of white rajah rule in Sarawak* (Kuala Lumpur, 1982)

Reese, T. *Australia, New Zealand and the United States: a survey of international relations, 1941–68* (1969)

Reynolds, D. *The creation of the Anglo-American alliance, 1937–1941: a study in competitive co-operation* (1981)
Britannia overruled: British policy and world power in the 20th century (2nd edn, 2000)

Rich, P. B. *Race and empire in British politics* (2nd edn, Cambridge, 1990)

Robbins, K. *Eclipse of a great power: modern Britain, 1870–1975* (1983)

Roberts, A. *Eminent Churchillians* (1994)

Roberts, A. D., ed., *Cambridge History of Africa*, vol. VII: *From 1905 to 1940* (Cambridge, 1986)

Robinson, K. *The dilemmas of trusteeship: aspects of British colonial policy between the wars* (Oxford, 1965)

Rogers, C. and C. Frantz, *Racial themes in Southern Rhodesia* (1962)

Rosberg, C. J. and J. Nottingham, *The myth of 'Mau Mau': nationalism in Kenya* (New York, 1966)

Rose, N. *The gentile Zionists: a study in Anglo-Zionist diplomacy, 1929–1939* (1973)

Roskill, S. *Naval policy between the wars*, vol. I: *The period of Anglo-American antagonism, 1919–1929* (1968)

Ross, R., ed., *Racism and colonialism* (Leiden, 1982)

Rotberg, R. I. *The rise of nationalism in Central Africa: the making of Malawi and Zambia, 1873–1964* (Harvard, 1966)

Rothwell, V. *Britain and the Cold War, 1941–1947* (1982)

Royal Institute of International Affairs. *British interests in the Mediterranean and Middle East: a report by a Chatham House study group* (Oxford, 1958)

Sachar, H. M. *Europe leaves the Middle East, 1936–54* (New York, 1972)

Sandbrook, D. *Never had it so good: a history of Britain from Suez to the Beatles* (2005)

Sarkar, S. *Modern India, 1885–1947* (1989)

Saville, J. *The politics of continuity: British foreign policy and the Labour government, 1945–1946* (1993)

Segev, T. *One Palestine, complete: Jews and Arabs under the British Mandate* (transl by H. Watzman, 2000, 2001)

Seldon, A. *Churchill's Indian summer: the Conservative government, 1951–1955* (1981)

Shay, R. P. *British rearmament in the Thirties: politics and profits* (Princeton, NJ, 1977)

Shepherd, N. *Ploughing sand: British rule in Palestine, 1917–1948* (1999)

Shlaim, A., P. Jones and K. Sainsbury, *British foreign secretaries since 1945* (1977)

Shonfield, A. *British economic policy since the war* (Harmondsworth, 1985)

Short, A. *The communist insurrection in Malaya, 1948–60* (1975)

Shwadran, B. *The Middle East, oil and the great powers* (1956)

Simelane, H. S. *Colonialism and economic change in Swaziland, 1940–1960* (Mbabane, Swaziland, 2003)

Simpson, A. W. B. *Human rights and the end of empire: Britain and the genesis of the European Convention* (Oxford, 2001, 2004)

Sithole, N. *African nationalism* (Cape Town, 1959)

Sklar, R. L. *Nigerian political parties* (Princeton, NJ, 1963)

Smith, Arnold, with C. Sanger, *Stitches in time: the Commonwealth in world politics* (1981)

Sorrenson, M. P. K. *Origins of European settlement in Kenya* (Nairobi, 1968)

Spencer, I. R. G. *British immigration policy since 1939: the making of multi-racial Britain* (1997)

Springhall, J. *Decolonisation since 1945: the collapse of European overseas empires* (2001)

Stockwell, A. J. *British policy and Malay politics during the Malayan Union experiment, 1942–1948* (Kuala Lumpur, 1979)

Ending the British empire: what did they think they were doing? (Inaugural lecture, Royal Holloway, Egham, Surrey, 1999)

Strachey, J. *The end of empire* (1959)

Strange, S. *Sterling and British policy: a political study of an international currency in decline* (1971)

Subritzky, J. *Confronting Sukarno: British, American, Australian and New Zealand diplomacy in the Malaysian-Indonesian Confrontation, 1961–65* (2000)

Tarling, N. *The sun never sets: an historical essay on Britain and its place in the world* (New Delhi, 1986)

The fall of imperial Britain in South-East Asia (Singapore, 1993)

ed., *Cambridge History of Southeast Asia* vol. II: *19th and 20th centuries* (Kuala Lumpur, 1992)

Thomas, H. *The Suez affair* (1966)

Thompson, F. M. L. *Gentrification and the enterprise culture: Britain, 1780–1980: the Ford Lectures, 1994* (Oxford, 2001)

Thorne, C. *The limits of foreign policy: the West, the League and the Far Eastern crisis of 1931–1933* (1972)

Allies of a kind: the United States, Britain and the war against Japan, 1941–1945 (1978)

Thornton, A. P. *The imperial idea and its enemies: a study of British power* (1959)

Throup, D. W. *Economic and social origins of Mau Mau, 1945–1953* (1987)

Tignor, R. L. *Modernisation and British colonial rule in Egypt, 1882–1941* (Princeton, NJ, 1966)

Tinker, H. *Separate and unequal: India and Indians in the British Commonwealth, 1920–1950* (1976)

Tomlinson, B. R. *The Indian National Congress and the Raj, 1929–42: the penultimate phase* (1976)

Political economy of the Raj, 1914–47: the economics of decolonisation in India (1979)

Tomlinson, J. *The Labour governments, 1964–70*, vol. III: *Economic policy* (Manchester, 2004)

Townshend, C. *Britain's civil wars: counter-insurgency in the 20th century* (1986)

Trevaskis, G. K. N. *Shades of amber: a South Arabian episode* (1968)

Trevelyan, H. *The Middle East in revolution* (1970)

Trotter, A. *Britain and East Asia, 1933–37* (1975)

Vatikiotis, P. J. *The modern history of Egypt* (1969)

Conflict in the Middle East (1971)

Wallace, E. *The British Caribbean from the decline of colonialism to the end of Federation* (Toronto, 1977)

Wallerstein, I. *The road to independence: Ghana and the Ivory Coast* (Paris and The Hague, 1964)

Wasserstein, B. *The British in Palestine: the mandatory government and the Arab-Jewish conflict, 1917–29* (1978)

Watts, R. L. *New federations: experiments in the Commonwealth* (Oxford, 1966)

Weisfelder, R. F. *The BaSotho monarchy: spent force or a dynamic political factor?* (Ohio, 1972)

Welsh, F. *A borrowed place: the history of Hong Kong* (New York, 1993)

Wheare, K. C. *Federal government* (4th edn, 1963)

White, N. J. *Business, government, and the end of empire: Malaya, 1942–57* (Kuala Lumpur, 1996)

Decolonisation: the British experience since 1945 (1999)

Wiener, M. J. *English culture and the decline of the industrial spirit, 1850–1950* (Cambridge, 1981)

Wight, M. *British colonial constitutions* (Oxford, 1952)

Wigley, P. *Canada and the transition to Commonwealth: British–Canadian relations, 1917–1926* (Cambridge, 1977)

Wilson, A. N. *After the Victorians* (2005)

Winter, J. M. *The Great War and the British people* (1985)

Wood, J. R. T. *The Welensky Papers: a history of the Federation of Rhodesia and Nyasaland* (Durban, 1983)

Woodward, P. *Condominium and Sudanese nationalism* (1979)

Young, J. W. *Britain, France and the unity of Europe, 1945–51* (Leicester, 1984)

Britain and European unity, 1945–1992 (1993)

The Labour governments, 1964–1970, vol. II: *International policy* (Manchester, 2003)

ed., *Foreign policy of Churchill's peacetime administration* (Leicester, 1988)

Youngson, A. J. *The British economy, 1920–57* (1960)

Zametica, J., ed., *British officials and British foreign policy, 1945–50* (Leicester, 1990)

4 SELECT LIST OF JOURNAL ARTICLES AND CHAPTERS IN BOOKS

Adamthwaite, A. 'Overstretched and overstrung: Eden, the Foreign Office and the making of policy, 1951–1955', *International Affairs*, vol. 64 (1988), pp. 241–59, repr in J.W. Young, ed., *The foreign policy of Churchill's peacetime administration, 1951–1955* (1988), pp. 1–28

'Suez revisited', *International Affairs*, vol. 64 (1988), pp. 449–64, repr in M. Dockrill and J.W. Young, eds, *British foreign policy, 1945–1956* (1989), pp. 225–45.

Adas, M. 'Contested hegemony: the Great War and the Afro-Asian assault on the civilising mission ideology', *Journal of World History*, vol. 15 (Hawai'i, 2004), pp. 31–63

Addison, P. 'The political beliefs of Winston Churchill', *Transactions of the Royal Historical Society*, 5th ser., vol. 30 (1980), pp. 23–47

Aldrich, R. J. and J. Zametica. 'The rise and decline of a strategic concept: the Middle East, 1945–51', in R. J. Aldrich, ed., *British intelligence, strategy and the Cold War, 1945–1951* (1992), pp. 236–74

Alexander, P. R. 'The Labour government, Commonwealth policy and the second application to join the EEC, 1964–1967', in A. May, ed., *Britain, the Commonwealth and Europe: The Commonwealth and Britain's applications to join the European Communities* (2001), pp. 132–55

Allan, C. 'Bureaucratic organisation for development in small island states', in R. T. Shand, ed., *The island states of the Pacific and Indian Oceans: the autonomy of development* (Canberra, Development Studies Centre monograph no 23, 1980), pp. 383–403

Ashton, N. J. 'A microcosm of decline: British loss of nerve and military intervention in Jordan and Kuwait, 1958 and 1961', *Historical Journal*, vol. 40 (1997), pp. 1069–83

Ashton, S. R. 'Introduction', in S. R. Ashton and S. E. Stockwell, eds., *Imperial policy and colonial practice, 1925–1945* (BDEEP, 1996), pp. xxiii–cii

'Introduction', in S. R. Ashton and D. Killingray, eds., *The West Indies* (BDEEP, 1999), pp. xxxvii–lxxx

'Introduction', in S. R. Ashton and W. R. Louis, eds., *East of Suez and the Commonwealth, 1964–1971* (BDEEP, 2005), pp. xxix–cxxxiii

'Ceylon' in J. M. Brown and W. R. Louis, eds., *The Oxford History of the British Empire*, vol. IV: *The twentieth century* (1999), pp. 447–64

'Keeping change within bounds: a Whitehall reassessment', in M. Lynn, ed., *The British empire in the 1950s: retreat or revival?* (2006), pp. 32–52

Bale, T. 'A "deplorable episode"? South African arms sales and the statecraft of British Social Democracy', *Labour History Review*, vol. 62 (1997), pp. 22–40

Ball, S. J. 'Harold Macmillan and the politics of defence: the market for strategic ideas during the "Sandys era" revisisted', *Twentieth Century British History*, vol. 6 (1995), pp. 78–100

'Harold Macmillan, the Second World War and the empire', in R. Aldous and S. Lee, eds., *Harold Macmillan: aspects of a political life* (1999), pp. 162–76

'Selkirk in Singapore', *Twentieth Century British History* vol. 10 (1999), pp. 162–91

'Banquo's ghost: Lord Salisbury, Harold Macmillan and the high politics of decolonisation, 1957–63', *Twentieth Century British History*, vol. 16 (2005), pp. 74–102

Ball, W. M. 'The Australian reaction to the Suez Crisis, July–December 1956', *Australian Journal of Politics and History*, vol. 2 (1957), pp. 129–50

Barber, J. 'The impact of the Rhodesian crisis on the Commonwealth', *Journal of Commonwealth Political Studies*, vol. 7 (1969), pp. 83–94

Bennett, G. 'Settlers and politics, up to 1945', in V. T. Harlow and E. M. Chilver, eds., *History of East Africa*, vol. II (Oxford, 1965) pp. 265–332

Boyle, N. 'Understanding Thetcherism', *New Blackfriers*, vol. 69 (1988), pp. 307–24, repr. in *Who are we now? Christian humanism and the global market from Hegel to Heaney* (Indiana, 1998), pp. 13–34

Bradlow, E. 'The evolution of "trusteeship" in Kenya', *South African Historical Journal*, vol. 4 (1972), pp. 64–80

Brady, C. 'The Cabinet system and the management of the Suez Crisis', *Contemporary British History*, vol. 11 (1997), pp. 65–93

Brailey, N. J. 'Southeast Asia and Japan's road to war', *Historical Journal*, vol. 30 (1987), pp. 995–1011

Brasted, H. V. and C. Bridge, 'Labour and the transfer of power in India: a case for reappraisal?' *Indo-British Review*, vol. 14 (1988), pp. 70–90

'The transfer of power in South Asia: an historiographical review', *South Asia: a Journal of South Asian Studies*, vol. 17 (1994), pp. 93–114

and J. Kent, 'Cold War, informal empire and the transfer of power: some "paradoxes" of decolonisation resolved?', in M. Dockrill, ed., *Europe within the global system, 1938–1960: Great Britain, France, Italy and Germany, from great powers to regional powers* (Arbeitskreis Deutsche England-Forschung, vol. 30, Bochum, 1995), pp. 11–30

Brecher, M. 'India's decision to remain in the Commonwealth', *Journal of Commonwealth and Comparative Politics*, vol. 12 (1974), pp. 62–90

Brinkley, D. 'Dean Acheson and the "Special Relationship": the West Point Speech of December 1962', *Historical Journal*, vol. 33 (1990), pp. 599–608

Brown, J. M. 'War and the colonial relationship: Britain, India and the war of 1914–18', in M. R. D. Foot, ed., *War and society: historical essays in honour and memory of J. R. Western* (1973), pp. 85–106

'India', in J. M. Brown and W. R. Louis, eds., *The Oxford History of the British Empire*, vol. IV: *The twentieth century* (1999), pp. 421–46

'Gandhi– a Victorian gentleman: an essay in an imperial encounter', *JICH*, vol. 27 (1999), pp. 68–85, repr in R. D. King and R. W. Kilson, eds., *The statecraft of British imperialism: essays in honour of Wm Roger Louis* (1999)

Bull, M. 'Indirect rule in Northern Nigeria, 1906–1911', in K. Robinson and A. F. Madden, eds., *Essays in imperial government presented to Margery Perham* (1963), pp. 47–87

Butler, L.J. 'Ambiguities of British colonial development policy, 1938–48', in A. Gorst *et al.*, eds., *Contemporary British history, 1931–61* (1991), pp. 119–40

'The winds of change: Britain, Europe and the Commonwealth, 1959–1961', in B. Brivati and H. Jones, eds., *From reconstruction to integration: Britain and Europe since 1945* (1993), pp. 157–65

'Britain, the United States and the demise of the Central African Federation, 1959–63', *JICH*, vol. 28 (2000), pp. 131–51

Cell, J. W. 'On the eve of decolonisation: the Colonial Office's plans for the transfer of power in Africa, 1947', *JICH*, vol. 8 (1980), pp. 235–57

Chege, M. 'Mau Mau rebellion, fifty years on', *African Affairs*, vol. 103 (2004), pp. 123–36

Coghlan, F. 'Armaments, economic policy and appeasement, 1931–39', *History*, vol. 57 (1972), pp. 205–16

Cohen, M. J. 'Appeasement in the Middle East: the British White Paper on Palestine, 1939', *Historical Journal*, vol. 16 (1973), pp. 571–96, and pt 2, 'The testing of a policy, 1942–45', *ibid.* vol. 19 (1976) pp. 727–57

'Genesis of the Anglo-American Committee on Palestine, November 1945: a case-study in the assertion of American hegemony', *Historical Journal*, vol. 22 (1979), pp. 185–208

Coleman, J. 'Nationalism in tropical Africa', *American Political Science Review*, vol. 48 (1954), pp. 406–24, repr. in J. H. Kautsky, ed., *Political change in under-developed countries* (New York, 1962)

Cooper, F. 'Mau Mau and the discourses of decolonisation', *Journal of African History*, vol. 29 (1988), pp. 313–20

Cowen, M. 'Early years of the Colonial Development Corporation: British state enterprise during late colonialism', *African Affairs*, vol 83 (1984), pp. 63–76

Creech Jones, A. 'Introduction', in Ruth Hinden, ed., *Fabian colonial essays* (1945)

Crook, R.C. 'Decolonisation, the colonial state and chieftaincy in the Gold Coast', *African Affairs*, vol. 85 (1986), pp. 75–105

Crowder, M. 'Indirect Rule: French and British style', *Africa*, vol. 34 (1964), pp. 197–205

'The 1939–45 War in West Africa', in J. F. A. Ajayi and M. Crowder, eds., *History of West Africa*, vol. II (1974), pp. 596–621

'The Second World War: prelude to decolonisation in Africa', in M. Crowder, ed., *Cambridge History of Africa*, vol. VIII: *From c. 1940 to c. 1975* (Cambridge, 1984), pp. 8–51

Crozier, A. J. 'Imperial decline and the colonial question in Anglo-German relations, 1919–1939', *European Studies Review*, vol. 11 (1981), pp. 207–42

Daly, M. W. and G. N. Sanderson, 'Egypt and the Anglo-Egyptian Sudan', in *Cambridge History of Africa*, vol. VII, pp. 742–879

Darby, P. 'East of Suez: a reassessment', in J. Baylis, ed., *British defence policy in a changing world* (1977), pp. 52–65

Darwin, J. 'Imperialism in decline?' *Historical Journal*, vol. 23 (1980), pp. 657–78

'British decolonisation since 1945: a pattern or a puzzle?' *JICH*, vol. 12 (1984), pp. 187–209

'Suez and the end of empire', *Contemporary Record*, vol 1 (1987), pp. 51–5

'Central Africa emergency, 1959', *JICH*, vol. 21 (1993), pp. 217–34

'An undeclared empire: the British in the Middle East, 1918–1939', *JICH*, vol. 27 (1999), pp. 159–76, repr. in R. D. King and R. W. Kilson, eds., *The statecraft of British imperialism: essays in honour of Wm Roger Louis* (1999)

'Decolonisation and the end of empire', in R. W. Winks, ed., *The Oxford History of the British Empire*, vol. V: *Historiography* (1999), pp. 541–57

'Was there a Fourth British Empire?', in M. Lynn, ed., *The British empire in the 1950s: retreat or revival?* (2006), pp. 16–31

Davidson, J. W. 'Current developments in the Pacific: the decolonisation of Oceania', *Journal of Pacific History*, vol. 6 (1971), pp. 133–50

Day, J. 'The creation of political myths: African nationalism in Southern Rhodesia', *Journal of South African Studies*, vol. 2 (1975), pp. 52–65

Deighton, A. 'The "frozen front": the Labour government, the division of Germany and the origins of the Cold War, 1945–47', *International Affairs*, vol. 63 (1987), pp. 449–65

Dewey, C. 'The end of the imperialism of free trade: the eclipse of the Lancashire lobby', in C. Dewey and A.G. Hopkins, eds., *The imperial impact: studies in the economic history of Africa and India* (1978), pp. 35–67, 331–8

Dias, R. W. M. '[Rhodesia:] Legal politics: norms behind the *Grundnorm*', *Cambridge Law Journal*, vol. 26 (1968), pp. 233–59

Dilks, D. 'Appeasement revisited', inaugural lecture, *University of Leeds Review*, vol.15, no.1 (1972)

Ekoko, A. E. 'British attitudes to Germany's colonial irredentism in Africa', *Journal of Contemporary History*, vol. 14 (1979), pp. 287–307

Elliot, M. 'Defeat and revival: Britain in the Middle East', in W. Kaiser and G. Staerck, eds., *British foreign policy, 1955–1964: contracting options* (2000), pp. 239–56

Ellison, J. R. V. 'Accepting the inevitable: Britain and European integration', in W. Kaiser and G. Staerck, eds., *British foreign policy, 1955–64: contracting options* (2000), pp. 171–89

Ferris, J. '"The greatest power on earth": Great Britain in the 1920s', *International History Review*, vol. 13 (1991), pp. 726–50

Fieldhouse, D. K. 'The Labour governments and the Empire-Commonwealth, 1945–51', in R. Ovendale, ed., *The foreign policy of the British Labour governments, 1945–51* (Leicester, 1984), pp. 83–118

Review of D. J. Morgan, *The official history of colonial development*, 5 vols., in *English Historical Review*, vol. 97 (1982), pp. 386–94

Fitzsimons, M. A. 'The continuity of British foreign policy', *Review of Politics*, vol. 21 (1959), pp. 301–22

Flint, J. E. 'Nigeria: the colonial experience, 1800–1914', in L. H. Gann and P. Duignan, eds., *Colonialism in Africa, 1870–1960*, vol. I: *History and politics of colonialism* (Cambridge, 1969), pp. 220–60

'Scandal at the Bristol Hotel: some thoughts on racial discrimination in Britain and West Africa and its relationship to the planning of decolonisation, 1939–47', *JICH*, vol. 12 (1983), pp. 74–93

'Planned decolonisation and its failure in British West Africa', *African Affairs*, vol. 82 (1983), pp. 390–410

Review of M. Lynn, ed., *Nigeria* (BDEEP, 2001), *JICH*, vol. 32 (2004) pp. 166–9

Furedi, F. 'Creating a breathing-space: the political management of colonial emergencies', *JICH*, vol. 21 (1993), pp. 89–106, repr. in R. Holland, ed., *Emergencies and disorder in the European empires after 1945* (1993)

Gallagher, J. A. 'Nationalism and the crisis of empire, 1919–1922', in C. Baker, G. Johnson and A. Seal, eds., *Power, profit and politics: essays on imperialism, nationalism and change in twentieth century India* (Cambridge, 1981), repr. from *Modern Asian Studies*, vol. 15 (1981), pp. 355–68

and A. Seal, 'Britain and India between the wars', *ibid*, pp. 387–414

Goldsworthy, D. '"Keeping change within bounds": aspects of colonial policy during the Churchill and Eden governments, 1951–57', *JICH*, vol. 18 (1990), pp. 81–108

'Britain and the international critics of British colonialism, 1951–1956, *Journal of Commonwealth and Comparative Politics*, vol. 29 (1991), pp. 1–24

'Introduction, in D. Goldsworthy, ed., *The Conservative government and the end of empire, 1951–57* (BDEEP, 1994), pt 1, pp. xxv–lxvi

Gordon, D. F. 'Mau Mau and decolonisation', in W. R. Ochieng' and K. Janmohamed, eds., *Some perspectives on the Mau Mau movement*, special issue of *Kenya Historical Review*, vol. 5 (1977), pp. 333–41

Gowing, M. 'Britain, America and the bomb', in D. Dilks, ed., *Retreat from power: studies in Britain's foreign policy of the 20th century*, vol. II *After 1939* (1981), pp. 129–38

Gupta, P. S. 'Imperialism and the Labour government of 1945–51', in J. M. Winter, ed., *The working class in modern British history: essays in honour of Henry Pelling* (Cambridge, 1983), pp. 99–123

Hargreaves, J. D. 'From strangers to minorities in West Africa', *Transactions of the Royal Historical Society*, 5th ser, vol. 31 (1981), pp. 95–114

Harper, T. N. 'Diaspora and the languages of globalisation', in A. G. Hopkins, ed., *Globalisation in world history* (2000), pp. 141–66

Hatzivassilou, E. 'Blocking "Enosis": Britain and the Cyprus question, March–December 1956', *JICH*, vol. 19 (1991), pp. 247–63

Hayes, F. 'South Africa's departure from the Commonwealth, 1960–1961', *International History Review*, vol. 2 (1980), pp. 453–84

Hazlewood, A. 'The economics of federation and dissolution in Central Africa', in Hazlewood, ed., *African integration and disintegration: case-studies in economic and political union* (Oxford, 1967), pp. 185–250

Hemming, P. E. 'Macmillan and the end of the British empire in Africa', in R. Aldous and S. Lee, eds., *Harold Macmillan and Britain's world role* (1996), pp. 97–122

Henshaw, P. J. 'Britain, South Africa and the Sterling Area, 1931–61', *Historical Journal*, vol. 39 (1996), pp. 197–223, repr. in R. Hyam and P. Henshaw, *The lion and the springbok: Britain and South Africa since the Boer War*, ch. 6

review of A. Megahey, *Humphrey Gibbs: beleaguered governor*, in *Canadian Journal of African Studies*, vol. 32 (1998), pp. 636–8

'South African territorial expansion and international reaction to South Africa's racial policies, 1939–48', *South African Historical Journal*, vol. 50 (2004), pp. 65–76

Hinds, A. E. 'Sterling and imperial policy, 1945–51', *JICH*, vol. 15 (1987), pp. 148–69

Holland, R. F. 'The imperial factor in British strategies from Attlee to Macmillan, 1945–63', *JICH*, vol. 12 (1984), pp. 165–86

'Ends of empire: some reflections on the metropole', *Round Table*, no. 317 (1991), pp. 81–8

'Never, never land: British colonial policy and the roots of violence in Cyprus, 1950–1954, *JICH*, vol. 21 (1993), pp. 148–76

Review of D. Goldsworthy, ed., *The Conservative government and the end of empire, 1951–57* (BDEEP, 1994), in *JICH*, vol. 23 (1995), pp. 543–7

Hopkins, A. G. 'Macmillan's audit of empire, 1957', in P. F. Clarke and R. C. Trebilcock, eds., *Understanding decline: perceptions and realities in British economic performance* (Cambridge, 1997) pp. 234–60

Horowitz, D. 'Attitudes of British Conservatives towards decolonisation in Africa', *African Affairs*, vol. 69 (1970), pp. 9–26

Howard, A. 'Iain Macleod: the "dark horse" at the back of the Tory field', *The Listener* (9 October 1980), pp. 457–8

Howard, M. 'Britain's strategic problem East of Suez', *International Affairs*, vol. 42 (1966). pp. 179–83

Hurwitz, S. J. 'The Federation of the West Indies: a study in nationalisms', *Journal of British Studies*, vol. 6 (1966), pp. 139–68

Hyam, R. 'Winston Churchill before 1914', *Historical Journal*, vol. 12 (1969), pp. 164–73

'Churchill and the British empire', in R. Blake and W. R. Louis, eds., *Churchill* (Oxford, 1993), pp. 167–86

'Africa and the Labour government, 1945–1951', in A. N. Porter and A. J. Stockwell, eds., *Theory and practice in the history of European expansion overseas: essays in honour of Ronald Robinson* (1998), repr. from *JICH*, vol. 16 (1998), pp. 148–72

'The British empire in the Edwardian era', in J. M. Brown and W. R. Louis, eds., *The Oxford History of the British empire*, vol. IV *The twentieth century* (1999), pp. 47–63

'Bureaucracy and "trusteeship" in the colonial empire', *ibid.* pp. 25–79

'The primacy of geopolitics: the dynamics of British imperial policy, 1763–1963', in *The statecraft of British imperialism: essays in honour of Wm Roger Louis*, repr. from *JICH*, vol. 27 (1999), pp. 27–52

'Winds of change: the empire and Commonwealth', in W. Kaiser and G. Staerck, eds., *British foreign policy, 1955–64: contracting options* (2000), pp. 190–208

'South Africa, Cambridge and Commonwealth history', *Round Table*, no. 360 (2001), pp. 401–14

Iliffe, J. 'TANU and the Colonial Office', *Tanzania Zamani: a Journal of Historical Research and Writing*, vol. 3, no. 2 (1997, Historical Association of Tanzania, Dar es Salaam), pp. 1–62

Jackson, A. 'Supplying war: the High Commission Territories' military–logistical contribution to the Second World War', *Journal of Military History*, vol. 66 (2002), pp. 719–60

'Governing empire: colonial memoirs', review article, *African Affairs*, vol. 103 (2004), pp. 471–92

'The British empire in the Indian Ocean', in D. Rumley and S. Chaturvedi, eds., *Geopolitical orientations: regionalism and security in the Indian Ocean* (New Delhi, 2004), pp. 34–55

Jeffery, K. 'Sir Henry Wilson and the defence of the British empire, 1918–1922', *JICH*, vol. 5 (1977), pp. 270–93

'The eastern arc of empire: a strategic view, 1850–1950', *Journal of Strategic Studies*, vol. 5 (1982), pp. 531–45

Johnson, H. 'The West Indies and the conversion of British official classes to the development idea', *Journal of Commonwealth and Comparative Politics*, vol. 15 (1977), pp. 58–83

'The British Caribbean from demobilisation to constitutional decolonisation', in *Oxford History of the British empire*, vol. IV: *The twentieth century*, pp. 597–622

Jones, Matthew, 'Creating Malaysia: Singapore, security, the Borneo territories, and the contours of British policy, 1961–1963', *JICH*, vol. 28 (2000), pp. 85–109

'A decision delayed: Britain's withdrawal from South-East Asia reconsidered, 1961–1968', *English Historical Review*, vol. 117 (2002), pp. 569–95

Kedourie, E. 'Suez revisited', in *Islam in the modern world* (1980), pp. 171–91, repr. from *Times Literary Supplement* (30 November 1979)

Kennedy, P. 'Strategy versus finance in twentieth-century Great Britain', *International History Review*, vol. 3 (1981), pp. 44–61, repr. in *Strategy and diplomacy, 1870–1945: eight studies* (1983)

'The logic of appeasement', *Times Literary Supplement* (28 May 1982), pp. 585–6

Kent, J, 'Anglo-French colonial co-operation, 1939–1949', *JICH*, vol.17 (1988), pp. 55–82

'Bevin's imperialism and the idea of Euro-Africa, 1945–49', in M. Dockrill and J. W. Young, eds., *British foreign policy, 1951–1956* (1989), pp. 45–56

'The Egyptian base and the defence of the Middle East, 1945–1954', *JICH*, vol. 21 (1993) pp. 45–65

'Introduction' to *Egypt and the defence of the Middle East* (BDEEP, 1998), pp. xxxv–c

Killingray, D. 'The idea of a British imperial African army', *Journal of African History*, vol. 20 (1979), pp. 421–36

Kirk-Greene, A. H. M. 'Introduction', to Witness Seminar on 'Decolonisation and the Colonial Office', *Contemporary British History*, vol. 6 (1992)

Klieman, A. S. 'The divisiveness of Palestine: the Foreign Office versus the Colonial Office on the issue of partition, 1937', *Historical Journal*, vol. 22 (1979), pp. 423–42

Krozewski, G. 'Sterling, the "minor" territories and the end of formal empire, 1939–58', *Economic History Review*, vol. 46 (1993), pp. 239–65

Kunz, D. B. 'The importance of having money: economic diplomacy and the Suez crisis', in W. R. Louis and R. Owen, eds., *Suez 1956: the crisis and its consequences* (Oxford, 1989), pp. 215–32

' "Somewhat mixed up together": Anglo-American defence and financial policy during the 1960s', in *The statecraft of British imperialism: essays in honour of Wm Roger Louis*, repr. from *JICH*, vol. 27 (1999), pp. 213–32

Kyle, K. 'To Suez with tears', in W. R. Louis, ed., *Still more adventures with Britannia: personalities, politics and culture in Britain* (Austin, Texas, 2003), pp. 265–84

Laracy, H. 'Marching Rule and the missions', *Journal of Pacific History*, vol. 6 (1971), pp. 96–114

Lerman, E. 'British diplomacy and the crisis of power in Egypt: the antecedents of the British offer to evacuate, 7 May 1946', in K. M. Wilson, ed., *Imperialism and nationalism in the Middle East: the Anglo-Egyptian experience, 1882–1982* (1983), pp. 96–122

Levine, P. 'Sexuality, gender and empire', in P. Levine, ed., *Oxford History of the British empire*, companion series, *Gender and empire* (2004), pp. 134–55

Lonsdale, J. M. 'The Depression and the Second World War in the transformation of Kenya', in D. Killingray and R. Rathbone, eds., *Africa and the Second World War* (1986), pp. 97–142

'Mau Maus of the mind; the making of Mau Mau and the remaking of Kenya', *Journal of African History*, vol. 31 (1990), pp. 393–421

'East Africa', in J. M. Brown and W. R. Louis, eds., *Oxford History of the British empire*, vol.IV: *The twentieth century* (1999), pp. 530–44

Louis, W. R. 'Appeasement and the colonies, 1936–38', *Revue Belge de Philologie et d'Histoire*, vol. 49 (1971), pp. 1175–91

'British imperialism and the partitions of India and Palestine', in C. Wrigley, ed., *Warfare, diplomacy and politics: essays in honour of A. J. P. Taylor* (1986), pp. 189–209

'American anti-imperialism and the dissolution of the British Empire', *International Affairs*, vol. 61 (1985), pp. 395–420, repr. in W. R. Louis and H. Bull, *The 'special' relationship* (1986)

'India and Africa and the Second World War', *Ethnic and Racial Studies*, vol. 9 (1986), pp. 306–20

'British imperialism and the end of the Palestine Mandate', in W. R. Louis and R. Stookey, eds., *The end of the Palestine Mandate* (Austin, Texas, 1986), pp. 1–31

'The Suez Crisis', books reviewed, *Times Literary Supplement* (31 October 1986), pp. 1207–9

'Libyan independence, 1951: the creation of a client state', in P. Gifford and W. R. Louis, eds., *Decolonisation and African independence: the transfer of power, 1960–80* (Yale, 1988), pp. 159–84

'Sir Alan Cunningham and the end of British rule in Palestine', in A. N. Porter and A. J. Stockwell, eds., *Theory and practice in the history of European expansion overseas: essays in honour of R. E. Robinson* (1998), repr. from *JICH*, vol. 16 (1988), pp. 128–47

'The coming of independence in the Sudan', *JICH*, vol. 19 (1991), pp. 137–58

'Churchill and Egypt, 1946–1956', in R. Blake and W. R. Louis, eds., *Churchill* (1993), pp. 473–90

'Hong Kong: the critical years, 1945–49', *American Historical Review*, vol. 102 (1997), pp. 1052–84

'Harold Macmillan and the Middle East crisis of 1958', *Proceedings of the British Academy*, vol. 94 (*1996 Lectures and Memoirs*, 1997), pp. 207–28

'The dissolution of the British empire', in J. M. Brown and W. R. Louis, eds., *Oxford History of the British Empire*, vol. IV: *The twentieth century* (1999), pp. 339–56

'The dissolution of the British empire in the era of Vietnam', *American Historical Review*, vol. 107 (2002), pp. 1–25, Presidential address

'The British withdrawal from the Gulf, 1961–1971', *JICH*, vol. 31 (2003), pp. 83–108

'Public enemy Number One: the British empire in the dock at the United Nations, 1957–71', in M. Lynn, ed., *The British empire in the 1950s: retreat or revival?* (2006), pp. 186–213

'Sir Keith Hancock and the British empire: the Pax Britannica and the Pax Americana', *English Historical Review*, vol. 120 (2005), pp. 937–62

Louis, W. R. and R. E. Robinson, 'The imperialism of decolonisation', *JICH*, vol. 22 (1994), pp. 462–511

Low, D. A. 'The Indian schism: a review article', *Journal of Commonwealth Political Studies*, vol. 9 (1971)

'The Asian revolutions', in P. Lyon and J. Manor, eds., *Transfer and transformation: political institutions in the new Commonwealth* (1983) pp. 265–77

'Sapru and the first Round Table Conference', in D. A. Low, ed., *Soundings in modern South Asian History* (1968), pp. 294–329

'The end of the British empire in Africa', in P. Gifford and W. R. Louis, eds., *Decolonisation and African independence: the transfer of power. 1960–80* (Yale, 1988), pp. 33–72

'Rule Britannia – subjects and empire: "The Oxford History of the British Empire"', *Modern Asian Studies*, vol. 36 (2002), pp. 491–511

and J. M. Lonsdale, 'Towards the new order, 1945–63', in D. A. Low and Alison Smith, eds., *History of East Africa*, vol. III (Oxford, 1976), pp. 1–64

and B. Lapping. 'Did Suez hasten the end of empire?' *Contemporary Record*, vol. 1 (1987), pp. 31–3

Low, J. 'Kept in position: the Labour Front-Alliance government of chief minister David Marshall in Singapore, April 1955–June 1956', *Journal of Southeast Asian Studies*, vol. 35 (2004), pp. 41–64

Ludlow, N. P. 'A mismanaged application: Britain and EEC membership, 1961–63', in A. Deighton and A. S. Milward, eds., *Accelerating, deepening and enlarging: the European Economic Community, 1957–63* (2000)

Lynn, M. ' "We can not let the North down": British policy and Nigeria in the 1950s', in *The British empire in the 1950s: retreat or revival?* (2006), pp. 144–63

Lyon, P. 'The Commonwealth and the Suez Crisis', in W. R. Louis and R. Owen, eds., *Suez, 1956: the crisis and its consequences* (Oxford, 1989), ch. 13

'The rise and fall and possible renewal of international trusteeship', *Journal of Commonwealth and Comparative Politics*, vol. 31, no 1, special issue on *Decolonisation and the international community: essays in honour of Kenneth Robinson* (ed. M. Twaddle, 1993), pp. 96–110

McIntyre, W. D. 'The admission of small states to the Commonwealth', *JICH*, vol. 24 (1996), pp. 244–77

'Britain and the evolution of the Commonwealth Secretariat', *JICH*, vol. 28 (2000), pp. 135–58

'Clio and Britannia's dream: historians and the British Commonwealth of Nations in the first half of the twentieth century' *Round Table*, vol. 93 (2004), pp. 517–40

McKeown, A. 'Global migration, 1846–1940', *Journal of World History*, vol. 15 (Hawai'i, 2004), pp. 155–89

Macleod, Iain. 'Trouble in Africa', *Spectator*, no. 7075 (31 January 1964), p. 127

'Blundell's Kenya: review of "So rough a wind" ', *The Spectator* (20 March 1964), p. 366

McMahon, D. 'A larger and noisier Southern Ireland: Ireland and the evolution of Dominion Status in India, Burma and the Commonwealth, 1942–49', in M. Kennedy and J. M. Skelly, eds., *Irish foreign policy, 1919–66: from independence to internationalism* (Dublin, 2000), pp. 155–91

Makin, M. 'Britain, South Africa and the Commonwealth in 1960: the "winds of change" reassessed', *Historia (Historiese Genootskap van Suid-Afrika/Historical Association of South Africa)*, vol. 41 (Pretoria, 1996), pp. 74–88

Markides, Diana Weston, 'Britain's "New Look" policy for Cyprus and the Makarios–Harding talks, January 1955–March 1956', *JICH*, vol. 23 (1995), pp. 479–502

Marshall, P. J. 'Imperial Britain', in Marshall, ed., *The Cambridge illustrated history of the British Empire* (Cambridge, 1996), pp. 318–37

Marston, G. 'Armed intervention in the 1956 Suez Canal Crisis: the legal advice tendered to the British government', *International and Comparative Law Quarterly*, vol. 37 (1988), pp. 773–817

Martin, G. W. 'The Irish Free State and the evolution of the Commonwealth, 1921–49', in R. Hyam and G. W. Martin, *Reappraisals in British imperial history* (1975), pp. 201–23

review of L. Freedman, 'The official history of the Falklands Campaign', *Round Table*, vol. 95 (2006), no. 383, pp. 153–7

Martin, L. W. 'The market for strategic ideas in Britain: the "Sandys era"', *American Political Science Review*, vol. 56 (1962), pp. 23–41

'British defence policy: the long recessional', *Adelphi Papers* no. 61 (Institute for Strategic Studies, 1969)

Mason, M. ' "The decisive volley": the battle of Ismailia and the decline of British influence in Egypt, January–July, 1952', *JICH*, vol. 19 (1991), pp. 45–64

Meredith, D. 'The British government and colonial economic policy, 1919–39', *Economic History Review*, vol. 28 (1975), pp. 484–99

Middleton, J. 'Kenya: changes in African life, 1912–1945', in V. T. Harlow and E. M. Chilver, eds., *History of East Africa*, vol. II (1965), pp. 333–94

Monroe, E. 'Mr Bevin's "Arab policy"', *St Antony's Papers*, no. 11 (1961)

Monson, L. 'The process of decolonisation', in W. Thornhill, ed., *The modernisation of British government* (1975), ch. 11, pp. 261–82

Morgan, K. O. 'Imperialists at bay: the British Labour Party and decolonisation', in R. D. King and R. W. Kilson, *The statecraft of British imperialism: essays in honour of Wm Roger Louis*, repr. from *JICH*, vol. 27 (1999), pp. 233–54

Morris-Jones, W. H. '36 years later: the mixed legacies of Mountbatten's transfer of power' *International Affairs*, vol. 59 (1983), pp. 621–8

Murphy, P. 'Intelligence and decolonisation: the life and death of the Federal Intelligence and Security Bureau', *JICH*, vol. 29 (2001), pp. 101–30

'Censorship, declassification and the history of the end of empire in Central Africa', *African Research and Documentation* no. 92 (2003), pp. 3–26

'The African queen? Republicanism and defensive decolonisation in British tropical Africa, 1958–64', *Twentieth Century British History*, vol. 14 (2003), pp. 243–63

'Introduction', P. Murphy, ed., *Central Africa* (BDEEP, 2005) pp. xxvii–cxvi

' "Government by blackmail": the origins of the Central African Federation reconsidered', in M. Lynn, ed., *The British empire in the 1950s: retreat or revival?* (2006), pp. 53–76

Nachmani, A. ' "It is a matter of getting the mixture right": Britain's post-war relations with America in the Middle East', *Journal of Contemporary History*, vol. 18 (1983), pp. 117–35

Nanda, B.R. 'Nehru and the British', *Modern Asian Studies*, vol. 30 (1996), pp. 469–79

Newton, C. C. S. 'The Sterling crisis of 1947 and the British response to the Marshall Plan', *Economic History Review*, vol. 37 (1984), pp. 391–413

Nicolson, I. F. and C. A. Hughes, 'A provenance of proconsuls: British colonial governors, 1900–60', *JICH*, vol. 4 (1975), pp. 77–106.

Northedge, F. S. 'Britain and the Middle East', in R. Ovendale, ed., *The foreign policy of the British Labour governments, 1945–1951* (Leicester, 1984), pp. 155–78

Ovendale, R. 'The Palestine policy of the British Labour government': I, '1945–6', *International Affairs*, vol. 55 (1979), pp. 409–31, II, '1947: the decision to withdraw', *ibid*, vol. 56 (1980), pp. 73–93

'Britain, the United States and the Cold War in South-East Asia', *International Affairs*, vol. 58 (1982). pp. 447–64

'Britain, the United States and the recognition of Communist China', *Historical Journal*, vol. 26 (1983), pp. 139–58

'The South African policy of the British Labour government, 1947–51', *International Affairs*, vol. 59 (1983), pp. 41–58

'Macmillan and the wind of change in Africa, 1957–60', *Historical Journal*, vol. 38 (1995), pp. 455–77

Owen, N. 'The Attlee governments: the end of empire, 1945–51', *Contemporary Record*, vol. 3 (1990), pp. 12–16

'Responsibility without power: the Attlee governments and the end of British rule in India', in N. Tiratsoo, ed., *The Attlee years* (1991)

' "More than a transfer of power": independence day ceremonies in India, 15 August 1947', *Contemporary British History*, vol. 6 (1992), pp. 415–51

'Decolonisation and the post-war consensus', in H. Jones and M. Kandiah, eds., *Myth of consensus: new views on British history, 1945–1964* (1996), pp. 157–81

'Critics of empire in Britain', in *The Oxford History of the British empire*, vol. IV: *The twentieth century* (1999), pp. 188–211

Parker, R. A. C. 'Great Britain, France and the Ethiopian crisis, 1935–1936', *English Historical Review*, vol. 89 (1974), pp. 293–332

Parmentier, G. 'The British Press in the Suez Crisis', *Historical Journal*, vol. 23 (1980), pp. 439–47

Parr, H. 'A question of leadership: July 1966 and Harold Wilson's European decision', *Contemporary British History*, vol. 19 (2005), pp. 437–58

Pearce, R. D. 'Governors, nationalists and constitutions in Nigeria, 1935–1951', *JICH*, vol. 9 (1981), pp. 289–307

'The Colonial Office and planned decolonisation in Africa', *African Affairs*, vol. 83 (1984), pp. 77–93

Peden, G. C. 'The burden of imperial defence and continental commitment reconsidered', *Historical Journal*, vol. 27 (1984), pp. 406–23

Peele, G. 'The revolt over India', in G. Peele and C. Cook, eds., *The politics of reappraisal, 1918–1939* (1975), pp. 114–44

Pelling, H. 'The Labour government of 1945–51: the determinants of policy', in M. Bentley and J. Stevenson, eds., *High and low politics in modern Britain: ten studies* (Oxford, 1983), ch. 9, pp. 255–84

Perham, M. 'A re-statement of Indirect Rule', *Africa*, vol. 7 (1934), pp. 321–34

Pfeiffer, R. 'New Zealand and the Suez Crisis, 1956', *JICH*, vol. 21 (1993), pp. 126–52

Pham, J. 'Ghost-hunting in colonial Burma: nostalgia, paternalism and the thought of J. S. Furnivall', *South-East Asia Research* vol. 12 (2004), pp. 237–68

'J. S. Furnivall and Fabianism: interpreting the plural society in Burma', *Modern Asian Studies*, vol. 39 (2005), pp. 321–48

Potholm, C. P. 'Changing political configurations in Swaziland', *Journal of Modern African Studies*, vol. 4 (1966), pp. 313–22

'Swaziland under Sobhuza II: the future of an African monarchy', *Round Table*, vol. 64 (1974), pp. 219–27

Potter, D. C. 'Manpower shortage and the end of colonialism: the case of the Indian Civil Service', *Modern Asian Studies*, vol. 7 (1973), pp. 47–73

Proctor, J. H. 'The effort to federate East Africa', *Political Quarterly*, vol. 37 (1966), pp. 46–99

Quartararo, R. 'Imperial defence in the Mediterranean, 1935', *Historical Journal*, vol. 20 (1977), pp. 185–220

Ranger, T. O. 'Connexions between "primary resistance" movements and modern mass nationalism in East and Central Africa', pts 1 and 2, *Journal of African History*, vol. 9 (1968), pp. 437–53, 631–41

Rathbone, R. 'The government of the Gold Coast after the Second World War', *African Affairs*, vol. 67 (1968), pp. 209–18

'Businessmen in politics: party struggle in Ghana, 1949–1957', *Journal of Development Studies*, vol. 9 (1973), pp. 391–401

'Introduction', in R. Rathbone, ed., *Ghana* (BDEEP, 1992) pt 1, pp. xxxi–lxxviii

Reece, R. H. W. 'A "suitable population": Charles Brooke and race-mixing in Sarawak', *Itinerario*, vol. 9 (Leiden, 1985), pp. 67–112

'European-indigenous miscegenation and social status in nineteenth-century Borneo', in V. H. Sutlive jr, ed., *Female and male in Borneo: contributions and challenges to gender studies*, Borneo Research Council Monograph Series, vol. I (Shangai, VA, 1991), pp. 455–88

Reinharz, J. 'The Balfour Declaration and its maker: a reassessment', *Journal of Modern History*, vol. 64 (1992), pp. 455–99

Reynolds, D. 'Eden the diplomatist, 1931–1956: Suezide of a statesman?', review article, *History*, vol. 74 (1989), pp. 64–84

Ridley, J. 'Edwin Lutyens, New Delhi and the architecture of imperialism', in P. Burroughs and A. J. Stockwell, eds., *Managing the business of empire: essays in honour of David Fieldhouse* (1998), repr. from *JICH*, vol. 26 (1998), pp. 67–83

Roberts, A. D., ed. 'The imperial mind', in *Cambridge History of Africa* vol. VII: *From 1905 to 1940* (1986), pp. 24–76

Robinson, F. 'The British empire and the Muslim world', in J. M. Brown and W. R. Louis, eds., *Oxford History of the British Empire* vol. IV: *The twentieth century* (1999), pp. 398–420

Robinson, R.E. 'Why "Indirect Rule" has been replaced by "Local Government" in the nomenclature of British native administration', *Journal of African Administration*, vol. 2 (1950), pp. 12–15

'The non-European foundations of European imperialism: sketch for a theory of collaboration', in R. Owen and B. Sutcliffe, eds., *Studies in the theory of imperialism* (1972), pp. 117–42

'Sir Andrew Cohen, 1909–1965', in L. H. Gann and P. Duignan, eds., *African proconsuls: Europeans in Africa* (Stanford and New York, 1978), pp. 353–64

'The moral disarmament of African colonial empire', in N. Hillmer and P. Wigley, eds., *The first British Commonwealth: essays in honour of Nicholas Mansergh* (1980), repr. from *JICH*, vol. 8 (1979), pp. 86–104

'Andrew Cohen and the transfer of power in tropical Africa, 1941–51', in W. H. Morris-Jones and G. Fischer, eds., *Decolonisation and after: the British and French experience* (1980), pp. 50–72

Roskill, S. W. 'Imperial defence, 1910–50', *Round Table*, diamond jubilee number (1970), pp. 449–61

Rotberg, R. I. 'The federal movement in East and Central Africa, 1889–1953' *Journal of Commonwealth Political Studies*, vol. 2 (1964), pp. 141–60

Sanderson, G. N. 'Sudanese nationalism and the independence of Sudan' in M. Brett, ed., *Northern Africa: Islam and modernisation* (1973), pp. 97–109

Sayer, D. 'The British reaction to the Amritsar massacre, 1919–1920' *Past and Present*, no. 131 (1991), pp. 130–64

Schenk, C. R. 'The sterling area and British policy alternatives in the 1950s', *Contemporary Record*, vol. 6 (1992) pp. 266–86

Siedentop, L. 'Mr Macmillan and the Edwardian style', in V. Bogdanor and R. Skidelsky, eds., *The age of affluence, 1951–1964* (1970), pp. 17–54

Singh, A.I. 'Keeping India in the Commonwealth: British political and military aims, 1947–1949', *Journal of Contemporary History*, vol 20 (1985) pp. 469–81

Smith, R. and J. Zametica. 'The cold warrior: Clement Attlee reconsidered, 1945–1947', *International Affairs*, vol. 61 (1985), pp. 237–52

Smith, Simon C. 'General Templer and counter-insurgency in Malaya: hearts and minds, intelligence and propaganda', *Intelligence and National Security*, vol. 16 (2001), pp. 60–78

Smith, Tony, 'A comparative study of French and British decolonisation' *Comparative Studies in Society and History*, vol. 20 (1978), pp. 70–102, repr. in P. Gifford and W. R. Louis, eds., *The transfer of power in Africa: decolonisation, 1940–60* (Yale, 1982)

Sorrenson, M. P. K. 'Land policy in Kenya, 1895–1945', in V. T. Harlow and E. M. Chilver, eds., *History of East Africa*, vol. II (Oxford, 1965), pp. 672–89

Spiro, H. J. 'Federation of Rhodesia and Nyasaland', in T. M. Franck, ed., *Why federations fail: an enquiry into the requisites for successful federalism* (New York, 1968), pp. 37–86

Stearn, R. T. 'G. W. Steevens and the message of empire', *JICH*, vol. 17 (1989), pp. 210–31

Stevens, R. P. 'Swazi political development', *Journal of Modern African Studies*, vol. 1 (1963), pp. 327–50

Stockwell, A. J. 'British imperial policy and decolonization in Malaya, 1942–52', *JICH*, vol. 13 (1984), pp. 68–87

'Introduction', in A. J. Stockwell, ed., *Malaya* (BDEEP, 1995), pt 1, pp. xxxi–lxxxiv

'Malaysia: the making of a neo-colony?', in P. Burroughs and A. J. Stockwell, eds., *Managing the business of empire: essays in honour of David Fieldhouse* (1998), repr. from *JICH* vol. 26 (1998), pp. 138–56

'Britain and Brunei, 1943–1963: imperial retreat and royal ascendancy', *Modern Asian Studies*, vol. 38 (2004), pp. 785–820

'Introduction', in A. J. Stockwell, ed., *Malaysia* (BDEEP, 2004), pp. xxxv–xcvi

Stockwell, S. E. 'Trade, empire, and the fiscal context of imperial business during decolonization', *Economic History Review*, vol. 57 (2004), pp. 146–60

Subritzky, J. 'Britain, *Konfrontasi* and the end of empire in Southeast Asia, 1961–1965', *JICH*, vol. 28 (2000), pp. 209–27.

Tarling, N. 'Britain and Sarawak in the 20th century: Raja Charles, Raja Vyner and the Colonial Office', *Journal of the Malay Branch of the Royal Asiatic Society*, vol. 43, no. 2 (1970), pp. 25–52

'Lord Mountbatten and the return to civil government in Burma', *JICH*, vol. 11 (1983), pp. 197–224

Thompson, G. 'Britain's plan to leave Asia', *Round Table*, vol. 58 (1968), pp. 117–23

Thompson, R. C. 'Conflict or co-operation? Britain and Australia in the South Pacific, 1950–1960', *JICH*, vol. 23 (1995), pp. 301–16

Thornton, A. P. 'With Wavell to Simla and beyond', in N. Hillmer and P. Wigley, eds., *The first British Commonwealth: essays in honour of Nicholas Mansergh*, (1980), repr. from *JICH*, vol. 8 (1979), pp. 175–86

Throup, D. W. 'The origins of Mau Mau', *African Affairs*, vol. 84 (1985), pp. 399–433

Tignor, R. L. 'Decolonisation and business: the case of Egypt', *Journal of Modern History*, vol. 59 (1987), pp. 479–505

Tinker, H. 'Colour and colonisation, *Round Table*, no. 240 (1970), pp. 405–16

'Introduction', in *Burma: the struggle for independence, 1944–48*, vol. I: *January 1944–August 1946* (1983), and in vol. II: *August 1946 to January 1948* (1984)

'Burma's struggle for independence: the transfer of power thesis re-examined', *Modern Asian Studies*, vol. 20 (1986), pp. 461–81

'The contraction of empire in Asia, 1945–1948: the military dimension', *JICH*, vol. 16 (1988), pp. 218–31

Tomlinson, B. R. 'India and the British empire, 1880–1935', *Indian Economic and Social History Review*, vol. 12 (1975), and pt 2, '1935–1947', *ibid*, vol. 13 (1976), pp. 331–52

'The contraction of England: national decline and the loss of empire', *JICH*, vol. 11 (1982), pp. 58–72

Tomlinson, J. 'The Attlee government and the balance of payments, 1946–51', *Twentieth Century British History*, vol. 2 (1991), pp. 47–66

'The decline of the empire and the economic "decline" of Britain', *Twentieth Century British History*, vol. 14 (2003), pp. 201–21

Tshokas, K. 'Dedominionization: the Anglo-Australian experience, 1939–45', *Historical Journal*, vol. 37 (1994), pp. 861–83

Twaddle, M. 'Decolonization in Africa: a new British historiographical debate?' in B. Jewsiewicki and D. Newbury, eds., *African historiographies: what history for which Africa?* (1986), pp. 123–38

Vereté, M. 'The Balfour Declaration and its makers', *Middle Eastern Studies*, vol. 6 (1970), pp. 48–67, repr. in E. Kedourie and S. G. Haim, eds., *Palestine and Israel in the nineteenth and twentieth centuries* (1982)

Warner, G. 'The United States and the Suez Crisis', *International Affairs*, vol. 67 (1991), pp. 303–17

Waters, C. 'Macmillan, Menzies, history, and empire', *Australian Historical Studies*, vol. 33 (2002), pp. 93–107

Weiler, P. 'British Labour and the Cold War: the foreign policy of the Labour governments, 1945–51', *Journal of British Studies*, vol. 26 (1987), pp. 54–82

Westcott, N. 'Closer union and the future of East Africa, 1939–1948, a case study in the "official mind of imperialism"', *JICH*, vol. 10 (1981), pp. 67–88

'The impact of the Second World War on Tanganyika', in D. Killingray and R. Rathbone, eds., *Africa and the Second World War* (1986), pp. 143–59

White, N. J. 'Government and business divided: Malaya, 1945–1957', *JICH*, vol. 22 (1994), pp. 251–74

'The business and the politics of decolonisation: the British experience in the 20th century', *Economic History Review*, vol. 53 (2000), pp. 544–64

Wight, M. 'Brutus in foreign policy: the memoirs of Sir Anthony Eden', *International Affairs*, vol. 36 (1960), pp. 299–309

Winks, R.W. 'On decolonisation and informal empire', *American Historical Review*, vol. 81 (1976), pp. 540–56

'A system of commands: the infrastructure of race conflict', in G. Martel, ed., *Studies in British imperial history: essays in honour of A. P. Thornton* (1986), pp. 19–30

Winter, J. M. 'The Webbs and the non-white world: a case of socialist racialism', *Journal of Contemporary History*, vol. 9 (1974), pp. 181–92

'Britain's "lost generation" of the First World War', *Population Studies*, vol. 31, (1977) pp 449–61

Wrigley, C. ' "Now you see it, now you don't": Harold Wilson's foreign policy, 1964–1970', in R. Coopey, S. Fielding and N. Tiratsoo, eds., *The Wilson governments, 1964–1970* (1993), pp. 123–35

Wylie, D. 'Confrontation over Kenya: the Colonial Office and its critics, 1918–40, *Journal of African History*, vol. 18 (1970), pp. 427–47

Yarwood, A. T. 'Overseas Indians as a problem', *Australian Journal of Politics and History*, vol. 14 (1968) pp. 204–18

Youé, C.P. 'The threat of settler rebellion and the imperial predicament: the denial of Indian rights in Kenya, 1923', *Canadian Journal of History*, vol. 12 (1978), pp. 347–60

Young, C. 'Decolonisation in Africa', in L.H. Gann and P. Duignan, eds, *Colonialism in Africa, 1870–1960*, vol. II *1914–60* (Cambridge, 1970) pp. 450–502

Young, J.W. 'The Wilson government and the debate over arms to South Africa in 1964', *Contemporary British History*, vol. 12 (1998), pp. 62–86

'Conclusion', in S. Kelly and A. Gorst, eds, *Whitehall and the Suez Crisis* (2000) pp. 221–23

Zweig, R. 'The Palestine Mandate', *Historical Journal*, vol. 24 (1981), pp. 243–51

Index